Lord E

and th

Marbl

Lord Elgin
and the
Marbles

William St. Clair

Oxford   New York
OXFORD UNIVERSITY PRESS
1998

Oxford University Press, Great Clarendon Street, Oxford OX2 6DP
Oxford New York
Athens Auckland Bangkok Bogota Bombay
Buenos Aires Calcutta Cape Town Dar es Salaam
Delhi Florence Hong Kong Istanbul Karachi
Kuala Lumpur Madras Madrid Melbourne
Mexico City Nairobi Paris Singapore
Taipei Tokyo Toronto Warsaw
and associated companies in
Berlin Ibadan

Oxford is a trade mark of Oxford University Press

First published 1967 by Oxford University Press
Second edition first issued, with
revisions, as an Oxford University Press paperback 1983
This edition first published as an Oxford Uiniversity Press paperback 1998

British Library Cataloguing in Publication Data
Data available

Library of Congress Cataloging in Publication Data
St. Clair, William.
Lord Elgin and the marbles / William St. Clair.—3rd rev. ed.
Includes bibliographical references and index.
1. Elgin marbles. 2. Elgin, Thomas Bruce, Earl of, 1766–1841.
3. Diplomats—Great Britain—Biography. I. Title.
NB92.S7 1988 733'.3'09385—dc21 97-50632

ISBN 0-19-288053-5 (pbk.)

1 3 5 7 9 10 8 6 4 2

Typeset by Best-set Typesetter Ltd., Hong Kong
Printed in Great Britain by
Mackays of Chatham,
Chatham, Kent

Preface to the Third Revised Edition

FIFTEEN years have passed since the last edition of *Lord Elgin and the Marbles* was printed in English, during which time public interest in all questions relating to cultural property, of which the Elgin Marbles remains the classic case, has steadily increased. I have been pleased to see that, since the book first appeared, it has held its place as the standard reputable historical account of the circumstances in which the sculptures of the Parthenon were acquired by Lord Elgin.

In the light of the considerable scholarly progress that has been made on many historical and archaeological questions concerning the Parthenon, however, and in the modern climate of postcolonial sensitivity and awareness of the changing cultural conventions within which all works of art are given meaning, it seemed inappropriate in this new edition just to reprint the previous test or to make additions. Bearing in mind, too, the shifts in emphasis and style that a greater authorial maturity might be expected to bring about, I therefore offer a fully revised and considerably expanded new version of the whole book, with the last four chapters and the two appendices entirely new.

In the revision, I have taken account of the large body of excellent new work relating to the Parthenon, its history and its changing meaning, which has been published in several countries in recent years. Drawing on my own researches, I also present new material on a number of aspects, mostly from previously unused and unpublished manuscript sources. As examples of the revision, this edition offers a full summary of the history of the Parthenon before Lord Elgin's time; adds to the account of what was actually done in Athens by Lord Elgin's agents in the light of newly found evidence; publishes new documents about Elgin's relationship with Byron; and carries the history of the Parthenon and of its sculptures through the nineteenth and twentieth centuries to the present day.

With respect to the Parthenon frieze I offer a summary of the exciting radical new interpretation of its mythological meaning suggested by Professor Joan Connelly. Connelly's interpretation is supported by quotations from a lost play by Euripides, some extensive and previously unknown fragments of which, discovered from an ancient papyrus, were first published by Professor Colin Austin after the first edition of this book appeared.

In revising the book I have aimed at presenting the events surrounding the Elgin Marbles in a wider European context and within a longer perspective of cultural change. The bibliography has also been extended and updated.

Since *Lord Elgin and the Marbles* is primarily a work of history, I do not wish to intervene directly in the polemic surrounding the possible return of the Parthenon sculptures to Greece. The extent to which Elgin had legal authority to remove antiquities from Athens is, however, one of many history issues which are relevant to this question, and one which has often been misunderstood and misrepresented. All discussion of legality must start with the second Firman issued by the Ottoman government in July 1801, under whose authority the Ottoman authorities in Athens permitted the first removals of sculptures from the Parthenon. The official translation into Italian which was provided, at Elgin's request, for the British Embassy in Constantinople and which was used to persuade the authorities on the spot in Athens, is now in my possession. The text of that document, the only version known to have survived, is published here in its entirety for the first time. In my account of the measures taken later to obtain condonation and legitimation of the removals which were undertaken under the claimed authority of the second Firman, I present newly found evidence about the extent to which bribes were paid and false assurances given, as well as other relevant historical material not included in the earlier edition.

Perhaps the most disturbing revelation which this edition offers to the public, and the one which might well have the most far-reaching consequences for the Elgin Marbles debate, is set out in Chapter 24. My researches have brought to light the facts of how, in 1937 and 1938, while in the stewardship of the British Museum, the Elgin Marbles were, over a period of at least eighteen months, and against the regulations then in force in the Museum, scraped with metal tools and smoothed with carborundum in an effort to make them appear more white. As a result, the historic surfaces of most of the sculptures were severely and irreparably damaged. With recourse to the official records to which access was repeatedly denied to me until 1996, I am here able to present the first full account of the circumstances in which the disaster occurred, and of the extent of the damage, which the official inquiry of the time, hitherto suppressed, said 'cannot be exaggerated'. I also describe the measures subsequently taken by the British Museum authorities to cover up, quite literally, the effects of the mistreatment, and then, by unlawfully denying access to the relevant public documents, to prevent the full facts from becoming known until now.

The damage done to the Elgin Marbles was far worse than has ever been publicly appreciated or acknowledged. As the suppressed official report noted, 'the surface of the sculptures, showing the evidences of two thousand years of exposure to the climate of Greece, was a document of the utmost importance. There being no possible doubt about the history of the Parthenon sculptures, they came to the Museum as authentic masterpieces of Greek work of the fifth century B.C. and for purposes of study and comparison they are of inestimable value.' As the members of the official inquiry appreciated, the damage not only changed the appearance of the sculptures, but impaired—and in some cases destroyed—all future opportunities for archaeological and scientific research into the nature, meaning, and history of the Marbles, and the artistic and carving techniques. The concealment and misrepresentation of the extent of the destruction have subsequently misled scrupulous archaeologists who believed that they were dealing with untouched original works, and, unless corrected, will continue to corrupt future research. Since claims that the British Musuem has exercised a careful stewardship continue to be made, I therefore suggest in that chapter the commissioning of a full and impartial inquiry into the present state of the Marbles, using both documentary sources and the light, laser, and other techniques which are now being successfully used in the study of Greek art in other countries. If confidence is ever to be restored, we need a full and reliable historical and scientific survey of what has actually happened to the Marbles, including a careful estimate what has been irreparably lost.

W. St. C.

March 1998

Acknowledgements

My greatest debt is to the late Mrs A. C. Longland of Abingdon, who unreservedly made me a present of a collection of papers relating to Lord Elgin's Embassy which belonged to her great-grand-uncle, Dr Philip Hunt. I am also grateful to the present Lord Elgin, who allowed me to examine the collections of papers relating to the seventh Lord Elgin which are preserved at Broomhall.

Professor Joan Connelly, whose suggestion for the interpretation of the Parthenon frieze is summarized in Chapter 6, has given me much help and advice for which I am deeply grateful. I should also like to record my warm thanks to Ms Irmgard Maassen for sharing her knowledge of European romanticism and for much other help.

For advice on the scientific evidence discussed in Chapter 24 I am grateful to Dr Richard Stone of the Metropolitan Museum, New York. I should like also to record my thanks to Dr Ian Jenkins of the British Museum, who has readily met all my requests for special facilities when I was making my inquires, and for much other help. Professor William Eliot has, over many years, given me information, help, and advice on many matters, for which I should like to record my gratitude. For help in understanding the wider legal implications and for much other help, I should like to thank Professor John Henry Merryman and my brother John St. Clair.

In addition to the individuals and institutions mentioned in the prefaces to earlier editions, I should like to record my thanks to many others who have given me information, help, and advice with the later research, including Colin Austin, Professor Benelli, Frau Brehme, Peter Cochran, Brian Cook, Frau Dido Demski, John Donaldson, Herr Dressler, C. W. J. Eliot, Guy Evans, Professor Hilary Gatti, John Goldsmith, the late Denys Haynes, Peter Hopkirk, the late A. C. Lascarides, Leslie A. Marchand, Dr Hanz Günter Martin, the late Mrs Melina Mercouri, Jane Millikan, Inge Morath, Virginia Murray, Dr W. A. Oddy, the late Anna Picken, Eleanor Picken, Robert Picken, Mme Christiane Pinatel, the late Dr H. J. Plenderleith and Mrs Plenderleith, Carol Potter, Sandra Raphael, Charles Martin Robinson, Michael Russell, David St. Clair, H. L. Schanz, Rodney Searight, Miranda Seymour, John Simmons, William Stewart, Eric Stockdale, Claudia Strasky, Brian

Thorne, Sir Guenther Treitel, Margrit Velte, Dyfri Williams, and
James Drummond Young.

Among the institutions which have given permissions or helped
in other ways, I should like to thank the Abgußsammlung, Berlin,
the Antiken Sammlung des Alten Museums, Berlin, the British
Museum, the British Museum Cast Service, the British Library, the
British School at Athens, the Bulova Center, New York, the
Gennadios Library, Athens, the former Greater London Council
Record Office, the Ipswich and East Suffolk Record Office, John
Murray (Publishers) Ltd., the Joint Library of the Hellenic and
Roman Societies, London, the Library of Lambeth Palace,
Magnum, the Museum of Classical Archaeology, Cambridge, the
London Library, the Metropolitan Museum of Art, New York, the
National Galleries of Scotland, the National Library of Scotland,
the Public Record Office, the Library of the Royal Academy, the
Royal Institute of British Architects, the Queens Museum, New
York, the Scottish Record Office, and the Victoria and Albert
Museum.

I should like to record my thanks to those at Oxford University
Press who have helped in the production of the book, including
George Miller, Rebecca Hunt, Shelley Cox, Elizabeth Stratford,
Carol Leighton Davis, Heather Watson, Rowie Christopher,
Lauren McClue, Janet Yarker, and Allison Jones.

Contents

List of Plates   xiii

1. An Embassy is Arranged   1
2. Great Events in the Levant   11
3. The Voyage Out   20
4. Reception at Constantinople   28
5. The Smith Brothers   35
6. Work Begins at Athens   43
7. In Search of Ancient Manuscripts   68
8. The Conquest of Egypt and its Results   80
9. The Firman   86
10. 'The Last Poor Plunder from a Bleeding Land'   98
11. Prisoner of War   119
12. Lusieri on his Own, 1803–1806   132
13. Homecoming   140
14. The Second Collection   151
15. Artists and Dilettanti   162
16. Elgin Offers his First Collection to
    the Government   173
17. Poets and Travellers   180
18. Later Years in Greece   201
19. Lord Elgin Tries Again   214
20. Tweddell J. and Tweddell R.   227
21. The Fate of the Manuscripts   238
22. The Marbles are Sold   245
23. 'An Aera in Public Feeling'   261
24. 'The Damage is Obvious and Cannot be
    Exaggerated'   281
25. The Parthenon since Lord Elgin   314
26. The Question of Return   332

Appendices
1. The Firman   337
2. The Damage to the Elgin Marbles:
   Extracts from Official Documents   342

Contents   xii

Notes   346
Bibliography   397
Index   411

List of Plates

1. The Central Scene of the Parthenon Frieze. From a photograph by Inge Morath, 1997.
2. The Acropolis of Athens in Lord Elgin's time, showing the fortifications, the Frankish Tower, the minarets in the town, and Haseki's wall. From Dodwell's *Classical and Topographical Tour*.
3. The Parthenon in 1801. From a water-colour by William Gell in the British Museum.
4. The south-east corner of the Parthenon after the removal of some of the metopes. From a water-colour by Lusieri in the National Gallery of Scotland.
5. The same corner after all the metopes had been taken, as shown in Hobhouse's *Journey*, 1813.
6. Lusieri on the Erechtheion. From a water-colour by William Gell in the British Museum.
7. A Tight-Rope Display in Athens, 1800, showing the Theseum and the fortifications of the Acropolis, from a drawing by Sebastiano Ittar. Private collection.
8. Lord Elgin's Marbles at Burlington House, 1816. From a drawing by an unknown artist, in the former Greater London Council Record Office.
9. Some of the Elgin Marbles in the courtyard of Burlington House, 1816. From a drawing by an unknown artist, in the former Greater London Council Record Office.
10. Protest at the waste of money in buying the Elgin Marbles in 1816. From a cartoon by Cruikshank.
11. Crowds in St James's jostle to see the drawings of the Elgin Marbles by Haydon's pupils, 1819. From a cartoon by Marks. Author's collection.
12. Helios, the sun god, in his chariot, breaking from the waves of the sea at dawn, from the corner of the east pediment of the Parthenon. The black and the white on Helios' neck shows the line between the historic and the scraped surfaces at the moment when the scraping was discovered and stopped. From a photograph by Inge Morath, 1997.

Line Drawings

Map of the Eastern Mediterranean   15
The Sculptural Decoration of the Parthenon   50

I

An Embassy is Arranged

IN November 1798 the Earl of Elgin had been advised to try warm sea-bathing for the benefit of his health. While at Brighton, England's nearest approach to a warm-weather resort, he sent an unequivocal letter to the Foreign Secretary, Lord Grenville.

I regret extremely that the attention I am obliged to pay to the means recommended for the recovery of my health prevents my having the honour of waiting upon your Lordship and mentioning in a more satisfactory manner than by letter what I now beg leave to lay before you.... It has occurred to me as possible that it may be in your Lordship's intention to send to Constantinople an English representative equal in rank and situation to the Imperial and French Ministers at that Court. Should that supposition be founded I would venture to bring myself under your notice for that embassy ... My health has, I confess, been one inducement with me for bringing forward the idea contained in this letter since I have much benefit to expect from a change of climate and a sea voyage.[1]

Lord Grenville thought Lord Elgin's idea an excellent one, discussed it with the King, and accepted it at once.[2] Within a few days, it was officially announced that Thomas Bruce, seventh Earl of Elgin and eleventh of Kincardine, had been appointed Ambassador Extraordinary and Minister Plenipotentiary of His Britannic Majesty to the Sublime Porte of Selim III, Sultan of Turkey.[3]

The idea of going to Constantinople was not entirely Lord Elgin's own, but had come originally from the King. Elgin had been attending a ball given by the fleet at Weymouth in August. He was dancing with Princess Augusta when the King came up, made a joke, and led Elgin aside into a bow window. There he explained that he thought the country should appoint an ambassador to Turkey and suggested that Elgin should apply for the post.[4]

Yet, however unusual the circumstances of his appointment. Lord Elgin could claim that he had experience enough for the job. Born into an ancient and distinguished family, he had inherited the earldom while still a boy and a splendid career had been open to him from the first. After an extensive education in Scotland, England, and France he had joined the army as an ensign in the Foot Guards.[5] He passed rapidly through the lower ranks and was soon in command of a regiment which he himself had raised, the Elgin Highland Fencibles. By the age of 29 he held the rank of lieutenant-colonel.[6]

Politics was his next profession. As a Scottish peer Elgin did not have an automatic entry to the House of Lords: he had to be elected as one of the sixteen representative peers for Scotland. But this proved to be no problem. In 1790, at the age of 24, he applied to Henry Dundas, who for many years regulated all the parliamentary elections in Scotland. Dundas was impressed and Elgin was duly elected.[7] He took his seat in the House of Lords and attended whenever his many other duties allowed, holding the seat for the next seventeen years.

Elgin's diplomatic career started one year later when he was 25, almost by accident. The Government was looking for a man to go to Vienna at short notice to try to take advantage of the accession of the new Emperor Leopold II. Dundas, impressed by the first speech that Elgin had made in the House of Lords, offered him the job and Elgin accepted it eagerly. The same day he was invited to dine with William Pitt, the Prime Minister. After dinner, at which Elgin was the only guest, the two men sat late discussing foreign affairs until at last Elgin felt obliged to rise and go. On his way out Pitt said that the sooner he left for Vienna the better, to which Elgin replied that he was ready to go as soon as he had his written instructions. Pitt immediately sent for writing materials and drafted out instructions there and then.[8]

Within twenty-four hours Elgin was on his way to Vienna as Envoy Extraordinary from the British government. He followed the new emperor on a tour of the Austrian territories in Italy. Although he was largely unsuccessful in his attempts to persuade the Austrians into a closer relationship with the British, he had established quite a diplomatic reputation by the time he returned to England in the summer of 1791.

The Government then debated whether to employ him again. As Dundas wrote of him to Lord Grenville, the Foreign Secretary:

Although not very rich he is easy in his circumstances and would not with a view to emolument alone wish for employment. But if he can be creditably to himself employed in the public service it would give him pleasure to be so. He thinks himself perfectly safe in that respect in the hands of the present government. He will never urge you to anything nor will he ever bring forward any pretensions, but you will at any time find him ready to obey any call made upon the grounds I have stated.

As Dundas was writing the letter, Elgin came into the room. Dundas read it over to him and Elgin, who was a good Tory, agreed that he had 'exactly delineated his sentiments'.[9] There was some discussion about which mission Elgin should be sent on. Berlin was suggested, but Elgin preferred Brussels as this would allow him to come back to England from time to time to pursue his political career in the House of Lords. Elgin went to Brussels as Envoy Extraordinary, acting as liaison officer with the Austrian armies which were trying to reconquer Belgium from the French. He stayed there with frequent absences for two years, eventually leaving when it was clear that they were not going to succeed.

It was not long before he had another, even more important, appointment. This time his dislike for Berlin was overruled. He was sent as British Minister Plenipotentiary to the Court of Prussia where he stayed for three years. At Berlin Elgin, as head of post, for the first time became thoroughly immersed in the diplomatic intrigues of Europe at war, trying to bring Prussia into alliance with Great Britain. The more secret aspects of the work came as a shock. He was surprised to learn that gathering intelligence was regarded as a normal part of his trade, and was horrified to discover that a British agent had been conducting separate negotiations with the Prussians without his knowledge.[10] Brought up in the days before the French Revolution when the nobility of Europe formed a close-knit club of like-minded aristocrats, Elgin's conception of his duties was already out of date. Nevertheless his straightforward approach to his task, although it impressed some as naivety, brought him success. He enjoyed greatly the pleasures and status of being an ambassador, although severe attacks of illness already made visits to spas and watering places a frequent interruption to his social life in the capital. At Berlin Elgin's house provided lavish entertainment to numerous English visitors most of whom found him a congenial host and cultured companion, if a little cold.[11] One of his visitors was a young scholar and traveller called John Tweddell, the cause of many later difficulties.[12]

When he heard that he was to go to Constantinople, Elgin had every reason to expect that his career which had begun so brilliantly, was only just beginning. At the age of 32 he had already made his mark in the three professions open to a British nobleman, the army, politics, and diplomacy. Before setting about his preparations, he made another request to the Foreign Secretary. The Duke of Hamilton, one of the Knights of the Thistle, he had heard, was dying—could he please be considered for the vacancy? But the Duke lingered on for another nine months and Grenville did not have to come to a decision.[13]

Elgin was still a bachelor. Since he had spent so much of his life abroad he had had few opportunities to find a wife. Perhaps his time at Berlin had shown him that bachelorhood was a disadvantage in an ambassador, although one of his visitors had complained that in the evenings Elgin's house was open to no one but 'a fair favourite, Madame Ferchenbeck'.[14] When he returned from Brighton to Broomhall, his magnificent new country house on the Fife side of the Firth of Forth, he did not take long to remedy the situation. Within a few weeks he had become engaged to marry a girl of good family from the other side of the Firth, Mary Nisbet of Dirleton.[15] She was 21, a beauty and an heiress, then enjoying the delights of society life in Edinburgh. She seems to have hesitated a little before committing herself. Certainly it was a difficult decision to leave home and set out at once on a long journey in time of war to what was regarded as a barbaric land. But Elgin's qualifications were overwhelming and her family had no doubts. The rich Nisbets—their fortune was said to be £8,000 a year—were happy to marry their daughter to a member of the nobility who was showing such promise.[16] Elgin was so eager for the connection that he offered to give up his embassy but no sacrifice was needed and the marriage took place in March. Elgin wrote to the Foreign Secretary shortly before, asking him not to send him on the embassy too quickly as he wanted to get used to married life.[17]

The new Countess of Elgin, to judge from her letters, was a rather silly girl, but full of good humour and intense interest in the exact details of everything and everyone around her. She was devoted to her parents and wrote them a series of cheerful gossipy letters about everything she did, confident, as an only child, that nothing she said about herself could fail to interest them. The parents promised to come and see her in Constantinople and this helped to make the departure from home more tolerable. Despite her good fortune, however, Lady Elgin remained a little afraid of her grand husband. Eggy and Poll, as they called one another, seemed to be an ideal couple. They were in love and their affection continued to grow.[18]

Yet, from the beginning, the marriage carried the suspicion of being one of convenience. The prospect of eventually adding the Nisbet estates to his own was of more importance to Elgin than he would perhaps have cared to admit. He was not a rich man and he was already in debt. He had pulled down the modest house in Fife which John Adam had built for his father and erected a bigger and more splendid country house, Broomhall, in its place. It was built by Thomas Harrison between 1796 and 1799 when Elgin was in Germany. Elgin had borrowed a large sum of money and was finding difficulty in meeting his bills.[19] With his marriage his money worries seemed to be over. Besides receiving at once a large marriage settlement, he could look forward in time to inheriting all the Nisbet fortune that was not bound by entail.

In the months that followed, Elgin began to select the staff to accompany him on his mission. For the embassy proper he decided to engage two private secretaries and a chaplain, as well as numerous lesser servants, and in all three he made an excellent choice. The first private secretary was William Richard Hamilton. He was 22 and this was the first step in a public career after his studies at Oxford and Cambridge. 'He has much good sense,' his sponsor wrote of him, 'and a great activity of mind; he is industrious and in the highest degree anxious to render himself useful. His manners are pleasing and his principles perfectly good so you may use him at once as your companion, your confidant, and your fag.'[20] Time was to bear out this judgement. The second private secretary was John Philip Morier, who was also 22 and in his first diplomatic post. He already knew something of the lands they were to visit and their languages—he had been born at Smyrna, where his father was consul, and had lived there before completing his education in England. He too was well qualified for a successful public career.

The chaplain was the Reverend Philip Hunt, aged 28, a clergyman under the patronage of Lord Upper Ossory. He greeted his opportunity with enthusiasm, writing to his father:

As the Turks have now made a common cause with us to stop the progress of French desolation, it has been thought expedient by our court to send a *splendid* Embassy to Constantinople in order to enter into certain treaties for the mutual advantage of both countries. The Earl of Elgin is appointed Embassador Extraordinary etc. to the Porte, and by the interest of my worthy and excellent friend the Reverend Mr. Brand, Rector

of Maulden, the situation of chaplain and private secretary to the
Embassador will most probably be filled by me; ... I have consulted Lord
Ossory and my other friends here who all concur in describing it as a most
brilliant opportunity of improving my mind and laying the foundation of
a splendid fortune ... I need only add that it is a situation to which the
younger son of a Nobleman might aspire; that it will be certainly attended
with great *present* advantages and most probably lead to an independent
fortune.[21]

While he was making these preparations Elgin saw a good deal
of the architect, Thomas Harrison, who was putting the finishing
touches to Broomhall. Harrison, who was an architect in the Greek
style, was the first to put the idea to Elgin which led eventually
to the collection of the Elgin Marbles. Elgin's embassy to
Constantinople, Harrison suggested, presented a unique opportunity of improving the knowledge of Greek architecture in Great
Britain. It was, he explained, now admitted that the best models for
classical architecture were in Athens, and not at Rome where he
and other architects in the classical style had studied. Although the
remains of the ancient buildings in Athens were now well known
to architectural students through engravings, architects could not
be fired by mere books. What was needed were plaster casts in the
round of the actual surviving objects.[22]

It was a sound suggestion with a modest aim, but Elgin took it
up with the enthusiasm of a crusader. He had been given an opportunity, he decided, of improving the whole level of artistic appreciation in Great Britain. Architecture, sculpture, painting, even the
design of ordinary household goods, would all be improved. The
grandiloquence of his language is astonishing but he never wavered
from it. To make his embassy 'beneficial to the progress of the Fine
Arts in Great Britain', to bestow 'some benefit on the progress of
taste in England', to improve 'the circumstances towards the
advancement of literature and the arts', these were the words he
used, without apology, time and again, to describe a plan to take
some drawings and plaster casts in Athens.[23] There was no suggestion at this time that the original remains themselves should be
removed.

A practical scheme was put to Lord Grenville that the
Government should equip the embassy with a professional artist
and a number of men qualified to take plaster casts and make
accurate architectural drawings. Elgin discussed the idea with
Grenville, Pitt, and Dundas, but he was unable to transmit his

enthusiasm. Their reaction was discouraging. 'With respect to architectural pursuits,' Lord Grenville wrote, 'I really believe all has been done by travellers and the magnificent publications of their discoveries that could reasonably be expected now, and I do not think that we could (at least from any funds at the disposal of the Foreign Department) defray with any propriety the expense of that encouragement which a person, qualified as you mention, would be entitled to expect for such an undertaking.'[24]

Although it was clear that if anything was to be done, it must be done at Elgin's own expense, he decided to go ahead. The President of the Royal Academy, the ageing Benjamin West, was asked to advise, and for a few weeks Elgin's scheme was a favourite topic in and around the Academy.[25] Various eager young painters offered themselves, including Thomas Girtin, Richard and Robert Smirke, and William Daniell, but with none of them was Elgin able to arrange acceptable terms. Girtin later claimed that after hanging about Elgin's hall for many hours he was offered only £30 per annum—half as much as Elgin's valet—and that apart from his main task he was to assist Lady Elgin in 'decorating firescreens, work tables and other such elegancies'.[26]

Then West suggested J. M. W. Turner, who was at that time only 24 and just beginning to make his name. Turner was willing to go, but among Elgin's conditions was that he should have the sole possession of every drawing and sketch that Turner made and that Turner should teach Lady Elgin to draw. These were hard terms for a man who already considered giving lessons beneath him and whose main purpose in going to the east would be to improve his own style by drawing the ruins. Turner demanded a salary of £400 per annum.[27]

It was too much and the negotiation was abandoned. Elgin had missed his chance of engaging the greatest English artist of the age. In describing this incident seventeen years later to the Select Committee on the Elgin Marbles, Elgin said: 'Turner...wished to retain a certain portion of his own labour for his own use; he moreover asked between seven and eight hundred pounds of salary, independently of his expenses being paid.'[28] No doubt Elgin's memory was at fault but whether at £400 or £800 Turner was too expensive. He had been told by Sir Robert Ainslie, a former British ambassador at Constantinople, that his travelling painter, a German, had been paid only fifty guineas per annum and one of his conditions of service was that the whole of his works, drawings, pictures, and sketches should be Ainslie's sole property.[29] After his unfortunate negotiations with the Academy, therefore, Elgin decided to postpone engaging someone until he reached Italy on the way out.

Although the Government had been unsympathetic to Elgin's proposals to take artists and architects, they did agree to pay for a different kind of cultural speculation suggested by the Bishops of Durham and Lincoln. A story had long been current in Europe that the libraries of the East contained manuscripts of ancient authors unknown in the West. It was decided to attach to Elgin's embassy a scholar who would attempt to find them. To the classically educated statesmen of the time, the prospect of finding, say, the lost works of Livy was irresistible.

The man the bishops suggested for this task was Richard Porson, but, for some reason, the idea fell through. Porson, it is now recognized, was one of the greatest of classical scholars, and, as with Turner, it is tempting to guess at how his genius would have developed if he had gone to Constantinople. As he now exercised his Cambridge professorship mainly in a London cider cellar and combined drunkenness with a vile temper and disgusting personal habits, he may not have been a success.[30]

In the end the man chosen was Joseph Dacre Carlyle, Professor of Arabic at Cambridge, a quiet scholarly man in holy orders who had published several learned books on Arabic and had a taste for composing poetry.[31] To the public he was known, if at all, as the author of a proposal to convert the inhabitants of Asia and Africa to Christianity by distributing to them a low-priced version of the Bible in Arabic, a scheme he hoped to start while in the East.[32] Carlyle too had high hopes of making his fortune by his attachment to Elgin.[33]

Apart from the costs of paying for his staff which by the custom of the day he had to find for himself, Elgin began to realize that his outlay on other things was greater than he expected.[34] Never slow to ask for favours, he wrote again to Lord Grenville to ask about his scale of allowances.

The arrangement rests entirely with you; I never did propose nor do I wish to propose anything on the subject. But I hope that the nature of my embassy, the assistance it is to hold out, at my expense, for researches of various kinds, the number of English officers naval as well as military who will naturally make my house their home, and the aid and support (always leading to much expense) which some Foreign Ministers in London assure me their governments expect from the English mission at Constantinople; these considerations, while they have guided me in the extent of my preparations, induce me to hope that your Lordship will put my embassy in point of appointments as well as in dignity on the footing of an extra-ordinary one.[35]

After some negotiation Elgin's salary was fixed at £6,600 per annum plus certain expenses and Grenville steadfastly refused to grant him any more.[36] This was far less than Elgin had hoped for and, as things turned out, a pittance compared with the grandeur of his schemes.

Hunt, the chaplain, was the first to feel the effect. He arrived at London and found himself having to borrow from his family and friends. He wrote to his father:

I had fondly indulged the idea that from the instant my connection with Lord Elgin commenced, I should cease to be under the necessity of apply-ing to you for money, but I have found a serious reverse, nor do I imagine I shall receive any part of my salary till after the conclusion of Our Embassy . . . I sincerely hope and I will use every exertion that the kind-ness of my friends may not be thrown away either by my indolence or ill conduct in a situation which certainly ought to lead to important improve-ment both for my instruction and emolument.

When Hunt set out he had only twelve guineas in his pocket.[37]

By August 1799, just nine months after the idea of the embassy was approved, the various members of Elgin's party began to assemble at Portsmouth where the Admiralty had provided a warship, HMS *Phaeton*, to take them to Constantinople. Elgin was already there when the news came through that the Duke of Hamilton had died. Although he had been made a Privy Councillor only a month before, Elgin hastened to renew his application for the vacancy among the Knights of the Thistle that he had made when the Duke first fell ill. The *Phaeton* was held up by order of the Admiralty, he told Lord Grenville; and there would just be time for the King to bestow the ribbon on him before she sailed. His request was not granted, the ribbon already having been promised elsewhere.[38] He put in another bid when the Duke of Queensberry fell ill the next year but again failed.[39]

HMS *Phaeton* was a frigate of thirty-eight guns under the command of Captain Morris. She had only one deck, and as fighting could be expected on the voyage out, she could not be made com-fortable. The party consisted of Lord and Lady Elgin, the secretaries Hamilton and Morier, the chaplain Hunt, McLean the physician, Carlyle the professor attached to the mission, Duff the courier, three personal maids for Lady Elgin, a few other female servants, and a number of Lady Elgin's dogs. The state room of the ship was divided into six compartments with green baize curtains. Lord and Lady Elgin had one each; the personal maids and other female servants had two; one was used as a mess; and the sixth was occupied by the five gentlemen (Duff was excluded). Hunt described the scene to his father:

In our little cabin twelve feet long, six broad and $6\frac{1}{2}$ high were five beds, five gentlemen, 13 large trunks, 8 small do., 6 basons etc., 6 hats, 5 dressing gowns, 5 great coats and boat cloaks, 3 servants getting ready our shaving apparatus and a cabin boy brushing shoes; 5 foul cloathes bags, 4 portmanteaux, 2 pewter bottles, 2 lanterns, 2 umbrellas, a travelling library, brooms, supernumerary blankets, quilts, brushes, carpets etc. in most glorious confusion, and an Eighteen Pounder with its tremendous apparatus of carriage tackles, iron crow, balls and grape shot.[40]

Elgin had arranged for the heavier luggage to be sent on by a merchantman. They included some carriages and pianos, numerous presents for the Turks, a complete set of ambassadorial gold and silver plate, and a great quantity of furniture. The merchantman also brought more servants, grooms, coachmen, and footmen.

By the beginning of September all was at last ready. Elgin had his last discussions with the Government and took his leave of the King. At one o'clock precisely on the 3rd Lord and Lady Elgin came aboard in the captain's barge to a salute of fifteen guns. The anchor was at once weighed and the embassy set sail.

2

Great Events in the Levant

LORD ELGIN's instructions on the purpose of his embassy run to twenty-six pages but, for the most part, they are both too wide-ranging and too limited to reveal the Government's true intentions On the one hand, he was to watch over the interests of His Majesty, promote trade, maintain British privileges, and look out for more, to protect all Christians 'particularly those of the reformed religion' and all the other generalities of the diplomat's rule book—the Foreign Office used this part of Elgin's instructions as a draft for the instructions to another ambassador to Turkey nine years later. On the other hand, Elgin was given certain specific objectives, to persuade the Turks to open the Black Sea to British trade, to obtain permission to cut timber there, to try to establish a British postal station at Suez, and so on.[1]

The main purpose of the embassy was, however, not stated. Perhaps at the time it was too obvious to need mentioning. Elgin was to help in every way he could to expel the French from Egypt and the eastern Mediterranean, and to keep the Ottoman Empire as friendly as possible to the British. Early in 1798 the Directory, which was then the government of France, had appointed the successful young general, Napoleon Bonaparte, commander-in-chief of the 'Army of England', a force which had been assembled on the coast of France with the intention of invading Great Britain. Bonaparte made a quick tour of inspection of the staging areas and reported to the Government that the project was impossible. He suggested instead that the forces should be used to invade Egypt and his suggestion was at once adopted.

In May a huge armada under Bonaparte's command set sail from Toulon, Genoa, and Ajaccio. It eluded the British warships in the Mediterranean and, without difficulty, captured Malta, where the Knights of St John of Jerusalem were still playing out the traditions of the Crusades. Malta was proudly incorporated into the French Republic and a garrison was established. In the middle of June the armada set sail from Malta, again escaped the British warships which went hurrying past it on a foggy night, and arrived in Egypt six weeks later. Without much opposition the whole force was quickly disembarked.

Egypt at the time was nominally part of the Ottoman Empire, as was most of the Middle East, Asia Minor, the Balkans, and the North African coast. But any real control which the sultans at Constantinople had exercised over Egypt had long since been lost. The Government, if government it could be called, was in the hands of the Mamelukes, who had originally been mercenary soldiers brought from the Caucasus by the sultans to help them keep down the Egyptians. First introduced to Egypt in the thirteenth century, the Mamelukes took over the government within a few years and remained in power for five centuries. They kept up their numbers and maintained their separateness by buying boys from the Caucasus for training as soldiers. The Mamelukes, who in 1798 numbered about 10,000, had spent their whole lives in the army and were a formidable force.

The pretence of Turkish authority was kept up most of the time. Whenever the Ottoman Porte appointed a new Pasha of Egypt, he was met at Cairo by the Mameluke leaders with impressive cere-mony, and conducted to the citadel. There he lived in virtual impris-onment until his term of office was over, his name invoked by whichever set of Mamelukes happened to control the citadel at the time as the legal authority for whatever they chose. The Ottoman authorities had tried to re-establish their authority at various times but had always failed.

Yet, however much superior the Mamelukes were to any force the Turks could put against them, they were no match for the French armed with modern European firearms and artillery. In the Battle of the Pyramids (which took place a considerable distance from the pyramids) the French were decisively victorious, with almost no casualties on their side, and the booty was enormous. Some days after the battle, the French made a conquerors' entry into Cairo with banners flying and bands playing. Bonaparte informed the French government that their ancient dream had become a reality. Egypt was now a French possession.

The sudden French conquest of Egypt put the Government at Constantinople in a quandary. They had no love for the Mamelukes, but they had no love for the principles of the French Revolution either, and were proud of being even the nominal rulers of Egypt. Ever since the sixteenth century France had been their staunchest ally and, as the Russians overran more and more of their vast empire in the north, France's importance had grown. The latest Turkish war with Russia had been more disastrous than most and since then France's support had been lavish and practical. A strong French military mission was sent to Turkey to train up the Turkish forces into some kind of European military discipline. Turkish cadets were sent to the French military academy. French engineers built shore defences at the Dardanelles, and French constructors began to supervise the building of a modern Turkish fleet. The Comte de Choiseul-Gouffier, who had been French Ambassador during this time, had enjoyed a specially intimate relationship with the Ottoman governments and, incidentally, as a token of gratitude, the Turks had allowed him to corner the market in classical antiquities.

At the very moment when Bonaparte was carrying out the invasion, Talleyrand, the French Foreign Minister, was to be sent to Constantinople to persuade the Turks that France was occupying Egypt in Turkey's own interest. But Talleyrand, with his genius for avoiding danger which was to keep him at the centre of power through the long vicissitudes of the Revolutionary and Napoleonic periods and beyond, had the sense to see that the Turks could scarcely be expected to swallow such a story and had managed to delay his departure until it was safely too late.

While this procrastination was the salvation of Talleyrand, it put Ruffin, the French Chargé d'Affaires at Constantinople, in an acutely embarrassing position. When the French invasion fleet was well on its way across the Mediterranean, Ruffin was sent for by the Turkish Foreign Minister, and interrogated for three hours on what the purpose of the fleet was. Poor Ruffin, unlike the Turks, did not know anything about it for no one had bothered to tell him. All he could do was bumble out the usual diplomatic platitudes that, if there were such a fleet, it was certainly not intended against the Ottoman Empire with whom the French wished to maintain the friendliest of relations, etc. A week after this interview Ruffin discovered the truth. He was told by Talleyrand to persuade the Turks that the invasion of Egypt was not intended as an unfriendly act but as a service to help Turkey. Seldom has a diplomat been given a less convincing brief to speak to. Besides knowing in detail about the invasion plans, the Turks had also heard of the schemes circulating in France for the complete dismemberment of the Ottoman

Empire. They knew too that Bonaparte had been negotiating with other pashas who paid as little heed to the government in Constantinople as the Mamelukes.

The Turks hesitated about what to do. On 6 August Ruffin was again summoned by the Turkish Minister. He was told he must remain within the walls of the French embassy, and if he had any communication to make to the Turkish government he must call at night. All Frenchmen were to avoid showing themselves in public. 'When I took my leave from him,' said Ruffin in his report, 'I was given neither sherbet nor perfume nor handkerchief. The absence of the marks of honour confirmed my impression that I had not had a conference but a ministerial scolding.'[2]

A month later, Ruffin was called yet again to the Turkish Foreign Minister. This time all the marks of honour were accorded and coffee was served. But this time the Turkish Minister was more strict. The Sublime Porte, he said, was pained to see an allied power seize without warning her most precious province, the navel of Islam. All diplomatic relations must be broken off at once. When coffee was finished the French Minister was escorted by a military guard to the insalubrious prison of the Seven Towers. A formal declaration of war followed a few days later. All Frenchmen in the parts of the Ottoman Empire over which the Porte exercised some control were arrested. They included Louis-François-Sébastien Fauvel, a French archaeologist living in Athens who had been helping the former French Ambassador to build his collection of antiquities.

The sudden stiffening of the Turkish attitude had an obvious cause. On 1 August, even before Ruffin's scolding by the Turkish Minister, the British admiral Horatio Nelson had utterly destroyed the French fleet. The Battle of the Nile (which was fought a considerable distance from the Nile) deprived the French army in Egypt of all means of returning home. Henceforth they were cooped up in Egypt and nothing the French government could do was likely to rescue or reinforce them. Since the British fleet had been withdrawn from the Mediterranean in 1796, to an outsider it must have seemed extremely unlikely that ships could be spared to go there now when the British Isles themselves were threatened. No doubt Bonaparte had counted on this. But the British Admiralty upheld the traditional naval principle that the first line of defence is the enemy's ports. Admiral St Vincent, who was blockading Cadiz, was ordered to strain every nerve and incur

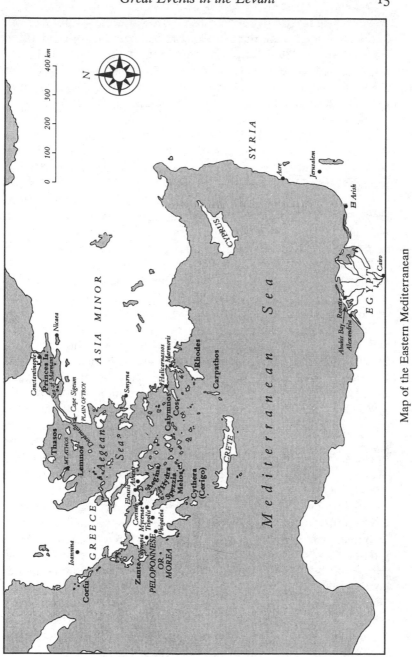

Map of the Eastern Mediterranean

considerable hazard by sending a squadron into the Mediterranean and he was advised to put it under the command of the promising officer Rear-Admiral Sir Horatio Nelson. St Vincent had already come to the same conclusion even before his instructions from home arrived and Nelson had sailed. He was then 39, had been in the Navy since he was 12, and commanded ships since he was 20. He had fought in every sea and had lost an eye and an arm in battle at different times. And, like Bonaparte, he considered that Almighty God had singled him out to be the instrument of His will.

When Nelson reached Toulon he found that Bonaparte had already gone. He at once set off in pursuit. There then followed a naval blind man's buff, with Nelson trying to guess where Bonaparte might be heading and rushing to try to cut him off. Nelson never did catch him before he reached Egypt although one night the fleets passed within a few miles of one another. Once ashore in Egypt Bonaparte thought he was safe. When Nelson suddenly attacked from the sea on 1 August, the French fleet was unprepared, and it was completely destroyed. The whole balance of power in the eastern Mediterranean was altered.

The Battle of the Nile and the subsequent Turkish declaration of war on France gave the British government a wonderful opportunity of securing another ally and of superseding France as the most favoured nation in the Ottoman Empire. They did not fail to take it. Hitherto Turkey had been regarded as a remote and unimportant country and Britain had not normally bothered to maintain an official government representative at Constantinople. Instead they had been content to leave British relations with Turkey in the hands of the Levant Company, an English chartered company, which had been given exclusive rights in the British trade with the eastern Mediterranean.

The Levant Company had been originally incorporated by Royal Charter in 1605 under the title of 'The Governor and Company of Merchants of England Trading to the Levant Seas' and since then it had been granted formidable privileges. It had the statutory right to appoint all British ambassadors, consuls, and deputies in the Levant, and to lay charges on its members—the 'Turkey merchants'—to support them. It had the right to impose fines, distrain goods, and send home under arrest anyone who offended against its monopoly. From time to time it ran its own fleet of warships. Although by Elgin's time the Levant trade had passed its peak, the company still supported consulates at Smyrna, Aleppo, Alexandria,

Algiers, and many smaller places, and it still maintained the fiction that it alone could appoint the ambassador to Turkey by formally electing the Government's nominee on the few occasions that the Government wished to intervene.[3] In 1799 the Government formally consulted the Levant Company about Lord Elgin's appointment.[4]

The last British Ambassador to the Sublime Porte, Robert Liston, had left Constantinople in 1794. Since then his private secretary, John Spencer Smith, an employee of the Levant Company, had been responsible for relations with the British, first as chargé d'affaires and subsequently as minister. Spencer Smith had satisfactorily conducted the commercial affairs of the Levant Company as well as such few diplomatic tasks as the British government gave him, when the French invasion of Egypt suddenly made his post one of the most politically sensitive in Europe.

Spencer Smith was told to start negotiations to try to conclude an alliance with Turkey at once. To reinforce his diplomatic effort, it was agreed that Britain could provide the Turks with some solid military help. Brigadier General Koehler along with seventy-six officers and men, mostly artillerymen and engineers, was sent from England to establish a British Military Mission and attempt the task of modernizing the Turkish forces on which the French had hitherto been employed. The Mission was accompanied by eighteen women and sixteen children.[5] It was naval help, however, that Britain was best able to provide. Nelson had returned to Sicily (and Lady Hamilton) after the battle of the Nile and only a small squadron was left to blockade Egypt. The British government had the excellent idea of sending out a dashing young naval captain to help the Turks. They chose Sir Sidney Smith, the brother of John Spencer Smith.

Sir Sidney Smith was a sailor from the same mould as Nelson. He was then 34 and had been in the Navy since he was 11, promoted captain at the age of 16. He had fought in many battles in many seas during the American Revolutionary Wars but when peace came he had found the life of a naval officer too dull. During a war between Russia and Sweden he disobeyed Admiralty instructions and accepted an invitation from King Gustavus to be his naval adviser, conducting the naval war personally from the King's yacht and being knighted for his services. On his return from Sweden, forgiven by the Admiralty, he had been sent on a fact-finding tour of Turkey, spending several years exploring the harbours and tides of the whole coastline from the Black Sea to the Nile Delta and making himself thoroughly familiar with the Turkish navy.

When war between France and Britain broke out in 1793 Sir Sidney Smith was at Smyrna. He bought a ship at his own expense, collected a scratch crew of unemployed sailors, and sailed to join the British Mediterranean fleet. The French, with some justice, branded him as a pirate, but the Admiralty regularized his status and he took part in the burning of the port of Toulon. His next adventure was to be captured by the French as he was raiding their shipping near Le Havre and he was imprisoned in Paris. But before long he had escaped back to England.[6]

In deciding to send Sir Sidney Smith to help the Turks in 1798 the Government thought they had made a brilliant stroke. They reckoned, rightly, that his intimate knowledge of Turkey, his bravery, and extravagant flamboyance would appeal to the Turks and make up for lack of ships under his command. And they also reckoned, rightly, that the Turks might allow him to command their own fleet. But the Government was even cleverer, or as it turned out too clever. They decided to give Smith a diplomatic rank as well as a naval one. He was appointed 'Minister Plenipotentiary' jointly with his brother Spencer Smith to help him to arrange the treaty of alliance with Turkey. To give an active service officer a political as well as a military task is a hazardous proceeding at any time. To do so with a man who had made his reputation largely through disobedience was dangerous in the extreme. Nelson, for one, saw this immediately, protested in the strongest terms, and threatened to resign and to take Sir William and Lady Hamilton home with him. But the Government insisted that the arrangement should stand. Nelson was soothed down despite a further disobedience of Smith in assuming, without authority, the rank of commodore. Sir Sidney Smith sailed through the Mediterranean with his one ship, the *Tigre*, and took up his station off the coast of Egypt to blockade the French. His success was so immediate and so tremendous that all was forgotten and forgiven.

Bonaparte, having conquered the whole of Egypt, led his army north against Syria. He captured Jaffa and one or two other towns, massacred their garrisons, and laid siege to Acre. Smith, with his usual gusto, flung himself into the battle. He landed men and guns from his ship and successfully resisted every attack that Bonaparte threw against the town. Bonaparte was compelled to give up the siege; he had suffered a major defeat and one which could not be concealed. The Egyptian expedition was now clearly doomed. Smith became a hero, almost the rival of Nelson. The picture of Sir Sidney Smith standing with drawn sword in the breach at Acre seemed destined to become a romantic image of the British at war to compare with Wolfe at Quebec. The nation was in no mood to listen to criticisms. Success in war was its own justification.

How far Elgin understood the complexities of the situation into which he had so eagerly thrust himself is difficult to judge. Nelson was at Sicily with the Neapolitan court and the Hamiltons. General Koehler was somewhere in Turkey trying to help the Turkish army. One Smith brother, an employee of the Levant Company, was in charge of British affairs at Constantinople; the other, a national hero, was off the coast of Egypt holding both naval command and diplomatic rank. General Bonaparte and a French army were in possession of Egypt but they had shown conclusively that they could not get out.

3

The Voyage Out

WHEN the *Phaeton* left Portsmouth in September Lady Elgin was already two months pregnant, and it became clear before they had been long at sea that she was going to have an extremely uncomfortable voyage. She became seasick the second day out and nothing Dr McLean could do succeeded in settling her stomach. It was decided, therefore, to stop for a few days at every suitable port of call to give her an occasional rest.[1] For everyone else the beginning of the voyage was remarkably pleasant. Captain Morris, who was to command a battleship at Trafalgar and retire from the Navy as a Vice-Admiral, had obtained funds from the Government to entertain his distinguished guests and his table was always well supplied with fresh meat and good wine. He invited the ship's officers, to dine in turn with the ambassador and his staff, and the conversation was said to be excellent.[2] Among the lieutenants was Francis Beaufort, soon to be a famous hydrographer, the inventor of the Beaufort scale for measuring wind strength.

Before long the strain of living in such a confined space produced some friction. Carlyle became Elgin's favourite and Hunt, always touchy on such points, felt that he was not being treated as well as his rank entitled him.[3] As he wrote to his father he began to have second thoughts about the whole enterprise:

I began to ruminate on the novelty of my situation and I must own I felt somewhat of a depression of spirits, when I considered that I was entering into a new sphere of life in which talents might be required that I do not possess and attainments which I have neglected to acquire; in which I might not be so fortunate as to meet friends who would overlook my failings or interest themselves in my favour: in short that every moment was increasing my distance from my family and all my early connections and rendering personal communication with them impossible ... that I might be weakening if not dissolving attachments of those from whom I have received happiness and the most flattering marks of attention; and forming others which may be productive of little comfort or advantage.[4]

Morier, too, confided in his diary that he detected 'a great indifference on the part of Lord Elgin towards those most immediately
dependent upon him'.[5] Already a certain coldness in the ambassador's manner which was later to cost him the loyalty of many of
his staff had begun to appear. His seriousness, partly caused
perhaps by the headaches from which he constantly suffered, contrasted sharply with the liveliness of his young wife. Besides, the
ambassador stood by and allowed everyone on his party to pay
their expenses and studiously avoided any mention of the subject
of money.[6] It soon became clear that no one would be paid until
the embassy was over. Lisbon was reached without incident and
after a few days of rest Lady Elgin stopped being sick.

A short distance out from Lisbon the *Phaeton* was joined in
company by a fast American frigate. This caused Captain Morris
great annoyance for the American consistently outpaced his ship,
but to the Elgins it was comforting to have a neutral vessel in
company in case they were attacked. As they approached the
Straits of Gibraltar the enemy could be expected, and the ship's
decks were cleared to be ready for action.

On 20 September a sail was sighted and, instead of escaping in
the other direction as might have been expected with so valuable
a party on board, Captain Morris set off in pursuit. The chase lasted
all day before the ship was overtaken and brought to with a shot
across her bows. Unfortunately for the crew of the *Phaeton*
who had high hopes of prize money, the ship turned out to be from
a neutral state in the Baltic and they had to let her go. The following day they chased another ship but she turned out to be another
neutral, an American this time, and they had to let her go too.[7]

The next port of call was Gibraltar, where the British garrison as
at Lisbon were hosts and guides. St Michael's Cave was specially
lit, and several grand parties were held in honour of the ambassador. The talk at Gibraltar was all about Nelson, Lady Hamilton,
and the court in Sicily. It was being rumoured that Nelson was
about to return to England with the King of Naples and the
Hamiltons, perhaps a leak of Nelson's threat to resign in disgust at
Sir Sidney Smith. But the general tenor of the stories was pretty
near the truth. 'They say,' Lady Elgin wrote to her mother, 'there
never was a man turned so *vainglorious* (that's the phrase) in the
world as Lord N. He is now completely managed by Lady
Hamilton.'[8]

All too soon they had to leave Gibraltar, much to the misery of

Lady Elgin. Neither calm nor storm agreed with her. She made an effort to attend the service on deck on the first Sunday at sea but it was no good. 'The calm I complained of so bitterly yesterday, was this morning succeeded by a brisk gale', she wrote.

We have been going 8 and 9 notts an hour but the sea was very rough and the ship roled and poor Poll was exceedingly sick. However I contrived to dress myself very smart and attended the service on deck; it was almost too much for me and I was ill when I came down again; you never saw anything conducted with so much decency as it was, all the sailors nicely dressed and listening with the greatest attention.[9]

Lady Elgin was continuously sick for the next three days as the *Phaeton* made her way to Sicily, lying in her cabin bathing her face in vinegar and expecting to die at any moment. At last, precisely a month after leaving Portsmouth, the ship arrived safely, to everyone's great relief, at Palermo harbour.

Meanwhile, another naval event, of greater importance, was occurring not far away. After his repulse by Sir Sidney Smith at Acre, Bonaparte finally realized the hopelessness of the French position in Egypt and decided that he personally must escape before it was too late. He reported all his defeats as glorious victories to the French government and announced to the army in Egypt that he was going on a tour of inspection. Instead of doing so, he waited until a large part of the blockading British squadron was replenishing in Cyprus and left Egypt secretly with four ships. He sailed along the North African coast to avoid Sir Sidney Smith's cruisers and then made a dash across the narrows to Corsica. On 30 September he must have passed within a few miles of the *Phaeton*. A few days later Bonaparte sighted the French coast and also a British fleet of twenty-two ships. The British admiral mistook Bonaparte's squadron for some of his own ships and did not give chase. Bonaparte reached France safely and, within a month, took over the government.

Elgin and his party knew nothing of Bonaparte's flight when they arrived at Palermo. They were more interested in meeting Nelson, Hamilton, and Lady Hamilton. As soon as the *Phaeton* dropped anchor one of Lady Hamilton's servants came on board to apologize for his mistress's absence because the Queen had sent for her. But the next day the Elgins were settled in a magnificent private palazzo near the Hamiltons' house, and were introduced to the unusual ménage.

In a letter to her family in Scotland, Lady Elgin described the dinner party the first night ashore.

We dined with Sir William Hamilton and I had the satisfaction of seeing her Ladyship and what is still more, heard her sing. I must acknowledge she is pleasant, makes up amazingly, and did all she could to make me accept of an apartment there, which I should have totally to myself. However I did not in the least scruple to refuse her Ladyship. She looked very handsome at dinner quite in an undress: my father would say 'There is a fine Woman for you, good flesh and blood'. She is indeed a Whapper! and I think her manner very vulgar. It is really humiliating to see Lord Nelson, he seems quite dying and yet as if he had no other thought than her. He told Elgin privately that he had lived a year in the house with her, and that her beauty was nothing in comparison to the goodness of her heart.[10]

When Captain Morris made his call at the Hamiltons' to see Nelson, he was met at the door by a little old woman with a white bed-gown and black petticoat whom he took for a servant, and whom he told off for asking inquisitive questions. She turned out to be Lady Hamilton's mother—it was perhaps incidents like this that had caused her to change her name from Duggins to Cadogan.

A few days later it was the birthday of the heir to the throne and the Court celebrated with a grand gala. In spite of the war and the loss of the best half of the kingdom to the enemy, they did not skimp. There was some difficulty about finding suitable clothes for the pregnant Lady Elgin but she was persuaded to take part. As she wrote to her family:

It was out in a garden and everything completely Chinese, innumerable numbers of round tables very well served, and a vast quantity of attendants all dressed like Chinese; they say the fête cost £6000; the whole garden lit with coloured lamps, one of the avenues I dare say at least a mile long, quite full of lamps, it really outdid the Arabian Nights.[11]

Sir William Hamilton is remembered nowadays chiefly as the husband of the famous Emma. But in his own day he had a great, and well-deserved, reputation as an antiquary. Ever since he had been appointed Ambassador to the Court of the Two Sicilies in Naples in 1764, he had been collecting classical antiquities. Unlike almost all the collectors of the time his taste did not run to marbles or bronzes but to vases. At the time, the black and red Greek vases were still known as 'Etruscan'—because most had been found in Southern Italy—and were not highly regarded as works of art.

Hamilton was one of the first to appreciate their true origin and to recognize their worth and interest. By 1772 his collection consisted of 730 vases, several hundred antiquities of various other kinds, and over 6,000 ancient coins.

By the time he discovered that his passion was proving financially ruinous and sold his whole collection to the British Museum, he had already described and illustrated most of it in four large volumes which he published in Naples at his own expense. Before long he had begun a second collection and for a few months he possessed one of the most celebrated of all classical antiquities, the Portland Vase.[12] Fresh excavations in the Naples area in 1789 and 1790 brought many more vases on to the market and Hamilton was unable to resist. Again he discovered quickly that his hobby was beyond his means and he was forced to sell. His second collection, which was bigger than the first, was eventually sold in England, although a third of it was lost at sea on the voyage.[13]

In 1799, when Elgin met him, Sir William Hamilton was a broken man. Palermo was no substitute for his beloved Naples, and, for the first time for over thirty years, he had no collection of antiquities of his own. He was delighted to meet a man who shared his enthusiasm and who intended to carry on the work. Hamilton had taught the world to appreciate a whole new field of classical art, but it was probably the more practical aspects of his successes that appealed to Elgin. Copies of Hamilton's book had passed into the hands of Josiah Wedgwood the potter. The engravings inspired him with new ideas for modern designs on the ancient model and the account in the text set him experimenting to revive the ancient technique.[14] Elgin intended to do for the arts of architecture and of sculpture what Hamilton had already done for pottery, to raise artistic standards in Great Britain.

Elgin discussed with Hamilton his scheme for sending professional artists, architects, and moulders to Athens which he had broached with so little success in England. The first essential, Hamilton advised, was to find a professional artist who would take charge of the whole enterprise. On Hamilton's recommendation Elgin engaged Giovanni Battista Lusieri, a well-known (at that time) Italian landscape painter who was then working at Taormina. Lusieri had enjoyed a successful private practice until the war with France obliged him to look for a permanent patron. He had been engaged by the King as a court painter and had been commissioned to sketch the antiquities of Sicily. With Hamilton's help the King of

Naples gave permission to release Lusieri from his engagement. His salary was to be £200 per annum, all found, and all his work was to be the sole property of Lord Elgin. The engagement was to last as long as Elgin's embassy, which was expected to be a few years at most.[15] In the end it lasted for over twenty years.

Elgin was delighted with Lusieri, 'the first painter in Italy', as he described him, and immediately made arrangements to look for the other men that he wanted.[16] He decided to send William Richard Hamilton (his private secretary, not to be confused with the ambassador) on a recruiting tour to Naples and Rome. Hamilton, therefore, was detached from the party.

The *Phaeton* stayed at Sicily for over a fortnight and everyone enjoyed himself or herself in their own ways. Elgin had long discussions with Nelson about the strategic situation, and with Hamilton about classical antiquities. Lady Elgin joined the social life of the court. McLean and Morier climbed Mount Etna, and the scholars to the party explored the ruins of Taormina and investigated the phenomenon of Scylla and Charybdis. But again, all too soon for poor, seasick, Lady Elgin, the *Phaeton* had to set sail. The ship called at several islands where they shot hares, partridges, and turtles, and eventually arrived at Tenedos, the small island at the entrance to the Dardanelles where ships were obliged to lie at anchor when the wind was unfavourable for the voyage upstream. Once they entered the Dardanelles they knew they would be in the hands of their Ottoman hosts.[17]

Meanwhile, William Richard Hamilton, Elgin's private secretary, and Lusieri his painter, were sent to Naples and then to Rome to try to recruit the other artists that he would need. But the French conquest of Italy had upset the artistic world as much as the political. The museums had been stripped and all the finest works of art sent to the Louvre. The ancient antiquities most famous in the eighteenth century, the Laocoon, Apollo Belvedere, and Venus dei Medici, had been taken, as well as a great many paintings. Artists were in great demand to help with the removals and it was very difficult to find anyone willing to go. Besides, many of the Italian artists had sided with the French during the Revolution and, as a result, Hamilton decided he would have to make inquiries about their political principles as well as their professional ability.

Before he left Elgin had drawn up a note of his requirements for Hamilton's guidance.

1. A man for casts
A painter of figures
To be under Lusieri. Their work to be entirely my property, and their labor
at my disposal—to be if possible at the second table—a fixed salary—say
about £50 per annum.
2. To procure materials for the Painters and casts.[18]

As usual Elgin had underestimated the difficulties and Hamilton
was obliged to depart considerably from his brief. As painter of
figures, he engaged Theodor Iwanovitch, a Calmuck or Tartar
from Central Asia, who was, according to Hamilton, the only man
of taste his nation had ever produced. Theodor had been captured
by the Cossacks as a child and taken as a slave to the court at St
Petersburg. A member of the Russian royal family gave him to his
German mother-in-law while she was on a visit to Russia, and he
went to live at the court of Baden. There his talents as a painter
were recognized and he was sent to Rome to study.[19] When
Hamilton met him his reputation as an artist was already considerable, and his salary was to be £100 per annum, far more than
Elgin had expected. He was known henceforward as 'Lord Elgin's
Calmuck'.

Hamilton had been asked to find an architectural draughtsman
to take measurements and make drawings of ancient buildings,
but he quickly discovered that he was obliged to engage two men,
Balestra who was experienced, and well recommended, and Ittar,
his student. Since Hamilton was partially crippled, he may have had
a natural sympathy with Balestra, who was a hunchback, insisting
to Elgin that Balestra's head and hand were not affected in any
way by his disability. The salary for the two together was to be £125
per annum. For the task of making plaster moulds Hamilton again
found that he had to recruit in pairs. Two men were engaged
at a salary of £100 a year each, and Hamilton was said to be
fortunate to get them even at that price since there were only six
moulders left in all Rome. All the rest were working for the French
in France.

The party of artists led by Hamilton, and also some musicians
whom he had recruited for Elgin's chamber orchestra, arrived at
Sicily in December after a good deal of difficulty in obtaining passports. But at Sicily they were stuck for four months waiting for
transport which was difficult to find in wartime. The architects and
moulders were accordingly set to work on the ruins of Agrigento
and Syracuse.[20]

Eventually, after a much interrupted voyage, Hamilton and Lusieri presented the team to Elgin at Constantinople in May 1800. Elgin found them all acceptable and Lady Elgin was overjoyed.

Mr. Hamilton and his long-expected Caro of Vertioso (is that right?)* arrived yesterday. Only think, he has absolutely brought 6 musicians, 6 painters, and 2 formatori. I will not say anything about them, but this I will say, that I think when my Dad hears the music he will be enraptured; I never heard anything equal to the first violin. He had the band at the Opera in Italy, and as for the painter—oh! Mother!!![21]

The artists and architects—all but Lusieri—were ordered to Athens at once to begin work. But such were the difficulties of transport that they did not arrive until August.

* Not quite. What she meant was 'Carro of Virtuosi'—cartload of artists.

4

Reception at Constantinople

WHEN the idea of Elgin's embassy had first been discussed in November 1798 its main purpose was clear. Sir Sidney Smith had been sent to help the Turks by sea; General Koehler to help by land. Elgin would make a formal treaty of alliance. But in January 1799 Spencer Smith had announced from Constantinople that he and his brother, the joint British Ministers, had already managed to achieve this.[1] It was decided, therefore, that Elgin's mission should be to ratify the treaty and he was given a secondary object, to persuade the Turkish government to open the Black Sea to British shipping and to British trade. But here also Elgin was too late. While he was in Sicily, Spencer Smith had secured this concession as well.[2] It is hardly surprising, therefore, if the Smiths thought that the appointment of Lord Elgin to a new position over their heads was unnecessary as well as unwelcome.

As soon as he heard of Elgin's appointment, Sir Sidney Smith wrote to Lord Grenville. The announcement, he said, had surprised everyone and paralysed the Turks with whom he and his brother were negotiating, by making them feel that all their work would have to be done again. His brother Spencer could no more revert to second place than he himself could become a lieutenant in his ship the *Tigre*. Spencer Smith must be given a new appointment. Perhaps, he suggested, his brother could take over from Sir William Hamilton at the court of Naples?[3] Spencer Smith himself wrote in similar terms to Lord Grenville.[4] But Grenville would not agree— Spencer Smith must stay on as Secretary of Embassy although retaining his honorary rank of Minister Plenipotentiary.

Sir Sidney Smith's first biographer tells a story of the reception of the news of Elgin's appointment at the Porte. It is perhaps a little too neat to be convincing.

When Sir Sidney Smith announced Lord Elgin's appointment to the Grand Vizier he was much grieved on his friend being displaced and asked 'But why should there be any change? we went on very well together; things went on very well.' Sir Sidney told him that the newly appointed ambassador was a great landed proprietor in Scotland, that he had great influence there, and that the English government were in the habit of conciliating such people by the appointment to high situations, as being the best things they had to bestow. The vizier then said 'Ah! then I understand that your government has also got its mountain chiefs to conciliate.' He then asked what he was called; what the name was. Sir Sidney told him the name in Arabic. 'Oh! but', said he, 'Elkin is very bad—it is evil genius—it is *the devil*. How could the English government send us such a person!'[5]

If the Turks were apprehensive about Elgin's arrival they certainly did not show it in their ceremony of welcome. At the Dardanelles lay the *Sultan Selim* of 132 guns, flagship of the Ottoman fleet, built by the French, and on board was the Turkish admiral the Capitan Pasha. After an exchange of salutes with the *Phaeton*, Elgin and his party were received on board. The sofas in the cabins, they found, were covered with yellow silk embroidered in gold, and the walls were decorated with swords and pistols, all embossed in gold. Dinner was served on fine Dresden china and coffee in diamond cups carried on a silver tray. The Capitan Pasha showed his visitors over the ship which impressed even Captain Morris, showing them his Japanese cabinets and candlesticks and two huge bowls of goldfish. Everything was covered with silk and cloth of gold. Then came the presents. The Elgins were given a model of the *Sultan Selim* made of diamonds with rubies and emeralds to represent the guns and flags, then some boxes of perfume, and rich Indian shawls. Twenty-five sheep and six oxen were driven on board the *Phaeton*, and new bread and fresh fruit were loaded into her in quantities far beyond anything the crew could be expected to consume.[6]

At the Dardanelles, Elgin also met the British Military Mission which had been sent out under the command of General Koehler to help the Turks against the French. Koehler had had a disappointing time. When he reached Constantinople the Grand Vizier was still assembling his army to march against the French in Egypt. Koehler immediately drew up a detailed strategic and tactical appreciation of the military situation, proposed an order of march for the Turkish army, and outlined the necessary command structure and division of the troops. With this plan, he was sure, it would not be long before Bonaparte was driven out of Egypt. He presented his plan to the Grand Vizier with a flourish and waited for his admiration. But Koehler had misjudged the Turkish character. The Grand Vizier thanked him politely, gave him all the honours of the court, and did nothing. Soon the Turkish army set off and despite all protests, Koehler and his mission were not even allowed to accompany it. Instead they were sent to the Dardanelles, far from the fighting and from the headquarters, instructed to help repair the shore defences that the French had built some years before.[7]

But although General Koehler was not to go down in history as the architect of victory over Bonaparte, to him does belong the small distinction of having collected the first of the Elgin Marbles. When the *Phaeton* had been held up by contrary winds at Tenedos the embassy party had gone on a day's expedition to the plain of Troy. Lady Elgin described it to her mother:

We took a basket of cold meat and eat our luncheon at 12 o'clock at a village called Sigamon [Sigaeum]; from thence E. and I, Captain Morris, Major Fletcher (who came with letters from General Koehler to E.), Masterman [one of her maids], Carlyle, Hunt, Morier, McLean and the Greek servant, mounted on asses. I could not get my own saddle so I was forced to ride on a Turkish one. We took guides and off we set to the supposed site of ancient Troy; we rode ten miles across the plain, saw camels grazing, and arrived at a romantic spot where they shewed us the ruins of the outside walls. And compleat ruins it is, for there are not two stones left one upon another, only it is visible there has been a great quantity of building. The Learned Men had taken Homer with them, and from examining the spot they agreed there was every appearance of its being the place. There being no twilight we were caught in the dark but only think of my riding 22 miles on a Turkish saddle too, without really being tired.[8]

Elgin was keen to inspect two famous monuments. Outside the village church at Yenicher were two slabs of ancient marble used as seats. The one on the left was a sculptured relief of mothers and children, the other a Greek inscription of unusual interest where the writing read from left to right and then right to left, 'boustrophedon', that is in the manner of an ox ploughing a field, so as to prevent later interpolation. Both these antiquities had been discovered about a hundred years before and had been coveted by European travellers since. Lady Mary Wortley Montagu could have had them for a small bribe in 1718 but the captain of her ship did not have the tackle to remove them. About the middle of the century another English traveller bid 400 Venetian sequins for them but the local inhabitants said they would destroy them rather than let them go, because once before they had sold a fragment and soon afterwards the village was infested with a plague. To show that they regarded the marbles as their own inalienable property, they broke off the heads of four of the five figures on the relief and defaced some of the letters on the inscription.[9] Later Louis XIV's Ambassador had offered a large sum, and so, more recently, had the Comte de Choiseul-Gouffier, both without success.[10]

Hunt was given an explanation by the local priest when he visited Sigaeum sixteen months later:

To explain this [veneration for the antiquities] it may be necessary to mention that during the winter and spring a considerable part of the neighbouring plain is overflowed, thus afflicting the inhabitants with agues; and such is the state of superstition at present among the Greek Christians, that when any disease becomes chronic or beyond the reach of common remedies, it is attributed to daemoniacal possession. The Papas, or priest is then called in to exorcise the patient, which he generally does in the porch of the church, by reading long portions of Scripture over the sufferer; sometimes indeed the whole of the four gospels. In addition to this, at Yenicher, the custom was to roll the patient on the marble stone which contained the Sigean inscription, the characters of which never having been decyphered by any of their Διδάσκαλοι [teachers], were supposed to contain a powerful charm. This practice had, however, nearly obliterated the inscription.[11]

When Elgin asked the Capitan Pasha if he could have these antiquities, his request was at once granted. A man who dispensed diamonds to his guest could hardly refuse a few pieces of battered marbles which were valued only by the ignorant village infidels. A party of soldiers from Koehler's military mission went to Sigaeum, and despite all the tears and protestations of the Greek priests, carried them to the coast, where they were loaded into the *Phaeton*. They eventually found their way to the port of Deptford on the Thames. The story of their medicinal properties was still being told locally twenty years later.[12]

About a week after leaving the Dardanelles the *Phaeton* arrived at Constantinople over two months after she had set sail from Portsmouth. Lord and Lady Elgin came ashore and were taken in golden chairs to the British Palace. Soon afterwards a Turkish officer arrived, accompanied by ninety servants, to present the Ottoman government's compliments on Elgin's arrival. When the flowers and fruit had been piled in the hall, the officer brought in eight trays with fine pieces of Berlin china, each cup filled with different sorts of sweets and covered with a different coloured handkerchief. A few days later another officer arrived with a similar gift from another Turkish dignitary but he only brought thirty servants. So the first fortnight passed with a succession of calls by important Turks all with some gift. Elgin had come well prepared to respond in kind. One officer who called was given a gold watch and chain set in diamonds, another a pair of English pistols, and another a ring set in diamonds. Everyone, including every servant, was given something.

These were only the preliminaries. The main ceremonies were Elgin's two presentations, to the Grand Vizier, and to the Sultan himself. The Turks did not admit women to their ceremonial, but Lady Elgin was determined not to be left out. Fortunately the Grand Vizier himself was away with the army in Syria and the more liberal Kaymacam, who was taking his place at Constantinople, agreed to let her come dressed as a man.[13] Lady Elgin was put down on the list as 'Lord Bruce, a young nobleman'. Lord Bruce was the family name given to the eldest son of the Earl of Elgin. A real Lord Bruce was born five months after the audience.

The audience with the Kaymacam was fixed for Thursday 21 November with a grand ball to follow. As Lady Elgin wrote to her mother the night before:

Is my dear Mother's expectation raised to the highest pitch? and is she dying to know what sort of pelisse [a fur coat which the Turks bestowed on important guests as a sign of welcome and high favour] *Lord Bruce* is in possession of? Know then, that when I had taken leave of you last night, I went to bed but not to sleep; for my brain was filled with Grand Turks, Viziers, Pashas, Pelisses—and then my ball came in for a share to occupy my thoughts. As for Eggy, he slept like a Top! tho' in the evening he had been modest, and affected to be annoyed at having a speech to make and particularly allarmed at *my* hearing him.[14]

The morning of the 21st was wet and windy and the audience was postponed. Much to Lady Elgin's consternation a great quantity of chickens, turkeys, and pastry prepared for the ball had to be thrown away. The audience took place a few days later. A large number of horses and boats were hired and several hundred soldiers and servants to form the ambassadorial procession. They crossed by boat to the walled palace of Topkapi Serai and were received by the Kaymacam Pasha. Elgin had ordered three brocade bags to be made, one to contain his credentials to the Grand Vizier, one for his credentials to the Sultan, and one for the instrument of ratification of the Treaty of Alliance. After short formal speeches of friendship on both sides the bags were handed over. Then Elgin, 'Lord Bruce', and the other members of Elgin's party were draped in their pelisses and introduced to the dignitaries and officials of the court. Elgin was then given a further present—a horse with gold trappings—and the ambassadorial party went in procession back to the British Palace.

The audience with the Sultan took place three days later. This time the foreign embassies at Constantinople were emptied for the day to provide the horses, carriages, boats, grooms, chamberlains, stewards, and soldiers that were required. Some 2,000 janizaries led the procession. The ceremony began before dawn and lasted nearly all day. The Turks insisted on keeping the ambassador's party waiting at a number of places to show their contempt for foreigners. It waited at the gate of the city, again outside the outer gate of the Serai, again outside the inner gate of the Serai, and finally for several hours outside the Sultan's chamber itself. Lord Elgin was also occasionally pushed roughly off the road by the janizaries. The Turks made quite clear, however, that these apparent insults were entirely a matter of etiquette. Yet more pelisses were bestowed and the whole party was given a meal of twenty-six courses, served on silver platters.

At last, with their shoulders and necks held by guards, Lord Elgin, 'Lord Bruce', and eleven others were led through rows of white eunuchs into the audience chamber, the room which Carlyle described as 'the abode of misery, and more frequently perhaps than any other place upon earth, the scene of guilt and horror'.[15] It was a small, dark room furnished solely with jewelled decorations. Even the windows looked out only into aviaries. The throne on which the Grand Seigneur was seated was, Lady Elgin wrote:

like a good honest English bed; the counterpane on which the Monster sat was embroidered all over with immense large pearls. By him was an inkstand of one mass of large Diamonds, on his other side lay his saber studded all over with *Brilliants*. In his turban he wore the famous Aigrette [a jewel from the Sultan's head-dress sometimes given to others as a mark of the highest honour], his robe was of yellow satin with black sable, and in a window there were two turbans covered with diamonds. You can conceive nothing in the Arabian Nights equal to that room.[16]

The short formal speeches were again delivered on both sides, although with some difficulty because Turkish etiquette forbade the

Sultan to cast his eyes on a foreigner or to speak to him directly. Then came the procession home and another ball.

Again Elgin followed the custom of distributing presents. To the Sultan he presented a huge chandelier, a large musical table clock, a gold enamel box, a bezoar stone and 350 Turkish yards of satin, brocade, velvet, and damask. To the Grand Vizier (in absentia) he gave a diamond box and two pieces of ermine worth 1,500 guineas. To the Kaymacam, a diamond box worth 500 guineas; to the Reis Effendi, diamonds and sables worth 1,250 guineas. To another dignitary, diamonds and furs worth 1,000 guineas; to another, a diamond box and ring worth 500 guineas; and so on to all the Turks that he met. He gave clocks, watches, pistols, and furs, but above all he gave pieces of cloth, silk, satin, brocade, velvet, and damask. Altogether he distributed about 1,300 yards of various materials and several hundred members of the court received gifts of one kind or another.[17]

Shortly after the two receptions Elgin submitted a claim to the Foreign Office for expenses incurred in his first fortnight. It totalled about £7,000 and it did not include the cost of about half the material and many of the other gifts which he had brought with him from England at his own expense. In Elgin's instructions on taking up the post of Ambassador Extraordinary to Turkey occurs the following sentence:

At your audience with the Grand Vizier you are to insist on being treated with the same ceremonies and respect that are or have been shewn to the ambassadors of any other crowned heads.[18]

No one could complain that in this respect Elgin had not done his best.

5

The Smith Brothers

IT became clear within days of Elgin's arrival that he and Spencer Smith were never going to agree. Spencer Smith began by declaring that he would help Elgin in every way he could but, whatever his intentions, he frustrated him from the start. Elgin discovered only by degrees how his subordinate was behaving.[1] First he was surprised that there were so few official papers, and, on inquiry, found that Smith had kept some from him. Next he discovered that Smith continued to deal direct with the Turkish government every day without telling him what he was discussing. Then he heard that Smith had ordered British officials in the Levant not to correspond with the ambassador. Then he heard from the Turkish government that Smith had made a complaint to them that Elgin was exceeding his powers in discussing tariffs, a subject on which only the Levant Company had the right to deal. Then the Turks began to give Elgin information in confidence on condition that he did not tell Spencer Smith.

As each of these irregularities came to light Elgin gave Spencer Smith increasingly severe scoldings and several times read over to him the exact terms of his appointment. Each time Spencer Smith promised to do better in future, but the conclusion is inescapable that he was trying deliberately to sabotage Elgin's efforts and restore the old monopoly of the Levant Company in diplomatic matters. Less than a month after Elgin's arrival there occurred an incident which Elgin regarded as the last straw. The Swedish and Danish Ministers and several other foreign representatives protested to him strongly that the British Consul at Aleppo had illegally seized some of their mail. Elgin at once asked Spencer Smith to show him the papers on the subject. After several days' delay Smith sent him a packet of papers accompanied by a note saying it contained all the information about one side of the question; when Elgin had read them he would send him the papers on the other side.[2]

As for Sir Sidney Smith, Elgin already knew and admired him. There were also family ties—Smith was a godson of Lady Elgin's grandmother and he 'always considered her a sort of relation.'[3] As soon as he arrived in Constantinople Elgin sent him a long friendly letter announcing the start of his embassy, a polite hint that matters would now be different. But Sir Sidney was no more willing to give up his place than his brother. The first thing that alerted Elgin was to see a letter signed by Sidney Smith as 'Minister Plenipotentiary' although he knew perfectly well that his diplomatic commission had ended with Elgin's arrival.[4] Then Elgin heard from the Turks what lay behind it.

After the escape of Bonaparte the Grand Vizier had taken the field with a huge Turkish army and was marching on Egypt. General Kléber, Bonaparte's successor, realizing that the French position was untenable, started to make secret overtures about the possibility of peace terms. Sir Sidney Smith, cruising in his ship the *Tigre* off the coast of Egypt, and seeing a chance of further fame, invited representatives of the French on board to discuss a possible evacuation of Egypt. Whether he had the legal power to do this is doubtful—governments seldom entrust questions of peace and war to naval captains however successful—but by the time of Elgin's arrival Smith had led the French to believe that he was negotiating with the authority not only of the British but also of the Ottoman governments. When the Turks protested to Elgin, he immediately sent his private secretary, Morier, to be his official link with the Grand Vizier's army and gave Sir Sidney Smith a sharp reprimand for exceeding his powers. He did not however—and this was his biggest mistake—forbid the negotiations explicitly, and to the Turks he could only apologize for the insubordination which he was unable to prevent.[5]

To complete his discomfiture Elgin had to deal with General Koehler. Elgin had insisted as soon as he arrived that the British Military Mission should be deployed on more active service than repairing the Dardanelles forts and General Koehler had returned to Constantinople. However his manner had made him unpopular with the Turks. He styled himself 'General Officer Commanding His Majesty's Land Forces in the Ottoman Dominions' although his force of seventy-six men was already depleted by disease, and, as Elgin said, 'he claimed to himself the respect paid to a Buonaparte and a Suvarov'.

Elgin reported all his difficulties in his official dispatches to Lord

Grenville. But after only six weeks of frustration he decided that his position was intolerable. He wrote privately to Grenville asking him to remove Spencer Smith and reprimand Sidney Smith. 'Seeing Englishmen in authority in Turkey,' he wrote, 'takes away all delight in reading Don Quixote.'[6] The details of all the bickering and jealousy were reported to Lord Grenville not only by the letters of complaint from Elgin but from letters protesting their own sides of the story from Spencer Smith, from Sir Sidney Smith, and from Koehler. At first he did not pay much attention, and it was mainly uncertainty about the status of the various British authorities in the Levant that led to one of the most disastrous muddles of the war.

At the end of January Sir Sidney Smith's negotiations with the French about terms to evacuate Egypt suddenly achieved success. At the Syrian town of El Arish, where the Grand Vizier was encamped with the Turkish army, he concluded, without reference to his superiors, the Convention of El Arish. Under the terms of this agreement the French army was to leave Egypt, neither victors nor conquered, conveyed back to France in British ships on condition that they did not fight against Turkey or Great Britain in the current war. Egypt was to be restored to the Turks. General Kléber ratified the convention on behalf of the French within a few days. On 16 February Elgin wrote to Lord Grenville:

I have infinite satisfaction in informing your lordship that on 24th ult. a capitulation was signed in the Grand Vizier's camp at El Arish, in consequence of which the French are to evacuate Egypt within the space of three months.[7]

The success of Sir Sidney Smith's negotiations had led Elgin to overlook the fact that Smith had entered into them without proper authority. Elgin also wrote at once to Nelson asking him to provide ships to help evacuate the French.[8] Soon afterwards he began to issue passports for the safe conduct of the French in Egypt back to France.

On 24 February, however, Elgin received an official dispatch from Lord Grenville dated 13 December, that is over a month before the Convention of El Arish was signed. This dispatch instructed Elgin in the strongest possible language that no arrangement was to be entered into with the French except on condition that they surrendered themselves as prisoners of war. The parole system, Grenville wrote, had been broken so often by the French that in future it would be forbidden. The dispatch also declared that precisely similar instructions had been sent to Lord Keith, the naval commander-in-chief in the Mediterranean, for passing on to Sir Sidney Smith. This dispatch rendered the Convention of El Arish null and void and invalidated the passports that Elgin had begun to issue: the whole agreement to clear Egypt of the French had been illegal from the start.

As soon as he received the fatal dispatch Elgin rushed to tell the Ottoman government and to try to arrange a graceful withdrawal from the convention. But, as luck would have it, it was the feast of Bayram and the Turks insisted that no business could be conducted until it was over. And so another vital fortnight passed before Elgin saw the Kaymacam Pasha.[9] When at last Elgin was given an audience and had explained what had happened the reaction of the Turks can be guessed. Sir Sidney Smith, they said, was a 'Minister Plenipotentiary' who had taken the initiative in promoting the negotiations. Poor Elgin could only confess that Smith had acted without instructions and that he was unable to control him.[10]

The Turks proposed that the arrangements for carrying out the Convention of El Arish should go ahead, but that when the French were safely aboard British ships on their way home, the convention should be disowned and the French seized as prisoners of war. Elgin, whose respect for the code of honour of international relations among European nations was exceptional even for his own times, refused even to discuss it.[11] But somehow a hint of it appeared in the papers of his private secretary Morier which later fell into the hands of the French.[12] On 28 March, to complete the muddle, Lord Grenville wrote again to Elgin. The British government, he said, had just heard of the Convention of El Arish; although it was quite contrary to the policy laid down in the dispatch of 13 December, they had decided to accept it after all.[13]

It was too late. Events in Egypt had taken their inexorable course. Soon after the ratification, the Grand Vizier with his large army had marched into Egypt to take over Cairo from the French in accordance with the convention. He was almost at Cairo when Lord Keith, the British commander-in-chief, received his copy of the British government's instructions of 13 December. Having had no instructions to the contrary from Elgin, he acted at once. On 18 March he wrote simply to Kléber that he could not now assent to any terms other than unconditional surrender. Kléber's reaction was equally straightforward. Within forty-eight hours he countermanded all orders about evacuation, and notified the Grand Vizier that the armistice was at an end. On 20 March he suddenly attacked the Turkish army, defeated them utterly, and drove the stragglers out of Egypt. Small parties of the Grand Vizier's army found their way back to Jaffa but large numbers of them were killed, taken prisoner, or died of thirst in the desert. The French were again in full possession of Egypt.

The muddle over the Convention of El Arish prolonged the war in Egypt for another fifteen months. Many thousands of French, British, Turks, and of course Egyptians were to be killed in the subsequent fighting and thousands more died of disease. In the end, the terms on which the French did eventually leave Egypt were almost exactly those which had been agreed at El Arish in the first place.

For Elgin himself the results of the fiasco were not as bad as one might have expected. He seems to have successfully persuaded the British government that he had done all he could and that he was not responsible, emerging from the episode with his reputation largely unscathed. But there was one man who did not exonerate Elgin so lightly. Napoleon Bonaparte became convinced that the convention and its subsequent disavowal was an elaborate plot personally engineered by Elgin. He was sure that Elgin wanted to deceive the French and seize them on their passage to France: there was even a story that the French were to be massacred as soon as they came into British power.[14] Bonaparte formed a strong personal hatred for Elgin whom he later described as 'one of the greatest enemies of the nation'.[15] He convinced himself that it was Elgin who caused the ill-treatment of the French prisoners in Constantinople and began to blame him for all the reverses of his Egyptian policy.[16] It is even said that he believed that Elgin sent the information that led to the destruction of his fleet at the battle of the Nile—an event that occurred fifteen months before Elgin arrived at Constantinople.[17]

But life at Constantinople was not all frantic diplomacy. There were the grand fêtes, the parties, the balls, the concerts, and the whist, perpetual whist. Spencer Smith later wrote a book on the game.[18] The missions of the foreign powers entertained one another in turn in their sumptuous palaces and vied with one another in their magnificence. Lady Elgin constantly complained of having to entertain large parties of 'hottentots', but she seems to have enjoyed it well enough. Only on Sundays were there no parties— alone of the missions the Elgins insisted that there should be no card-playing or dancing on that day. Lady Elgin struck up a friendship with the sister of the Capitan Pasha and began to pay her frequent visits. When the Capitan Pasha was at home his sister kept house for him; when he was away she served her turn in the Sultan's harem. Lady Elgin went both to the Capitan's and to the harem. On one occasion Elgin found her dressed in Turkish costume with the other ladies when he called to see the Capitan on business. And she began to teach the ladies of the harem the delights of Scottish country dancing. Very soon Lady Elgin was a great favourite of the Turks and the object of great jealousy among the other foreign ladies at Constantinople.

In April the Elgin's first child was born, and being a boy received the family title of Lord Bruce. Shortly afterwards Lady Elgin's mother and father, Mr and Mrs Nisbet, arrived from Scotland to stay with their daughter for a holiday. As they had promised at the time of her marriage they had made the long and dangerous journey only four months after their daughter left. They were to stay at Constantinople and in Greece for nearly a year before returning home.

Elgin himself, despite the El Arish episode, became more and more popular with the Turks. Further presents were heaped upon him—horses, jewellery, furs, fabrics, and a 200-ton yacht for his private use if he wanted to explore the Greek Islands. The Capitan Pasha set a new precedent in Turkish etiquette by himself calling at the British Palace to play whist, an occasion captured by the pencil of Lusieri, and other Ottoman officials began to abandon the attitude of arrogance towards the British which the court had previously insisted upon as a matter of routine.[19] As an ambassador Elgin was highly successful, but his days were long and tiring. He worked hard, tolerating with good grace the lengthy ceremoniousness of Turkish business, and fighting helplessly against Smith and the Levant Company merchants. For weeks on end he struggled at his business leaving Lady Elgin very much on her own.

Contrary to his expectation the climate of Constantinople did not help his bad health but made it worse. He suffered severely, as did Lady Elgin, from the fevers which regularly swept the city. Worst of all he contracted a severe skin disease of the face and an extremely painful tic. As Lady Elgin wrote to her mother:

I am very miserable about Elgin. I dread his nose will be marked. As yet the doctors do not think the bone is touched and they hope to prevent it but they do not say they positively can save it . . . I trust the flesh alone is cut and that it may heal.[20]

The disease ate into his face until he lost the whole of the lower part of his nose.[21] He was monstrously disfigured for the rest of his life.

Elgin had suffered from smallpox while a child, and all his life he was to devote great efforts to encouraging the new invention of inoculation against the disease, but smallpox, if survived, seldom recurs, and Elgin's enthusiasm for smallpox prevention may have been something of a show. In his time it was regarded as part of the normal education of a boy of his high rank that he should consort with prostitutes, both at school and on his visits abroad, and as a young man Elgin had built something of a reputation for sexual promiscuity.[22] At the time of his engagement to Mary Nisbet, he was already showing signs of his so-called rheumatism, and the wedding service was halted for a while to allow the bride an opportunity to say something important to the officiating bishop, although in the event she kept her silence.[23] The reports of Elgin consuming large quantities of mercury at Constantinople suggest that he knew that the illness he was suffering from was syphilis, a disease which frequently attacks the nose.[24] Lady Elgin too is said to have suffered badly from the asthma and rheumatism which was how Elgin's illness was described.

Elgin's first son, Lord Bruce, born in 1800 when, it appears, the attacks of Elgin's disease were particularly strong, seemed for a while to be normal. By his teens, however, he had developed signs of what was referred to as epilepsy.[25] By his early twenties he needed continuous care as the attacks became more frequent and more violent, and he was to die at the age of 40, to the relief of his family, after a long period of what was described as tortured imbecility.[26] Although the symptoms of hereditary syphilis usually make themselves apparent at an early age, Lord Bruce too may have been a victim of his father's syphilis, or have been regarded as such by Lady Elgin and others. There is no recorded evidence of hereditary illness among the other children of the marriage, and the eldest son of the second marriage, who was to outlive his brother and succeed to the title, was to pursue a public career of extraordinary vigour.

Despite the diplomatic successes, Elgin's relations with the Smith brothers did not improve. Sir Sidney Smith continued to see himself as the one man who could bring about a settlement with France. Lord Keith, the naval commander-in-chief, kept a close watch on him and Koehler was sent to the Grand Vizier's army partly to act as a counterweight. Elgin's private secretary, Morier, went to and fro between Constantinople and Syria keeping Elgin informed of what Sir Sidney was up to.

Spencer Smith was harder to deal with. He could not get used to being in second place and the long tale of disobedience, intrigue, and spite was soon repeated. In March there was a complete breakdown. Elgin refused to see him altogether and would not even correspond with him. He wrote again and again to Grenville asking for Smith to be removed and the arrangement with the Levant Company to be terminated. In May speaking terms were resumed as a result of a stiff letter from Grenville to Smith, but the rapprochement did not last long. There were virtually two independent British Missions at Constantinople and the British community in the Levant sided with one or the other as they chose.[27]

At last the situation at Constantinople became so notorious and Elgin pressed so hard that in October it was discussed by the British Cabinet. The first words of common sense on the whole matter came from Dundas. 'Either Lord Elgin or the Smiths should come away,' he wrote to Grenville, 'for the public service never can go on with any effect or even safety in the hands of such jarring and discordant instruments.'[28]

It was decided to leave Sir Sidney Smith but to ask the Levant Company to recall Spencer Smith and hand over responsibility for their affairs to Elgin. At long last, in January 1801, to Elgin's intense relief, Spencer Smith received his order of dismissal. He was replaced, at Elgin's request, by 'a very pleasant lively man and a most capital whist player' called Alexander Straton.[29] On his way home Spencer Smith made a tour of Levant Company establishments and paid a visit to his brother's naval squadron. Everywhere he went he proclaimed that he had been done down by the wicked Earl of Elgin and spread as much slander about him as he could.[30] Shortly after his return to England he entered Parliament. Elgin had made his second enemy, not perhaps to be compared with Napoleon Bonaparte, but dangerous nevertheless. Smith departed from the scene with bad grace and time did not soften his anger.

6

Work Begins at Athens

IN August 1800 Lord Elgin's artists arrived in Athens to begin the work that was to improve the arts in Great Britain. They paid their respects, with the usual presents, to the Ottoman authorities and established themselves in lodgings ready for a long stay. The British Consul Logotheti took them under his protection.[1]

Athens was then a small town, and like many in the Ottoman Empire, inhabited by a mixed population drawn from the many religions and cultures of the eastern Mediterranean.[2] About half the population of about 10,000 were Greek-speaking Orthodox Christians; a quarter, Turkish Muslims. Most of the Turks spoke Greek as their main language, with many knowing no Turkish.[3] Among the others were ethnic Albanians who divided between both main religions, plus some Muslims of African origin, Jews, and Roman Catholics. There were half a dozen families of western European nationalities, 'Franks' as they were collectively called, mainly moneylenders long settled in the town, and, to an increasing extent, travelling gentlemen, visiting artists, and officers and sailors from the naval squadrons of the warring European nations.

The Athens of 1800, illustrated in Plate 2, probably contained no more than thirteen hundred houses in all, mostly clustered on the northern and eastern slopes of the Acropolis.[4] The town was entirely enclosed by a ten feet high wall which had been hurriedly built in 1778 after it was plundered by a roving armed gang of a few hundred Muslim Albanians.[5] A Western traveller recorded that a brisk walk round the whole perimeter wall took less than forty-five minutes. The Acropolis was nominally a military fortress but its few guns were dismounted and mainly for show. The few dozen soldiers of the garrison lived with their families in houses on the Acropolis so badly built that some crumbled whenever there was a heavy shower of rain.[6] They were rarely paid, and seldom troubled by military duties. Athens, with its palm trees, its camels, and its mosques, was an oriental town, the forty-third city of European Turkey.[7] The size of the population had scarcely changed since the town was surrendered to the Ottoman invaders in 1456.[8]

For most of the three and a half centuries of Ottoman rule Athens had been the property of one of the lesser dignitaries of the Ottoman court, the Chief of the Black Eunuchs, and its revenues had gone to support the Imperial harem at Constantinople. Most Western travellers, who mainly relied for their information on books which were long out of date, still believed that Athens was owned by the Chief of the Black Eunuchs, a thought which gave a special poignancy to their meditations on ancient civilization engulfed by eastern barbarism. In 1760 Athens lost its privileged position. Henceforth a lifetime right to certain of its tax revenues was sold by the Ottoman government for a lump sum to a rich private individual Turk who, in effect, was buying an annuity.[9] The successive owners then deputed the actual collection to a local governor, or Voivode, who also normally had to pay a lump sum for the privilege.

Hadji Ali Haseki, the first Voivode appointed under the privatized system, ruled in Athens from 1775 until 1795. The wall which he built to protect the town from bandits and corsairs also made it easier to control the movements of the local population and to tax their moveable goods. Haseki, who took 10 per cent of the revenues he collected on behalf of his master in Constantinople, is said to have hanged, drowned, poisoned, or otherwise put to death several prominent local Turks and Greeks who opposed him, as well as imprisoning others, in a long career of shameless extortion. He built a fine official residence for himself and his harem, and, by taking into his possession lands seized by confiscations, he built up a private property containing 12,000 olive trees which he worked by forced labour. Petitions of complaint which were made from time to time to the Ottoman government in Constantinople by the Turks and Greeks of Athens were listened to sympathetically but, in practice, with a weak central government, protests usually simply brought heavy reprisals on the heads of the petitioners. At last in 1795, when about half the population had left Athens to take refuge in the surrounding villages, an order arrived from Constantinople requiring Haseki to go into exile in Cos, where, shortly afterwards, an executioner arrived to cut off his head. Haseki's head was publicly exposed at Constantinople as a warning to others, one of the few ways by which the Ottoman authorities could proclaim its waning power.

By the time Lord Elgin's artists arrived in 1800 the worst extortions had ceased, civic stability was restored, and the economy had begun to recover. The six gates in Haseki's wall, formerly closed at night, were removed altogether. The properties in Athens and in the surrounding countryside which Haseki had seized were gradually auctioned off by the state. Many of them were bought by absentee Turks, including the Grand Vizier of the day and the Sultan's mother, and they seem to have taken an interest in preventing a recurrence of over-exploitation.[10] But although by the time Elgin's artists arrived, the more normal, more lax, standards of Ottoman administration had been re-established, everyone in Athens, Turk and Greek, governors as well as governed, could remember the terrible decades which had recently ended. They also knew that, in an empire where the central authority was always weak and uncertain, such times could easily return.

The Imperial Ottoman power was represented by two Turkish officials, the Voivode or governor, and the Disdar, the military governor of the Acropolis. The Cadi, or Judge, administered the Muslim civil law and the Mufti the Muslim religious law over the minority Turkish population. The majority Christian Greek population normally enjoyed a good deal of autonomy in both civil and religious matters. Tax collection was in the hands of twelve local Greek archons, whose posts seem to have become almost hereditary in a handful of families, and who were an essential part of the Ottoman administrative system. The Archbishop of Athens, with responsibilities for education and welfare as well as social matters, exercised extensive powers over the personal lives of the Christian clergy and Christian peoples, with the right to impose fines, to inflict the bastinado, and to impose any penalty other than death on his own authority. The Archbishop, whose palace was bigger and more impressive than that of the Voivode, maintained his own episcopal prison.

Under their separate regimes, the communities mixed freely. The Turks of Athens, many travellers remarked, were exceptionally courteous, and the Voivode had a Greek wife. France, Great Britain, and a few other European countries appointed consuls, normally local Greeks, to help with the modest export trade in olives, to look after travellers, and to keep their respective flags flying. As visitors from western Europe became more frequent, the consuls had standing arrangements for accommodating them in local houses. The French were usually able to find accommodation with the Capuchin Friars who had been established in the town since the seventeenth century. The widow Macri, favoured by the British, let out a sitting-room with two bedrooms opening on to a courtyard with lemon trees. Her three daughters were to be commemorated in the travel accounts of innumerable visitors including Lord Byron.

Among the modern houses of Athens, with their pretty tiled roofs and vined gardens, there stood out, in sharp contrast, the remains of its magnificent ancient buildings. On the Acropolis, the rocky hill that rises in the middle of the Attic plain, and which had been from the earliest times both the fortress and the religious centre of the people of Athens, stood the ruins of three buildings of the fifth century, the Parthenon, the Erechtheion, and the Propylaea. In the lower town stood another monument of the classical period, now known to be a temple of Hephaistos, but at the time commonly known as the Theseion or, in its Latinized version, the Theseum. Also to be seen were several well-preserved monuments of a later date, the Octagonal Tower of Andronikos Cyrrhestes, commonly known as the Tower of the Winds, the Choragic Monument of Lysicrates, commonly known as the Lantern of Demosthenes, and the Monument of Philopappos. The arch built by the Emperor Hadrian in the first century to mark off the city of Hadrian from the city of Theseus still stood, as did some pillars of the later gigantic temple to Olympian Zeus begun by Hadrian and completed by Antoninus, the remains of an aqueduct, and other monuments of the Roman period.[11] The remains of the ancient Stadium and of the Odeion of Herodes Atticus were visible, although they were as yet unexcavated, and there were occasional signs of other ancient buildings peeping above ground.

The exact status of the various surviving ancient ruins in Athens under the local law in Lord Elgin's time is not known, but since the time of the Ottoman conquest the whole Acropolis area appears to have been regarded as a publicly owned military complex over which the Sultan and the Ottoman government had the sole and final legal authority.[12] Direct responsibility rested with the Voivode and the Disdar. Other ancient buildings and sites had a variety of owners, public and private. The Theseum was an Orthodox church. The Monument of Lysicrates belonged to an order of French Capuchins who used it as a storeroom and library. The Tower of the Winds was the holy place of the Whirling Dervishes.

The Turks living on the Acropolis built their houses, gardens, and fortifications round about the ruins or made use of them as it suited their purpose. Inside the Parthenon was a small mosque, and the spaces between the pillars of the Propylaea were half bricked up to provide castellation for the guns. The Erechtheion contained a gunpowder magazine. Everywhere it was obvious that for centuries the ancient ruins had been a main source of building materials. Slabs of crisp-cut marble were built into the rude modern walls, and here and there pieces of sculpture could be seen among the fortifications. Many of the houses in the town had an ancient fragment set above their door or standing in their garden.

It was the Parthenon which exercised the strongest fascination for all Western visitors to Athens. Although the main outlines of the building's history and present state were known from accounts in ancient authors and from reports by modern travellers, it was only as a result of the researches of the Frenchman Le Roy, whose *Les Ruines des plus beaux Monuments de la Grèce*, was published in Paris in 1758, and of James Stuart and Nicholas Revett, the second volume of whose more detailed *The Antiquities of Athens* was published in 1787, that western Europeans had become aware of how extraordinary a monument it was and how much of it still survived. When Lord Elgin's artists arrived in 1800, they were reasonably well informed, but they knew far less than is available now as a result of two intervening centuries of accumulating modern research. Apart from what had been collected in *The Antiquities of Athens*, they had little knowledge of the history of Athens and of its monuments during the long Byzantine, Frankish, and Ottoman centuries. Their main sources for the topography of Greece continued to be Pausanias, who wrote in the second century of the Christian era, and Sir George Wheler, whose *Journey into Greece* was first published in 1682 and never reprinted; and these remained the standard works available in England.[13]

In the year 490 before the Christian era, and again in 480, the city states of mainland Greece had been invaded by the armies of Darius and Xerxes, kings of the huge Persian empire. During 480, when the people of Athens abandoned their city, the Acropolis sanctuary was occupied, burned, and desecrated by the invading armies. All the existing temples, statues, dedications, and other monuments, including an unfinished temple to Athena which was then under construction, were thrown down and destroyed, the heat caused by the burning of the wooden scaffolding splitting much of the marble beyond repair.[14]

After the war, and the final defeat and retreat of the Persians, the city states of Hellas, including Athens, left their holy places desolate for a generation. They had, according to a later account, sworn not to rebuild their temples for thirty years, but there were practical military and economic as well as religious reasons for the postponement. The first priority was survival. There were no resources for non-essential works. When the broken marble from the older temples was used to rebuild the walls of the Acropolis, care was taken that the column drums could be seen from the city as a perpetual reminder, visible to the present day, of what Athens had suffered. When the time came to rebuild, rather than restoring the older buildings in replica or reviving the designs for new buildings started before the invasion, the Athenian authorities, under the leadership of Pericles, decided to rebuild the whole sacred area afresh, treating the Acropolis as a unity, and making use, whenever possible, of scattered pieces of marble from earlier ruined structures.

The Temple of Athena Parthenos, the Temple of Minerva as she was usually called in the Latinized version by visitors from the West, was built between the years 447 and 438, as a dedication to the eponymous protecting deity of the city of Athens. The building was constructed in the Doric order of architecture, with a porch at each end which leads into two chambers of unequal size. The starkness of the Doric style was softened by fluted columns and many decorative features. The larger room in the temple was the site of the cult statue, a huge image of Athena, made from gold and ivory by the sculptor Phidias. The other room, known as the Parthenon, 'the Room of the Maiden' or 'the Room of the Maidens', was used to house the Athenian treasury, and the name Parthenon was later applied to the whole building.[15]

Despite its appearance of regularity, no two columns of the Parthenon were the same, and numerous other refinements were included in the architectural design of the building in order to enhance the effect on viewers. Some of these refinements were noticed in the eighteenth century, others in the nineteenth, and others have only recently been discovered as a result of the restoration works which began in the 1980s.

The Parthenon was built throughout of local marble from the ancient quarries on Mount Pentelikon the remains of which are still visible on the side of the mountain. Blocks of marble were selected, cut, transported to the Acropolis, and carved or finished on site, before being hoisted into place. According to Plutarch, writing five hundred years later but with access to sources now lost, the sculptor Phidias was in charge of the overall programme and, we may confidently assume, of the overall design. The building was designed by the architects Ictinos and Callicrates.[16]

Substantial fragments of the financial accounts, which were carved in marble and set up in a public place on the Acropolis for anyone to inspect, were not known in Lord Elgin's time.[17] For such a huge project, involving the skilled carving of innumerable pieces of marble to extremely fine specifications, many masons, sculptors, painters, gilders, and other artists must have been employed, recruited, we can guess, from all over the Hellenic world. The whole project was completed with astonishing speed.

By the time the decision to build was taken, the Persian menace had been beaten back. The city of Athens had put herself at the head of an alliance of other cities, the Delian League, which pooled their resources to protect the Greek cities of the Aegean against invasion and to carry out raids into Persian-held territory. By the 460s the allied cities had become, in effect, part of an Athenian empire, prevented by Athenian military and naval power from resigning from the League, and forced to see their tax revenues centralized in a treasury in the Acropolis of Athens in accordance with tribute lists.[18]

The main focus of attention for all visitors to the Parthenon was the cult statue and the various sacred objects and dedications preserved inside, all of which are completely lost. The sculptures with which the Parthenon was decorated on the outside of the building commemorated the local traditions of the city preserved in its local myths. The illustration on p. 50 shows where they were placed. The largest and most visible were in the pediments, the triangular spaces at either end of the building. Originally there were probably about fifty large statues, carved in the round and hoisted into place when they were complete. Pausanias records that the east pediment showed the birth of Athena—Athena springing fully armed from the head of Zeus was probably its central event. The west pediment, Pausanias records, illustrated the contest of Athena

PEDIMENT

METOPES

FRIEZE

The Sculptural Decoration of the Parthenon

and Poseidon for the land of Athens and Attica. The two foundation myths which the pedimental compositions commemorated
were, to the Athenians of the fifth century, not only very ancient
but, we can be sure, directly relevant to a proud people who
claimed to be autochthonous, that is sprung from the native earth
(unlike other Hellenic cities which had been colonized by settlers
from other places in historical times), and whose economic pros-
perity manifestly depended both on the land and on the sea.[19]

The columns of the building supported a marble beam, or architrave, on which rested a series of panels known as metopes sculpted in high relief. Since the carving of the metopes could not have been done when the blocks were in place, far above the ground and under an overhanging cornice, the metopes must have been carved before the cornice and the roof were completed, and then hoisted into place. Not only artistically but structurally the metopes were thus a fully integral part of the building.

The subject of the metopes is different on each side. Those on the east represent the battle between the Gods of Olympus and the Giants who tried unsuccessfully to overthrow them. On the west side are scenes of the struggle between Greeks and opponents wearing oriental dress, probably Amazons. On the north side the main subject appears to have been scenes from the fall of Troy; and on the south, battles between men and the mythical half-men, half-horse figures known as centaurs. The four subjects were favourite decoration of religious buildings elsewhere in the Hellenic world. They are all mythic celebrations of the ongoing struggle of the civilized Hellenes against oriental barbarism, highly topical to a people who had only narrowly survived the Persian invasions of 490 and 480.

Under the ceiling of the colonnade and running round all four sides was a continuous sculptured frieze carved in low relief. By carving each slab a little more deeply at the top than at the bottom, so that the frieze, in effect, leans forward, the ancient sculptors helped the viewer on the ground to see it more clearly despite the sharp angle of vision. Some features in the sculpture, such as wreaths and horses' bridles, were made from metal, others added in paint, all of which made the frieze more easily seen and understood by viewers on the ground. The whole composition, like other special parts of the building, was probably painted in bright colours against a blue background.

The fact that paint was used on ancient temples was first remarked upon by Stuart and Revett in the 1750s and made public in the first volume of *The Antiquities of Athens* published in 1762. The discovery caused surprise, disbelief, and disappointment among many Western artists and connoisseurs who for long afterwards, and against mounting evidence to the contrary, continued to assume that 'classical' sculptures were made of plain white marble, with the eyes vacant, as appeared from the famous ancient statues which had been shown since the Renaissance in the museums in Italy.[20]

The long length of the frieze relative to its height, about 160 metres long but less than one metre high, limited the choice of subject. Some other temples of the time showed random battle scenes, which could be made to fill any space, but the designers of the Parthenon chose to illustrate a procession which they conceived, designed, and executed as a single unity. At the west end the viewer saw the preparations for the procession which can then be seen moving along both the long north and south sides to meet at what is evidently the central event which takes place on the east frieze. Both the north and the south friezes showed numerous horsemen and chariots, some of whom are naked and others wearing helmets and other indications that they are soldiers. Male figures lead animals for sacrifice, mainly cattle but also sheep, and there are other distinctive groups in the procession, women carrying trays and pitchers, musicians, elders, stewards, and other participants in what is evidently a great festival involving all the people of Athens, old and young, citizens and residents from abroad, men and women.

At the time when the Parthenon was built, visitors to the Acropolis approached the sanctuary along a narrow steep road which zigzagged up the hill. It then led through the Propylaea, a large marble ceremonial gateway, to the open ground of the Acropolis. The approach ensured that visitors to the Acropolis would see the Parthenon as soon as they passed through the Propylaea and not before. If they looked up at the frieze, they would see the preparations for the procession on the west frieze and then be able to follow it with the eye, as it quickened its pace, along the north frieze, and then slowed down. As visitors rounded the corner to approach the building by the east doorway they would then see the central event above the main doorway.

Seated figures, who are carved far larger than the other figures on the frieze, represent the gods and goddesses of the Olympian Pantheon. They are arranged in two groups. On the viewer's left, in the place of honour sits Zeus on his throne opposite Hera who draws back her veil as the sign that she is his bride. Hermes is identified by his travelling hat and herald's staff, and Dionysos, Demeter, Ares, and the Iris, the winged messenger, by traditional iconographic attributes readily recognized at the time. On the other side the place of honour is taken by Athena, for it is her temple, on this occasion shown without her helmet but with her identifying aegis on her lap. Next to her is Hephaistos, the long stick which he uses as a crutch reminding viewers that he was lame, and Poseidon, Apollo, Artemis, and Aphrodite with Eros. Some standing male figures on either side of the two groups of gods, who are carved larger than the other human figures but smaller than the gods are evidently also of particular importance. They probably represent the eponymous heroes of the tribes into which the citizens were divided for voting and other purposes, the use of visual representation of myth again emphasizing that the whole free citizenry of Athens are present and actively participating. The gods seem strangely indifferent to the solemn event being acted out in their presence, turning their backs and refusing, it would seem, even to let their gaze rest upon it. Maybe they are far away on Olympus, unseen by the men and women and indifferent to what is going on.

The central scene consists of five figures more widely spaced than any others on the frieze so giving a sense of solemnity and stillness after all the bustle and movement of the procession. A photograph of the central slabs as they appear today is at Plate 1. An older man, dressed as a priest, appears to be presenting a large folded cloth to a young boy or girl who is dressed in a loose-fitting dress which reveals his or her nakedness. An adult women faces towards two younger women each of whom appears to be carrying a long-legged cushioned stool or a tray with legs. The battered condition of the sculptures, with the loss of some features which were added in metal or picked out with paint, makes it difficult to be certain what these sacred objects are, and the damage may give a misleading impression to the modern eye.

No ancient author has left an explanation of what the central event is which the frieze commemorates. In the 1787 volume of *The Antiquities of Athens* Stuart and Revett conjectured that it represents the Great Panathenaic festival, which was held in Athens every four years, during which the cult statue was ceremonially robed in a new garment or 'peplos'. It was a brilliant conjecture and has been accepted for so long that, until recently, most writers on the Parthenon have forgotten that it is only a conjecture. There are, however, severe difficulties with this explanation. For example, the events shown on the frieze do not match what is known of the Panathenaia from ancient authors. There is no trace of the ship which was drawn to the temple as part of the procession. The frieze shows horsemen, but no foot-soldiers who were the foundation of the city's citizen army, and there are other problems. Under the Panthenaia theory, the two widely spaced female figures can only be explained as attendants, and it is hard to believe that the designers and artists of the frieze, whose skill in packing figures and meanings into limited space has never been equalled, decided to allot nearly half the central scene to, whatever their importance in the ceremony were, essentially minor temple servants moving furniture. And there is another worry. If the Parthenon frieze represents a fifth-century ceremony, it would be the only ancient temple to break the strict convention that sacred buildings are decorated with scenes from the myths which lay at the heart of Hellenic religion.

In recent years Professor Joan Connelly has suggested an alternative, and to many scholars, a more convincing, explanation of the Parthenon frieze.[21] The event being commemorated, she suggests, is the sacrifice of the daughters of Erechtheus. According to the local Athenian legend, King Erechtheus of Athens, faced with an invasion by barbarian Thracians, had been told by the oracle at Delphi that if the city was to be saved he must sacrifice one of his daughters. His three daughters had sworn that if one should die the others would share her fate.[22] The daughters submit themselves to death, not reluctantly but willingly and proudly. If the men of Athens give their lives as soldiers, the women too, so they proclaim, can put city before self. In the ensuing battle the Athenians won, but Erechtheus was killed. The central scene of the frieze, Connelly argues, shows Erechtheus dressed as a priest, and accompanied by his wife, about to perform the sacrifice of his three daughters. The piece of cloth is a shroud, and the other daughters bring their shrouds on head trays. As was a convention in Greek art and literature, the horror of the event is made more bearable by showing the anticipatory moment rather than the act of violence itself. In Greek religion the immortal gods may not look on human death, which is a pollution. The turning away of the gods which appears to the modern eye as indifference may signify the presence, or the imminence, of human death.

The Erechtheus story is well documented as one of the founding myths of Athens which symbolized and reinforced its civic cohesiveness. It is a common theme in Athenian art. The tomb of King Erechtheus was located in the Erechtheion near by, which, most unusually, shared an altar with the Parthenon, and the visitor to the Parthenon passed between the two. Human sacrifice is intrinsic to Greek religion and myth—Iphigeneia is a direct parallel—and, even if the story was no longer credited in literal terms by the sophisticated citizens of fifth-century Athens, it was a common theme in their drama, an archetypal narrative which could be endlessly reused and reinterpreted to give meaning to current situations.

As it happens, a substantial number of new fragments of a lost play by Euripides, the *Erechtheus*, have been recovered from the papyrus used for wrapping an Egyptian mummy in the Sorbonne. They were first published by Professor Colin Austin in 1968, and published again along with the fragments known from other sources in 1995.[23] Connelly's suggested explanation for the Parthenon frieze does not depend upon the evidence of the play, but the new material provides further direct evidence of the religious and cultural attitudes of the fifth-century Athenians who commissioned, paid for, and built the Parthenon, and who then saw it as they went about their business in the city every day of their lives. The play was probably written some time between 432 and 421, about ten years after the completion of the Parthenon.

Euripides was a highly regarded and much performed playwright with a reputation reaching all over the Hellenic world. It is said that some of the Athenian soldiers captured in Sicily during the Peloponnesian war obtained their freedom by reciting passages from his plays.[24] The *Erechtheus* was evidently among the most popular, being so much quoted that some of its lines became proverbial tags. If it had been among the eighteen plays by Euripides which have survived into modern times out of ninety which he is known to have composed, the story would be as familiar to Western culture as, say, that of Oedipus. Freud would probably have written an essay about its deep psychological significance.

By an amazing piece of good fortune in which the Greeks would have seen the hand of a friendly god, the recently recovered fragments include the justificatory speech of Erechtheus' wife Praxithea in which she offers the sacrifice of her daughter. The following are a few extracts:

ἐγὼ δὲ δώσω παῖδα τὴν ἐμὴν κτανεῖν.
λογίζομαι δὲ πολλά. πρῶτα μὲν πόλιν
οὐκ ἄν τιν' ἄλλην τῆσδε βελτίω λαβεῖν.
ἧι πρῶτα μὲν λεὼς οὐκ ἐπακτὸς ἄλλοθεν,
αὐτόχθονες δ' ἔφυμεν. αἱ δ' ἄλλαι πόλεις
πεσσῶν ὁμοίως διαφοραῖς ἐκτισμέναι
ἄλλαι παρ' ἄλλων εἰσὶν εἰσαγώγιμοι.

ὅστις δ' ἀπ' ἄλλης πόλεος οἰκήσηι πόλιν,
ἁρμὸς πονηρὸς ὥσπερ ἐν ξύλωι παγείς,
λόγωι πολίτης ἐστί, τοῖς δ' ἔργοισιν οὔ.
  ἔπειτα τέκνα τοῦδ' ἕκατι τίκτομεν,
ὡς θεῶν τε βωμοὺς πατρίδα τε ῥυώμεθα.
πόλεως δ' ἁπάσης τοὔνομ' ἕν, πολλοὶ δέ νιν
ναίουσι. τούτους πῶς διαφθεῖραί με χρή,
ἐξὸν προπάντων μίαν ὕπερ δοῦναι θανεῖν;
εἴπερ γὰρ ἀριθμὸν οἶδα καὶ τοὐλάσσονος
τὸ μεῖζον,†ἑνὸς† οἶκος οὐ πλέον στένει
πταίσας ἁπάσης πόλεος οὐδ' ἴσον φέρει.
  εἰ δ' ἦν ἐν οἴκοις ἀντὶ θηλειῶν στάχυς
ἄρσην, πόλιν δὲ πολεμία κατεῖχε φλόξ,
οὐκ ἄν νιν ἐξέπεμπον εἰς μάχην δορός,
θάνατον προταρβοῦσ'; ἀλλ' ἔμοιγ' εἴη τέκνα
<ἃ> καὶ μάχοιτο καὶ μετ' ἀνδράσιν πρέποι,
μὴ σχήματ' ἄλλως ἐν πόλει πεφυκότα.
τὰ μητέρων δὲ δάκρυ' ὅταν πέμπηι τέκνα,
πολλοὺς ἐθήλυν' εἰς μάχην ὁρμωμένους.
μισῶ γυναῖκας αἵτινες πρὸ τοῦ καλοῦ
ξῆν παῖδας εἵλοντ' ἢ παρήινεσαν κακά.
καὶ μὴν θανόντες γ' ἐν μάχηι πολλῶν μέτα
τύμβον τε κοινὸν ἔλαχον εὔκλειάν τ' ἴσην.
τῆμῆι δὲ παιδὶ στέφανος εἰς μιᾶι μόνηι
πόλεως θανούσηι τῆσδ' ὕπερ δοθήσεται,
καὶ τὴν τεκοῦσαν καὶ σὲ δύο θ' ὁμοσπόρω
σώσει. τί τούτων οὐχὶ δέξασθαι καλόν;

I shall give my daughter to be put to death. I take many things into account and first of all that I could not find any other city better than this. To begin with we are an autochthonous people, not introduced from elsewhere: other communities founded as it were through board-game moves, are imported, different ones from different places. Now someone who settles in one city from another is like a peg ill-fitted in a piece of wood—a citizen in name, but not in his actions.

Secondly our very reason for bearing children is to safeguard the altars of our gods and our homeland. The city as a whole has just a single name, but its inhabitants are many. How can it be right for me to destroy the many when I can give one girl to die for all? If I can count and can distinguish larger from smaller, one person's family does not lament more if a disaster occurs than a whole city, nor is the amount of suffering the same.

If my family had produced male children instead of females, and the flame of war was gripping our city, would I be refusing to send them out to battle for fear that they would be killed? No. Give me sons who would not only fight but be outstanding men, not mere useless figures who return no benefit to the city which raised them. When children see mothers' tears, many men are made less hard as they leave for battle. I detest women who choose life rather than righteous courage for their sons, or encourage them to be cowards. And sons, if they die in battle earn a common tomb and equal glory shared with many others; my daughter, though, will be awarded one crown for herself alone when she dies for this city, and will save her mother, and you, and her two sisters. Which of these things is not a fine reward?[25]

In the final speech of the play the goddess Athena calls upon her rival god Poseidon, having had his sacrifice, to stop the destruction of her city. She commands Praxithea, the mother whose daughters have been sacrificed, to bury them in a common tomb. She instructs the citizens of Athens never to forget them but to honour them every year with sacrifices of animals and festivals of dances. When in future the soldiers of Athens are about to go into battle, she commands, they are to make their first sacrifices to the daughters of Erechtheus, avoiding wine but confining themselves to honey and spring water. And the Athenians are to prevent the enemies of the city from secretly making sacrifices there. To commemorate Erechtheus Athena commands that a holy precinct be built in the centre of the city, where Praxithea, who has rebuilt the foundations of the city, shall be priestess with the right to make animal sacrifices.[26]

On the Parthenon frieze we see the sacrificial animals, the water carriers, and the honey carriers. Some of the horsemen wear Thracian caps, tokens of their victory over the Thracian invaders defeated as a result of the sacrifice of the daughters of Erechtheus. Greek art mixes gods with mortals, the living with the dead, the past with the present, the seen with the unseen. The Parthenon of Athens was, at the time it was conceived, built, and first viewed, not a celebration of Hellenic civilization as a whole. It was a local Athenian temple which used local myth to proclaim the majesty, the power, and the distinctive local culture of a single Hellenic city. To contemporary Hellenes from other cities, the Parthenon was probably a humiliating reminder of the hegemony of Athens over dozens of other Hellenic cities whose freedoms had been quashed.

Contemporaries could also see that the Parthenon made exaggerated, if not quite false, claims. The most powerful city of the Hellenic world in the age of Pericles and for long afterwards continued to be Lacedaimon or Sparta, which had provided the military forces which had been decisive in both 490 and 480, and whose militarized citizens despised both the artistic aspirations and the democratic system of government practised in Athens. The Athenian historian Thucydides, writing in about 430 when the classical buildings of Athens were at their most splendid, offered some perceptive advice to modern archaeologists and modern mythmakers.

Λακεδαιμονίων γὰρ εἰ ἡ πόλις ἐρημωθείη, λειφθείη δὲ τά τε ἱερὰ καὶ τῆς κατασκευῆς τὰ ἐδάφη, πολλὴν ἂν οἶμαι ἀπιστίαν τῆς δυνάμεως προελθόντος πολλοῦ χρόνου τοῖς ἔπειτα πρὸς τὸ κλέος αὐτῶν εἶναι (καίτοι Πελοποννήσου τῶν πέντε τὰς δύο μοίρας νέμονται, τῆς τε ξυμπάσης ἡγοῦνται καὶ τῶν ἔξω ξυμμάχων πολλῶν. ὅμως δὲ οὔτε ξυνοικισθείσης πόλεως οὔτε ἱεροῖς καὶ κατασκευαῖς πολυτελέσι χρησαμένης, κατὰ κώμας δὲ τῷ παλαιῷ τῆς Ἑλλάδος τρόπῳ οἰκισθείσης, φαίνοιτ' ἂν ὑποδεεστέρα), Ἀθηναίων δὲ τὸ αὐτὸ τοῦτο παθόντων διπλασίαν ἂν τὴν δύναμιν εἰκάζεσθαι ἀπὸ τῆς φανερᾶς ὄψεως τῆς πόλεως ἢ ἔστιν.

If the city of the Lacedaimonians should be deserted, and nothing should be left of it but its temples and the foundations of its other buildings, posterity would, I think, after a long lapse of time, be very loath to believe that their power was as great as their renown. (And yet they occupy two-thirds of the Peloponnese and have the hegemony of the whole, as well as of their many allies outside.) But as their city is not compactly built, and is not provided with costly temples and other edifices, but is built like the villages that Hellenes used to live in, its power would appear less than it is. Whereas if Athens should suffer the same fate, people would, from what appeared of the city's ruins, guess its power to be double what it is.[27]

Isocrates, writing in the fourth century, and recalling the great days of Periclean imperialism which he hoped could be revived, praised the statesman who 'so adorned the city with temples, monuments, and other projects of beauty that, even today, visitors who come to Athens think her worthy of ruling not only the Hellenes but all the world'. But for Plato, who feared the corrupting power of art, the Parthenon was simply part of the unnamed trash with which the leaders of the previous century had filled the city and which had contributed to its subsequent sharp decline.

By Hellenistic times, when Athens and the other Greek cities were incorporated into larger political entities and had lost much of their local independence, the meaning of the monument to viewers was already changing. A succession of non-Athenian Greeks, led by Alexander the Great, of Macedon, endowed their own dedications, drawing on the prestige of the monument to help legitimate their own claims to be the successors of the fifth-century Athenians.[28] In the year 304 the people of Athens gave a successful war-lord, Demetrios Poliorcetes, the 'liberator of Athens', the right to use the Parthenon, the sacred house of the virgin Athena, as his private residence, where he is said to have kept free-born Athenians as well as prostitutes of both sexes for sexual purposes.

Plutarch caught much of the sense of wonder and spirit of nostalgia for an imagined lost golden age which already by his time surrounded the monument.

κάλλει μὲν γὰρ ἕκαστον εὐθὺς ἦν τότε ἀρχαῖον, ἀκμῇ δὲ μέχρι νῦν πρόσφατόν ἐστι καὶ νεουργόν. οὕτως ἐπανθεῖ καινότης ἀεί τις ἄθικτον ὑπό τοῦ χρόνου διατηροῦσα τὴν ὄψιν, ὥσπερ ἀειθαλὲς πνεῦμα καὶ ψυχὴν ἀγήρω καταμεμιγμένην τῶν ἔργων ἐχόντων.

Every work of the time of Pericles had from the moment of its creation the beauty of an ancient masterpiece, but yet it retains its freshness and newness to this day. There is a certain novelty that seems to bloom upon them which keeps their beauty untouched by time, as if they had perpetual breath of life, and an unageing soul mingled in their composition.[29]

During the Roman conquests a succession of generals looted Athens of its main moveable statues. But when lasting peace was established in the first century Athens enjoyed a privileged position as an acknowledged cultural centre for the whole Roman Empire. The Emperor Augustus, who visited the city in the year 20, is said to have met Virgil on the foothills of the Acropolis where the poet was trying to complete the *Aeneid*. In another attempt to appropriate the Parthenon to current imperial cultural and political purposes, Augustus built a small temple dedicated to Rome and Augustus directly in front of the temple. In the second century, the Emperor Hadrian made a great show of 'restoring' Athens, financing an imperial building programme as ambitious as that of Pericles.

When in the fourth century the Emperor Constantine proclaimed Christianity the official religion of the empire, Athens was among the places which suffered worst. Although Paul of Tarsus had preached there, the number of Christians remained small. The prestige of Athens as an intellectual and cultural centre, with its schools of philosophy serving as universities for the élites of the empire, was inextricably associated with the ancient paganism with its multiple deities and absence of dogma. The Emperor Julian, who tried to reverse Constantine's decrees, had studied in Athens. But although, after the Christianizing of the empire, Constantinople gradually supplanted Athens, it was not until the forcible closure of the philosophy schools in the year 529 that the traditions of classical Athens were finally extinguished.

On the death of Theodosius in 395 Alaric the Goth invaded the empire, burning and plundering whatever came his way. When the Gothic hordes reached Athens, however, Alaric made a peaceful entrance, and caused no damage to the Acropolis and its temples. According to later legend he took the sight of the bronze shield of a statue of Athena flashing the reflected light of the sun as a warning from the gods. Lord Elgin, it was often to be said later, was more of a barbarian than Alaric the Goth.

Early in the sixth century, the Parthenon was converted into a Christian church, dedicated first to the Holy Wisdom and then, in an attempt to appropriate the traditions of Athena, to 'Our Lady of Athens'. As part of the building's conversion, the east pediment was torn down and its sculptures destroyed. During this time there appears also to have been some deliberate defacement of some sculptures of the frieze which, probably through misinterpretation of what they represented, particularly offended the new theocratic orthodoxy. For nearly six centuries after that time Athens remained a provincial centre of the Byzantine Empire, until, in 1204 the Crusaders from western Europe, having invaded and destroyed Constantinople, also occupied Athens. The Burgundian Othon installed himself in the Acropolis as the new ruler. As Athens settled into a long period of rule by a succession of Franks from the West the Parthenon now became the Roman Catholic church of Notre Dame. When the Turks took possession in the fifteenth century they converted the Parthenon into a mosque and built a minaret on top.

What is astonishing from a modern perspective is not the fact that the Parthenon was gradually being destroyed but that it survived for so long. The cult statue disappeared in the early centuries as did all the treasures and dedications which had been kept within the building. The interior was stripped and reshaped many times to match the needs of the changing religious observances. But for nearly a thousand years the main fabric of the building, including its roof and most of its decorative sculpture, remained intact. Western travellers who saw the Parthenon in the later seventeenth century were amazed to find the building nearly complete, and some wrote descriptions and made sketches. In 1674 the French ambassador to Constantinople obtained permission for an artist associated with Jacques Carrey to make sketches of the sculptures, and although they were sketched hurriedly from a distance and are incomplete, they are an invaluable record of much that is now lost.

For most of the seventeenth century, the Turks were being hard pressed militarily by the Venetians, with islands, towns, and fortresses in the eastern Mediterranean being fought over and changing hands more than once. In 1645 during a battle in Athens the Propylaea, which was being used as a gunpowder magazine, was struck by lightning and exploded. Henceforth it was a ruin. In 1686 the little temple of Athena Nike was deliberately thrown down by the Turks to clear the bastion for an artillery position. Then on 26 September 1687 the Parthenon was struck.

The Venetians, under a general called Morosini, were laying siege to the Acropolis. The Parthenon, which had now taken the place of the Propylaea as the gunpowder magazine, received a direct hit from one of the Venetian cannon and the whole building exploded. The roof was blown off; a huge gap was torn in the long colonnades on either side; and much of the sculpture was utterly destroyed. The Erechtheion too was badly damaged by the blast. When the garrison surrendered and Morosini took possession of the Acropolis he decided to take home to Venice as a trophy of his conquest the large group of sculptures from the west pediment which had survived the explosion. But when his engineers were lowering the massive statues their cables broke and the whole group was shattered. A head from one of the pedimental figures, now in Paris, was taken back to Venice by Morosini's secretary. Two heads from a metope, now in Copenhagen, were taken by another officer of his army. The following year Morosini was compelled to withdraw from Athens, leaving the Acropolis a heap of marble rubble. More damage was done to the Parthenon in one year than in all its previous history.

After the explosion the marble fragments that had been thrown to the ground lay in heaps where they had fallen providing ready-to-hand building materials. Being of fine marble, they were also suitable for burning into lime which was also needed for building. From 1687 until the middle of the eighteenth century, it has recently been ascertained, these marble ruins were the main source of repair work to the walls of the Acropolis. The rendering down of the marble continued until there was none left within the inside of the temple, at which time part of the building was demolished. The marble from the original floor paving was also torn up for building works, although the portion which lay under the new mosque survived.[30] There was also another practical use for the ancient ruins. The lead which the original builders had used to join the drums of columns could be extracted to make bullets, particularly in times of siege, another incentive to throw down any parts of columns which remained standing.

Elsewhere in Athens the story was the same. An Ionic temple on the banks of the Ilissos which was still well preserved in the 1750s was destroyed completely in order to provide materials for the building of Haseki's wall in 1778, as was an ancient bridge. The surviving columns at Sounion and Corinth became fewer and fewer. The last remains above ground of the Temple of Zeus at Olympia disappeared. In Asia Minor in at least two places the Turks built lime kilns within the columns of a temple so as to be near their materials.

During the eighteenth century, the monuments of Greece began to face a new danger. More and more travellers from western Europe began to find their way to Greece. These travellers were prepared to pay handsomely for pieces of original sculpture which, now that it had a market value, was seldom used for lime. On the Acroplis of Athens Voivode after Voivode and Disdar after Disdar were successfully bribed to allow sculptured fragments to be taken away. The Turkish soldiers of the Acropolis garrison realizing that small, easily transportable, fragments found a ready market, began deliberately to break off choice pieces from the buildings. Occasionally, to help encourage sales and to raise prices, they deliberately defaced the sculptures to emphasize their contempt, as can be seen in the sculptures that still survive. Some Turks, mystified at how foreigners could attach such value to broken pieces of marble, concluded that gold must be hidden in them and joined hopefully in the destruction. The travellers, avid for even the smallest piece by the hand of Phidias to show off to their friends at home, convinced themselves that their souvenir-hunting was rescuing ancient art from Turkish barbarism.

There thus began a steady export to all parts of Europe of the fragments found on the Acropolis. Unfortunately the pieces that were thus saved from the Turks were, all too often, lost to the world. On their return the souvenir hunters frequently lost interest in their acquisitions, or their heirs dispersed or jettisoned their collections.

All means of tracing them quickly disappeared. Apart from pieces removed in 1687 small fragments of the Parthenon sculptures have subsequently come to light in Palermo, Padua, Paris, and Karlsruhe, all brought from Athens in the eighteenth century. Three pieces found their way to the cellar of the Vatican Museum. A large slab of the frieze obtained somehow in 1744 was in the possession of the Royal Academy in London. Other fragments lay in English country houses—Chatsworth and Marbury Hall each had their precious morsel. The Society of Dilettanti had another. A part of the frieze was dug up in a garden in Essex in 1902—how it got there is not known. Three fine pieces known to have been obtained by the traveller Chandler in 1765 have disappeared.[31]

During the last years of the eighteenth century the antiquity market at Athens was successfully cornered by one man. The French antiquary Louis-François-Sébastien Fauvel was by profession a painter and, with the architectural draughtsman Foucherot, he had accompanied the young French nobleman, the Comte de Choiseul-Gouffier on a Hellenic tour in 1780.[32] Their names can still be read, carved on the Monument of Philopappos at Athens.[33] When Choiseul-Gouffier was appointed French Ambassador to the Ottoman Porte, he established Fauvel at Athens as his full-time agent with explicit permission to draw and make casts. Choiseul-Gouffier's motive had been almost exactly the same as Elgin's now was with Lusieri. Choiseul-Gouffier, however, had his eyes on more than drawings and casts: he set Fauvel to collect for him as many original antiquities as he could.

His instructions were clear enough: 'Enlevez tout ce que vous pourrez', he wrote. 'Ne négligez aucune occasion de piller dans Athènes et dans son territoire tout ce qu'il y a de pillable. N'épargnez ni les morts ni les vivants.' (Take all you can. Do not neglect any opportunity to pillage anything that is pillageable in Athens and its territory. Spare neither the dead nor the living.)[34] Choiseul-Gouffier had the good luck to be French Ambassador at the time when French influence at Turkey was at its height and there was little that the Turks refused him. A sizeable collection of sculptures was collected at Athens and elsewhere in Greece and shipped back to France. The British Ambassador of the time protested vigorously and ineffectively to the Ottoman government against the export even of the casts.

Choiseul-Gouffier's greatest ambition was to obtain some of the sculpture from the Parthenon but here the Turks drew the line.

In spite of constant requests they refused categorically to give him permission to remove any from the building. By judicious bribing of the Disdar Fauvel obtained at different times a fine slab of the frieze and a metope that were dug up among the ruins. These two pieces were dispatched to France and arrived safely a few years later. In 1788 Fauvel bought another metope that had fallen from the building during a storm and had broken into three pieces.[35]

Choiseul-Gouffier was never to enjoy the collection of marbles and casts from the Parthenon that he had built up with great pain. He was a nobleman of one of the great families of France and when the Revolution came he remained loyal to the Royalist cause. The French government disowned him as a traitor and he was compelled to go into exile in Russia. The antiquities that had reached France, including the two pieces from the Parthenon, were declared national property. The casts were for the most part destroyed. The metope that had come down in the storm was left behind at Athens.

Despite his patron's downfall, Fauvel stayed on at Athens. He took possession of the antiquities that still remained there, including the metope, as recompense for arrears of his pay, and accepted money from the French government to keep them for the national collection. He also began to build up a collection of his own. With such an old campaigner on the spot the casual travellers found it more difficult to buy fragments: anything that came up for sale went straight to Fauvel's store-room. For example, in 1795 the English traveller J. B. S. Morritt of Rokeby made a secret agreement with the Disdar to buy a metope and part of the frieze, but before they could be got away, Fauvel heard about the scheme and threatened to denounce the Disdar.[36] In 1798, however, his fortunes took a plunge. When Turkey declared war on France after Bonaparte's invasion of Egypt all the French subjects in the Ottoman Empire were arrested and put into prison. Fauvel was no exception and, although later set free, he was again out of the way when Lord Elgin's artists arrived in Athens. His antiquities were sequestrated.

When Lusieri and Elgin's other artists arrived, they knew little of the lively trade in sculpture fragments that had supplemented the incomes of successive Voivodes and Disdars in recent years. They had not come to take anything away. Their remit was quite clear—they were to draw and mould and measure. Elgin was interested in acquiring original sculptures, but the artists were given this very much as a secondary task. They were merely to keep their eyes open for any pieces that could be purchased.

The first priority was to set to work on drawing and moulding the Parthenon but at once they ran into difficulties. The Disdar refused to allow the artists on to the Acropolis on the grounds that when they climbed the buildings they would overlook the Turkish homes and spy on their women. The Acropolis, as a military fortress, could be visited on payment of a fee, but no one would be allowed to record the details of its fortifications. It was clear that, if the artists were to do what they had come to do, they would need a firman, that is a letter from the Ottoman government in Constantinople which would overrule the decisions of the local officials. Letters were sent to Elgin asking him to arrange for a firman to be sent.

While they were waiting, the artists decided to set to work on the chief monuments outside the Acropolis, the Theseum and the Monument of Lysicrates. A drawing of the Theseum made by Sebastiano Ittar is reproduced as Plate 7. Permission was readily given, but there were other snags. Lusieri discovered that they could not obtain timber for scaffolding, or even ropes for lifting their materials, in Athens. Timber was sent for from the island of Hydra, but for the ropes and other tackle they had a windfall. Fauvel, when working for the Comte de Choiseul-Gouffier had brought from Toulon some excellent equipment including a large cart big enough to transport heavy materials. Since Fauvel was now in gaol the Turks were happy to give all these things to the agents of the British Ambassador.[37]

At long last work began, and good work it was. The drawings of Theodor the Calmuck and of the architects, now in the British Museum, are elegant, well finished, and remarkable for their extreme attention to detail, but they were not necessarily accurate. The drawing made of the south side of the Parthenon, for example, showed the metopes but not in the order in which they stood in the building.[38] Taking to heart that his master's purpose was to improve the arts at home, the Calmuck rose above simple representation; he drew the sculptures in the state of decay in which he found them but also offered lively restorations on paper of how they must have looked in their original condition.

For Lusieri's drawings were unfortunately mainly have to rely for our knowledge on contemporary accounts since all but a few of the wonderfully accurate drawings he made in Athens were destroyed.[39] One is reproduced as Plate 4. Lusieri specialized in large panoramas, seven or eight feet long, with the outlines of every detail of the landscape delineated in pencil and then coloured in water-colours.[40] He had several views in preparation at the same time so that he could work comfortably on one of them, whichever way the wind was blowing. His meagre figure sitting drawing under an umbrella (see Plate 6) became one of the familiar sights of Athens. The detail of his drawing was so intricate that many people thought he used a telescope and it seems quite probable that he did. Unfortunately he was a slow worker and often he had to rub out part of a view he was working on because the growth of trees and the alteration of buildings had made it out of date before the rest of the picture was complete. Besides being slow at his drawing Lusieri was inclined to leave his drawings half-finished or uncoloured. He excused himself by saying that if he once began colouring he would be so fascinated that he would not have patience to return to the dry details of outline.[41] But these faults were in the right direction. There is no doubt that for the purpose of obtaining an exact record of the buildings of Athens Elgin had found the right men.

In February 1801, that is six months after their arrival in Athens, the artists were allowed on to the Acropolis for the first time. They did not yet have a firman but they obtained permission in the usual Turkish way. They paid. Every day they entered the fortress they paid the equivalent of £5 to the Disdar. Because of the highly favourable exchange rates, most visitors from western Europe felt very rich when they visited Greece, but for some privileges they paid highly.[42] For £5 Elgin's agents could have hired sixty-three labourers or forty men, each with two bullocks, for a day.[43] Since they had no alternative Elgin reckoned it was worth the price and Lusieri, the Calmuck, and the architects went up daily to make their drawings. So they continued happily for several months.

Then suddenly there was a change. The time had come for the first of the mouldings of the Parthenon sculpture to be taken. The scaffolding was all erected and the moulders were ready to begin work. At that very moment the Disdar announced that all access to the Acropolis for all the artists was forbidden. Bribes were of no avail. The Disdar was quite immovable. Nothing less than a special firman from the Porte would persuade him. He had been told by the Porte that a French force was again gathering at Toulon and all military installations were to be closed to foreigners. The Turks, after their experience of the Egyptian expedition of Bonaparte, believed that the Toulon force was directed against some other part of the Ottoman Empire. The artists therefore returned sadly to their work in the lower town.

7

In Search of Ancient Manuscripts

SINCE the time of the Renaissance, scholars in western Europe had wanted to explore the libraries of the Ottoman Empire Many felt sure that the libraries known to exist in Constantinople and in the other parts of the former Eastern Roman Empire must contain manuscripts of classical authors, probably of works that had not survived in the West. Ancient authors told of a vast body of Greek and Latin literature of which only a tiny proportion had survived. The three great tragedians, Aeschylus, Sophocles, and Euripides, for example, were known to have written over three hundred plays but only thirty-three still existed. Livy had written a history of Rome in one hundred and forty-two books, of which only thirty-five had been handed down. Some ancient authors had only survived in a single manuscript. After the Ottoman conquest, the Turks had, for the most part, allowed the Christian communities in their empire to remain unmolested. The Greek Patriarchate had an unbroken tradition going back to the time of the early Christian emperors, as had many churches and monasteries. Greek was still spoken, in some cases recognizably classical, and some of the Greek families of Constantinople considered themselves the heirs of the old Byzantine aristocracy.

The greatest hope, in most scholars' minds, was that there were manuscripts in the Topkapi Serai at Constantinople. The Serai had been the palace of the Byzantine emperors before the conquest and the Turks had taken it over and adapted it as the centre for their new empire. Since the Serai was known to contain many buildings from before the conquest, it was reasonable to hope that at least a remnant of the imperial library might have survived as part of the Sultan's Ottoman Library, but it was absolutely closed to all Christians and to most Muslims. Two years before Elgin's embassy set out, a book on Constantinople by James Dallaway, a former chaplain to the Levant Company at Constantinople, was published in London. It was this book, written by a man who seemed to know what he was talking about, which revived interest in the subject of the Library of Topkapi Serai in the minds of the English bishops. 'By comparing the accounts of different relators,' wrote Dallaway, 'it is evident that many manuscripts both Greek and Latin as well as oriental are kept in confused heaps without arrangement or catalogue.' Dallaway also asserted as a fact that the Turks preserved with due veneration no less than one hundred and twenty manuscripts in folio, chiefly New Testament and commentaries, which had belonged to the Emperor Constantine.[1]

It was to look for classical manuscripts—and above all to obtain access to the Library of Topkapi Serai—that Professor Carlyle had been attached to Lord Elgin's mission at public expense. As a professor of Arabic, Carlyle also wanted to acquire manuscripts of unpublished works in oriental languages, and also old manuscripts of the Bible in any languages which might help to reconstruct the tradition of the text. As soon as the embassy arrived at Constantinople, Elgin put in a request for Carlyle to be admitted to the Library of Topkapi Serai. What was needed was a firman, that is a special letter of permission from the Ottoman government. The Government declared they were eager to be helpful, but weeks passed and no firman was forthcoming. In January plague broke out in old Stamboul, a signal for all foreigners to retire within their palaces in the European quarter. Access to the Serai became out of the question until the last traces of the plague had gone. Carlyle spent the first weeks, therefore, in exploring the other libraries at Constantinople of which there were about a dozen. He also searched the bazaars for oriental manuscripts and bought a great number.

The Patriarch of Constantinople, leader of the large Greek community, lived in splendour in the Turkish style—inevitably Carlyle compares his palace to the *Arabian Nights*—and received the representative of the English bishops with great friendliness. He wrote letters of introduction to his ecclesiastical colleagues in the Ottoman Empire and promised to be as helpful as he could. Carlyle discussed with him his plans to distribute the Bible in Arabic as part of English schemes to convert the Muslims, but he was given no encouragement. The Patriarch, it was intimated, whether truthfully or tactfully, had heard nothing of a first consignment of 5,000 volumes that had been sent from England many months before. The Patriarch of Jerusalem, another of the leaders of the Eastern Orthodox Church who also lived in Constantinople, received

Carlyle with equal friendliness. He too had heard nothing of the consignment of Bibles that had been sent to Alexandria and after this disappointment Carlyle seems to have abandoned this part of his plan. As the patriarchs knew, the good relations between the different religious communities who made up the Ottoman Empire depended on continuing mutual respect and unspoken no-poaching understandings. For a Muslim to convert to Christianity was a capital offence.

At the end of December Carlyle, by Elgin's influence, was given permission to look for manuscripts in the Church of St Sophia. The great church of Justinian had been converted into a mosque after the Turkish conquest and infidels were now only occasionally admitted. There was hope that somewhere in the vast building there might be the remains of a library. Carlyle and Hunt had been allowed to visit at the time of Elgin's reception as an Ambassador and the superintendent had pointed out to them a compartment secured with a very heavy lock which, he said, had formerly been a chapel. According to the superintendent, a priest and a boy had been in the chapel at the time of the capture of Constantinople celebrating mass; the door had been shut tight by an earthquake and had not been opened since. After some negotiation Carlyle and Hunt were allowed into this chamber. They went to St Sophia in great secrecy to avoid being seen by the Turks and the rusty lock was forced. But there were no manuscripts and no skeletons of priests or boys. All they found of interest were some very badly defaced wall-paintings and mosaics.[2]

In January Elgin persuaded the Turks to allow General Koehler to go from Constantinople to join the Grand Vizier's army in Syria. He had been determined all along that the British Military Mission should be employed on more active service than repairing the Dardanelles forts but he had now another reason. He wanted Koehler to act as a brake on Sir Sidney Smith's disobedience, and he gave him authority, if necessary, to order Smith back on board his ship. Spencer Smith, out of loyalty to his brother, had encouraged the Turks in their opposition to letting Koehler go. To make sure, therefore, that Koehler's departure was not delayed at the last moment on some pretext it was arranged that he should leave Constantinople secretly and suddenly with only a few of his staff and make the journey as far as possible by land, the rest of the mission following later by sea.[3] Carlyle, realizing that his hopes of entering the Serai Library in the near future were remote, asked if he could join the party in order to visit the monasteries of the Holy Land on the way.

In 1800 much of the area they were to pass through was almost unknown to Europeans, but over the next two years nearly all of Elgin's party did a great deal of travelling in dangerous areas, and Carlyle was one of the most adventurous of them all. After their first round of journeys Carlyle and Hunt drew up some notes for use as hints to their successors.

Preparations for a tour from Constantinople
Unless you mean to visit the interior parts of the country the adoption of the Oriental dress is not necessary: but if you do, the Tartarian or Polish dress will be found the most convenient. In this case a defence for the eyes will be wanted; and the best is made with a piece of paste board cut into the shape of a crescent, covered with green silk and bound round the front of the cap by means of a silk ribband.

The best European dress consists of a white hat with a broad brim, a light-coloured broadcloth greatcoat, silk and cotton mixed waist-coat, trowsers or loose pantaloons of Manchester or Nankeen and strong roomy half boots. A large Venetian mantle or German cloak would prove a useful and salutary companion at night. A portable bed frame would conduce much to comfort in a country so full of vermin, particularly if furnished with a Moskito curtain, but if so much baggage be thought too cumbersome, a small hair Mattrass, and a carpet to spread it on, cannot well be dispensed with.

Three dozen of clean shirts must be taken for there are very few places where our mode of washing linen is understood. The bedding and the rest of the baggage ought to be divided into such portions as are fit for conveyance on horseback. An English saddle (made very hollow in the back) should be taken with you, or at least a Turkish saddle accommodated as much as possible to our mode of riding. It is necessary to provide yourself with kitchen utensils, a portable furnace, and (in your voyages) with a quantity of charcoal, also with table linen, plates etc. An Armenian or Greek servant must be hired for cooking your victuals.

On the mode of conveyance by land
Horses are to be hired in most places of the continent but if the country is very rocky and mountainous it would be advisable to chuse mules. In the Isles of the Archipelago in general you must be contented with Asses . . . The usual rate of going is about 3 geographical miles per hour. The horse hire varies from two to three piastres a day for each beast including all expenses. There is usually a man to every two horses who accompanies them on foot and receives a backshish or gratuity of 20 paras a day.

Your guides, if their horses are hired by the day will devise various pre-
texts for detaining you on the road such as the distance of good night quarters etc. They will also endeavour to prevail on you not to visit many
interesting spots either because they fear the roads will cripple their horses
or because they know the price of barley there is high. You must be on
your guard against all such interested manoeuvres.

In general it is best to avoid associating with you in these tours officious
Greeks or Franks [Europeans] of the Towns whose only object as best is
to live well for a few days and take a pleasant ride at your expense, and
who, of course, will endeavour to detain you as long as possible on the
road, especially at such places as afford good eating and drinking.

The best night quarters are in the Greek monasteries which are to be
found almost everywhere. On your departure pay the full value of the provisions which you have consumed and leave a few piastres as a present to
the church. In default of a monastery, a peasant's cottage neatly swept out
is infinitely preferable to a Turkish Konak—for in the former you will be
well protected from the night air and feel no material inconvenience but
from fleas: in the latter you will be exposed to the wind on all sides and
devoured by bugs. . . .

Immediately upon your arrival at a new place visit the chief thereof,
whether Turk or Greek, and present your firman. He becomes then responsible for your safety and good treatment but would otherwise be piqued
at your neglect. A Turkish guard is always an incumbrance and attended
with considerable expense but is frequently expedient by way of protection from insult or from robbery. In the first case a single attendant is
sufficient but in the second the force necessary for your protection varies
with the danger from two to twenty men. . . .

Your firman will have more or less authority in proportion as the
province or district has more or less dependence on the Porte: for in some
provinces that dependence is very slight indeed and in a few virtually null.
It is here you must have recourse to the other means of protection such
as presents. . . .

Useful Hints
Avoid having the air of examining Turkish fortresses. If you should be
questioned about the motives of your tour, you may reply that it is the
custom of your country, and that you have read much of Greece in ancient
books, of which you may exhibit a proof that will serve to amuse. The most
current notion is that you are in search of hidden treasure, it being impossible for them to conceive that you travel merely to examine the mouldering ruins of ancient towns and temples . . . The national character differs
extremely in the various parts of the Empire. In the first place a great line
of distinction must be drawn between the European and Asiatic Turks. The
former corrupted by too much power and by their intercourse with the
Greeks are perfidious, and proud. The latter are more simple in their

manners and trustworthy. Among the Greeks the Islanders of the Archipelago and in general the inhabitants of large towns are a very selfish insidious and perfidious people...

Presents of money are always expected by the attendants of the persons whom you visit whether Greeks or Turks and these in fact constitute their wages. But it is best to distribute this yourself instead of employing a deputy. At every house you are treated after the fashion of the country with pipes and coffee and the attendants when you retire expect their fee at the door.

When you travel thro' a country suspected to harbour the plague you will, of course, ask questions at every village about its existence; but it never happens that you can hear the real truth so much is the interest of every place affected by the reputation of harbouring the disorder. If you ask directly whether the plague exists there and receive a positive denial of it, the answer is by no means to be relied on; but if you ask whether there is any sickness in the village and receive for answer that there is a feverish complaint but which they assure you is not the plague, you have then very strong reasons for suspecting it. In which case suffer no intercourse with the villagers but what is accompanied with every precaution, and by no means suffer your servants to stroll into the bazar for brandy or on any pretence whatever.[4]

The party set off in January 1800. Apart from Carlyle, it consisted of Koehler, two of his officers, a military draughtsman, and thirty attendants. All were dressed as Turks and were well armed. The plan was to strike straight across Asia Minor from north-west to south-east. No European had been that way for about a hundred years and the journey took them through the territory of many warlike pashas. Some turned out to be hospitable, others unfriendly, depending largely on their current relations with the Porte.

All the members of the expedition were interested in classical antiquities and they made many diversions to look at ancient remains. They copied numerous inscriptions and the draughtsman drew the more interesting buildings. They also tried to make a rough map of their route, noting anything of geographical interest, and attempting to identify ancient cities from the names of the modern villages. The journey took about a month, at first on horseback, latterly on camels. Carlyle kept a detailed diary of the journey and he also indulged his taste for writing verses. His poetic manner, which affected his prose as much as his verse, made him rather a joke with the soldiers but they seem to have liked him well enough. The following passage, written among the ruins of Nicaea, now

Iznek, the place where a council of the Church formulated the
Nicene creed, is a typical example of his style.

Just as the sun appeared we emerged from the dell in which we had been
for some time travelling; when as sweet a scene opened upon us as can be
conceived. In front was the lake of Nicaea bending through its green valley.
Immediately between us and the lake rose up a woody hill, which, by inter-
cepting the centre of the prospect seemed to divide the expanse of water
before us into two separate reaches. Along the opposite side of the lake
ran a range of dark mountains, scarce yet, except on their most prominent
parts, illuminated by the sun—the snowy summits of Olympus empurpled
by the reflection of the morning clouds, terminated the view. To the left
the minarets of Nicaea were seen peeping out of the water at the extremity of the lake. To the right the lake stretched itself till it was lost amongst
the windings of the mountains.

It is not possible to form an idea of a more complete scene of desolation than Nicaea now exhibits:—streets without a passenger, houses
without an inhabitant, and ruins of every age, fill the precincts of this once
celebrated city. The deserted mosque, whose minaret we ascended in order
to obtain a general notion of the plan of the place bore evident marks of
having been erected from the remains of a Christian church and many of
these upon a closer inspection shewed clearly that they had formerly
belonged to a Pagan temple:—our Mohammedan mosque was falling to
decay and like its predecessors in splendour must soon become a heap of
rubbish—what a *generation* of ruin was here![5]

> Nicaea hail! renown'd for fierce debate,
> > For synods bustling o'er yon silent spot.
> For zealous ardour—for polemic hate—
> > For truth preserv'd, and charity forgot.
>
> Full oft, th'historic record as I've scann'd
> > Has fancy's touch those solemn scenes pourtray'd,
> Bid thy proud domes display the mitred band,
> > Thy streets unfold the long-drawn cavalcade.
>
> Those scenes are past—thy streets no longer shew
> > Their busy throngs—yet is there breast so cold
> As calm can trace, without one trilling glow,
> > What thought has pictur'd and what fame has told?
>
> Those scenes are fled—those domes are swept away—
> > Succeeding domes now totter to their fall,
> And mouldering mosques on moulder'd fanes decay
> > While desolation bends to grasp them all.[6]

From Asia Minor Carlyle crossed to Cyprus where he met Sir
Sidney Smith. When Smith told him about the Convention of El

Arish he decided to leave Koehler, and cross to Egypt in the belief that peace was restored. When his ship was off Alexandria, however, he and Sir Sidney Smith heard of the disowning of the Convention by the British government and the subsequent battles. Despite the renewal of the war he went ashore under a flag of truce with an officer of Sir Sidney Smith's staff and met the French generals. They gave him dinner and showed him the sights of Alexandria. He was introduced to some of the French scholars and scientists who had accompanied the expedition and also—laid on specially for his benefit—saw some of the best French troops on parade.

From Alexandria Carlyle made a journey to Jerusalem and visited the ancient monastery of St Saba. Only a fortnight before some Bedouin bandits had attacked the monastery, set fire to part of it, and killed a number of the monks. But Carlyle was not daunted. The Governor of Jerusalem furnished him with an escort of the same bandits to protect him from their friends. Carlyle was permitted to examine the library but found little of interest. As he wrote to the Bishop of Lincoln:

Except twenty-nine copies of the Gospels and one of the Epistles, this celebrated library does not contain anything valuable. . . . I was permitted by the Superior to bring along with me six of what I judged the oldest Mss. viz. two copies of the Gospels, one of the Epistles, two books of Homilies and apostolic letters, which I took for the sake of the quotations, and a copy of the Sophist Libanius, the only work like a classic author that I met with. I hope the Patriarch will allow me to convey them to England.[7]

From Jerusalem Carlyle went to the Grand Vizier's headquarters which were now established at Jaffa and then made his way back through the Greek Islands to Constantinople. Back at Constantinople Carlyle renewed his efforts to gain admittance to the Library of Topkapi Serai. The Turks, as before, hummed and hawed, and the stories about ancient manuscripts became more and more confusing. The Turks began to say that there was no library in the Serai at all; then that there were two; then they suggested that Carlyle might look in a building near St Sophia that they said had been shut ever since the Turkish conquest. Carlyle himself met a Frenchman who declared that his brother had personally seen Greek and Latin manuscripts in the Serai Library.

While awaiting the results of the negotiations, Carlyle, with Hunt's assistance, explored every Greek monastery in Constantinople and in the nearby Princes Islands. He also examined thoroughly the library of the Patriarch. In none of them did he discover a single fragment of any unknown classical author, the libraries consisting almost entirely of religious works. The monks attached little value to manuscripts, much preferring printed editions, and Carlyle was able to buy a number of those he thought the most interesting. The Patriarch of Jerusalem also allowed him to borrow some from his library to be sent to England to be collated. Altogether he collected about twenty-eight manuscripts, mostly written in medieval times.

At last, on a day in November 1800, almost a year after his arrival at Constantinople, Carlyle accomplished the object of his mission. Unlike all the other libraries he had visited, the Library of Topkapi Serai was carefully looked after. The books were arranged with titles showing in padlocked cases in a small cruciform building near the Serai Mosque. Carlyle was permitted to look at every one. But the result was bitterly disappointing. As he reported to the Bishop of Lincoln.

The whole number of Mss in the Library amounts to 1294 much the greatest part of which are Arabic; these are however most of the best Persian and Turkish writers but alas, not one volume in Greek, Hebrew or Latin! ... Such, my Lord is the famous Library of the Seraglio! respecting which so many falsehoods have been advanced; but which, I am now very clear both from the manner in which it is secured, the declarations of the Turks, and the contradictory accounts of the Franks, was never before subjected to the examination of a Christian.[8]

Carlyle had wanted (since the Black Sea was now open to British ships) to make a journey along the north coast of Asia Minor to Trebizond examining the monasteries on the way, but the long delay in negotiating with the Turks made that impossible. He decided to go home. He had, however, one last hope. In the rocky promontory of Mount Athos there were twenty-four monasteries that had survived the Turkish conquest as a virtually independent community. Perhaps in the Holy Mountain he might yet find an ancient manuscript? He decided, therefore, to visit Athos on his way back and, if possible, to examine other monasteries of mainland Greece.

Armed with numerous firmans and letters of introduction the two travellers set off in March 1801. They stopped at the Dardanelles on their way to examine the plain of Troy and make their contribution to the controversy that was then raging in academic circles about the exact location of ancient Troy. Hunt visited the church from where the first of the Elgin collection of marbles had been removed by Koehler's soldiers in 1799 and also, with the help of the local pasha, obtained a number of other statues and inscriptions on behalf of his employer. Carlyle continued his meticulous journal and composed poems appropriate to the romantic spots they visited.

Carlyle and Hunt spent about three weeks in the Troad, Homer in hand, tracing on the ground the scenes of the *Iliad*. They came to the conclusion that Homer was often wrong but, as Hunt wrote modestly in his diary, 'It would be an invidious task to attempt destroying any of the enthusiasm that is felt in reading some of the immortal works of the ancient writers by shewing in what instances they have deviated from geographical precision in their allusions to local scenery.' Another party of British travellers led by Edward Daniel Clarke of Cambridge was exploring the Troad at the same time, and rivalry broke out.[9]

Carlyle and Hunt then crossed to Tenedos and Lemnos and, after very nearly perishing in a storm at sea, arrived at Athos.[10] The first monastery they visited, Batopaidi, turned out to be more like a fortress than a religious retreat. It was surrounded by high walls interspaced with towers, and cannon lay in the embrasures. The outer gate was doubly plated with iron, and there were three more gates to be negotiated before they could enter. At each stage they saw more cannon mounted on carriages, ready to be brought forward to the defence.

Despite their warlike appearance, the monks, of whom there were about two hundred and fifty, received the travellers with great kindness. They showed them over the twenty-seven churches attached to the convent and their farms and vineyards. They would have paid more attention to their guests but it was Easter and the peninsula was crowded with thousands of pilgrims. These pilgrims were of all Balkan races, Albanians, Bulgarians, and Wallachians, and for the most part were professional bandits. They brought their arms with them and shot off their muskets perpetually in celebration. Whenever these bands of robbers made a successful raid or act of piracy, they came to Athos, received absolution, and handed over part of their spoils. At Easter all the 'pilgrims' arrived together and arranged for liturgies to be said for themselves during the coming year. The economy of Mount Athos was largely dependent on their contributions.

Carlyle and Hunt asked to be allowed to see the library. For a few days all they could get were evasive answers. At last Carlyle, becoming impatient, invoked his letter from the Patriarch and insisted that he should be shown the library. The visitors were thereupon taken to a damp dark cellar where they found a large number of manuscript volumes lying about on the floor in disorder. Most of the covers had been torn off and all were eaten by worms and rats and mouldy with damp. Most turned out to be ecclesiastical works, gospels, liturgies, and polemical theology, but, for the first time in any library the two scholars found a substantial number of classical authors, Homer, Plato, Aristotle, Hippocrates, Galen, and others. None was of any unknown work but their hopes were greatly raised. They offered to buy some of the oldest copies, but the Abbot—more scrupulous than his colleagues in monasteries they had so far visited—declared he could not sell any church property without the express approval of the Patriarch.

After Batopaidi the travellers visited every one of the twenty-four monasteries on Athos. They examined every library and made a detailed catalogue of each but again they were to be disappointed. In none of them did they find a single unknown classical fragment. The libraries were generally in much the same condition as at Batopaidi, sometimes even in the open air. Everywhere the monks attached more value to the printed editions. But although there was nothing new, some of the libraries did contain valuable ancient copies of the New Testament and other works in which Carlyle was interested. He soon learnt to offer his money in private to the Abbot and so overcome his scruples about selling church property. In one monastery the Abbot said a substantial number of their manuscripts had already been sold to the Venetians.[11]

From Athos Carlyle and Hunt went by sea to Athens, having abandoned the plan to search for manuscripts in mainland Greece because of the danger from bandits. They arrived at about the same time as Lady Elgin's mother and father, who were now on their way home after their holiday at Constantinople. All the new visitors had expected to find Lusieri and the artists hard at work on the Acropolis, but nothing had been done. The Disdar, or Military Governor, continued to refuse them permission. Carlyle and Hunt made various attempts, in Elgin's name, to persuade the Disdar to change his mind but without success. The Disdar, it turned out, was prepared to let the ambassador's friends visit the fortress but not his artists—working on the same principle that nowadays sometimes forbids photography in the vicinity of military installations. It was clear that only a strong firman direct from the Disdar's superiors in Constantinople would offer any hope of a change.

At the end of May Mr and Mrs Nisbet left Athens for Malta and home. They had arranged to have sent on, as a decoration for their house, a number of pieces of coloured marble and porphyry which they had noticed at various ancient sites and also an ancient marble throne with which they had been presented by the Archbishop of Athens. Carlyle also went home, taking with him a few dozen manuscripts collected from various monasteries and several hundred oriental manuscripts which he had bought in the bazaars. He was a disappointed man. Not only had he failed to find what he had come for, but he had spent a large sum of money and ruined his health in the process. His expectation that Elgin would help pay his expenses proved unfounded and the early friendship gave way to dislike.[12] He returned to his quiet life of scholar and churchman and died shortly afterwards.

8

The Conquest of Egypt and
its Results

IN the fourteen months since he landed secretly on the south coast
in November 1799, Napoleon Bonaparte had made himself undisputed leader of France, had put down a rebellion in the Vendée,
established a new constitution, made far-reaching economic
reforms, and laid the foundations of a new legal system. He had
overcome the resistance of all the countries opposed to France with
the exception of Britain and Turkey. In January 1801 he turned his
attention at last to the army shut up in Egypt and began to gather
a force at Toulon to reinforce it. It was put under the command of
Admiral Ganteaume who had been on the first expedition to Egypt
but whose principal distinction was his successful command of the
squadron that brought Bonaparte secretly home.

The British had watched their allies crumble away one by one
with only the capture of Malta to console them. But they did not
repeat the mistake of withdrawing from the Mediterranean which
they had made when the first alliance against Revolutionary France
had collapsed. Instead they made preparations to send their own
expedition to Egypt to expel the French by force. An army of 17,000
under General Sir Ralph Abercromby began to assemble at Malta
at the same time as the French relief force of Admiral Ganteaume
was getting ready at Toulon. In addition a smaller British force
assembled at the Cape of Good Hope, ready if need be, to attack
Egypt from the Red Sea.

Abercromby made his preparations well. The force was taken by
sea to Marmaris on the coast of Asia Minor opposite Rhodes. It
was then allowed to recuperate from the voyage and was put
through a full programme of training in amphibious landings to
prepare it for the invasion of Egypt. Abercromby brought most of
his supplies with him but he was still in need of food, horses, and
various other stores. For these he applied to Lord Elgin, who was

not only the chief British authority in the area but a friend and neighbour at home in Scotland.

Vast quantities of stores were purchased. Asia Minor was scoured to provide horses. Special shipyards were established to build boats, and grain ships were sent all over the eastern Mediterranean to buy supplies. Elgin paid and ran up bills of many thousands of pounds on behalf of the British government, reducing the rate of exchange of the pound and the local value of his salary and allowances.[1]

General Menou, who had succeeded General Kléber as Commander-in-Chief of the French in Egypt, was much more interested in trying to colonize Egypt than in the military side of his job. Although well warned that an invasion was imminent, he did nothing to reinforce his units stationed near the coast, and even after the invasion fleet was sighted off Aboukir, he stayed in Cairo for ten days before going to the coast. Ganteaume's relief force at Toulon had set sail for Egypt in February but returned to port after a few days without even making contact with the enemy. Bonaparte was furious and ordered him to sea again, but Ganteaume, more afraid of the British than of Bonaparte, returned to Toulon for a second time after sighting a British naval squadron. He and his fleet were safely at Toulon when the decisive battle for Egypt took place.

The British Expeditionary Force landed at Aboukir Bay in Egypt on 8 March. The French on the coast were quickly overcome and the force moved inland. Menou continued to make every possible military mistake. Having waited until the British were consolidated ashore, he attacked with only a fraction of the forces at his disposal and was severely defeated and forced to retire to Alexandria. The British were now able to bring in reinforcements by sea and to concert plans with the Turkish army which had again lumbered down from Syria.[2] In early April the ancient dykes around Alexandria were breached so that the sea poured in round the outside of the city. The British and Turks were then able to put the city under siege. By June the main body of the rest of the French forces were compelled to retire within the gates of Cairo and it too was put under siege. Without reinforcement by sea, it could only be a matter of time before they would be forced to surrender.

Bonaparte had ordered Ganteaume at Toulon to sea for the third time. The Toulon force, according to Bonaparte's strategy, was to sail to Libya and land 5,000 troops from where they were then to make their way to Egypt through the desert. That Bonaparte expected these troops to achieve this feat of endurance after three months on board ship is perhaps a measure of the boldness of his strategic imagination but, fortunately for them, Ganteaume was still not a hero. He did set sail for the third time from Toulon and some of his ships actually reached the Libyan coast, but the locals looked hostile and he scurried back yet again to the safety of Toulon. The French in Egypt had no hope left.

Seven days after declaring he would fight to the end, Menou capitulated and the last French resistance in Egypt came to an end. The terms he obtained were those he had denounced as shameful and treasonable when his countrymen besieged in Cairo had capitulated not long before. They were the same as those of the Convention of El Arish. In September the French forces in Egypt were conveyed back to France by the Royal Navy. Egypt was completely in the hands of the British and the Turks. For the first time for some hundreds of years Egypt returned actually as well as nominally to Ottoman rule.

When the news came through of the final triumph in Egypt the Turks arranged a splendid national celebration. For seven days Constantinople was illuminated. There were firework displays, music, and salutes of guns every evening. Scenes from the Egyptian war were acted out in miniature by the warships in the harbour.[3] On the first night of the celebrations it rained and the fireworks did not go off very well. The Turks therefore immediately banished the man in charge and appointed someone else in his place. Fortunately for him the weather kept fine for the rest of the week. The Elgins hired a special ship over which a huge illuminated star and crescent was to be hung, but the celebrations had caused a complete sell-out of all the lamps in Constantinople. 'It was the most beautiful night you can imagine,' Lady Elgin wrote home, 'both sides of the Bosphorus illuminated, rockets, guns, cannon going off at all corners, all sorts of music, and a sort of masquerade, and all the Turks were as merry as Christians. . . . I think they might have conquered Egypt over and over again had they but fired half the number of cannon in earnest they are now firing in joke.'[4]

The climax of the celebrations was the Sultan showing himself to his people. He lay on a silver sofa in the Green Kiosk of the Serai surrounded by hundreds of attendants. An immense concourse of people on shore and in boats prayed that he should 'conquer all his enemies and reward all his friends'.[5] The women prayed that he should have a son and the priests conferred on him

the title of 'Selim the Conqueror'. While Elgin was at a conference
Lady Elgin rowed about and looked at all the sights. She did not
realize that it was forbidden to pass near the Sultan and ordered
the sailors to row past him. The Sultan, who not long before
regarded it as intolerably degrading to cast his eyes on a foreigner,
nodded amiably to her and, when she had gone past, picked up a
telescope and watched her into the distance. Lady Elgin noticed
that the discipline of the Serai had been relaxed for the occasion.
She saw some of her friends, the ladies of the Harem, looking out
of the windows and waving to her although the black eunuchs kept
a close watch on these improprieties.

Lord Elgin, the ambassador of the nation who had brought about
the triumph, immediately became the most influential foreign representative in Constantinople. The Turks could not do enough to
show their appreciation. Elgin was given (again) all the honours of
the Ottoman court. He was presented with an aigrette from the
Sultan's turban, the Order of the Crescent (set in diamonds), more
pelisses, and more horses. He was put through all the elaborate
ceremonial that he had received when he first arrived. He was now
so much more practised at it than the majority of the Turkish
participants that he was able to put them right when a mistake in
etiquette occurred.[6] Lady Elgin too was given the unprecedented
honour of being received by the Sultan's mother, to whom she was
conveyed by a large escort of black eunuchs.[7]

All British warships were given free provisions and refitting facilities in Turkish ports. The captain of one which happened to be
in Constantinople at the time of the celebrations received a
diamond snuff box and the other officers a gold one. All the officers
who took part in the Egyptian Expedition, some eighteen hundred
in all, were given a gold medal and, needless to say, a pelisse.
General Hutchinson's brother who was in Constantinople acting as
a messenger from Egypt, received a pelisse, a diamond aigrette, a
watch set in diamonds worth £2,000, twenty-five purses of money,
a diamond snuff box, and shawls and embroidered stuffs worth
£7,000.[8]

Another gift was the release of Maltese slaves. For centuries the
Knights of St John had employed Maltese as crews for their ships
as they conducted their latter-day crusades against the Turks. Many
had fallen into Turkish hands to be kept chained as slave workers
in the Constantinople dockyard. But now Malta was British and
the Maltese British subjects. Elgin persuaded the Porte to release

them from slavery. One hundred and sixty were discovered and given freedom. Most had been in captivity for six or eight years but a few had been there much longer and two for forty-eight years. Tents were pitched for them in the grounds of the British Palace until they could be taken back to Malta, and the Capitan Pasha, who was responsible for the dockyard, even gave them 48 piastres each as they left his service.[9]

Elgin persuaded the Turks to release all the French subjects who had been put in prison in all parts of the Ottoman Empire.[10] It was contrary to the usage of civilized nations, he argued, to imprison mere civilians and Ruffin, the French Chargé d'Affaires, emerged from the Seven Towers where he had been held since 1798. But this produced another problem and another opportunity. Since 1799 Elgin and the British embassy had lived in the French Palace while the rightful owners were in the Seven Towers. Another embassy building was clearly necessary. Elgin persuaded the Turks to grant him a site of land suitable for building a permanent British Palace, and at the same time he persuaded the British government and Levant Company to put up the money for the building. He brought over the architect Balestra, one of the artists who were working for him at Athens, and set him to work on a design. The result was a close copy of Elgin's fine new neo-classical country house in Scotland, Broomhall.[11] Unfortunately the building was burnt down in one of Constantinople's frequent fires in 1831.

Lord Elgin enjoyed a position of influence at Constantinople such as no Christian ambassador had ever approached. The Government at home were well pleased with his success and congratulated him in an official letter.[12] All the aims of the embassy had been achieved and Britain was now the dominant power in the eastern Mediterranean. However successful the French might be on the continent of Europe this was one sizeable victory that could be claimed against them. Elgin, at the height of his career, might well look forward to further advancement even though his old friend Lord Grenville, who had helped him so far, had now been replaced as Foreign Secretary by Lord Hawkesbury. But apart from the official letter of commendation there was no sign from home that the Government wanted to do more for him. There was no knighthood, no United Kingdom peerage that would save him from having to be elected as a Scottish Representative Peer. Elgin was never constrained by modesty in these matters. He drew up a 'Memorial to the King' and sent it to the Foreign Secretary with a request that it should be submitted. The Memorial gave a blow by blow account of his career to date setting out the various successes and emphasizing the huge personal expense that they had involved him in. It finished with a straightforward request for a mark of royal favour.[13] But no public honour was forthcoming. A few months later Elgin wrote to Lord Keith, the naval Commander-in-Chief, asking him to explain to the Government in his dispatches what an important part Elgin had played in the conquest of Egypt. He deserved an honour, he wrote, adding disingenuously: 'I have never had one mark of favour nor ever asked one in my life.'[14] But it was no good. The prize which he passionately desired all his life escaped him at his moment of greatest triumph.

9

The Firman

THE first firman which gave privileges to Lord Elgin's agents in Athens was prepared at his request and issued by the Ottoman government in May 1801.[1] Exactly what it said is not known, but it probably required the Ottoman officials in Athens to give permission to Elgin's artists to enter the Acropolis, to draw, to erect scaffolding, and to make moulds. The first firman appears to have been sent direct to the Ottoman officials in Athens through Ottoman channels. It took so long time in the post that by the time it arrived it was of no use.

When the French forces under Admiral Ganteaume's command began to gather at Toulon the British intelligence system got to work. Last time a naval force had gathered there they guessed that the French were preparing to invade Ireland, but the expedition had gone to Egypt. This time they guessed the French were about to invade Greece. When Elgin passed this information to the Turks they sent out an order to all the military governors in the European provinces telling them to put their fortresses into a state of readiness. Among those who received the order was the Disdar of Athens and his first, and perhaps only, action was to forbid Lusieri and Lord Elgin's other artists from entering the Acropolis to draw and mould the sculptures.

The prohibition came into force in May 1801 shortly before Carlyle and Hunt, and Lady Elgin's parents, Mr and Mrs Nisbet, arrived in Athens, and before the first firman arrived. Logotheti and Lusieri both wrote to Elgin asking him to obtain a new firman to enable the artists to continue their work, but it was mainly the Nisbets that persuaded Elgin to persevere. He had been half-inclined to abandon the whole enterprise because of the constant difficulties but, when they wrote to him about the wonderful work that had been done before the prohibition, he decided to ask for a new firman.[2] He opened negotiations with the Capitan Pasha on 14 June, the day he received their letter.[3] A few days earlier Hunt arrived back at Constantinople from Athens and was able to give Elgin another direct eyewitness account of what was happening and what was needed.

Hunt drew up a memorandum which listed the main features of a second, clearer and more comprehensive, firman which he believed was necessary if Lord Elgin's aims were to be achieved.

July 1, 1801. Mr. Hunt recommends that a Ferman should be procured from the Porte, addressed to the Voivode and Cadi [Chief Justice] of Athens, as well as to the Disdar, or Governor of the Citadel; stating that the artists are in the service of the British Ambassador Extraordinary, and that they are to have not only permission but protection in the following objects:—

(1) to enter freely within the walls of the Citadel, and to draw and model with plaster the Ancient Temples there.

(2) to erect scaffolding and to dig where they may wish to discover the ancient foundations.

(3) liberty to take away any sculptures or inscriptions which do not interfere with the works or walls of the Citadel.[4]

The emphasis is on Elgin's original objectives—the artists were to be allowed to draw, to model, and to take away for Elgin's collection any scattered pieces they found lying about. The request for permission to dig was new compared with the existing firman, and the exception in the last section was evidently intended to forestall any Turkish fears that removing antiquities built into the walls would affect the military strength of the fortress. There is nothing in the British Embassy document about seeking permission to take sculptures, or indeed anything, from the ruins of the buildings, as distinct from taking detached pieces lying on the ground or dug up in excavations.[5]

The granting of the firman was negotiated by Pisani, the dragoman, that is the official interpreter, of the British Embassy. Since few people from western Europe knew Turkish and the Turks regarded it as undignified to learn foreign languages, the embassy dragomans did much of the diplomatic work. As intermediaries whose words could not be easily checked by either side, they could wield great power and were much feared. As the Constantinople proverb put it, comparing them to the packs of fierce, wild, and filthy scavenging dogs which infested the city,

> Dio mi guardia dei Dragomani
> Io mi guardero dei Cani.

God save me from the Dragomans, and I will save myself from the Dogs.[6]

On 6 July Pisani, the official British dragoman, reported to Elgin:

I have already got a most complete letter from the Caimacam relative to the artists wh. I wish much to see translated for yr. lordship's and Mr Hunt's observation.[7]

As was the case with many official Ottoman documents of the time, the official translation was given in Italian, at the time the lingua franca of the eastern Mediterranean. A copy was supplied to the Embassy soon afterwards. As Philip Hunt explained to the Select Committee of the House of Commons which investigated the circumstances in 1816:

I advised Lord Elgin to apply to the Porte for a fermaun embracing the particular objects I pointed out to him; and as I had been before deceived with respect to the pretended contents of a fermaun, I begged that this might be accompanied by a literal translation, and that translation I now possess. It is left at Bedford, and I have no means of directing any person to obtain it; I would have brought it if I had been aware I should be summoned before this Committee before I left Bedford.[8]

Hunt evidently made the document available to the Select Committee, and an edited, and in some minor respects inaccurate, translation into English was published among the supporting documents in its report.[9] All subsequent accounts of Lord Elgin's activities before the publication of the first edition of the present book were dependent on this derived English version. The actual document remained in the family among the Hunt papers where I discovered it, and it is now in my possession.[10] The official Italian version is published in full for the first time, 1998, in Appendix 1.

On 17 June General Hutchinson received the surrender of Cairo and the success of the British expedition against the French in Egypt was finally assured. On 6 July Elgin obtained the firman he had asked for.[11] These two events were intimately connected: indeed, allowing for the time news took to travel, one followed at once after the other. Elgin himself acknowledged that he was making little progress in the negotiations for a firman until suddenly the Turks began to shower their British allies with favours. The granting of the second firman was just another gift to be compared with the aigrettes, pelisses, horses, snuff boxes, and medals.

The second firman was a letter addressed to the Governor and Chief Justice of Athens and issued over the seal of Seged Abdullah, the senior official who was acting as deputy, or Kaymacam, for the Grand Vizier during the latter's absence with the army in Egypt. It is in two parts, the first stating the request of Lord Elgin, the second granting it point by point. It is so closely modelled on Hunt's memorandum of 1 July as to be little more than a recasting of the memorandum into official language. The caveat in Hunt's memorandum to limit the works to those which did not affect the military strength of the fortress was omitted, so giving more than was asked for. Whoever was the translator wrote good Tuscan, with some archaisms, but appears to have had difficulty finding the appropriate Italian words for some expressions in the Turkish original which were presumably themselves translations from the English of Hunt's memorandum. The version we have is the result of a translation from English to Turkish and then to Italian.

Although in some places the firman takes the form of a request, it was, as the text makes clear, a direct command from the highest level of the Ottoman Empire made for reasons of official state policy, and it allows no discretion. Despite its appearance of being exact and comprehensive, it becomes a little ambiguous at a crucial point. There can be little doubt that it confers authority for Elgin's agents to enter the Acropolis freely without having to pay, to erect scaffolding, to view and draw the buildings and sculptures, to make moulds, to remove obstructions from the monuments, and to conduct excavations, taking away anything of interest which the excavations yielded. Compared with the terms of the first firman, the explicit permission to dig was new.[12]

The firman confers no authority to remove sculptures from the buildings or to damage them in any way. On the contrary it seems certain that the Ottoman government, if they considered the point at all, only intended to grant permission to dig and take away, which is all they had been asked for in Hunt's memorandum. Nor is there is any indication that at the time either Elgin or any of his entourage believed that the firman gave permission to make removals from the buildings. 'I am happy to tell you,' Lady Elgin wrote on 9 July to her parents:

Pisani has succeeded à merveille in his *firman* from the Porte. Hunt is in raptures for the *firman* is perfection and P. says he will answer with his whiskers that it is exact.

It allows all our artists to go into the citadel to copy and model everything in it, to erect scaffolds all round the Temple, to dig and discover all the ancient foundations, and to bring away any marbles that may be deemed curious by their having inscriptions on them, and that they are not to be disturbed by the soldiers etc. under any pretence whatever. Don't you think this will do? I am in the greatest glee for it would have been a great pity to have failed in the principal part after having been at such an expence.[13]

Lord Elgin wrote at once to Lusieri, urging him to seize the moment. It is clear that he too had no intention at this stage of touching the buildings.

Besides the general work (by which I mean that which had been begun at the departure of Mr. Hunt) it would be very essential that the *Formatori* should be able to take away exact models of the little ornaments or detached pieces if any are found which would be interesting for the Arts... Besides you have now the permission to dig, and there a great field is opened for medals, and for the remains both of sculpture and architecture.[14]

Governments have only themselves to blame if they draft ambiguous instructions which are then misinterpreted by their officials. If one believes, however, that the Turks had any interest at all in preserving the Parthenon, they had bad luck. The removals from the buildings only took place as a result of a series of interrelated contingencies all of them involving the Reverend Philip Hunt. First of all, the firman would not have been drafted in the form it was if Philip Hunt had not happened to be in Athens in May when the trouble started and in Constantinople in July when the good news from Egypt came through. Secondly, the firman would not have been given the interpretation that was later put on it if Hunt had not happened to be the man who was chosen to carry it to Athens and was on the spot to see it implemented, an unusual situation which was also linked to larger events.

While Admiral Ganteaume's squadron still lay at Toulon, the British government became more and more convinced that the French were intending to invade mainland Greece. Elgin decided, therefore, on advice from London, to send someone to Greece to visit the Ottoman governors in the area, to warn them of the consequences if they were tempted to collaborate with a French invasion, to report on their military strength, and to make preparations for the country to receive a garrison of British troops if this should prove necessary. Elgin would normally have sent one of his private secretaries on such a mission, but since Hamilton was in Egypt and Morier was in England on other missions, the only man available for the job was the chaplain and Hunt was appointed temporary private secretary for the purpose.[15]

Since Hunt was going immediately to Athens on his diplomatic mission it seemed sensible that he should be asked to convey the firman to the Voivode, and the Ottoman government agreed to this arrangement. As is confirmed by a phrase in the letter as well as by other direct evidence, the second firman was not sent by Ottoman channels as the first had been. Hunt acted as courier for the Ottoman government, carrying both the original letter and the Italian translation.

Hunt left Constantinople in the middle of July. Besides having the firman for the Voivode of Athens, he carried letters of introduction from the Ottoman government commending him to the authorities of all the places he was due to visit. In addition to the usual retinue of servants, he was accompanied by a senior official of the Ottoman government, Rachid Aga, whose duty, we can guess, was not only, as Hunt was told, to ensure that he was accorded the right treatment, and that his firmans were obeyed, but to keep an eye on what the British were up to. Hunt took with him a large collection of the wherewithal of diplomacy, chandeliers, firearms, telescopes, jewellery, pieces of cloth, and other presents. He arrived in Athens on 22 July, having picked up some inscriptions and statues at the Dardanelles on the way and having survived an encounter with pirates. He was met by Logotheti and put up in his house as the only other quarters in the town were taken by a party of English travellers including Edward Dodwell and William Gell, both of whom he knew from their days at university.

The situation had changed since Hunt was last in Athens. About a month beforehand Logotheti and Lusieri had succeeded, without any new firman, in obtaining permission for the artists to enter the Acropolis from time to time. The normal daily fee, according to another visiting artist, was five pounds of coffee and five pounds of sugar.[16] Even so, Elgin's artists were subjected to constant insult, interruption, and extortion from the soldiers, the Disdar, and the Disdar's son. Dodwell and Gell who were also trying to make drawings on the Acropolis were subjected to the same treatment, reluctantly paying a large daily fee.

Hunt immediately called on the Voivode, to make a protest, to hand over the firman, and to invoke its terms. The Voivode was the superior of the Disdar, and the official of the Ottoman government who accompanied Hunt, if not formally the superior of the Voivode, was a man with huge potential influence over careers. Hunt began by demanding that all Englishmen should be allowed to visit the Acropolis at any time they wanted without interference. The Voivode, after reading the firman, said he was mortified to hear that the Disdar had treated any Englishman with disrespect or had demanded money. The Disdar's son was then sent for, his father being ill. He came in barefooted and trembling and the Porte official announced at once that he was to be sent into exile from Athens. Hunt then interceded and obtained a pardon for him, but the Porte official hinted strongly that if there was another complaint, he would be sent as a slave to the galleys. The effect was immediate. The conference ended with assurances that the Acropolis would be open to all Englishmen from sunrise to sunset and that Lord Elgin's artists would have all the facilities which the firman conferred.

After the interview, Hunt immediately pressed home his advantage. A labour force of Greeks was hired, and men brought from a ship in Piraeus to supervise them. All the inscriptions lying about the Acropolis were collected, including the Athenian Treasury lists and other prime documents of the fifth century; extensive excavations were begun, and the Caryatid porch of the Erechtheion was cleared of its modern obstructions. Then, a few days later, Hunt made the decisive move. He asked the Voivode for permission to take down one of the metopes from the Parthenon. At the time five columns at the east end of the south colonnade were still standing, complete with the architrave, seven metopes, eight triglyphs, and parts of the cornice. The seventh metope, at the corner was already loosened. Although the Parthenon was a ruin, removing sculptures that had fallen to the ground was one thing, removing sculptures from their original places on the surviving building was another.

As Hunt noted in a letter to Elgin a few days later:

Much management was necessary to obtain leave to take them down but the death of the old disdar, which happened a few days ago, facilitated our operations because the son who hopes to succeed him in the office (which has been hereditary in the family above a century) feels how much reason you have to oppose his views and is now submissive to all our views in hopes of your speaking favourably for him to the Porte. He tells me Choiseul gave his father 800 piastres...

Since the choice was between the Disdarship and the galleys his change of attitude is understandable, and when he was appointed Disdar not long afterwards, it was made clear to him that only the entreaties of the English had saved him.[17]

Logotheti, the British Vice-Consul, also had doubts, initially at least. Although, according to Gell, he had shared in the income from bribes taken by the Disdar, he was, as Hunt reported to Elgin, 'timid'.

As archon of Athens, he did not enter *con amore* with the idea of taking the sculptures from the Parthenon and ventured to hint that the Voivode durst not extend the firman to such a point. However Mr Pisani's excellent translation of the Caimacam's second letter and the rumour of the fall of Cairo inspired me with confidence. I spoke in a determined tone and succeeded, I trust, without exacting the least disgust in any party.

It appears to have been the Voivode who decided the outcome. He was soon persuaded to believe that the firman granted permission to remove from the buildings or that at any rate he had the power to grant the permission himself. On 31 July the ship's carpenter with five of the crew mounted the walls of the Parthenon and with the aid of windlasses, cordage, and twenty Greeks succeeded in detaching and lowering down without accident the seventh metope, one of the best surviving. As Hunt reported:

The Voivode behaved with uniform politeness. I did not even mention my having presents for him till the Metopes were in motion.[18]

And so, the vital twist to the firman was given. A sketch made by William Gell in the evening light of that day, reproduced as Plate 3, shows that the seventh metope has already gone, but the sixth was still in its position with a block of the cornice above. The next day the cornice block was thrown to the ground and the sixth metope removed.[19] In Gell's picture the Disdar can be seen wagging his finger at Lusieri, presumably in protest. Lusieri, his arms folded, leans nonchalantly against a column, unmoved by the Disdar's pleas.[20]

The two metopes were taken at once with the aid of a gun carriage to the yard of the British Consul where the Calmuck was given the job of drawing them. They were then conveyed, with the help of the large cart that had once belonged to Fauvel, along the four-mile track to Piraeus and were put on board the ship. Within a few weeks the ship had sailed. Hunt wrote in delight to Lord Elgin:

These admirable specimens of Greek sculpture which have been repeatedly refused to the gold and influence of France in the zenith of her power, I have now embarked with other precious fragments of antiquity on board the ship that brought me here. I trust they will reach England in safety where they must prove of inestimable service in improving the National Taste.[21]

The two metopes were, Hunt declared, the 'chef d'oeuvre' of sculpture.[22] Lusieri said there was nothing so perfect of their kind in the whole universe.[23] But the enthusiasm of the agents on the spot was nothing to that of Lord Elgin. 'The object that I had in view...', he wrote from Constantinople when he heard the news,

now seems to promise a success beyond our most ardent hopes. I venture to flatter myself that my purpose will be attained in a fashion to put the names of my artists on an elevation that no one has approached since the time of the originals whose perfection you are about to revive.[24]

Some of Hunt's answers to questions from the Select Committee when the legality of Elgin's actions was being investigated fifteen years later, confirm that both he and the Voivode realized the terms of the firman were being exceeded. 'Do you imagine,' Hunt was asked, 'that the firmaun gave a direct permission to remove figures and pieces of sculpture from the walls of temples, or that must have been a matter of private arrangement with the local authorities of Athens?' 'That was the interpretation', Hunt answered, 'which the Vaivode of Athens was induced to allow it to bear.'

'In consequence of what was the Vaivode induced to give it this interpretation?'

'With respect to the first metope, it was to gratify what he conceived to be the favourable wishes of the Turkish Government towards Lord Elgin, and which induced him rather to extend than contract the precise permissions of the firmaun.'[25]

Earlier in the hearing before the Select Committee Hunt was asked: 'Was there any difficulty in persuading the Vaivode to give this interpretation to the firmaun?' He replied 'Not a great deal of difficulty.'

Hunt was asked about the extent to which bribes had been paid either in obtaining the firman in Constantinople or in applying its terms in Athens, but he pleaded that he had 'Nothing sufficiently precise to enable me even to conjecture the amount.'[26] He did admit to having made presents of 'brilliant cut glass lustres, fire arms, and other articles of English manufacture'.[27] An English traveller who visited Athens in 1803 after Hunt had left, and who knew Lusieri and Fauvel, tells a different story. For every fragment of sculpture Elgin's agents took, he noted in his diary, they had to pay four, five, or six hundred piastres.[28] At current rates of exchange that would have been roughly equivalent to £45 to £65 a piece.

In his answers, Hunt emphasized the enthusiasm with which the Voivode had co-operated and the readiness of Greek workmen to be employed on Elgin's projects. When asked if there had been 'any opposition shewn by any class of the natives', he answered 'None.'[29]

Whether, under the system of law prevailing at the time in Athens, the Voivode and the Disdar had the legal authority to exceed the powers given by the firman, or to give permission for the removals on their own authority, is unknown. The probability is that they did not.[30] Robert Smirke, who visited Athens in 1803, in discussing how Elgin's agents bent the terms of the second firman, says that 'this power was extended to every part of Greece where the property was the Grand Signor's', that is to all public lands, but there is no other mention in the documents that survive.[31] But, even more than the men from the West, the men of the East knew the difference between law and power. As the career of their predecessor Haseki had shown vividly, the Ottoman service offered high rewards for high risks, and the political situation in Constantinople was constantly changing. No provincial Voivode would willingly risk offending a European ambassador or his agents.

As far as Hunt was concerned, questions of legality or of propriety scarcely arose. In his mind he was taking advantage of a moment of good fortune to perform an act of rescue. 'It grieved me to the heart,' he wrote to Lord Upper Ossory when the first metopes were taken down, 'to see the destruction made daily by the Janizaries of the fortress. They break up the finest bas-reliefs and sculptures in search of the morsels of lead that unite them to the buildings after which they are broken with wanton barbarity.'[32] Lusieri reported the same story to Lord Elgin and it is confirmed by the accounts of many travellers who were unsympathetic to Lord Elgin.

It was the travellers as much as the Turks who now posed the main danger. With the closing of the Continent to British visitors, many moneyed young men who might previously have gone on the Grand Tour to France, Switzerland, and Italy, now ventured further afield. Officers from the large British military and naval forces in the eastern Mediterranean liked nothing better than to spend part

of their leave visiting the sights. As Lord Elgin himself said in his
defence to the Select Committee in 1816:

Every traveller coming added to the general defacement of the statuary in
his reach: there are now in London pieces broken off within our day. And
the Turks have been continually defacing the heads; and in some instances
they have actually acknowledged to me that they have pounded down the
statues to convert them into mortar: It was upon these suggestions, and
with these feelings, that I proceeded to remove as much of the sculpture
as I conveniently could; it was no part of my original plan to bring away
any thing but my models.[33]

The sculptures themselves offered ample confirmation that he was
right. In 1749 the traveller Dalton drew twelve figures in the west
pediment of the Parthenon. By the time Lusieri arrived in 1800
there were only four. Five slabs of the frieze drawn by Stuart
between 1750 and 1755 had completely disappeared. The two
figures in the left corner of the west pediment still had their heads
when they were drawn by Pars in 1765. By the time Lusieri arrived
both heads had gone. One slab of the frieze of which a mould had
been taken by the Frenchman Fauvel as recently as 1790 had been
utterly destroyed. The metopes tell a similar story of constant,
rapidly increasing, erosion.[34] As one traveller noted:

If the progress of decay should continue to be as rapid as it has been for
something more than a century past, there will, in a few years, be not one
marble standing upon another on the site of the Parthenon.[35]

As the first metope was being lowered from the Parthenon the
Disdar's son told Hunt that Choiseul-Gouffier had given his father
800 piastres for the adjoining metope, but that as it was being taken
down the rope broke and the metope was dashed to a thousand
pieces.[36] This story was untrue—Choiseul-Gouffier never succeeded in obtaining any sculptures from the building.[37] It was,
however, just the sort of story to suit Elgin's book and he never
doubted it.[38] The excuse that it was the French who had started
it carried great weight with British public opinion which, as the
war went on, began to regard anything the French did with deep
loathing.

By 1839, when the Elgin Marbles were safe in London, the
author of the official British Museum catalogue could let his imagination loose. Choiseul-Gouffier was the first to remove a sculpture
from the Parthenon, he said. 'The machinery he first used was
defective, the ropes failed and the marble was broken to pieces;

fresh tackle was then procured from Toulon and the removal proceeded satisfactorily.'[39] This was all unfair on Choiseul-Gouffier
whose motives were as honourable, and his methods as efficient, as
those of Elgin. Nevertheless the story does illustrate a more general
point. If the accessible sculptures of the Parthenon had not been
taken by Elgin they might equally have been taken by the French.
In 1801 it must have seemed only a matter of time before someone,
French or British, acquired the right combination of opportunity
and resources to attempt large-scale removals whether in the name
of rescue, of scholarship, or of a desire to improve the arts of
modern Europe.

10

'The Last Poor Plunder from a Bleeding Land'

THE first excavations on the Acropolis produced a rich harvest. Beneath the west end of the Parthenon, where the house of a Turkish soldier was bought and pulled down, the diggers uncovered some of the huge figures of the west pediment that had been thrown to the ground and broken by the explosion of 1687. Excavations were then begun on the south side and a number of other fragments from the pediments and some parts of the south frieze were recovered. The central slab of the frieze which shows the mysterious handing over of the cloth, and which is the key to the possible understanding of the whole monument, was found built into the south wall of the Acropolis. It had been removed from its place on the building at some early time, probably when the temple was converted into a Christian church (Plate 1). Since all the frieze sculptures had been carved direct on to the full-size marble blocks from which the building was constructed, the backs of the marble blocks were sawn off with saws specially obtained from Constantinople.

There were evidently limits, both legal and practical, to the extent to which the local Ottoman authorities could legally interfere with property rights even on the Acropolis. When at another site on the Acropolis the owner was unwilling to sell his house, a firman for a compulsory purchase order was obtained from Constantinople to buy it compulsorily. The excavations, which went down to the bedrock, yielded nothing. The Turk whose house it was declared laughingly that he had used the marble from the statues found on that spot to make the mortar.[1]

As was pointed out not long after, this story if true must have referred to events of long before. By the beginning of the nineteenth century, pieces of sculptured marble, which could be sold to tourists, were unlikely to have been used for making lime, and in any case the walls of the houses on the Acropolis were made with clay, which gave better protection against earthquakes.[2] It was, however, a good story and one which has stuck. When in 1965 a Member of Parliament repeated that the Elgin Marbles had been rescued from the Turks who were turning them into mortar, Harold Wilson, the Prime Minister, quipped that questions on the cement industry were for the Minister of Works.

Once the initial step to allow removals was taken, all the authorities in Athens, whether Turk or Greek, civil, military, or religious, co-operated fully and enthusiastically. As Hunt wrote to Elgin:

During the whole of my residence in Athens, I am happy to inform your Lordship that there was not an individual, either among the Officers of the Porte, or the Greeks of the city, who did not sem to vie with each other in gratifying your wishes, particularly the voivode, the archbishop, and our agent Logotheti, who conjointly possess all the power of the place.[3]

With high prices being paid, the people of Athens who used to guard the ancient fragments built into their houses were, it was said, now delighted to sell any fragments of carvings or inscriptions that they possessed or found in diggings.

Besides the general firmans obtained from Constantinople, there are references to many other firmans for more limited purposes having been issued locally, on their own authority, by the Voivode of Athens and other Ottoman governors in Greece. Many were to permit digging and removals in sites in Athens outside the Acropolis area. The Archbishop of Athens, who co-operated fully with Elgin's agents, also gave permissions for removals from buildings which were the property of the Orthodox Church.[4]

According to Hunt, no one made any objection or expressed any regrets.[5] Elgin encouraged the work from Constantinople, urging his agents not only to copy and to dig, but also now to take specimens of architecture from all the surviving ruins.

I should wish to have examples in the actual object, of each thing, and architectural ornament—of each cornice, each frieze, each capital—of the decorated ceilings, of the fluted columns—specimens of the different architectural orders and of the variant forms of the orders,—of metopes and the like, as much as possible. Finally everything in the way of sculpture, medals, and curious marbles that can be discovered by means of assiduous and indefatigable excavation. This excavation ought to be pushed on as much as possible, be its success what it may.[6]

When the Caryatid porch of the Erechtheion was first cleared of its modern accretions Hunt suggested that the whole building could be removed and rebuilt in England. 'If your Lordship', he wrote, 'would come here in a large Man of War that beautiful little model of ancient art might be transported wholly to England.'[7] Elgin at once wrote to Lord Keith to ask for a naval ship.

I have been at a monstrous expense at Athens where I at this moment possess advantages beyond belief. . . . Now if you would allow a ship of war of size to convoy the Commissary's ship and stop a couple of days at Athens to get away a most valuable piece of architecture at my disposal there you could confer upon me the greatest obligation I could receive and do a very essential service to the Arts in England. Bonaparte has not got such a thing from all his thefts in Italy. Pray kindly attend to this my Lord.[8]

For the time being no ship could be spared and, for the time being, the Caryatid porch survived, the artists contenting themselves with sawing off choice pieces of the cornice selected to illustrate details of the Ionic order. The Erechtheion episode also showed that there were limits to the power of the firman. When Hunt suggested removing the whole Caryatid porch there were murmurs. 'The Turks and the Greeks are extremely attached to it', Lusieri reported, and the only hope of securing it for Elgin was to obtain a special additional firman from Constantinople.[9] As for the Monument of Lysicrates, another building small enough to be considered for removal *in toto*, it belonged to the French Capuchins. The only hope of getting the necessary permission, Lusieri suggested, was to offer money to the head of the monastery who lived in Constantinople.[10]

For those parts of the architecture and the sculpture which Elgin's artists decided not to remove, scaffolds were erected so as to enable the moulders, architects, and artists to make a detailed record. When the moulders had difficulty in making satisfactory moulds with the earth to be found near Athens, Elgin chartered a vessel to bring a more suitable type from the island of Melos.[11] Gangs of carpenters, diggers, porters, and others were taken on to Elgin's payroll, and his agents gathered in inscriptions, vases, coins, and other antiquities. Logotheti made Elgin a present of some antiquities that had been lying in his yard for many years.

Meanwhile Philip Hunt had gone on his diplomatic tour of the Greek mainland to encourage the local pashas to resist the French. Accompanied by Rachid Aga, he visited many of the famous clas-

sical sites, looking for removable antiquities wherever he went. Ali
Pasha of Ioannina promised to send any antiquities discovered in
his province and said he had recently broken up some statues that
'only seemed to want breath' to make them real.[12] At Thebes Hunt
obtained an ancient cameo of a female centaur suckling her infant.
At Mycenae, helped by the Voivode of Nauplia, he cast covetous
eyes over the Lion Gate but decided regretfully that it was too far
from the sea for there to be hope of removing it. At Eleusis, the
site of the Temple of Demeter and home of the Mysteries, he saw
what he thought was a colossal statue of Demeter and suggested
that it was worth taking away.

The aims continued to be utilitarian. All the work, whether
drawing, moulding, or collecting actual specimens of sculpture and
architecture, was intended to help to improve the arts in Britain.
As Elgin wrote to Hunt:

The very great variety in our manufactures, in objects either of elegance
or luxury, offers a thousand applications for such details. A chair, a foot-
stool, designs or shapes for porcelain, ornaments for cornices, nothing is
indifferent, and whether it be in painting or a model, exact representations
of such things would be much to be desired.[13]

Neither Elgin nor his agents were interested much in archaeology
as a study of the past for its own sake, nor in collecting antiquities
which might illustrate the different periods and changing styles of
Greek art. Only the best would do, and for their purposes the best
meant the high classical period of the fifth century. Outside Athens,
there were few places which they regarded as worth considering
apart from Olympia 'where the arts of Greece had been advanced
to the highest degree of perfection'.[14] When Hunt viewed the
remains of the temples at Aegina and at Bassae he decided not to
waste any resources even on copying them. As he wrote after his
reconnaissance of the sites of the Peloponnese:

I have found nothing so far that needs a formatore, still less a figure
painter ... It is well known that the true models and all the refinements of
the [Doric] order are met with in the Temple of Minerva at Athens.[15]

While Hunt was on his travels Elgin engaged one of the survivors
of the Koehler mission to act as supervisor at Athens. Thomas Lacy,
a captain in the Royal Engineers, accepted the job mainly as a
means of escaping from Egypt and the ill-fated assignment that he
had been sent on three years before. 'Congratulate me,' he wrote

to Hunt, 'I have at length found means to escape from the Mission and shall now be at leisure to devote myself to my friends. In two days I embark for Athens to plunder temples and commit sacrilege, a proper finish to my diplomatic career.'[16] But Lacy quarrelled with Lusieri and soon went off on a tour of the classical sites, returning to England not long afterwards.

Lacy's engineering knowledge would have been useful. As the experience with the first two metopes from the Parthenon had shown, it was impossible to remove the metopes and frieze, which were an integral part of the structure of the building, without causing a good deal of further damage. Some of the removals were not skilful. The traveller Edward Dodwell, who had benefited from Hunt's firman, spent his days sketching on the Acropolis. He was now on the best of terms with the new Disdar, to whom he gave a bottle of wine whenever his dinner was sent up. He was in Athens when the first two metopes were removed in 1801, and again in 1805 when he saw the results of what was done later. The description which he gave in a book published in 1819 ran together some of his memories:

During my first tour to Greece I had the inexpressible mortification of being present when the Parthenon was despoiled of its finest sculpture, and when some of its architectural members were thrown to the ground. I saw several metopae at the south east extremity of the temple taken down. They were fixed in between the triglyphs as in a groove; and in order to lift them up, it was necessary to throw to the ground the magnificent cornice by which they were covered. The south east angle of the pediment shared the same fate; and instead of the picturesque beauty and high preservation in which I first saw it, it is now comparatively reduced to a state of shattered desolation.[17]

Another eyewitness was Edward Daniel Clarke, who arrived in Athens in the course of his long tour in October 1801. Since his quarrel with Carlyle and Hunt in the Troad he had been to Cyprus, the Holy Land, Egypt, and the Greek Islands. Although his antipathy to Hunt was great, his account has the ring of plausibility.

Some workmen, employed under his [Lusieri's] direction for the British Ambassador, were then engaged in making preparation, by means of ropes and pulleys, for taking down the metopes, where the sculptures remained the most perfect. The Disdar himself came to view the work but with evident marks of dissatisfaction; and Lusieri told us that it was with great difficulty he could accomplish this part of his undertaking from the attachment the Turks entertained towards a building which they had been accustomed to regard with religious veneration and had converted into a mosque. We confessed that we participated in the Mahometan feeling in this instance and would gladly see an order enforced to preserve rather than destroy such a glorious edifice. After a short time spent in examining the several parts of the temple one of the workmen came to inform Don Battista that they were then going to lower one of the metopes. We saw this fine piece of sculpture raised from its station between the triglyphs: but the workmen endeavouring to give it a position adapted to the projected line of descent, a part of the adjoining masonry was loosened by the machinery; and down came the fine masses of Pentelican marble, scattering their white fragments with thundering noise among the ruins. The Disdar, seeing this could no longer restrain his emotions; but actually took his pipe from his mouth, and letting fall a tear, said in a most emphatic tone of voice 'telos' ['The end!' or 'Never again!'] positively declaring that nothing should induce him to consent to any further dilapidations of the building. Looking up we saw with regret the gap that had been made; which all the ambassadors of the earth, with all the sovereigns they represent aided by every resource that wealth and talent can now bestow, will never again repair.[18]

Clarke later told the story to Lord Byron, who incorporated it in a note to *Childe Harold's Pilgrimage* which was published in 1812.[19]

If we compare the drawing made by Gell in 1801, shown as Plate 3, with the one in a book by Hobhouse made in 1810, shown as Plate 5, we can see the extent of the change. By 1810 not only the metopes but the cornice had entirely disappeared. All that was then left was a series of jagged blocks sticking up like broken teeth. On the south side, all that was left was the metope at the extreme west, one of the finest and best preserved of all. Until it was taken down and replaced by a replica, that metope remained in solitary splendour, a last example of the sculptor's and architect's skill. One reason it was left until recent years was the sheer physical difficulty of removing it. It is surmounted by a huge block which forms part of the pediment. To have removed it by the methods available to Elgin's agents would have required irreparable damage to a vital part of the building which was still in good condition.

Two pedimental sculptures which could have been removed without much difficulty were allowed to remain in place on the building, even although the sculptures on either side were taken away. The two seated embracing figures, which are now believed to represent Cecrops, the legendary first king of Athens and his daughter, were in as good a state of preservation as the rest, but had suffered badly in recent years.[20] As recently as 1795 both

figures still kept their heads, with one exception, the only pedimental sculptures to do so. Sometime soon after that date one of
the heads was broken off by a British sailor.[21] In 1801 the other was
still in place but it disappeared from the statue soon afterwards.[22]

When the Englishman Sir George Wheler and the Frenchman
Dr Spon visited the Acropolis in 1671, at a time before the explo-
sion in the Parthenon when the whole pediment was still in place,
Wheler remarked on the two figures:

> my companion made me observe the next two Figures sitting in the Corner
> to be of the Emperour Adrian and his Empress Sabina, whom I easily knew
> to be so by the many Medals and Statues I have seen of them.[23]

Spon's own account offered his explanation for his opinion:

> Ceux figures des deux frontons n'étoient pas si anciennes que le corps du
> Temple bâti par Pericles, & il n'en faut pas d'autre argument, que celuy de
> la statuë d'Hadrian qui s'y void, & le marbre qui en est plus blanc. Tout le
> reste n'a pas été touché.

> These figures on the two pediments were not as old as the body of the
> Temple built by Pericles, and there must be no argument about the one of
> the statue of Hadrian which one sees there and whose marble is more
> white. All the rest have not been touched.[24]

What Wheler and Spon suggested was, at best, a speculation for
which there was no ancient or other documentary authority, and
they saw the sculptures at a distance from the ground. Nevertheless
the story that the two figures were Roman additions intended to
flatter Hadrian and Sabina, the emperor and his wife who had instituted the rebuilding of Athens, entered the tradition of both
English and French travellers. When Stuart and Revett carelessly
included it as a fact in *The Antiquities of Athens*, the error could
not easily be reversed. Fauvel believed it.[25] It was accepted without
question by Philip Hunt, and it was because they were believed to
be inferior works, that after Elgin's agents had taken their pick
these two sad fragments were the only reasonably complete pedimental sculptures to be deliberately left on the building.[26] They too,
having suffered further in the meantime, were taken down in the
1980s and have been replaced by replicas as part of the recent conservation programme. Both the heads are now lost.

Clarke too was an eager collector. At Alexandria he had found
a sarcophagus which he convinced himself was the tomb of
Alexander the Great.[27] His judgements about the many antiquities
he obtained in Greece were equally imaginative. The piece he was

most proud of was an inscription which, he said, he 'bought of a consul from under the very nose of the ambassador's chaplain and his host of gothic plunderers'.[28] But the Euclid whose tombsone he had found was not the famous geometer.

Clarke also obtained a small marble relief which, with his usual confidence, he pronounced to be 'nothing less than a fragment of one of the metopes belonging to the Parthenon and there-fore...the undoubted work of Phidias'.[29] It was difficult to take anything from the Acropolis except into Elgin's storehouse, but Clarke persuaded the Disdar to give it to him secretly. In fact the fragment is not from the Parthenon at all but is a coarsely carved piece of an old gravestone. Clarke later felt some embarrassment that he had obtained his own fragment of the Parthenon, but per-suaded himself that his piece was 'the solitary example of sculpture removed from the Parthenon without injuring what time and the Goths had spared'.[30] The Disdar also sold him some architectural fragments from the Erechtheion, but, like the Dodwell fragments, these too are now lost.[31]

Clarke's greatest antiquarian triumph was to secure the colossal statue from Eleusis that Hunt had pronounced worthy to be added to the Elgin collection. This much battered bust of a woman with a basket on her head was, like many surviving antiquities, held in veneration by the local inhabitants, and like many antiquities it had been much sought after by collectors, including Choiseul-Gouffier. Eleusis in ancient times was a shrine of Demeter, the goddess of corn and fertility, and the behaviour of the modern Eleusinians seemed living proof that the pagan tradition of worship of Demeter was still flourishing. A traveller who visited Eleusis in 1765 reported that the local inhabitants regarded the fertility of the land as depending on the statue and Clarke found that they lit a lamp before it on festival days.[32] They told him that as often as foreigners came to remove the statue some disaster occurred and that the arm of any person who touched it with violence would fall off.[33]

Clarke acted quickly and secretly to forestall Elgin's agents. As he wrote with the usual contempt for the protests and beliefs of the local inhabitants:

I found the goddess in a dunghill buried to her ears. The Eleusinian peas-ants, at the very mention of moving it, regarded me as one who would bring the moon from her orbit. What would become of their corn, they said, if the old lady with her basket was removed? I went to Athens and made application to the Pacha, aiding my request by letting an English telescope glide between his fingers. The business was done.[34]

The English telescope which did the trick Clarke had obtained from Lusieri, who temporarily abandoned his loyalty to Elgin and connived with Clarke for the purpose.[35] Clarke was just in time. Shortly afterwards Elgin sent Lusieri a telescope made by the best maker in London as a gift for the Voivode. His instructions were, 'Make good use of it. I still hope you will find the means to procure for me the colossal bust of Ceres at Eleusis.'[36]

Ropes and poles were obtained from Athens and the jetty at Eleusis had to be repaired. And the local inhabitants had to be persuaded. On the night before the statue was due to be removed an accident occurred which seemed to confirm the opinions of the Eleusinians. While they were conversing with the Turkish officer who brought a firman from the Voivode of Athens, one of the oxen broke loose from its yoke and butted violently at the statue with its horns, and then ran amok over the plain of Eleusis, bellowing loudly. The Eleusinians joined in the clamour and there was nearly a riot. They had always been famous for their corn, they shouted, and the fertility of the land would cease if the statue was removed.

Next day the Eleusinians agreed to obey the Voivode's decree. The local priest, arrayed in full vestments, struck the first blow to remove the rubbish. After many hours' work a force of one hundred men and fifty boys eventually succeeded in hauling the statue to the shore, where it was loaded into a ship Clarke had chartered. Elgin generously forgave Clarke for 'plucking the jewel from his crown', and allowed it to go home in a warship from Smyrna.[37] It was a damaged piece, Lusieri assured Elgin, reminding him of his artistic objectives, 'more interesting to antiquaries than to artists'.[38]

In the first year the crop was good and the Eleusinians believed that their goddess would return. In the next year it was not so good and they feared she must have deserted them. Gradually they convinced themselves that only witchcraft could have carried her off. The goddess did, however, have some revenge. The ship taking her to England foundered off Beachy Head and it was only with great difficulty that she was recovered from the sea-bed.[39] She now stands in a corner of the Fitzwilliam Museum at Cambridge. An object which had been venerated over a longer continuous period than any other from the ancient world is now regarded as a second-rate architectural fragment and hardly engages the attention of the casual visitor.

In the spring of 1802 Lord Elgin decided to pay a personal visit to Greece to see the situation for himself. He had asked London for permission to be away from the capital in 1800 but the Egyptian expedition and troubles with Spencer Smith had intervened.[40] He asked again in July 1801 on the day after the firman was obtained, and this time permission was granted.[41] His second child was born in August 1801 and Lady Elgin was pregnant for the third time when they set off, but it was necessary to press ahead quickly before the French could persuade the Turks to withdraw their permission. Lady Elgin produced another reason: 'If it were not for leaving the little girl this would be the most desirable tour possible; for travelling through this country while Elgin's ambassadorial titles and pomp remain, is certainly a very great advantage. We mean to take a number of servants to cut a dash.'[42] The ambassadorial party arrived at Athens at the beginning of April 1802. During the stay two British warships lay in the harbour.

Elgin was delighted with everything Hunt and Lusieri had achieved.[43] Gifts were showered on the Voivode and other Turkish officials, and Lusieri was given authority to increase the already vast expenditure. Elgin did not himself see many of the Parthenon sculptures as most had already been packed up for shipping, but he was on the spot when the horse's head of the chariot of the waning moon was taken from its corner in the east pediment. He urged his agents on, telling them to dig and buy and take away. No effort or money was to be spared to get what was wanted from the Acropolis, and that work was to have priority over everything else. In a letter of 19 May Lady Elgin gives an unguarded vivid glimpse of the unscrupulous exercise of raw power:

Yesterday morning the Voivode sent word to the Disdar that he was going to ye Acropolis to see what we had got and what more we wanted. Upon which the Disdar told Lusieri that he was *frightened* the Voivode wd. find fault with him. This was a good opportunity for Lusieri who *whissled* in his *lug* that he need be under no sort of uneasiness for if the Voivode said anything to him he might inform him that *I* had in *my* possession firmans which if necessary would settle everything. This I told Lusieri to *let off* upon some convenient occasion. I suppose the Disdar had let the Voivode into this *Secret* for in the evening when Logotheti went to ye Voivode to pay 170 ps [Piastres] for the statue the Voivode sent him to me with a thousand compts to beg *I* would accept of it.[44]

Which particular statue Lady Elgin is referring to is not known, but it evidently belonged to a Greek who was unwilling to give it up. Three days later Lady Elgin was able to report:

I have got George's statue price 170 piastres. I think enormous but he expected to make his fortune and would not part with it so today he was taken before the Voivode and as Lusieri says *forced* to give it.[45]

This appears to have been an exercise of unofficial pressure rather than of legal power.[46]

By 2 June Lady Elgin was able to announce, 'We yesterday got down the last thing we want from the Acropolis so now we may boldly bid defiance to our enemies.'[47] In the ten months since Hunt first arrived with the firman more than half of the Parthenon sculptures which were to form the Elgin collection had been taken. They included at least seven metopes, about twenty slabs of the frieze, and almost all the surviving figures from the pediments so far found.

With everything being done in Athens that could be done, Elgin spent several weeks on a tour of the classical sites of Greece. Everywhere he went he collected more antiquities and sent back streams of instructions to Lusieri. The monasteries round Athens were to be searched, columns were to be taken from Daphne, and excavations were to be started at Eleusis. The architects, if they could be spared from the Acropolis, were to be sent to supervise diggings at various parts of the Peloponnese, and the feasibility of large-scale excavations at Olympia was to be looked at again. At Mycenae Elgin was so impressed by the ruins that, with the authority of a firman issued by the local Voivode, he ordered excavations to be started at once and was able to obtain some ancient pillars as well as some vases.

In the course of the tour the Ambassador and his party made a ceremonial entry into Tripolis to pay his respects to the Pasha of the Peloponnese, or the Morea as it was called at the time. Even in the remote provinces Turkish magnificence was not stinted. Lady Elgin gave her usual vivid description.

Three Parade Horses were sent for Elgin, Mr. Hunt and Dr. Scott besides a great many led Horses all with the most brilliant furniture, the Lieutenant Governor and the first Chamberlain riding by their side, the Dragoman of the Morea preceding, and a train of at least six or seven hundred on Horseback following. All the Inhabitants of the Town in their best dresses and well armed lined the Avenues to the Gate, and as we approached, the Great Cannon were fired from every Fort round the Walls of the City. One man out of a large embroidered box kept flinging money to the Children and poor People on the road. There was something extremely grand in that. In the Evening we alighted at the house of the Dragoman of the Morea which was assigned for our residence, and were waited on by the officers of the Pasha and Bey to congratulate us on our arrival, and an immense Supper of 30 or 40 dishes dressed in the Turkish style were sent from the Pasha's Seraglio.[48]

The next day the audience with the Pasha took place and there were the usual gifts of pelisses, shawls, and horses. More important for Elgin, whose collection of these commodities must by now have exceeded his wants, the Pasha gave approval for excavations and removals anywhere in his province.

In the middle of June Elgin left Athens in HMS *Narcissus* on his way back to Constantinople. He left behind instructions that would keep his army of diggers busy for years. He sailed round to Marathon, where he ordered more digging, and then set off across the Aegean, calling at several islands to pick up antiquities. These was no temptation to hurry back to Constantinople. Not only had plague broken out but the Pasha of Central Greece, or Roumelia, was in revolt and reported to be only twenty-four hours' march from the capital. Lady Elgin as usual was almost continuously seasick. Near Delos the *Narcissus* sighted a pirate ship attacking a British merchantman. They gave chase but the pirates landed on the island and started to fire at the *Narcissus* from the cliffs. The Captain ordered the *Narcissus* to fire at the ship until she sank and then sent a party of marines ashore to attack the crew. Twenty-five were captured.[49]

On 1 August Elgin arrived at Smyrna and stayed for a while with the Levant Company merchants who were settled there. Not only was it so hot that plague was expected, but he took ill before they arrived and there was already an epidemic of whooping cough among the children. The Smyrna merchants who hated the intervention of the Government in their affairs had, it turned out, believed all Spencer Smith's complaints, and they received Elgin with marked coldness. Many of them had been profiteering out of the Egyptian war.[50] At last at the beginning of September, after a tour that had lasted six months, Lord and Lady Elgin arrived back to the comparative safety of Constantinople, having escaped bandits, plague, and insurrection.

They were just in time for the birth of their third child. But Elgin had now had enough. He was tired of the East and his health had not improved as he had expected. All the diplomatic objectives of the embassy had been achieved and his own schemes had succeeded far beyond his most optimistic hopes. It was time to return to England to promote his political career and to put his collection of marbles in order. Permission to end the Embassy Extraordinary was given by the Government and it was arranged that he should leave Constantinople for home in January 1803.

During the summer and autumn of 1802 six continuous slabs of the Parthenon frieze were taken from the building and two more metopes. Another slab of the frieze was discovered in excavations. Four slabs of the frieze of the Temple of Athena Nike were discovered built into the fortifications of the Acropolis and successfully removed. Examples of all the architectural details were taken, capitals, bases, cornices, and pieces of pillar from the Parthenon, the Propylaea, the Erechtheion, and the Temple of Nike. The Parthenon capital selected to be the example of that feature of the architecture had to be sawn in two before it could be moved. The colossal headless statue of Dionysos which stood above the Monument of Thrasyllos on the south side of the Acropolis was removed on the day the Voivode was given a horse and green cape.

The haste with which everything was done caused more casualties. On 16 September Lusieri reported 'I have, my Lord, the pleasure of announcing to you the possession of the 8th metope that one where there is the Centaur carrying off the woman. This piece has caused much trouble in all respects and I have even been obliged to be a little barbarous.'[51] Another slab of the frieze, the great central slab on the east side showing the central event was taken from the Acropolis wall in to which it had been built many years before (Plate 1). On its way down to Piraeus it broke into two pieces in a line down the middle. Fortunately it broke at a place where there was no carving. The money seemed inexhaustible, and horses, telescopes, and shawls were heaped on the Voivode and Disdar until even they must have had enough.

On his return to Constantinople Elgin obtained from the Ottoman government letters which confirmed that the Government approved of all that the Voivode and Disdar had done. Elgin thus obtained an official legitimation, after the event, of any illegalities perpetrated under the terms of the firman of July 1801. Although in a constantly changing political situation there were no guarantees, the documents provided a measure of protection to the Voivode and Disdar that, if and when official policy changed, they would not be blamed, dismissed, imprisoned, sent to the galleys, summoned to Constantinople for public beheading, or quietly done away with by official assassins. Lusieri handed over the documents to the two men, much to their relief, in October 1802.[52]

At about the same time a high official, mou bashir, from Constantinople accompanied by Engineer Calfi, arrived in Athens to inspect the defences of the Acropolis. Successive Voivodes and Disdars had repeatedly pleaded that repairs were urgently needed, while quoting such terrifying large sums as their estimate of the expenditure needed that the local Greeks trembled at the thought of the taxes. As Hunt reported to Elgin:

It is supposed by the Turks here, that as the English and French have lately shewn so much interest about the Antiquities of Athens, as if it were like Mecca to the Mahometans or Jerusalem to the Crusaders, this will be the first place of Attack in case of a War with either the French or with us. The Greeks, on the contrary, think, that as so many Franks visit Athens, who go to no other part of the Turkish Empire, it is intended to repair the fortress to Strike Travellers with a grand idea of their Military Establishments.[53]

It is not known what, if any, works were actually carried out on the Acropolis at this time. It is fair to conclude, however, that one of the purposes of the visit was for the Ottoman government in Constantinople to obtain first-hand information about what exactly Elgin's agents were doing in Athens. The fact that his operations were allowed to continue is further confirmation that the Ottoman government knew what was going on and condoned it.

As time passed and Elgin's schemes became ever more ambitious another threat to his activities, more dangerous than the protests of disgruntled travellers, appeared on the horizon. The French were on their way back. With the withdrawal of their army from Egypt it was only a matter of time before peace between France and Turkey was restored. If a French Ambassador re-appeared at Constantinople Elgin could be sure he would do everything in his power to put an end to the removals at Athens —even if only to keep open the possibility that the antiquities might later be taken by France.

At Athens Louis-François-Sébastien Fauvel, who had dominated the antiquarian scene before the arrival of Lusieri, was expected to return, and no one could have any doubt about what his attitude would be. Fauvel had been in prison when Elgin's artists first arrived in 1800, but even from there his influence had still been felt. The Calmuck and the architects were suspected by Lusieri of concealing drawings and measurements with the intention of selling them to Fauvel, and had to be regularly searched. In July 1801 the French prisoners at Athens, including Fauvel, were sent to Constantinople—the ship in which they were carried passed the one bringing Hunt and the firman outside Piraeus.[54] But although Fauvel was out of the way during the critical initial removals, the French found ways of sabotaging the operations. A French doctor who had managed to escape internment by claiming Danish citizenship, cut off the water supply to Lusieri's store. Lusieri also protested that the doctor 'has made and continues to make efforts to stop our acquisitions by sowing foolish ideas in the weak minds of the Turks'.[55]

While the Franco-Turkish war continued the French property at Athens was in theory sequestrated. This had not prevented the Turks from giving Lusieri the large cart and tackle that had belonged to Choiseul-Gouffier and subsequently to Fauvel. As they were the only effective equipment in all Athens it is doubtful if Lusieri could have removed the Parthenon marbles without them. But besides this tackle, there still remained in the cellars of the Capuchin Monastery the collection of antiquities that Fauvel had in his possession when he was arrested. They included the metope from the Parthenon that he had obtained for Choiseul-Gouffier when it fell from the building in a storm fourteen years before. Lusieri, whose antipathy to Fauvel was stronger than his enthusiasm for Lord Elgin, suggested various schemes to seize the collection by force or to buy it, but he did not succeed.[56] Choiseul-Gouffier later accused Elgin's agents of having taken some of his antiquities from another storehouse at Piraeus, but there is no evidence that Lusieri ever succeeded in doing so.[57]

The news that Fauvel was coming back, and this time as an official representative of the French government, brought dismay to the British camp. Lusieri suggested that another cart should be specially made at Naples. He also recommended that the Calmuck should be sent away from Athens as he was too unreliable when Fauvel was around. The French abbot of the Capuchin Monastery was afraid he would incur official displeasure for having allowed

Elgin's agents to mould the frieze of the Monument of Lysicrates. Fauvel reached Athens in January 1803.

The French influence also reappeared at Constantinople. Peace between France and Turkey was concluded in October, and Elgin, as expected, had to hand back the Embassy building. In December 1802 Count Sébastiani arrived as the personal agent of First Consul Bonaparte. As Lady Elgin noted:

There is a smart French Beau just arrived from Paris to sign a treaty of Peace with the Turks, he arrived two days too late. He has called upon us and was excessively civil; there is another young man come with him, they are both equipped *parfaitement à la mode* and are both handsome: I wish you could see the fuss everybody makes of them.[58]

With Turkish gratitude to the British already on the wane, Elgin had better seize his moment at Athens while it lasted. Removing the marbles from the Acropolis to the storehouse in the town was one thing. Transporting them to Piraeus and shipping them to England was another. There were many British warships and merchantmen in the eastern Mediterranean as a result of the Egyptian campaign but not many of them called at the Piraeus, and their captains, understandably, were not eager to weigh down their ships with heavy cases. When peace came in March 1802 matters were easier, but even then the British were under treaty to evacuate Malta by midsummer and Malta was an essential staging post.

No one questioned Elgin's right to use Royal Navy ships and British government transport vessels to carry home his collection of marbles even although they were private property, but he was obliged to use whatever vessels he could find. The first two metopes that Hunt obtained with the help of the second firman were, for example, taken to Egypt in a Ragusan merchantman, the *Constanza*, and when the ship was obliged by the weather to put into Halicarnassos and Cnidos Hunt carried off more antiquities from both places. The captain of HMS *Cynthia*, on the other hand, refused to take any cases on board and sailed after only thirty-six hours in harbour. The marbles in Elgin's collection reached England by a variety of routes, usually after long delays, mostly by way of Alexandria or Smyrna. Almost all were unloaded at Malta and found their way from there as opportunity offered.

It was probably as a result of his difficulties with the Navy, and because of the increasing threat from the French, that Elgin decided to use his own ship, the small brig *Mentor*, which he had originally bought to take him on his tour of Greece. The *Mentor*'s first task in December 1801 was to take ten cases of marbles and moulds from Piraeus to Alexandria, not a large cargo, and only a fraction of the cases already piling up in Athens, but all she would take. Elgin wrote to Malta to try to buy a bigger ship but for some reason nothing came of this idea, although he managed to charter a small brigantine, the *Dorinda*, which later took away a few cases. In March 1802 the frigate HMS *La Diane* took some cases and in May HMS *Mutine* some more, but the cases continued to pile up more quickly than they could be taken away. As emerges from a notice prepared by Lusieri, everything was to be sent to Elgin care of the Foreign Office in London:

If any of the articles require being cased it would much oblige Lord Elgin to make cases for them similar to the others; and if any of the cases etc are without Direction, it will be esteemed a great Favour to make them in strong letters with the Name of His Excellency The Earl of Elgin, Ambassador Extraordinary and Plenipotentiary at the Porte, Downing Street, London.[59]

Lady Elgin was in Athens when HMS *Mutine* came in, and it was she who persuaded Captain Hoste that he must oblige. As she told Elgin who was on his tour:

I began by saying as the Capt. was going straight to Malta & there being no Enemies to encounter I ventured to propose his taking them. It would be doing me a very great favour as you were extremely anxious to get them off & *I* shd feel so proud to tell you how well I had succeeded during your absence—*Female* eloquence as *usal* succeeded, the Capt. sent me a very polite answer, & by peep of Day I send down the three cases.[60]

Later in the same day Lady Elgin wrote that she had persuaded Captain Hoste to take two more cases largely by giving him and his friends lavish hospitality and by giving what she called 'Backcheses' to the workers. The next day she wrote again in triumph:

But in hopes that I shall be the *first* to tell you what I have done for your ——Know that besides the 5 cases I have already told you of I have prevaled on Capt. Hoste to take *Three* more, two are already on board & the third will be taken when he returns from Corinth. How I have faged to get all this done, do you love me better for it, Elgin? . . . And *how* I have pushed Lusieri to get cases made for these three large packages! I beg you will shew delight (Lay aside the Deplomatic Character) to Capt. Hoste for taking so much on board. I am now *satisfied* of what I always thought; which is how much *more* Women can do if they set about it than Men. I will lay any bet had you been here you would not have got half so much on board as I have. As for getting the other things you wished for down from the Acropolis it is *quite impossible* before you return. Lusieri says Capt. Lacy was, upon his *first* coming here, against the things being taken down but at last he was keener than anybody & absolutely wished you to have the whole Temple of the Cari-something, where the Statues of the Women are.[61]

When the *Mentor* returned to Piraeus to pick up her second cargo in June she had on board William Richard Hamilton, Elgin's private secretary, who now became Elgin's principal agent. Hamilton had been sent to Egypt in June 1801, exactly a year before, to help superintend the evacuation of the French (Elgin did not want to risk a repetition of El Arish), but the evacuation had gone so smoothly that he had been able to go on a tour of Upper Egypt with Clarke.

When he was in Egypt Hamilton had assisted in securing for the British government another archaeological treasure, the Rosetta Stone, a slab of black basalt which contains an inscription of a decree of 196 before the Christian era, repeated in three languages, Greek, Demotic Egyptian, and Hieroglyphs. The stone was uncovered by Bonaparte's engineers in July 1799 as they were repairing fortifications, and the French generals immediately took possession of it. Its potential importance as a clue to the decipherment of ancient hieroglyphics was recognized at once and, in fact, it was by comparing the three scripts, starting with the proper names, that Young and Champollion were later able to reconstruct the language.[62] After the successful British invasion of Egypt General Hutchinson, on Hamilton's advice, insisted on writing into the terms of capitulation that the Rosetta Stone and certain other antiquities should be handed over to the British.

When the news of the cease-fire came through, Hamilton rushed to Hutchinson to press on him the importance of securing the stone. It was concealed in General Menou's own house from where Hamilton, accompanied by a detachment of gunners, broke in and removed it.[63] By the time of Hamilton's death in 1859 the story of his exploit had so grown that his obituary said he rowed out in a small boat to a plague-infested French warship and, at great personal danger, succeeded in removing it.[64] The Rosetta Stone is now one of the most visited antiquities in the British Museum.

Hamilton arrived in Athens with the *Mentor* just in time to see
Elgin before he left for Constantinople at the end of his Greek tour.
He was immediately put in general charge of the operations and
asked to supervise the loading of the *Mentor* for a second shipment.
He had instructions from Elgin to put on board everything that the
captain could be persuaded to accept without endangering the ship
and, if possible, to charter other vessels to get the marbles out of
Ottoman jurisdiction as soon as possible.

On 16 September, after several weeks of intensive work making
and packing the cases, transporting them to Piraeus, and loading
them into the ship, the *Mentor* sailed. She had on board seventeen
cases including fourteen pieces of the Parthenon frieze, four pieces
of the frieze of the Temple of Athena Nike, and various other
marbles including the ancient throne given to the Nisbets by the
Archbishop of Athens. The *Mentor* did not, however take any of
the largest sculptures, the figures from the pediments, as Captain
Eglen could not be persuaded to enlarge his hatches to get them
in. When Elgin heard that Captain Eglen was unwilling to do this
he at once wrote a peremptory letter to say he was sending the
captain of HMS *La Diane* to overrule Captain Eglen's opinion if,
in his view, the hatches could be enlarged without danger.

Captain Eglen's... conduct in that respect has been unpardonable. The
officers of the frigates at Smyrna assured him that this opening might be
made without injury to the vessel. It is troublesome, it is true, but nothing
in comparison with the object.... It is only his obstinacy that would have
found the difficulties that he raised at Athens. My brig is come from
England for my acquisitions. That is its purpose.[65]

Two days from Athens the *Mentor* ran into a storm and struck a
rock at the entrance to the harbour of the island of Cythera.[66] She
sank at once. Hamilton and the crew managed to scramble ashore.
No lives were lost, but some of the finest sculptures of the
Parthenon were now at the bottom of the sea in twelve fathoms of
salt water. Hamilton, who had hoped to return to England, immediately made plans to have the vessel salvaged and the marbles
recovered. It was to be a long, frustrating, and expensive business.[67]

In November HMS *La Victorieuse* was sent from Constantinople
to see if she could lend a hand at Cythera. Philip Hunt took passage
in her as far as Athens and, before she had left for Cythera, he
managed to get a few more cases away.

There are twelve or fifteen cases of Sculpture at the Piraeus, ready for embarking, but many of them are too large for the hatchway or Stowage of such a Ship as the Victorieuse: but Captn. Richards observed that if his decks had not been so encumbered by the spars he has on board for weighing the Mentor, he could have taken some of the Smaller ones. It is not easy to describe how much our Commander required being humoured. His Hobby horse seems to be that every action of his life shall appear to originate from himself; and he is more jealous than can be conceived of the most trifling requests or even suggestion coming from anyone but such as the strict rules of service authorize a Superior Officer to give him. On my first hinting to him the danger your acquisitions here were in on any change of Interests in Turkey, he mentioned a number of difficulties and concluded by saying he had been unable even to take Lady Elgin's chest on board at Constantinople, but after a walk with me among the ruins of Athens, he melted into good humour, and has taken two cases on board containing parts of the Frieze of the Parthenon in good preservation, and which Lusieri ranks with the most valuable in your Lordship's possession.[68]

Next day Hunt emulated Lady Elgin's efforts with the *Mutine* and persuaded the *Victorieuse* to take another case.

But although about fifty cases of sculptures had thus left Piraeus by various means, there were still about fifty left at Athens including the heaviest and most difficult ones containing the pedimental sculptures, seventeen cases of the frieze, and two metopes. The danger of losing them to the French seemed to be growing. A French Ambassador, in addition to Sébastiani, was already on his way to Constantinople with an escort of five warships, and the Chief of the Capuchin Monastery, so far from agreeing to sell the Monument of Lysicrates, as had been contemplated at one time, was told to withhold all co-operation of any kind.

Then on Christmas Eve 1802 Hunt had a stroke of luck. HMS *Braakel*, a troopship under the command of Captain Clarke, brother of 'Eleusinian' Clarke, ran aground at Piraeus. She was in imminent danger of sinking for lack of hands to unload her and pull her off. In the middle of the night Hunt hurried to see his old friend the Voivode and demanded that he should send a hundred men to Piraeus at once. The Voivode was hesitant but Hunt insisted that the gates of his palace should be immediately shut and 'the requisite number of men pressed for service out from the gaping multitude of Greeks and Albanians who were in the courtyard'.[69] After a night of excitement during which the whole of Athens seems to have gone to Piraeus to watch the spectacle, the *Braakel* was pulled off the rocks and saved. As Hunt wrote:

A Naval person can hardly believe that the *Braakel* ran smack on a boldish shore with a wind *off* the land—in a clear night, and fine weather. It is attributed to a terrible obstinacy on the part of the Master who had the Midnight watch when it happened.[70]

Captain Clarke, ashamed of having endangered his ship, and well aware of the consequences of the court martial that might have followed, was so grateful to his brother's enemy that he agreed to take all the cases he could. He landed his crew to help in bringing the marbles to Piraeus, built a special raft to float the heaviest pieces out to the ship, and kept his ship at Piraeus for five weeks solely to take the marbles.[71] No less than forty-four cases were embarked— by far the biggest shipment to date and by far the most important. But for Captain Clarke's bad seamanship it is doubtful if the most important part of the Elgin collection would have left Athens.

In the eighteen months between the obtaining of the second firman and his departure for home Lord Elgin had done all that he had set out to do and far more. As he was often to say in later years, the indifference of the Turks, the jealousy of travellers, and the intrigues of the French had all been overcome. The buildings of Athens had been drawn, measured, and moulded in detail never before attempted, and much of the best surviving sculpture had been moved into his storehouses. Some was already on its way to England, and there was good hope of recovering the rest, including the cases still at the bottom of the sea.

The financial cost had been enormous, and almost all had been met from his personal pocket with money borrowed on his personal credit.[72] In his last dispatch to the Foreign Office Elgin made another despairing plea, using almost exactly the same words as he had done in a letter to Lord Grenville in May 1799. He asked yet again that his appointment might 'be placed on the footing of an extraordinary embassy in respect to salary as it has been in rank, display, business, and expense.'[73] In one of his last letters to Lusieri he urged him to more removals and more excavations. 'If I had still three years', he wrote, 'and all the resources I have had, I would employ them all at Athens. . . . The slightest object from the Acropolis is a jewel.'[74]

Lord Elgin left Constantinople with his family and suite for the last time in HMS *La Diane* on 16 January 1803.

Prisoner of War

PEACE between France and Great Britain was signed at Amiens on 25 March 1802, but few expected that it would last. French interference in Ireland, British refusal to give up captured colonies, and many other issues caused continuing distrust, but one especially concerned Lord Elgin. Although Sébastiani on his arrival in Constantinople in December 1801 had been named as French 'commercial agent' in the Levant, he was in reality on a political and military reconnaissance. He was reporting to Paris on whether it was feasible for the French to invade Egypt for a second time and also to send an army into the Balkans.

Although Elgin kept on close personal terms with Sébastiani, frequently inviting him to dine when he was at Constantinople, he sent Philip Hunt to Greece to keep a watch on him on his travels there. Hunt arrived at Athens in the *Victorieuse* at the end of November and darted about Greece trying to 'counteract such impression as he may have attempted to make on any class of the inhabitants contrary to the interests of Great Britain and the Ottoman Porte'. 'The loss of the *Mentor*', he wrote to Elgin, 'and your lordship's antiquarian researches will furnish me with reasons sufficiently plausible for my journey.'[1]

Although the British government were thus kept secretly informed of what Sébastiani was up to, they need not have taken the trouble. In January 1803 Sébastiani's report was published in the official Paris newspaper the *Moniteur*. Dropping all pretence that the mission had been commercial, the report set forth the opportunities that would be open to France in the eastern Mediterranean if there was a war immediately. Six thousand men, it said bluntly, would be enough to reconquer Egypt and the British general was mediocre.[2] The publication of Sébastiani's report added to the tensions between the two countries, and after protracted negotiations, war broke out again in May 1803.

Lord Elgin knew little of the frantic diplomatic activity that was

taking place between London and Paris when he left Constantinople for home in January. As far as he was concerned peace
had at last returned after years of war, and he was as anxious to
enjoy it as anyone. His ship called at Athens, at Cythera (where he
saw the wreck of the *Mentor*), and at Malta and then went on to
Italy. He spent Easter at Rome, and decided to make the rest of
the journey by land by way of Florence, Marseilles, and Paris. He
arrived in France early in May.

On 18 May war was declared. On 23 May came a decree of the
First Consul.

All the English enroled in the Militia from the age of 18 to 60 holding a
commission from his Britannic Majesty, who are at present in France, shall
be made Prisoners of War, to answer for the Citizens of the Republic who
have been arrested by the vessels or subjects of his Britannic Majesty
before the declaration of war. The Ministers, each as far as concerns him,
are charged with the execution of the present decree.

French officials, on instructions from the First Consul, showed
unusual zeal. They interpreted the decree to apply not only to those
actually holding a commission in the militia, but also to those who
might conceivably do so in the future. Since all British male subjects had a liability to serve if the country was invaded and all could,
in theory at least, become officers, this meant that every male
British subject was considered a prisoner of war. Lord Elgin, an
officer in the Fencibles, was included.

'We intended remaining a week or ten days at most at Paris when
we arrived from Constantinople', wrote Lady Elgin bitterly.

I must have made some sad mistakes in writing to you if you did not always
understand that. We were most positively assured by all the French
Generals and Commanders and Ministers between Leghorn and this, that
even should war be declared, we might go through France in the utmost
security. We only knew war *was* declared at Lyons, it was then too late to
go back—and with assurances, how could one imagine that an ambassador
would be arrested; never since the world began was such a thing done
before. The night we arrived here, E. finding Lord W. gone [Lord
Whitworth, the British Ambassador; the departure of the Ambassador was
a sign that war was imminent], immediately wrote to M. de Talleyrand to
ask whether he had better set off for London instantaneously, or whether
we might remain a few days to rest after our long journey. M. de
Talleyrand's answer (which unfortunately I lost in my Imperial, or I would
have sent it you) was that we might remain as long as we pleased and that

we should have our passports whenever we pleased. The very next morning Elgin was declared prisoner of war. Who could expect that?[3]

It is difficult to imagine the horror with which this latest outrage of Bonaparte was greeted all over Europe. One of the conventions of the wars of the eighteenth century had been that only the armed forces of the contesting monarchs took part. Civilians were exempt and carried on business as usual. During the eighteenth-century wars the Dover to Calais packet had usually continued to run uninterrupted, and gentlemen on the Grand Tour suffered only minor inconvenience. Whether or not the British had illegally seized French ships, Bonaparte was forcing one more step towards total war.

The decree produced a good bag of prisoners. After ten years of war, the English upper and middle classes could not wait to get back to the Continent. In the few months of peace it is estimated that no less than two-thirds of the then House of Lords visited Paris, including five dukes, three marquises, and thirty-seven earls. No wonder the French called the visitors Milords. The decree netted about five hundred prisoners, of whom about half were aristocracy and gentry and the remainder professional men and merchants. Many of those detained, the *détenus*, were rich, and apart from their value as hostages, they contributed to France's invisible exports.

On 27 May Elgin gave his parole that he would not attempt to escape and the children were allowed to go on their way to England. At this stage he was confident that he would soon be released. He appealed to everyone of importance within reach, including his old friend the King of Prussia.[4] Ironically his greatest hope lay in Count Sébastiani, the French agent with whom he had played cat and mouse in the East, and whose report in the *Moniteur* had been one of the causes of the war. As Lady Elgin wrote to her mother:

Sébastiani professed everything, came repeatedly to us, and stayed hours talking politicks. We have been anxiously expecting him these two days but alas! no Sébastiani has appeared. What is that a sign of, Ma? We heard today from good authority that this evening he was to make his great push for us, so probably tomorrow morning we shall see him. He told me that Madame B[onaparte] interested herself extremely for me and that she said she would use all her influence for us?[5]

Sébastiani was unable to help his old rival, and Elgin had a letter from Talleyrand confirming that he must stay. Elgin then called on the Chief Justice and reminded him of how scrupulously he had respected the capitulation in Egypt—giving passports to the returning French in his own name. But nothing could be done. The decision was Bonaparte's own and he would not change it. Lord and Lady Elgin therefore settled down to wait. Life was not unpleasant. Having given their parole they were at liberty to lead their own lives, reporting to the authorities every now and then.[6]

In July all the British were obliged to leave Paris. As his health was not good, Elgin obtained permission to move to Barrèges, a fashionable spa near the Pyrenees.[7] There he settled down to take the cure and Lady Elgin amused herself in entertaining the international society. As she wrote:

Barrèges . . . is the most dreary place I ever saw, immense high hills without a tree. There is but one ride that one can call practicable and that one continues going down hill for an hour and a half, there are many beautiful spots at an hour or two's distance from this, but Barrèges itself is most miserable. However I firmly believe it has saved Elgin's life, he gets better every day; he gets up at six or seven o'clock in the morning and goes out a shooting for four or five hours with the Duke of Newcastle [Another detained prisoner], then about one o'clock he goes out a riding with me. He has now begun to take the baths twice a day, when he returns from shooting, and at 11 o'clock at night; he remains almost an hour each time.[8]

The evenings were spent at dinner parties, concerts, and whist. Social life at the spa was little different from life at home, or indeed from life at Constantinople. At Barrèges Lord Elgin was joined by Philip Hunt. After his shadowing of Sébastiani in Greece he had joined Elgin's ship at Athens but he had left him at Malta and he had made his way to Venice independently. There he decided to come home by land, and although, like Elgin, he received assurances that he could travel safely through France, he too was detained and obliged to give his parole.[9]

At Barrèges there also appeared the man whom Elgin had long regarded as a rival and whom he had never expected to meet. As usual Lady Elgin is the source for this account of their first meeting.

Le Comte de Choiseul-Gouffier is here, he is very pleasant. Poor man he has been most unfortunate; after having lost almost all he possessed, he had just money enough to buy a Villa near Paris and set his heart upon the idea of placing the marbles etc he had collected at Athens: he has just received information that the Frigate on board which his Antiquities were placed, has been taken by the English. The tears were really in his eyes when he told me. He said after having lost his fortune and very nearly all the Antiquities he had with so much trouble and expense collected at Constantinople [actually mainly at Athens] ... and having hid these for so many years, and having now sent for them, he is completely overcome by the loss. It is very hard upon him, he has been entreating Elgin to write to Ld Nelson about them.[10]

Choiseul-Gouffier had returned from exile to France in 1802, forgiven along with other aristocrats for his temporary disloyalty to France, but his titles and fortune were gone. His only interest in life was his collection of antiquities. He succeeded in reclaiming most of the sculptures, including the Parthenon metope that had been seized by the Government during the Revolution, but the Louvre insisted on retaining the slab from the Parthenon frieze.[11]

This slab, his most precious piece, had lain in the cellars of the Louvre from the time of its arrival in France until January 1802 when it was suddenly brought into prominence by Bonaparte himself. At one of his periodic inspections to see how the Louvre was filling up with the looted treasures of Europe he asked Visconti, the Director, if the Museum possessed any work by Phidias. Visconti replied that the only monument which could reasonably be attributed to that artist was a relief taken from Athens by Fauvel. The First Consul expressed his astonishment that so precious a piece was not yet on exhibition but Visconti replied that it was too mutilated and must first be restored. The work of restoration was immediately put in hand (fortunately without too much damage to the original) and the slab took a prominent place in the Louvre where it still remains.[12]

With the First Consul himself displaying such a lively interest in the sculptures of the Parthenon, the French government decided to help Choiseul-Gouffier to recover the rest of his collection that still lay at Athens, including the Parthenon metope that had come down in the storm. Fauvel, who had returned to Athens in January 1803 just in time to meet Elgin, had taken repossession of Choiseul-Gouffier's collection. He decided to attempt the same trick on Lusieri that had been played on him while he was in prison, and seize the marbles belonging to his British rivals, and only the lack of shipping prevented him from doing so.[13] In May 1803, however, the French frigate *l'Arabe*, sent by Bonaparte's express command, arrived at Piraeus to pick up the collection belonging to Choiseul-Gouffier.

To Lusieri's disappointment and Fauvel's delight the whole collection was successfully put on board and the ship sailed into international waters. The French glee soon turned out to be premature, for war broke out before *l'Arabe* could reach France, and on 14 June 1803 she was captured and taken as prize by HMS *Maidstone*. By the law of prize, the value of any enemy property captured was divided among the crew of the ship which made the capture. *L'Arabe* herself was sold at Malta but Nelson directed that the cases of marbles be sent unopened to England in case the Government wanted to buy them. He wrote to Sir Joseph Banks, the President of the Royal Society, asking him to advise the Government on whether to buy them.

One of our frigates has taken...some cases of I know not what but I suppose things as choice as Lord Elgin's.... As they are the property of the lowest seamen they cannot be presented, as I would have been truly happy to have had it in my favour to give them to the Royal Society or to the Academy of Arts.[14]

The cases arrived in due course at the Customs House in London but the Government declined to buy them. A duty was levied on them and the owners were advised by the auctioneers, Messrs Christie, that they were not worth taking away.[15] The cases were therefore left at the Customs House to await a clearance sale. They were still there in 1806 when they were rediscovered by Lord Elgin.

When Elgin met Choiseul-Gouffier at Barrèges in August 1803 he knew nothing of these events. Choiseul-Gouffier for his part knew only the barest outline. Nevertheless it is astonishing that he should appeal to Elgin. After all, it had been from Elgin's agents that he had been hiding the marbles for so many years. And he probably knew something at least of Elgin's schemes to seize them by force. A few months before, Fauvel had reported that Elgin's agents had stolen the piece of marble which he had years before sawn off the back of the Parthenon slab (now in the Louvre) in order to reduce its weight.[16] In another letter, reporting gleefully the loss of 'the barbarian Elgin's' ship at Cythera, Fauvel accused Elgin's agents of breaking up sculptures for the sheer pleasure of doing so.[17]

The two noblemen met at a time when their two nations and

their two agents at Athens were engaged in a bitter rivalry, but there was no personal acrimony. They were both European noblemen with a common interest in classical archaeology. They were true to the standards of the old regime which the Revolution and Napoleon had swept away. Besides, Elgin's possession of Greek marbles was one of the few bargaining counters which he had to offer in seeking his release. Elgin wrote to Nelson on Choiseul-Gouffier's behalf asking that the Parthenon metope should be sold back to Choiseul-Gouffier. Unfortunately for the Comte the collection was already in England when Nelson received the letter and he could do nothing. Choiseul-Gouffier, for his part, added his efforts to try to get Elgin released.

When the season finished at Barrèges the Elgins moved to the nearby town of Pau. Life there began pleasantly enough too but, as the months went by, events took a sinister turn. Many of the detained British were obtaining their release by bribery or influence, but it was clear that Elgin was being treated as a very special case. Elgin thought at first that he was being kept in case Bonaparte wanted an unofficial ambassador—and this was also Sébastiani's explanation—but the real reason lay in the personal animosity of Bonaparte. Many untrue stories had grown up about Elgin's activities at Constantinople. It was said, for example, that he had attempted to double-cross the French at El Arish—on the contrary, he was one of the few who came out of the muddle with honour. It was also said that he had deliberately ill-treated the French interned in Turkey and had caused a French diplomat called Beauchamp to be put to death. This too was untrue. Elgin had intervened successfully with the Ottoman government to relieve the sufferings of the French in the Seven Towers and, so far from causing Beauchamp's death, he had rescued him from being beheaded as a spy by Sir Sidney Smith.

Bonaparte at first seems to have believed some of these stories although his dislike of Elgin did not depend on their being true. For a time the French government deliberately spread them and they appeared in the newspapers. Before long Lady Elgin reported that at Pau everyone was saying, 'Ah, c'est ce Milord Elgin qui a si maltraité nos compatriotes à Constantinople!' (Ah, that is Lord Elgin who so mistreated our countrymen at Constantinople.)[18] Luckily Elgin had a powerful advocate in Sébastiani, and Lady Elgin wrote:

He swore positively that there was not the least ill will to E. personally, but on the contrary his conduct to the French in Turkey had gained him great good will. S. said for his own part he would declare whenever he was called upon, that E.'s behaviour to the French was certainly handsome, and that many Frenchmen had told him so—the first Consul was perfectly acquainted with it—and we know for certain that Sébastiani has said this in two or three Assemblies.[19]

Nevertheless it was wartime and a war that became more brutal every day. The stories persisted. Another story sprang up. It was said that a French general called Boyer who had been captured in the West Indies and was now a prisoner of war in England was being ill-treated in prison. This too was untrue—General Boyer was enjoying a quite comfortable life on parole. But true or false the stories had their effect. On 9 November Bonaparte issued an order that an officer of Boyer's rank should be arrested in reprisal for the ill-treatment of General Boyer.[20] Lord Elgin was the officer selected and was arrested a few days later and taken to the fortress of Lourdes.

At the time of the arrest Lady Elgin was in Paris trying to arrange for a visit home for herself and to counteract the false stories. She went straight to Talleyrand, saw him several times, and corresponded through him with Bonaparte She also sent out streams of letters to all her acquaintances, English and French, whom she thought might help. Talleyrand said it was now accepted by the French government that Elgin had not been responsible for the ill-treatment of prisoners at Constantinople, but that it was Spencer Smith. After some negotiations with Bonaparte, Talleyrand offered to release Elgin altogether if the British would release General Boyer in exchange, but it was no good. Lady Elgin wrote a long plaintive letter to the Foreign Secretary and asked her father to stir up political support for the move, but the British government took their stand on the principle that a genuine prisoner of war (Boyer) could not be exchanged for a civilian illegally detained (Elgin). There was no exchange.[21]

Meanwhile Lord Elgin himself had gone into prison at Lourdes.[22] The commandant of Lourdes was a friend with whom he had spent three months at Barrèges the previous summer where both were on the social round. At Lourdes, however, to Elgin's great surprise and mortification, he received his prisoner with studied coldness and austerity, and made him pay for the furniture of his cell. The Prefect of the Department, on the other hand, when he heard of

Elgin's arrest, protested 'J'aurais volontiers donné cinquante mille écus de ma poche que ceci ne fut pas arrivé chez moi' (I would have willingly given fifty thousand écus from my own pocket to have prevented this from happening in my province) and immediately came and passed the whole day with him accompanied by members of his suite.[23]

A few days later a sergeant of the guard came mysteriously to Elgin's cell and gave him a letter. The letter purported to be from a fellow prisoner and said that if Elgin wanted to talk to him he could do so at the window. Elgin tore the letter to pieces, gave the sergeant a louis d'or, and told him that if he or anyone brought another unofficial letter he would at once deliver it to the commandant. The commandant occasionally spoke to Elgin of the mysterious fellow prisoner and seemed to be keen that Elgin should speak to him.

After only a fortnight Elgin was released from Lourdes and returned to Pau. Soon afterwards, when he was at breakfast, the woman of the house where he was lodging brought him a packet of letters which he saw was from the man who had tried to communicate with him at Lourdes. One letter said the writer had been caught in an attempt to set fire to the French fleet at Brest. It asked Elgin to forward the other letter to the Comte d'Artois who was the leader of the anti-Bonapartist *émigrés* in England. The plan to sabotage the French fleet was to be revived. Elgin kept the woman in the room, threw all the letters in the fire, and told her that he refused to receive any letters except by the official post. He then told the whole story to the Prefect.

When Elgin had left Lourdes the commandant had immediately dropped his air of sternness and seemed disposed to renew their friendship on the old terms. He told Elgin that his speedy liberation was due to the failure of the attempts he had been ordered to make to entrap him into some anti-Bonapartist intrigue. The letters had been written in Paris, and sent down by confidential agent, in the expectation of seizing them when they were in Elgin's possession. Elgin himself, with his respect for the old-fashioned codes of honour, only half-believed that the French government, which included so many of his friends, were implicated in the trickery, but in this he was probably wrong. He was only one of a number of British diplomats that Bonaparte attempted to discredit or entrap in the interests of propaganda. Among the others was John Spencer Smith, who had recovered from his disgrace at Constantinople and was British Minister in Württemberg. The French tried to plant on him documents addressed to *émigrés* recommending the assassination of Bonaparte.

After Elgin's release from Lourdes, he and his wife settled down to a normal life at Pau waiting patiently for permission to return to England. They lived for a time at Orléans but in the summer they returned to Barrèges for the season. The Empress (Bonaparte had now become the Emperor Napoleon) was expected there and society was grander and more glittering than it had been even in the days of the *ancien régime*. In the winter the Elgins returned as before to Pau and settled down again to enjoy country life. As Lady Elgin wrote:

The situation is most delightful, such a variety of beautiful rides and drives, you would be quite enchanted. As E. and Hunt were here so long before, we are allowed to remain perfectly quiet—they only go to town to present themselves occasionally to the Authorities. I have not seen a soul; almost all the families are in the country, but in winter Pau is the greatest of places, balls, great dinners and suppers, and plenty of card playing tho' unfortunately only for sous. E. with all his ill luck, says of a long evening he could never contrive to lose more than half a crown.[24]

In the spring of 1805 they were allowed to return to Paris. To bid farewell, the Prefect and the local general each gave a grand dinner in their honour. Lady Elgin was by now bored with the Bordeaux road so they went on a tour by way of Toulouse, Lyons, and Nîmes. The journey took nearly a month.

No sooner had they arrived in Paris than disaster struck. The Elgin's fourth child, who had been born at Barrèges just over a year before, suddenly died. Lady Elgin was desolated and wrote home:

Pray for me, my dearest Mother, take me in your arms; Your prayers will be heard tho' mine were not listened to. I have lost my William, my angel William—my soul doated on him, I was wrapt up in my child. From the moment of his birth, to the fatal night it pleased God to call him, I have devoted myself to him. I am resigned to the Will of the Almighty but my happiness is destroyed for ever... *My William, my adored William is gone... gone... and left me here.* Bless your miserable child.[25]

Lady Elgin was already pregnant with a fifth child and her health was feared for. Elgin persuaded Napoleon, on humanitarian grounds, to allow Lady Elgin to return to Britain to bury the dead child in the family vault, and she left France, accompanied by Philip Hunt, in October 1805.[26] Elgin himself was not permitted to go.

About the time of Lady Elgin's return, Robert Ferguson of Raith, a rich young man, heir to a large neighbouring estate in Fife, was also released.[27] The Elgins had met Ferguson in Paris soon after the decree in 1803 and both recognized an old childhood friend. In the close-knit society of the British prisoners in Paris they were thrown very much together and Lady Elgin wrote that he lived 'constantly with us'.[28] Ferguson was named as the godfather of the child who died. When Lady Elgin was on her own in Paris trying to negotiate Elgin's release from Lourdes it was natural that she should turn to him for help. He was again there to comfort her when her child died.

Even before Lady Elgin had left for England Napoleon struck at Lord Elgin again. He was suddenly arrested for a second time and sent to prison at Melun. 'When I was in Paris a prisoner in the year 1805,' he told the Select Committee eleven years later, 'living in Paris, perfectly tranquilly with my family, I received a letter from an English traveller, complaining of Lusieri's taking down part of the frieze of the Parthenon. The next morning a common gens d'arme came and took me out of bed, and sent me into close confinement away from my family. Such was the influence exercised by the French to prevent this operation.'[29]

Elgin later claimed that he could have obtained his liberty at any time he chose and named any price he wanted, if he would only agree to cede his collection to the French government.[30] Napoleon, who bought, seized, and extorted works of art from all over Europe to make the Louvre (temporarily) the greatest collection ever likely to be assembled in one place, was quite capable of making such an offer. Although Elgin and Napoleon both wanted to possess the sculptures of the Parthenon the motives of the two men were different. Napoleon wanted a collection of original works of art of all periods from all over the known world to emphasize the power and grandeur of the imperial city of Paris. Elgin still clung to his ambition to improve the modern art of Great Britain by making examples of the best ancient art accessible to artists.

Lady Elgin's return to England was the start of another series of attempts to get Elgin released. The King of Prussia, who had interceded unsuccessfully two years before, tried again, and so did the Emperor Alexander of Russia but without success. *The Times*, on recounting this news, remarked:

One of Bonaparte's confidential ministers is said to have declared at the time that such high intercession was only calculated to prolong his

Lordship's captivity as Bonaparte could not deny his pride and
gratification of rejecting it; and it was observed that if the application had
come from any learned Society in this country on the ground that his
Lordship was an enlightened and liberal patron of the arts and had recovered many remains of antiquity at a great expense it is not improbable that
the application might have succeeded as he affects to be a friend of the
Arts.[31]

The confidential minister, one suspects, was Choiseul-Gouffier, or
Talleyrand reported by Choiseul-Gouffier, and the source of the
story Lady Elgin. A letter was drawn up by the Royal Society of
Antiquaries and the Royal Academy addressed to the Institute of
France.

The rage of war ought not to interrupt the intercourse of men of science
and we rejoice in the progress and success of your labours. Being always
ready on our part to lend assistance to your scientific men who may visit
this country we beg leave to represent the following case to your
consideration.
    A British Nobleman, an Ambassador, embued with the love of the arts
and sciences, has, at a great expense, remitted to England a very large collection of ancient monuments of Grecian art. But these precious remains
have neither been published nor exhibited, to the great disappointment of
artists and the learned world, because in his absence it is impossible to form
any arrangements for that purpose. These noble fragments of antiquity
remain packed in large cases and moulder in obscurity, exposed to the
dangers of negligence and various accidents. Withdrawn from the destructive ignorance of the Turks who have already converted into lime too many
similar monuments of Grecian genius, they have passed into learned and
civilized Europe without conferring any of the numerous advantages that
might otherwise have been expected to arise from their study and inspection, to sculpture, architecture, painting, and the sciences in general.[32]

This approach too failed like the others. It is uncertain why the
French at last changed their mind. There had been an increase in
the number of prisoners unofficially exchanged although neither
the French nor the British government abandoned the principle on
which each had taken its stand. Perhaps it was easier for the French
to let Elgin go in an unofficial secret exchange because he was an
ambassador, or perhaps they simply gave in at last to pressure of
opinion. The approach which finally did the trick was one direct to
Napoleon from Lord Grenville during his few months as Prime
Minister.
    But even in releasing Elgin the French managed to do him a dis-

service. When Talleyrand brought the passports he also brought a document for Elgin's signature which made him promise that he would return to France whenever the French government required. This parole was never rescinded and Elgin, ever true to the principles of *noblesse oblige*, regarded himself as bound by it right up to the moment of Napoleon's downfall.[33] Elgin finally reached England in June 1806. It was a most unhappy homecoming.

Lusieri on his Own, 1803–1806

WHEN Elgin and his family left to return home in January 1803 all the artists except Lusieri left with him. Most of the moulds and drawings which Elgin wanted had already been made, and not much more work needed to be done on the spot. The main task was now to have the drawings finished and engraved for publication, a step as vital to Elgin's aim of improving the arts of his country as the making available of originals and casts.

In Greece the main job to be done was to try to salvage the *Mentor* and her cargo of marbles which lay at the bottom of Cythera harbour. Hamilton, who was on board the ship when she sank, established himself ashore there for several months. By offering money to passing ships, and by recruiting sponge divers from Calymnos and other sponge islands in the south-east Aegean, he soon succeeded in recovering four out of the seventeen cases of marbles which were known to have been on board. Quite independently, Elgin, in one of his last acts before he left Constantinople had dispatched an Italian messenger called Pietro Gavallo with elaborate instructions, the gist of which was that any naval vessel he came across was to be ordered at once to Cythera, and that no effort or expense was to be spared to salvage the *Mentor*. Elgin also made a contract with a Greek shipowner from Spezzia called Basilio Menachini by the terms of which Basilio became British Vice-Consul at Spezzia in exchange for lending ships and aid to recover the *Mentor*. Besides all this activity, Philip Hunt, who was on his mission following Sébastiani, started to do what he could from Athens. It is perhaps hardly surprising, with so many masters trying to direct the salvage operations from different places, that a muddle occurred.

HMS *La Victorieuse* was the first Royal Navy ship to arrive at the scene at Cythera. It had been arranged that she should rendezvous there with one of Basilio's ships and that between them they should try to raise the *Mentor* entire. The *Victorieuse* lay at

Cythera for thirteen days waiting for Basilio's promised ship to arrive from Spezzia but she did not come. At last, as she could wait no longer, the *Victorieuse* attempted to raise the *Mentor* by herself. But when she had lifted the wreck two fathoms from the bottom the cables gave way and the *Mentor* fell back to the bottom. The *Victorieuse* then sailed away.[1]

Only two hours after she had gone Basilio's ship at last arrived. As Hunt wrote to Hamilton from Athens to explain what had happened:

It is not easy to describe my vexation on receiving a letter from Mr. Basilio, our Vice-Consul at Spezzia, saying that he was ready to sail for Cerigo with two large ships and 120 men to co-operate with the Brig of War agreeable to Lord Elgin's written instructions, when Mr. Pierre, Corriere Straordinario di S.M.B. etc dissuaded him most strongly by saying the *Mentor* had gone to pieces ('e tutto perso, e tutto dispatto').[2]

How Pietro Gavallo got hold of the false information is unknown. It was probably a rumour returning full circle from some story he himself had told about the sinking of the *Mentor*. His incompetence cost Elgin dear. By the time the muddle was sorted out, it was well on in December and too cold for the divers. All hopes of raising the *Mentor* before the winter storms dashed her to pieces had now to be abandoned.

The divers returned to Cythera the following spring and worked there all through the summer. As expected the *Mentor* was now quite beyond salvage and holes had to be cut in her decks to get at the cases of marbles inside. We may be grateful that the heavy figures from the pediments were not on board, as Elgin had instructed, for they would probably have had to be abandoned at the bottom of the sea. And the great slab of the frieze which had broken in two as it was taken to Piraeus would probably not have been recovered if it had been packed in one piece. In 1803 five out of the thirteen remaining cases were all that could be rescued. As the marbles were recovered they were half-buried on the beach and covered with seaweed, brushwood, and heavy stones, in an effort to protect them from further erosion by wind, weather, and salt water. In the spring of 1804 the divers returned to Cythera and worked there for the whole of the second summer. At last in October, over two years after the *Mentor* first sank, the remaining eight cases of marbles were brought ashore. The last was the ancient throne which the Archbishop of

Athens had given to Mr and Mrs Nisbet when they were in Athens in 1801.

Nelson, to whom Elgin had written from France, ordered a ship specially to Cythera to pick up the collection on the beach and all the marbles found their way safely to England. The whole operation had cost Elgin about £5,000. If any proof is needed that he had a genuine concern for preserving the Parthenon marbles and was not simply, to use Clarke's favourite phrase, looking for material 'to decorate a Scotch villa', the episode of the *Mentor* alone would provide it.[3]

Meanwhile Lusieri was still busy at Athens. Elgin had obtained permission from the King of Naples to prolong his employment at Athens and he was overjoyed. By now he was so immersed in Elgin's schemes and so fond of Greece that he could imagine no other life. As he wrote to Elgin shortly before Elgin left:

Here, My Lord, is my plan! It is to execute here the best works of my life, and to devote myself to them with all my strength in order to succeed. I must do more still and I much want to try it, so that some barbarisms that I have been obliged to commit in your service may be forgotten. I must work quietly. When the work of collecting is going on so furiously, how can I find the time to draw, or have the head for it?[4]

In the first few months when he was on his own, Lusieri secured from the Parthenon another long run of the frieze and three more metopes. Among the witnesses of his operations was Robert Smirke, the architect, one of the candidates whom Elgin had rejected in 1799 when he was trying to engage an English artist to accompany him to the East. Smirke had again met Elgin at Rome on his way to Greece, but when he arrived in Athens he said nothing to Hamilton and Lusieri about the opportunity he had let slip four years before. Although, for the most part, Smirke approved of Lusieri's efforts to send the Parthenon marbles to England, yet, like Dodwell and Clarke earlier, he too was distressed at the destruction to the Parthenon which the rescue operation involved. As he wrote in his journal:

It particularly affected me when I saw the destruction made to get down the basso-relievos on the walls of the cell [the frieze]. The men were labouring long ineffectually with iron crows to move the stones of these firm-built walls. Each stone as it fell shook the ground with its ponderous weight with a deep hollow noise; it seemed like a convulsive groan of the injured spirit of the Temple.[5]

When Smirke left the Acropolis he was careful to take a few choice pieces of the Erechtheion with him. As with so many smaller items collected at this time by travellers, they are now lost.

It was in early 1803 that Lusieri took one of the Caryatids of the Erechtheion, as well as one of the columns and other pieces, so causing a more obvious destruction to a well-loved monument than any other of Elgin's acquisitions. The gap where the Caryatid had stood was filled with a crude bare brick pillar to prevent the roof falling down. The pieces from the Erechtheion, as well as some sculptures from the Parthenon and other items of the Elgin collection were shipped from Athens in HMS *Medusa*, the naval ship which brought Elgin's successor Drummond to Athens on his way to Constantinople.[6]

But Lusieri's difficulties became greater and greater. Drummond, despite having given help with the shipping, seems not to have fully approved of what he had seen being done in Athens in the name of his predecessor. As far as Lusieri was concerned, it was virtually impossible to communicate with Elgin in France. Hamilton too returned to England as soon as he had organized the salvage operations at Cythera. Morier, alone of the initial members of Elgin's Embassy, remained in the Ottoman territories—he went to Ioannina as British Consul-General—but Elgin's relations with him were cool after he had published an unauthorized account of the Convention of El Arish.[7] Lusieri's status with the Turks, now that he was deprived of a powerful protector, fell lower and lower and his status with Elgin's bankers fell too. He found it increasingly difficult to obtain money or credit even at exorbitant rates.

Elgin and his agents were always well aware that the Voivode and the Disdar who had connived at the removals from the buildings were at risk of being severely punished if the authorities in Constantinople should ever decide to change the general policy and to disown what they had done. In the spring of 1802 when Elgin and Lady Elgin visited Athens, Lady Elgin ordered Lusieri to put about a false story that she had powerful new firmans.[8] In the autumn of 1802, when Elgin was preparing to leave Constantinople at the end of his appointment, he obtained two documents from the Vizier aimed at giving them some protection if circumstances should change.[9] The exact status of these documents is unclear. They were not, it would seem, firmans addressed to the officials concerned but letters to Elgin from the Ottoman government which commended the two officials for what they had done. They thus gave some official approval from the central government, after the event, to any stretching of the legal powers of the second firman with which they had co-operated. The two documents were sent by Elgin to Lusieri, who gave them to the officials concerned. As he wrote:

The Voivode and the Disdar have been much pleased with the letters that your Excellency has procured and sent to them, and I have thought it necessary to give them to them today, in order to encourage them [to continue to give approval for Elgin's operations].[10]

In 1804, as a result of repeated representations by the French, the permissions in the second firman under which removals from the buildings had continued, more or less continually, for several years were rescinded.[11] What form the new decision took is not known, and it may have been a local one. But, to judge from the form of the ban on removing statues and columns which followed not long afterwards, it may have been a communication from the Ottoman government to the British Ambassador, who then passed it by letter to the British Consul Logotheti. The decision to put a stop to further removals threw no doubt on the legality of the removals made previously. In the successive withdrawals of permissions of 1804 and 1805, there is no evidence of any official Ottoman attempt to claim back the cases of marbles over which Elgin's agents claimed ownership which still lay at Athens and Piraeus.

The French were quick to take advantage of the change of fortune. At the very moment when Elgin and Choiseul-Gouffier were becoming the best of friends in France, Lusieri and Fauvel were engaged in a bitter struggle in Athens. Fauvel, who arrived back in Athens in January 1803, again planned, with the agreement of the French Ambassador at Constantinople, to seize those of Elgin's cases which were still at Athens, and again only the lack of shipping prevented this from happening.[12] He also constantly urged the Ottoman authorities to issue a firman ordering that all removals, other than his own, should be banned.

For the first time others besides Lusieri and Fauvel now joined the game of firmans and bribery. Athens was now frequently visited by travellers of several European countries, some of whom were very wealthy. As Lusieri wrote in September 1803:

Two very rich English gentlemen were on the point of offering as much as 50,000 piastres [about £5,000], to obtain the frieze. Happily I was told of it, and I made them see that it was impossible, that it was necessary to have firmans, but that in any case I would not have let Your Excellency be second to anybody. In consequence they did nothing and will do nothing. I will work at this new acquisition with all the necessary vigour, and, I hope, My Lord, that the frieze will be yours.[13]

This part of the frieze was secured for the Elgin collection. It was probably one of the rich travellers that Lusieri had frustrated who wrote the complaining letter to Elgin which he believed sent him to prison at Melun.

Another visitor to Athens was a future prime minister, the Earl of Aberdeen, then aged 20, another man who knew the power of money. He conducted large-scale excavations near the Acropolis and spent money freely in building up a collection of antiquities. He was shown round Athens both by Lusieri and by Fauvel and at the Parthenon noted 'the devastation which is indeed continual'.[14] It is likely that he had a hand in making the offer to the Voivode for part of the frieze. Among the antiquities that he sent to England were a foot from a metope sculpture, and pieces from the Parthenon, the Propylaea, and the temples at Sounion and Eleusis. These, like so many of the fragments taken by other travellers at this time, one need hardly add, are now lost.[15] Later Lord Aberdeen was to join the group of connoisseurs who attempted to denigrate the artistic quality of the Parthenon sculptures.

By the beginning of 1804 Lusieri was obliged to stop all further removals from the buildings. As he wrote:

I must stop. Fauvel has frightened all the Turks. After a number of extravagant fanfarronades he told the Disdar that he had received an order from his Ambassador to take a note of all the marbles that your Excellency has taken and to send it to him. Let him do whatever he likes, though he may get firmans empowering him to take, I very much doubt his succeeding without his paying. Then we shall see.[16]

Without a new firman, which would overrule the local Ottoman authorities, he was confined to digging.[17] Lusieri started excavations at many sites in Athens, Piraeus, and Attica. A fine collection of vases was accumulated including some of marble and one of bronze, along with coins and ancient jewellery. But time was running out. Drummond not only made no effort to obtain a renewal of the firman for removals from the buildings, but in the middle of 1805 Consul Logotheti received a letter from the British Embassy saying that no more statues or columns were to be taken away. Henceforth Lusieri was only allowed to take away ceramic vases, coins, and minor antiquities.[18]

Dodwell had now reappeared, combining as before condemnation of Elgin with aggrandizement of his own collection, and so had William Gell, who had drawn the picture of Elgin's first removals.[19] As Lusieri wrote of them:

They conduct themselves in such a way as to disgust everybody, and I think that those who come after will not find the same civility either here or at Argos. These gentlemen have wanted to undertake diggings without firmans, without asking permission of the Voivode, or of the landowner, and without making any return. The Voivode has been so much disgusted that he has stopped them from going on, letting all know that he would not allow anyone whatever to dig except me.[20]

Lusieri's relief was short-lived. In October 1805 the Voivode ordered a complete ban on all diggings whether by Lusieri or by anybody else.[21] Gell seems to have had a hand in this decision. He told Fauvel that Lusieri's activities were disapproved of by the British Ambassador and they immediately told the Voivode. The Voivode had arrived to take up office after the last of the Parthenon sculptures was taken down but found himself accused nevertheless of having accepted a bribe of 150 purses for allowing the removals. He was being asked to repay that sum, equivalent to 75,000 piastres or about £8,000. From his point of view a total ban certainly seemed the best policy.

And so in October 1805 Lusieri's operations came to a complete halt. Removals and excavations were both forbidden. All he could do was draw, the purpose for which he had originally been engaged, but he was short even of drawing materials. In the same month, Elgin's bankers at Constantinople, having been refused further credit by Elgin's bankers in London, refused to advance him a piastre more. Lusieri's position was desperate. He repeated his pleas to Drummond the British Ambassador but without success, and Morier, Elgin's former private secretary who was now Consul-General at Ioannina, refused to help him. It must have been particularly galling to receive about this time one of the few letters from Elgin in France that reached him. This urged him to further excavations in Attica, Eleusis, Megara, Corinth, Argos, Epidauros, Salamis, and Aegina. Lusieri only kept himself alive by borrowing money at extortionate rates of interest.

Meanwhile the case of marbles collected earlier still lay at

Piraeus. Apart from the few taken from Cythera which were salvaged from the *Mentor*, and some others taken to Constantinople
by Drummond, no marbles left Greece during all the time that
Elgin was in France. In 1806 forty cases containing many of the best
of the Parthenon sculptures as well as the results of all Lusieri's
labours in 1804 and 1805 lay at Piraeus, a perpetual invitation to
Fauvel and to any other person who thought he could organize the
necessary mixture of political influence, local permission, threats,
briberies, and shipping. Lusieri dutifully mounted guard over this
second Elgin collection. In the autumn of 1806, to his great relief,
he heard of Elgin's release.

13

Homecoming

WHEN Elgin returned to England in 1806 he was full of renewed high hopes. He was still only 40 and, although he had been abroad for nearly seven years, there was no reason to suppose that his career, which had begun so brilliantly, should have suffered more than a temporary set-back from the wasted years in France. But as soon as he returned home he sustained a series of cruel misfortunes.

The first was the loss of his family life.[1] Lady Elgin had returned to England nearly nine months before her husband and had lived first with her parents in Portman Square and later by herself in Baker Street. In January 1806, while Elgin was still in France, her fifth child was born and it was then that he had his first indications that something was wrong. Lady Elgin wrote to say 'that she had suffered so much from this event that she would never subject herself again to that intercourse with him which might be productive of such effects'.[2] When Elgin returned from France a few months later Lady Elgin continued to deny him what were then regarded as his conjugal rights.

Lady Elgin had been pregnant in every year of their marriage, and had lost one child in infancy. How far she was aware of the risks she and her children were running from Elgin's earlier syphilis can only be guessed at. It had become clear that their eldest son was severely epileptic and unlikely to live to be a suitable heir. Now that another son was born, Elgin's fear that his title and lands would pass outside his family at his death was, to some extent, alleviated. Shortly after his return, however, some letters came into his possession which left no doubt that his wife was involved in an affair with Robert Ferguson of Raith. 'You must exasperate him,' ran one of Ferguson's letters, 'you must consider his approach as a violation of your person, and force him to a separation.'[3] Lady Elgin's letters were even more conclusive. In one she wrote:

He [Elgin] was very much agitated indeed, but he said nothing—after tea he got up suddenly and went into his room for a couple of hours. He coughed dreadfully which he always does when he is annoyed. I told him of my wish to go and see where my beloved William is laid—and that I wished to go alone. Friend, it was you that placed that adored angel there. There is something... I cannot account for but I feel as if he was our own. E. went out early this morning. I have not met him. I must do him the justice to say he has taken upon himself to keep his promise, but I hardly think it possible he can go on with it... What a desperate horrible idea that nothing but death can make us free. I shudder when I dare think of it and too thoroughly I feel I cannot live without you.[4]

There was much more in the same vein and long precise instructions about how the secret correspondence should be continued. Several of Elgin's friends were helping to pass letters, including Alexander Straton whom Elgin had promoted to the post of secretary at Constantinople when Spencer Smith was dismissed.

Elgin decided he must divorce his wife. Under English law of the time this could only be done by a civil action for damages against Ferguson, followed by a (very expensive) private Act of Parliament. Divorce on grounds of adultery was, however, permitted by Scots law. Elgin decided on two actions, first a civil action under English law, then a divorce action in Edinburgh. The first trial took place in London in December 1807. Elgin's counsel brought in Hamilton, Morier, and several others to testify how happy the Elgin family had been right up until the last months in France. Of Ferguson it was said, 'He was indeed a very dangerous inmate [of Elgin's family] after he had planned a scheme of seduction; his manners were soft and alluring; he had been accustomed to study all the weaknesses of the female heart and the methods of taking advantage of them; and was well practised in the arts which render gallantry successful.'[5] Ferguson's lawyers, in his defence, could only claim that no adultery had taken place in France 'even in the voluptuous and fascinating capital of the French Empire where temptation is ever busily at work' but that, when Lady Elgin was alone in England 'without the protection of her husband and possessing sweetness that might rivet an anchorite—charms that could command and fascinate the coldest heart—he, all alive to such unequalled excellence and beauty, fell a devoted victim to such a shrine'.[6] No hint was given about the nature of Elgin's illness. He was awarded damages of £10,000. The broadsheet sellers found a lively market as the people enjoyed the disgrace of a noble family.[7]

The second trial took place in Edinburgh, in March 1808. Lady Elgin's lawyers first tried to claim that one of Lady Elgin's servants who was in hospital in London was too ill to give evidence even by proxy. Another servant, who could have been an important witness, was quickly sent out of the country to prevent her having to give evidence. Then they claimed that Elgin had condoned his wife's adultery, and had even obtained a large sum of money from her as the price of condonation. Lord Elgin was only able to obtain his divorce after a long succession of servants and hotel chambermaids had proved the adultery in humiliating detail.

The second blow was the virtual termination of his public career. When he was first in France it had been suggested that he might go as Ambassador to Russia, and he had welcomed the idea more as a means of regaining his freedom than because he was attracted by the prospect.[8] Later, while still in France, he was urging his friends to press for him to be appointed Ambassador to Austria but, in the end, no diplomatic post was offered.[9] The parole which Talleyrand had exacted as the price of Elgin's release was a cruel limitation. As long as the war with France lasted no government could take the risk of employing a man who was under such a restraint.

There still remained the other two careers on which he had embarked as a young man, the army and politics, but here too the story was the same. He had been promoted colonel in 1802, but there was no real prospect of success in the army for a man who had seen no active service, who was in chronic bad health, and who had given a parole to the enemy. As for politics, in 1807 Elgin lost his seat in the House of Lords which he had held since 1790 as one of the sixteen representative peers for Scotland. The only life that was open to him was that of a country nobleman.

There was one indication that he had not been entirely forgotten. Lord Grenville offered him the green ribbon of the Knights of the Thistle, the honour that Elgin so eagerly wished for and which had so often been refused, but he was denied even this crumb of comfort. Grenville left office before the honour could be bestowed and his successor did not renew the offer. The only honour that Elgin ever received after his return from Turkey was the Lord Lieutenancy of Fife and even this he was allowed to enjoy for only two months.[10]

Elgin was now deep in debt, and his divorce had deprived him of the prospect, on which he seems to have relied, of eventually adding the Nisbet fortune to his own. By the standards of some noblemen he had never been rich, nor was it really true, as Dundas had said many years before on launching him on his career, that he was 'easy in his circumstances'.[11] The income from his Scottish estates was only £2,000 a year—a paltry sum for a man of his class and one which would scarcely have appealed to the plainest of Jane Austen's heroines.[12]

Elgin had never during his diplomatic career expected to live within his salary nor could he ever have hoped to do so. Nevertheless he paid higher than most for the privilege of public service. His salary at Constantinople was £6,600 but, to take one item only, the domestic expenditure in the British Palace during the first year of the embassy had been £8,500.[13] Elgin had still to pay the salaries and expenses of his numerous staff, the upkeep of a large house he rented outside Constantinople, the cost of couriers and postage, and all the other multifarious expenses of a large and important embassy. Furthermore, the vast expenditure made necessary by the British invasion of Egypt had caused a decline in the exchange-rate of the pound, reducing the value of his salary to about £4,400; and Elgin had spent many thousands of pounds buying supplies for the army in Egypt, not all of which he had recouped from the Government before he left Constantinople.[14]

Although on his return from France in 1806 the Government gave Elgin a further £10,000 this was only a part of what he had spent out of his own purse on tents, horses, gunboats, medical supplies, and other equipment.[15] Elgin never ceased to complain that the sum was inadequate and ten years later he was still pestering the Government for recompense, claiming, with justice, that if he had been permitted to return to England in 1803 when his success was in everybody's mind, he would never have been treated so shabbily.[16]

What made matters worse, nobody in authority believed that he was really short of money.[17] For years the story was current that Elgin had made a fortune in Turkey in the style of a Nabob in India, a result, no doubt, of exaggerated accounts of the lavish expenditures in Athens and of the diamonds, pelisses, and caparisoned horses that he had received as part of diplomatic life. Nelson, for example, warning his brother off a diplomatic career in 1804, wrote:

Corps Diplomatique is road to ruin. I never knew or heard of anyone who made a fortune at it and it is very easy to spend one: indeed without much more prudence than is considered right a minister cannot exist upon his salary. We must not judge because perhaps Lord Elgin at a particular moment got money at Constantinople, and even a Scotchman I dare say would have been richer with his interest if he had set up as a master tailor.[18]

Elgin's original plan of making drawings and taking casts of the buildings in Athens was to have cost only £620 per year in salaries with something similar for expenses and materials. As his schemes had become more ambitious, his expenditures had grown in proportion. For the period when he himself was in Constantinople, that is excluding any liabilities Lusieri had incurred in his name since 1803, Elgin estimated his expenditure on his collection as follows.

Pay and Expenses of the Artists over three and a half years	£9,200
Conveyance of the Artists to and from the East and their journeys there	£1,500
Pay of Workmen employed at Athens and elsewhere	£15,000
Storage of Marbles at Malta	£2,500
Cost of the *Mentor* and Salvage Operations	£5,000
Cost of landing, moving and arranging the collection in England	£6,000
TOTAL	£39,200[19]

Gradually, in the months after his return from France, Elgin's financial affairs were sorted out. When all the bills were totted up the full extent of his difficulties was brought home to him. It came as a shock. As he wrote later:

All the money I had drawn upon public account, the whole proceeds of my patrimonial estate, my wife's fortune, and every private fund at my disposal had been absorbed; and a debt was awaiting me of about £27,000 accumulated during my foreign life.[20]

Philip Hunt, who had played the most decisive part in the collecting of the marbles and who, because he had stayed behind to help with the salvaging of the *Mentor*, had also been detained in France, was one of many who were also brought down by Elgin's financial difficulties. All the hopes of setting himself up with an independent fortune with which he had entered Elgin's service were now gone. It is doubtful whether he received any money at all. In bitter disappointment he broke off relations with his former patron and transferred his services to the Duke of Bedford. As a conscientious magistrate for many years, he reformed the running of the Bedford prison.[21] One by one, Elgin's other former colleagues lost touch. Of the party which had set out in the *Phaeton* with such high hopes seven years before only the amiable Hamilton now remained to help Elgin in his difficulties.

The question of what to do about the marbles now pressed ever more urgently. The main cargo, mostly those that Hunt had put on board the *Braakel*, had arrived in England in January 1804. Since Elgin was in France, his mother the Dowager Countess had accepted responsibility for them, and they were taken first to the house of the Duchess of Portland in Westminster and then moved near by to the Duke of Richmond's. From France Elgin at one stage had told his mother to hand the collection over unconditionally to the British government as a way of saving further trouble and expense, but she had not done so. Another idea, to put the marbles on public exhibition in London, had also fallen through. When Elgin returned the cases still lay unopened.[22]

Besides the main cargo, smaller lots had also arrived at different times and still lay at the various ports where they had been landed. Agents were sent to look for them and they were soon collected in. At the London Customs House one of Elgin's agents bought twenty-six unidentified cases of antiquities at a clearance sale at a cost of one pound each, thinking they must be Elgin's. Most of the cases contained casts or original marbles of lesser interest, but when one of them was opened it was found to contain a metope from the Parthenon. Although Elgin did not realize so at the time, these were the cases that the Comte de Choiseul-Gouffier had been so concerned about when he met Elgin at Barrèges. They had lain at the Customs House awaiting a buyer ever since Nelson had sent them as prize after the capture of the French frigate which was taking them to France. And so the metope which had had such an eventful history since it fell from the Parthenon in 1787 now joined the Elgin collection.[23]

The Duke of Richmond, understandably, was unwilling to have fifty huge cases containing 120 tons of marbles lying in his house and garden for any longer than was necessary. Elgin, for his part, was equally anxious to remove the collection which had already cost him so much into a place where it could be both sheltered and seen. After all he had not yet seen the collection himself and was eager to open his parcels. No doubt arguing to himself that it was too late to skimp now, he plunged into further expenditure. He rented a large house at the corner of Piccadilly and Park Lane which had a large garden behind which he built a spacious shed.

It took three months to build the shed and a further four to unpack and arrange the marbles. A rare fungus found growing in the sawdust of one of the cases was examined at a meeting of the Linnaean Society.[24] The shed where the marbles were exhibited was about fifty foot square and the marbles were arranged to form a symmetrical picturesque composition to face the visitor as he entered. There was no attempt to lay out the collection systematically or chronologically. Sculptures, inscriptions, and architectural fragments were piled indiscriminately on one another. In the centre stood the Caryatid from the Erechtheion and all the other marbles were arranged around her according to size. The torso from the Parthenon pediment, perched precariously on an inscribed column, was balanced at the other side of the room by the horse's head of the chariot of the moon on top of a piece of pillar from the Erechtheion. The total effect resembled a vignette of classical ruins common in the travel books of the time. This temporary museum was finally ready in June 1807.

If Elgin was to continue with his plan to improve the arts of his country the next need was to have engravings made. As *The Antiquities of Athens* prepared by Stuart and Revett had already shown, engravings could inspire an appreciation of the arts of antiquity among persons who had no hope of ever seeing the original works. That book had not only shown the ruins of Athens as romantic reminders of lost glory, but gave the exact measurements and proportions needed if architects were to make convincing adaptations. It had also opened the way towards new theories of what constituted the essence of ancient art and architecture. Although the fact was not yet appreciated, it was only because the Parthenon had been blown to pieces in the explosion of 1687 that it had become possible for western Europe to anatomize, to classify, to copy, and to appropriate it for their own modern artistic and ideological purposes.[25]

After Elgin left Constantinople, Ittar, one of the architects, had been employed for a further year in Italy to make fair copies of his drawings. They were duly finished and sent to England without incident. (Every time Ittar came to copy 'Egina', as in Italian he called the island of Aegina, he made a Freudian slip and wrote 'Elgina'.)[26] Theodor the Calmuck too had also been engaged to go to England to complete his drawings and engrave them. Unfortunately, without supervision, the Calmuck's drinking limited his output and, despite two years on Elgin's payroll, he never completed the engraving of the drawings.[27] This essential part of Elgin's original purpose had therefore to be postponed indefinitely.

Another important decision had still to be taken. Were the marbles to be restored? In the eighteenth century, as earlier, it was the universal practice when an ancient statue was discovered, to repair the battered nose, add the missing limbs, and generally to give the imagination free play to restore the statue in entirety to what it once may have looked like. In Italy a flourishing industry produced numerous detailed and artistic compositions from unlikely collections of oddments. A restored statue looked better as an ornament to a room and invariably fetched a higher price than a mutilated one. The best Italian sculptors were employed in making restorations and many a famous antique statue contained more modern than ancient parts.[28] With the technology available at the time, in order to tack a new piece of marble on to a weathered or battered surface the rough surface had first to be filed smooth. There was thus no going back either at the time or later. If a restored piece was wrong it could not subsequently be taken off without exposing the smooth modern joints.

When Elgin's sculptures were being collected in Greece it never occurred to him or to Hunt or Lusieri that they would not have to be sent to Italy for restoration. One danger of doing that, as Hamilton advised Elgin, was that if they went there they might easily fall into the hands of the French. Once the war was over that objection might lose its force, and there were sculptors capable of doing the work well in other countries. The slab of the Parthenon frieze in the Louvre, for example, had been restored in Paris. But Hamilton now introduced a new argument. Restoration, he suggested, was wrong in any circumstances:

Few would be found who would set a higher value on a work of Phidias or of one of his Scholars, with a modern head and modern arms than they would in their *present* state.[29]

The study of ancient art, as it had developed in Europe in the eighteenth century, had been seen primarily as a humanizing educational enterprise. By contemplating works of ancient art, so it was believed, the modern observer would begin to share in the minds of the ancients, and to become more aware, and more civilized as a result. For Winckelmann and the other, mainly German, writers whose theories were influential over the whole of Europe, the classical ideal was implicit in the artistic forms which had been brought to a state of perfection in the ancient world and never been equalled. Aristocrats and artists who could afford to go to Italy would have their humanity enlarged by studying the works of ancient art preserved in the museums there. For those who were obliged to stay at home, plaster casts which preserved the ideal forms could be almost as effective. Winckelmann, who had had the opportunity to go to Greece to see for himself the remains of actual ancient Greek art which in his time were becoming known from the accounts of travellers, thought it was unnecessary to do so.[30]

As it happened, at the very time when Lord Elgin's marbles arrived in England, the new romantic aesthetic was beginning to take its hold in Western culture. Great works of literature and of art, it was increasingly asserted, were 'created' by unique men and women of special genius, who shared a spark of the divine creativity and were inspired to express an inner individual and personal essence. The romantic approach, in its attitudes to literature and art, shifted the emphasis from the reader to the author, from the viewer to the artist. The fact that the Parthenon marbles were battered and incomplete, far from being a loss, was now seen as a manifestation of their aura of authenticity. In the new romantic aesthetic, the notion of a fragment, a broken relic from the ruins of time, exercised a powerful attraction in its own right. To keep the marbles as fragments was to be true to the artists who created them. In another unrelated thought, fragments were also, romantics tended to believe, a truer expression of the disjointed, unpredictable, and fragmentary nature of actual experience.

If, as Elgin assumed in accordance with the older tradition, the main purpose of his collection was to influence the arts of the modern world, then his marbles should be restored. If, by contrast, as Hamilton was suggesting in accordance with the newly emerging romantic aesthetic, the marbles were works of supreme genius created by a supreme artist and which stood outside time and place irrespective of their effects on viewers, then restoring them would, paradoxically, damage or destroy their integrity, their uniqueness, and their authenticity. Neither approach, as is clearer to our own generation, appreciated the extent to which the sculptures of the Parthenon, although designed as a unity, were essentially collaborative, with many agents other than the designer contributing to the result, including the quarrymen who selected the marble blocks, the engineers who transported and hoisted them, the masons who carved them, the sculptors who executed the designs, and the inspectors who accepted the work, as well as the people of Athens and their officials who, through their collective institutions, commissioned, approved, and authorized the continuing expenditure.[31]

Homecoming   149

Nor did either the humanistic or the romantic approach appreciate the extent to which the meaning of the Parthenon in its own
time was culturally constructed by viewers whose sense of identity,
whose religion, whose attitudes to images and to the conventions
of art, and whose understanding of the world in which they found
themselves, were essentially different from those of modern
Europe.

When Elgin left Greece it was his firm intention to have his
sculptures restored in Italy and this seems to have been one of his
chief reasons for going to Rome on his way back. Characteristically
he decided that nothing but the best would do and he offered the
work to the most famous sculptor in Europe, Antonio Canova.
Canova, although he worked in the neo-classical style, creating
many statues in the whitest of marble in the tradition of the
Graeco-Roman statues of Italy, was also at the same time much
influenced by the new romantic approach. He is reported to have
said:

That however greatly it was to be lamented that these statues should have
suffered so much from time and barbarism, yet it was undeniable that they
had never been retouched; that they were the work of the ablest artists the
world had ever seen; executed under the most enlightened patron of the
arts, and at a period when genius enjoyed the most liberal encouragement,
and had attained the highest degree of perfection; and that they had been
found worthy of forming the decoration of the most admired edifice ever
erected in Greece: That he should have had the greatest delight and
derived the greatest benefit from the opportunity Lord Elgin offered him
of having in his possession and contemplating these inestimable marbles.
But (his expression was) it would be sacrilege in him or any man to
presume to touch them with a chisel.[32]

Canova had gone on to say, however, that if Elgin was insistent on
having the marbles restored there was a man in England who could
do the job as well as he, and that man was his own pupil, John
Flaxman.[33]

So the question remained during the three years of Elgin's detention in France, but he was too much a man of his generation to
depart so quickly from the ideology in which he had been brought
up. As Canova had suggested, he now offered the work to 'the
English Phidias', John Flaxman. Flaxman was willing to do the
work but was hesitant. The restored parts would be inferior to
the original, he said modestly, and would be a constant source of
disputes; the job would be long and, even when finished, might not

increase the financial value of the collection. Most important of all, from Elgin's point of view, Flaxman estimated the cost of the work at over £20,000.[34]

We may be glad, for once, that Elgin was deep in debt. Lavish though he was in pouring out money on his precious marbles he could not possibly afford sums of that magnitude. The scheme was shelved and though it was later revived (Elgin wanted to offer a prize to the best suggestions for restoration) he was persuaded to drop it.[35] The fragmentary sculptures of the Parthenon, rescued from Turkish misgovernment and from tourist pilfering, narrowly escaped the restorer's chisel.

14

The Second Collection

STORING, arranging, and displaying the antiquities that had reached England was only part of Elgin's problem. At Athens there still lay a second large collection of marbles, vases, coins, and other antiquities almost as fine as the first, over which Lusieri was still loyally standing guard. Harassed by the Turks, conspired against by the French, largely abandoned by the official British authorities, and cut off from all supplies of money, Lusieri by 1806 was in a pathetic state. Elgin's release in the middle of the year was just in time to save him.

Money and materials began to flow again, and although there could now be no question of further removals of sculpture from the buildings, excavations were restarted, despite the absence of authority, by the usual stratagem of bribing the current Voivode. The famous cart which had been taken from Fauvel in 1800 was again repaired and brought into service. Lusieri proposed that he should go for a time to Naples to have the best of the vases cleaned and restored by the skilled men that had worked for Sir William Hamilton. Before anything could be decided, however, Lusieri's fortunes suddenly took a further plunge. He was forced to fly for his life as larger political events again intervened.

In 1806 the period of Anglo-Turkish friendship and alliance that Elgin's Embassy had inaugurated came to an abrupt end. While Napoleon was engaged in fighting the Russians in Germany the French Ambassador in Turkey (Elgin's old friend Sébastiani) persuaded the Turks to break their treaty with Russia in favour of France. War between Russia and Turkey broke out and Britain tried to prop up her failing ally Russia by declaring war as well. A British fleet (including Sir Sidney Smith) sailed through the Dardanelles to make a demonstration of force outside Constantinople, but Sébastiani used the confused period of negotiations that followed to put the Dardanelles forts into a state of readiness, and the Turks inflicted heavy damage on the British ships as they returned through the straits. A small British force made an attempt to invade Egypt but little was achieved. Within a few weeks all Lord Elgin's diplomatic successes of five years before were swept away. The Turks were more hostile to the British than ever before.

When the news of the outbreak of war reached Athens, Lusieri decided to leave. It was out of the question that he could take any of the marbles with him but he did make arrangements with the Voivode to take some of the best vases. At the very moment when the vases were about to be embarked the Voivode changed his mind. The vases were seized and Lusieri had to flee secretly at night to avoid arrest. He eventually reached Malta without any money or even spare clothes. From Malta he returned to Sicily where, characteristically, he still had drawings to finish that he had begun before 1799.

As usual the French prospects rose as the British sank. The departure of Lusieri was the signal that Fauvel had been waiting for. The two rivals had been casting covetous eyes on one another's collections ever since Fauvel's return in 1803, and each had planned, on at least one occasion, to seize the other's by force. Fauvel now had the best chance of his life. He took repossession at last of the cart he had lost in 1800 and made plans for the second time to seize Elgin's collections at Athens. The cases containing the vases were broken into and the vases sent overland to Ioannina for forwarding to the Louvre. But the real prize, the sculptures, presented a far more difficult problem. The muleteers from Ioannina declared decisively that such heavy loads could not be taken across country by land. Fauvel could only wait therefore until a French ship could call. There could be no doubt that sooner or later Napoleon would arrange this, if only in revenge for the loss of Choiseul-Gouffier's collection in *l'Arabe*.[1]

Elgin, after all his efforts, was not going to allow his precious collection to fall into the hands of the French without a struggle. If Britain was at war with Turkey, then the use of force was legitimate. Elgin wrote to the Governor of Malta and to the First Lord of the Admiralty, asking them to send a warship to Piraeus and a transport ship big enough to embark the marbles.[2] To Sir John Stuart, the military Commander-in-Chief, he suggested another idea, in a letter from Broomhall:

The only combination which occurs to my mind from hence is supposing it possible that a secret communication could be made to the authorities at Athens, I mean the Voivode, making it worth his while to permit, or connive at, the removal of such of the effects as were easily transported to the Port—Perhaps then a demonstration of disembarking a few marines, especially if there were more than one ship of war in the offing, might justify his compliance, and could easily be done, while there was not a possibility of any resistance being made.[3]

To strengthen his plea Elgin promised that he would hand over any marbles thus rescued free to the British Museum. The naval officers who were engaged in a desperate war against French cruisers were, however, not enthusiastic about sending their warships to pick up cargoes of marbles which would slow their sailing and cause them to sink immediately to the bottom in any unlucky encounter with the enemy or bad weather.

In April 1808, despairing of finding a warship, Elgin decided to send an agent of his own to the East to supervise matters on the spot. He engaged Stephen Maltass, an employee of the Levant Company who knew Greece and Turkey well, to go to Sicily and concert with Lusieri on how best to get the collection away from Athens. The main hope was still to persuade the naval authorities to send a ship but another more daring scheme was to be suggested, the seizing of Fauvel and the Athenian magistrates by force and holding them as ransom while the marbles were embarked. Maltass was equipped with a large sum of money, silver pistols, and English watches in case an opportunity occurred of bribing the Turks, and he was instructed to ensure that any warship that went to Athens had in company a strong transport ship, horses, tackle, and, of course, a large cart.

Maltass arrived in Sicily in July. The British military authorities there continued to hesitate to send a ship to Athens but Lusieri was keen. He even began to build a cart. If a seizure by force was to be attempted, however, Lusieri declined to take part. Maybe, as Elgin suggested, it was because he had 'formed a tender connexion' in Athens and did not want to jeopardize his chances of returning.[4] But there is no reason to doubt Lusieri's own explanation.

Perhaps in their vexation they [the Turks] might break or burn everything in the stores and at my house; and that is the best there is. Three metopes, the best preserved, and the best pieces of the frieze, of the most picturesque part of the procession, making a sequence of several slabs, are in the town ... One of these reliefs, which they cannot find, though they have made holes in all the corners of my house, is the despair of the Vice-

Commissary [Fauvel]. They have opened all the other boxes on purpose to find it. It is finer and better preserved than all the rest.[5]

All such schemes were soon abandoned. When Russia suddenly decided to ally herself with France, Britain found herself in the uncomfortable position of being at war with both the belligerents, and had to make a hurried peace with at least one of them. On 29 August 1808 Lusieri wrote to Sir Robert Adair, who was appointed to conduct the peace negotiations with Turkey on behalf of the British, setting out a list of the firmans he now needed.[6] He asked for firmans as a kind of amnesty for the protection of himself and of the Greeks and others who had worked for him, firmans that would enable him to repossess all sequestrated goods, including antiquities, firmans permitting free entrance to the Acropolis and the right to draw and to excavate. He did not, it seems, ask for a firman to undertake further removals from the buildings, but he did seek explicit permission to export the antiquities that had so far been collected. Issuing an official document to allow the export of these antiquities would, he knew, have been further legitimation of any alleged illegality committed when they were acquired.

When peace was signed in January 1809, Maltass went at once to Constantinople and in April obtained for Lusieri a firman allowing him to return to Athens but as yet nothing else. Lusieri did not go direct to Athens in spite of a ship's being specially provided to take him, but decided to take the long land route by way of Ioannina. The Ottoman officials now in charge in Athens were, in practice and perhaps in law, subordinates of Ali Pasha of Ioannina who had used the troubled times to extend his power over much of mainland Greece. Lusieri knew where the power lay. When Elgin heard of this decision his impatience at last got the better of him and he let fly at Lusieri:

Heavens! why the delay? How at a time like the present can you believe in the possibility of a lasting peace? What is the use of the cruel experience we have had already? For the love of God dont lose another instant at whatever cost. Take any ship that you can possibly get, either from Smyrna or Malta, to get the things into a place of safety. When you have once made them secure, then we will go forward with more confidence and calmness. But remember all I have suffered for the last six years. Think of all the opposition you have met with and that you still have to fear. Think of all the delays inseparable from one's object in those countries. Recall the entire trust that I place in you: that I send you all the means that you can desire or that I can procure for you. Think of all that we have done;

of the marvellous work at which we labour. Give yourself up entirely to the *impetuosity* of your character, as the object itself, our past success, and in short everything unite in requiring.[7]

Elgin added that he himself had decided to come to Athens in the autumn—an intention he never carried out.

Lusieri reached Athens at the end of August 1809. He took repossession of his sequestrated house. The doors were broken open. A ladder was placed permanently against the garden wall to enable anyone who wanted to go in and out at will. Everything of any value that could be easily moved had been stolen. All the vases were gone as were a collection of presents for the Turks, all his stores, scaffolding, ropes and tackle. But the marbles still remained.

There then began a period of frantic activity to try to get the marbles away. At Elgin's request Hamilton again urged the naval authorities in the Mediterranean to send a ship to Athens, reiterating the earlier promise that any marbles thus recovered would belong to the nation and not to Elgin privately.[8] But at Athens Lusieri, taking his master's exhortations to heart, had already chartered a large vessel from the island of Hydra and obtained the permission of the Voivode to embark the collection. The marbles were actually on board and the ship was about to sail when an order arrived from the Porte forbidding them to go. There was no alternative: the marbles had to be unloaded again, as Lusieri reported, 'in such a fashion as to cause the greatest possible pleasure to our enemies'.[9] Shortly afterwards, in response to Elgin's repeated pleas, a British warship at last arrived at the Piraeus—specially sent to take off the marbles, but it was no good. The Voivode refused absolutely to let them go. Only a firman from the Porte countermanding the first would persuade him to change his mind. The warship waited patiently for a while and then retired in disgust.

The scene of the contest to get the marbles away turned to Constantinople. The British Ambassador, Robert Adair, as a result of constant pressure from Lusieri, Elgin, and the Foreign Office in London, began to apply constant pressure to the Ottoman government to obtain a firman. But such discussions could always be relied upon to produce surprises. The Turks now declared that Lord Elgin had never had permission to remove any marbles in the first place. The activities of his agents at Athens that had been going on, with interruptions, for over eight years had, they declared, been illegal from the start.[10]

When peace between Britain and the Ottoman Empire was formally restored on 5 January 1809, no decisions about the status of the marbles in Athens had been taken. Although in some respects life in Athens returned to normal, neither the Ottoman officials nor Lusieri were willing to risk shipping them without explicit authorization from the Ottoman government in Constantinople and they were in no hurry to agree. Once the marbles were exported, they could no longer be useful to the Turks in their political strategy of playing off the British and French.

It was only a matter of time, Adair knew, before the political tide would begin to turn. On 18 February 1810, nearly six months from the time he began negotiating on this subject, he reported to the Foreign Secretary 'with great satisfaction' that the Turks were now thoroughly dissatisfied with their new-found friendship with France and were again veering strongly towards an alliance with Great Britain.[11] Presents amounting to 1,480 piastres, over £100, were given to Ottoman officials in addition to a present to the Kaymacam the size of which is not recorded.[12] A few days later Adair was able to announce:

I have at length succeeded in obtaining an order from the Caimacam to the Voivode of Athens, for the embarkation without further detention of the antiquities collected by Lord Elgin and now lying at Athens.[13]

It had been a letter from the Kaymacam to the Voivode that was the original authority for removing the sculptures of the Parthenon. Now a precisely similar authority was granted to allow those that still remained in Ottoman territory to be exported. The granting of the firman allowing the marbles to leave Ottoman jurisdiction implied condonation, if not approval, of all the actions and abuses committed under the authority of other firmans granted earlier.

In 1816 the Select Committee of the British House of Commons, which included opponents of Lord Elgin, was asked to consider four questions, including;

The First . . . relates to the Authority by which this collection was acquired; The second to the circumstances under which that Authority was granted.[14]

In answer to the first question the Committee made no direct judgement but contented itself with summarizing the evidence they had collected from the replies of witnesses:

He [Philip Hunt] stated further, that no remonstrance was at that time [the time of the first removals from the Parthenon under the authority of the

second firman] made, nor any displeasure shown by the Turkish government, either at Constantinople or at Athens, against the extensive interpretation which was put upon this fermaun; and although the work of
taking down and removing, was going on for months, and even years, and
was conducted in the most public manner, numbers of native labourers, to
the amount of some hundreds, being frequently employed, not the least
obstruction was ever interposed, nor the smallest uneasiness shown after
the granting of the second fermaun.[15]

In answer to the second question, the Committee noted that only
the Turkish ministers concerned could give an authoritative answer.
The Committee agreed with the comment that:

A British subject not in the situation of Ambassador, could not have been
able to obtain from the Turkish Government a fermaun of such extensive
powers.[16]

The Committee noted the attempts by French ambassadors to
obtain permission to make removals. If the marbles had not been
taken by Lord Elgin, it was, the Committee agreed, probable that:

at no great distance of time, they might have been removed by that government from their original site, if they had not been taken away, and
secured for this country by Lord Elgin.[17]

Although the actions of the various Ottoman officials were, to
a large extent, arbitrary, politically driven, and, in many cases,
decisively influenced by threats and by bribery, modern experts in
international law who have studied the case have usually agreed
that Elgin's actions were probably technically lawful in the circumstances of the time, that his claim to personal ownership and
right to sell were valid in law, and that any action by Greece, as successor government, to try to recover the marbles in an international
court would probably fail.[18]

  The main interest in ancient antiquities shown by the Ottoman
authorities was in what use could be made of them to win friends
or distress enemies, in other words as a minor instrument of foreign
policy. The firmans and counter-firmans about the Parthenon
marbles emanating from Constantinople between 1784 and the
establishment of Greek independence are an accurate barometer
of whether the French or British were uppermost in Turkish
favours, but they show little consistency otherwise. As far as Elgin
and his agents were concerned, questions of legality and illegality
scarcely mattered. They had no difficulty in justifying what they did

against what they saw as their higher duty of rescue. And the same was true of the British government, who devoted huge diplomatic and naval resources to what was still claimed as a matter of private property.

The firman obtained by Adair reached Athens on 20 March and Lusieri lost no time in putting it into effect. By spending over £200 he succeeded in loading up his Hydriote ship by the evening of the 21st. A British warship, HMS *Pylades*, was sent specially from Smyrna to act as escort. At long last it looked as if the collection was saved. But even now Fauvel would not admit that he was beaten, and made his last bid to prevent the marbles from slipping for ever from his grasp. John Galt, the Scottish novelist, who was then in Athens in the course of a business speculation, described the final hours. He was obviously torn between a desire to join in the general condemnation of Elgin and pride in his own part in obtaining the marbles for his country.

Two circumstances occasioned this interference on my part; an Italian artist, the agent of Lord Elgin, had quarrelled about the marbles with Monsieur Fauvelle the French consul . . . Fauvelle was no doubt ambitious to obtain these precious fragments for the Napoleon Museum at Paris; and certainly exerted all his influence to get the removal of them interdicted. On the eve of the departure of the vessel, he sent in a strong representation on the subject to the governor of the city, stating, what I believe was very true, that Lord Elgin had never any sufficient firman or authority for the dilapidations that he had committed on the temples. Lusieri, the Italian artist alluded to, was alarmed, and called on me at the monastery of the Roman Propaganda where I then resided; and it was agreed that if any detention was attempted I should remonstrate with the governor and represent to him that such an arrest of British property would be considered an act of hostility.[19]

The presence of the *Pylades* would no doubt have given credibility to the implicit threat. But fortunately there was no need for the marines. Fauvel's protests were rejected and the Hydriote ship set sail with all her cargo on 26 March. Lusieri wrote at once in triumph to Lord Elgin:

Covering up all my past woes with eternal oblivion I wholly give myself up to joy, when I see the antiquities on board the polacca ready to set her sails for Malta. I regret that I cannot follow them as I am obliged to stay here as a surety for paying what I owe and carrying out my promises to the Voivode.[20]

The last point had not been lost on Galt, who had taken passage on the ship as far as Hydra. Knowing that Elgin's bankers at Malta might refuse to pay Lusieri's bills when the ship arrived, he wrote to his own banker there to instruct him to buy up the marbles if an opportunity occurred. 'Here was a chance,' he confessed later, 'of the most exquisite relics of art in the world becoming mine, and a speculation by the sale of them in London that would realise a fortune.'[21] Luckily, when the ship reached Malta, Elgin's bankers paid up and the marbles remained in his possession. What fate a collection of 'Galt Marbles' might have suffered is anyone's guess.

Lusieri's joy at the dispatch of the Hydriote ship was heartfelt, but his problems were not over. The ship had taken forty-eight cases of marbles, including most of the Parthenon sculptures, but she had not been large enough to take them all. Five of the heaviest cases had to be left behind and they were to prove almost the most difficult of all. It was over a year before they could be got away.

During these months Greece had been filled with English visitors driven by the war from the more usual haunts of the Grand Tour. John Galt came and went, as did Lord Guildford, Lord Sligo, Lady Hester Stanhope, and many others less well known. In particular, Athens was visited on two occasions by Lord Byron. In the controversy between Lusieri and Fauvel these visitors took sides, mostly against Lusieri—and the local Greek community of Athens joined in. 'It was during our stay in the place', wrote Byron's friend Hobhouse, the mildest of the visitors, 'to be lamented that a war more than civil was raging on the subject of my Lord Elgin's pursuits in Greece, and had enlisted all the Frank settlers and the principal Greeks on one or the other side of the controversy. The factions of Athens were renewed.'[22]

The Fauvel party were determined to stop the last of the Parthenon sculptures, the five cases left behind by the Hydriote ship, from being shipped away. They declared again and again to the Voivode that his actions were illegal and that he would be disowned, and they exaggerated what Elgin had done, especially the damage to the buildings. Lusieri countered by saying that Fauvel wanted to take away the whole Theseum, but perhaps, when one remembers that he himself had hoped for the whole Caryatid porch and for the Monument of Lysicrates, that is not so preposterous a piece of engineering as it seems now.[23] Most effective of all, the visitors attempted to sap Lusieri's self-confidence by insinuating that Elgin was ruined and would never pay him or his bills. Lusieri, reassured on the last point, calmly continued his excavations.

Among the many foreign visitors to Athens was Lord Byron, then aged 22. Shortly before he left England, Byron had published his satire *English Bards and Scotch Reviewers*, which included a few swipes at Lord Elgin and the collection of marbles which were already on view in London.[24] *Childe Harold's Pilgrimage, A Romaunt*, the poem which was shortly to make him famous, was still being written when he was in Greece.

Byron was on the best of terms with both Fauvel and Lusieri, inspecting and comparing their collections of antiquities and drawings, and using them in turn as guides on his explorations round Athens and the vicinity. Lusieri had married the daughter of Madame Giraud, the widow of a French merchant with whom he lodged, and Byron had a sexual affair with Nicolo Giraud, then aged about 15, the young brother of Lusieri's wife.[25] Nicolo went with Byron on his travels in Greece (helping him with his Greek and Italian) and was still writing him passionate letters five years later. Byron showered the boy with presents and included him in his will for £7,000.[26]

It was in April 1811, a year after the dispatch of the Hydriote ship, that Elgin's agents in Malta at last persuaded the Navy to send another transport, called confusingly the *Hydra*, to pick up the last of the marbles. Since Byron was then in Athens waiting for an opportunity to go home, it was agreed that he should take passage in the *Hydra* as far as Malta. He sailed from Piraeus with the last cargo on 22 April 1811. Also on board were Lusieri and Nicolo Giraud.

When the *Hydra* reached Malta the party broke up and Byron proceeded to England. At Lusieri's request he acted as messenger for a letter which Lusieri wanted to send to Elgin, and on his return to London he forwarded the letter to Elgin as he was asked. When Elgin offered to call on him personally to thank him, Byron was embarrassed. In another letter Elgin asked again to call, and said he attached much value to Byron's opinion of the researches at Athens. The two men never met, but Byron did feel obliged to give Elgin an indication of his real opinions and to warn him that he was intending to publish an attack on him.[27] How Elgin reacted to the warning is not known, but he may have agreed with Hamilton to whom he sent Byron's letter for advice. As Hamilton wrote:

I do not consider him [Byron] a very formidable enemy in his meditated attack and I shall be much surprised if his attack on what you have done do not turn out one of the most friendly acts he could have done. It will create an interest in the public, excite curiosity, and the real advantage to this country and the merit of your exertions will become more known and felt as they are more known.[28]

If this is what Elgin thought, it was a disastrous misjudgement.

15

Artists and Dilettanti

By June 1807 the first collection of Elgin Marbles in the shed behind Piccadilly was unpacked ready to be exhibited. It was now time to begin the improvement of the arts in Great Britain which had been the original aim. A number of prominent artists, sculptors, and connoisseurs were permitted to view the collection and make drawings. The effect was startling.

The sculptor John Flaxman, who had been asked to advise on possible restoration, was one of the first to make a visit. The pupil of the famous Canova, his models of perfection were the Apollo Belvedere, the Laocoon, the Medici Venus and the other famous copies of lost Greek originals to be seen in Italy which were then regarded as incorporating the purest spirit of the classical world. Mainly as a result of the writings of Winckelmann, which were influential all over Europe, these works were believed by many to represent the summit of artistic achievement, the greatest masterpieces from the ancient world which had never been, and never could be, surpassed. In the eighteenth century, in addition to the belief in their humanizing qualities, a theory of what constituted 'Ideal Beauty' had been constructed from a study of their form and technique.

Flaxman's reaction to his first sight of the Parthenon sculptures is a tribute both to his honesty and to his perception. For the first time he was looking at statues which were undoubtedly original Greek works of the fifth century brought directly from Greece, and the differences from his previous models, both in their artistic spirit and in their technical competence, were as immediately apparent to him as they had been to his master Canova.[1] He at once declared that the Elgin Marbles were 'very far superior' to all the treasures of Italy, virtually admitting that the standards on which he had based his art and whose study had brought him to the top of his profession had now to be abandoned.[2] From the first day he never wavered from his opinion and no praise of the Elgin Marbles was too high.

Compared with the figure then known as the Theseus, the Apollo Belvedere was a dancing master, he told Hamilton.[3] 'The hand of Phidias was on that,' he would say as he showed visitors round.[4]

Benjamin West, the President of the Royal Academy, who had tried to find Elgin an English artist before he set out for Constantinople, was equally enthusiastic. The marbles were, he said 'sublime specimens of the purest sculpture'. He wished he was 20 instead of 70 years of age, he declared, so that he could begin his career again, knowing what he now knew. As it was, as soon as it was warm enough to spend time in Elgin's cold shed, he intended to start an intensive study, and this is what he did, sketching the marbles and incorporating the results in his huge historical paintings.[5] West then composed a long letter of thanks to Lord Elgin which he hoped the Royal Academy would publish.

I have found in this collection of sculpture so much excellence in art (which is as applicable to painting and architecture as to sculpture) and a variety so magnificent and boundless, that every branch of science connected with the fine arts, cannot fail to acquire something from this collection. Your Lordship, by bringing these treasures of the first and best age of sculpture and architecture into London, has founded a new Athens for the emulation and example of the British student.

By allowing him to draw from these works of art, West declared, Elgin had given him an advantage not enjoyed by Raphael. His letter closed with a resounding vindication of Elgin's achievement as rescuer and benefactor expressed in the new romantic discourse of genius and creativity:

In whatever estimation the arts of the present day shall be held by those of future ages, your Lordship must be remembered by the present, and be recorded by those to come, as a benefactor who has conferred obligations not only on a profession but upon a nation; and as having rescued from the devastation of ignorance and the unholy rapine of barbarism, those unrivalled works of genius, to be preserved in the bosom of your country, which a few centuries more might have consigned to oblivion. . . . And may the materials from which those sublime sculptures have been produced be preserved from accident, that men of taste and genius yet unborn may be gratified with a sight of them; and that the admiring world may revere the Author of all things, for having bestowed on man those peculiar powers of his mind and hand.[6]

The Royal Academy were unwilling to publish this letter, considering it too full of 'self-panegyrick'.[7] Elgin himself published it shortly afterwards.

The landscape painter Farington on his visit thought the marbles were 'the highest quality of Art, a union of greatness and nature'.[8] The portrait painter Sir Thomas Lawrence became a regular visitor. The eccentric old sculptor Nollekens, who had learned his art from the masterpieces of Italy, was at first inclined to be lukewarm, but he too soon changed his mind and joined the other artists applying for permission to sketch.[9] Richard and Robert Smirke, and William Daniell, who had all been rejected by Elgin in 1799, had to admit that they had missed a great opportunity.[10] Turner, another rejected candidate, wrote enthusiastically to 'pay my homage to your lordship's exertions for this rescue from barbarism'.[11]

Artists, sculptors, statesmen, ambassadors, and members of London fashionable society begged to be allowed to visit Lord Elgin's cold shed, and permits to draw were in such great demand that they had to be rationed. The Elgin Marbles were the talk of the town.[12] William Hamilton, Elgin's former private secretary, acted as curator when Elgin was in Scotland, but in 1809 he was made Under-Secretary of State at the Foreign Office. A full-time curator was appointed and a catalogue of the exhibits printed for the use of visitors.

In June 1808 the prizefighter Gregson agreed to stand naked in the museum and pose for two hours in various attitudes so that his anatomy could be compared with that of the statues. A number of artists and gentlemen each contributed five shillings (some a guinea) to witness the perfect match between nature and art.[13] A month later another such show was held in the presence of eighteen gentlemen. This time three actual boxing matches were arranged between the best professional prizefighters of the day. The physique of Dutch Sam was much admired and so, no doubt, were the marbles.[14]

On another occasion Elgin invited West and Lawrence, the two best-known artists of the day, to meet the great tragic actress Mrs Siddons at his museum. The experience of the Parthenon sculptures was not only visual, but could elevate the human mind like the performance of a great play. As Lawrence wrote:

Mrs. Siddons can nowhere be seen with so just accompaniments as the works of Phidias, nor can they receive nobler homage than from her praise. She is of his age, a kindred genius, though living in our times.[15]

Mrs Siddons did her best to live up to the occasion. According to Elgin, the first sight of the Three Fates, 'so rivetted and agitated the feelings of Mrs Siddons, the pride of theatrical representation, as actually to draw tears from her eyes'.[16]

Among the artists who came to pay homage to the Elgin Marbles was the young historical painter Benjamin Robert Haydon. A man of colossal energy, passionate feelings, and some vanity, he was probably manic depressive, exulting in his occasional successes with a joy that few human beings ever touch but thrown by his more frequent misfortunes of debt and imprisonment into correspond- ing misery. Although disadvantaged by poor eyesight, he believed sincerely that he was destined by God to found a new and brilliant school of English historical painting, an ambition for which he was to struggle in vain for sixty years. Eventually he was to commit suicide.

In the spring of 1807 Haydon was struggling with a picture of a Roman army being ambushed in a rocky pass and, as with most of his pictures, he was making little progress, perpetually rubbing out and repainting in frustration. When, along with his fellow student, David Wilkie, who had obtained a pass, he set off to visit the Elgin Marbles, the two men had little idea of what they were to see. As he wrote in his autobiography the effect was dramatic.

To Park Lane then we went, and after passing through the hall and thence into an open yard, entered a damp, dirty pent-house where lay the marbles ranged within sight and reach. The first thing I fixed my eyes on was the wrist of a figure in one of the female groups, in which were visible, though in a feminine form, the radius and the ulna. I was astonished, for I had never seen them hinted at in any female wrist in the antique. I darted my eye to the elbow, and saw the outer condyle visibly affecting the shape as in nature. I saw that the arm was in repose and the soft parts in relaxation. That combination of nature and idea, which I had felt was so much wanting for high art, was here displayed to midday conviction. My heart beat! If I had seen nothing else I had beheld sufficient to keep me to nature for the rest of my life. But when I turned to the Theseus and saw that every form was altered by action or repose—when I saw that the two sides of his back varied, one side stretched from the shoulder blade being pulled forward and the other side compressed from the shoulder blade being pushed close to the spine as he rested on his elbow with the belly flat because the bowels fell into the pelvis as he sat—and when, turning to the Ilissus [the other reclining pedimental figures], I saw the belly protruded, from the figure lying on its side—and again, when in the figure of the fighting metope I saw the muscle shown under the one arm-pit in that instantaneous action of darting out, and left out in the other arm-pits because not wanted— when I saw, in fact, the most heroic style of art combined with all the essential detail of actual life, the thing was done at once and for ever. Here were principles which the common sense of the English people would understand; here were principles which I had struggled for in my first picture with timidity and apprehension; here were the principles which the great Greeks in their finest time established, and here was I, the most prominent historical student, perfectly qualified to appreciate all this by my own determined mode of study... perfectly comprehending the hint at the skin by knowing well what was underneath it!

Oh, how I inwardly thanked God that I was prepared to understand all this! Now I was rewarded for all the petty harassings I had suffered.... I felt as if a divine truth had blazed inwardly upon my mind and I knew that they would at last rouse the art of Europe from its slumber in the darkness.[17]

Haydon's autobiography shows how he was affected both as an artist and as a professional student of artistic technique. Like Flaxman he recognized at once that here was sculpture which did not depend for its effect on a slurring over of anatomical detail or 'idealization' of natural features characteristic of the ancient 'classical' statues of Italy. That evening Haydon rushed home and 'dashed out the abominable mass', from the picture of the battle he was trying to paint. All night he dozed and dreamed about the marbles and woke at five in the morning in a fever of excitement. For the next few days he tried to sketch them from memory, rejecting attempt after attempt to recapture the forms he had seen.

Shortly afterwards he obtained a pass to view the Elgin Marbles on his own account and rushed off—Haydon always rushed—to find another of his friends, the Swiss painter Henry Fuseli. Fuseli's father had collected money for Winckelmann when he was in financial difficulties, and Fuseli himself had translated Winckelmann's most influential works into English.[18] The two men drove headlong along the Strand, upsetting a coal cart and a flock of sheep on the way, and at last reached Park Lane. 'Never shall I forget his uncompromising enthusiasm', wrote Haydon of Fuseli's reactions. 'He strode about saying "De Greeks were godes! de Greeks were godes!".... To look back on those hours has been my solace in the bitterest afflictions.'[19]

With some difficulty Haydon obtained permission to draw at Elgin's museum. His patron was sceptical whether this would do his painting any good but Elgin took the larger view, remembering, no doubt, his original object of improving the progress of art. For months afterwards Haydon spent every spare moment drawing, sometimes for ten or fifteen hours at a time, and continuing by candlelight until the porter came to close up at midnight. In his autobiography he says:

Then often have I gone home, cold, benumbed, and damp, my clothes steaming up as I dried them; and so spreading my drawings on the floor and putting a candle on the ground, I have drank my tea at one in the morning with ecstacy as its warmth trickled through my frame, and looked at my picture, and dwelt on my drawings, and pondered on the change of empires, and thought that I had been contemplating what Socrates looked at and Plato saw—and then, lifted up with my own high urgings of soul, I have prayed to God to enlighten my mind to discover the principles of those divine things—and then I have had inward assurances of future glory, and almost fancying divine influence in my room, have lingered to my mattress bed, and soon dozed into a rich balmy slumber.[20]

Some typical entries in Haydon's diary give an idea of how he worked in these tempestuous months:

8 September 1808. Drew at Lord Elgin's from ten till $\frac{1}{4}$ past two and from three till $\frac{3}{4}$ past five—walked about and looked at those matchless productions. I consider it truly the greatest blessing that ever happened to this country their being brought here.[21]

31 October 1808. Drew at Lord Elgin's from $\frac{1}{2}$ past nine to five, without intermission, perhaps I got up twice, say I lost ten minutes or 15—dined, at the Academy as usual from six to eight—9 hours and a quarter absolute drawing, not at all fatigued, not at all sore, but rather damp & cold.[22]

1 November 1808. I have begun this new month by rising early, praying sincerely and studying industriously: let this be the character of this month for Jesus X sake and the character of the remainder of my existence. Drew at Lord Elgin's from $\frac{1}{4}$ past nine to $\frac{3}{4}$ past 4—at the Academy $\frac{1}{2}$ past 6 to 8.[23]

The entry for 5 November would surely have pleased Lord Elgin:

November 5—Drew at Lord Elgin's—6 hours. My taste thank God is improved wonderfully.[24]

But if the artists who wielded the brush and the chisel were unanimous in their praise and had unanimously adopted the new romantic discourse, the rich noblemen and gentlemen who commissioned the artists took a different, more traditional, view. The chief spokesman for the art collectors, the art patrons, and the art connoisseurs was Richard Payne Knight, the 'arbiter of fashionable virtu'.[25] As a young man a diary Payne Knight wrote of a journey to Sicily so impressed Goethe that he translated it into German and published it. Shortly afterwards Payne Knight became a Member of Parliament, but his main interests lay elsewhere. His first printed work was a treatise on phallus worship which had to be withdrawn. He then published a long didactic poem, its ponderous humour explained in meticulous footnotes, satirizing the activities of Capability Brown and other landscape gardeners whose romantic aesthetic of turning nature into art was rapidly superseding the formal classical style.

In 1805 Payne Knight's essay on aesthetics, *An Analytic Inquiry into the Principles of Taste*, which drew heavily on Winckelmann was an immediate success. After considering in turn Sense, Ideas, and Passions, and various concepts such as the sublime, the pathetic, the novel, and the ridiculous, he concluded, against the prevailing view, that even if Ideal Beauty did not exist, there were consistent and reliable standards.

There are certain standards of excellence which every generation of civilized man subsequent to their first production has uniformly recognised in theory how variously soever they have departed from them in practice. Such are the precious remains of Greek sculpture which affords standards of real beauty, grace and elegance, in the human form and the modes of adorning it, the truth and perfection of which have never been questioned.[26]

Payne Knight's private collection of classical antiquities included some marble statues from Italy, along with coins, gems, and pieces of ancient jewellery, but it chiefly consisted of bronzes. During a long stay with Sir William Hamilton in Naples, he had bought all the finest bronze statues, statuettes, and pieces of armour that appeared on the market there. As soon as a fine piece of bronze work appeared anywhere in Europe, and in time of war many private collections were being dispersed, every dealer knew that Payne Knight would buy. When Knight heard of a find of bronzes in Greece that had been taken to Russia, he immediately sent an agent there who bought them all. A Hermes with a golden necklace found near Lyon passed through the hands of three Frenchmen before Knight eventually secured it.

Ancient writers on sculpture left no doubt that free-standing sculpture in bronze was, in the estimation of the ancients, a higher form of art than free-standing sculpture in marble. The great Greek sculptors whose names have come down to us, Myron, Polycleitos, Phidias, Praxiteles, and others, had all, according to the sources, made their masterpieces of bronze and in more precious materials such as gold and ivory, although it was known that they also worked in marble. Although Payne Knight's bronzes were for the most part small, and copies of full-scale works which had long since been lost, he considered, with some justice, that his collection was more representative of the types of statues which the ancients most admired than the heavy, much restored, marble copies, mainly of the Roman period, that English noblemen and gentlemen who had been on the Grand Tour were importing from Italy to decorate their houses and gardens.

Ten days after Lord Elgin arrived back in England from captivity in France in 1806 he met Payne Knight at a dinner. At this time Payne Knight had not seen Elgin's marbles which were still in their packing cases, but this did not prevent him from stating his opinion. 'You have lost your labour, my Lord Elgin. Your marbles are overrated: they are not Greek: they are Roman of the time of Hadrian.'[27] Within hours Payne Knight's pronouncement was the talk of London. The Elgin Marbles which many connoisseurs had read about in reports from Athens and elsewhere were already condemned, and condemned unseen. Payne Knight was to spend ten years proclaiming that the sculptures of the Parthenon were inferior works, mere architectural decoration, not highly regarded even in its own time, scarcely to be compared with the free-standing bronzes.

Payne Knight was right to combat the idea, which was already taking hold, that the sculptures which decorated the Parthenon had been carved by the genius of Phidias working alone with his own hands. As one who had read what the ancient authors had written on the subject of art, he recognized the anachronism of the emerging romantic aesthetic, and felt he knew the correct criteria of excellence. His charge that the Parthenon sculptures were of Roman date was, however, simply a misreading of the erroneous speculation about the two white pedimental figures suggested by Spon and Wheler in the seventeenth century and then repeated by Stuart and Revett in the eighteenth.[28] Benjamin West, although in general one of Elgin's most enthusiastic supporters, told one of the artists at the Academy that some parts of the Elgin Marbles had been 'very badly restored probably about the time of Adrian but it was at once seen that these parts were not the original work'.[29] This was a difficult argument to sustain since the allegedly Hadrianic pieces had been left behind on the building in Athens. Payne

Knight, a classical scholar, ought to have known better. If Payne Knight had read the modern authorities, he would have seen that none had ever suggested that the frieze, the metopes, or the other figures in the pediments were other than original.

Unfortunately for Lord Elgin, Payne Knight had a ready audience for his opinion that the Elgin Marbles were inferior works. The Society of Dilettanti, founded in about 1732, began as a mainly social club for rich young men, and its original antiquarian activities consisted largely of meeting once a month in the Star and Garter and drinking toasts to 'Grecian taste and Roman spirit'. From its earliest days members of the Society returning from the Grand Tour in Italy brought home with them quantities of 'classical' statues, making the country houses of England one of the greatest repositories of Graeco-Roman art and stimulating a booming industry in Italy to excavate, reconstruct, and restore statues for the English market.[30]

By mid-century, the English were outbidding the Vatican Museums in buying any marbles and other antiquities that came on the market in Italy. Charles Townley, a prominent member of the Dilettanti, built up an impressive collection which in 1772 he brought to London. But it was also the Society of Dilettanti who had financed Stuart and Revett to go to Athens in the 1750s in order to make an accurate and detailed record of the surviving ancient buildings and sculptures of Athens. The result was the publication in 1762 of the first volume of *The Antiquities of Athens*, a magnificent folio work whose beauty and craftsmanship were enhanced by a level of scholarship and accuracy never before attempted in classical archaeology. Two more volumes of *The Antiquities of Athens* appeared in 1787 and 1794 and a fourth was in preparation. And other expeditions to other classical sites intended to retrieve the remains of Greek as distinct from Graeco-Roman art and to publish the results were under way.

Towards the end of Elgin's time at Constantinople, when he found himself running short of money, he had turned to the Dilettanti for help. It was only natural to expect that the Society which had commissioned *The Antiquities of Athens* should wish to help in bringing home the Parthenon marbles and perhaps welcome Lord Elgin himself among their ranks. Thomas Harrison, the architect who had first suggested attaching artists to Elgin's embassy, succeeded in interesting some members of the Society on Elgin's behalf and obtained an offer of a 'handsome remittance' for

Lusieri. In the event the Dilettanti did nothing. At the meeting in February 1803 when the proposal was discussed someone, probably Payne Knight, vetoed it.[31] His much publicized remark at the dinner in 1806 confirmed the breach between Lord Elgin and the men who were most able to help him.

In 1809 Payne Knight spoke again. The next of the Dilettanti Society's magnificent folios, *Specimens of Antient Sculpture*, which had been in preparation since 1799, was finally published. It contained engravings of sixty-three works of art in the possession of members of the Society of which no less than twenty-three belonged to Payne Knight. In the accompanying text, which Payne Knight also wrote, appeared a comment on the Elgin Marbles. Characteristically the dismissive author did not even mention Elgin by name.

Of Phidias's general style of composition, the friezes and metopes of the Temple of Minerva at Athens, published by Mr. Stuart and since brought to England, may afford us competent information; but as these are merely architectural sculptures executed from his designs and under his directions probably by workmen scarcely ranked among artists, and meant to be seen at the height of more than forty feet from the eye, they can throw but little light upon the more important details of his art. From the degree and mode of relief in the friezes they appear to have been intended to produce an effect like that of the simplest kind of monochromatic painting when seen from their proper point of sight; which effect must have been extremely light and elegant. The relief in the metopes is much higher, so as to exhibit the figures nearly complete, and the details are more accurately and elaborately made out, but they are so different in their degrees of merit, as to be evidently the works of many different persons, some of whom would not have been entitled to the rank of artists in a much less cultivated and fastidious age.[32]

Payne Knight had changed his ground considerably from his earlier statement that the marbles were of the time of Hadrian. In spite of himself his artistic perceptiveness shines through in some of his judgements. The Elgin Marbles are indeed architectural sculptures, and it is true that the quality of the metopes is irregular. Knight was careful to make no mention of the pediment sculptures. Nevertheless the total effect is to damn with faint praise.

Many of the Dilettanti followed Payne Knight's lead, as did others. William Wilkins, later architect of the National Gallery in London, was the most contemptuous. In a book on the antiquities of Athens Wilkins hardly bothered to argue his case, but merely quoted the passage from *Specimens of Antient Sculpture*. 'Supported by such authority', he wrote, 'we may venture to check that mistaken enthusiasm which venerates the sculptures as the works of Phidias.'[33] Others, such as Lord Aberdeen, who had been willing to spend a huge amount of money to buy the marbles himself, found it prudent to be unenthusiastic.[34]

When Charles Townley died in 1805 his will required that a special gallery should be built to house and exhibit them, and in 1805 an Act of Parliament was passed which enabled the British Museum, of which Townley had been a trustee, to buy most of the collection for £20,000. A further payment of £8,200 was made, under another Act of Parliament, in 1814. The new Townley Gallery built at the British Museum, opened to the public in the spring of 1808.[35] In 1809, uniquely in London as a result of the simultaneous opening of the Townley Gallery and of Elgin's museum, it was for the first time possible for artists to compare the Graeco-Roman Townley Marbles with the Elgin Marbles from the Parthenon.

The contest was over almost before it had begun. The practising artists, old as well as young, the moment they saw the Elgin Marbles, deserted the old aesthetic in their droves. Even if the Elgin Marbles were architectural ornaments they revealed a technical competence never before seen. From the beginning the Payne Knight party, by contrast, appeared as out of date, defensive, and grudging. As undoubtedly original works, the Elgin Marbles also silently condemned the whole enterprise of importing Graeco-Roman sculptures from Italy. In the new romantic discourse the ancient marbles which lined the galleries of the British Museum and of the noble houses of England, being essentially mere copies, could never be more than second-rate. Greece had conquered Rome, romanticism had superseded the aesthetic ideal.

16

Elgin Offers his First Collection to the Government

AFTER his return from France in 1806 Lord Elgin's way of life changed completely. Cut off from all public life by the loss of his seat in the House of Lords and by his parole to the French government, he rarely visited London. The disfigurement of his nose made him shy of company, but even country life was not what it might have been in happier circumstances. He could no longer afford to run Broomhall, his country house in Fife, on the scale on which Harison had built it in the 1790s and much of it remained unfurnished. Most of the servants were discharged and Elgin lived as quietly and economically as he could in one wing of the building.

In 1810 Elgin married again. His second wife, Elizabeth Oswald of Dunnikeir, daughter of a neighbouring landowner, was perhaps a more stable, if less interesting, woman than the first countess. Eight children were born of this second marriage and, since Elgin still had the four surviving children of the first marriage to look after, his financial burden continued to grow. The former Lady Elgin had duly married Robert Ferguson of Raith and settled in his estate not far from Broomhall. Occasionally the four children were sent to their grandmother's home across the Firth so that their mother could visit them.[1]

It became increasingly clear that Elgin could not afford to keep the house in London where the marbles were stored. On the other hand, there seemed no prospect of being able to sell the house until the marbles were removed. The collection which had already cost him so much, and it was still only the first collection, was rapidly becoming a millstone round his neck. All idea of bringing the marbles to Broomhall had long since been abandoned and even the scheme to have engravings published, an essential part of the project for the improvement of the arts, was put off indefinitely for lack of funds. There seemed no alternative but to try to sell the collection to the Government. In May 1809 Hamilton suggested in a letter to Elgin that a number of 'respectable men, Artists, Amateurs, and members of the House of Commons' should be appointed to fix a fair price based on Elgin's actual expenses, and he named among possible members, West, Flaxman and Nollekens, Lord Aberdeen and Payne Knight.[2] As Under-Secretary at the Foreign Office, Hamilton was well placed to know what the Government were thinking and soon afterwards (after two rejections) he was elected to the Society of Dilettanti, whose members were bound to be involved in any decision.

But Elgin was still unwilling. In 1803, at the time when he had asked the Dilettanti for help, he had also approached the Government, through Flaxman, to consider building an extension of the British Museum to house his collection.[3] Since at the time their main focus of attention was on the Townley marbles, they had refused and Elgin was unwilling to risk further humiliation. Another scheme was investigated whereby the shed at Park Lane would be replaced by a more substantial structure and a permanent private museum established to which admittance charges could be levied, but this scheme too was found to be uneconomic and impracticable. A new museum could be built at a cost of between £1,500 and £2,000 but it would probably have to be pulled down at the end of the lease and the admittance charges were unlikely to cover the expense. A year went by after Hamilton's suggestion and still the Park Lane house remained unsold and Elgin's debts continued to mount.

In the summer of 1810 Elgin came at last to the painful decision that he would have to sell his collection. Overtures had been received from the British Museum asking what his intentions were and public opinion, if not the opinion of the Dilettanti, seemed to be moving in his direction When Elgin's friends urged him to seize the opportunity, he came to London and saw the Librarian of the Museum, and also the Speaker of the House of Commons, one of the principal Trustees of the British Museum. It was agreed to suggest to the Trustees that the collection should be purchased by the nation.

The next meeting of the Trustees was fixed for November 1810, more than three months from the time that Elgin saw the Librarian. Elgin decided to use the intervening months to present his case to the public in the most favourable light possible. Some people had

begun to question whether the marbles were indeed Elgin's legal
property to sell, seeing that he had held an official post and used
official influence when he obtained them and had been allowed to
use naval ships to bring them to England. It was necessary to clear
away such doubts and also to offer some reply to the assertions of
Payne Knight. Elgin decided to publish his own account of his activities in Greece.

The anonymous *Memorandum on the Subject of the Earl of
Elgin's Pursuits in Greece* was printed late in 1810. Although published for sale in the normal way as a book, many copies were distributed as gifts to potentially influential friends and colleagues.
The *Memorandum* begins with a short, plain, and modest history
of how, from the first, Lord Elgin had wished his Embassy to be of
service to the arts, how he had been discouraged by the
Government but had gone ahead at his own expense, and how,
having seen the destruction perpetrated by the Turks and realized
the greedy designs of the French, he had used his influence to
remove to safety all the sculptures he could obtain. There then followed a brief description of the chief antiquities he had collected
and of the praises lavished on them by the artists. While offering
a plain factual account of what Lord Elgin had done, the
Memorandum was also a piece of self-vindication.

It is not known whether Elgin wrote the *Memorandum* himself
or employed an editor to draft the book under supervision. Either
way, Elgin, who had not been at Athens when the marbles were
acquired, relied for his account of the main facts on a long letter
which Philip Hunt had composed in captivity in Pau in 1805, even
repeating the preciosity of Hunt's prose style.[4] The Caryatid porch,
for example, was a '*concetto* in architecture', the Monument of
Lysicrates 'a most precious little *bijou* in architecture'.

The *Memorandum* admits frankly that Elgin had wished to have
his marbles restored until dissuaded by Canova and it reasserts that
it was still his object to make his collection beneficial to the arts of
his country by having engravings made that artists could buy at a
reasonable price. It then offers two practical suggestions on how
the marbles might be used to improve the arts: first, that a competition should be held among artists for the best restorations executed on casts, and second, that artists should be invited to witness
athletic exercises performed in the presence of the marbles so that
'the variety of attitude, the articulation of the muscles, the descriptions of the passions; in short everything a sculptor has to

represent' could be understood and copied. The pamphlet finishes with this thought:

Under similar advantages, and with an enlightened and encouraging protection bestowed on genius and the arts, it may not be too sanguine to indulge a hope, that, prodigal as Nature is in the perfections of the human figure in this country, animating as are the instances of patriotism, heroic actions, and private virtues, deserving commemoration, sculpture may soon be raised in England to rival the ablest productions of the best times of Greece.

The *Memorandum* makes no mention that Elgin wanted to sell his collection to the nation. It does, however, by implication, deal several blows to the opinion of the Dilettanti. Benjamin West's effusive letter of thanks for being allowed to sketch is quoted in full as an appendix, and the *Memorandum* itself emphasizes that much of the excellence of the sculptures derives from an intimate knowledge of anatomy, so discounting the notion that 'Ideal Beauty' was already available in other works.

The first edition soon ran out.[5] Elgin immediately put in hand a second edition. Hamilton, who recognized the style as examples of his former friend's 'fanciful flights of eloquence' suggested that they should be cut out, and in the second edition the whole text was sharpened up to make it more persuasive in the political as well as in the artistic arena.[6] More appendices were added, including a reprinting of an article recently published in France which showed the French regarded the single slab from the Parthenon frieze which they possessed as one of the great treasures of the Musée Napoléon.[7] Besides fortifying the judgement of the many British artists who might still secretly feel inferior to their colleagues in France and Italy, the article lent weight to Elgin's claim that, when he was in France, he could easily have sold his collection in exchange for his freedom and that only his patriotism had stopped him from doing so.

Greatly encouraged by the success of his pamphlet Elgin threw himself wholeheartedly into the negotiations. After some hopeful discussions it was decided that he should write a formal letter to Charles Long, the Paymaster-General, giving the Government a detailed account of his expenses in collecting the marbles. It was agreed that this should provide a basis for the price. Elgin wrote this letter on 6 May 1811.

Elgin's letter referred Long to the *Memorandum*, so in effect turning it into a public document, compulsory reading for all involved in the decision. It noted again the opportunities Elgin had turned down of selling the collection advantageously in France, the universal admiration of the artists, the benefits the arts of the country could expect to derive from the public possession of his collection. If an independent commission of artists and 'men of taste' had been asked to advise, they would, Elgin felt sure, endorse his view. And as he had done so often before he begged for a public honour.

And while they would have awarded a fair reimbursement of my expenses, which the state of my family and my affairs would not justify me in fore-going; they would at the same time have stamped the transaction as wholly differing from a pecuniary bargain, and would have pronounced on the service I had been the means of conferring on the Country, in a way to have presented a powerful recommendation and claim in my favour, for some mark of Royal approbation.[8]

The last part of Elgin's letter contained his estimate of his expenses. They were huge. The cost of the artists and workmen, the storage of the collection at Malta, and the salvaging of the *Mentor*, he put at £39,200.[9] Since much of this money had been borrowed he thought it fair to include interest on this amount at 5 per cent for fourteen years, that is from 1797, two years before he set out for Constantinople, so adding another £23,240. Expenses of moving the marbles to Westminster and then to Park Lane he put at £6,000. The grand total of identifiable expenses was thus £62,440. Three of the items on his list he did not put a figure to, agency fees in Turkey, money borrowed in Turkey at 12 or 14 per cent and 'a variety of minor expenses': these he left to the Government to fill in, perhaps hoping that the Government would round the sum up to £70,000.

The same day as he wrote this letter to the Paymaster-General Elgin wrote another to the Prime Minister, Spencer Perceval. Apart from omitting the estimate of his expenses this letter was for the most part the same, word for word, as the other. But when he reached the place where he had mentioned the 'mark of Royal approbation' Elgin became more explicit. 'To a Scotch peer,' he declared roundly, 'nothing could be so desirable as a British peerage . . . I need hardly add that such an arrangement would be in the highest degree gratifying to my own feelings.'[10] He finished by suggesting, if a peerage was conferred, that he would be prepared to accept payment by instalments, or partly by annuity, if this would be more convenient.

Elgin's hopes of thus restoring his finances and, at the same time, re-entering political life were badly misplaced. The next few weeks were to be among the most uncomfortable in his life. The Prime Minister's reply came first. Far from using the proposed peerage to negotiate terms of payment, Spencer Perceval administered a sharp snub.

In reply to the observations conveyed in your Lordship's letter respecting the peerage, I must candidly say that I should feel it quite impossible to recommend any arrangement of that nature as connected in the remotest degree with the purchase of your Lordship's collection.[11]

The Paymaster-General's letter was equally mortifying. The Government, Long said, were prepared to recommend to Parliament that the collection should be bought for £30,000—less than half of what Elgin had claimed, and even allowing for some exaggeration in the claim, clearly less than he had spent. If the Government agreed to buy the marbles, the letters implied, it would be done grudgingly, as a hard bargain in a buyer's market, with Elgin presented not as the nation's benefactor, as Townley had been when his collection was bought after his death, but as someone who had brought misfortune on himself and his country.

Elgin at once declined the offer as 'wholly inadequate either to the expenses incurred, or to the acknowledged value of the collection'.[12] More letters passed in the next few days between Elgin and the Government but the Government refused firmly to depart from their offer. The Speaker too, from his knowledge of the views of 'Leading Persons unconnected with Government'—meaning the Dilettanti who would need to be content with any decision—could hold out no hope. Elgin's situation was now desperate. At long last a buyer had appeared for the Park Lane house, the Duke of Gloucester. It was urgent that the marbles should be moved out as soon as possible to ensure the sale. Elgin immediately offered his collection for exhibition to the British Institution, the rival of the Royal Academy, but they declined for lack of room.

Elgin was saved, for the present, by a timely offer of the Duke of Devonshire to store the marbles in the enclosed space at the back of Burlington House. This could only be a temporary arrangement, the Duke warned, but Elgin accepted thankfully. In July 1811 he began to cart the marbles to Burlington House in Piccadilly, their fourth London home. But there was no end to Elgin's bad luck. While the marbles were still in transit, the Duke of Devonshire died and there was an anxious waiting period while it was ascertained if the new Duke would agree. Fortunately he did and the removal continued. The cost of carrying the 120 tons of marbles a quarter of a mile along Piccadilly was £1,500. The new site was too small for proper storage, and some of the larger marbles had to be left out in the open air, but it was something. Two drawings made in 1816 are reproduced as Plates 8 and 9. At the end of July Elgin wrote plaintively to Spencer Perceval that his debt (which was £27,000 in 1806) had now risen to £90,000.[13] And the second collection still lay at Malta attracting heavy expenses every day.

After the failure of the negotiations Elgin retired unhappily to Broomhall. The summer passed but Hamilton reported that there was no likelihood of the Government increasing its offer. Elgin's bankers were pressing him to settle for the smaller sum and Hamilton reluctantly began to agree. Schemes were suggested to try to sell the collection to the Prince Regent or to induce the Duke of Devonshire to build a more permanent museum at Burlington House, but nothing was done. On 11 May 1812 Spencer Perceval, the Prime Minister, was shot dead in the lobby of the House of Commons. For the time being further negotiations about Lord Elgin's marbles were out of the question.

17

Poets and Travellers

LORD BYRON was 21 and not yet famous when he wrote *English Bards and Scotch Reviewers* shortly before he set out on his voyage to the Mediterranean.[1] Since there was scarcely a single contemporary writer, famous or obscure, who escaped his satirical scorn, the manuscript was turned down by ten or more regular London publishers.[2] Eventually Byron contracted with James Cawthorn, a fringe publisher, for an edition of 1,000 copies to be published anonymously. Byron later authorized a second edition with amendments, then a third and a fourth, each of 1,000 copies, all of which acknowledged his authorship.

Soon after his return from his travels, when he realized that *English Bards and Scotch Reviewers* had been unfair to many authors who were now his friends, he refused Cawthorn permission to print a fifth edition, and ordered the poem to be suppressed. This made little difference. The price of second-hand copies soared. An advertisement of 1818 by a Paris pirate publisher claimed that 'this work is so scarce in London that copies have been sold for five guineas and upwards'.[3] Shelley's friend Thomas Jefferson Hogg noted that the book 'became so exceedingly scarce that a large price was often given for a copy, and some curious people even took the trouble to transcribe it'.[4] Many manuscript copies written by professional copyists appeared on the market.[5] When an Irish publisher put on sale a printed pirated edition Cawthorn took legal proceedings to have him stopped. But the real pirate was Cawthorn himself. Denied permission to print a fifth edition, he went on reprinting third and fourth editions. About twenty such fakes have been identified, all claiming on the title-page to have been issued in 1810 or 1811, but all reprints, and all manufactured from paper on which the manufacturing dates of 1812, 1815, 1816, 1817, 1818, and 1819 are clearly visible in the watermarks.[6]

Over the first ten years after publication Cawthorn probably sold about 20,000 copies of *English Bards*. By the standards of the day, the poem was a runaway best-seller. Many of the readers, we can be sure, were the members of London fashionable society who patronized the large circulating library in London which was Cawthorn's main business. Indeed there can have been few men or women among the upper and middle classes who did not read it. By the 1820s, because the ownership of the copyright was uncertain, *English Bards and Scotch Reviewers* was reprinted by other publishers and became available to an even wider readership in innumerable cheaper editions.

Towards the end of the poem, as an aside from the scorn at the writers, Byron took a swipe at the antiquarians:

> Let Aberdeen and Elgin still pursue
> The shade of fame through regions of virtu;
> Waste useless thousands on their Phidian freaks,
> Misshapen monuments and maim'd antiques;
> And make their grand saloons a general mart
> For all the mutilated blocks of art.

In a footnote he added 'Lord Elgin would fain persuade us that all the figures, with and without noses, in his stoneshop are the work of Phidias! "Credat Judaeus!" '

Few readers of the poem outside art circles are likely to have realized that Byron was endorsing the Payne Knight view that the claims made for the Parthenon sculptures were exaggerated. Byron's sneer at Lord Elgin's syphilitic nose, on the other hand, probably caused titters and sniggers among those in the know. Another rhyme about Lord Elgin's noseless marbles is known to have been widely repeated, and perhaps invented, by Byron.

> Noseless himself he brings here noseless blocks
> To show what time has done and what the pox.[7]

On his way back from Greece in 1811 Byron acted as courier for a letter from Lusieri to Elgin. On 29 July 1811 Elgin paid a personal call on him at his hotel in order to thank him, and when he found him not at home, wrote a letter asking for a meeting:

I did myself the honor of calling upon your Lordship this morning, to thank you for the letter you was so good as [to] bring for me from Malta—and with a desire of enquiring into the nature of Lusieri's late acquisitions & operations at Athens, in regard to which I have not received any recent information. If your Lordship would do me the favor of naming any time, when I could, without inconvenience to you, wait upon you for that purpose, I should be greatly indebted to you.[8]

Byron responded to this request from his fellow peer in a letter, now lost, in which he gave a report about Lusieri's activities. Something of the contents and friendly respectful tone of the letter can be deduced from a second letter which Lord Elgin wrote in reply on 31 July:

I am under a very great obligation indeed to your Lordship for the trouble you have taken on my application to you. And I have extreme reluctance in being further importunate, but in truth, the circumstance of your not being a collector makes me attach double value to the opinion you may have formed on the objects of the researches still carrying on for me at Athens, and I confess I should esteem it a very essential favor to be allowed a few minutes conversation with your Lordship in those matters.—If you would therefore permit me, & I hear nothing to the Contrary from you— I would beg leave to do myself the honor of waiting upon you about Eleven o'c tomorrow forenoon; otherwise at any other time you might prefer.[9]

It was on that day or the next that Byron received news that his mother was seriously ill and he left London immediately. He probably never met Elgin, nor had he any wish to do so. As he wrote to his friend Hobhouse on 31 July when he was still in London and after he had received Elgin's second letter:

Lord Elgin has been teazing to see me these last four days, I wrote to him at his own request all I knew about his robberies, & at last have written to say that, as it is my intention to publish (in Childe Harold) on that topic, I thought proper since he insisted on seeing me, to give him notice, that he might not have an opportunity of accusing me of double-dealing afterwards.[10]

Whatever the warning was, there was little that Elgin could do, not he could never have guessed that the young lord who had used his painter as his guide to Athens and had sailed in his ship from Greece to Malta was destined to do him more damage than Payne Knight or Napoleon Bonaparte.

Childe Harold's Pilgrimage, a Romaunt, the long poem which Byron had been composing during his travels, was turned down by Longman and by Constable, the two leading literary publishers of the time, because it contained attacks on Lord Elgin. William Miller, who published Elgin's *Memorandum*, also turned it down, and there may have been others.[11] It was only with the help of a friend with connections in the literary world that, after some months of disappointment, Byron managed to place it with John Murray, who was then still an outside publisher with little to lose.[12]

The result was one of the most astonishing events in English literary history.

Within three days of the book's publication on about 1 March 1812 the first edition of 500 copies was sold out. Over the next two years 13,000 copies were printed and sold, mostly to members of the British aristocracy and gentry, to circulating libraries, to book clubs, and increasingly abroad.[13] With *Childe Harold*, as he used to say, Byron woke up and found himself famous. The hostesses of London crowded him with invitations, fashionable young ladies vied for his attentions, the Prince Regent joined in the congratulations, and the literary world at once forgave the youthful excesses of *English Bards*. The scurrilous versifier had become a great romantic poet, and *Childe Harold's Pilgrimage* was eagerly read in every drawing-room in England. It was to become one of the most admired and most read poems of the nineteenth century.[14]

Only once in the body of the poem did *Childe Harold's Pilgrimage* attack a living individual. At the beginning of Canto II Childe Harold has arrived in Greece. Sitting upon a 'massy stone, the marble column's yet unshaken base' and contemplating the ruins of the Parthenon, his melancholy gives way to anger.

> But who, of all the plunderers of yon fane
> On high—where Pallas linger'd, loth to flee
> The latest relic of her ancient reign;
> The last, the worst, dull spoiler, who was he?
> Blush, Caledonia! such thy son could be!
> England! I joy no child he was of thine:
> Thy free-born men should spare what once was free;
> Yet they could violate each saddening shrine,
> And bear these altars o'er the long-reluctant brine.

> But most the modern Pict's ignoble boast,
> To rive what Goth, and Turk, and Time hath spared:
> Cold as the crags upon his native coast,
> His mind as barren and his heart as hard,
> Is he whose head conceiv'd, whose hand prepar'd,
> Aught to displace Athena's poor remains:
> Her sons too weak the sacred shrine to guard,
> Yet felt some portion of their mother's pains,
> And never knew, till then, the weight of Despot's chains.

> What! shall it e'er be said by British tongue,
> Albion was happy in Athena's tears?
> Though in thy name the slaves her bosom wrung,

Tell not the deed to blushing Europe's ears;
The ocean queen, the free Britannia, bears
The last poor plunder from a bleeding land:
Yes, she, whose gen'rous aid her name endears,
Tore down those remnants with a Harpy's hand,
Which envious Eld forbore, and tyrants left to stand.

Where was thine Aegis, Pallas! that appall'd
Stern Alaric and Havoc on their way?
Where Peleus' son? whom Hell in vain enthrall'd,
His shade from Hades upon that dread day,
Bursting to light in terrible array!
What! could not Pluto spare the chief once more,
To scare a second robber from his prey?
Idly he wander'd on the Stygian shore,
Nor now preserv'd the walls he lov'd to shield before.

Cold is the heart, fair Greece! that looks on thee,
Nor feels as lovers o'er the dust they lov'd;
Dull is the eye that will not weep to see
Thy walls defac'd, thy mouldering shrines remov'd
By British hands, which it had best behov'd
To guard those relics ne'er to be restor'd.
Curst be the hour when from their isle they rov'd,
And once again thy hapless bosom gor'd,
And snatch'd thy shrinking Gods to northern climes abhorr'd![15]

  With the publication of these verses, the controversy over the
Elgin Marbles moved to a new battlefield. No longer did the conversation turn on the dry academic question of whether the
marbles were truly 'Phidian' or not. Now the question was what
right had Elgin to remove the precious heritage of a proud nation,
what right had he to raise his hand against a building that had stood
for over two thousand years. The Elgin Marbles had now become
a symbol, of Greece's ignominious slavery, of Europe's failure to
help her, and of Britain's overweening pride. The land of Greece,
with its intensely beautiful landscape and clear atmosphere, offered
a powerful romantic fantasy—classical ruins with goats in the foreground, turbaned pashas, inscrutable and cruel, smoking their long
pipes, black-eyed girls, young, passionate, and open. The mixture of
ancient classicism and oriental exoticism made a strong appeal to
the peoples of Northern Europe and North America who could
visit the Mediterranean only in their imaginations.
  After *Childe Harold* Byron published a rapid succession of other

poems with Greek themes, *The Giaour, The Bride of Abydos, The Corsair, The Siege of Corinth*, all of which were immensely popular both at home and abroad, then and later. By the time the battle of Waterloo brought the long wars to an end in 1815 Byron was a European figure, almost as famous as Napoleon.

Much of the poem is about the present condition of the countries through which the poet made his pilgrimage. The Greeks are slaves, Byron proclaimed. And it is no good the Greeks looking to foreigners to help them, what Greece needs is a violent revolution. The Greeks will never be free until they imitate their ancient ancestors.

> When riseth Lacedaimon's hardihood,
> When Thebes Epaminondas rears again,
> When Athens children are with Arts endued,
> When Grecian mother shall give birth to *men*,
> Then may'st thou be restored, but not till then.

There is contempt for the Modern Greeks for their ignorance and lack of patriotism:

> Shrine of the mighty! can it be
> That this is all remains of thee?
> Approach, thou craven crouching slave,
> Say is this not Thermopylae?
> These waters blue that round you lave,
> O servile offspring of the free—
> Pronounce what sae, what shore is this?
> The gulf, the rock of Salamis!

No need to remind a European readership of the associations of these names. The Modern Greeks, it is implicitly assumed, are the descendants of the Ancient Greeks, degenerate slaves, passively accepting their humiliation among the monuments of their former greatness. The word 'lave' exists in romantic poetry mainly to provide a rhyme for 'slave'.

Byron was an example of a type which was already a familiar feature of the Greek scene, the milordos or travelling gentleman. Greeks and Turks could understand how it might be necessary, from time to time, to go to the trouble, expense, and considerable danger of travel for the sake of business or to make a pilgrimage. But to travel for pleasure, or to look at ruins, that was a western European madness. The travellers, whether British, French, or from other countries necessarily saw the country through eyes that had been pre-set by their education in the classics. Clutching their copies of Plutarch and Pausanias, they mostly knew nothing of the history of the country after the death of Alexander the Great. They simply assumed that the Modern Greeks were the linear descendants of the ancients, although much debased by foreign occupation, without bothering too much about the facts or the implications. They looked carefully at Greek faces to see if they could find the Grecian profiles shown in ancient vases. They wondered whether Modern Greek customs, such as the siesta and love of arguing, were survivals from ancient times.

Byron's ideas about Greece were not new. They had been constructed by a succession of travellers and writers, mainly British and French, during the eighteenth century.[16] The notion that Greeks might overthrow their Turkish rulers and take their place among the nations of modern Europe was also already a commonplace among the literatures of Europe, and had been adopted by some prominent Greek writers living abroad. But not until Byron had the ideology of philhellenism been expressed with such power or carried so widely all over the Western word. Byron shared in the glamour of Greece, but Greece in its turn was carried along by the glamour of Byron, with innumerable paintings and engravings giving a visual reinforcement to the philhellenic myth.[17]

Under the conventions of the long romantic poem, as it was developed in Scotland and England by Sir Walter Scott, Lord Byron, Thomas Moore, and others, it was the custom to complement the verse part of the poem with explanatory and historical prose notes which were not only of direct interest to readers in their own right but added authority and legitimacy to the verse. With the verse appealing to the emotions, and the prose to the intellect, a long romantic poem could thus not only address the whole mind of the reader, but it could also offer cumulative, and occasionally alternative, ways of reading and of understanding the main text. In the case of *Childe Harold's Pilgrimage, a Romaunt*, more than half of the book was taken up with writings other than the verse narrative. Although contemporary readers of *Childe Harold's Pilgrimage* could thus, if they wished, read the work as an impassioned polemic, it appeared at the same time as a carefully considered and researched factual account by a highly educated traveller who had been on the spot and who knew both ancient and modern Greek.[18]

Many of the notes in *Childe Harold's Pilgrimage* related to Lord Elgin.

We can all feel, or imagine, the regret with which the ruins of cities, once the capitals of empires, are beheld; the reflections suggested by such objects are too trite to require recapitulation. But never did the littleness of man, and the vanity of his very best virtues, of patriotism to exalt, and of valour to defend his country, appear more conspicuous than in the record of what Athens was, and the certainty of what she now is. This theatre of contention between mighty factions, of the struggles of orators, the exaltation and deposition of tyrants, the triumph and punishment of generals, is now become a scene of petty intrigue and perpetual disturbance, between the bickering agents of certain British nobility and gentry. 'The wild foxes, the owls and serpents in the ruins of Babylon' were surely less degrading than such inhabitants. The Turks have the plea of conquest for their tyranny, and the Greeks have only suffered the fortune of war, incidental to the bravest; but how are the mighty fallen, when two painters contest the privilege of plundering the Parthenon, and triumph in turn, according to the tenor of each succeeding firman! Sylla could but punish, Philip subdue, and Xerxes burn Athens; but it remained for the paltry Antiquarian, and his despicable agents, to render her contemptible as himself and his pursuits.

In another passage, written on 3 January 1810, before Lusieri's ship had sailed he declared:

At this moment besides what has been already deposited in London, an Hydriot vessel is in the Piraeus to receive every portable relic. Thus, as I heard a young Greek observe in common with many of his countrymen— for, lost as they are, they yet feel on this occasion—thus may Lord Elgin boast of having ruined Athens. An Italian painter of the first eminence, named Lusieri, is the agent of devastation; and, like the Greek *finder* of Verres in Sicily, who followed the same profession, he has proved an able instrument of plunder. Between this artist and the French Consul Fauvel, who wishes to rescue the remains for his own government, there is now a violent dispute concerning a car employed in their conveyance, the wheel of which—I wish they were both broken upon it—has been locked up by the Consul, and Lusieri has laid his complaint before the Waywode. Lord Elgin has been extremely happy in his choice of Signor Lusieri. During a residence of ten years in Athens, he never had the curiosity to proceed as far as Sunium, till he accompanied us in our second excursion. However, his works, as far as they go, are most beautiful; but they are almost all unfinished.

Childe Harold's Pilgrimage is, among much else, a political poem. In the verse part Byron's view is an uncompromising reassertion

of the philhellenic myth. Ignoring two thousand years of intervening history, Byron asserts an identity between the Modern Greeks
of the nineteenth century and their putative ancestors, the Ancient
Greeks of the classical age. The Modern Greeks are a degenerate
enslaved nation who will only be freed when they begin to imitate
their ancestors and start a violent revolution. The rich Westerners
coming to visit the birthplace of civilization invariably drew melancholy comparisons between the glories of ancient Greece and her
modern degradation. It was a pleasing antithesis especially as they
and their readers were in no doubt that their own countries now
represented the acme of modern civilization.

> And lo! he comes, the modern son of Greece,
> The shame of Athens: mark him how he bears
> A look o'eraw'd and moulded to the stamp
> Of servitude.[19]

So wrote William Haygarth and most of the travellers agreed with
him. That the Greeks were a thoroughly contemptible race was, it
was said, the only point on which Fauvel and Lusieri were agreed.[20]
Byron alone was of a different opinion. In his notes to *Childe
Harold* he declared

They are so unused to kindness that when they occasionally meet with it
they look upon it with suspicion, as a dog often beaten snaps at your fingers
if you attempt to caress him. 'They are ungrateful, notoriously, abominably
ungrateful!'—this is the general cry. Now, in the name of Nemesis! for what
are they to be grateful? Where is the human being that ever conferred a
benefit on Greek or Greeks? They are to be grateful to the Turks for their
fetters, and the Franks for their broken promises and lying counsels. They
are to be grateful to the artist who engraves their ruins and to the antiquary who carries them away: to the traveller whose janissary flogs them,
and to the scribbler whose journal abuses them! This is the amount of their
obligations to foreigners.[21]

In the prose notes Byron offers an alternative, even a contradictory, discourse, to the rhetoric of the verse. The Greeks will never
be independent, he notes, and in any case it is nonsense to discuss
the problems of contemporary Greece in terms of their putative
ancestors. That is like discussing the future of Peru in terms of the
Incas.

   As a guide to the contemporary political situation in Greece, the
notes to *Childe Harold* are more reliable than the verse. And it was
by no means obvious that the future of a land inhabited for hun-

dreds of years by peoples of different traditions and religions in conditions of social harmony lay in driving out the minorities and trying to establish a homogeneous nation state. Capodistria, the most eminent Greek of the time, put his faith in a gradualist approach, relying on the spread of education to liberalize the institutions of the Ottoman state. Others looked forward to the day, which did not seem far distant, when the Greeks would supersede the Turks as the dominant group within the Ottoman empire, would gradually take over more and more of the positions of power, and establish a new Byzantium. The educated Greek classes, who, apart from a large diaspora in western Europe, mostly lived in Constantinople were strong upholders of the Ottoman system in which they filled many positions of power and wealth.[22] Few of the Greeks living in the territory of present-day Greece shared the views set out in the verse part of *Childe Harold's Pilgrimage*, and would not have understood his allusions. They did not, in Elgin and Byron's time, think of themselves in nationalist terms. They were not Hellenes, but the Orthodox Christian inhabitants of a large multicultural empire. When Western travellers heard stories about the great men and women of ancient times, they thought they had picked up a genuine continuous tradition, but in most cases, it is likely that they were repeating back stories derived from previous travellers.[23]

Even before the custom began of leaving out the prose notes, it was the message of the verse which readers wanted to hear. In the decades after 1812 the fame and influence of Byron's Grecian poems helped to consolidate and strengthen the philhellenic fallacy first in Europe, and soon, increasingly, in Greece itself. And, from the beginning the Parthenon became an integral part of the construction of the Modern Greek sense of national identity, a visible and tangible manifestation of the continuity which the myth required and asserted.

Some weeks before *Childe Harold's Pilgrimage* was due to be published Byron received a letter from Edward Daniel Clarke, the Cambridge professor who had quarrelled with Carlyle and Hunt in the Troad in 1801 and had subsequently witnessed the taking down of the first sculptures from the Parthenon. Clarke reported that Lord Aberdeen wished to propose Byron for membership of the Athenian Club, a club of rich young men who had visited Athens, almost an offshoot of the Dilettanti.

The letter put Byron in a dilemma. On the one hand, he seems to have been genuinely flattered to be invited. On the other, he was afraid of how the Athenian Club would receive the attacks on Lord Elgin in his forthcoming poem. In his reply to Clarke, Byron remarked

In the notes to a thing of mine now passing through the press there is some notice taken of an agent of Ld. A's in the Levant, *Grossius* by name, & a few remarks on Ld. Elgin, Lusieri & and their pursuits, which may render the writer not very acceptable to a zealous Antiquarian.—Ld. A's is not mentioned or alluded to in any manner personally disrespectful, but Ld. Elgin is spoken of according to the writer's decided opinion of *him* and *his* . . . Truth is I am sadly deficient in gusto and have little of the antique spirit except a wish to immolate Ld. Elgin to Minerva and Nemesis.[24]

Lord Aberdeen was prepared to overlook the remarks on anti-quarians but Byron did not join the Athenian Club. The exchange of correspondence with Clarke did, however, reveal that he too was an old enemy of Lord Elgin and an alliance directed against Elgin's reputation grew up between the two men. In writing to congratu-late Byron on the publication of *Childe Harold's Pilgrimage*, Clarke told him the story of the damage caused to the Parthenon cornice when the first metope was taken down and of how the Disdar had wept when he saw it. Byron gratefully incorporated the story with due acknowledgement in the notes to subsequent editions of his poem.[25] Clarke, in his turn, asked permission to quote from *Childe Harold's Pilgrimage* in the enormous book of *Travels* on which he was then engaged and obtained Byron's thanks for 'preserving my relics embalmed in your own spices &—ensuring me readers to whom I could not otherwise have aspired'.[26]

In his huge multi-volume *Travels in Various Countries of Europe, Asia, and Africa* Clarke attacked Elgin mercilessly for 'want of taste and utter barbarism'.[27] The Parthenon sculptures removed from their original setting, he said, lost all their excellence. Elgin was compared to 'another nobleman who being delighted at a Puppet Show, bought Punch and was chagrined to find when he carried him home, that the figure had lost all its humour'.[28] Clarke's narrative (which described proudly the numerous removals of antiquities which he himself had accomplished and includes several views drawn by Lusieri and the Calmuck which had improperly come into his possession) provides ample confirmation of Elgin's view that the Parthenon was being quickly destroyed and that the Turks were incapable of preventing it even if they had wished. The British public knew nothing of what lay behind the scenes. To them it seemed simply that the opinions of the passionate poet were being confirmed by the painstaking researches of the scholar.

Byron was being a little disingenuous in telling Clarke that it was only Elgin that he wished to attack. At a late stage before publication the manuscript of *Childe Harold's Pilgrimage* contained the following lines:

> Come then ye classic Thieves of each degree,
> Dark Hamilton and sullen Aberdeen,
> Come pilfer all that pilgrims love to see,
> All that yet consecrates the fading scene—
> Ah! better were it ye had never been
> Nor ye nor Elgin nor that lesser wight
> The victim sad of vase-collecting spleen
> House furnisher withal one Thomas hight
> Than ye should bear one stone from wronged Athena's site.[29]

Dark Hamilton is probably Sir William Hamilton, who had bought many antiquities while ambassador in Naples, although it was William Richard Hamilton, Elgin's private secretary, who had been involved in the Elgin collecting. Lord Aberdeen too had removed pieces of sculpture from the Parthenon and fully deserved the charge of pilfering. 'One Thomas hight' is Thomas Hope, another prominent member of the Dilettanti, author of a book on ancient furniture, who had obtained a sculptured fragment from Athens several years before which he exhibited in his London house as a fragment of the Parthenon.[30]

In another rejected stanza Byron suggests:

> Or will the gentle Dilettanti crew
> New delegate the task to digging Gell

and comments 'According to Lusieri's account he [Gell] began digging most furiously without a firman but before the resurrection of a single sauce-pan the Painter [Lusieri] counterminded and the Waywode countermanded and sent him back to bookmaking'.[31]

In the notes to *Childe Harold's Pilgrimage* as it was published Lord Aberdeen is not mentioned by name. He is 'Lord——' exempt from even the usual partial identification of asterisks. He is, compared with Elgin, 'another noble Lord [who] has done better because he has done less'. Georg Gropius, who acted as Lord Aberdeen's agent in collecting antiquities although he pretended to be only a painter, quarrelled with Lusieri over the ownership of some vases, each claiming them for his master. In the early editions of *Childe Harold's Pilgrimage*, Byron tells a story that Lusieri challenged Gropius to a duel and asked Byron to arbitrate. In later editions Byron withdrew even these heavily veiled criticisms of Lord Aberdeen in an unnecessarily profuse apology.

Byron at one time considered making a reference to Elgin's nose and to his wife. A rejected passage declared:

> Albion! I would not see thee thus adorned
> With gains thy generous spirit should have scorned,
> From Man distinguished by some monstrous sign,
> Like Attila the Hun was surely horned
> Who wrought this ravage amid works divine
> Oh that Minerva's voice lent its keen aid to mine.[32]

Besides Clarke, more and more travellers returning from Greece took up their pens and, since the war had put a stop to the Grand Tour of Italy, more travellers found their way to Greece in the early part of the nineteenth century than ever before. Almost without exception they had something disparaging to say of Elgin although equally they were all full of praise for Lusieri. F. S. N. Douglas, who wrote a book comparing the Ancient and Modern Greeks, while admitting most of Elgin's arguments in the *Memorandum*, concluded:

It appears to me a very flagrant piece of injustice to deprive a helpless and friendly nation of any possession of value to them ... I wonder at the boldness of the hand that could venture to remove what Phidias had placed under the inspection of Pericles.[33]

Dodwell, himself a despoiler of the Parthenon, wrote of Elgin's 'insensate barbarism' and of 'his devastating outrage which will never cease to be deplored'.[34] Thomas Hughes, another visitor to Athens, wrote of Elgin's 'wanton devastation' and 'avidity for plunder'.[35] J. C. Eustace in a popular *Classical Tour through Italy* condemned Elgin fiercely without having been to Athens and seen the circumstances there.[36] French travellers combined indignation at Elgin with regret that the marbles had not gone to the Louvre.[37] Chateaubriand joined in the condemnation although, when he left Athens, he too had a piece of the Parthenon in his pocket.[38]

During the centuries when the Parthenon was a Christian church, the names of the bishops of Athens were inscribed on one of the columns. In 1802, in a new form of cultural appropriation, the names Elgin and Mary Elgin with the date of their visit were carved deeply and clearly about half-way up one of the columns of the Parthenon in a place which Hunt had specially reserved in May 1801.[39] Elgin's name was soon deliberately erased but that of Mary Elgin could still be read in 1826.[40] Byron's name could be seen carved on several monuments which he had visited, at Sounion, in the quarry at Pentelikon, on the wall of the monastery at Delphi, on the Monument of Lysicrates, and hidden in one of the capitals of the Erechtheion.[41]

On one of the surviving original Caryatids some wit from the West wrote 'Opus Phidiae' (the work of Phidias). On the crude brick pillar substituted for the Caryatid removed by Elgin's agents, he wrote 'Opus Elgin' (the work of Elgin).[42] Another traveller, familiar with the ancient Greek convention of signing works of art, wrote, in Greek, 'Elgin Made Me.'[43] A better joke could be seen carved on a wall inside the Erechtheion. There some donnish wit, recalling the story that even Alaric and his Visigoths had respected the monuments of Athens, wrote the Latin rhyme 'Quod non fecerunt Goti, hoc fecerunt Scoti' ('What was not done by the Goths was done by the Scots').[44] Travelling gentlemen would have recognized the echo of the older tag about the Popes of Rome who used bronze from the Pantheon in the building of St Peter's. 'Quod non fecerunt barbari, fecerunt Barberini' ('What barbarians did not do, was done by Barberini'). These jibes, clearly intended to impress other travellers and not the Greeks or Turks, were gleefully recounted by travellers and taken up by the newspapers and literary reviews at home. Within a few years the stories current among the foreign colony in Athens were so confused that Elgin was soon being blamed for actions he never committed.[45] Indignation at the Turks waned in proportion.

The most bitter attack of all was *The Curse of Minerva* by Lord Byron. Like the first part of *Childe Harold's Pilgrimage* some of it was composed when Byron was in Athens, but it appears to have been mostly written on his return to England.[46] Originally it was intended that the two poems should be published together in 1812 along with some other of Byron's satires. At the last moment, however, owing to the intervention of one of Elgin's friends, Byron decided not to publish the *Curse* and the full version did not appear under his name until some years later.[47]

Byron had not the heart to suppress it entirely. In 1812 a few copies were printed and sent to Byron's friends. To Clarke, for instance, in thanks for the story about the Disdar, Byron wrote

'I have printed 8 copies of a certain thing, one of which shall be yours'.[48] Samuel Rogers had another, and no doubt many people had an opportunity of reading it.[49] In 1815 a pirated copy, much mutilated, appeared in the *New Monthly Magazine* and other versions began to circulate some months later.[50] Although Byron attempted to disown the pirated versions, his authorship was clear.[51] Another poem called *The Parthenon* published by James and Horace Smith in 1813 bears evidence of having been paraphrased from the *Curse of Minerva*.[52]

The Curse of Minerva begins with a beautiful descriptive passage on the evening in Greece which Byron used again in *The Corsair*. The poet (as in *Childe Harold's Pilgrimage*) sits alone and friendless within the walls of the ruined Parthenon when suddenly Minerva herself appears. She is hardly recognizable. Her aegis holds no terrors, her armour is dented, and her lance is broken.

> 'Mortal!'—'twas thus she spake—'that blush of shame
> Proclaims thee Briton, once a noble name;
> First of the mighty, foremost of the free,
> Now honour'd *less* by all, and *least* by me:
> Chief of thy foes shall Pallas still be found.
> Seek'st thou the cause of loathing?—look around.
> Lo! here, despite of war and wasting fire,
> I saw successive tyrannies expire.
> 'Scaped from the ravage of the Turk and Goth,
> Thy country sends a spoiler worse than both.
> Survey this vacant violated fane;
> Recount the relics torn that yet remain:
> *These* Cecrops placed, *this* Pericles adorn'd.
> *That* Adrian rear'd when drooping Science mourn'd.

Byron claimed in a footnote that he was referring to the Temple of Olympian Zeus built by Hadrian, not here subscribing to the Payne Knight view that the Parthenon sculptures were Hadrianic. The poem continues:

> What more I owe let gratitude attest—
> Know, Alaric and Elgin did the rest.
> That all may learn from whence the plunderer came,
> The insulted wall sustains his hated name:
> For Elgin's fame thus grateful Pallas pleads,
> Below, his name—above behold his deeds!
> Be ever hailed with equal honour here
> The Gothic monarch and the Pictish peer:

> Arms gave the first his right, the last had none,
> But basely stole what less barbarians won.
> So when the lion quits his fell repast,
> Next prowls the wolf, the filthy jackal last:
> Flesh, limbs, and blood the former make their own,
> The last poor brute securely gnaws the bone.

Minerva then observes that another goddess has helped to avenge her.

> Yet still the gods are just, and crimes are cross'd:
> See here what Elgin won, and what he lost!
> Another name with *his* pollutes my shrine:
> Behold where Dian's beams disdain to shine!
> Some retribution still might Pallas claim,
> When Venus half avenged Minerva's shame.

To those in the know, Elgin's syphilis, his cuckolding, and his divorce are a punishment for his sacrilege.

To this outburst from Minerva the poet dares to make some reply. Do not blame England for this terrible deed, he says. England disowns him, the plunderer was a Scot. Just as Boeotia was the uncivilized part of Greece, so Scotland is the uncivilized part of Britain:

> And well I know within that bastard land
> Hath Wisdom's goddess never held command;
> A barren soil, where Nature's germs, confined
> To stern sterility, can stint the mind;
> Whose thistle well betrays the niggard earth,
> Emblem of all to whom the land gives birth;
> Each genial influence nurtured to resist;
> A land of meanness, sophistry, and mist.
> Each breeze from foggy mount and marshy plain
> Dilutes with drivel every drizzly brain,
> Till, burst at length, each wat'ry head o'erflows,
> Foul as their soil, and frigid as their snows.
> Then thousand schemes of petulance and pride
> Despatch her scheming children far and wide:
> Some east, some west, some everywhere but north,
> In quest of lawless gain, they issue forth.
> And thus—accursed be the day and year!—
> She sent a Pict to play the felon here.

It was necessary for the argument that Elgin's Scottishness should be stressed. But Byron was conscious of his own Scottish origins, and obviously did not want to be included in his own condemnation. His solution was very neat and contains one of the few hints of humour in the poem. Just as Boeotia managed to produce a Pindar, he said, so there was hope for a few Scotsmen, 'the letter'd and the brave', provided they were prepared to shake off the sordid dust of their native land.

Minerva curses not only Elgin but his children. The only surviving son, Byron knew, was mentally retarded. As for his other children, from what had been said about Lady Elgin at the divorce trial, could Elgin be sure that he was really their father?

> First on the head of him who did this deed
> My curse shall light—on him and all his seed:
> Without one spark of intellectual fire,
> Be all the sons as senseless as the sire:
> If one with wit the parent brood disgrace,
> Believe him bastard of a brighter race:
> Still with his hireling artists let him prate,
> And Folly's praise repay for Wisdom's hate;
> Long of their patron's gusto let them tell,
> Whose noblest, *native* gusto is—to sell:
> To sell, and make—may shame record the day!—
> The state receiver of his pilfer'd prey.
> Meanwhile, the flattering, feeble dotard, West,
> Europe's worst dauber, and poor Britain's best,
> With palsied hand shall turn each model o'er,
> And own himself an infant of fourscore.
> Be all the bruisers cull'd from all St. Giles'
> That art and nature may compare their styles;
> While brawny brutes in stupid wonder stare,
> And marvel at his lordship's 'stone shop' there.

After some amusing remarks about the embarrassment of the young ladies of London at seeing such huge naked manly statues Minerva pronounces her curse. Lord Elgin, like Eratostratus who set fire to the Temple of Diana at Ephesus, will be for ever hated. 'Loathed in life nor pardoned in the dust.' Vengeance will pursue him far beyond the grave 'In many a branding page and burning line'.

Elgin's deed is so terrible that it is not enough that he alone should be punished. Britain herself must suffer the penalty. The terrible war on which she has embarked will soon destroy her. In the Baltic and the Peninsula she will be defeated. In the East the Indians will 'shake her tyrant empire to its base'. At home Minerva will strike. Trade will languish, famine break out, the Government become powerless. The country itself will be invaded and ravaged. And, says Minerva, no one will be sorry. It is too late. The country has brought all this upon herself.

Childe Harold's Pilgrimage and *The Curse of Minerva* have coloured the world's view of Lord Elgin's activities ever since they first appeared. And it is no criticism of a satirist to say that he gives only one side of an argument. On the other hand, the indignation of satirists which appears to be spontaneous and heart-felt is often little more than a literary exercise, an attempt to recapture the spirit of Juvenal and of Pope. When Byron was in Athens John Galt was writing voluminously both in prose and verse. As his letters show, Galt clearly recognized that the antiquities of Greece were being quickly destroyed by the travellers and by the Turks and that if Elgin had not removed the Parthenon marbles the French certainly would.[53] Nor was he averse from acquiring them himself if he had had the chance.[54] While he was staying at the Capuchin Convent, however, Galt knocked out a satire on Lord Elgin which he called the *Atheniad*.[55] He showed this to Byron, who kept the manuscript for several weeks before returning it by way of Hobhouse. On his return to England Galt intended to publish his poem but, like Byron, he was dissuaded by one of Elgin's friends, in this case Hamilton.[56] It was not published until 1820.

The *Atheniad* is an amateurish piece of mock heroics, good-humoured enough on the whole. Where the *Curse* becomes bitter against Lord Elgin, the *Atheniad* merely shows bad taste. It was clearly never intended to be more than a literary exercise. In Galt's satire, the gods of Olympus, dejected by the oppression of Greece, are consoled somewhat by the memory of the former glories of Athens and by the contemplation of her ruins. Then Fate takes a hand. Mercury is sent back to earth disguised as a man called 'Dontitos' (Don Tita Lusieri). 'Cadaverous, crafty, skilled in tints and lines, A lean Italian master of designs', Dontitos seeks out a nobleman called 'Brucides' (Lord Elgin) and tells him he will be famous if only he will rescue the Parthenon sculptures from the Turks. Brucides falls for this trap and sets to work.

> With ready gold he calls men, carts, and cords,
> Cords, carts and men, rise at the baited words.
> The ropes asunder rive the wedded stone,
> The mortals labour and the axles groan,
> Hymettus echoes to the tumbling fane,
> And shook th' Acropolis—shakes all the plain.

Suddenly the gods of Olympus realize what is happening and one by one they take their revenge. First Neptune conjures up a storm and sinks Brucides' vessel at Cythera. Minerva inspires Brucides with delirious fancies so that his diplomatic dispatches are filled with talk of 'basso-relievos' and 'marble blocks' instead of military and political affairs—Brucides at once loses his ambassadorship. One the way home, however, Brucides makes a partial recovery. He lingers in Italy and France and, 'still has sprightly pleasures left'. But Minerva soon has the better of him. She drives to Paris in her golden chariot and disguising herself as Talleyrand, she persuades Napoleon to arrest all the British in France and so to possess Brucides 'a prize more precious than the Greeks of old, From Ilion stole'.

Meanwhile Mars too is taking his revenge. In order to effect the transfer of a very useful cart from 'Fouvelle' (Fauvel) to Dontitos, he stirs up wars in Egypt, Russia, and Spain, and finally, in a delight-ful piece of bathos, causes a conflict in Athens over the wheel of this cart, which by 1810 had changed hands between Fauvel and Lusieri at least four times. Next Venus in her turn takes her revenge on Brucides, but the poet is reluctant to speak of it—he is forbid-den by Juno. Those in the know would detect the usual references to syphilis and cuckoldry. Cupid's revenge is to thrust a flaming torch into Elgin's face disfiguring him to look like a noseless antique bust. And finally Apollo vents his wrath by inspiring John Galt to record these great events 'in epic strains'.

> Thus wrought the gods in old Athenia's cause,
> Avenged their fanes, and will'd the world's applause.

The Curse of Minerva clearly owes some of its ideas to the *Atheniad* although its whole tone is different and Galt was never able to per-suade Byron to acknowledge any debt.[57] Most probably it was the idea itself that Galt inspired. Perhaps Byron on reading Galt's lit-erary effort, decided that he could do much better than his tedious companion and dashed off the *Curse*. It may be a literary extrava-ganza. *Childe Harold's Pilgrimage*, too, undoubtedly owes much to its literary predecessors. Its main theme—that of a reborn Greece rising against the Turks—was far from new when Byron wrote: it was already a well-known literary genre.[58] A long anonymous poem on this theme—*A Letter from Athens addressed to a Friend in England*—appeared almost simultaneously with the first two cantos of *Childe Harold's Pilgrimage*.[59] Another—William

Haygarth's *Greece*—was actually being written when Byron was in Athens and he knew and liked its author. All three poems show similarities of idea if not of style. Haygarth's *Greece* also has a few resemblances in construction to *The Curse of Minerva*.

Is then Byron's indignation against Elgin purely literary? Was he being no more serious in attacking Elgin than he was in his satire against the *English Bards and Scotch Reviewers*, much of whose unfairness he later regretted? Was his main objection Elgin's 'robbery of Athens to instruct the English in sculpture'.[60] Or was there something about Elgin personally which roused his anger, his Scottishness, for example, or his Toryism, or his apparently typical British contempt for foreigners? The cruelty of *The Curse of Minerva* is unusually personal. Possibly the answer lies in Byron's sheer perverseness, his wish to be different from the careful moderation of Hobhouse and Galt. Writing of *Childe Harold's Pilgrimage* in September 1811, some months before it was published, he declared boldly that he had been forced into the attack by the contemptuous review of his first poems which had appeared in the *Edinburgh Review*:

I have attacked De Pauw, Thornton, Lord Elgin, Spain, Portugal, the *Edinburgh Review*, travellers, Painters, Antiquarians, and others, so you see what a dish of Sour Crout Controversy I shall prepare for myself. It would not answer for me to give way now; as I was forced into bitterness at the beginning, I will go through to the last. *Vae Victis!* If I fall I shall fall gloriously, fighting against a host.[61]

Byron's attack fell on a man who was already almost broken by his misfortunes. Lord Elgin, trying desperately to restore his finances in his Scottish retreat, was strangely silent. The world's reception of *Childe Harold's Pilgrimage* coming so soon after his rebuff from Spencer Perceval seemed merely another in the long series of misfortunes to which he was now almost accustomed. After *Childe Harold's Pilgrimage* it seemed to Elgin that every time he opened the *Edinburgh* or the *Quarterly Review*, yet another book of travels had been published with its inevitable sneers and accusations. What could be the meaning of it all? What had he done to deserve such treatment? He had only done what men of his class had been doing for over a hundred years, the exception being that his interest in antiquities had been so genuine that it had ruined him. There must be some explanation, Elgin felt. The world could not be so unjust without some cause.

Who could the arch conspirator be? Could it be his hated neighbour Robert Ferguson of Raith, the man who had run away with
his wife and whom he had successfully sued for £10,000? Possibly.
Ferguson, who sat in Parliament as a Whig, might have persuaded
his friends in those days of increasing political bitterness to attack
a prominent Tory.[62] Could it be Clarke? His hatred of Elgin seemed
to be unlimited, despite the many kindnesses he had accepted at
Constantinople. This too was a possibility, although it was unlikely
that a mere Cambridge don could exert so much influence.

But there was a man who held his grudge against Elgin more
deeply than either of these. John Spencer Smith could not forget
the disgrace of being superseded by Elgin as minister in Turkey and
then of being dismissed for incompetence and disobedience. He
could not forget too that the accusations which Napoleon had
levelled against Elgin in 1804 of mistreating the French in
Constantinople had subsequently been transferred by the French
government to himself; and that, partly as a consequence, he was
bundled out of his last diplomatic appointment in Württemberg.
Here, Elgin suspected, was his conspirator. Spencer Smith's tongue
was active against him in England and the merchants of the Levant
Company were maligning him to travellers, English and French,
in Greece and Constantinople. The Levant Company had an interest in preventing any more ambassadors extraordinary being
appointed to Constantinople to break their precarious monopoly.
And had not Byron had an affair with Spencer Smith's wife in
Malta on his way to Greece and commemorated the event in *Childe
Harold's Pilgrimage*?[63]

Elgin was wrong in thinking his misfortunes were the result of a
conspiracy. His detractors were too numerous and, for the most
part, too independently minded to be so carefully disciplined. What
looked like a conspiracy can be seen in retrospect to have been
simply a conjuncture of events, the discovery of Ancient Greece
and its triumph over Rome, the cultural shift in Western attitudes
to works of art and literature known as romanticism, and the
increasing power of western European notions of national identity
and how it should be constructed, celebrated, and reinforced both
in western Europe and, increasingly elsewhere.

Later Years in Greece

LUSIERI meanwhile, undisturbed by the controversies in England, still continued in Lord Elgin's employment. After reaching Malta in the *Hydra* in April 1811 with Byron, Nicolo Giraud, and the second Elgin collection, he spent a few months reconditioning the cases in which the marbles were stored and negotiating new credits with Elgin's bankers. Early in July he returned to Athens.

During his absence his own archaeological activities had been put in the shade by a new discovery. A young architectural student, Charles Robert Cockerell, had arrived in Greece some months before on a tour of the Levant that was to last several years.[1] He had obtained a British government commission to carry dispatches as a result of his friendship with Hamilton at the Foreign Office, but once they were safely delivered he applied himself to an exhaustive and meticulous study of every ancient building he could find. The day that the *Hydra* left Piraeus Cockerell was crossing to Aegina in a local vessel. Recognizing the *Hydra* he went alongside and sang a favourite song of Byron whom he had met in Constantinople. Byron and Lusieri invited them on board and the two parties enjoyed a glass of port together before going their separate ways. A few days later Cockerell and his party engaged local Greek workmen to dig the temple of Aphaia, then known as the Temple of Jupiter Panhellenius, which stood outside the town. As he wrote later, the results were beyond his imaginings:

On the second day one of the excavators working in the interior portico, struck on a piece of Parian marble which, as the building itself is of stone, arrested his attention. It turned out to be the head of a helmeted warrior, perfect in every feature. It lay with the face turned upwards, and as the features came out by degrees you can imagine nothing like the state of rapture and excitement to which we were wrought... Soon another head was turned up, then a leg and a foot, and finally, to make a long story short, we found ... no less than sixteen statues and thirteen heads, legs, arms etc, arms etc, all in the highest preservation not three feet below the surface of the ground.[2]

Cockerell's party had discovered a magnificent example of a period of Greek art hitherto virtually unknown. The Aegina marbles, all pedimental sculptures, date from some years before the Parthenon in the transitional period between archaic and classical.[3]

The leading men of the island presented petition to Cockerell protesting that terrible misfortunes would fall on their land if the marbles were removed, and imploring him to stop. Cockerell took this merely as an invitation to treat, and after some negotiation, he and his companions bought the marbles outright for the equivalent of about £40 sterling. It is not clear whether the travellers had permission to dig or the Aeginetans to sell, but the transaction was confirmed by a legal receipt.[4] Remembering the difficulties Lusieri had suffered with the Parthenon marbles, Cockerell then conveyed the collection in great secrecy, at night, to Athens, to await shipment out of Ottoman jurisdiction.

The four men who had bought the marbles were Cockerell, his friend Foster, who was also English, Haller von Hallerstein, who was travelling as agent of Prince Ludwig of Bavaria, and Linckh, his painter. The foreign community of Athens, which included the German Baron von Stackelberg, the Danish archaeologist Brönstedt, and other travellers and artists from different countries of Europe as well as Fauvel, was given a peep at them. As Cockerell wrote on 13 May, they could not bring themselves to acknowledge that the aesthetic of Ideal Beauty had suffered another blow:

Our council of artists here considered them as not inferior to the remains of the Parthenon and certainly in the second rank after the Torso, Laocoon and other famous statues. We conduct all our affairs in respect to them with the utmost secrecy for we sadly fear the Turks may either reclaim them or put some sad difficulties in our way. The few friends we have here and consult, such as they are, are dying with jealousy, literally one who intended to have farmed Aegina of the Capitan Pasha is almost ill on the occasion. Fauvel, the French consul hardly recovers the shock, although an excellent man, he does not suffer his envy to prevail against us. On the contrary he is on all occasions most obliging and has given most excellent advice to us. You may imagine the finding of such a treasure has tried everyone's character most powerfully.[5]

The Aegina marbles were still at Athens when Lusieri returned from Malta. There is a hint of sour grapes as well as sound historical appreciation in his report on them to Lord Elgin. 'They are respectable for their antiquity, there are some fragments that are very fine and some that are very curious. They want the perfection and elegance of the age of Phidias.'⁶ As had been the case from the beginning Elgin and his agents were only interested in one period of the past which they privileged above all others, including their own.

As far as Cockerell and his friends were concerned, the sooner their prize could be exported from Ottoman territory, the better. But what was to be done? There were four owners, two English and two German, each eager that their country should possess them but equally determined that the collection should not be split. It was soon clear that, whatever happened, they would each make a killing on their £10 investment. The two Germans, who knew the prices paid for ancient marbles in Rome, talked of a price of £6,000 to £8,000 for the whole collection. Two visiting English gentlemen, Gally Knight and Fazakerly, made a specific offer of £2,000 to buy out the Germans' share and, with Cockerell and Foster waiving their claims, the promise to present the whole collection to the British Museum, but it was not accepted.⁷ Fauvel, on behalf of the French government made an offer equivalent to about £6,500 but, remembering the fate of Choiseul-Gouffier's collection which had been captured at sea in 1803, he stipulated that the bulk of the money should not be paid until the marbles had arrived safely in France. His offer too was declined. At last, on Fauvel's advice, it was decided to ship the collection to Zacynthos (one of the Ionian Islands then known as Zante and at the time under British occupation) and hold a public auction there on 1 November 1812. The Aegina marbles left Athens soon afterwards.

Cockerell's father, as soon as he received news of his son's discovery, persuaded the Prince Regent to make an immediate offer of £6,000 for the Aegina Marbles. He also persuaded the British government to send a warship to Athens to pick them up. HMS *Pauline*, with a heavy transport in convoy, duly arrived at Piraeus in November 1811 only to discover that the marbles had already gone to Zacynthos. The captain, although angry at his wasted journey, agreed to take on board some cases of marbles for Lord Elgin that Lusieri had collected, and also to go to Zacynthos and transport the Aegina marbles to the greater safety of Malta, which he did.

Meanwhile, with the forthcoming sale advertised in the newspapers of Europe, the connoisseurs and artists of the various countries pressed their sovereigns and governments to acquire them. In London the Dilettanti Society, with an enthusiasm never shown for the Parthenon marbles, persuaded the Government through Hamilton that Britain must possess them at virtually any cost. It was agreed to send Taylor Combe of the British Museum to attend the auction with full powers to buy. When he reached Malta he found the Aegina marbles had been brought there by the *Pauline* and assumed, on wrong advice, that the venue of the sale had been changed to Malta.

Taylor Combe was still at Malta on 1 November 1812 when the sale at Zacynthos took place. Two bidders presented themselves, one on behalf of the French government, the other representing Prince Ludwig of Bavaria. The French repeated the conditional offer made by Fauvel but this was not accepted. The marbles were knocked down to Prince Ludwig for the equivalent of £8,000.[8]

Some months before, Lord Elgin's second collection of marbles, the ones brought by the *Hydra*, left Malta on board a transport ship which reached the port of Deptford near London in May 1812. The port authorities who were expecting the arrival of the ship bringing the Aegina marbles for the Prince Regent were horrified to find that her cargo consisted solely of yet more marbles for Lord Elgin. There was some acrimonious argument about the ownership of the collection although Lord Elgin's claim was indisputable. But, as had happened before, some of the blame for an event for which he was in no way responsible seemed to rub off on Lord Elgin.[9] His second collection at long last was united with the first in the courtyard of Burlington House.

Gradually the story of the muddle over the Aegina marbles came out. Attempts were made to prove that Taylor Combe had been deliberately misled and to sequestrate the marbles at Malta, but the legality of the sale at Zacynthos was finally upheld. The Aegina marbles were sent to Munich where they still remain.[10] Unfortunately, they suffered the fate from which the Parthenon sculptures were saved by Elgin's poverty. They were restored by the neo-classical sculptor Thorwaldsen, and although the work was done carefully and most of the restorations have since been removed, the historical surface has been damaged.

Cockerell's second discovery occurred in much the same way as the first. While he was waiting for the sale of the Aegina marbles Cockerell made a tour of ancient sites in Greece. In Arcadia while visiting the remote temple near Phigaleia he saw a fox darting out of the heap of stones that lay inside the ruins. Cockerell crept into the foxhole and at the bottom discovered a beautiful and well-preserved marble relief. He realized at once that this temple too, although built of stone, had once been decorated with a sculptured frieze which had been covered in the ruins when the roof fell in. He let the other members of the party into the secret (they were the same as the Aegina party with some others) and it was agreed to seek permission to remove them.

With the usual presents the Ottoman government in Constantinople was prevailed upon to grant a firman but as usual, in remote Greece, a firman was only permission to negotiate with the local authorities. It was accordingly agreed with the Governor of the Morea that he should have half-profits of the sale of anything that was discovered and excavations began in the summer of 1812. The excavators uncovered an almost complete, well-preserved, frieze in high relief depicting battles of Amazons and of Lapiths and Centaurs, a fine example of architectural sculpture of the classical period, although of lesser quality than those of the Parthenon. The excavators also discovered that the temple contained the first known example of the Corinthian order of architecture. One solitary Corinthian pillar had stood in the interior. For three months an army of between fifty and eighty men was employed digging out these sculptures. In August 1812 they were on their way to the sea.

At the last minute the whole expedition almost ended in disaster. The Ottoman governor of the Peloponnese was bitterly disappointed that no gold had been found but, when he heard that he had been superseded in his command, he accepted £400 as his share of the spoils. The local Greeks were not so easily assuaged. A strike occurred among the porters and it was only after great delays that the marbles reached the coast. All the marbles were embarked with the exception of the unique Corinthian capital when the new pasha arrived with a party of armed troops to stop them going. The excavators had to put out to sea leaving the capital lying on the beach half in and half out of the water. They had the mortification of seeing the Turkish troops hack it to pieces.[11] The Phigaleian marbles, as they came to be called, reached Zante safely where they were bought by the local British general on behalf of the British government for £15,000. They arrived in London at the very time that Elgin was trying for the second time to sell his collection, providing a useful benchmark not only for artistic quality but for market price.

Lusieri remained at Athens. But ever since the last of the

Parthenon marbles had been successfully sent off, his life had changed. He was no longer the undisputed leader of the foreign artists in Athens but one of many. He no longer had the resources to carry on his researches. The price of the few antiquities that still appeared on the market was constantly rising as a result of the numbers of visitors. By about 1810, the whole of Attica had been virtually exhausted of anything ancient above the surface that could be bought for money. The main source was now digging. In 1812 Lusieri made a bargain with the Governor of the Peloponnese (the one that had attacked Cockerell's party) to dig at Olympia but the initial cost (500 sequins and a gold watch) was more than Elgin's bankers would allow, to say nothing of the cost of labour and transportation that would follow. Lord Elgin's collecting days were over.

Gradually digging too was abandoned. Occasionally a new item was added to Lusieri's collection for Lord Elgin, and occasionally he took up his pencil to work on his numberless uncompleted drawings, but the old enthusiasm was gone. It was so much easier to accept money for acting as guide to the travellers and to sit late telling them about the past.[12] With advancing age and growing ill health, Lusieri, who had only occasionally been energetic, did less and less. The old rivalry with Fauvel continued. The great war between Great Britain and France was fought out in miniature by the two parties in Athens, each side giving a feast to celebrate the news of military victories, and it continued after Waterloo brought an end to the larger conflict. Their two houses, each within sight of the other on the slopes of the Acropolis and each proudly flying the flag of the warring nations were the first places in Athens that travellers invariably made for. The names of Fauvel or Lusieri, the two doyens of Athens, were passport enough for any Turkish official.

In 1813 for the last time Lusieri set the politics of Athens alight. Years before, in an attempt to sweeten the Turks towards his activities on the Acropolis, Elgin had promised to present a town clock to Athens. This suggestion was seized upon and never forgotten. Probably the only other provincial town in the whole Turkish empire which had a clock was Thebes and the Thebans were far more proud of their town clock than of any ancient buildings. Turks everywhere, it was said, liked to stop foreigners who might have a watch to ask them what time it was, and watches and clocks were among the most effective of presents to sweeten a negotiation. Like all lazy people, the travellers sneered, the Turks were concerned to measure the amount of time they were wasting.[13]

The clock, ordered in 1806, arrived in Athens in 1813 to great excitement. But immediately argument broke out about where it should be sited. Lord Guildford, a visiting member of the Dilettanti, offered money to have the tower built in the lower town, but Lusieri, with more loyalty than tact, insisted otherwise. The clock would be erected at Lord Elgin's expense, he said, and nowhere else but on a prominent site on the Acropolis. It seemed that, as one traveller said, Lusieri wished to remind the Greeks of the despoiler of the Parthenon at every hour of the day.[14] In the end a tower was built, amidst considerable murmuring among the Greeks, at public expense in the bazaar near the Tower of the Winds.[15] A marble slab from the Parthenon bore an inscription in Latin, the one language that the multilingual inhabitants of a multicultural empire could not read:

> TOMAS COMES
> DE ELGIN
> ATHENIEN. HOROL. D.D.
> SPQA EREX COLLOC
> AD MDCCCXIV

Thomas Earl of Elgin presented this clock to the people of Athens. The Senate and People of Athens erected it and sited it here, 1814.

As so often, what Elgin saw as an act for which he deserved to be honoured was soon regarded, as attitudes changed, to be adding insult to injury. Scurrilous verses about Lord Elgin's clock were composed in Greece as early as 1817 but the clock tower continued to dominate the skyline.[16] During the Greek Revolution the clock itself was destroyed, but the tower remained in use as a prison.[17] It stood until 1884 when it was destroyed in a fire, but the marble inscription is preserved in the National and Historical Museum in Athens.[18]

The argument about Lord Elgin's clock was a symptom of a more profound change that was occurring in Greece, the growth of neo-Hellenic nationalism.[19] In the larger towns the ancient Greek language was beginning to be taught, and there was increasing talk of a possible revolution.[20] What is striking, however, when one reads the contemporary accounts of local opposition to the activities of Elgin's agents, is the absence of a nationalist element in the way in which the opposition was formulated. When Elgin and Koehler took the first antiquities from the Troad in 1799, the inhabitants protested that the loss would bring ruin on the local community. The same argument was heard when Clarke took the statue of Demeter from Eleusis, when Cockerell found the Aegina sculptures, and at other times.

The travellers and collectors, on whose reports we largely depend, usually reported the reactions of those who opposed them in a discourse of colonial condescension towards ignorance and superstition, and were quick to notice the mercenary eagerness with which the local people disposed of the antiquities to buyers from the West. As Byron said, the travellers condemned the Greeks as a nation on much the same grounds that a Turk in England would condemn the English because he was wronged by his lackey and overcharged by his washerwoman.[21] But even allowing for the mentality of most of the writers of the sources on which we are obliged to rely, it is striking that during the years of the greatest depredations there is no record of any local Greek community claiming that they were the descendants of the ancients and the heirs to their heritage. They simply did not yet think in those terms.

The main removals of the Parthenon sculptures occurred between 1801 and 1805, and Lord Elgin's agents were visible and active for long after. After Byron, virtually all travellers from western European countries felt it necessary to condemn Lord Elgin, even when they acknowledged that the monuments were being rapidly eroded and joined in the random plundering. Surely, during those years of rising nationalist feeling, some Greek must have raised his voice against the destruction of the most famous monument surviving from antiquity and the export of its sculptures? But, even allowing for the bias of most of the sources, for the lack of records about local Greek opinion, and for the climate of fear which may have existed in Athens, the evidence is sparse.

Logotheti, it is recorded, had some initial qualms when the first removals from the Parthenon were proposed, but they were not formulated in nationalist terms and he seems to have overcome his doubts soon enough. Philip Hunt, who knew more about the first decisive removals than anyone else and who could speak Greek, declared later that no opposition to the scheme was made by any class of the natives of Athens.[22] Hamilton, who also spoke Greek, went further in answer to a similar question. Not only, he said, did the removals create 'no unpleasant sensation' among the Athenians but 'they seemed rather to feel it as a means of bringing foreigners into the country and of having money spent amongst them'.[23]

Even those travellers who wished to claim that Lord Elgin's activities were opposed by the Greeks found it difficult to find examples, and almost none were couched in terms of a national heritage. One story, constantly repeated, was that when the Caryatid was removed from the Erechtheion the whole town was filled with doleful sighs and lamentations as the remaining Caryatids mourned 'their ravished sister'.[24] Hobhouse, one of the most thorough, independent, and careful recorders of what he saw, says the 'common Athenians' regarded the statues as:

real bodies, mutilated, and enchanted into their present state of petrifaction by magicians, who will have power over them as long as the Turks are masters of Greece. The spirit within them is called an Arabim, and is not unfrequently heard to moan and bewail its condition. Some Greeks, in our time, conveying a chest from Athens to Piraeus, containing part of the Elgin Marbles, threw it down, and could not for some time be prevailed upon to touch it, again affirming, they heard the Arabim crying out, and groaning for his fellow-spirits detained in bondage in the Acropolis. The Athenians suppose that the condition of these enchanted marbles will be bettered by a removal from the country of the tyrant Turks.[25]

In his unpublished journal for 6 January 1810, on which he drew for his book, Hobhouse added a few details but made no mention of the political point.

Lusieri also mentioned a singular superstition of the Greeks. They consider that the *statues antiques* in Greece are men and women enchanted by some magician and that they will at some future time recover their pristine form. Some men employed in loading my lord Elgin's marbles a few days past refused to put one of the chests on board saying that it was an *Arabim* or had a spirit within. And some Greeks who conveyed two busts to Captain Leake declared they heard an *Arabim* groan and scream most piteously within them. Some of these statues, they say, have been heard to bewail at leaving their friends and fellow marbles in the Acropolis. In the well of Lusieri's house there is also an *Arabim*.[26]

Even in the late nineteenth century, by which time Greek anger against Lord Elgin had become part of the national history, it was mainly variations of this story which were repeated to travellers when they looked for evidence that Elgin had been opposed.[27]

In Athens there were a few Greeks who had resurrected a knowledge of the classical Greek language and who knew the history of their country. In Lord Elgin's time, Ioannes Benizelos, a teacher who wrote a history of Athens under the Turks, ran a school maintained from funds invested in Venice. When Venice fell to the French, Benizelos' school had to close for lack of money. Despite poverty and exile, Benizelos survived just long enough to see the revival of ancient Greek teaching which began in Athens, with the assistance of western Philhellenes, at the beginning of the nineteenth century. Philip Hunt, whom knew him well, described him as 'the sole representative of all the ancient philosophers of his country'.[28]

In January 1803, shortly before Elgin's Embassy sailed for home, Benizelos wrote a long letter to Hunt. His letter described how Athens was prospering under a benevolent voivode; and how prices were falling. In conclusion he wrote, in neo-Hellenic Greek:

ἕν ὅμως ἤθελε σᾶς λυπήση οὐ μετρίως, καθώς καί ὅλους ἐκείνους ὁποῦ ἔχουσιν ὁπωσοῦν ἰδέαν τῶν τοιούτων, ἡ τελευταία καί ἀξιοδάκρυτος γύμνωσις τοῦ ναοῦ τῆς Ἀθηνᾶς ἀν τῇ ἀκροπόλει, καί ἄλλων λειψάνων τῆς ἀρχαιότητος, ὥσπερ μιᾶς εὐγενοῦς καί πολυτελοῦς νύμφης ὁποῦ ἀπέβαλεν ὅλα της τά διαμαντικά καί στολίδια. ὦ πόσον πρέπει ἡμεῖς οἱ Ἀθηναῖοι νά ἐνθυμούμεθα αὐτό τό συμβεβηκός, καί πόσον χρεωστοῦμεν νά ἐπαινοῦμεν καί νά εὐφημίζωμεν τούς παλαιούς ἥρωας τῆς ῥώμης Πομπήϊον καί Ἀδριανόν, βλέποντες ταῦτα.

One thing only would make you sad as it does all those who have some understanding of these things—the last deplorable stripping of the Temple of Athena on the Acropolis and of the other relics of antiquity. The temple is like a noble and wealthy lady who has lost all her diamonds and jewellery. Oh, how we Athenians must take this event to heart, and how we must praise and admire the ancient heroes of Rome, Pompey and Hadrian, when we look on these things.[29]

Pompey and Hadrian had used their power to preserve Athens. The British, the modern Romans, had stripped her. It was a gentle rebuke but a rebuke nevertheless. Benizelos' letter seems to be the first recorded sign of protest among educated Greeks. In his *History of Athens Under the Turks* Benizelos recorded briefly the activities of Elgin's agents on the Acropolis. The removal of the statues from the Parthenon, he said, caused 'shock and consternation among all the travellers'.[30] Significantly, he makes no mention of any reaction among the Greeks or Turks.

It was at Ioannina, which at the time contained more educated Greeks than Athens, that Hobhouse, Byron's companion, had a conversation which showed unequivocally that philhellenism was

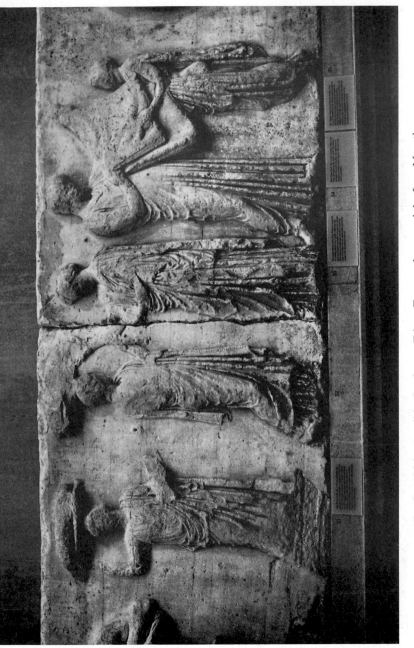

1. The Central Scene of the Parthenon Frieze. From a photograph by Inge Morath, 1997.

2. The Acropolis of Athens in Lord Elgin's time, showing the fortifications, the Frankish Tower, the minarets in the town, and Haseki's wall. From Dodwell's *Classical and Topographical Tour.*

3. The Parthenon in 1801. From a watercolour by William Gell in the British Museum.

4. The south-east corner of the Parthenon after the removal of some of the metopes. From a watercolour by Lusieri in the National Gallery of Scotland.

5. The same corner after all the metopes had been taken, as shown in Hobhouse's *Journey*, 1813.

6. Lusieri on the Erechtheion. From a watercolour by William Gell in the British Museum.

7. A Tight-Rope Display in Athens, 1800, showing the Theseum and the fortifications of the Acropolis, from a drawing by Sebastiano Ittar. Private collection.

8. Lord Elgin's Marbles at Burlington House, 1816. From a drawing by an unknown artist, in the former Greater London Council Record Office.

9. Some of the Elgin Marbles in the courtyard of Burlington House, 1816. From a drawing by an unknown artist, in the former Greater London Council Record Office.

10. Protest at the waste of money in buying the Elgin Marbles in 1816. From a cartoon by Cruikshank.

11. Crowds in St James's jostle to see the drawings of the Elgin Marbles by Haydon's pupils, 1819. From a cartoon by Marks. Author's collection.

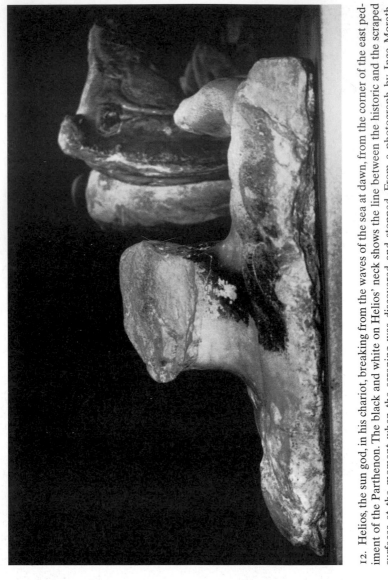

12. Helios, the sun god, in his chariot, breaking from the waves of the sea at dawn, from the corner of the east pediment of the Parthenon. The black and white on Helios' neck shows the line between the historic and the scraped surfaces at the moment when the scraping was discovered and stopped. From a photograph by Inge Morath, 1997.

making progress among local Greeks as well as among expatriates and foreigners.

I have said nothing of the possiblity of the ruins of Athens being, in the event of a revolution in favour of the Greeks, restored and put into a condition capable of resisting the ravages of decay; for an event of that nature cannot, it strikes me, have ever entered into the head of anyone who has seen Athens, and the modern Athenians. Yet I cannot forbear mentioning a singular speech of a learned Greek of Ioannina who said to me 'You English are carrying off the works of the Greeks, our forefathers—preserve them well—we Greeks will come and redemand them.'[31]

Lusieri failed to recognize the signs of change. It probably never occurred to him that the time was not far off when the Greeks could want to preserve every relic of antiquity as a precious heirloom and have the ability to do so. But even if he had recognized the signs, Lusieri would not have acted any differently. For the justifications which had prompted the first removals remained as powerful as ever.

Between 1805 when Lusieri had to cease his operations on the Acropolis and 1821 when the Greek Revolution broke out, every monument in Athens suffered more or less severely. The destruction of the Erechtheion during this time has been closely documented, with most of the pieces known to have been taken now lost and others turning up in unexpected places from unknown sources.[32] A glance at the drawings of the monument of Philopappos made at different times during this brief period shows a steady attrition of arms and legs, to say nothing of a general destruction of the sculptured surface.[33]

In 1813 Thomas Hughes, an English traveller, records that one day he noticed that Lusieri had a shivering fit. This was not, he recounted, due to ill health

but, as he observed to us, he is always thus attacked whenever an English or a French frigate anchors in the Piraeus. The young midshipmen are then let loose upon the venerable monuments of Athens, and are seldom deterred by the religion of the place from indulging in the most wanton devastation of statues, cornices and capitals, from which they carry off mementoes of their Athenian travels.[34]

H. W. Williams, later known as Grecian Williams from the neo-classical buildings he designed in Edinburgh, was in Athens in 1817. 'Some midshipmen', he noted, 'on visiting the Acropolis, chipped and broke the drapery of one of the caryatids... The Disdar, on perceiving this, was much in wrath, and threatened vengeance if he could find them.'[35] A later traveller, Laurent, gives another instance:

The last time I visited the citadel . . . I was much displeased at seeing an English traveller, an officer of the navy (for such his uniform bespoke him to be) standing upon the base of one of the Caryatids, clinging with his left arm round the column, while his right hand, provided with a hard and heavy pebble, was endeavouring to knock off the only remaining nose of those six beautifully sculptured statues. I exerted my eloquence in vain to preserve this monument of art.[36]

As usual, it was the Parthenon, as the most famous building, which suffered worst. The two heads from the west pediment, those wrongly believed to represent the Roman Hadrian and Sabina, disappeared entirely, one going to Dodwell, the other to Fauvel, and both are now lost.[37] Two slabs of the frieze fell to the ground in the few weeks between Byron's two visits to Athens.[38] The Turks, keen to profit from the ready market in easily transportable relics, resumed their old practice (virtually suspended during the supremacy of Fauvel and Lusieri) of chopping off small pieces, such as heads of the frieze.

The plaster casts of the west frieze which Lord Elgin's moulders made in 1801 and 1802 reveal many features including heads of horsemen which were broken off or defaced from the originals shortly afterwards. In some cases the originals were almost entirely obliterated and Elgin's casts are our best record of what they once looked like. It was during this period that Fauvel, despairing of sending any more sculptures to the Louvre while the war and British naval power lasted, began to sell off to passing travellers some of the antiquities from the enormous collection he had amassed during his long stay at Athens. Thus Fauvel too began to encourage the dispersal he had earlier done so much to prevent.[39] Four fragments which he sold were later obtained by the British Museum.[40] But, as in the earlier period, no doubt many others are now permanently lost.

For the most part the pieces sold were small, and easily lost. Few travellers could afford the enormous bribes now demanded for larger pieces or the cost of carriage; and it is doubtful if they could have obtained firmans to remove openly from the Acropolis. When Cockerell was about to leave Athens for the last time in 1814, the Disdar gave him a present. He invited him to bring a cart to the foot of the Acropolis at a certain time of the night, it being unwise, he said, to make the gift in daytime for fear of offending the Greeks. When Cockerell arrived with his cart there was a shout from above, and part of a slab of the Parthenon frieze was bowled down the cliff, breaking into three pieces on the way. Cockerell took it to Piraeus, shipped it at once, and later presented it to the British Museum. The other half of the slab remained in Athens.[41]

Helpless to prevent the continuing destruction, Lusieri remained at Athens increasingly debilitated by rheumatism and old age. His own researches became more and more desultory and latterly he abandoned even his pencil. Hamilton, who had once told a traveller that 'he had never met anyone to whom he felt really attached to as a friend except Lusieri the Italian artist', now advised Lord Elgin to read his latest letters only on a very fine day.[42] Lusieri, he said, 'has finished nothing—nor indeed *done* anything *to the purpose* in any way whatever for the last four or five years'.[43]

Lusieri's presence at Athens now merely served as a constant reminder to travellers to moralize about the spoliation of the Parthenon. Fauvel too was ever ready to talk of the great destruction of many years before, and the indignation at the barbarian Elgin spread to the Greeks.[44] When the Princess of Wales visited Athens she stayed with Fauvel in preference to any of the English colony and indulged in the usual sneers against Elgin.[45] Even the Turks remembered. In 1816, far from Athens at Askalon in Palestine, Lady Hester Stanhope led an expedition of Turks to look for hidden gold among the ruins of Astarte's Temple. When they discovered not gold but an exquisite marble statue, Lady Hester ordered it to be broken up and thrown into the sea to emphasize how much she differed from her countrymen who dug only for stones.[46]

19

Lord Elgin Tries Again

THE second collection of Lord Elgin's marbles arrived in England in May 1812 just as the enthusiasm for *Childe Harold's Pilgrimage* was approaching its height. His promise to give the British Museum any marbles brought home by naval vessels was conveniently forgotten and the whole collection was taken to Burlington House. Under Flaxman's superintendence the newly arrived marbles were unpacked and arranged and were available for inspection at the end of the year.

The museum at Burlington House now consisted of a small, irregular, half-timbered outhouse which stood in the yard at the back of the house. There were no windows and the marbles could only be seen with difficulty even in daylight. Some had to be left outside in the open air. The large architectural fragments, the pieces of Parthenon columns and architraves, and miscellaneous pieces from the other buildings of Athens, were piled higgledy-piggledy on top of one another. As can be seen from the two drawings reproduced in Plates 8 and 9, even some of the slabs of the sculptured frieze were left outside to the mercies of the English weather and soon grass began to grow round them.[1] Although, compared with this, the draughty museum at Park Lane had been a palace, the aim of improving the arts in Great Britain was not forgotten. Nollekens, West, Flaxman, and Haydon continued to spend long hours sketching in the new museum, and West arranged for the medallists of the Royal Academy school to go there as part of their studies.

Lord Elgin remained at Broomhall waiting patiently for his luck to change. But the enmity of the Dilettanti Society continued, exacerbated by an unfortunate misunderstanding in 1814. After many decades of preparation, the last volume of the great *Antiquities of Athens*, which had begun with the work of Stuart and Revett in 1750 and 1751, was at last ready for publication. The final volume, which had been completed by other artists, was to contain engravings of some of the sculptures of the Parthenon taken from drawings made in Athens many years before Elgin's Embassy. The editor, naturally enough, wrote to Elgin to ask if he could be given the opportunity of comparing the engravings with the originals now at Burlington House. Unfortunately the wording of his letter was not clear and Elgin misunderstood it. He thought that the Dilettanti had somehow made engravings of his marbles without his permission and were about to forestall him in his long-cherished scheme of publishing them. Deeply affronted he gave the Dilettanti a curt refusal, which was recorded in volume iv of *The Antiquities of Athens* published shortly afterwards.[2]

At last in April 1814 came the news that Elgin had been waiting for. Napoleon abdicated from the throne of France and the long war came to an end. After eight years Elgin was freed from the crippling parole which he had given to Talleyrand in 1806 as the price of his freedom. If he could but restore his finances, in other words dispose of his marbles for a good price, there might still be hope of saving his ruined public career. He realized that the only hope of persuading British official opinion to overrule the dismissive stance taken by Payne Knight and the Dilettanti was to obtain an authoritative foreign opinion. In 1811 his case had been greatly strengthened by pointing to the example of the Choiseul-Gouffier piece of the frieze. Now that the war was over he was able to do even better.

As soon as peace was declared he set off for Paris to meet Ennio Quirino Visconti, the Director of the Louvre. Visconti had been director of the Capitoline Museum at Rome and had followed the masterpieces of Italy to Paris, and it was he who, at Napoleon's instigation, had brought the Choiseul-Gouffier fragment into prominence. Acknowledged as the greatest art historian and connoisseur in Europe, he now presided over the greatest accumulation of works of European art that the world is ever likely to see under one roof. Besides many thousands of paintings taken from all over Europe, the Louvre boasted all the ancient sculptures from Italy which had constituted the canon of ideal beauty, including the Apollo Belvidere, the Medici Venus, the Discobolus, the dying Gladiator, the Laocoon, and more than sixty other sculptures from the Vatican and Capitoline museums. After some negotiation Elgin struck a bargain with Visconti under which he would come to London to see the Elgin Marbles for a fee of £120. He would stay for a fortnight, and on his return, prepare a memoir on the marbles, the fee for which was to be settled later.

Elgin also took the opportunity of his visit to Paris to try to settle some other unfinished business. This was the affair of Choiseul-Gouffier's metope which he had bought at a Customs House sale in 1806. A misunderstanding had arisen between Elgin and Choiseul-Gouffier about this metope and Elgin now paid a call on his old friend and rival to try to sort it out. Soon after he had bought the metope (and other lesser antiquities) at the sale in 1806, Elgin realized that this was one of the antiquities that Choiseul-Gouffier had told him about at Barrèges in 1803. It was the metope that Nelson had captured from *l'Arabe* and sent to England as prize. With his usual magnanimity, and in gratitude for Choiseul-Gouffier's help to him while he had been a prisoner in France, Elgin at once wrote to him offering to give it back. This was an act of kindness since his own legal title to the metope under the international law of war at sea was indisputable.

Choiseul-Gouffier, however, did not respond with the same generosity. He had somehow heard a story that Nelson himself had not sent the antiquities from *l'Arabe* to England but had directed that they should be kept at Malta to be returned to Choiseul-Gouffier after the war. Nelson, of course, had no power to do this even if he had wanted to. Nevertheless, despite Elgin's letter giving him the true story, Choiseul-Gouffier remained convinced that his lost collection still lay at Malta.

Although on his visit to Paris in 1814 Elgin was able to convince his friend that the metope was indeed his, Choiseul-Gouffier could not believe that there was no collection waiting for him at Malta. When enquiries on the spot there showed finally that there was nothing there, he turned on Lord Elgin. Elgin's agents at Malta, he wrote shortly after Elgin's visit, must have stolen them, just as Elgin's agents in Athens had stolen the antiquities which Fauvel had hidden in a warehouse in Piraeus.

Fauvel and Lusieri, it was true, had made many attempts to steal the collections of their respective patrons, but there is no evidence that either ever succeeded.[3] In the second volume of *Voyage Pittoresque de la Grèce*, published in 1809, Choiseul-Gouffier wrote of a marble throne which he had seen in Greece and which had been taken by Elgin.

J'ai vu ce monumen devant la porte de l'évêque, qui s'y plaçoit en certains jours de fête, et l'avait consacré à la religion; cette destination a contrarié toutes les tentatives que j'ai faites pour l'acquerir. Lord Elgin, plus heureux, a su profité du crédit qui lui donnoient la présence d'une escadre victorieuse, la conquête de l'Egypte, et la restitution de cette importante possession pour obtenir de la Porte des complaisances qu'en d'autres temps ses ministres les plus faciles et les plus bienviellans n'eussent jamais osé se permettre. Lord Elgin a fait, dans toute la Grèce, une riche moisson de précieux monumens, que j'avois longtemps et inutilement désirés; il m'est difficile de les voir entre ses mains sans un peu d'envie; mais ce doit être une satisfaction pour tous ceux qui cultivent les arts, de savoir ces chefs d'oeuvre soustraits de la barbarie des Turcs, et conservés par un amateur éclairé qui en fera jouri le public.

I saw this monument in front of the door of the bishop who put it there on certain festivals and had thus consecrated it to religion. This dedication thwarted all my attempts to acquire it. Lord Elgin, more fortunate than I, knew how to profit from the influence given him by the presence of a victorious fleet, the conquest of Egypt, and the restitution of that important possession. He thus obtained from the Porte an acquiescence which at other times even the most easy-going and benevolent ministers would never have dared to allow themselves. Lord Elgin has collected all over Greece a rich crop of precious monuments which I had long and vainly desired. It is difficult for me to see them in his hands without a touch of envy; but it must be a source of satisfaction for all who love the arts, to know that these masterpieces have been rescued from the barbarity of the Turks and are preserved by an enlightened connoisseur, who will give the public an opportunity of enjoying them.[4]

Choiseul-Gouffier added a more personal touch. Elgin's agents had also taken a cart and some other tackle which belonged to him. 'They did well,' he wrote magnanimously, 'I would have been delighted to lend them to you.'[5] For all their differences, the French Count and the British Earl shared the view that the best place for the antiquities of Athens was in western Europe.

Visconti's visit to London took place in October 1814. On his return to Paris the letter to Hamilton which he wrote as a first instalment of his promised memoir surpassed all Elgin's expectations. None of the engravings, the casts, or the few originals which he had seen in Paris, Visconti wrote, had been able to give him the idea of the works of Phidias that the sight of the Elgin marbles had done. The frieze, the metopes, the pediments, all showed every perfection, as excellent in every way, as the famous statues of Italy. There could be no doubt, he claimed, that the Parthenon sculptures had been executed under the superintendence of Phidias himself. And, he went on, if the classical statues of Italy had been an inspiration to the Michelangelos and Raphaels of the sixteenth century, would not the Elgin Marbles inaugurate a new era for the progress of sculpture of England.[6]

Visconti's letter was just what Elgin needed to start a new campaign to sell his collection, and he at once ordered it to be published at his own expense. The list of those who received free copies can be read as Elgin's assessment of the men who would decide his fate.[7] His own *Memorandum on the Subject of the Earl of Elgin's Pursuits in Greece* was revised and sent to the press for a third edition with yet more appendices. Hamilton began to take soundings among the Government about how a new offer to sell the marbles would be received and he heard a hint that £80,000 might be forthcoming. The international scramble to acquire the Aegina and then the Phigaleian marbles showed that European nations had found a new form of rivalry. Although by 1814 the Parthenon marbles were not yet a focus of nationalism in Greece, they had already become so in the countries of western Europe.

Then suddenly, when for the first time since 1811 Elgin's prospects began to look promising, everything was again thrown back into the melting-pot. On 1 March 1815 Napoleon landed at Antibes and the Hundred Days had begun. With a desperate war once more on their hands the Government could hardly be expected to have much time to consider the claims of Greek art for a share of public funds. It seemed as if, yet again, Elgin was to be a helpless victim of political upheaval.

Just before he heard of Napoleon's landing, bad news affecting him more personally reached Elgin. While looking over the newspapers at Broomhall on 4 March he read a report that the Duke of Devonshire had sold Burlington House, and the new owner, Lord George Cavendish, intended to rebuild the whole structure, beginning work within a few weeks. It was now imperative that the Elgin Marbles should be moved at once. But where? Could a fifth London home be found at a few days' notice for several hundred tons of marbles? The situation was desperate. It would cost about £1,000 to move the marbles, even if a site could be found, and then probably another £1,000 to move them to the British Museum if a bargain could be concluded. The obvious solution was to seek to move them to the British Museum with the option to move them out again if the sale fell through. Such a move would obviously weaken Elgin's negotiating position, but he had little alternative. Despite the preoccupation of the Government with the war he set to work.

Hamilton pressed Lord George Cavendish to delay the rebuilding of Burlington House as long as possible to give time to man-
œuvre, and at once opened formal negotiations with the Speaker
of the House of Commons and the Trustees of the British Museum.
The first results were not hopeful. The Speaker (one of the principal trustees) said he did not believe the Government would have
the courage to offer more than the £30,000 proposed in 1811 by
Spencer Perceval. And Elgin's inevitable suggestion that a British
peerage should be bestowed on him as part of the transaction was
firmly discouraged.

On 8 April a meeting of the Trustees of the British Museum was
held to consider Lord Elgin's overtures. To his consternation they
decided to set up a committee consisting of Charles Long, Lord
Aberdeen, and Richard Payne Knight to conduct the Museum's
negotiations with Elgin on behalf of the Government. From Elgin's
point of view there could hardly have been a worse choice. Payne
Knight had never made any secret of his hostility and Aberdeen
was widely regarded as his obedient disciple. Charles Long had
been closely associated with the abortive negotiations of 1811.

Soon afterwards Hamilton heard from Lord Aberdeen what had
occurred at the first committee meeting. The members had agreed
to recommend accepting the marbles, but could not spend money
on building a shelter. As for a price, Long had talked of £35,000 at
the very outside. Payne Knight, on the other hand, wished to draw
the line at £15,000 or £20,000. Payne Knight had also declared that
if Elgin tried to sell his collection abroad, an Act of Parliament
should be passed to keep it in England. It came to light that he had
made his pronouncements without even having seen the second
collection.

In the course of this conversation with Aberdeen, Hamilton mentioned that Visconti's letter had been printed and was ready for
publication. Aberdeen's reply was deflating. There could be no
doubt, he observed, 'that Visconti was the best practical Antiquary
in the world and that his independent unbiassed opinion would be
of great weight everywhere, but that it was equally well known that
he would write anything he was asked for £10'.[8]

Elgin was bitterly disappointed. After all his patience it seemed
as if he might receive less for his total collection than he had
refused for the first part of it four years before. But there could be
no going back. By April the building operations at Burlington
House had begun and Elgin's agent had to rearrange the marbles

within the yard: Cavendish began to press him hard to remove them altogether. Yet as long as Payne Knight and Lord Aberdeen remained members of a Committee of three no improvement on the offer could be expected.

At the end of May Elgin came to London to confer with Hamilton about the next move. The only way of averting Payne Knight's hostility that they could think of was to sell him Elgin's collection of ancient coins which he and Lord Aberdeen had long wanted, but Elgin was determined not to appease his enemies.[9] It was probably at Hamilton's suggestion that he decided on a new approach. He wrote a formal letter to the Chancellor of the Exchequer suggesting that the direct negotiations with the Government and the British Museum should be discontinued. Instead, he proposed, consideration of the whole affair should be referred to a Select Committee of the House of Commons who could then investigate the circumstances in which the collection had been obtained and advise on whether, and at what price, the nation should acquire them. Elgin was, by this move, virtually throwing himself on the mercy of Parliament. The Government, relieved perhaps at not having to make up their own minds, accepted Elgin's suggestion with eagerness. Even Payne Knight made a point of calling personally on Elgin to say that he welcomed the move although at the same time, Elgin recorded, 'he exposed all his plan of hostility'.

The *Petition of the Earl of Elgin Respecting his Collection of Marbles* was presented to the House of Commons on 15 June.[10] It described briefly the circumstances in which the petitioner had acquired his collection and begged that the House should institute an inquiry on the advisability of transferring it to the nation. The *Petition* was then the subject of a short debate. The Chancellor of the Exchequer accepted the proposal on behalf of the Government and made some remarks on the excellence of the collection. Others also praised it but some clearly took their brief from *Childe Harold's Pilgrimage*. 'It seemed to have been reserved for an ambassador of this country,' said Sir John Newport, 'to take away what Turks and other barbarians had always held sacred. It was the duty of the House to ascertain the truth of these matters; for otherwise in case they should consent to purchase the collection they would evidently sanction acts of public robbery.' Several members felt that the matter should be deferred until the next session so that Lord Elgin's right to the collection could be fully investigated. The

Chancellor, knowing Elgin's difficulties, urged speed. Lord George Cavendish intervened in the debate to say that he would allow the marbles to stay at Burlington House for a short time. At the end of the debate the matter had not been settled: Elgin's *Petition* was to lie on the table.

Three days after the House of Commons debated the Elgin Marbles Napoleon was finally defeated at the Battle of Waterloo. Lord Elgin rejoiced with the rest, but it soon became clear that time to discuss his case would not be found before 1816. The session ended in the middle of July. The next session would not begin until February. The marbles would have to spend another winter in the yard of Burlington House. Even in his defeat Napoleon seemed to have interfered successfully in the affair of the Elgin Marbles. There was, however, an unexpected bonus.

One of the first questions which the victorious allies decided to settle was what should become of the works of art that Napoleon had assembled in the Louvre. For the most part these had not been looted or seized by force, but handed over, with due legal process, as part of agreed peace terms and treaties with the countries and cities with which the French armies had been at war.[11] Unless these treaties were superseded by other agreements of equal legal validity, the French could claim legal ownership.

The armistice agreements of 1814 which involved Napoleon's abdication made no mention of the works of art taken by France during the wars. By implication therefore the treaties and agreements by which the works of art had come to Paris still stood. After Waterloo the French tried to include a clause in the Convention of Paris guaranteeing 'the integrity of museums and libraries', but this time the allies refused. As Lord Liverpool wrote to the British representative in Paris, emphasizing the dangers to international peace of the new nationalist attachment to works of art:

It is most desirable, in point of policy, to remove them if possible from France, as whilst in that country they must necessarily have the effect of keeping up the remembrance of their former conquests and of cherishing the military spirit and vanity of the nation.[12]

When the Prussian army marched into Paris in July, one of the first things the commanding general did was to demand back all the works of art taken from Prussia and other north German states. By 13 July they were packed and ready to go. The Dutch and Austrians were quick to make similar demands. Only Russia among the major countries opposed the proposal for a complete repatriation—it has since been discovered that the Tsar had made a secret agreement with Napoleon's relatives to buy some of the works of art for the Hermitage in St Petersburg.

Britain, being virtually the only country which had not been invaded, had lost nothing to the Louvre, but did not escape suspicion. The Prince Regent, realizing late in the day that Britain was poor in these modern status symbols, let it be known that he favoured splitting the Louvre collection among the victorious allies or at least buying some of them from their former owners. As the Director of the Louvre wrote to Talleyrand:

There remains only England, who has in truth nothing to claim, but who, since she has just bought the bas relief of which Lord Elgin plundered the Temple at Athens, now thinks she can become the rival of the Museum [the Louvre] and wants to deplete this museum in order to collect the remains [for herself].[13]

The discourses by which the French had defended their acquisitions in the first place and which were now repeated, in more muted form, in an attempt to retain them in Paris, were remarkably similar to those used by Lord Elgin. In 1796, at the time of General Bonaparte's first conquests in Italy, a petition signed by all the leading French artists of the day, had argued without shame, that:

The more our climate seems unfavourable to the arts, the more do we require models here in order to overcome obstacles to the progress thereof ... The Romans, once an uncultivated people, became civilized by transplanting to Rome the works of conquered Greece ... The French people, naturally endowed with exquisite sensitivity, will ... by seeing models from antiquity, train its feeling and its critical sense ... The French Republic, by its strength and superiority of its enlightenment and its artists, is the only country in the world which can give a safe home to these masterpieces. All other Nations must come to borrow from our art as once they imitated our frivolity.[14]

Works of art previously held by Roman Catholic countries, had, others claimed, been 'soiled too long by slavery'. Men of genius of all ages, General Bonaparte wrote from Milan in 1796, 'are French, no matter in what country they may have been born'. The works of art, books, and manuscripts, taken from foreign collections, especially those in places inhabited and ruled by 'degenerate' Roman Catholics such as the Pope, were not being seized or exported by the French, they were being brought home. The French conquests were conquests made on behalf of the arts and sciences. They were triumphs of liberty over tyranny, and philosophy over superstition.[15]

Combining the rhetoric of the Enlightenment with that of the newly emerging romantic notion of the autonomy of works of art, the French removals wrenched paintings, sculptures, and parts of buildings not only from their places of origin but from their context. As Quatremère de Quincey protested, the greatest works of art were the Coliseum, the Sistine Chapel, the Farnese Palace, the rooms of the Vatican, and the churches where the paintings and sculptures had previously been admired. But the Western drive to isolate and aestheticize continued unabated.

Statesmen and connoisseurs of the different countries gathered in Paris in August 1815 to discuss the question of what to do about the Louvre. Canova represented the Pope. Hamilton and Charles Long represented the British government. When in the end it was decided that everything should be returned to its place of origin, this meant that Britain got nothing. Until the end the French argued that the works of art had been acquired legally, that the allies could not abrogate private and public contracts, that the break-up of the unique collection assembled in the Louvre would be an act of vandalism, and that they had 'rescued' the works of art for civilization, not least from British travellers and connoisseurs who were able to strip Italy by the superior power of their purses.

Among these debates it was inevitable that the Elgin Marbles should be discussed. It so happened that Visconti's *Memoir* which Elgin had commissioned on his visit to Paris the previous year was ready just at that time when the main decisions were being taken. Visconti delivered it to a meeting of the French Institute on 18 August and it was quickly printed.[16] Visconti's assessment, which was long and scholarly, surpassed even his letter in its enthusiasm. He even took trouble to disprove in detail Payne Knight's assertions that the Parthenon sculptures could not be by Phidias and that they were Hadrianic. He concluded one section

In their new situation in the midst of an enlightened nation particularly disposed to afford encouragement to sculpture, they will rouse the talents of the young artist to exertion and will direct him in the road which leads to perfection in his art. We have only to regret that the noble idea which induced Lord Elgin to rescue them from the daily ravages of a barbarous nation was not entertained a century and a half earlier by some rich and powerful amateur.[17]

Visconti was also heard to declare that until he had been to London
he had seen nothing. Like the artists in England the artists in
France were already deserting the old canon of ideal beauty. The
sculptures of Italy which Napoleon had regarded as the centre-
piece of the Louvre, and which were now on their way back to Italy,
were, it now seemed only second-rate works. The British diplomats
need not be too disappointed at having failed to secure any tro-
phies from the Louvre. The best sculptures from the ancient
world were, the leading international critics seemed to be saying,
already in London, even if not appreciated by the London art
establishment.

Canova too was delighted at Hamilton's diplomacy in helping to
secure the return of the papal collections to Rome. He became a
personal friend and considered himself under a strong obligation
to him for the rest of his life. Canova, the other connoisseur with a
European reputation, agreed to come to England in the autumn to
see the Elgin Marbles of which he had seen only a small part in
1803. There was every prospect that he too would endorse
Visconti's judgement. In his quarrel with Payne Knight Elgin had
made a diplomatic coup.

Canova's visit to London took place in November 1815. He was
treated as an honoured guest by the Government and invited to all
the great houses. Everywhere he went he spoke admiringly of the
Elgin Marbles. They were the finest collection in Europe, he said,
with the exception of course of the Apollo, the Venus, the Laocoon
and the other ideal beauty models which had determined his own
style and career and over whose return to Italy he had presided.
The Elgin Marbles were worth coming all the way from Rome to
see; they had opened his eyes to the real principles of ancient art;
they should create a new era in the art of sculpture.[18] Haydon followed Canova around gleefully, prompting him to confirm what
he himself said about the Elgin Marbles and exulting in the
discomfiture of the Payne Knight party.[19] Canova's enthusiastic
letter of thanks to Lord Elgin when he left was yet another valuable piece of ammunition for the battle to be fought in the next
session.[20]

Shortly before Canova's visit to London the Phigaleian Marbles
which the Government had bought from Cockerell arrived at the
British Museum.[21] The Payne Knight party, who had done much to
secure their purchase, seized the opportunity of disparaging the
Elgin collection yet again. The Phigaleian Marbles, said an article

in the *Morning Chronicle*, 'are believed to be the only examples extant of entire subjects of the admirable school of Phidias and exhibit the sublimity of poetic imagination united to the boldness and power of execution resulting from extensive practice in the greatest school of antiquity'.[22] Haydon was quick to respond to the implied slur and wrote in another newspaper:

This is written, I suspect, by the same hand who said the Elgin Marbles were the work of journeymen not worthy the name of artists in a less fastidious age. Now so far from these Phygaleian Marbles being the only works of Phidias, they have not the slightest pretensions to be considered by his hand at all ... As to the taste of those who hesitated to acknowledge the beauty of the Elgin Marbles and decided at once without hesitation on the Phygaleian ones, nothing need be said ... There are one or two groups very fine in these Phygaleian Marbles but still approaching to manner; and in most instances they are entirely mannered. United with the Elgin collection their errors will do no injury to the student and both together will form the finest museum in Europe.[23]

Canova, invited by the Government to give his opinion, left the issue in no doubt. The Phigaleian Marbles were very good, he said, but if they were worth £15,000 (the price paid by the Government), then the Elgin Marbles were worth £100,000.[24]

Yet another foreign admirer of the Elgin Marbles, who had visited England some months before, was Ludwig the Crown Prince of Bavaria. It was he who had bought the Aegina Marbles in 1812 as a result of the muddle over the sale and he was eager to increase his collection. He showed his admiration in a very practical way. He deposited a large sum of money in a London bank and it soon became known that if the British government declined to buy Lord Elgin's collection he was eager to step into the breach.[25] With Visconti, Canova, and Prince Ludwig, Elgin's plan of obtaining authoritative foreign advice to pit against the prejudice of Payne Knight and his followers was succeeding beyond his most hopeful expectations.[26] He had successfully mobilized British nationalism.

Meanwhile, during the winter of 1815/16, the Elgin Marbles themselves still lay, scarcely visited, at Burlington House, covered with dust and dripping with damp.[28] The building operations had begun and it was necessary to move them from place to place within the courtyard to give the builders room. It was during this period that one or two smaller pieces were stolen from the collection.[29] They included two votive reliefs which had been catalogued by Visconti and, perhaps, for all we know, some fragments of the

Parthenon. None has ever been found. There was also another casualty. Lord Elgin's agent, who was engaged in packing the collection into boxes for transportation, failed to recognize the small pieces of the moulds of the Theseum frieze and inadvertently destroyed them, although the casts themselves were preserved.[30]

Lord Elgin now commissioned a full catalogue to be prepared of all his collection using Visconti's memoir as a basis. A further consignment of miscellaneous marbles arrived at Burlington House from Lusieri after Visconti's visit. They were not included in the main collection and were shipped to Broomhall. All was now ready for the Select Committee's investigation due to begin in February 1816.

20

Tweddell J. and Tweddell R.

To Lord Elgin, therefore, 1815 was more than the year of Waterloo. As a result of careful planning and patient negotiation great advances had been made in the campaign to establish the artistic excellence of his collection. The Payne Knight view was now definitely on the defensive. Elgin's judicious republication of his *Memorandum*, with the letter from Visconti for which he had paid handsomely, had redressed the balance against the attacks of his enemies. The sale, on which depended all his hopes of private comfort as well as public vindication, seemed at last to be near. For the first time for many years the outlook was distinctly promising.

It was at this delicate juncture in his affairs that Elgin's reputation was struck a cruel and premeditated blow on a front that had so far not been attacked. His enemies chose their hour well. Their attack had nothing to do with the Elgin Marbles. In 1815 appeared a stout quarto volume, price three guineas, by the Reverend R. Tweddell, AM, under the apparently innocuous title of *Remains of John Tweddell, late fellow of Trinity College Cambridge, being a Selection of his Correspondence, a republication of his Prolusiones Juveniles, An Appendix containing some account of the Author's Collections, Mss, Drawings etc. and of their Extraordinary Disappearance, preceded by a Biographical Memoir of the Deceased, and illustrated with Portraits, Picturesque Views and Maps*. On the face of it this was just a work of piety to a dead brother, yet another of the travel books for which the Regency public seemed to have an insatiable appetite.

Tweddell's *Remains* was not all its title suggested. It contained an appendix of no less than 255 pages (over half the book) devoted entirely to accusations against the Earl of Elgin. The main charge was simple. Lord Elgin, it was alleged, had made use of his position as Ambassador at Constantinople to steal a large and valuable collection of drawings and journals which had belonged to John Tweddell. Other charges were thrown in, for example, that Elgin had neglected his ambassadorial duties and behaved in an arrogant and irresponsible way to the British residents at Constantinople and to travellers; that he had allowed his staff, in particular Philip Hunt, to plagiarize Tweddell's papers; that he himself intended to pass off Tweddell's drawings as the work of his own artists; and that he had so far met all inquiries with a prevarication of lies and contradictions to avoid having to give up the stolen property. For good measure it claimed that Elgin's Embassy had been quite unnecessary in any case since the treaty of alliance with Turkey and the opening of the Black Sea to the British flag had been agreed before he arrived.

An extract from the index of the *Remains* gives a clear idea of the tenor of the argument.

ELGIN (Earl of)

Mr. Tweddell's watch seen in his possession by Papa Simeon 440, 441, 450

Attached Mr. Tweddell's *Athenian drawings and Mss* in November 1799 without allowing Mr. J. S. Smythe to receive them notwithstanding they had been consigned to him 348

His officious interference with Mr. Smythe 356, 413

This interference stigmatised by the Levant Company as informal and illegal 586 note

Ordered Mr. Tweddell's *Athenian drawings and Mss* to be unpacked Jan. 26 1800 349

These drawings and Mss seen in Lord Elgin's palace at Pera by Mr. Barbaud 433

Also by the Comte de Ludolf 434, 435

And by Papa Simeon 440, 441

Ordered Mr. Thornton to deliver up Mr. Tweddell's *Mss and drawings relative to the Crimea and his tour in Switzerland etc* to himself 353, 432

And had them under his care 370, 415

They were seen in his possession *eight* months afterwards by Professor Carlyle 457, 458

At which time all Mr. Tweddell's Mss including the Tour to Switzerland were entire 353, 372, 374

And exactly in the state in which they had been left by Mr. Tweddell 382

Mr Tweddell's. trunks all in good condition when consigned by Mr. Thornton to the British Chancery at Constantinople 431

Was informed of their arrival in the British Chancery 431

But ordered no inventory to be taken of them ibid

Lord E. returned to Mr. Thornton Mr. Tweddell's trunks, which only contained wearing apparel 354, 374

And retained the drawings etc. 378, 413

So it goes on. The entry under Elgin alone in the Index runs to nearly four columns. Philip Hunt is treated equally severely.

Tweddell's *Remains* caused a first-class scandal. Almost every review (and this was a golden age of lengthy review articles) related Tweddell's story at great length, calling on Elgin to give an explanation. Most were openly hostile, making no secret of their belief in all that Tweddell claimed. 'The case is a strong one,' wrote the *Edinburgh Review*, 'In performing this . . . task, the Editor deserves almost unmingled praise.'[1] The *Christian Observer* concluded that 'if the impression which will be felt by all the readers of this work be unjust and unfounded, seldom has it fallen to the lot of a human being to be placed in a more cruel situation than the noble lord'.[2] The *New Monthly Magazine* went further. 'Most men of simple judgement and honest hearts will be apt to think that the spoliation of Athens and the loss of the Tweddell papers must be considered as a lamentable drawback on the national character.'[3] With one stroke Elgin's reputation fell deeper than it had ever been even in the first days of *Childe Harold's Pilgrimage*.

The story of John Tweddell's papers was a complex one. John Tweddell, a young man of exceptional academic promise, had set out alone in 1795 on the grandest of grand tours, intending to visit Switzerland, Germany, Russia, Turkey, the Holy Land, Egypt, and Greece. In the course of his tour he composed and collected a prodigious quantity of material—in the East alone 5 books of journals, 4 notebooks, 4 volumes of Greek inscriptions, 7 portfolios containing 364 drawings, 8 other books of drawings, and much more besides. He engaged Preaux, a painter who had once worked for Choiseul-Gouffier and later for Clarke, and kept him busy from dawn to dusk for many months. He had also bought some drawings from Fauvel. Without doubt he would in due course have produced the biggest and most learned of travel books, matching even Clarke in the mass of miscellaneous information he would have incorporated.

In 1799, after four years' steady work, he died of a fever in Athens. His friend Fauvel buried him in the Theseum hoping in the course of the digging to uncover the tomb of Theseus. Part of Tweddell's papers had been left at Constantinople in the possession of Thomas Thornton, a banker of the Levant Company, but they were largely destroyed in a fire that ravaged the city soon afterwards. The other part which was at Athens was sent by

Logotheti to John Spencer Smith, the British Minister, to be forwarded to Tweddell's heirs. Unfortunately the ship in which they
were sent was wrecked in the Sea of Marmara. Some boxes were
recovered but reached the chancery in a wet and damaged
condition.

Shortly after Tweddell's papers arrived, Lord Elgin reached
Constantinople to supersede Spencer Smith as British Minister and
the long period of bitterness between the two men began. Spencer Smith, as we have seen, refused absolutely to recognize Elgin's
authority and continued to behave exactly as if he were still British
Minister. Elgin struggled vainly to impose his authority until
Spencer Smith had eventually to be dismissed. When he heard
of the death of Tweddell (whom he had known at Berlin) Elgin
ordered his papers to be laid out in his cellar in an attempt to dry
them out, and Hunt and Carlyle were given the opportunity of
sorting them and salvaging what was still useful. Elgin then gave
orders that the recovered papers should be packed up and sent
home (at his own expense) to Tweddell's family in England.

Unfortunately here some mistake was made. The papers seem
never to have been properly packed or dispatched although both
Elgin and Hunt later recollected that they were sent in some merchant ship, whose name they could not remember. Some drawings
were certainly sent home by the hand of Mr Nisbet, the father of
Mary Elgin, when he returned from his visit to Turkey in 1801.

Spencer Smith as part of his feud with Elgin wrote to Tweddell's
family complaining of Elgin's interference but making no more
serious allegations. As a result of this letter Edward Daniel Clarke
('Eleusinian' Clarke who had captured the statue of Demeter)
undertook to make some inquiries on behalf of the family when he
started on his journey to the East. When he mentioned the subject
to Elgin in 1801, Elgin told him that the papers had been sent home.
When Clarke persisted with his questions, Elgin seems to have told
him to mind his own business.

Here the matter of Tweddell's papers rested for nearly ten years.
But Tweddell himself was not forgotten. The romantic theme of the
young scholar dying amongst the ruins of his beloved Athens
attracted the poets of the time.

> Such the fair pile where shrin'd in holy cell
> The slumb'ring ashes of the mighty dwell;
> Where Tweddell, youthful shade, to classic rest
> Sinks, like a wearied child, in science' breast.

So ran an Oxford prize poem on the Theseum.[4] Haygarth, too, could not resist the thought, in some of his less happy verses:

> Pause on the tomb of him who sleeps within,
> Fancy's fond hope, and Learning's fav'rite child,
> Accomplish'd Tweddell—but weep not, his death
> Was kind although untimely, for he rests
> Upon the shores to Taste and Genius dear.[5]

Tweddell's grave in the Theseum became a place of pilgrimage for the English travellers to Athens. Elgin himself went there in 1802 on his visit to Greece and told Lusieri to erect a suitable tombstone. He sent Lusieri a long Latin inscription but Lusieri had not much confidence in his patron's Latin grammar and sent it to Italy to be checked. But in 1810 he had still done nothing about committing it to marble.

In that year a number of English travellers were in Athens, including Lord Byron, and the question of Tweddell's tombstone was raised again. Byron's party had come armed with an eight-line Greek epitaph composed in Cambridge, but Lusicri was insistent that Lord Elgin's Latin version must have pride of place. He had obtained a suitable piece of marble from the Acropolis, sawn from the back of a slab of the frieze, and offered to allow Byron's party to carve their inscription on it under Lord Elgin's. But this offer was turned down and they decided to act independently of him. The Disdar offered to sell them a piece of marble from the Acropolis but Lusieri had the only cart capable of carrying it. After a search in the town they found a suitable piece and in two days' hard work dragged it to the Theseum. Lusieri had the only saws in the town capable of cutting the marble but, with Fauvel's help, they managed to hammer it smooth. After another week's work the inscription was cut and the completed tombstone installed in the Theseum. Lusieri had been beaten in the race but he persevered with his Latin inscription.

Soon there were two rival epitaphs over the bones of the unfortunate Tweddell.[6] Parts of Lusieri's version can still be seen (wrongly restored) in the wall of the English Church in Athens. Others were found in the excavations in the Agora. The Greek version seems to have disappeared in its entirety.[7]

The affair of Tweddell's papers had lain dormant from the death of their author in 1799 until 1810. In that year appeared the second edition of a book of reminiscences by Thomas Thornton, the Levant

Company banker at Constantinople, called *The Present State of Turkey*. It was a dull book, factious, quarrelsome, and inaccurate. Its main claim to be remembered is the stinging attack on it included by Lord Byron in his notes to *Childe Harold's Pilgrimage*. In making the usual eulogy to the memory of the lamented Tweddell, Thornton remarked that, if his papers had been collected by the hand of Friendship, they might have formed a monument to rescue his memory from unmerited oblivion. Thornton's book was reviewed anonymously in a journal, the *Naval Chronicle*, by John Spencer Smith, three years after it first appeared.[8] Smith, still nine years later smarting under the humiliation of his dismissal by Elgin, made some biting but mysterious observations about Elgin's part in the dispersal of Tweddell's papers, hinting that much more was known if only he and Thornton were prepared to speak out. In a footnote Smith gave away his identity and the source of his discontent by remarking on the scandal of replacing a Minister who had negotiated a treaty by an Ambassador-Extraordinary to ratify it.

Spencer Smith could hardly have guessed what he was unleashing. The article attracted the attention of Tweddell's brother, the Revd Robert Tweddell, and he decided to reopen the whole matter. The energy of the Reverend Robert was equal to that of the lamented John. He began by writing a polite, almost servile letter to Lord Elgin asking him to relate the circumstances of the loss of his brother's papers: he claimed that this was to help with a biography he was writing. When Elgin wrote, recounting what he could remember of the incident, Tweddell promptly wrote again asking for elucidation of certain points arising. When Elgin replied he wrote again for more, and by this procedure obtained a number of letters from his unwary victim. After six months Elgin's suspicions were aroused by a hint in one of Tweddell's letters and he asked for copies of the letters he had previously written. This was refused and the correspondence came to an abrupt end.[9]

Robert Tweddell adopted the same tactics towards Thornton, towards Philip Hunt, and towards a friend of Carlyle who might have been expected to contribute something. By this persistence he extracted a large number of letters containing the recollections of the various actors in an event nearly fourteen years old. He set to work on this material as if he were editing an ancient text, comparing and contrasting the various accounts, checking any points that could be confirmed by outside evidence, and documenting

every step with great care. Not unexpectedly, he uncovered numerous inconsistencies. He then engaged a lawyer to turn this mass of
evidence into a memorandum to the Levant Company. As a result the Levant Company in 1813 conducted its own investigation
on the spot in Constantinople. Another mass of documents was
produced and put into Tweddell's hands, copies of correspondence,
statements of witnesses, fragments of reminiscence, and titbits of
gossip. This second corpus was subjected to the same tendentious
scrutiny.

The man who lay behind the unusual diligence on the part of the
Levant Company was John Spencer Smith. Smith decided that here
was the opportunity for taking his revenge on Elgin that he had
long looked for. Through the instrument of the indefatigable
Tweddell, Spencer Smith could clear his own name of the stigma
of dismissal by disgracing Elgin. Tweddell's *Remains* bears unmis-
takable signs of his influence and direction, being full of irrelevant
panegyrics on Spencer Smith, long tedious dissertations about the
laws and usages of the Levant Company, and gratuitous information about how he had been hated by Napoleon. In an anonymous
review of the *Remains* in the *Naval Chronicle* Spencer Smith
boasted openly that he had been responsible for its publication.[10]
The whole affair was a full-scale conspiracy to defame Elgin
concocted by Spencer Smith and Tweddell. And the great Levant
Company connived more or less openly at this disgraceful and
underhand attack, no doubt reckoning that its ancient monopolis-
tic privileges could not survive many embassies like Elgin's.

Eleusinian Clarke, whose brother was editor of the *Naval
Chronicle*, soon joined the conspirators. In the volume of his en-
cyclopaedic *Travels* published in 1814 he wrote cryptically of John
Tweddell

That the literary property of this gentleman after being in the undisputed
possession of the British Ambassador at Constantinople should absolutely
have disappeared *in toto* and eluded the most diligent inquiries of his
family and friends presents a subject for the deepest regret, and is a circumstance of the most unaccountable nature. Upon this point, however,
the author refrains from saying all that he might in the expectation of
seeing this strange mystery unfolded by a kindred hand which may justly
aspire to the best information.[11]

In his next volume, published almost simultaneously with the
Remains, he went further, implying that the papers had been deliberately stolen.

Thus every doubt is done away as to this mysterious transaction. It is to be feared that if any other part of Mr. J. Tweddell's observations upon Greece ever see the light, it will only be in the garbled form of extracts made from his writings by those who had the ransacking of his papers which will be published, as perhaps they have been already, without any acknowledgement being made of their real author.[12]

An attempt was also made to enlist Byron, and Tweddell was nearly joined by those immortalized in the later editions of *Childe Harold's Pilgrimage*. Writing in 1813 about 'The Parthenon', an attack on Elgin in verse by James and Horace Smith, not, as far as is known, related to Spencer Smith, Byron suggested:

I wish I had the pleasure of Mr. S[mith]'s acquaintance as I could communicate the curious anecdote you read in Mr. T's letter. If he would like it, he can have the substance for his second edition; if not I shall add it to our next, although I think we already have enough of Lord E[lgin].[13]

'Mr. T.' we can confidently guess is the Reverend Robert Tweddell.

While Tweddell's *Remains* was being prepared for the press the conspirators indulged in some sniping in the reviews. In 1815 the *New Monthly Magazine* published an article by Hamilton, under the pseudonym Philalethes, which praised Elgin's efforts in saving Greek marbles from destruction. This produced a long, rambling, and obscure reply from 'T.' which concluded, 'I feel there is not a nobleman in England and but one in Scotland who has accomplished so much in some respects as the Earl of***** towards the depression of the arts "and I may add painting" in particular as also towards the suppression of literature.' Philalethes responded at once. 'Philalethes would be very much obliged if T. would have the goodness to put his observations on Lord Elgin's collection of marbles which appeared in your paper of 29 last into English or any other intelligible language in order that his meaning may be known and that his notions upon that subject which appear to be very confused may be set right.' T. replied with a quotation from Byron: 'The last the worst dull spoiler etc.'[14] It was not a constructive discussion and the meaning of the dark hint about suppression of painting was not disclosed.

Neither Hamilton nor Elgin guessed the identity of T. and they thus knew nothing of what Tweddell and Spencer Smith were preparing.[15] The publication of Tweddell's *Remains* at the most delicate stage of Elgin's negotiations for the sale of his marbles thus

came as a complete surprise to him. His first news of it came when
he read a review of it, praising Tweddell and condemning himself,
in the *Edinburgh Review*.

Stung with indignation at the unfairness of the article he could
not wait until he had seen the book itself before launching his
defence. He hurriedly composed a *Letter to the Editor of the
Edinburgh Review* and had it published in pamphlet form in
Edinburgh and London. In the *Letter* Elgin denied all the allegations. He was able to show from his own records that Tweddell had
suppressed a number of letters inconvenient to his side of the story;
that the importance of Tweddell's papers had been exaggerated;
and, so far from seizing them, he himself had acted properly and
generously throughout.

The *Letter* did something to restore the situation. As soon as he
had obtained a copy of Tweddell's *Remains* he followed it with a
Postscript to a Letter to the Editor of the Edinburgh Review which
he also published. This was a more formidable defence, demon-
strating, with great restraint, that Spencer Smith's animosity lay
behind the whole story and that it was largely through Spencer
Smith's negligence that the papers had been so badly damaged.
Elgin finished with a burst of indignation against the *Edinburgh
Review*, couched in his usual ponderous style.

If ever you shall again be tempted to trespass beyond your province and
to arraign the moral conduct of a private individual who has not even, as
an author, subjected himself to your jurisdiction; remember—and let the
recollection restrain you—that your pages must go where no answer or
refutation can follow them; and that, if you lend them to the gratification
of revenge and malignity—nay, even if you scatter firebrands and call it
sport,—your *Review* is the most intolerable nuisance that can exist in a
civilized country.[16]

Meanwhile, at Bedford, Philip Hunt, long estranged from Elgin,
was also stung to action. He began by writing to the *Christian
Observer* but soon he too felt obliged by the mounting tide of criticism and abuse to publish his own pamphlet.[17] *A Narrative of
What is Known Respecting the Literary Remains of the Late John
Tweddell* is also a convincing account. It did, however, have one
great weakness. Hunt now admitted, for the first time, that he had
copied some notes from Tweddell's journals, hoping they would be
useful on his visit to Greece. There was obviously no improper

intention in this and Hunt had made no secret of it at the time, but it did tend to support Tweddell's claims.

Within a few months of the first, a second edition of Tweddell's *Remains* appeared, greatly enlarged, in which the publications of Elgin and Hunt were subjected to the same nitpicking as their earlier letters. The scandal grew and with it the rumours. By the middle of 1816 the claims and counter-claims in the argument had become so complex and numerous that hardly anyone could have had the energy to take an objective view. Those who did take the trouble, for example they Tory *Quarterly Review*, which instinctively opposed its rival the Whig *Edinburgh*, were inclined to acquit Elgin of all the main charges.[18] But few men can afford to have their affairs paraded in such detail before the public and hope to escape unscathed.

Hunt's admissions caused great glee in the Tweddell camp, and even Elgin's explanations had some curious features.[19] Why, for example, had he not done more to exert his authority over Spencer Smith? Why was it Elgin seemed to have aroused the hostility of everyone he came in contact with in the Tweddell affair? For, almost without exception, Elgin had to admit sadly that all the main actors were now on bad terms with him or had been when they died—Spencer Smith of course, and Thornton, and Mr Nisbet his former father-in-law, but also Clarke, Philip Hunt, and Carlyle. Surely a man who made so many enemies must have something unpleasant about him?

The impression against Elgin seemed to be confirmed by a discovery arising from the dispute. Mr Nisbet uncovered a number of drawings in his home which he had brought back from Constantinople. On examination some of them turned out to have belonged to Tweddell. Mr Nisbet had brought them back but lacking instructions, or forgetting them, he had assumed they belonged to Elgin. When Elgin's marriage to his daughter broke up he forgot about them. The 'Elgin Box' containing the Tweddell drawings was opened in the presence of solicitors in November 1816 and the drawings delivered to Robert Tweddell. The Tweddell–Spencer Smith party were then able to hail this as a 'triumphant vindication' of all their claims and accusations.[20]

So this sterile and unsavoury affair came to an end. It had done untold harm to Elgin's reputation. Breaking out just at the crisis in his affairs when events at last seemed to be moving in his favour, it continued all through the negotiations for the sale of the Elgin

Marbles to the Government. Just what the effect was it is impossible to say, but surely it ruled out for ever the possibility of a British peerage on which Elgin had so long set his heart. For the conspirators it was sweet revenge.

21

The Fate of the Manuscripts

WHILE the Tweddell controversy was raging, another criticism of Lord Elgin's Embassy began to break through. This concerned the collection of ancient manuscripts which Professor Carlyle had brought back from the East in 1801.

As always the nose for scandal of Eleusinian Clarke led him early to the scene. In his 1816 volume of his *Travels*, he wrote in his usual sneering style that

as he has reason to believe that the *theft* of a Greek Manuscript which was committed in one of the monasteries [of Mount Athos] by persons who had seen Mr. Tweddell's Journals was owing to intelligence therein contained, he will not remain altogether silent as to the *fact*. The subsequent death of one who was principally concerned in that transaction, precludes the possibility of his communicating more upon this subject.[1]

Philip Hunt in his *Narrative* about Tweddell's *Remains* retorted brusquely,

If Dr. Clarke means to insinuate that any manuscript was taken by me from Mount Athos or elsewhere, I explicitly deny the charge. If the observation be meant to apply to my deceased friend, I beg leave to refer Dr. Clarke to the Archbishop of Canterbury's Library at Lambeth, in which all the Greek manuscripts he had procured in Turkey were deposited by his executrix after his decease.[2]

Nevertheless in this case Clarke did seem to have a point. It was well known that it was almost impossible to obtain any manuscripts legally from Greek monasteries. All alienation of Church property was forbidden unless with the authority of the Patriarch himself, or in some cases, of the local bishop. All Greek monks were bound by an oath, administered to them when they were first admitted, to preserve the property of their monastery, and it was largely because this rule had been rigidly enforced for hundreds of years that any property remained to them at all. If any manuscripts had come from Greek monasteries as a result of Elgin's Embassy, and it was undeniable that some had, then there was a case to answer that they had been obtained irregularly. Clarke was well qualified to speak of these matters since, in direct competition with Carlyle, he had himself brought home a collection of manuscripts which he sold to the Bodleian Library for £1,000.[3]

As always the consciousness of his own guilt did not hinder Clarke from condemning other people. He had, however, ferreted out only a small part of the story of the Carlyle manuscripts and an unimportant one. Had he known more he would no doubt have made more accusations. The story, as usual, was a complex one.

Professor Carlyle had been attached to Lord Elgin's Embassy by the Government for the specific purpose of looking for ancient manuscripts. Although he was unsuccessful in his main aim, that of discovering manuscripts of unknown classical Greek and Latin works, he did bring home, besides many Arabic manuscripts bought in the bazaars, thirty-seven ancient manuscripts, some of which were valuable for the study of the text of the New Testament.[4] They ranged in date from the tenth to the fifteenth century.

Carlyle obtained them in various ways. Six he brought from the monastery of St Saba near Jerusalem.[5] Four or five others came from the Library of the Patriarch of Jerusalem at Constantinople.[6] To none of these manuscripts did Carlyle have any legal title. They were lent to him, at his own insistent request, to allow them to be collated in England and to help with the production of a revised edition of the New Testament. Before he left Constantinople for the last time in March 1801 Carlyle signed a declaration prepared by the Patriarch promising to return the manuscripts to the Patriarch at Constantinople 'when the purposes for which they were borrowed were completed or whenever the Patriarch should demand them'.[7] Philip Hunt, as a secretary to the Embassy also signed the declaration, thus making the British government a party to the promise.

The remainder of the manuscripts which Carlyle brought to England were bought. Some were bought in the monasteries of the Princes Islands near Constantinople which Carlyle visited in the spring of 1800, sometimes with Hunt, sometimes by himself. The others were bought later that year when Carlyle and Hunt visited Mount Athos. Special techniques were found to circumvent the ecclesiastical rules. 'All *direct* offers of purchasing manuscripts', wrote Carlyle to the Bishop of Lincoln, 'must and will be rejected by these communities especially if they be made in too public a manner for, in this case, the rigid scruples of a few members will counteract the pliancy of the rest'. But there were other means.

It may not be difficult to procure cession of some of the old vellum books which lie neglected in an obscure chamber of the building, especially if the negotiation be conducted with that degree of secrecy and delicacy which is necessary to avoid the worldly consequences of such a measure and to furnish a casuistic argument for quieting the consciences of the more timid members of the community. The transaction, for instance, may be disguised under the form of an exchange of presents and the Manuscripts may be given and received as a trifling acknowledgement for a pecuniary donation to the Panagia. The above hints are applicable to most cases which will occur to a traveller who is in search of Greek Manuscripts, but they will occasionally prove superfluous for there are a few Monastic Communities in this country so sordidly immersed in ignorance and barbarity as to permit a traveller to pocket a Tetravangelion almost with as much indifference as if it were a bundle of waste paper.[8]

Carlyle's techniques for evading church rules had been used by travellers and monks for centuries before Carlyle, and were to be used long afterwards. They were a form of conspiracy to steal as was noted at the time.[9]

Carlyle returned home with his manuscripts in 1801 and resumed the quiet life of priest and scholar in which his adventures in the East had been a hard interlude. Although he had failed to make his fortune and had parted on bad terms with Elgin, his manuscripts turned out to be more useful than he had thought. 'I believe,' he wrote, 'they amount to near a tenth part of all mss of the new Testament that have yet been examined in Europe.'[10] It was therefore decided that, with their help, he should prepare a new edition of the New Testament. The Arabic version which was to help convert the heathen was to follow later. In addition he wanted to publish a book of verses and journals from the voluminous notes he had made during his travels.

For the New Testament edition, Carlyle gathered round him a number of scholars and clergymen and set them to work on the huge task of collation. To help them he had printed a memorandum entitled *Hints and Observations which Mr. Carlyle takes the liberty of suggesting to the consideration of the gentlemen who have kindly promised their assistance in collating the Greek Mss of the New Testament.*[11] This was a rough catalogue of part of the collection with some notes on where they had come from. Five were marked 'S' as coming from Syria; four marked 'C' for

Constantinople; and eighteen, 'I' for Princes Islands. The provenance of the others, which were manuscripts other than of the New Testament, was not identified. Carlyle mentioned in the *Hints* that some of the manuscripts belonged to the Patriarch, but, unfortunately, he did not make clear precisely which.

In April 1804, before the work of collation had gone far, Carlyle died. His heirs received a great disappointment. The journey to the East had made severe inroads into the Carlyle fortune and all there was to show for it was the collection of manuscripts. Carlyle's sister, Miss Carlyle, his executrix, immediately put in hand a posthumous edition of his poems and this was published, with a public subscription of some of the great names of the land (including Elgin and the Smiths), in 1805.[12] She also decided to sell the manuscripts.[13] The Arabic collection was sold to the East India Company and is still in the India Office Library. The others did not all belong entirely to Carlyle. Apart from those borrowed from the Patriarch, which Miss Carlyle identified as the four marked 'C', she knew that Philip Hunt had a claim on some of the others. When she wrote to Hunt, who was still in captivity in France, about how they should be disposed of, Hunt suggested depositing them with the Archbishop of Canterbury in the Library at Lambeth. Miss Carlyle then replied,

As to the manuscripts I think that as the survivor you have an undoubted right to dispose of those brought from Constantinople in any way you please; nor could you have fixed upon any place more agreeable to me to deposit mine in than under the patronage of the Archbishop of Canterbury.... It would give me great pain to separate what has cost us so dear to collect together. At the same time I do not conceive myself authorised to refuse any compensation for them which the Archbishop, after inspection, may think proper to make me. My brother, the day before he died, said to me that, as his unfortunate journey had been attended with a great pecuniary loss to his family, I must make what I could of his manuscripts for the benefit of his daughter.[14]

Hunt thereupon resigned all claim he might have had to any of the manuscripts and the whole collection was sold to the Archbishop, with the exception of one, a manuscript of Eutropius, which Miss Carlyle kept as a memento. The four manuscripts marked 'C' were not entered in the library catalogue since it was considered that they belonged to the Patriarch.

On his release from France, Hunt called on the Archbishop to tell him that he had given up his share and to remind him of his arrangement with the Patriarch. He did not specify which manuscripts were involved thinking that Miss Carlyle had been able to identify them. Shortly afterwards, he went to Ireland as secretary to the Duke of Bedford.

So the matter rested for nine years. The manuscripts lay at Lambeth admired by many although little work seems to have been done on them. Then in 1813 Hamilton at the Foreign Office received a letter from the British Ambassador at Constantinople saying that the Patriarch of Jerusalem had formally asked for his borrowed manuscripts to be returned. Hamilton, after some delay, referred the matter to Hunt, who immediately wrote to the Archbishop of Canterbury asking him to return the manuscripts to Constantinople. The Archbishop made no reply. Hunt wrote again, and wrote also to Hamilton, but two years passed and still nothing was done.

Then in June 1816 when the question of the Elgin Marbles still lay in the balance, and when the Tweddell affair was at its height, another, stiffer letter arrived from the British Embassy at Constantinople. The Ambassador declared that the 'National character suffers by this neglect and that the Patriarch looks on the transaction as a breach of confidence.'[15] This time the charge of theft levelled at Lord Elgin's Embassy was fully justified.

When he heard of the second letter from Constantinople Hunt immediately called on the Archbishop again to tell him that the manuscripts must be returned. At long last some action was taken, but soon another difficulty arose. The Archbishop had thought that only the four manuscripts marked 'C' belonged to the Patriarch: but the Patriarch's request was for no less than eleven. Contrary to what Hunt had presumed, but not checked, in 1805 there was no sure way of telling which belonged to the Patriarch, and Miss Carlyle had made the assumption most favourable to herself. An attempt was now made to find the Patriarch's missing manuscripts.

The Patriarch asked for two copies of the Gospels, three copies of the Acts, and a Libanius, all from St Saba; and two Gospels, two Psalters, and a Eutropius from his library at Constantinople. The Libanius and the Eutropius were easily picked out, and there were only two Psalters in the whole collection so it was assumed they must be his: the four marked 'C' consisted of three Gospels and one Acts and they were also clearly his. This left one more Gospels and two more Acts to be found. Since the only Acts remaining were in the series marked 'I' meaning bought in the Princes Islands it was assumed that Carlyle must have made a mistake. One of the Acts and two of the Gospels were, therefore, taken from the 'I' series. So the numbers were made up to the eleven the Patriarch had asked for. In 1817, after Miss Carlyle had paid back the Archbishop for the manuscripts he was returning, these eleven manuscripts were delivered at the Foreign Office for sending on to Constantinople. This complicated incident at last came to an end with little credit to anybody.

It seems certain that the wrong manuscripts were sent. Although Carlyle had been careless about marking the manuscripts not containing the New Testament, in his *Hints* he had been quite specific about those which did—the ones that were to be farmed out to scholars for collation. His cataloguing was as follows:

'S' for Syria: i.e. borrowed from St Saba   2 Gospels
'C' for Constantinople   3 Acts and Epistles
   3 Gospels
   1 Acts.[16]

The Patriarch's request was for:
From St Saba   2 Gospels
   3 Acts
   Libanius
From Constantinople   2 Gospels
   Eutropius.[17]

If we exclude the non-New Testament manuscripts excluded from Carlyle's catalogue the two are remarkably similar. For the manuscripts from St Saba we also have the evidence of one of Carlyle's letters to the Bishop of Durham of July 1800. 'I was permitted to bring away with me to Constantinople six of what I judged to be the most curious Mss—viz two of the oldest copies of the Gospels and only one of the Epistles and Acts; two copies of Apostolic letters, and a copy of Libanius.'[18] The lists for St Saba thus coincide exactly. One would have thought that Hunt and the Archbishop would have seen that Carlyle intended all marked 'S' to be returned to St Saba. As for the others Carlyle was more likely to be right than the Patriarch. He kept such detailed journals of every day's events as to be a joke among his friends and it is easy to believe that he was permitted to borrow a few more manuscripts after the agreement with the Patriarch was drawn up.[19]

The Archbishop ought to have returned (at least):

1. The five manuscripts marked 'S'
2. The four marked 'C'
3. The two Psalters
4. The Libanius
5. The Eutropius.

Instead he returned:

1. Three marked 'I'
2. The four marked 'C'
3. The two Psalters
4. The Libanius
5. The Eutropius.

The five manuscripts from St Saba, all vary valuable, are still at Lambeth. Perhaps if he could find the three from the Princes Islands which are not strictly his, the Patriarch of Jerusalem might still reclaim them.

Lord Elgin was only indirectly concerned with the affair of Carlyle's Greek manuscripts. Most of the blame for the carelessness which was undoubtedly shown throughout fell, rightly, on Carlyle and Hunt, Miss Carlyle, and the Archbishop of Canterbury. One would be surprised, nevertheless, if some members of the Government and others who knew the long sad story did not hold Elgin responsible for at least some of the muddle.

22

The Marbles are Sold

As soon as the new Parliamentary session began in February 1816, Lord Elgin again presented his *Petition* asking the House of Commons to appoint a Select Committee. He asked again that the Committee should investigate the circumstances in which he had obtained the collection and advise on whether, and on what terms, it should be sold to the Government.[1]

The Petition was debated on 23 February.[2] The Chancellor of the Exchequer, on behalf of the Government, proposed to accept it. 'It was certainly one of the most wonderful events of the day', he was reported as saying, 'that the works of Phidias should become the property of a native of Caledonia. The desire of conferring honour on the arts as well as on the arms of this country was the object of his motion; for, of all the arts, sculpture was at present the least flourishing in England.' Eleven other speakers took part in the debate. Several spoke of the value of the collection but the House was by no means inclined to accept the proposal without reservation. Several members queried whether Lord Elgin had been right to use his position of ambassador to acquire the collection, and one was concerned that 'if ambassadors were encouraged to make these speculations, many might return in the character of merchants'. The cries of 'spoliation' which owed much to Byron were repeated.

Lord Brougham, a prominent contributor to the *Edinburgh Review*, attacked the proposal on grounds of economy. If there was public money available to be spent, he said, it should go towards alleviating the distress of men discharged from the Navy. If the country could not afford to 'give them bread, we ought not to indulge ourselves in the purchase of stones'. He had a point. After the victories, hundreds of thousands of men were discharged from the Navy and later the Army without any support. It was a time when the climate in Britain was the most severe since the 1690s.[3] A cloud of volcanic dust settled in the upper atmosphere giving rise to the wonderful orange sunsets painted by Turner and perhaps adding to the romantic vision of the Acropolis of Athens as bathed in a warm golden evening glow.[4] All over Northern Europe the glaciers advanced, the sea froze, the summer came late and ended early, and harvests failed. The price of bread, the main component of the cost of living, was at its highest level ever in real terms in the history of British bread.

After two divisions, Lord Elgin's petition was agreed to, and a Select Committee was appointed. It consisted of eighteen MPs of all shades of opinion. Among the members were the Chancellor of the Exchequer and Charles Long, who had played an important part in the earlier negotiations. There were two Members of Parliament who knew Greece well, F. S. N. Douglas, who had written a book which included an attack on Elgin, and J. H. Fazakerley, who had been concerned with Cockerell in the affair of the Aegina Marbles.

The Select Committee began its hearings on 29 February with a two-day examination of Lord Elgin.[5] On the first day, in answer to a series of questions, Elgin recounted in simple straightforward terms, the now familiar story of how, before he had left England, the idea had been suggested to him of helping the arts of his country; how the Government had refused to help and he had gone ahead at his own expense; and how, when he saw the great destruction being perpetrated at Athens, he had obtained a firman allowing him to rescue everything that he could. The Committee pressed him about the exact legal authority for his operations, how far the French were involved in similar schemes, and how far his position as ambassador had been responsible for his extraordinary privileges. The questioning was thorough and fair. To every question Lord Elgin was able to give honest and convincing answers.

In the course of his examination about the activities of the Comte de Choiseul-Gouffier, Elgin told the story of how Choiseul-Gouffier's metope had come into his possession through an accident of war, and how he had recently offered to give back all antiquities that once belonged to Choiseul-Gouffier. He made it clear that he still wanted to give them back. 'He has never yet sent about them,' Elgin said, 'and I do not know what he means to do at all; but there they are, marked among my things as belonging to him.'[6]

The next day Elgin was asked about the expense of making his collection. He began by presenting several documents which he had prepared for the Committee's consideration to help settle certain questions that had been raised. They included a memorandum which argued forcefully, from examples such as that of Sir William Hamilton and his collection, that the Elgin Marbles belonged exclusively to Lord Elgin despite his having been an ambassador at the time they were collected, a copy of the letter which had formed the basis for negotiations in 1811, and a letter explaining in mild terms the hostility he had endured from the Dilettanti Society ever since 1806. He also presented a long letter setting out his estimate of the expenses he had incurred.[7]

In the negotiations of 1811 Elgin had assessed his expenditure to date at £62,440. He now added the money that had been spent since that time, emphasizing that about eighty more cases of marbles had since arrived at Burlington House. For the later years in Greece Elgin was able to produce detailed accounts. They showed that, despite his precarious financial state, he had not skimped. Presents to the authorities in Athens, for example, between 1803 and 1815 amounted to over £6,000. The interest rate paid at Malta on the large sums borrowed there was 17.75 per cent. The grand total of expenditure was £74,240. In submitting this enormous figure to the committee, Elgin observed,

I beg once more to repeat, that I do not offer this view of my expenses as a criterion of the intrinsic value of my Collection. I ever have been persuaded that, in justice to the Public, that should be calculated on other grounds. But it is, I trust, sufficient to prove, that in amassing these remains of antiquity for the benefit of my Country, and in rescuing them from the imminent and unavoidable destruction with which they were threatened, had they been left many years longer the prey of mischievous Turks, who mutilated them for wanton amusement, or for the purpose of selling them piecemeal to occasional travellers; I have been actuated by no motives of private emolument; nor deterred from doing what I felt to be a substantial good, by considerations of personal risk, or the fear of calumnious misrepresentations.[8]

From one who had suffered much, it was a dignified defence. If the test of a man's enthusiasm is the price he is willing to pay, then Lord Elgin had certainly established his bona fides. The figures also disposed of another point. At various times Elgin had offered to cede at least part of the collection free to the British government, asking only for his expenses. With expenses like these it was cheaper to buy the marbles than to accept them as a free gift.

The next major witness was William Richard Hamilton, loyal as always to Lord Elgin's cause, but universally respected as a man of standing in his own right, especially after his part in the negotiations for the return of works of art from Paris. Hamilton was able to confirm almost all of Elgin's story from his own experience and had checked other parts from the Foreign Office files. When he was asked his opinion about the value of the Elgin Marbles, he quoted the example of the Aegina marbles which had been sold for £6,000 and the Phigaleian marbles which had cost £19,000, and then made a comparative valuation of the Elgin collection. The principal parts of the pediment he put at £4,000 each, the metopes at £10,000 altogether, and the frieze at £400 a piece. The total value of the collection according to Hamilton was £60,000.

At the beginning of the next week the Committee took evidence on the artistic value of the collection. All the eminent sculptors of the day were called in, the aged Nollekens, Flaxman, Westmacott, Chantry, and Rossi, and two famous painters, Sir Thomas Lawrence and Benjamin West, although the latter was too ill to attend and sent his answers in writing.

To all the artists the Committee put the same general questions—in what class of art did they place the Elgin Marbles? Were they as good as the Apollo Belvedere, the Laocoon, and the other masterpieces of Italy? Did they have more 'Ideal Beauty'? Did the close imitation of nature which the marbles showed detract from their excellence? Were they less valuable for not having been restored? Behind these questions lay the assumptions of the day, the view that true classical art was idealized, that it not conform closely with nature. Their aesthetic was that of Winckelmann, of the Dilettanti, of the great English collectors before Elgin, of Byron, and (until they had actually seen the Elgin Marbles) of Canova and Visconti. It was the taste of men taught to regard the restored Graeco-Roman statues of Italy as the finest remaining works of antiquity.

The answers of the artists, all of whom had been educated in the same tradition, showed that, in a few short years, the Elgin Marbles had already transformed their appreciation. These large mutilated marbles with the intimate knowledge of anatomy that they revealed had set an entirely new standard in ancient art. The artists answered in their different characteristic ways and some offered reservations, but on the main points, they spoke with one voice. The Elgin Marbles, said Nollekens, were 'the finest things that ever came to this country'.[9] 'The finest works of art I have ever seen', said Flaxman.[10] 'Infinitely superior to the Apollo Belvedere', said Westmacott, because they have 'all the essence of style with all the truth of nature; the Apollo is more an ideal figure'.[11] 'There is in them', said Lawrence, 'an union of fine composition and very grand form, with a more true and natural expression of the effect of action upon the human frame than there is in the Apollo or in any of the other most celebrated statues.'[12] All the artists agreed that it was right that the Elgin Marbles had not been restored, and that for the nation to acquire them would lead to great improvement in the arts in Great Britain. Unfortunately for Elgin, none of the artists felt it was his place to put a monetary figure on the value of the collection: that was a job for the patrons, not for the artists they employed.

After the artists came the connoisseurs. Richard Payne Knight, still regarded as the foremost authority in the country, was asked more questions than any other witness except for Elgin himself. His performance was a dismal one. Not only did he try, helplessly, to maintain the old-fashioned artistic criteria which the artists had so decisively rejected, but his hostility to Elgin and his deep-seated prejudices shone through. From the beginning his answers were unenthusiastic and supercilious.

Are you acquainted with the Elgin Collection—Yes: I have looked them over, not only formerly, but I have looked them over on this occasion with reference to their value.

In what class of art do you place the finest works in this Collection?—I think of things extant, I should put them in the second rank—some of them; they are very unequal; the finest I should put in the second rank.

Do you think that none of them rank in the first class of art?—Not with the Laocoon and the Apollo and these which have been placed in the first class of art; at the same time I must observe, that their state of preservation is such I cannot form a vary accurate notion; their surface is gone mostly.

Do you consider them to be of a very high antiquity?—We know from the authority of Plutarch that those of the Temple of Minerva, which are the principal, were executed by Callicrates and Ictinus, and their assistants and scholars; and I think some were added in the time of Hadrian, from the style of them. . . .

In what class do you rank the fragments of the draped female figures?— They are so mutilated I can hardly tell, but I should think most of them were added by Hadrian: they are so mutilated I cannot say much about them: they are but of little value except from their local interest, from having been part of the Temple.[13]

The Committee asked him to substantiate his opinion that most of the sculptures were added by Hadrian. He replied:

From no other authority than Spon and Wheler having thought one of the heads to be of that Emperor, and later travellers having found no symbols of deity upon it; also from the draped trunks, which seem to be of that complicated and stringy kind of work which was then in fashion; that is a mere matter of opinion; there is no authority as to the time when particular articles were made.

When pressed to explain in greater detail the evidence of Spon and Wheler, of Nointel, and of Stuart and Revett, and the others who had investigated the Hadrian story Knight had to admit that he had not looked at the books recently. When asked to identify the figures which Spon and Wheler had thought Hadrianic, the only direct piece of evidence for the damaging story which he had done his best to spread for ten years, he could only admit:

I can give no opinion on this point, having misunderstood Lord Aberdeen, from whose conversation I had formed an opinion.

Payne Knight, faced with even the simplest questions, came across as ill-prepared, unscholarly, arrogant, and bumbling.

From his answer to the first question, it was obvious that Payne Knight was keen to pronounce on the value of the collection. When eventually he was asked, he delivered a paper to the Committee in which a figure was put against the main items of the collection. The two large recumbent figures from the pediment he put at £1,500 each. The total for the frieze £5,000; for the metopes £7,000. The Caryatid and the horse's head of the chariot of the waning moon he put at £200 and £250 respectively, but suggested £300 for a granite Egyptian beetle that had somehow become mixed up with the Greek sculptures, and £500 for a coarse, undistinguished, sarcophagus.[14] He went on to suggest more for the architectural fragments, and even for unadorned blocks of marble and porphyry, than for the sculptures themselves.

Three capitals and part of a column from the same Temple [i.e. the Parthenon]	£500
Various shafts and blocks of marble	£350
Do. of Porphyry	£350

Payne Knight's grand total was £25,000 for the whole collection, which, he said, was far more than twice what they would fetch on the open market. The scale of values which this estimate revealed, insulting though it was to Lord Elgin, was allowed to pass by the Committee. But he did not go completely unscathed.

After Payne Knight came two more witnesses who were generally expected to support his line. William Wilkins, the architect,
admitted that the marbles had some merit but was unenthusiastic.
The most he would say was that they helped to show off the architecture. Lord Aberdeen, however, to everyone's surprise, took a different line and admitted that the marbles were 'extremely valuable'
and almost certainly of the time of Phidias. He refused, however,
to admit it was possible to judge the excellence of the work by
examining the sculptures alone. Like Payne Knight he declared that
the surface was too corroded to allow a judgement and he timidly
based all his aesthetic appreciation on the testimony of the ancient
authors. Apart from Hamilton and Payne Knight, Lord Aberdeen
was the only witness who ventured to put a monetary value on the
collection. He suggested £35,000 for the whole, refusing to break
the figure down into individual items.

Besides taking evidence on the artistic merit of the marbles, the
Select Committee made many inquiries into the conditions prevailing at Athens when they were collected. Wilkins and Lord
Aberdeen, who had both been in Athens while the removals were
taking place, were able to confirm that all the monuments were
being damaged by the Turks, by the French, and by other travellers.
Aberdeen said nothing about his own contribution to the dispersal
of the Parthenon sculptures. Another witness, John Morritt, admitted frankly that, when he had been in Athens in 1795, he had bribed
the Disdar to allow him to take some pieces of the frieze and a
metope but had been prevented by Fauvel. John Fazakerley, himself
a member of the Committee, told the story of the Aegina marbles.
Finally Philip Hunt, who happened to be in London on other business, was called in unexpectedly and was able to confirm Elgin's
story in all its main particulars and to add to it. He later produced
the copy of the translation of the second firman which he had kept
in his possession after his break with Elgin and sent it to the
Committee.[15]

After two weeks of examining witnesses, the sittings of the Select
Committee came to an end. Throughout the hearings Benjamin
Haydon had stood patiently by, waiting to be called. Elgin obtained
a promise that he would be called but he was not asked for his view,
a decision he put down to their fear of offending Payne Knight.[16]
When the sittings came to an end, Haydon, passionate as always,
could not restrain himself. Three days after the Committee rose, a
long letter signed by him appeared in *The Examiner* and other

newspapers, entitled *On the Judgment of Connoisseurs being preferred to that of Professional Men*.[17] It was a savage indictment of
the Select Committee's work, written, said Haydon, in the fear that
they would be influenced by the opinion of Payne Knight and the
connoisseurs rather than by artists.

In no other profession is the opinion of the man who has studied it for his
amusement preferred to that of him who has devoted his soul to excel in
it. No man will trust his limb to a connoisseur in surgery; no minister would
ask a connoisseur in war how a campaign is to be conducted; no nobleman
would be satisfied with the opinion of a connoisseur in law on disputed
property; and why should a connoisseur of an art, more exlusively than any
other without the reach of common acquirement be preferred to the professional man?

Haydon drew his own excited picture of the overwhelming excellence of the marbles and of Payne Knight's earlier attempts to dis-
parage them.

These are the productions which Mr. Payne Knight says may be original!
May be! There are some men who have that hateful propensity of sneering at all which the world holds high, sacred or beautiful; not with the view
of dissipating doubt, or giving the delightful comfort of conviction, but to
excite mysterious belief of their own sagacity, to cloak their own envy, to
chuckle if they can confuse, and revel if they can chill the feelings: according to them love is nothing but lust; religion is nothing but delusion; all
high views and elevated notions, wild dreams and distempered fancies.

Haydon's article was widely reported as were numerous replies
and rejoinders. It was translated into several European languages.[18]
Haydon for a time enjoyed the reputation of a fiery rebel. The
sculptors and artists who had modestly declined to value the Elgin
Marbles were put to shame. Perhaps artists, if not quite independent creative geniuses as romanticism wished to see them, were
more than mere trade craftsmen after all.

The Select Committee's Report was soon prepared. Apart from
a passage proving the authenticity of the marbles from ancient and
modern authors, it was a short but comprehensive document. It
examined Lord Elgin's claims in four parts, first, the authority by
which the collection was acquired, secondly, the circumstances in
which the authority was granted, thirdly, the merit of the marbles
as works of art and their prospects of promoting the fine arts in
Great Britain, and lastly, their value as objects of sale. With all parts
except the last, Lord Elgin had every reason to be satisfied. The

Report, without giving any explicit endorsement, vindicated him from the main charges of illegality, misuse of ambassadorial powers, unnecessary damage to the monuments, desire to make money, and other accusations that had been levelled against him.[19] Its narrative of the circumstances in which the collection was obtained was almost a précis of Elgin's own *Memorandum on the Subject of the Earl of Elgin's Pursuits in Greece.*

The Report became almost lyrical about the improvements to the arts that could be expected if the marbles were bought. Elgin's only cause for complaint was the price recommended for the marbles. After considering recent sales of Greek sculpture, Elgin's expenses, and the likely market elsewhere, the Select Committee recommended £35,000 for the collection, the figure named by Lord Aberdeen. The Committee recognized that this represented less than half Elgin's expenses, and was only £5,000 above the figure refused in 1811 before the second collection arrived. They tried to soften these apparent illogicalities by pointing to the change in the value of money since then.

The full version of the Select Committee's Report, including a verbatim report of the replies of witnesses, became available to the public early in April.[20] Payne Knight's reputation as a connoisseur was instantly and finally destroyed. He was severely attacked in the press, and although he attempted to defend himself by replies, he now stood convicted by his own evidence.[21] The *Examiner* composed a ditty on the evidence of the connoisseurs to the Select Committee:

> Nay some, unconscious of remorse,
> Prefer a Beetle to a Horse,
> > And worship Egypt's models,
> Composed throughout of granite rare
> In substance hard, in outline square,
> > The type of their own noddles.
> Envelop'd by the shades of *Knight*
> Still must Athenian genius bright,
> > Be doom'd to shine unseen;
> To shew the depth of Art's rich mines
> No northern light from Glasgow shines
> > Nor yet from *Aberdeen.*[22]

In a less playful comment the *Examiner* exposed the pettiness of the Dilettanti. 'The great cause of all the animosity against Lord Elgin arose chiefly from the mean passions of collectors. . . . their vanity was deeply wounded at the prospect of a new era being effected in Art by works too dirty for their drawing-rooms.'[23] At the Royal Academy the talk among the triumphant artists was all about Payne Knight's downfall. 'It was gratifying to us,' wrote Farington, 'to see that Mr. Payne Knight had so fully and publicly committed himself in the opinion he gave of the Elgin Marbles. . . . Thus will the judgement ignorance of this presumptuous connoisseur be recorded.'[24] The Academy decided immediately to omit Payne Knight's name from its list of invitations that year.[25]

Haydon, certain in his own mind that he had been responsible for the recognition of the Elgin Marbles, filled his diary with accusations against the Select Committee and contempt for their judgement.[26] His earlier prophecy was now to be soon fulfilled.

Remember, Mr. Payne Knight, the fame of the Elgin Marbles will encrease with our knowledge and treble with time. Remember that, when all thy works are sunk into oblivion . . . thou wilt be only recollected by thy presumption in disbelieving their beauty.[27]

Lord Elgin, severely disappointed at the price offered, decided after some hesitation that he had no alternative but to accept.[28] The Government accordingly applied to Parliament for the sum of £35,000 to be voted.

The debate took place on 7 June 1816.[29] With the Select Committee's Report now available to the House the standard of debate was higher than in the earlier discussion, but still the old charges of spoliation and breach of ambassadorial duty by bribery were freely made. Lord Elgin's case was ably put by the Government and by some other members who pointed out the risks of the collection being broken up and sold piece by piece or sold abroad to some foreign prince who would value them. Despite the Government's support, the motion voting the money was passed by the narrowest of majorities, 82 to 80.

A cartoon by Cruikshank, reproduced as Plate 10, shows a long-nosed Lord Elgin persuading a starving John Bull to buy his stones. 'Here's a Bargain for you, Johnny? Only *£35,000*!! I have bought them on purpose for you! Never think of **Bread** when you can have **Stones** so wondrous cheap!!' The advertisement on the wall is a reference to Elgin's *Memorandum* 'Just Published. Speculation!! or Travels in the east in search of ruinous fragments of stone for John Bull by Lord Elgin.' On the ground are papers noting the extravagance of expenditure for the royal family, the increases in taxes, and the price of bread.

An interesting contribution to the debate, in view of the later history of the Elgin Marbles controversy, was a proposal by a Mr Hugh Hammersley. 'It was to be regretted,' he said, 'that the government had not restrained this act of spoliation; but, as it had been committed, we should exert ourselves to wipe off the stain, and not place in our museum a monument of our disgrace, but at once return the bribe which our ambassador had received, to his own dishonour and that of the country.' Hammersley proposed an amendment which, after a long preamble, read:

This committee, therefore, feels justified, under the particular circumstances of the case, in recommending that £25,000 be offered to the earl of Elgin for the collection in order to recover and keep it together for that government from which it has been improperly taken, and to which this committee is of opinion that a communication should be immediately made, stating that Great Britain holds these marbles only in trust till they are demanded by the present, or any future, possessors of the city of Athens; and upon such demand, engages, without question or negociation, to restore them, as far as can be effected, to the places from whence they were taken, and that they shall be in the mean time carefully preserved in the British Museum.

Greece, Catherine the Great had suggested, might one day be liberated from Ottoman rule by a Russian invasion and it was this possible future Russian government which Hammersley had in mind. As was pointed out in the debate, it would be odd to hold the marbles in trust to reward some future conquering invader to encourage his ambitions and reward his aggression.

In due course an Act of Parliament was passed transferring the ownership of the Elgin Marbles to the nation.[30] By the terms of the Act, Lord Elgin and his heirs were to be trustees of the British Museum, a privilege which they enjoyed until 1963. Of the £35,000 the Government immediately claimed £18,000 in payment for a debt which one of Elgin's creditors had shrewdly succeeded in transferring to them.[31] The remainder was quickly disbursed to other creditors. In August the Elgin Marbles were moved to the British Museum where a temporary structure had been built to receive them. At long last Elgin was free of the fateful marbles which had hung round his neck for over ten years and had been the ruin of his life.

The relief was partial only. Elgin's honour had been officially vindicated but he still was deep in debt. He still had no prospect of renewing his public career. A few months after the controversy over the marbles had died down, Elgin reverted to a familiar theme. He wrote a long and detailed letter to the Prime Minister relating, blow by blow, the disasters that had fallen on his innocent head, and imploring him to grant him a British peerage.[32] The letter makes sorry reading. He was just about to return in triumph from Constantinople in 1803, he said, when suddenly he was seized in France and 'persecuted with the most vindictive animosity' by Bonaparte.

It was while suffering under these severities and separated from all but the most constrained communications from my family in England, that the foulest and most insidious intrigue was darkly at work here, preparing the ruin of my domestic peace, creating prepossessions in regard to my official conduct, which however I had subsequently the good fortune to remove at least from Mr. Perceval's mind: nor were the true motives of this undefined, unavowed, yet most injurious, persecution brought home to its real source in disappointment and jealousy till Mr. Spencer Smith, finding a willing instrument in Mr. Tweddle to distort one of the most ordinary incidents in foreign stations, could not refrain from standing prominently forward in the publications that then appeared against me. And presuming upon the ill will against my operations in Greece in which some late travellers had indulged, he actually transmitted anonymous abuse against me to the newspapers at the moment when the House of Commons was entering upon the subject of my marbles; one of which attacks in Mr. Spencer Smith's handwriting is now in my possession.

The Prime Minister may have sympathized, but there was no peerage. He had got the money but he had been only partially vindicated.

After the transfer of the marbles Lord Elgin returned once more to the quiet life of Broomhall and to his ever growing family. He devoted himself patiently to the development of his estates in an attempt to relieve the huge debts which still encumbered them. His claim for expenses for his Embassy Extraordinary to Constantinople was not finally brought to account until 1818. Instead of the expected substantial addition to the £10,000 granted in 1806, the Government, to Elgin's consternation, calculated that he had been overpaid and successfully reclaimed £38. 11s. 11d.[33] His army half-pay went entirely to paying arrears of the Elgin Fencibles long since disbanded. All Elgin had to live on was a Foreign Office

pension. Oblivious to the irony he even wrote and published a treatise *On the Present State of Pauperism in Scotland.*

In 1817 news came from France that his old friend and rival, the
Comte de Choiseul-Gouffier, had died. For the final time the question arose of the ownership of the metope which Elgin had accidentally obtained at the Customs House sale in 1806. Elgin had
deposited it with the rest of the collection in the British Museum
but it was accepted on all sides that Choiseul-Gouffier could have
it back for the asking. He had not reclaimed it before he died. In
1818 it was claimed by his heirs but the Trustees of the British
Museum decided that Elgin's offer to Choiseul-Gouffier had rested
on personal friendship alone and did not extend to his heirs. The
claim was rejected.[34]

Choiseul-Gouffier's heirs decided to sell his collection of Greek
antiquities including the other metope which Choiseul-Gouffier
had obtained from Fauvel in 1788. The British Museum bought
several pieces but were unable to secure the metope, which was
bought by the Louvre for 25,000 francs, the only piece of sculpture
from the Parthenon which they had other than the piece of frieze
that Bonaparte had confiscated from Choiseul-Gouffier. Unfortunately the generosity towards Lord Elgin which had character-
ized Choiseul-Gouffier despite their rivalry did not descend to his
heirs. They filled their published account of his collection with lies
and accusations against Elgin which Choiseul-Gouffier would
never have allowed.[35] Yet a curious accident turned this incident to
Elgin's advantage. Although Elgin was then a trustee he refused to
take any part in the publication of his former collection. The British
Museum Catalogue of the Elgin metopes, published in 1835, by
confusing the history of the two metopes, invented a pleasing story.

The fourteenth [metope] had been previously removed by Monsieur le
Comte de Choiseul Gouffier, and having been captured on its way to
France, was purchased at a Custom House sale in London by Lord Elgin,
and with a liberality, of which it is to be lamented there are so few examples, was restored to its former owner. After the death of M. Choiseul, it
was purchased by the French Museum against a strong competition from
the British Government for the sum of twenty-five thousand francs or
about one thousand guineas.[36]

This fictitious tale with the seeming authority of the British
Museum behind it, entered the Elgin story and was repeated in
several accounts until exposed by A. H. Smith in 1916.[37] By this

curious accident the memory of Elgin's generosity to Choiseul-Gouffier, which was indeed great, was preserved.

Meanwhile Lusieri continued in Athens at Lord Elgin's expense. His work had long since been virtually abandoned not only because of his natural laziness but also because he was increasingly afflicted by rheumatism. Perhaps because he knew the effects of this disease so well himself, Elgin was unwilling to terminate Lusieri's contract although reports from travellers were far from encouraging. He himself planned to go again to Greece but never carried out his intention. In 1817 the British Ambassador at Constantinople told Elgin that the ugly pillar which had been built to replace the Caryatid of the Erechtheion was still causing offence and suggested that a plaster copy of the original should be sent to replace the pillar. Elgin readily agreed, but a copy of artificial stone had already been sent by Lord Guildford.[38] When it arrived in Athens the Turks declared that it was the original Caryatid returned to its place because it could not be made to stand erect in England.[39] It was never put on the building. Travellers went to see its broken pieces lying abandoned in a yard and deduced, against all the evidence, that the Turks and the Greeks cared so much for their monuments that they were too proud to accept mere substitutes.[40]

Although a few more antiquities continued to arrive from Lusieri, including a case of 610 Greek vases, Elgin decided in the middle of 1819 that he could not afford to support Lusieri any longer. He wrote him a sad letter asking him to put his accounts in order and to arrange the drawings he had made.[41] Yet, what with the delays in correspondence and difficulties in reconciling accounts, Lusieri managed to put off the evil day. Hamilton, who had followed his more famous namesake as Minister to Naples, attempted to arrange a personal meeting with him to discuss the final winding-up of the artistic mission, but nearly two years passed and nothing was achieved. Lord Elgin, despite his own financial difficulties, could not bring himself to cast off the old man who had once served him so well. Then suddenly on 1 March 1821 Lusieri was found dead in his house, surrounded by his unfinished drawings.[42] He had been in Lord Elgin's service for nearly twenty-two years.

Lusieri was buried in the grounds of the Capuchin Convent and the English colony at Athens subscribed to erect a marble monument to him. It can still be seen alongside the tombstone he had carved for John Tweddell, in the wall of the English Church at

Athens. Within a few years Greek indignation against Lord Elgin's activities had grown so great that the following tale was recorded by a credulous English traveller:

Signor Lusieri . . . died by the breaking of a blood-vessel. The feeling of the people ran so high against him that he thought it necessary to barricade his home at night, particularly as he lived quite alone. The day of his death, the neighbourhood, surprised at his non-appearance, forced the door, and found him extended on the floor, his blood about him, and a huge black cat seated on his breast, which the people to this day believe to have been the avenging spirit, the punisher of his crimes, or else the form assumed by his own black soul; according to this latter notion, the animal was instantly killed.[43]

In the contract signed with Elgin in Sicily in 1799 Lusieri had agreed that all his drawings and sketches should be the property of his patron. When he died he had completed only two drawings— one of the Parthenon and one of the Monument of Philopappos: innumerable others were in various stages of completion. The picture of the Monument of Philopappos eventually reached Lord Elgin and is still in the possession of the Elgin family. The others, ironically, suffered a similar fate to those of John Tweddell over twenty years before. Sealed by the British Consul in Athens in March 1821, they were moved first to Cythera and then to Constantinople. Seven years passed before the persistent efforts of Elgin and Hamilton caused them to be sent home, but the ship that was bringing them to England sank in the Mediterranean and they were lost. All Elgin had to show from Lusieri's twenty-one years' drawing at Athens was a single watercolour of the least distinguished of the antiquities of Athens.

In 1820 Elgin returned to the House of Lords as one of the representative peers for Scotland and held the seat for the remainder of his life. In 1821 he was, with the long-hated Byron, one of the first to subscribe to the Philhellenic Committee to support the Revolutionary Forces in Greece.[44] But he was never able to resume his public career. From time to time he renewed, despairingly, his request for a British peerage, begging to be allowed to bequeath something to his family besides his debts, but it was never granted.[45]

Despite his efforts his debts still pursued him, his assets were put into trust, and eventually he was obliged to live in France to escape his creditors. He died in Paris on 4 November 1841. Broomhall was put under care and maintenance, the eighth earl was obliged to spend most of his life abroad, and the debts were not finally paid off by his family until another thirty years had passed. The affair of the marbles had left a bitter legacy.

Yet in his last years Lord Elgin was granted a grain of comfort. Payne Knight was dead and the Dilettanti at last recognized their fateful mistake in condemning his collection.[46] In July 1831 the ever loyal Hamilton, now the Secretary of the Society, wrote to Elgin to say he had been elected a Member of the Dilettanti. His letter reached Lord Elgin at Leamington where he had gone, as to so many spas, in an attempt to relieve what he called his rheumatism. Lord Elgin's reply to Hamilton, in his familiar involved style, dignified and without bitterness, expressing yet again the honest aims that had caused his downfall, is a fitting end to his story.

No-one knows more intimately than you do, that the impulses which led me to the exertions I made in Greece were wholly for the purpose of securing to Great Britain, and through it to Europe in general, the most effectual possible knowledge, and means of improving, by the excellence of Grecian art in sculpture and architecture. My success, to the vast extent it was effected, will never cease to be a matter of the utmost gratification to me. If, when it was made known to the public, twenty-five years ago, or at any reasonable time afterwards, it had been thought that the same energy would be considered useful to the Dilettanti Society, most happy should I have been to have contributed every aid in my power. But as such expectation has long since past, I really do not apprehend that I shall be thought fastidious if I decline the honour now proposed to me at this my eleventh hour.[47]

The consignment of antiquities which arrived after the 1816 catalogue was prepared remained in the possession of the Elgin family at Broomhall. Some pieces were later sold, including some, in recent years, to the Getty Museum in Malibu, California. The last collection contained nothing from the Parthenon. Elgin also retained the collection of ancient jewellery, rings, bracelets, earrings, and other pieces mainly gold, which his agents had bought or excavated from tombs in Greece. The fifty-six items, which range from the Mycenaean to the Roman periods, included a fifth-century gold myrtle spray found in 1804, with some human ashes, inside a bronze vase which was itself inside a marble vase in the so-called Tomb of Aspasia on the road to Piraeus. The jewellery collection was on loan to the British Museum from 1926, and in about 1960 was bought with the aid of a grant from the National Art Collections Fund.[48]

23

'An Aera in Public Feeling'

LORD ELGIN's collection of antiquities, now officially called the Elgin Marbles, was entrusted to the British Museum on 8 August 1816. By January 1817 a temporary building had been erected, and the British public, their new owners, were admitted to see what they had bought.[1] The crowds were bigger than the Museum had ever received, soon more than a thousand a day.

Lord Elgin's purpose from first to last had been to improve the arts and manufactures of Great Britain, an aim which, he believed, justified all that he had done and all he had suffered since 1799. It had been that argument which had convinced the Select Committee that the British taxpayer could be asked to buy them, and it was that argument which now caught the public mood. After Waterloo, 'England', as the whole United Kingdom was usually called by its citizens, was supreme and unchallenged, politically, commercially, and industrially. In the sustained assault on Christian civilization begun by the French Revolution—as most of the country's political leaders regarded the recently ended war— England had triumphed. Like Athens after Salamis, she was ready to scale new heights of achievement and to celebrate them in her literature and public art.[2] As Wordsworth proclaimed in one of the many poems written to celebrate the peace:

> Victorious England! bid the silent Art
> Reflect, in glowing hues that shall not fade,
> Those high achievements; even as she arrayed
> With second life the deed of Marathon upon Athenian walls;
> So may she labour for thy civic halls;
> And be the guardian spaces
> Of consecrated places
> As nobly graced by Sculpture's patient toil;
> And let imperishable Columns rise
> Fixed in the depths of this courageous soil;
> Expressive signals of a glorious strife,

And competent to shed a spark divine
Into the torpid breast of daily life.[3]

Mrs Hemans, in her poem *Modern Greece* also published in the
year of the Elgin Marbles, echoed the popular wish:

And who can tell how pure, how bright, a flame,
Caught from these models, may illumine the west?
What British Angelo may rise to fame,
On the free isle what beams of art may rest?

A spate of books of engravings were quickly published, all aimed
at the improvement of public taste and the instruction of artists.[4]
As the author of one of them remarked:

That a spirit is already kindled in the bosom of our native artists which, if
fanned by the breath of public approbation, may some day shine forth in
such immortal works as those which have perpetuated the glory of ancient
Athens; that spirit of fruitful emulation, even to enthusiasm has already
been excited—we need not hesitate to affirm.[5]

The British Museum, picking up the long-planned project which
Elgin had been forced to abandon for lack of money, itself began
a multi-volume publication, with detailed engravings of great skill
and beauty.[6] These volumes were evidence in themselves, one of
the editors claimed, of the rapid progress in the arts which was
already occurring as a result of the nation's purchase.[7]

The editor of the first volume, Charles Robert Cockerell, the man
who had acquired the Phigaleian Marbles and who was now a
famous neo-classical architect, was another to proclaim the new
age. Athens, though a small city, had risen to greatness through the
genius and energy of its citizens. Athens, blessed with free institutions, had achieved an immortal glory when the remains of other
greater empires of the ancient world merely illustrated the tran-
sience of human vanity. England, with its free institutions, was now
the modern successor to that tradition, steward both of the memory
and of the relics.

No country can be better adapted than our own to afford an honorable
asylum to those monuments of the school of Phidias, and of the administration of Pericles; where secure from further injury and degradation, they
may receive the admiration and homage to which they are entitled, and
serve in return as model and examples to those who by knowing how to
revere and appreciate them, may learn first to imitate, and ultimately to
rival them.[8]

The national consensus was almost complete. Byron, whose contempt for Lord Elgin never diminished, declared publicly from his exile in Italy:

I opposed—and ever will oppose—the robbery of ruins from Athens to instruct the English in Sculpture—(who are as capable of Sculpture as the Egyptians of skating) but why did I do so?—the ruins are as poetical in Piccadilly as they were in the Parthenon—but the Parthenon and its rock are less so without them.

But in *Childe Harold's Pilgrimage, Canto the Fourth* published in 1818, Byron too now listed the sculptures of the Parthenon alongside the Apollo Belvedere, the Laocoon, the Venus dei Medici, and the other masterpieces of the older aesthetic which he had since seen, admired, and celebrated.[9]

The British Museum galleries were designed to enable artists and art students to draw and sketch the sculptures from all angles with the maximum daylight. Some of the pedimental pieces were mounted on swivels so that they could be easily rotated.[10] In the first year of opening, over two hundred passes were issued, and the numbers continued high for the next ten years.[11] In January 1819, although by this time the public could see the original sculptures if they wished, Haydon arranged an exhibition of chalk drawings of the Elgin Marbles done by two of his pupils which were put alongside copies of the Cartoons of Raphael from the royal collection. Interest was so intense that St James's Street was blocked by the carriages of the fashionable. The satirical print reproduced as Plate 11 shows Haydon standing beside a taller man who is probably Lord Elgin as they watch the crowds jostling to get in. The pupils later made other full-size drawings of the Elgin Marbles, two of which were ordered by Goethe and can still be seen in his house in Weimar.[12]

The numbers of artists drawing might have been higher but for a rule of the Royal Academy which required that when students offered a drawing of a statue for their examination, it must be of a perfect, that is of a complete, work. For the purposes of professional advancement, therefore, it was better for artists to draw from the casts of the Graeco-Roman sculptures which were anatomically complete, even if only made so by some recent Italian marble mason. As late as 1857 the Keeper of Antiquities at the British Museum told a Parliamentary Commission:

Though I think the Elgin Marbles are more valuable than all the sculptures in the world as a school of art, yet they were never much used by students . . . It was quite dreadful to see a thing they called a drunken faun (though it was not really a drunken faun) which was regularly wheeled into the room. Whenever I saw it, I knew that admission to the academy was approaching.[13]

The revival in the arts was to be a national enterprise involving all the people of the three kingdoms. The Society for the Diffusion of Useful Knowledge, which existed to bring education to the newly literate skilled working classes through Mechanics Institutes and Libraries, published an excellent cheap two-volume book with engravings.[14] Readers of the book were advised that 'Tuesdays and Thursdays in every week, and the whole month of September in every year, when daylight is usually the steadiest and strongest, are now exclusively devoted to artists and students in the Elgin and Townleyan Galleries in the British Museum.'[15]

Elgin himself, always more interested in improving the design of manufactures than in the fine arts, would have preferred the Marbles to be exhibited in some public place which was less élitist than the British Museum of his day, a place where they would be seen by 'every idler as well as every connoisseur'.[16] Only then, he believed, would the Elgin Marbles make their proper impact on the nation's industries. As matters turned, many of the visitors to the Museum were indeed from classes of society who did not normally or previously frequent museums or art galleries. As one newspaper reported:

It is quite amusing to listen to the remarks of the people: unaccustomed to such works, they seemed eager and curious, and without the least affectation of taste, say things which, however homely, shew them to be sound at the core. 'How broken they are! a'ant they?' said a decent man to another. 'Yes' answered the other, 'but how *like life*?' The profoundest artist, after years of thinking, could not have uttered a truer conclusion.[17]

Elsewhere in Europe the same chorus of admiration could be heard.[18] The Elgin Marbles, the supreme masterpieces of the ancient world, would help to usher in a new renaissance in the modern. In France the *Memoir* which Enrico Visconti had written in order to help Elgin's cause before the Select Committee was republished in a fuller version in French. He was in no doubt, Visconti declared, that the sculptures had been executed under the supervision of Phidias and that as works of art they had never been surpassed.[19] In Italy, Canova, echoing the sentiments which were already becoming something of a cliché in England, declared that his works would have been different if he had been given the chance to study the sculptures of the Parthenon when he first began his career. The Bavarian neo-classical architect Leo von Klenze delivered a lecture in 1821 to the Academy of Sciences in Munich, emphasizing the humanizing, as well as the artistic (and monetary) value of the Aegina Marbles which had recently arrived in the city. The rescue work of Choiseul-Gouffier and Elgin, he declared, by bringing Europe for the first time into contact with original Greek sculptures, had inaugurated a new period in the history of art.

By the end of 1816, requests for sets of casts had been received from the Royal Society of Arts, the Academy of Arts in Edinburgh, the Committee of Fine Arts of the Dublin Society, the three main training centres for artists in the three kingdoms. Inquiries had also arrived from the King of Württemberg and from some private connoisseurs at home and abroad. Although the Louvre already had a regular service able to supply casts of all their main sculptures on demand to museums in France and elsewhere, as far as Britain was concerned this was something new. But the logic was clear. If the Elgin Marbles were to improve public taste and raise the level of artistic production, plaster casts were more useful than books.

The British Museum arranged for Westmacott the sculptor to produce a set of moulds from which plaster casts could be made, and soon afterwards established a regular service to supply casts on demand. Within a few years casts of the Elgin Marbles had been sent all over the country to museums, to public buildings, and to country houses. As early as 1819, conscious of the growing potential for foreign policy purposes, the British Treasury authorized the gift of sets of casts to the courts of Rome, Naples, and Prussia. Russia, Bavaria, and Württemberg had to pay. By the middle of the century most major cities in Europe or America possessed casts of some at least of the Elgin Marbles.

After 1834, the British Museum made arrangements with the newly independent Greek state to acquire casts of every new piece of sculpture from the Parthenon that was discovered in successive excavations. Casts of other pieces and fragments held in museums everywhere were also gradually gathered in London as part of a world-wide enterprise to reassemble, to reconstruct, to understand, to educate, as well as to provide models for copying. For most of the nineteenth century the great museums of Europe and America showed the sculptures of the Parthenon, casts and originals (if they had any) side by side.

For the humanizing as well as the training purposes of art, many people believed, plaster casts which showed the ancient shapes and forms and the ancient facial expressions in their presumed original whiteness were at least as good as original sculptures, if not better. Winckelmann's *Gedancken über die Nachahmung der griechischen Werke in der Mahlerey und Bildhauer-Kunst* (Reflections concerning the Imitation of the Grecian Artist in Painting and Sculpture), first published in 1755 before he had been to Italy, was mainly based on a study of the casts of the masterpieces of Italy recently brought to Dresden. Although there were a few genuinely ancient pieces from Italy near Dresden, Winckelmann appears to have visited them only once. It was of the arrival of the casts that he wrote:

Die reinsten Quellen der Kunst sind geöffnet: glücklich ist, wer sie findet und schmecket. Diese Quellen suchen, heißt nach Athen reisen; und Dressden wird nunmehro Athen für Künstler.[20]

The purest springs of art have been opened. Happy the man who finds and drinks at them. In search of these springs we must journey to Athens, and Dresden henceforth will be the artist's Athens.

Later, when Winckelmann was in Italy, he confirmed the ideas which he had drawn from seeing the casts by studying the famous marble Graeco-Roman statues in Rome and Florence from which the casts had been made. More than once when in Italy Winckelmann was given an opportunity to pay a visit to Greece and see Athens and the Parthenon sculptures which were now becoming known from books, but he declined. It is doubtful if he ever saw any ancient statue which was not a later Graeco-Roman adaptation.

Schiller also drew his Hellenic inspiration from plaster casts. Of the statues in the Gypssaal at Mannheim which he visited in 1784, he wrote;

Meine ganzes Herz ist davon erweitert. Ich fühle mich edler und besser ...Empfangen von dem allmächtigen Wehen des griechischen Genius trittst du in diesen Tempel der Kunst. Schon deine erste Ueberraschung hat etwas ehrwürdiges, heiliges. Eine unsichtbare Hand scheint die Hülle der Vergangenheit vor deinem Aug wegzustreifen, zwei Jahrtausende versinken vor deinem Fußtritt, du stehst auf einmal mitten im schönen lachenden Griechenland, wandelst unter Helden und Grazien, und betest an, wie sie, vor romantischen Göttern.[21]

My whole heart is enlarged. I feel myself to be a nobler and a better man
... Entering this temple of art you are received by the almighty spirit [*literally wind*] of the Greek Genius. Even in your initial astonishment there
is something dignified, holy. It is as though an invisible hand gently
removed the veils of the past from before your eyes, two thousand years
fall away before your footsteps and you are suddenly standing amidst
beautiful laughing Greece, and walking among the heroes and the Graces
and worshipping romantic Gods as they do.

Goethe, whose interest in all aspects of antiquity was intense, was
an early admirer of the Parthenon as well as of the earlier models.
As early as 1787 when he was in Rome, he remarked of drawings
of the frieze shown him by a returning English traveller that they
were:

Arbeiten des Phidias. Man kann sich nichts Schöneres denken als die
wenigen einfachen Figuren.[22]

The work of Phidias. It is impossible to imagine anything more beautiful.

Like Winckelmann, Goethe's knowledge and his appreciation of
Greek art was almost entirely derived from drawings, engravings,
and plaster casts. In 1816 he followed every detail of the Elgin
Marbles debate, reading all the books about them published in
England, and himself writing about them frequently. Of a set of
plaster casts, brought from London to Weimar, he wrote in a letter
of October 1817:

Von England sind uns die kostbarsten Sachen zugekommen ... Die Elgin
Marbles mit dem ganzen Gefolg, immer wieder und wenigstens bequemer
dargestellt, sind uns beynah so bekannt als wenn wir sie gesehen hätten.[23]

Some very precious things have come to us from England ... The Elgin
Marbles and all the rest, depicted so many times, are as familiar to us as if
we had the originals before us.

On the last day of 1816 Haydon wrote in his diary: 'This year the
Elgin Marbles were bought and produced an Aera in public
feeling.'[24] Of the year 1818 Goethe repeated the same sentiment,
by now being heard all over Europe:

Für die Einsicht in höhere bildende Kunst begann dieses Jahr eine neue
Epoche.[25]

This year was for Great Art the beginning of a new age.

When, in his evidence to the Select Committee in 1816, Payne
Knight valued Elgin's collection of casts at half the value of the

whole Parthenon frieze, he was ostentatiously displaying his contempt for what he regarded as architectural decorations of the
Hadrianic period.[26] But when, in 1819, the Louvre offered to
exchange their one original metope for a set of casts of the Elgin
Marbles, they were, in effect, genuinely putting a value on casts not
far below that of originals. The British Museum's counter-offer to
supply casts to the value of £1,200, a figure almost exactly equivalent to the 25,000 francs which the Louvre had paid for their
metope, implied an even narrower premium.[27] In 1840, in the spirit
of bringing together fragments which had been separated by the
accidents of souvenir-collecting, the Louvre made a free gift of the
head of a horseman from the Parthenon frieze which had been
taken from Athens in 1814 after the slab to which it belonged had
already gone to England.[28]

However, the classical aesthetic which saw the ancient masterpieces primarily as ideal models to be copied, and which could
therefore put a high value on casts, was already in retreat. In March
1817, soon after the Elgin Marbles went on public show in London,
Haydon took his new friend John Keats, then aged 21, to see them.
The two sonnets which Keats immediately wrote and sent to
Haydon for publication in *The Examiner*, strongly reminiscent in
many ways of the enthusiasm of others, also show the emergence
of a new way of looking.

TO HAYDON, WITH A SONNET WRITTEN ON SEEING THE ELGIN MARBLES

  Haydon! forgive me that I cannot speak
   Definitively on these mighty things;
   Forgive me that I have not Eagle's wings—
  That what I want I know not where to seek:
  And think that I would not be over meek
   In rolling out upfollow'd thunderings,
   Even to the steep of Heliconian springs,
  Were I of ample strength for such a freak—
  Think too, that all those numbers should be thine;
   Whose else? In this who touch thy vesture's hem?
  For when men star'd at what was most divine
   With browless idiotism—o'erwise phlegm—
  Thou hadst beheld the Hesperean shine
   Of their star in the East, and gone to worship them.

ON SEEING THE ELGIN MARBLES

  My spirit is too weak—mortality
   Weighs heavily on me like unwilling sleep,

And each imagin'd pinnacle and steep
Of godlike hardship tells me I must die
Like a sick Eagle looking at the sky.
    Yet 'tis a gentle luxury to weep
    That I have not the cloudy winds to keep
Fresh for the opening of the morning's eye.
Such dim-conceived glories of the brain
    Bring round the heart an indescribable feud;
So do these wonders a most dizzy pain,
    That mingles Grecian grandeur with the rude
Wasting of old Time—with a billowy main—
A sun—a shadow of a magnitude.

'He went again and again to see the Elgin Marbles,' wrote the biographer of his friend Severn, who was a painter, 'and would sit for an hour or more at a time beside them rapt in revery. On one such occasion Severn came upon the young poet with eyes shining so brightly and face so lit up by some visionary rapture, that he stole quietly away.'[29]

It is hard to imagine Keats writing his sonnets about plaster casts. For the young poet who knew no Greek, as for the German poets, the Elgin Marbles opened a vision of a lost Hellenic world. But they were not just models to be learned from and copied. Indeed it made little difference whether the sculptures were appreciated, or even observed, by modern mortals. Like the aura of holiness which earlier generations felt was exuded by the holy relics of the saints and the martyrs, the Elgin Marbles now began to carry and to emit an aura of artistic originality. Casts, however accurate they might be in showing the forms of the statues from which they were made, being mere copies, could never therefore be works of art. The final stanzas of Keats's *Ode on a Grecian Urn*, written shortly afterwards, which draw their imagery direct from particular slabs of the Parthenon frieze, are explicit:

Who are these coming to the sacrifice?
    To what green altar, O mysterious priest,
Leadst thou that heifer lowing to the skies?
    And all her silken flanks with garlands drest?
What little town by river or sea shore,
    or mountain-built with peaceful citadel,
    Is emptied of this folk, this pious morn?
And, little town, thy streets for evermore
    Will silent be; and not a soul to tell
Why thou art desolate, can ne'er return.

    O Attic Shape! Fair attitude! with brede
        Of marble men and maidens overwrought,
    With forest branches and the trodden weed;
        Thou, silent form, dost tease us out of thought
    As doth eternity: Cold Pastoral!
    When old age shall this generation waste,
        Thou shalt remain, in midst of other woe
    Than ours, a friend to man, to whom thou say'st
        'Beauty is truth, truth beauty,'—that is all
        Ye know on earth, and all ye need to know.

To the romantic imagination the Elgin Marbles were the supreme example of great art as creation, the nearest to the divine to which human beings could aspire. The Elgin Marbles were masterpieces, unsurpassed and unsurpassable, exempt from the contingencies of time, of place, and of history.

    At the time the Elgin Marbles first went on show, the British Museum was also beginning to exhibit sculptures taken from Egypt. It may have been the head of Rameses seen on a visit to the Elgin Marbles which Percy Bysshe Shelley had in mind in composing a poem published in 1817 in *The Examiner*.

OZYMANDIAS

I MET a traveller from an antique land,
Who said, 'two vast and trunkless legs of stone
Stand in the desert. Near them on the sand,
Half sunk, a shattered visage lies, whose frown,
And wrinkled lip, and sneer of cold command,
Tell that its sculptor well those passions read,
Which yet survive stamped on these lifeless things,
The hand that mocked them and the heart that fed;
And on the pedestal these words appear:
My name is OZYMANDIAS, King of Kings.'
Look on my works ye Mighty and despair!
No thing else beside remains. Round the decay
Of that Colossal wreck, boundless and bare,
The lone and level sands stretch far away.[30]

Another cultural shift was occurring, another face of romanticism. The ancient Hellenes had appropriated, improved, and civilized the arts of carving in stone which they found being practised in ancient Egypt and in the other neighbouring eastern empires. It was now the turn of that Hellenic art to be appropriated by the countries of modern Europe who, in their turn hoped to match it and surpass it.[31] Like the mythic fights of civilized Hellenes and barbarous Centaurs re-enacted on public buildings all over Europe, the museums now contrasted the pure, beautiful, freedom-loving white of the Hellenic marble with the spotted, ugly, coloured granite which was unchangingly oriental, alien, oppressive, and barbarous.

It was one thing to proclaim a new era in art, another to create it, yet another to found a new school or arts and manufactures based on the archaeological knowledge now being retrieved. In describing his first sight of the Elgin Marbles some years before they went on public exhibition, the sculptor John Henning wrote:

It struck me forcibly that from the superior excellence they might some time or other become such an object of public curiosity that models of them, while they might be very improving to myself, might become objects of pecuniary advantage.

Copies of Henning's restoration of the frieze were made from white plaster and sold in boxes that could easily be passed from hand to hand. Every gentleman could, if he wished, have his own miniature set of part of the Elgin Marbles.

Henning also prepared a full-scale restoration of the frieze which was directly copied to decorate the Hyde Park Corner Arch, the Athenaeum, the Royal College of Surgeons, Terling Place, Essex, and other buildings elsewhere in Great Britain.[32] William Threed incorporated copies of the head of Selene's horse in several of his monuments.[33] The vase in Buckingham Palace Gardens which commemorated Waterloo owes much to the horsemen of the Parthenon frieze as does Pistrucci's medal for the same battle.[34] The Parthenon frieze was a common motif of Regency wallpaper.[35] Some of the efforts to respond to the official challenge to create a new era in art were straightforward.

By the 1820s it had been established beyond any reasonable doubt that the sculptures of the Parthenon had, in part at least, been painted in bright colours. The more ancient statues that were discovered in excavations, the more overwhelming became the evidence. Imaginative reconstructions of what a painted Parthenon might have looked like were published in several countries, and meetings of architects and artists were held to consider the implications.[36] But, for all their professed conversion to the cause of truth to the Greek originals, this was a discovery which neither artists nor their patrons could easily come to terms with. 'A very doubtful exhibition of taste, as judged by modern standards,' was a

common reaction.[37] Most of the works of the sculptors of the nineteenth century remain more reminiscent of the cold white neoclassicism of Canova than of the Elgin Marbles.

For a modern sculptor to paint his work would be to vulgarize
it, to make it like a waxwork in a fair or like the garish totems of
primitive peoples being brought to Europe by anthropologists and
sailors. In Great Britain no modern sculpture was ever coloured.
No modern sculptor even dared to add paint to the cold lifeless
eyes of marble portraits. As a compromise with historical authenticity the designers of the new neo-classical British Museum building intended that the background to its pediment should be painted
a pale blue, but the blue was never added.[38]

In the field of painting, West, Haydon, and others made specific
claims that some of their pictures owed their inspiration and composition to the study of the Elgin Marbles. They had, they claimed,
founded a new school of historical painting. However, their styles
of painting, with the frequent direct depiction of violence, showed
little of the restraint of the Greek tradition with its convention of
displaying the anticipatory moment rather than the actual event.
No one would guess the influence of the Parthenon sculptures on
their paintings if the fact had not been documented by the artists
themselves.[39]

Apart from the professional restrictions of the Royal Academy,
there was, furthermore, something in the emerging new romantic
aesthetic which made it hard for artists to copy the Parthenon
sculptures direct. If it was true, as the new consensus proclaimed,
that the artists of the Parthenon had achieved their sublimity by
copying Nature, why should modern artists not do the same? A
well-dressed riding master could sometimes be seen standing by
the frieze of the Parthenon teaching his pupils how to sit elegantly
on horseback.[40] Should not artists who wished to catch the spirit of
the Marbles study the forms of real human beings and of real
horses? Artists under training at the Royal Academy drew from
live nude models who posed, shivering, among the casts. Landseer
designed the bronze lions in Trafalgar Square by sketching a real
dead lion obtained from the London zoo.[41]

There were other worries. The Parthenon sculptures were incomplete and fragmentary. They had been battered by time, lost, and
rescued. These were all features which romanticism valued and
celebrated. But surely no modern sculptor could deliberately set
out to produce an incomplete and fragmentary work of art? If the

Parthenon sculptures were perfect, autonomous, and timeless, unmatched and unmatchable, was it not artistically sacrilegious for modern successors to presume even to try to capture their spirit? As a modern scholar has put it, 'Latent in Romanticism is an inner existential anxiety which is absent from the Olympian serenity of Classicism.'[42]

With architecture, direct copying from ancient models was less problematical than with sculpture. The Grecian style, already strong a generation before the arrival of the Parthenon sculptures, continued to thrive.[43] The many architectural fragments in the Elgin collection were joined by another collection of architectural fragments from the Parthenon and the Erechtheion, removed from Athens by the architect Inwood in 1819 and bought by the British Museum for £40. Caryatids appeared early in the architecture of Sir John Soane, and two replicas of the whole Caryatid porch still stand incongruously outside Euston Station in Inwood's St Pancras Church. All over Britain there are buildings of the time reminiscent of the Erechtheion, the Propylaea, the Theseum, and, perhaps most common because smallest, the Monument of Lysicrates. Elgin had lent his drawings of the Theseum to the architect of the new Royal Observatory which was to be built at Edinburgh. Other Scottish architects, notably 'Grecian' Williams who had been to Athens and written a book about his experiences, helped to turn the New Town of Edinburgh into a proud neo-classical city.[44] But with architecture too there were strict limits to the extent to which artists and their patrons were willing to have their preconceptions about classical buildings corrected by archaeological discoveries. In Great Britain no neo-classical building was ever given any colouring on the outside, even to pick out details.

In Germany too the classical style reigned supreme. If Edinburgh saw itself as the Athens of the North, Berlin would be the Athens on the Spree. The Brandenburg Gate, begun in 1791, and soon the symbol of the city, had been inspired by the drawings of the Propylaea published in the 1788 volume of Stuart and Revett's *Antiquities of Athens*. Metopes were added later when knowledge of the Parthenon sculptures became more easily available.[45] The Altes Museum in Berlin, completed in 1825, and drawing on features from the Pantheon in Rome as well as some from the Parthenon, was intended by its architect Schinkel as a temple dedicated to the worship of great art as well as being a display of ancient statues for copying. The collections, which were mainly casts not originals, were therefore not arranged in chronological order. When the Neues Museum was opened in 1859, the whole of the first floor was filled with casts, now arranged to display historical and artistic development.[46]

In architecture however, as in sculpture, there was a shying away from the ultimate challenge. In the United States, it became common to see a private bank or insurance company office as well as a public town hall or court-house with features copied from the Parthenon. In Europe, by contrast, only monuments intended to commemorate and express national unity and national sacrifice on the grandest and most sublime scale were permitted to copy the supreme building which, more truly than the nineteenth century was able to appreciate, had served the same purposes in Periclean Athens.[47] Although proposals were occasionally put forward to build replicas of the Parthenon, the few designs that were offered, such as that for the monument to Frederick the Great, were not built. In Germany as in Britain it was easier and safer for architects and their patrons to capture a touch of Athens by topping their buildings with replicas of the Monument of Lysicrates or by adding a few pilasters to the frontage.

The original proposals for the German National Monument, the Valhalla, prepared for King Ludwig of Bavaria in 1807, drew principally on the Pantheon in Rome. The Valhalla was to contain busts of the most eminent Germans in history ranging from Alaric—one of whose finest achievements was to have spared Athens—to Mozart, Schiller, and Goethe. In 1809, at the behest of the architect Karl von Fischer, who had recently returned from Athens, the Pantheon was synthesized with the Parthenon, and by 1810, in a further revision, the Parthenon predominated. When, after the Battle of the Nations in 1813, which marked the defeat of the French invaders, Ludwig announced a national competition, Baron Karl von Hallerstein, who had played a large part in outwitting Cockerell, Lusieri, and Fauvel in bringing the Aegina Marbles to Munich, proposed something near to a full-scale replica of the Parthenon, to stand on its own acropolis, the whiteness of its marble sculptures contrasting with the honey-coloured building into which they were set.[48] In the end the design chosen and executed was that of von Klenze which aimed at illustrating the common roots of ancient Greeks and modern Germans, who like the British, the French, and the Americans, now also claimed to be the true inheritors of their spirit.[49] Although externally the Valhalla was strikingly similar to the Parthenon, the interior was entirely German, with Valkyries holding up its iron roof and a narrative display of the epic romance of the Nibelungen.

In Great Britain too it was decided that the victory should be commemorated in a National Monument modelled on the Parthenon. The first design, by Thomas Harrison the architect who had first suggested to Lord Elgin that his embassy to Turkey could be used to improve the arts, also, like the German Valhalla, combined features both from the Pantheon of Rome and from the Parthenon of Athens. Funds for the project were never voted and it fell through. At Lord Elgin's suggestion it was then decided that a National Monument to the Scottish heroes of the wars should be built in Edinburgh. A Christian church in the form of a full-scale 'facsimile' of the Parthenon would stand on Calton Hill, Edinburgh's other acropolis being already occupied by Edinburgh Castle.[50] Cockerell was appointed architect, and a start was made, but in 1829 the money ran out and the project was abandoned. If the monument had been completed it is difficult to imagine how it could have escaped the bathos of pastiche. As events turned out, its twelve stark columns on the eastern skyline, surrounded by other neo-classical monuments to the poets and philosophers of Scotland, were more true both to the civic art of Athens, to the notion of enlightenment, and to the emerging romanticism than any completed version would have achieved.[51]

For a time it looked as if Elgin's enterprise was succeeding. For a generation the Elgin Marbles helped to make the classical style the norm for public buildings in Britain. In a published letter to his former patron, William Richard Hamilton listed the Courts of Justice at Newcastle, Chester, Gloucester, Hereford, and Perth, the Council House at Bristol, the Royal High School in Edinburgh, the Bank, the Exchange, and the County Hall in Glasgow, the Custom House at Liverpool, the Town Halls at Manchester and Birmingham, the Post Office in London, St George's Hospital in London, London University, King's College, Covent Garden Theatre, the National Gallery, and the British Museum. He might have added the thousands of factories, shops, and houses which softened the starkness of their utilitarianism with a pediment or a pillar. Modern Britain, the most commercial, most international, and most individualistic society that had yet existed, offered a public art which proclaimed the virtues of citizenship, emphasized its debt to its ancient teacher, and declared that its heritage was shared with the rest of the Western world.

In 1836, however, Lord Elgin had the mortification of hearing that architects submitting plans for the new Houses of Parliament were to be confined to two styles only, the Gothic or the Elizabethan.[52] The supreme monument of the British Empire, the country's political leaders had decided, was to be nationalist. Sir Walter Scott whose novels appealed 'to all our feudal and ancestral recollections', had, Hamilton speculated, reinforced the delusion that the antiquities of Britain had as much value as those of Greece and Italy. It was deeply to be regretted, he wrote in a last despairing attempt to reassert and save the identity of Hellenism and modern European humane values, that:

Some unfortunate combination of prejudices, or a doubtful view of useless consistencies, may possibly throw us back into the middle ages, and may tell us that all we have been learning, all the progress we have made, all the principles our artists have been taught to look up to, as the best and only guides in their profession, are to be of no avail; that gothic barbarism is again to be allowed to triumph over the master-pieces of Italy and Greece, and that Britons are henceforth to look for the model of what is sublime and beautiful in art, to the age of ignorance and superstition.[53]

As it happened, 1836 was also the peak year for the number of artists applying to draw from the Elgin Marbles. After that, the numbers began a long decline. By the 1860s they were scarcely a quarter of those drawing earlier.

In the 1870s and 1880s there was a new surge of interest in the Elgin Marbles which took the numbers of artists who attended the Museum in order to draw to higher levels than they had ever been. During those decades there was a surge of reprints of the works of the romantic poets, including Byron, Keats, and Shelley, which came out of copyright at that time. Many of the books which, for the first time, brought the English romantic poets to classes of society who had not previously been able to afford them, were illustrated in a dreamy, naked, vaguely Grecian, style.

Grecian themes also featured frequently in the most famous paintings of the time, particularly those of G. F. Watts and of Frederick Leighton, who dominated late Victorian high art.[54] Copying ancient statues was a sure way of spoiling one's taste for form, Watts consistently advised his pupils, with the single exception of the Elgin Marbles.[55] Leighton too, who, like Watts, kept casts of some of the Elgin Marbles in his studio, took his admiration further. When President of the Royal Academy, he delivered an address to the pupils, 'On The Relation in which Art stands to Morality and Religion'. After dismissing the arts of the other ancient peoples in accordance with contemporary notions about the characteristics of inferior torpid oriental and semitic races, he turned to Greece:

Let me now look, for a moment, and in conclusion, at an Art which whatever was best in them rose to a fuller and nobler life, an art which we can compare no longer to a broad and sluggish stream, but which is as the sudden up leaping of a living source, reflecting and scattering abroad the light of a new and a more joyous day; a spring at which men shall drink to the end of all days and not be sated: the Art of Greece.[56]

The perfect balance of intellectual ability and physical beauty, of truth and nobility, which Leighton saw in the Elgin Marbles, and which he tried to recapture in his own work, he attributed to the Aryan element, 'of which the only parallel I know of is sometimes found in the women of another Aryan race—your own'.[57] 'Through art,' wrote Cecil Rhodes, 'Pericles taught the lazy Athenians to believe in Empire.'[58] The rhetoric of national liberty which had clustered round the Elgin Marbles since they were first acquired had, by late Victorian times, slipped into a justification of an imperial race.

As the nineteenth century progressed, the British Museum's collections of ancient sculptures grew rapidly. Although after independence Greece did not permit the export of antiquities, there were plenty of original Greek works to be found beyond the political borders. For most of the century the Ottoman authorities allowed British, French, and German archaeologists to take what they wanted, either as part of an international agreement or using much the same mixture of permissions, bribery, and exchange of political influence that had served Elgin so well. The British Museum secured a huge haul from Lycia, another from the Mausoleum of Halicarnassos, as well as innumerable lesser additions. After ancient Greece came ancient Egypt and ancient Assyria, the arts of India, of the Maya, of the Chinese, and many others.

As, one by one, the civilizations of the ancient world yielded up their secrets, the ships of the Royal Navy brought examples of their carvings in stone to London to join the Elgin Marbles in Bloomsbury. As the old and the newly discovered lands round the world were opened to exploration and to science, specimens of their natural history were exported to the great repository in London. The British Museum Library collected every book published in the country as well as buying up book collections being dispersed elsewhere. As the century progressed it was increasingly hard to regard the British Museum as a school for artists or a repository of models of excellence. It was an imperial and universal museum of nature and of man, dedicated to the ideas, artistic endeavours, and written records of all peoples of all ages.

By the middle of the century, when the burgeoning collections were already larger than the British Museum building could comfortably accommodate, it was clear that something had to be done. But what? One solution would be to split the collections. But how? Were the antiquities primarily a historical archive, an illustrative record of the artefacts of mankind? Did they reveal the implicit progress in art and civilization from the earliest Middle Eastern cultures through Greece and Rome to its modern European flowering? If so they should be kept together. Or were they still models of excellence? If so the best could be separated from the others without loss. Once again the Elgin Marbles became the site of a contest between competing aesthetics and ideologies on which a practical question now forced a resolution.

Sir Richard Westmacott, the sculptor who had advised the Select Committee in 1816, appearing before a Parliamentary Inquiry in 1852, was asked if the Elgin Marbles were as much the subject of interest and admiration now as they were in former years. He replied:

With all persons conversant with art they must be and will always, because these are the finest things in the world: we shall never see anything like them again.[59]

Westmacott, an advocate of the older ideal, favoured bringing together the nation's finest art collections in one place. The Elgin Marbles should go to the National Gallery to join the Old Masters in a temple dedicated to the best painting and the best sculpture. But where did that mean for the Egyptian and Assyrian sculptures? Would exhibiting them in public cause public taste to deteriorate? Westmacott, with consistency, said he was opposed to artists studying Egyptian, let alone Chinese, art. However, in accordance with the racial commonplaces of the time, he also believed that anyone who had gazed upon and understood the beauty of the Elgin Marbles would remain pure in his artistic sensibilities, no matter what barbarisms his eyes might see elsewhere.[60]

It was Charles Newton, who had obtained the Mausoleum sculptures for the British Museum, who provided a way through. The Elgin Marbles, he advised, were the keystone without which the arch would fall:

we cannot appreciate art aesthetically unless we first learn to interpret its meaning and motive, and in order to do this we must study it historically; that if a series of specimens be arranged by schools and periods, according to the time and place of their production, the merit of the more beautiful works of art will be enhanced, not diminished, by contrast and comparison with the rest.[61]

It was decided to keep the collections of ancient art together, the natural history collections going to a separate museum elsewhere in London. For most of the later nineteenth and early twentieth centuries the Elgin Marbles were displayed as part of a historical arrangement of the monuments of the great ancient civilizations, linking them with what was known of the lives of the peoples who made them, and showing the progress and development of artistic styles. By the end of the century the Elgin Marbles had ceased to be primarily regarded as models to be copied.

Lord Elgin, William Hazlitt had noted in 1816 in reviewing the Select Committee's Report, had claimed that the Elgin Marbles were only 'bits of architecture, loose pieces of stone', but:

no sooner do they get into the possession of our glorious country than they are discovered to be infinitely superior to the Apollo, the Venus, and the Laocoon, and all the rest of that class which are found to be no better than modern antiques.[62]

Hazlitt distrusted the official talk of firmans, legality, and rescue. Like Byron he had a keen nose for official cant. But he was also expressing a more general point which became clearer as the century proceeded. It had been scholars from western Europe who had retrieved a knowledge of ancient civilization, rediscovered and made available the ancient literature, and resumed and then advanced the ancient traditions in history, philosophy, and science. It was the French, the British, and the Germans who sent expeditions to study, record, and excavate the ruins of ancient Greece, who published the results, who wrote theoretical and practical histories of ancient art, who drew the lessons both aesthetic and archaeological, and who tried to take the lessons into their own public art. The sculptures of the Parthenon came from Greece, but it was the countries of modern Europe which gave them their fame, their iconic status, and their constantly changing meaning, as well as their new name. The Elgin Marbles were physically constructed in Athens, but, until the time of Greek independence, they were culturally constructed in Dresden, London, Paris, Rome, and Weimar.

24

'The Damage is Obvious and Cannot be Exaggerated'

THE sculptures of the Parthenon as they existed in Lord Elgin's time had been smashed and scattered by war, invasion, religion, fire, earthquake, explosion, looting, vandalism, neglect, and souvenir hunting. In one respect only were they intact. For at least fifteen hundred years their surfaces had remained unaltered by the hand of man. Most had probably not received any maintenance or repair since long before the building ceased to be in active use as a temple some time in late antiquity.[1] As for the backs of the large pedimental sculptures which had remained inaccessible from the time they were first placed in position, they were, when Elgin's agents removed them, exactly as they had been left when first put in place by the original artists in the fifth century before the Christian era.

The main change to the surfaces of the sculptures was in their appearance. Most of the paint had long since gone. The metal attachments which were probably also painted or gilded had likewise gone, although there were many holes in the marble which showed where they had been fitted, and on the Iris figure from the west pediment, a large metal plug remained in place. In a few places, particularly where they had been protected from the weather, the sculptures still showed where they been highly polished to give a glassy reflective surface, a sight which Winckelmann would have recognized and admired. For the most part, however, the surfaces as they existed in Elgin's day were covered with a patina, in some places smooth, in others scaly, in a rich mixture of white, brown, orange, and occasional black, the result of long exposure to the open air.

In 1750 and 1751 the architect James Stuart made a number of coloured drawings of the ruins of Athens.[2] He showed the marble in varying degrees of whitish grey and orange brown, the variegated tinted appearance contrasting sharply with the bright white paper of the artist whom he sometimes showed sketching in a corner of his pictures. Stuart and his colleague Nicholas Revett, who saw the sculptures close up on the building, were the first to publish the fact that the Parthenon had been painted in ancient times and that the building still carried clear traces of the painted designs and decoration.

The water-colours made by Robert Smirke, another architect in the neo-classical tradition who was in Athens in 1803, also show the marble of the monuments in whites and browns.[3] When Smirke was allowed to examine the sculptures recently removed from the Parthenon by Elgin's agents which were then in a storeroom awaiting shipment, he remarked 'they are executed very flat which, I should think, while the marble retained its original whiteness, revealed a great delicacy of effect'.[4] Like many others then and later, Smirke, a prisoner of his artistic education in the Winckelmann ideal, was reluctant to accept that Greek sculptures could ever have been anything but white.

The man who knew the Parthenon and its sculptures best before the first modern attempts at preservation and restoration began in the 1830s was Louis-François-Sébastien Fauvel, who was both an archaeologist and an artist. As far as Fauvel was concerned there was no doubt that the Parthenon had been painted both outside and inside. Remains of painted ornament could, he told visitors, still be seen 'on the fillets above the triglyphs and upon the upper mouldings of the inside of the Portico'. To Fauvel the monuments of Athens were 'a rich brown gold'.[5] His painting of the west front of the Parthenon made in 1790 before the pedimental sculptures were removed by Elgin's agents shows the whole structure, architecture and sculptures, in this colour.[6]

The engravings in *Les Ruines des plus beaux Monuments de la Grèce* and *The Antiquities of Athens* which first took knowledge of the monuments of Athens across Europe, being in black and white, gave no indication of the actual colours. The water-coloured engravings and lithographs in the books by Dupré, Dodwell, Hobhouse, and others, although unlikely to be as accurate a record as the colour in original pictures, also show the monuments as brown or honey-coloured.[7] William Haygarth, whose book on Greece was written during his visit in the winter of 1811, used brown ink for his engravings and then covered them with a brown wash.[8]

The impression made by the Parthenon on the observer differed, depending upon the state of the light, whether it was summer or winter, morning, midday, or evening. The brown which was so universally remarked upon by travellers and artists in the early nineteenth century may have owed something to actual climatic conditions—during those years a cloud of volcanic dust settled in the upper atmosphere causing spectacular sunsets as well as severe winters all over Europe—but it probably owed more to changing Western ways of seeing than to any actual change.[9] As early as Stuart's time, western European artists, already imbued with the philhellenic myth, tended to see the Athens of their time as the evening which followed the high noon of ancient civilization, the calm autumn after the glories of summer. Although Stuart had no tradition of colour illustration of Greece to guide or influence him in looking at the ruins of Athens, there were plenty of coloured pictures of the ruins of Rome which adopted the convention of evening autumnal light. Edward Dodwell, who visited Athens in 1801 and again later, noticed how:

the Parthenon, which once sparkled with the chaste but splendid brilliancy of the Pentelic marble, is now covered with the warm and mellow tint of an autumnal sun-set.[10]

Orange brown was not only the authentic actual colour—it also matched the romantic aesthetic of the ruins of ancient civilization.

In the 1990s, with the publication of more reliable colour reproductions of many original pictures which were painted by different artists from different countries at different times, it is possible for the first time to appreciate the extent to which visitors from western Europe saw and presented the Parthenon through eyes culturally conditioned by changing Western ideologies. During the eighteenth century, when the main aim was to record the antiquities as models to be copied by modern artists, the ruins of Athens were seen and illustrated as mostly white, their presumed original colour. With the advance of romanticism, and the romantic view of ruins, they became browner an browner.[11] By the later nineteenth century, by which time the monuments were increasingly seen, presented, and represented as archaeological remains, the public images began to turn white again. The recent programme of restoration, which incorporates newly cut marble into the ruins has made them more white.

The local Pentelic marble from which the Parthenon and its

sculptures were carved contains iron, magnetite, and other miner-als. Although the marble is clear white when freshly cut and uncom-fortably dazzling in the summer sun, the chemical interaction of moisture with the ores within the marble later produces a surface patina of variegated colour. The pervasive brown colour is, in the opinion of many experts, mainly due to ferrous minerals reacting with rain-water and with moisture in the atmosphere.[12] The black patches may owe something to the remains of lichens reacting with the marble and with rain-water, and perhaps also to the effects of smoke and to the precipitation of particles of burned olive oil released into the air from lighting and cooking. The surface of some of the sculptures, especially those in the pediments, has also been affected by water running or dripping from higher parts of the building. The effect has been, in some cases, to cover some of the historic surface with a layer of calcium carbonate, incipient stalag-mites, which has pitted and obscured the original surface, but also to seal the original surface beneath a protective layer. Similar slow changes seem to have occurred to those sculptures which fell to the ground in the explosion of 1687 and which remained buried among the marble rubble until they were excavated in the nineteenth century.

Until the 1960s the atmosphere in Athens was mainly dry and unpolluted and the change to the historic surface and to the visual appearance of the marble was extremely slow. Two and a half thou-sand years had probably affected the surface to a depth of less than a millimetre, although the extent of the change was different even on the same piece depending upon its chemical composition, the degree of its exposure, and the extent to which it had been affected by water. The careful architect and archaeologist F. C. Penrose, who studied the monument in 1846 and 1847, noted that:

the marks made by the cannon balls on the Parthenon in the last war (1820) were as white as the freshest fracture of the marble in the quarry, not having acquired the slightest tint in thirty years. Even the Venetian shot marks of 1680, though partially tinted by time, were still very white.[13]

In 1858, more than thirty years after the end of the fighting, the American traveller Bayard Taylor remarked on the 'tawny gold of two thousand years staining its once spotless marble, sparkling with snow-white marks of shot and shell'.[14]

As the ancient artists may have appreciated, the patina forms first on the rough surfaces and in the crevices, where surface water and lichens last longest, leaving the polished surfaces relatively untouched. The effect is therefore to enhance, and gradually to replace, the contrasts brought about by the paint. The hair of the Demeter of Cnidos, for example, a superb work of the fourth century which was acquired by the British Museum from its original site in 1859, was then a different colour from the face. The differing colours of the patinas on the drapery had reinforced the effects of the original paint as it was gradually eroded.

From the time of Stuart and Revett, many scholars realized that studies of the historic surfaces of the Parthenon sculptures might yield vital information about the true nature of Greek art. In 1815 Canova noted that remains of the metal attachments which formed an integral part of the sculptures were still to be found in the many holes and grooves in the sculptures.[15] Colour was also to be seen. In 1830, in the first official publication of the Elgin Marbles by the British Museum, Cockerell noted that:

indications of colour . . . are apparent in several portions both of the sculpture and architecture after an exposure of more than 2,000 years to the inclemencies of the weather . . . and many of the remains of Grecian architecture, on their first discovery from the earth, show the colours in all their freshness.[16]

Describing the polished back of the reclining river god from the west pediment, traditionally called the Ilissos, Cockerell remarked that:

A colour which appears to have covered every part of the work is still discoverable in this statue.[17]

The special importance of the surface of the Helios group from the east pediment piece shown in Plate 12 was also quickly recognized. As Cockerell wrote in the Museum's official publication:

The unsparing diligence exhibited in the execution of this fragment confirms the conjecture that these works were subjected to a rigorous public examination before they finally occupied their destined position . . . The superincumbent cornice has preserved the original polish of this figure, from which a judgement may be formed of the elaborate execution of the other portions of the pediment.[18]

The flesh parts of all the sculptures of the Parthenon, the early scholars concluded, were probably highly polished as well as painted in ancient times.[19]

The moulders employed by Fauvel and by Lord Elgin applied their wet plaster to parts of the frieze and to some of the metopes while the sculptures were still on the building in Athens.[20] In 1815 in London Haydon contrived to have some moulds hurriedly made by a commercial plasterer before he was stopped.[21] Many of the sculptures were moulded again on the orders of the British Museum in 1819.[22] In 1836 William Richard Hamilton, by that time one of the Trustees of the British Museum, voiced his alarm that every time new moulds were made, any remaining traces of colour were likely to be further eroded.

A committee of artists and scientists, including Michael Faraday, examined the sculptures for paint but could find nothing. The Museum's moulder, too, it was reported, had never found any traces of paint on the sculptures. When he added that 'the whole surface of the Marbles had been twice washed over with soap lyes as that, or some other strong acid, is necessary for the purpose of removing the soap which is originally put on the surface in order to detach the plaster of the mould', Faraday and his colleagues came to the conclusion that this alone would be enough to remove any vestiges which might have existed until then.[23] Metal traces in the holes and grooves would also have been affected.

For a time the lesson was well learned. It was decided, when the moulds of the Elgin Marbles became eroded by use and new moulds had to be made, they were to be made from casts specially preserved for the purpose rather than from the original Marbles. At this time too, although many slabs of the frieze, some metopes, and the larger pedimental figures in the collection had been moulded, some more than once, there were a number of more fragmentary pieces, including the Helios group from the east pediment and the Iris from the west pediment which, because they were not much in demand as models for artists, had not been moulded.[24] However, when, in the late 1830s museums and art schools abroad began to request sets of the complete Elgin Marbles, almost the whole collection was moulded or remoulded, with the possibility of further erosion. By the end of the nineteenth century the moulds were worn and patched and customers were complaining. In about 1901 the Museum authorities, again, it seems, without worrying about causing possible further damage to the historic surfaces, ordered the manufacturing of a new set of moulds from the originals, a programme which was substantially completed by 1912. The old moulds, with the possible exception of a few which were still regarded as serviceable, were then destroyed. Among those destroyed were the original moulds made by Lord Elgin's moulders.[25]

As the Ilissos figure exists today there is no visible trace of the colour that Cockerell saw. In the light of later knowledge, however, the losses caused by moulding may not have been so severe as Faraday believed. Although the place on the back of one of the other pedimental pieces where he and his colleagues scraped for paint is visible, their eyes, mistaking change of colour for dirt, failed to notice a large trial brush stroke of paint immediately below on the same statue.[26] Since that statue was among those which had stood undisturbed and inaccessible in the pediment until Lord Elgin's agents took it away, the paint must be the original paint of the fifth century.

On the reclining male figure from the east pediment traditionally called the Theseus, the fifth-century masons had to cut away some of the excess marble at the back of the completed statue in order to enable it to be exactly fitted into its place in the pediment. In contrast to the rest of the statue, there is no patina on the surface of the marble which the masons cut away. These differences provide further direct evidence, according to Jenkins and Middleton, two experts who have made a recent study of the surfaces, that an artificial coating of some kind was applied to the statue, and probably to the whole Parthenon, in ancient times. If they are right, the pervasive brown or honey colour may have been, in part at least, the result of a conscious decision by the ancient artists to coat the building, perhaps with the aim of reducing the uncomfortable glare of freshly cut white marble. Any traces of paint or of ancient wax coating which survived into modern times either lay beneath the patina or the patina itself contained them. Among the Elgin collection are a number of architectural fragments from the Parthenon whose meander and other patterns added in paint are obvious to the casual naked eye at the present day. Other painted patterns can still be seen on the building. The paint appears to be sealed into the patina.

The patina also preserves, indeed in many cases makes more visible, the surface texture of the original fifth-century marble where it has not been eroded. Chisel marks can be seen, for example, on parts of the Helios group, as shown in Plate 12. A line of tiny drill holes, which emphasize the outlines of the figures and help to achieve the illusion of depth are to be seen on one of the blocks of the frieze.[27] Elsewhere on the frieze, the patina, where it survives, reveals tiny lines where the surface was smoothed until the ancient artists were satisfied that they had achieved their desired final effects.[28]

Contrary to what was assumed in Elgin's time, ancient Greek methods of carving marble were very different from those used since the Renaissance in modern Europe. The Greek sculptors, for example, seem to have worked on every side of a statue at the same time, never allowing any one part of the carving to go ahead of the rest, and so preserving their sense of the artistic unity of the whole composition as each tiny layer of marble was removed.[29] The ancient sculptors learned some of their techniques for working marble from Egypt. Others, such as the use of the running drill, they invented for themselves at different historical times in antiquity which recent research has made it possible to pin-point. But much still remains mysterious.[30]

It is not known, for example, how the artists achieved such an amazingly fine exactness both in the sculptures and in the architectural blocks, each of which is unique, in such a short time. As Sheila Adam, author of the standard work on the techniques of Greek sculpture, has remarked:

The drapery in some of the pedimental figures from the Parthenon is carved in a wealth of deep and richly variegated folds. The sculptor has made no attempt to save himself trouble; the design was all-important and technique must be stretched to accomplish it. Literally thousands of holes of different sizes must have been drilled in the carving of these draped figures . . .[31]

Manolis Korres, the architect of the current programme to preserve the Acropolis monuments, who has studied the marble of the building more closely than any predecessor since the fifth century, has written of his sense of wonder at the technical skills of the ancient marble workers, among whose greatest achievements, he believes, were their metal tools.

Judging from the quality of the marks left by these tools on the marble, they must have been of a quality much higher than that of their modern counterparts. It would appear that in antiquity certain craftsmen had, after much systematic experimental research, discovered unsurpassed metallurgical processes. Knowledge of the contents of these processes is denied to us today along with so many other secrets that were lost with the decline of the ancient world.[32]

Among the inscriptions found on the Acropolis are building accounts for the Erechtheion which show the payments made to the sculptors who executed single figures on the frieze. The accounts for the Parthenon record payments to the sculptors who worked on the pediments in 434–433.[33] Adam believed that she could begin to identify some of the individual masons and sculptors practising in Greece from their distinctive styles. In the slow work of advancing our understanding of ancient art, the historic surfaces of original works, with their tool marks, their traces of polish and paint, and their metal residues, are a prime source.

Apart from effects of moulding, the Elgin Marbles may have lost some of their historic surfaces as a result of their time at sea (and in some cases under the sea), in the long periods of storage in salty seaports, and when they were in the open air in London. Writing in a book published in 1819, three years after they were acquired for the nation, Edward Dodwell, who had admired the patina in Athens, wrote:

Upon some parts of the statues from the tympana [pediments] of the Parthenon, and upon the architectural fragments of the Erechtheion, which are in the British Museum, remains of this golden patina are still visible, though much diminished since their removal from Athens.[34]

Nevertheless it is evident that when the Elgin Marbles were transferred to the British Museum in 1816, their ancient patina was still largely intact. An oil painting of the Temporary Elgin Room officially commissioned to commemorate the opening in 1819, shows the Marbles as honey-coloured.[35] In a water-colour made by a professional artist exhibited in 1818 they are a deeper brown.[36] The same shades of brown can be seen in the many other pictures painted during the nineteenth century.[37] When in 1880 Lord Leighton, the President of the Royal Academy, painted his self-portrait standing in front of the Parthenon frieze, he showed it in the same rich brown as he used in his many paintings.[38]

From the beginning some viewers were uncomfortable with what they saw. Ancient marble statues had been white, western Europe had come to believe over the centuries since the time of the Renaissance, and modern sculptures should be the same. Nor was the presumed whiteness of classical sculpture merely an archaeological error which could be put right as knowledge developed and spread. It was an essential component of the prevailing theories of art which were accepted all over Europe. Winckelmann, for example, believed that ancient marble statues were normally white, the colour of purity, and smoothed in wax.[39] As he wrote in his chapter 'Von dem Wesentlichen der Kunst' (On what is Essential of Art), in his *Geschichte der Kunst des Altertums* (History of Ancient Art):

Die Farbe aber sollte wenig Antheil an der Betrachtung der Schönheit haben, weil nicht sie, sondern die Bildung das Wesen derselben ausmachet, und über dieses werden sich Sinne, die erleuchtet sind, ohne Widerspruch leicht vereinigen. Da nun die weisse Farbe diejenige ist, welche die mehresten Lichtstrahlen zurükschiket, folglich sich empfindlicher machet: so wird auch ein schöner Körper desto schöner sein, je weisser er ist . . .

For the essence of beauty consists not in colour but in shape, and on this point enlightened minds will at once agree. As white is the colour which reflects the greatest number of rays of light, and consequently is the most sensitive, a beautiful body will, accordingly, be the more beautiful the whiter it is.[40]

Italian marble, from which the statues which Winckelmann saw were made, contains less iron than Greek marble, and it remains white for longer. The brown colour of the Parthenon, it was frequently noted by visitors to Greece throughout the nineteenth century, gave a pleasing impression of age, but it detracted from what was seen as the original purity.[41] The grand neo-Hellenic buildings with which Athens was adorned in the years after independence were invariably built in a glittering dazzling white, further emphasizing the differences between the old and the new, the weathered and the unstained.[42]

Until the 1950s the atmosphere of London was heavily polluted with soot. Fogs were frequent, and even on good days the daylight was poor. The Elgin Marbles, removed from Athens, were a variegated patchwork of white and browns, with patches of black especially in the folds of the draperies. In some places there were unexplained encrustations. In the strong Mediterranean sun, the patinated surfaces absorbed and reflected the light. In drab London, though frequently washed, the Elgin Marbles looked dingy and dirty.[43] Plaster casts of the Elgin Marbles, by contrast, were uniformly white, with varnish giving a touch of apparent translucency. If the arrival of the Marbles had dealt a blow to some aspects of the Winckelmann aesthetic, the later proliferation of casts at home and abroad tended, paradoxically, to pull public expectations back towards it. To many who had known the Marbles already from casts or pictures, a visit to the British Museum could be a disappointment. The reproductions were more like what Greek statues were expected to look like than the originals.

With public expectations differing from the experiences the public actually received, the British Museum authorities were under pressure to bring the two more into line. Attempts were made from time to time to brighten the exhibits by colouring the walls. They began as a rich red, as in the Uffizi in Florence, where the Venus dei Medici had long been displayed, or in a Victorian picture gallery. Visitors were later offered a touch of the Mediterranean sky with bright blue. But there was always pressure to do more, and not only from the ignorant. 'Mere stains' was the comment of the sculptor Westmacott, son of the whiter than white neo-classical sculptor of the same name, and long a dominant figure in the British Museum, as late as 1864 when yet more overwhelming evidence was discovered that ancient statues had been painted.[44]

In 1921 Jacob Epstein, a celebrated sculptor in marble, protested at what he saw as the damage being done to the Demeter of Cnidos by men who knew little about the properties of marble.[45] To judge from a water-colour of 1880, from old photographs, from what Epstein and others remembered, and from the present appearance of the statue, the Museum authorities of the day ordered the surface to be stripped of its surface patina, leaving the statue a uniform white.[46] However, it seems to have been partly at least due to the scandal of the damage to the Demeter that new arrangements were brought into force. 'All the officers of the [Greek and Roman] Department knew several years ago', it was reported in 1938, 'that it is dangerous to let masons clean sculpture because they are inclined to prefer their own trade processes to our scientific ones'. The washing of the sculptures in the Museum, it was said, was previously done periodically by the labourers 'with ordinary water and hard brushes'.[47] In 1934 the British Museum set out its new policies in a published book. They had been devised and implemented some years earlier:

Marble monuments . . . are ill adapted to withstand washing, as the surface is absorbent; water containing soap or caustic soda attacks the binding material, and in time causes the crystals to fall away like so much granulated sugar, leaving rough white patches on the sculpture which is a great disfigurement.

The Marbles are gone over regularly with a feather duster. About once per annum they receive a thorough dusting by brush and are then washed with [a solution of soft soap and ammonia]. They are sponged immediately

afterwards with fresh water, and rubbed down with a clean soft cloth . . .
It is not desirable to try to get a uniform surface all over the work, but
only to clean off direct action dirt, and not to remove the natural discol-
oration of the material. The hollows and cavities need only have the loose
dirt removed.[48]

Arthur Holcombe, one of the mason's labourers employed by the
Museum, was trained to carry out the washing in the newly
approved manner with the proper brushes and distilled water. He
was kept on long after the normal retirement age. 'No other person
washed or cleaned sculpture for the next four years,' it was reported
in 1938, 'and no washing was done except by the Keeper's order
and under his supervision.'[49] The change came in time to save the
Phigaleian sculptures, the Mausoleum sculptures, and some others.
The Elgin Marbles too, saved from the restorer's chisels by the
modesty of the sculptors of the early nineteenth century, narrowly
escaped being powdered, granulated, and waxed by the zeal of the
museum keepers of the early twentieth.

Conservation was always a matter for official self-congratulation.
The British, it was proclaimed, had not only saved the Elgin
Marbles, they had preserved them. In London they were, as the first
official publication boasted, 'secure from further injury and degradation'.[50] As early as 1851 it was urged that 'in as much as England
was the means of removing the sculptures of the Parthenon from
the original site, she has a point of honour to maintain, not only in
assuring their safe custody, but in doing all that may be done to
further and facilitate their study'.[51] Whatever the Greeks themselves might say, the British authorities were sure that it was best
for Greece that the Marbles were in London.[52] Alongside the
justification of imperial rescue marched an assertion of imperial
stewardship. Nor were such claims without foundation. During
much of its history, to the despair of the Western democracies, the
Greek state took part in an apparently unending succession of
wars, often as the aggressor. Athens was frequently shaken by political instability, by military coups, by civil unrest, and by riots. In
1916, during the First World War, an Anglo-French landing force
fought a bloody engagement with Greek forces positioned in front
of the Acropolis which resulted in heavy casualties on both sides.[53]
Shells were fired from French warships, some of which damaged
the royal palace in central Athens. The allies were forced to retreat
leaving their dead unburied, and Athens was given over to revenge
massacres.

In the 1920s as a result of the restoration work on the Acropolis, it emerged that the sculptures which had been left on the Parthenon had been damaged to a far greater extent than had been expected. For some parts of the frieze, Lord Elgin's casts preserved features which were lost from the originals by casual vandalism. For the frieze of the Theseum or Hephaisteion, from which Elgin's agents had taken nothing original, his casts now provided a record superior to that of the originals. Unlike the modern Greeks who could not even look after what they still had, it was now said, the British were the true respecters of the classical heritage and its best guardians. What a pity he had not taken more when he had the chance. To many in the West, and not a few in Greece, it seemed to be only a matter of time before the monuments of Athens would again be further damaged or destroyed in some conflict or other. The Elgin Marbles, thankfully, were safe in London.

In 1928 the British government accepted an offer from Sir Joseph Duveen, a millionaire picture dealer, to finance the building of new exhibition galleries at the Tate Gallery and the British Museum. In the debates and decisions about the design of the new Duveen Gallery, we see the Elgin Marbles becoming the site of another cultural contest. When they first arrived in England the main purpose of the display was to enable modern artists to copy and to learn from them. The Elgin Marbles were displayed as models. Later, as modern knowledge of the ancient world became more complete, they were seen as archaeological remains, survivals from the extraordinarily rich period of the ancient civilization to which modern Europe owed most. As such, it was the duty of the Museum authorities to offer viewers a sense and understanding of the original architectural context, by providing pictures, diagrams, and models of the building and displaying casts of those many parts of the sculptures which existed elsewhere. The display in the 1920s and 1930s was 60 per cent originals, 40 per cent casts.[54] If, however, according to the aesthetics of romanticism, the Elgin Marbles were 'works of art', as the public now tended to regard them, and as the new generation of museum professionals now also proclaimed, then they should be offered for admiration and worship, as objects and forms in their own right, in a specially designed secular shrine, where their uniqueness would be emphasized. In the new Duveen Gallery, it was decided, the Elgin Marbles from the Parthenon would be kept free from any intrusion of objects not regarded as 'art', such as the architectural fragments, casts, models, or photographs, all of which would be banished to preparatory ante-rooms.

Sir Joseph Duveen's fortune had been built by buying old pictures in Europe and selling them in the United States. In the years following the First World War, many families in Britain and elsewhere in Europe were glad to ease their financial problems by selling their inherited pictures. Across the Atlantic there were rich men eager to buy. Duveen, it was suspected at the time and is now known for certain, shamelessly modified the pictures he bought to make them more attractive to his potential clients, and they, for the most part, did not know or care that they were being deceived. Old masters were stripped, touched up, repainted, prettified, and coated with varnish, and Duveen would deny that there had been any intervention.[55] Bernard Berenson, an art historian with whom Duveen had a secret financial partnership supplied misleading professional attributions. If a picture was not good enough to be passed off as a Botticelli, it was attributed to the unknown 'master' Amico di Sandro. If, as was pointed out, the Duveen Dürer carried more new paint than old paint, well, he would explain, it had been a Dürer once.[56]

By flattery, lies, gifts, and bribery, and by employing a well-rewarded staff whom he made party to his conspiracies, Duveen was used to getting his way. Having become indispensable to King Edward VII as a supplier of funds and of well-funded friends, he did the same for his son, giving £10,000 to King George V for a 'Leonardo'—which he knew was nothing of the kind—that hung in Windsor Castle. He cemented the relationship with frequent large gifts to the King's private secretary. Duveen had contrived to have himself appointed a Trustee of the National Gallery while being allowed to remain an active, much feared, unscrupulous, dealer. He had secured a knighthood and was shortly to secure a peerage.[57] When the Nazis came to power in Germany he set up a front company to help them sell pictures from German galleries. Duveen is said to have had 'a curious, machine-gun like and hypnotising way of talking, assuming your agreement with what he was saying, which needed real knowledge to stand up to.'[58]

The Trustees of the British Museum knew the man they were dealing with. 'Duveen lectured and harangued us,' Lord Crawford, one of the Trustees, noted in his diary about a meeting at which Duveen's schemes were discussed, 'I suppose he has destroyed more old masters by overcleaning than anybody else in the world, and now he told us that all old marbles should be thoroughly cleaned—so thoroughly that he would dip them into acid.'[59]

Because of problems connected with the buying of the land, which it took time to overcome, it was not until 1936 that actual work on the new gallery began.[60] By that time Duveen was suffering from a terminal illness and he was in a hurry to secure his immortality. As the gallery was being built, the Elgin Marbles were removed from public exhibition to be prepared for their new setting. Duveen and his agents bombarded the authorities with proposals for making the Marbles look more attractive to the public. Coulette, a French moulder employed by Duveen, was permitted to make experiments with the Parthenon frieze aimed at filling in gaps and producing a more uniform colour.[61] Under normal circumstances the Keeper or a member of his curatorial staff was expected to inspect the Elgin Marbles at least once every day. Instead they stopped supervising altogether.

Duveen's agents, against all the professional ethics of the curatorial profession, were given their own keys, so that they could go in and out of the galleries whenever they chose.[62] They also gave orders direct to the Museum staff, especially to Holcombe, the foreman mason. As Berenson admitted after Duveen's death, with the residual shame of an insider who had shared in the conspiracies and the spoils, he 'stood at the center of a vast circular nexus of corruption that reached from the lowliest employee of the British Museum right up to the King'.[63]

It was a long time before anyone in authority discovered that anything was wrong. Harold Plenderleith, the scientist who had devised and recommended the new washing procedures but who had no direct managerial responsibility, told the author that on one occasion at lunchtime, he noticed that metal tools were being used, and told the masons to stop.[64] On the evening of Thursday 22 September 1938, the Director of the Museum, John [later Sir John] Forsdyke, was told about the 'somewhat raw appearance' of parts of the frieze, and next day he instructed Roger Hinks, who was then temporarily in charge of the Department, to 'ensure that improper methods were not being used'.[65] What, if anything Hinks did is not recorded, but on Sunday 25 September the Director 'happened to have occasion to pass through the basement of the Department'. As the official report records:

He was surprised to find there the Helios group in process of cleaning. On the bench he observed a number of copper tools and a piece of coarse carborundum, and from the appearance of the sculptures he at once saw that the tools had been used on the sculptures. On Monday morning 26 September the Iris was found by Mr Hinks to be undergoing similar treatment in an annex to the new Duveen Gallery, and the Selene horse's head was in the Foreman Mason's workshop. The Director ordered all further cleaning operations to be stopped and instituted an inquiry into what had occurred.[66]

To use metal tools on the surface of an ancient statue defied all notions of conservation, then as now. Carborundum, an artificial substance made at intense heat in incandescent furnaces, was at the time, next to diamond, the hardest substance known to science, used for grinding steel tools and for polishing the hardest granite.[67] The Selene horse's head, the most perfectly surviving piece in the whole Elgin collection, had been transformed from brown to white. The Helios group and the Iris, both of which had also been scraped, were now a patchwork of scraped and unscraped surfaces. The three pieces had, in the words of the Director's immediate report, been 'greatly damaged'.[68]

The ultimate responsibility for preserving the national collections entrusted to the British Museum rested with the Board of Trustees in whom authority was vested by Parliament and by the law. However, it was the convention that all the important business of the Museum was handled by a Standing Committee under the chairmanship of the Archbishop of Canterbury, which usually took its lead from, and followed the advice of, the permanent staff. It was also the custom that the Keepers of the various departments reported direct to the Trustees rather than through the Director. A meeting of the Standing Committee was hurriedly summoned to consider the crisis. They immediately decided to set up an internal Board of Enquiry made up of four of their own number 'to consider the nature of the damage and the policy of the Trustees in regard to publication of the facts, to determine responsibility for the damage, and to advise upon the necessary disciplinary action'. From the beginning, the secret of the damage was kept within a small circle who were able to control what was said to their colleagues as well as to outsiders.[69]

The Board was asked to investigate the cleaning of the Selene horse's head, of the Iris, and of the Helios group, that is the three pieces from the pediments which were in the process of being cleaned when the Director discovered what was happening and ordered a stop. The Board of Enquiry was not asked to investigate possible damage to the other pedimental sculptures, to the metopes, or to the frieze, and they did not do so, although they made a remark about the damage to these sculptures in their report. Why the terms of reference should have been so restrictive, and why the Board of Enquiry should have been content to accept them in this form, has not been explained. It seems likely that the Director, with the approval of the Trustees, was already looking for ways of protecting himself. He had been appointed Director of the British Museum in 1936. Before that he had himself been Keeper of Greek and Roman Antiquities. Apart from war service, he had spent his whole career in the Department, including the time when the Demeter scandal occurred. According to a colleague who knew him when he was Director, he 'hated everyone', was much feared, and was effective in getting his way.[70]

The cleaning of the three pieces which he had discovered was, it quickly emerged, not an isolated incident, but part of an operation that had been going on for at least a year and a half and probably longer. If the Board of Enquiry's investigation covered the general question of the cleaning of marble antiquities, it would have to go back to the time when he himself had carried direct departmental responsibility as Keeper of Greek and Roman Antiquities. If the investigation was confined to the cleaning of the Elgin Marbles the Board of Enquiry would still need to examine a long period when he, as Director with a special knowledge, had not ensured that the Department was properly staffed and managed.

The Board of Enquiry, in a series of interviews with those principally concerned, including the masons, quickly established the main facts. Frederick Pryce, the Keeper, who had the direct departmental responsibility, was absent on leave when the discovery was made. He, it emerged, had an alcohol problem, had been 'drinking himself to death' as one of his colleagues remembered, and was frequently ill and absent. Holcombe too was a heavy drinker.[71] Although he at first denied that he or his team had used copper tools, the Board decided that he was not telling the truth.

Before the Marbles were cleaned, Holcombe declared, they were as black as the soot in the grate.[72] Since copper was softer than marble, he claimed, it could never do damage, although, as Epstein was to point out, comparative softness had not prevented the feet of the bronze statues in Italian churches from being worn away by the kissing lips of pilgrims. Holcombe's defence in some ways resembles that of Lord Elgin's agents in Athens when accused of exceeding the powers of the firman. If he had exceeded his authority, he claimed, he was only doing what he and others had done elsewhere. He had made no effort to conceal what he was doing over many months, and the tools he used were lying exposed to full view on the bench when the Director found them. If the Museum authorities had had any doubts they could have called a halt at any time. Holcombe was only doing what he believed was expected by Lord Duveen.

Daniel, a mason employed by Duveen, had urged him and his team to make the sculptures as white as possible. When the cleaning of one of the frieze slabs was completed, he told the Board, Daniel complained that it was not white enough for Lord Duveen's new gallery. The masons were asked to 'brighten it up', and it was accordingly 'recleaned'. 'One or two of the slabs of the frieze came up rather white,' Holcombe said later, 'and I am afraid they caused the trouble. But anyone who knows anything about marble knows that if you treat two slabs in exactly the same manner, it is possible that they will come up a different colour.'[73] The Board of Enquiry also discovered that Daniel had made illegal cash payments to the Museum's masons to thank them for their work, although they did not consider that they amounted to bribery.

When Duveen had ordered the stripping and repainting of old master paintings to make them more acceptable to his clients, it could be said in his defence that, at least, the paintings which he damaged were, mostly, his own property. The Elgin Marbles, according to the stewardship claim, were unique and priceless masterpieces held by the British nation in perpetuity on behalf of the whole civilized world. It was Pryce, the Keeper, who gave the professional opinion on the extent of the damage which the Board included in its report.

The effect of the method employed in cleaning the sculptures has been to remove the surface of the marble and to impart to it a smooth and white appearance. Mr Pryce described the Selene's horse's head as having been 'skinned.' The surface of the sculptures, showing the evidences of two thousand years of exposure to the climate of Greece, was a document of the utmost importance. There being no possible doubt about the history of the Parthenon sculptures, they came to the Museum as authentic masterpieces of Greek work of the fifth century B.C. and for purposes of study and comparison they are of inestimable value. The damage which has been caused is obvious and cannot be exaggerated.

Having learned the horrifying facts, the Standing Committee had to decide on what to do, and what, if anything, to say. It was now December 1938. The Duveen Gallery was nearly ready and due to open in May 1939. The King was due to perform the opening. The day when the Elgin Marbles would have to be put on public display again could not long be postponed. If the facts were known a storm of protest could be expected. It would be obvious that not only the Director and the Keeper, but the Trustees too had failed catastrophically over a long period. The Government too would be furious that, through sheer incompetence and mismanagement, the British Museum had thrown away the British claim to be exercising a wise stewardship, one of the main justifications in the continuing dispute with Greece. Urged by Stanley Baldwin, the former prime minister who had recently been elected a Trustee, the Archbishop and the Standing Committee decided that their best course was to say as little as possible and to pretend that nothing much had happened.[74] The greatest disaster in the history of the British Museum, they decided, was to be shrugged off as a temporary lapse in the supervising of the workmen.

The Marbles had left the galleries a warm brown. Most were now a dull unpolished white. As for the three pieces where the cleaning had been interrupted, the extent of the scraping, the skinning, and the whitening cried out for an explanation. How could the dramatic change in the appearance of the Marbles, now obvious to the most inexpert observer, be explained? It was not only the facts which needed to be covered up.

A solution was to hand. As the minutes of the meeting of the Standing Committee record:

They have learned with satisfaction that remedial measures applied by the Director and Dr Plenderleith have mitigated to a considerable extent the evidence of the treatment which the three pedimental sculptures have received so far as the eye of the general public is concerned but to the expert the damage will remain discernible.

What the 'remedial measures' were is not recorded in the papers. But there is no doubt about what happened. The Director, with the advice of his scientific adviser, covered up the Marbles with some kind of coloured coating. If brown had been taken off, brown could be put back on.[75]

In dealing with the staff, the Standing Committee foresaw another danger. If anyone were to be dismissed, that would be an admission that what had gone wrong was more serious than they were willing to admit. Under questioning the official version might unravel.[76] The Trustees, Baldwin advised, must at all costs avoid giving anyone the sack. Who should take the blame? Pryce, the Keeper, was given early retirement on medical grounds. Holcombe was finally retired at the age of 74. But was that enough? If, as had been obvious for years, the Keeper was incapable of doing his job, it was the responsibility of the Director to make sure that the work of his Department did not suffer. Instead of taking the responsibility himself, Forsdyke fixed his eye on the unfortunate Hinks, the Assistant Keeper, who was persuaded to believe that the disaster was primarily his fault. The Standing Committee decided that Hinks should be reprimanded, deprived of ten years' seniority with loss of pay, matters which did not need to be publicly announced or defended, but he was also told that, if he did not make a fuss, the decision would later be quietly reversed. If, however, Hinks were to decide to resign of his own accord, he was told that 'it would not be to his disadvantage'.[77] When, to the Trustees' delight, Hinks resigned, there was no public need for even the mild disciplinary measures, and they were all dropped. Soon afterwards the Director felt able to make a public denial that the recent staff changes in the British Museum were connected in any way with the cleaning of the Elgin Marbles.[78] If Hinks had failed to save the skin of Selene's horse, he could still save the skins of the Archbishop, of the Trustees, and of the Director.

In May 1939 the rumours began. 'Elgin Marbles (Worth £1,000,000) Damaged in Cleaning' ran a headline in the Daily Mail. 'Reports of irreparable damage to the Elgin Marbles . . . have been whispered in art circles during the past few weeks.' Ingenious methods have been used to conceal the state of the damage, wrote a reporter for the Daily Telegraph who visited the Museum. The frieze was on show, but none of the metopes, and the three pedimental pieces which were partly cleaned and partly not had been replaced by casts. Epstein, who saw them at this time, and who knew about the use of metal tools, protested in The Times that the Elgin Marbles were 'permanently ruined'.[79]

In the new display the public was prevented from taking too close a look. Bernard Ashmole, the professor of archaeology at

London University, and an undoubted expert, was among the few
who saw the display at this time. Some of the metopes, he noted:

were at eye level, but railed off so that a close view was impossible, but
they did look unnaturally white; I ought to have realised that something
was wrong but didn't.[80]

The separating rail was, along with the artificial coating, among the
so-called 'remedial measures' which 'mitigated the evidence' to all
but the 'experts'. There had been no rail in the approved design for
the Duveen Gallery.[81]

A public statement made in response to the outcry was reported
in the press:

Yesterday the trustees of the British Museum issued a Statement that they
found unauthorised methods were being introduced in some instances and
that this was done without the knowledge of the officers of the Museum
who were responsible for the cleaning. The Statement added that the
effects of the methods used were imperceptible to any one but an expert
and concludes 'The Trustees do not allow any departure from their
approved methods, and at once took the necessary steps to ensure that no
such innovations should be adopted at the Museum.'[82]

Far from admitting that anything had gone badly wrong, the
Trustees now tried to take credit for the firmness and speed of their
response. By describing as 'innovations', methods of cleaning
marble which would have disgraced a municipal cemetery, they
gave the impression that they were solid, reliable, old-fashioned,
conservatives who could be safely trusted not to be seduced from
their duty by the wizardry of modern science.

Sir George Hill, who had been Keeper at the time of the
Demeter scandal, spread black propaganda in *The Times*, at that
time a mouthpiece of the Government. Epstein, Hill sneered, must
have been looking at a cast of the Demeter, 'which less expert
critics than himself may well have taken for an original', not at the
real statue. Epstein might be the most famous marble sculptor of
the day, but as a Jewish American, he needed to be put in his place.[83]
Hill's final paragraph, apparently given with all the authority of the
steadfast Trustees, is a masterpiece of the pompous diversionary
indignation often used in cover-ups:

I may be allowed to add that no such thing as 'restoration' of the Parthenon
Marbles has been or will be undertaken as long as the authorities of the
British Museum have them in their keeping; and no 'cleaning' other than

simple washing with neutral soap and distilled water is authorised in the Museum.[84]

Sir George Hill took care to say that no restoration or drastic cleaning was authorized. He did not say that they had not taken place.

The answers given in the House of Commons by a Treasury Minister, on the advice of the Trustees, continued the policy of stonewalling and obfuscation. Some questions the minister refused to answer on the grounds that they were matters for the Trustees.[85] On others the minister claimed that the responsibility did not lie with the Director.[86] Some of the follow-up questions are typical of 'inspired' questions offered to compliable government supporters by the party whips in order to blunt the criticism and to use up the allotted time.[87] On the main point, the minister's answers were so economical with the truth as to be seriously misleading.

The Marbles are in the process of transference to the new Gallery, but none of them have suffered in any way by the removal. So far as cleaning is concerned, I am informed by the trustees of the British Museum that there has been some unauthorised cleaning of some of the marbles but that it is not yet possible to determine precisely what the effect has been. I am assured however that the effects are imperceptible to anyone but an expert and I think it follows that the intrinsic beauty of the marbles has not been impaired.[88]

All that I can say about that is that if any damage has been done, it is completely imperceptible to ordinary people like ourselves, and I very much doubt whether it is very obvious to experts.[89]

The Trustees and the Director, locked in a tacit agreement to save one another's skins, had now drawn the Government into the conspiracy. It is not known whether the Greek government made any protest at this time. A Foreign Office file of 1939, labelled 'Treatment of Elgin Marbles: use of copper wire brushes to clean the marbles thus damaging the surface', has been destroyed.[90]

By the summer of 1939 everyone knew that war was imminent and that air raids on London were to be expected. The first task of Ashmole, the hurriedly appointed temporary Keeper, was to move the sculptures as close to the walls of the gallery as possible, roof them over with corrugated iron and heavy timbers, and protect them with sandbags.[91] Soon afterwards the slabs of the frieze were put in cases and carefully stored in an unused section of the London Underground at the Aldwych Station. The metopes and pedimental sculptures were taken from the gallery to the Museum's vaults.

In 1940, by which time Lord Duveen had died, the gallery suffered minor bomb damage, but the antiquities were safe, and in 1945, when the war ended, it was confirmed that the Elgin Marbles had not been damaged by enemy action. The Trustees, however, were in no hurry to return to the unfinished business of 1939. Three years after the end of the war the Elgin Marbles were still in storage. By September 1948, Epstein and others began to question whether the nation was ever going to see them again.[92] A generation of artists, archaeologists, and art historians had been deprived of an essential part of their education. At last in November 1948 the cases were brought back from the Aldwych and the vaults and in September 1949, nearly four and a half years after the end of the war, the Elgin Marbles were at last again put on public view in the British Museum. The Forsdyke brown, as well as some of the dirt accumulated during the years of storage, was apparently allowed to remain, and the Marbles again appeared darker than the surrounding gallery walls as they had before 1938.[93]

Apart from the brief appearance of the frieze in 1939, it was more than twelve years since the Marbles had last been publicly seen. By 1949 only a few people could remember what they had looked like before the events of 1938. No statement was made, nothing was published, the relevant papers were closed to the staff as well as the public, and the scandal remained contained. Scholars and archaeologists who knew what had happened, many of whom felt a deep sense of shame, were willing to whisper. But details were few. Gradually the memory faded.

In 1948 a British team of scholars and archaeologists, including Sir John Forsdyke, went to Greece to assess the extent of the war damage to the monuments there. In December 1944 British forces had landed in Athens to restore the monarchist government, and took part in fighting in central Athens. Most of the buildings on the Acropolis, including the Parthenon, the team reported, had been chipped and scarred by bullets and by mortar fire, with some large pieces being dislodged. The British troops had used pieces of broken marble, including some from the Parthenon, to build fire positions, but, according to the report, they put them all back when the fighting ended. The report concluded, with some smugness:

The Acropolis rock of Athens, which was occupied by British troops, easily absorbed the thirty two mortar bombs directed against it by the Greek rebels. In a few years' time when the flecks, which still glisten white, have been toned down by wind and weather, historians will look in vain for traces of the operations which clouded Anglo-Greek relations for a time.[94]

Although in 1948 the Elgin Marbles were still hidden in their packing cases deep under London, the discourses of rescue and stewardship were already back on the surface on full public display.

For over twenty years the war-damaged Duveen Gallery stood like a gigantic gloomy tomb ready to receive the Elgin Marbles into their final resting place. In hopes that Duveen's heirs might pull out of the deal, or that the building could be redesigned, successive post-war Keepers put off the repairs and the reopening for as long as possible, but excuses ran out and the gallery opened for the second time in 1961, much as Duveen had wanted it.[95] The name of Lord Duveen occupied the most prominent place on the wall, those of Phidias and of Lord Elgin being dropped altogether.[96] The plan to exhibit the banished casts in another room was never carried out.[97]

Although, in its rectangular shape, the Duveen Gallery is vaguely reminiscent of the inside of a Greek temple, it gives a misleading idea of the size, shape, and colour of the Parthenon. The central scene of the frieze, which in its original place on the temple was set above the entrance on the short east side, was placed on one of the long sides of the gallery. Reinforcing the misleading impression of the dedication inscription that the gallery contains 'THE PARTHENON SCULPTURES' and not just a portion of them, the Marbles were arranged in a false symmetry giving a misleading impression of completeness. The central scene, which on the temple was flanked on each side by representations of the twelve Olympian gods arranged in two groups, was now interrupted on the right, where the relevant slab remained in Athens, by a large fake wooden door.

In ancient Athens the sculptures faced out, the observer looked in. The frieze as designed offered a changing narrative to the citizens of ancient Athens as they moved round the outside of the building until they reached the culmination. As now presented, following a modern European aesthetic which would have dismayed the people of ancient Athens, it was the observer who was now the centre, not the sacred building of the goddess. The whole frieze, and what remained of both pediments, could now be appropriated in one sweep of a westernizing gaze. Wrenched from their original context by Lord Elgin, the sculptures were now wrenched into a fake context by Lord Duveen.

In preparation for the second opening, the Elgin Marbles were washed. Beneath the Forsdyke coating of 1939, the conservators found a raw granulating surface described as 'milky' or 'hazy'. To offset this effect the Marbles were again coated with a wax-like substance.[98] Forsdyke's barrier rail, which prevented viewers from seeing the exhibits too closely, although moveable and not shown in official photographs, also became a permanent feature, and the Elgin Marbles are still the only exhibits which are so cordoned. In recent decades, coloured spotlights prevent viewers from ever seeing the Marbles in natural or plain light, which in the Duveen Gallery is, in any case, particularly poor. By exaggerating the shadows, the coloured lights give further encouragement to viewers to see ancient Greek art through the anachronizing eyes of nineteenth-century romanticism. By giving an impression of brown where it no longer exists, they help to offset the dull waxed white, neither original nor historic, which will be Lord Duveen's most enduring legacy.

Since 1949, when the Elgin Marbles first went back on view, the Trustees of the British Museum have published a succession of guides, booklets, and books about the Parthenon and its sculptures, most of which deal with its later as well as with its ancient history. Not one of them has made any mention, however muted or oblique, of the fact that the Elgin Marbles were damaged. Even the fact of the cleaning has never been mentioned.[99] The pretence that nothing much happened has continued to the present day. A recent book-length study of the changing aesthetics of the display of antiquities in the British Museum between the years 1800 and 1939, scholarly, well illustrated in colour, and excellent in all other ways, is entirely silent on the biggest change that occurred to the Elgin Marbles during the period discussed, indeed the biggest change since 1687.[100]

Denied access to the facts, and taking past public statements at face value, the scholarly and scientific staff of the British Museum, and their colleagues at home and abroad, came to accept a revised version of the stewardship argument. Those who cleaned the Elgin Marbles before the war, it has come to be believed, were only following what was regarded as best practice at the time.[101] In 1983 in a debate in the House of Lords about the British Museum, a minister declared that the Elgin Marbles 'had been well cared for by the British Museum'.[102] As recently as January 1997, a letter in *The Times* could claim, without much risk of contradiction, that in

London the Marbles had been 'meticulously cared for'.[103] Even Melina Mercouri, who as a Minister of the Greek Government campaigned for the return of the Parthenon sculptures, acknowledged 'the excellent care given to the Marbles by the British Museum'.[104]

After his resignation from the British Museum in 1939 Hinks made a career in the British Council and died in 1963. In 1984 extracts from his diary were published which gave some facts about the cleaning episode which at that time were unknown.[105] Having been asked to review the book in which the extracts appeared, I asked to see the official records but was told by the Secretary of the Museum that, under the terms of the Public Records Acts, they were closed to the public until 1 January 1998.[106]

Until 1958 there was no general provision for public access to public records, each government department and non-departmental public body such as the British Museum having the right to decide, case by case, in what circumstances to grant access. In 1958 the Public Records Act established the so-called Fifty Year Rule, which was amended by a subsequent Act of Parliament in 1967 to the Thirty Year Rule. Under these laws, all public records enter the public domain thirty years after they are created, with certain highly limited exceptions which require the personal authorization of the Lord Chancellor. As the legislation was passing through Parliament the Ministers of the day gave a number of assurances, stressing that the provisions for exceptions would only be used in highly exceptional circumstances, and not simply to avoid political embarrassment. As far as can be judged, and in the opinion of many professional historians, these promises have been honoured. The papers relating to the Suez fiasco of 1956, for example, have been released.

By the terms of the legislation government departments and most other public bodies are required by the law to deposit their records with the Public Records Office, whose duty it is to ensure that the law is adhered to. The British Museum, since it is regarded as a public body dedicated to historical inquiry and is itself a custodian of many national public records, was, exceptionally, as a matter of convenience, permitted to retain its own archives.

The public records relating to the cleaning of the Elgin Marbles were created in 1938 and 1939. Until 1996, all applications to exercise what researchers were advised by legal experts were their statutory rights, were turned down by the British Museum authorities. In 1984 the Director at the time, Sir David Wilson, alleged 'security implications' as the reason for denying access, although all departures from the Thirty Year Rule on security or other grounds can only be authorized by the Lord Chancellor personally, and no approach had been made to seek such an exemption. Sir David also implied that he was bound by the statute not to grant access, although nothing in the statute would have prevented the Museum authorities from giving access if they had chosen to do so.[107]

In subsequent correspondence the Museum authorities claimed that they had a legal justification for refusing access based on a subsection relating to the dating of documents in files and assemblies of papers.[108] Their claim that the papers were deliberately kept together in order to constitute the Museum's 'corporate memory' implies that the authorities were aware of what they contained.[109] According to legal experts who specialize in administrative law, given the intentions of the Act as a whole as emphasized by Ministers, a court would be likely to regard it as unreasonable for the Museum to read the subsection in a way which would defeat the purposes of the Thirty Year rule.

The Museum authorities have denied that there has been any manipulation of the records aimed at postponing the date when they would be obliged to expose the events of 1938 and 1939 to historical inquiry.[110] If their interpretation of the subsection were accepted, every new document which was added to the assembly of papers gained the Museum another thirty years of secrecy. Volume 7, in which the relevant documents are pasted, is a heavy wood and leather ledger. It bears the ticket of the suppliers, 'Barclay and Fry, Contractors to His Majesty', which implies that it was purchased before 1952, the year of the death of George VI. Some papers of 1944 appear to have been cut out without explanation. Comparing the time span which the volume covers with that of the other volumes in the series reveals the extraordinarily long period of time it covers.[111]

Volume 4, 1876–1892	16 years
Volume 5, 1892–1915	23 years
Volume 6, 1916–1932	16 years
Volume 7, 1932–1967	35 years
Volume 8, 1968–1971	3 years

So many papers have been bound in that Volume 7 has become a thick, triangular wedge, so unwieldy, and so unlike a normal volume in shape, that it cannot stand on a shelf alongside other normal-sized volumes, without taking up the space of three.

In 1995, when I again complained in a letter to the Secretary of the Museum that, in refusing me access, the Museum authorities were denying my statutory rights, I was approached by one of the Trustees. As we walked round an Oxbridge quad like characters in a novel by C. P. Snow, I had the strong impression that he was offering to negotiate with me. In 1996, after some further months of delay, I was finally given access to the papers which reveal the facts described in this chapter.

In an official guide to the British Museum's collections published in 1989, the former director drew a picture of the steadfast Museum upholding scholarly standards against ignorant outsiders:

The Museum is governed by a body of Trustees who act truly in the sense of that title, protecting it from ephemeral media pressure and political clamour . . . Without the protecting and caring interests of the series of most distinguished members of the Board of Trustees, the British Museum would be a poorer place than it is today. The Museum is buffetted from time to time by uninformed clamour, and it needs the backing of such powerful figures . . .[112]

The history of the Elgin Marbles suggests a different interpretation. The damage done to the Marbles by the Museum's employees continued, without interruption, over a number of years, despite warnings and protests. When the disaster was eventually discovered, rather than face up to their public statutory responsibilities, the Museum authorities clutched at any excuse, quibble, dubious device, or diversionary slur, that might postpone the day when the truth could no longer be concealed. The policy of avoiding public accountability by slow retreat, inch by inch, and yielding only under irresistible pressure, has been continued over the years right up to the last hour.

Sixty years after the event, it is at last possible to offer some initial judgements about the scale of the damage done. As far as can be judged from comparing the present state of the sculptures with what is thought to have been their prior condition as recorded by witnesses and as shown in old photographs, all the metopes, 80 or 90 per cent of the frieze, and about half the pedimental sculptures of the Parthenon were damaged by overcleaning at some time before the halt was called.[113]

Apart from the minority of pieces which were not cleaned, or were only partially cleaned, the Elgin Marbles are now a dull white or grey. Their surfaces are now different from the surfaces of the sculptures which remained in Athens which still show the scaly surfaces, the variegated brown patinas, and the occasional shining surface textures which were formerly present on the sculptures now in London.[114] The damage is both archaeological and aesthetic.

On the frieze of the Mausoleum, exhibited in a nearby gallery of the British Museum, and not railed off, the naked eye can see the bright red of a plume and some blue on the background. On another statue there appear to be traces of gold. On the Phigaleian sculptures, which also escaped overcleaning, a recent analysis made with the help of an electron microscope has detected traces of a gypsum plaster coating probably applied in ancient times after the sculptures were put in place on the building.[115] As has been repeatedly shown in the recent history of archaeology, traces, even minuscule traces, can sometimes allow larger questions to be solved, including the making of discoveries not yet within our current research capabilities or horizons. The prospect of recovering similar evidence from the Parthenon sculptures, whether of paint, other coatings, or of metal, has been severely reduced, perhaps lost. The damage which has destroyed the evidence of the past, has also destroyed possibilities for the future.

Among the sculptures from the Parthenon in London there are obvious differences between those which were casualties of the 1930s and those which survived. Most of the large groups of the east pediment, for example, have, mercifully, come through with their historic surfaces largely intact, and appear to be in much the same condition as they were when Elgin's agents removed them. The Ilissos from the west pediment also appears largely as it was, apart from the earlier loss of its paint. On the other hand, most of the smaller pedimental figures from the west pediment appear to have been stripped. On the figure of Amphitrite, from which the black which lay within the deep folds of the drapery has been scraped out, the valleys in the marble are now whiter than the peaks, so that the Amphitrite looks like a film negative among a display of positives.[116]

The historic surface has also been removed from most of the frieze, and the exceptions are revealing. The large patch of brown on one of the slabs of the maidens of the procession, for example, on which the delicate lines of the artists' smoothing tools can still be seen, shows vividly what has been lost elsewhere.[117] Why that slab should have escaped is unknown, but it may have been regarded as so badly damaged that it was left behind to the last—like the lame boy in the story of the Pied Piper of Hamelin, it was saved by its injuries. On a few of the other slabs which have been stripped of most of their patina, it can be seen that those who did the scraping, perhaps fearing to go too near the jagged line, have left a thin raised ribbon of patina near the edges.[118] Again these may be traces of unfinished business postponed to the last. In photographs of the pieces taken before 1938 there are no signs of these lines.[119]

The long slab of the frieze which shows the central event of the handing over of the cloth (reproduced as Plate 1), retains a good deal of patina on the lower half. This piece was not taken from the building by Elgin's agents but found among the fortifications of the Acropolis wall. As the slab was being moved it broke into two parts, opening up two long jagged edges of raw white marble. As the slab is at present exhibited no attempt has been made to conceal the break line with plaster, as was usual in the past, and as Duveen's men wanted, but the broken edges are not white, as one would expect, but the same brownish colour as the top half of the slab. These edges have presumably since been coated and coloured.

After it left Athens in 1802 the two pieces spent two years at the bottom of the sea when the *Mentor* sank, exposed to the salt water and to the corroding sands of two seasons of winter and summer storms. After being salvaged from the sea in 1804, they spent another five months buried under seaweed and brushwood on the beach at Cythera and eight years in store in Malta, and were not unpacked until they reached England in 1812. Despite these vicissitudes, the historic surfaces of the two pieces of the broken central slab are better preserved than those of the many other slabs which came straight from Athens without mishap but which were later scraped.

The metopes have suffered more. As far as the naked eye can judge, there is now no trace of historic patina on any of them.

The most vivid evidence for the extent of the damage is in the three pieces which were still being cleaned when Sir John Forsdyke discovered what was going on in September 1938, the Helios, the Selene horse's head, and the Iris. In the case of the Helios group and the Iris the historic surfaces and the scraped surfaces can be seen side by side.

As far as the Helios is concerned, Plate 12 shows vividly what Holcombe and his team of 'six hefty men' had been doing at the moment the 'cleaning' was stopped.[120] On the right side of the god's neck, as it exists today, there still remains the original fifth-century surface, now black but still shiny from its original polishing. On the left side, the polished surface has now been scrubbed away, leaving a dull matt white surface. On Helios' right shoulder there remains the black shining surface, now rough and gnarled by time. On his left shoulder, on the other side of the cessation line, the surface is now a dull, unpolished, Duveenian white. On the right side of Helios' lower neck innumerable indentations made by the chisels of the original artists, some quite deep, can still be clearly discerned. On his left side, across the cessation line, there are scarcely any such traces.

The British Museum store contains a plaster cast of the Helios group which derives, directly or indirectly, from a mould made from the original in the nineteenth century. The surface of this cast appears to show tool marks on both sides of the cessation line. Another cast of the Helios in Cambridge also seems to reveal impressions of tool marks which are no longer detectable on the original.[121] The conclusion is inescapable. The scraping of 1938 removed a layer of marble from the original surface so deep that the original tool marks have been lost.

Of the Selene horse's head Canova wrote, in 1815, that 'it is of the finest possible workmanship, and its surface has been very little injured', a view publicly endorsed by Cockerell in 1830.[122] When the halt was called in 1938, the 'cleaning' was evidently nearly completed, and there are no obvious cessation lines. However, comparing the original, as it exists now, with earlier photographs and casts, it looks as if in addition to skinning off the patina, Holcombe removed some of the calcareous incrustations.[123] A case can be made for removing such incrustations, which are additions to the original surface, although not by entrusting the work to a mason who had no knowledge of what was original surface and what was incrustation. Incrustations on the frieze and metopes seem also to have been scraped off.

The Iris had one of the most fragile historic surfaces of all the Elgin Marbles. The Museum's standing orders required that, when it received its annual wash in distilled water, the conservation

experts should be consulted and the actual washing closely super-
vised by the curatorial staff.[124] Instead, the Iris too appears to have
been scraped with wire brushes, metal tools, and carborundum. The
white left leg, where a patch of residual patina had not yet been
removed when the halt was called, looks as if it had been smeared
in dog dirt. In Berlin, by a stroke of fortune, there survives a cast
which was probably made from the first moulds taken from the
original in 1838. Unlike most other surviving casts, the Berlin cast
appears to be in the same state as it was when it arrived from the
moulds in London. Although some parts are lost, the cast retains
all of the original join lines, and appears to be unvarnished and
unpainted.[125] On one of the folds of the drapery of the Berlin cast
there can be discerned a group of wavy parallel impressions, like
an enlarged fingerprint, of which there is now no obvious trace on
the original.[126] Although these marks may have been caused when
the moulds or the casts were made, it is possible that, as on the
Helios group and elsewhere, they are impressions of tool marks
now lost from the surfaces of the originals.

Adam found few tool marks of any kind on the Parthenon sculptures compared with the numbers to be found on other sculptures
made at the same time.[127] 'Once the marble has been worked with
the flat,' she wrote of the flat chisel, 'its surface is almost completely
level, and it does not take long to remove any remaining tool marks
with rasp or emery.'[128] 'The Parthenon sculptures reveal as little
about the work of the flat as of most other tools,' she noted with
some surprise.[129] Since Adam did not know about the extent of the
damage done to the surfaces in the late 1930s, her surprise may
have been more perceptive than she could have guessed. Adam
may also have been led by the present matt surfaces into believing
that sculptures of the classical period had not been generally polished unlike those made before and after the classical period.[130]
Here too she may have been misled by the changes made to the
surfaces in the 1930s. By suppressing the facts about what actually
happened, it would seem, the British Museum authorities have polluted the prime sources of research and have caused errors about
the nature of Greek art to be given a wide, apparently authoritative, currency.

Whether the British Museum authorities before 1996 acted
improperly or unlawfully, whether they took decisions inconsistent
with their statutory and trusteeship duties, and whether they
misused their powers, can be left to the competent authorities to

determine. As far as the Elgin Marbles are concerned, what seems to be needed now is for the Government to insist on a full, open, international study of the historic surfaces as they stand at the present day. The aim of the inquiry would be to establish, as far as can now be known, what has been taken off, what has been put on, and generally to assess the extent of the damage to the sculptures from the time when the Elgin Marbles were first entrusted to the Museum's care, and report on their present state. The inquiry should be asked specifically to consider the effects of the scrapings of the 1930s.[131] Although the damage done to the sculptures of the Parthenon cannot be reversed or remedied, publishing the results of an honest study into their present state would be the first step towards restoring the Museum's reputation.

25

The Parthenon since Lord Elgin

IN 1822, the year after the outbreak of the Greek Revolution, the town and Acropolis of Athens were captured by the Greek revolutionary forces. When in 1826 an Ottoman army retook the town and laid siege to the Acropolis, the Greek forces made several attempts to force a way through, but all without success, and the Acropolis was surrendered back to the Turks in June 1827. In October of that year the fleets of Britain, France, and Russia destroyed the Ottoman fleet at Navarino. The allied powers had not meant to go to war, but their action effectively prevented a full reconquest of Greece by the Ottoman armies.

When the fighting came to an end, the line separating the Greek and the Ottoman-controlled areas lay to the south of Athens. As elsewhere during the war, the fighting there had been marked by massacres, counter massacres, broken agreements, atrocities, and the forced driving out of populations. There had also been much destruction of property.

T. Abercromby Trant, a captain in the British Navy, who visited Athens in 1829, was shown round by Georg Gropius, who was now the leading foreign archaeologist resident in the town. The Choragic Monument of Thrasyllos, from which Elgin's agents had removed the statue, was, Trant records, totally destroyed. The Monument of Lysicrates still stood—Gropius had financed emergency work to prevent it from collapsing—but part of its frieze and one of its columns had recently been badly damaged by visitors.

The Theseum, which had been converted from a church into a stable for Turkish cavalry, had survived without major structural damage, one of the few buildings to do so in all Athens. A few months before Trant's visit, a swarm of bees had built a hive in the crevices of the eastern pediment. Some Turkish youths, finding they could not easily get at the honey, threw down half the pediment. The sculptures, particularly the metopes, had also suffered recently, a Lapith losing a leg and a Centaur a head, but 'these injuries are

the works of *virtuosi*.[1] The casts of the Theseum made by Elgin's
agents preserve many features irreparably lost from the originals.

Since, even after the end of the fighting, the Acropolis of Athens
was a military fortress not far from the armistice line, the Turks
were reluctant to allow visitors, and there are few accounts of what
happened to the monuments there in the years during and after the
war. The Erechtheion was badly damaged by cannon fire. As for
the Parthenon, the recent discovery of a photograph taken before
1842 has revealed that the damage done to the walls during the
siege of 1822 was far greater than had previously been believed.
Desperate for their lives, the besieged Turks, it is now known,
demolished a long section of the wall in order to extract the ancient
lead joints for use as bullets. Some five hundred and twenty ancient
blocks of the Parthenon were moved out of position of which about
two hundred were cut up for use as makeshift fortifications.[2]

In 1833, after a prolonged period of international negotiations,
Greece was formally recognized as an independent nation state to
be governed, on the European model, under the protection of the
three allied powers, Britain, France, and Russia. Otho, a relative of
the strongly philhellenic King Ludwig of Bavaria, was appointed
king, and the Bavarians were given special privileges to help with
the defence, the reconstruction, and the modernization of the new
nation. It was also agreed that the Kingdom of Greece should
include Athens as its capital city.

In April 1833 Christoph Neezer, the Bavarian officer who
accepted the surrender of the Acropolis from the Turks on behalf
of the new state, described what he found:

Ich aber ging dann ein wenig später auf der Akropolis umher und be-
trachtete die bunt durcheinander aufgehäuften Marmorstücke. In diesem
Chaos, zwischen Säulenkapitellen, zertrümmerten Säulen, kleinen und
großen Marmorstücken, fanden sich Geschützkugeln, Splitter von
Kartätschenkugeln, menschliche Schädel und Gebeine, von denen viele
hauptsächlich bei den anmutigen Karyatiden des Erechtheions aufgehäuft
waren.

But then a little later I walked about on the Acropolis and observed the
heaps of jumbled marbles. In this chaos among column capitals, smashed
columns, marbles large and small, were to be found bullets, splinters of
cannon balls, human skulls and bones, many of which were mainly heaped
up near the graceful Caryatids of the Erechtheion.[3]

For many years afterwards visitors to the Acropolis remarked
on the white gashes where the shooting had scarred the

monuments. As late as the 1840s one of the main sights was the pyramid of fifteen hundred human skulls of the Turks and the Greeks who had died in the sieges, alongside a heap of their commingled bones.[4]

The work of establishing the new state with its own distinctive identity, which had been talked about before and during the war, started the moment the Turks left and was vigorously carried through by successive governments for the next hundred years. The use of an artificially archaized and purified form of Greek was encouraged. Piastres gave way to drachmas. Greek officials assumed ancient titles, such as ephor. Boys who would previously have been christened Constantine or Georgios or Anastasios became Miltiades, Pericles, or Aristoteles. Among innumerable changes in the names of places, Napoli di Romania became Nauplia, Negropont reverted to Chalcis, and Cerigo to Cythera. The street map of the rapidly expanding Athens offered a lengthening catalogue of the gods, goddesses, and heroes of ancient mythology and of ancient history.

Emergency repair work to the monuments on the Acropolis began the moment the Turks left.[5] A garrison of Bavarian troops established their headquarters in the mosque, the only building with a roof. Permits to visit the ruins were issued free of charge to Greeks and to foreigners, and, for the first time in many centuries, the people of Athens were able to feel that the rock was, if not yet quite in their own possession, at least free of enemies.

In 1834 the Bavarian neo-classical architect Leo von Klenze was invited to Athens to advise the new government on a policy for the future of the Acropolis. Like Elgin and most of his contemporaries, von Klenze admired the Athens of the fifth century above all other periods of the past. He proposed that Greece should repair the surviving monuments, using a mixture of old marble and modern imagination. They would, however, remain as ruins, romantic and picturesque, a lasting reminder of what had been lost and what had been regained.

A different vision lay behind the proposals of another leading German neo-classical architect, Karl Friederich Schinkel. Instead of leaving the Acropolis as a monumental ruin, Schinkel proposed the building of a magnificent marble neo-classical royal palace which would stand parallel to the Parthenon, dominating it in scale if not quite in height.[6] The government buildings and gardens which formed part of the scheme would have given life to the Acropolis which, under the von Klenze plan, was deprived of any contemporary purpose. But the Schinkel project would have cost too much and it remained a fantasy. It was von Klenze's plan which was accepted.

From the beginning, it was determined that the artistic, historical, and archaeological heritage would be won back, celebrated, treasured, and preserved, stone by stone, statue by statue, inscription by inscription, vase by vase. At a ceremony in 1834, attended by the young king, von Klenze declared that:

Die Spuren einer barbarischen Zeit, Schutt and formlose Trümmer werden, wie überall in Hellas, auch hier verschwinden, und die Ueberreste der glorreichen Vorzeit werden als die sichersten Stützpunkte einer glorreichen Gegenwart und Zukunft zu neuem Glanze erstehen.[7]

The vestiges of a barbarous age, the rubbish and shapeless rubble will disappear from here, as from all Hellas, and the remains of the glorious past shall shine with new splendour as a firm base for a glorious present and future.

As part of the ceremony two fallen columns of the Parthenon were re-erected, using modern mortar to rejoin marble drums which were to be found lying scattered near the building.

The excavations and searches among the ruins, which also began the moment the Turks left, produced a rich harvest, but the problems grew with the finds. To approach the west side of the Parthenon visitors soon had to brave a narrow lane through the heaps of marble piled head-high on either side. Ancient inscriptions and pieces of sculptures stored in the open air were a constant invitation to thieves and vandals.[8] The earth which was removed in the course of the excavations was dumped over the side of the Acropolis, so that what had been a sheer drop, picturesque and romantic, became a mere slope of tipped rubbish.[9] As the excavations proceeded, with the destruction of virtually all vegetation, the whole Acropolis came to resemble a huge marble quarry made up of 'broken columns, friezes, cornices, bases, blocks of every shape, remnants of statues and bas-reliefs, with numberless other pieces of sculpture collected together in various parts'.[10] This original marble, it was intended, would eventually be used to reconstruct part at least of the broken monuments.

H. B. Young, a British naval officer who visited the Acropolis a few weeks after the Bavarians marched in, records a particular incident:

Though shot and shell have done their work even on the Parthenon itself, yet it remains as grand & glorious as ever ... Though I wished to have seen the Temple in its pristine and perfect state, yet the damage it has sustained in these late wars and the ruthlessness of even its present guardians will fully exculpate his Lordship [Elgin]: one of the Metopes only remains in the S.W. Corner, another had been lately found, among the rubbish either forgotten or unintentionally covered by Lord E: as it must have been taken down by him & was very perfect till a day or two before we saw it where some of the Bavarian (Barbarian?) guard had broken the horse's legs and knocked off other parts of the figure: two or three very beautiful pieces of the frieze had also been found & some stones with inscriptions of great interest.[11]

Contrary to what was believed at the time, that metope had not been taken down from the Parthenon by Elgin's agents. In drawings made of the building in the mid-eighteenth century, it was already absent.[12] As the metope survives today, it lacks the centaur's legs and some of the other parts which could be easily broken off.[13] In 1835 another of the fallen metopes could still be seen built into the fortress wall. The traces of colour which were then visible have, however, since disappeared.[14]

In March 1835, as part of the von Klenze plan, the Acropolis was declared a national monument, and, for the first time for many centuries, perhaps for the first time in its whole history of human settlement, the Rock of Athens ceased to be a military fortress. When the soldiers of the Bavarian garrison departed, a force of Greek pensioned veterans was given the task of defending the monuments, from Greeks now as well as from foreigners. The custodians followed the visitors closely.[15] Nothing was to be taken away. Even to pick up a marble pebble to look at it, one visitor noticed, caused an immediate reaction.[16]

But still the erosion continued. During the Greek Revolution many nations had sent naval squadrons to Greek waters. In 1824 an Austrian ship removed several column drums from the ruined temple at Sounion, commemorating its visit by painting the inscription BELLONA AUSTRIACA 1824 in large black paint along the frieze so as to be seen from several miles out to sea.[17] In 1826 one of the fourteen remaining standing columns was thrown down.[18] As soon as Greece was free and the Acropolis of Athens opened to visitors, every warship which anchored at Piraeus could send its vandals and its hooligans on a destructive run ashore. As Trant wrote of the situation he found in 1829 before the Turks left:

The mania for destruction which activates all those who visit Athens is incredible. Every youngster who obtains leave to have a cruise on shore thinks it necessary to carry off a piece of marble as a relic: if the head or leg of a statue, so much the better. A stone is seized and applied as a hammer to one of the finest bas-reliefs; off flies a fragment, and on board starts the midshipman with his prize. Some years since, a letter was picked up at Athens, written by one of the midshipmen of a man-of-war stationed at the Piraeus, to his messmate who was in Athens, requesting him to knock off another piece from the Caryatides, as he had lost the marble he took with him.[19]

In another incident in the 1830s, when the Greeks had taken control, a party of midshipmen from the British Navy deliberately broke off parts of a recently excavated statue. When, at the insistence of the Greek government, the British admiral held an inquiry, one of the culprits turned out to be the nephew of a duke.[20]

As conditions in Greece became more settled, the British TGs— 'Travelling Gentlemen' or 'Travelling Gratis' as the British Navy called them—also returned in large numbers, later joined by an increasing number of French, Germans, Americans, and others.[21] A visit to the Acropolis soon developed its own rituals. Visitors were encouraged to pay their respects to the monuments first by day and then by night, to meditate on the ruins of a great civilization, and to consider the future of Modern Greece. Special permits were issued on nights when the moon was full. The visitors enjoyed seeing the little owls which still fluttered around the Acropolis under the protection of the owl goddess Athena, a visible link with the ancients, and watching the camels lumbering along the road to Piraeus, a touch of exotic orientalism.[22] Reading a passage from Lord Byron would help to focus the feelings, and also from Chateaubriand if you were French. You could buy a copy of Byron's works and hire a telescope from an Indian trader, and towards the end of the century you could have your photograph taken.[23]

The export of antiquities was strictly forbidden. Even before formal independence, Capodistrias, the provisional President, had intervened to interrupt the French army from taking away sculptures discovered during excavations at Olympia. Fauvel was refused permission to export the fifty-four cases in which he had gathered the fruits of his long career of digging and collecting. However, since the Greek government offered no compensation to the finders of antiquities but merely demanded that they should be

surrendered, the law was difficult to enforce. As Edmond About
wrote in 1854:

Les courtiers se livrent à un commerce clandestin et cachent sous leur
manteau toute leur marchandise. Si quelque marbre est trop grand ou trop
pesant pour être transporté en cachette, ils le mettent en morceaux, et l'on
débite une statue comme un mouton, pour le vendre.[24]

The brokers carry on a clandestine business and hide all their merchan-
dise under their cloak. If a marble is too big or too heavy to be secretly
transported, they cut it up into pieces and retail a statue like mutton.

For the inspectors of antiquities, as it was for the singing policemen
in Offenbach's operetta, it was their unlucky fate, always to arrive
too late.[25] The Aphrodite of Melos, known also as the Venus de
Milo, was bought by a French government agent from the Greek
who found it. Later, when large numbers of ancient gravestones
and hoards of terracottas were discovered in Athens, many were
dispersed by dealers to museums and collectors in Europe and the
United States.

The contrast with what had gone before, and with what the Turks
continued to allow in the Greek-speaking territories still under
their control, was striking. A proposal by the British government
to finance repairs to the Propylaea was rejected by the Greeks, who
feared the English even bringing gifts.[26] An American millionaire
who offered to buy a Caryatid was surprised to find that no amount
of money would be enough.[27] By the middle of the century, when
the various European countries began to establish resident schools
of archaeology, it was made an invariable condition that nothing
they excavated should leave the country. The illegal export of antiquities was not only a crime, it was a betrayal of the ideals of
the new Hellas.

However, with the exchange rate continuing to be highly
favourable, the travelling gentlemen and the tourists were able to
pay bribes, many prided themselves on their classical learning, and
some carried hammers. One British visitor who picked up a marble
foot, a fragment from the Parthenon frieze, decided, he records,
after a number of hesitations, to put it back.[28] 'Once I was tempted
to knock off a corner [of the Erechtheion]', wrote an American
tourist, 'and bring it home as a specimen of the exquisite skill of
the Grecian artist, which would have illustrated better than a
volume of description; but I could not do it; it seemed nothing less

than sacrilege.'[29] Another American is said to have filled his pockets before being caught.[30]

On the Acropolis, Ludwig Ross, the first ephor of the antiquities of Athens, and Pittakis, his Greek successor, did what they could to gather up the most important pieces and lock them away, first in the mosque, and later in the cisterns and the cellars. Some larger pieces were built back into the walls and secured with cement in order to stop them from being stolen.[31] By the time the first inventory was made in 1850 there were ten secure depositories.[32] But there was simply too much for everything to be collected, let alone guarded. As late as 1872, the British consul found thirteen fragments of Parthenon sculptures which, he believed, had been lying about on the Acropolis since Lord Elgin's time.[33]

Like Elgin and their other predecessors, Ross and Pittakis took little interest in pieces of marble without carvings or inscriptions. The marble debris with which the Acropolis surface area was covered, including the blocks from which Elgin's agents had sawn off parts of the frieze, were cut up for use as building materials by the masons for makeshift repairs. Pieces of marble without carving or inscriptions were sold to visitors, with official approval. In 1845, to help heal a rift in American–Greek relations, the Greek government donated a block from the Parthenon to be built into the Washington Monument in Washington.[34] Only in 1874 when all the main antiquities discovered on the Acropolis were gathered into a museum specially built for the purpose, did the losses of fragments come more or less to an end.[35]

Von Klenze's proposal to keep the Acropolis as an ancient monument was acted upon by successive Greek governments, with scarcely a challenge, throughout the nineteenth century.[36] In accordance with the plan, the non-classical buildings were gradually removed. First to go was the small town of houses and shops where the Turkish garrison had lived for over three hundred years. The storks, whose nests had been protected by the Turks, left soon after.[37] Between 1836 and 1838 the remains of the medieval palace in the Propylaea were stripped out. The mosque came down in 1844 and its minaret in 1889. In 1852 the ancient gate at the foot of the Acropolis was cleared of the immense Roman, Byzantine, and Frankish bastions with which it had been covered since ancient times. In 1856 the water reservoir which had shown its value through many sieges was taken away, and in 1862 the apse which had been built into the Parthenon in Byzantine times.

Finally in 1875 the huge Frankish Tower, which had stood at the entrance to the Acropolis since the thirteenth century, and which even von Klenze wanted to keep, was dismantled, with the help of money given by the excavator of Troy, Heinrich Schliemann. The Frankish Tower marred the harmony of the Acropolis, it was claimed. Priceless remains of the classical period, it was suggested, would be revealed if it were demolished. Many of the nineteenth-century travellers, when invited to subscribe to the costs of demolition, debated the issue when they wrote their books. Which was more important, they asked, the gain to art or the loss to history? In the education of the human race, they were inclined to conclude, some ages are worth nothing, and others worth everything.[38]

The real reason why the Frankish Tower had to go lay more with the demands of nationalism. All the governments which Athens and Greece had endured or enjoyed during its long history since the end of the classical period were by now described as forms of foreign occupation. The whole period between the death of Alexander the Great and the uprising of March 1821 was now to be seen as a regrettable and forgettable interlude. With the removal of the Frankish Tower, the Parthenon became the highest building on the Acropolis, rivalled only by the flag-pole of the Modern Greek state.

The Temple of Athena Parthenos, which in the fifth century had originally enshrined the distinctive identity of the people of Athens as they defined their Athenian identity, now stood as the supreme unifying symbol of all Modern Greece and all Modern Greeks. The Parthenon would help to marry the new state of nation, at that time still more oriental than Western, to the nations of western Europe under whose guidance and protection its regeneration was to take place. From the time of the Crimean War, when the Parthenon was the venue for a dinner for the officers of the allied armies, the Acropolis of Athens has been the chosen site for all of Greece's most symbolic international gestures.

Greece's narrative of national continuity, like those of the many other countries which invented their traditions in the nineteenth century, was more myth than history. Greeks speak a language with a rich and continuous spoken and literary tradition going back three or four millennia to the most ancient recorded times. As the travellers also constantly emphasized, the Greeks whom they met seemed to share many of the characteristics of their putative ances-tors. They were as intelligent, as sharp, and as enterprising, and if, in other respects, they did not match nineteenth-century Europe's conceptions of what Hellenes should be, the flaws could be put down to the centuries of slavery and degeneration.

As for continuity of race, another favourite nineteenth-century category used for defining European national identities, the Modern Greeks, it was sometimes claimed, looked like the Ancients portrayed on sculptures and vase-paintings. On the other hand the land of Greece had seen many settlements of non-Hellenes during the centuries.[39] As recently as the War of Independence some communities of Albanian-speaking ethnic Albanians became Greek-speaking neo-Hellenes. When J. Ph. Fallmerayer, a German historian, suggested in the 1830s that many Greeks were likely to be ethnically Slav, the resulting storm con-tinued for many decades.[40] By drawing attention to the factual fragility of the national blood narrative, the Fallmerayer contro-versy revealed why it was so highly valued. As Byron, a citizen of a more confident nation, had pointed out long before, 'What Englishman cares if he be of Danish, Saxon, Norman, or Trojan blood? or who, except a Welchman, is afflicted with a desire of being descended from Caractacus.'[41]

Apart from the language, it was the sharp cultural discontinuities which Greek history revealed. The early Christians had closed the philosophy schools, had neglected, condemned, and failed to pre-serve the ancient Greek literature, had co-opted the monuments of the defeated ancient gods to their own religious and civic purposes, and had imposed a uniform and static system of belief and con-formity where previously there had been a sceptical progressive diversity.[42] The Orthodox Church, the main institution which had given the Greeks their sense of identity since that time, had pre-served its cultural monopoly throughout the Ottoman centuries. Only in the decades immediately preceding the outbreak of the Greek Revolution in 1821 is there evidence of a revival of neo-Hellenic sentiment, and that came mainly from Greeks living in western Europe. At the time of Lord Elgin's removals the Orthodox Patriarchs were engaged in a long and losing battle to try to stop it.[43] Although in western Europe the Greek Revolution of 1821 was almost invariably presented in philhellenic terms, most of those who took part in the fighting probably did not yet think of themselves as Hellenes.[44]

After independence, Athens, where St Paul had preached, attracted an influx of missionaries from the West, eager to take part in the regeneration of the new nation by reversing what they saw as the superstitions of the Greek Church. Now that he had seen the Parthenon, wrote an American churchman who visited Athens soon after the Turks left, he could 'willingly yield up his breath'.[45] Athens, for many visitors from northern countries, was less upsetting than Rome, whose ruins and churches proclaimed the power and long endurance of papal domination.[46] But if Greece looked more ripe for cultural colonization than the other Mediterranean countries, the missionaries had little success.[47] Greece remained firmly loyal to its Orthodox past.

Despite its Western origins, its questionable historicity, and the encouragements to intolerance which lay beneath some of its assumptions, the neo-Hellenic national story was adopted with enthusiasm not only by philhellenic romantics abroad but by the official and educational institutions of the people of Greece. Soon after the establishment of the Greek state it overcame all other conceptions of group identity which had existed in Greece before 1821. Those who protested at the deliberate destruction of the non-classical monuments in their city risked being accused of disloyalty. With every act of demolition, the people of Greece were invited to increase their ignorance of two thousand years of their historical experience.

Set on its Acropolis high above the capital city, visible from the windows of every house, the Parthenon became the supreme unifying symbol of the national narrative. The sight of the ancient monuments built by their ancestors, had, it was said, sustained the Greek national spirit through the long centuries of subjection.[48] The first guidebook to the antiquities of Athens published by the Greek state set out a version of the history of Lord Elgin's actions which owed more to Byron and to neo-Hellenic mythologizing than to an honest assessment of what had happened a generation before:

Jamais nous n'avons senti plus vivement la tyrannie des barbares que lorsque nous nous vîmes trop faibles pour empêcher un Ecossais d'enlever ce que les Goths, les Turcs, et les siècles avaient épargné.

Never did we feel the tyranny of the barbarians more keenly than when we saw ourselves unable to prevent a Scotsman taking away what the Goths, the Turks, and the centuries had spared.[49]

One of the first shots of the war of independence, visitors were told, had smashed the column of the Parthenon where he and Lady Elgin had carved their names.[50] A curse on Lord Elgin, the plunderer, was one of the rituals of a visit to the Parthenon or, if you were British, at least a twinge of shame.[51] When Bayard Taylor was told of what Elgin had done by a lady of his party, he records:

The strong Anglo-Saxon expression I then made use of, in connexion with Lord Elgin's name, was not profane, under such provocation, and was immediately pardoned by the woman at my side.[52]

In the words of Melina Mercouri, the people of Greece came to regard the Parthenon as the 'soul of Greece'.[53]

During the nineteenth century the frontiers of Free Greece were advanced to the north, the east, the west, and the south [54] With each territorial acquisition the minority non-Greek-speaking non-Christian populations were encouraged to leave or to conform. By the end of the century the territorial area of Greece, which had not long before been a patchwork of peoples of several religions, languages, and cultures living in proximity in relative harmony, had become, to a large extent, the paradigm of a nineteenth-century nation state, with the majority of its people regarding themselves as forming a single ethnic group, with a single language, a single religion, a largely homogeneous culture within its own geographical frontiers, pockets of minorities obstinately resisting official pressure to assimilate, and an aggressive nationalistic foreign policy aimed at realizing some vision of long-lost historic frontiers. With every political change, the national myth of continuity and identity on which the new Greek nation state had been founded was reasserted, reaffirmed, and reinforced.

By 1890, when the whole area of the Acropolis had been excavated to the rock and the results of the digging gathered into museums, it was no longer possible for anyone to say that the best Greek sculpture was in London. But this was of little comfort. Slabs of the frieze had been split between the two countries. Heads and legs of men and of horses were separated from their bodies in London. Dozens of small fragments whose original place on the monument was unknown lay unsorted in the storerooms. As in the British Museum, plaster casts could help to fill gaps by showing what had survived elsewhere, but the patchwork display of originals and casts in the Acropolis Museum, reciprocating the patchwork of casts and originals in the British Museum, also exacerbated the Greek sense of national anger and humiliation.

By 1890, the last remains of the Byzantine, Frankish, and Ottoman centuries had all been demolished. As the General Ephor of Antiquities announced, making a claim more often heard from the British Museum or the Louvre:

In this final form Greece bequeaths the Acropolis to the civilized world—a testimony to the Greek genius, a venerable monument cleansed at last of barbaric remnants, a unique repository of exquisite works of art from the ancient world, a constant inducement for all civilized peoples to work together in friendly emulation.[55]

And so at last, when virtually everything had already gone, the so-called 'purist' approach to the Acropolis came to an end. The Parthenon was now a badly ruined building of the fifth century. The Acropolis was a fully dug archaeological site.

As the century progressed and the missionaries gave up and left, visitors from the West too began to see the monument with new eyes. Before independence, they might have been mainly interested in looking at the ruins, but they could not ignore the modern Greeks whose lives took place in and around them. With the progressive dismantling of the non-classical monuments, Athens now became a city of the very ancient and the very modern, an empty archaeological site and a bustling commercial city. Increasingly the books which they carried invited them to visit Ancient Hellas, a land of the imagination, without being too much concerned about the country in which the monuments happened to be situated.[56] As the Acropolis was progressively stripped back to its fifth-century ruins, Western visitors were left to their philhellenic meditations, undisturbed except by the other visitors, of whom there were only a few. What need of books, of guides, or of history, they came to believe, when the monuments spoke for themselves?[57] On the Acropolis, which was free both of charges and of pestering guides, the visitor could imagine his or her ideal civilization, untouched by tainting commerce.[58]

With beauty went truth, and with truth virtue. As Penrose and other archaeologists uncovered yet more details about the Parthenon's subtle curves and gradients, the building too approached ever nearer towards an ideal of absolute perfection. Viollet-le-duc, for France, declared that 'the Greeks were capable of anything in the sphere of art; their sense of sight enjoyed pleas-

ures which we are too uncouth ever to be able to appreciate'.[59]
Ruskin, for the English-speaking world, noted that the eye is most
influenced by what it cannot detect. Mrs Russell Barrington, who
had been brought up surrounded by casts of the Elgin Marbles, on
seeing the Caryatids, was reminded, as well she might be, of the
paintings of Watts and Leighton.[60]

With the aestheticizing came secularization, or rather the sacral-
ization of romantic notions of beauty. Bayard Taylor, an American
visitor in 1858, when reminded that Ruskin had called Greek architecture 'atheistical', exclaimed:

God has no better temple on earth than the Parthenon ... Are not the triumphs of human art the sublimest praises of Him who created the human
mind? What ancient or modern Saint dares to sneer at *Heathen* Greece,
where Socrates spake, and Phidias chiselled, and Ictinus built, glorying God
through the glory of Man for all time to come.[61]

The temple of the Goddess of Wisdom which for more than a thousand years, according to one traveller, had languished as a place for
the worship of a Jewish peasant and an Arab camel driver, had at
last been returned to its true purpose.[62] The Ancient Greeks, it was
frequently repeated, had conferred on the world the three gifts of
beauty, wisdom, and liberty, and the Parthenon, their supreme
monument, embodied all three in perfection.

From the beginning the von Klenze plan involved restorations as
well as removals. The Temple of Athena Nike, most of whose original pieces were in reasonable condition and easily identifiable was
rebuilt. The Caryatid porch was restored, using a replica for the
figure removed by Elgin's agents. In the 1840s a number of columns
of the Parthenon were re-erected complete with capitals, and
others were rebuilt to about two-thirds of their original height. No
less than one hundred and fifty-eight marble blocks which had
fallen from the cella walls were put back in place. A number of
further repairs were made in 1872, using bricks and iron bars to
prop up lintels and parts of the west frieze, but they were not part
of any comprehensive plan or theory of conservation, and no
records were kept.

But, for most of the nineteenth century, the Greek authorities
were more confident about what should be destroyed than about
what should be restored. Who would dare to touch the Parthenon?
Just as Canova and Flaxman hesitated to restore the sculptures,

successive Greek governments shied away from restoring the building. As with the debates about displaying the sculptures in the British Museum conflicting cultural ideologies clustered round questions which at first sight appeared straightforward. The Parthenon was an old building, much damaged by the vicissitudes of history, which needed urgent repair. That much was agreed. But which Parthenon should be restored? Was it legitimate to try, even partially, to redress the catastrophe of 1687? Could modern marble worked by inferior modern hands be laid side by side with marble carved by the Phidian artists of the fifth century? To treat the Parthenon purely as a sacred building of high archaeological and artistic interest would risk downgrading its modern purpose. If, on the other hand, the building was merely a romantic ruin, would not Greeks and foreigners be confirmed in attitudes of wistful hopeless nostalgia? And where would the Greek state find the money?

It was only when the strong earthquake of 1894 shook many pieces to the ground, and it was feared that the whole structure might collapse, that decisions became unavoidable. Between 1898 and 1902, and again between 1923 and 1933, Nikolaos Balanos, the Prefectural Engineer, carried out a massive works programme largely of his own devising and largely free from criticism. The aesthetic which lay behind his interventions was to restore some of the Parthenon's fallen grandeur, to make the building appear more like it had done in ancient times, but at the same time to give it a stronger modern image both for Greeks and for foreigners. Balanos had little interest in the historical authenticity or continuity of the building or in the discoveries of research. He used scattered original marble, newly cut replicas, occasional reinforced concrete, cement, and iron. The marble lying about on the Acropolis was treated as a common quarry from which pieces of carved marble could be selected and cut to fit.

Under Balanos's regime, nine columns of the north colonnade which had been thrown to the ground in the explosion of 1687 were re-erected, along with their architraves, triglyphs, and the backing blocks from which Elgin's agents had taken the metopes, using mostly original marble. By 1933 the appearance of the Parthenon had been drastically transformed. It was still a ruin, but less of a ruin than it had been since 1687, and from the town it almost looked complete. It is Balanos's partially restored Parthenon, a twentieth-century Parthenon, which has since become iconic, reproduced and re-imagined in countless schoolbooks and posters throughout the world, and increasingly presented, in accordance with another cultural shift, as a monument to Western liberal democracy.

Many of Balanos's aesthetic decisions have since been regarded as successful. His engineering decisions too are understandable as the best practice in the circumstances of their day. However, as a Greek expert has recently noted, he 'deprived [the building] of historical documentation, he adulterated its details, and he paved the way for serious damage to occur in the near future'.[63] In 1944 the first cracks appeared in some of the re-erected columns. The iron bars which had been used in the rebuilding had expanded and were bursting the marble drums. Although the effects of rusting iron were well known and the ancient artists never used it, Balanos had paid no attention.

Worse was soon to follow. In the 1960s, with the rapid, largely uncontrolled, industrialization of Greece, the air in the Athens basin became seriously polluted. Previously unusually moistureless, it was now humid. Recently clean and clear, it was now full of sulphur and other impurities. The days when visitors could count the columns of the Parthenon from ships at sea or from the quayside at Piraeus had gone for ever. Highly acidic when previously it had been neutral, the now polluted air bit into the exposed patina of the marble, destroyed the surface detail, and continued to bite. The iron which Balanos used in his reconstructions rusted more quickly, causing more bursting, and pieces of masonry fell from the building ever more frequently.

The damage caused by the many previous disasters which had struck the Parthenon had been immediate, obvious, and limited. The damage caused by air pollution was constant, insidious, and pervasive. The man-made catastrophes had knocked down, damaged, and scattered the marble blocks from which the building was constructed, but had not necessarily destroyed the marble itself. Air pollution eroded the surface of every piece of marble from which the Parthenon was built. Within a few years air pollution had done more damage to the essential constituents of the Parthenon than any single previous catastrophe. As Richard Economakis, editor of an officially prepared book on the subject, wrote in 1994:

Any visitor to the Acropolis can see for himself the disastrous effects of acid rain and the increasing amounts of pollutant fuel emissions on the once perfect surfaces of the marble buildings; delicate mouldings unrecognisable under coats of black soot, layers of marble flaking off or bursting, smooth surfaces crumbling like sugar at the touch of a hand. At the same time the oxidisation of the exposed and uncoated iron clamps that were ignorantly or unwisely incorporated by older restorers have resulted in numerous new fractures, ruptured members, and grotesquely discoloured stone surfaces.[64]

In 1970 UNESCO prepared a report which detailed the deterioration which was apparent at that time. In 1975 the Greek government set up the Committee for the Conservation of the Acropolis Monuments, a group of experts from many disciplines with a broad remit to take urgent measures and to devise longer term solutions. A large number of studies were set in hand, drawing on experience from Greece and elsewhere. In 1981, as in 1894, a severe earthquake provided another pressing reminder of the urgency of doing something quickly. By the mid-1980s the whole Acropolis had been transformed into a building site full of scaffolds, cranes, crowd barriers, and busy artists, craftsmen, and workmen. The project is due to continue far into the twenty-first century, becoming more difficult and potentially more controversial as it proceeds.

From the beginning of the crisis, the Greek authorities have drawn on scholarly and scientific advice from countries outside Greece, and have consulted widely before every new intervention. The last sculptures left outdoors have been taken down and, in some cases, replaced with replicas. Every detached fragment of original marble has been carefully recorded, and some have been put back on the buildings. Each of the monuments is, in effect, being partly dismantled and re-erected, block by block, to enable the broken marble to be repaired, joined with new marble, and treated with an inorganic protective coating. Walkways now protect the ancient pathways from the eroding feet of the tourists. The iron in the columns is being replaced with titanium. The errors in the positioning of columns made by earlier restorations are being corrected. In accordance with the Charter of Venice, which sets out internationally approved principles of conservation, all the interventions are the minimum believed to be needed, are carefully recorded, are visible, and are, if it should ever become necessary, reversible. Cumulatively the changes are more radical than anything done hitherto and workmen have already been on the Acropolis longer than it took to build and carve the monuments in the fifth century. So far the main work has been on the Erechtheion, on the Propylaea, on the Acropolis rock, and to a more limited extent on the Parthenon.

The care and reverence with which the Greek authorities have approached the formidable problems are impressive. But there is a more general worry which recent reports do little to allay. The air pollution in the Attic basin is as bad as ever, with no realistic prospect of much improvement in the foreseeable future. The only two solutions which would really conserve the ruins of Athens, either stopping the air pollution or enclosing the whole Acropolis under a protective canopy, both look politically impossible. Could it be that all the current work, admirable though it may be in its own terms, will turn out to have been at best a palliative, at worst a diversion from the main task?

26

The Question of Return

As long as the land of Greece was part of the Ottoman Empire, the idea of returning the Parthenon sculptures to Athens made no sense. The Ottoman government, by whose authority they were removed, had not valued them, had not been able to protect them, and for many years afterwards continued to allow Greek antiquities to be exported from territories under its jurisdiction. The Turks had seized the land of Greece by force, but for many centuries the Ottomans had been internationally accepted as the legitimate government, and in Lord Elgin's time there had been no reason to expect any political change. In the debates of 1816, a few British voices advocated that the Parthenon sculptures should be held in trust in London, not permanently annexed. Nobody suggested that they should be sent back.[1]

By 1833, however, with the establishment of the modern Greek state, many of the arguments which were decisive in the past no longer held good. There was now a government in Greece determined to join the community of Western countries, internationally accepted and guaranteed as the legitimate successor to the Ottoman authorities. If the Greeks appeared indifferent or unconcerned about the Parthenon and its sculptures in the years before independence, their successors now regarded them as their own property, stolen by a foreign ambassador who had made a shady deal with an alien occupying power. Even if, as many admitted, Lord Elgin had, in the circumstances of his time, performed an act of rescue, then what was required in the new circumstances was an act of restitution.

At the time of independence only a minority of Greeks lived within the territory of free Greece. As every visitor to Athens could see, the Parthenon too was incomplete. For decades gaping white gaps in the structure showed the places from where the sculptures had been cut away by Elgin's agents, and the ground around the Acropolis was strewn with their discarded debris. Like the Greek

people the Parthenon cried out to be reunited. One of the first
British visitors to the Acropolis when it was vacated by the Turks
suggested that England should return what had been taken.[2]
Shortly after King Othon arrived in his newly independent
kingdom, one of his soldiers declared in an open letter to the
British Parliament that he had heard the ghost of Lord Byron on
the Acropolis calling on his countrymen to restore the exiled sculptures to their homeland.[3]

In the first guide to the antiquities of Athens published by free
Greece, Pittakis, the first Greek classical archaeologist, linked the
claim for the Elgin Marbles directly to the national history.

Je crois que dans l'état d'independance où nous entrons, nous aurons le
droit de réclamer auprès de la nation Anglaise les chefs d'oeuvres de
nos ancétres, pour les remettre à la place que le divin Phidias leur avait
choisie.[4]

I believe that in the state of independence we are entering we will have
the right to reclaim from the English nation the masterpieces of our ancestors to put them back in the place which the divine Phidias chose for them.

When in 1835 the British Museum first offered to provide plaster
casts of the Elgin Marbles in exchange for casts of the Parthenon
sculptures still in Athens, the response of the Greek government
was to ask for the return of the originals.[5]

The request has been repeated many times since. Greek hopes
rose after 1864 when Britain transferred sovereignty of the Ionian
Islands to Greece, one of the few examples of a nineteenth-century
empire voluntarily giving up territory. 'If England gave up the
Ionian Islands, worth several millions sterling,' it was suggested,
'why should they not give back the marbles which, if put up to
auction in lots, would scarcely fetch a million.'[6] Ioannes Gennadios,
for many years the Greek Minister in London, suggested in 1890
that the architectural fragments at least might be returned, and
many people who were not necessarily sympathetic to a general
restoration have felt a particular twinge of guilt that the Caryatid
was separated from her sisters in the Erechtheion porch, but only
casts were sent. The centenary in 1924 of the death of Lord Byron
at Missolonghi in the cause of Greek freedom seemed another pro-
pitious moment in Anglo-Greek relations, but if things were going
well, why should they be changed? From the beginning the Greek
claims have been supported by influential voices in Britain and
elsewhere.

The occasions when a change of policy on the part of the British government have looked most likely have been those when wider political considerations were at stake. In 1940/1, for example, after the fall of France, the British Foreign Office prepared the draft of a scheme to return the Elgin Marbles to Greece after the war. The hope was to stiffen Greek resistance to the invading Italian and German armies.[7] During the Cyprus insurgency of the 1950s the British government hinted that the Greeks might have the Elgin Marbles back if they would call off their support for the terrorist campaign against the British colonial government in the island.[8] In the early 1970s there was talk that a return of the Marbles might feature in an international political package to end the military dictatorship in Greece. Like the Ottoman government from whom they negotiated the original export, the British government has been willing to negotiate a return of the Marbles, but a sufficiently large political price was never found. Neil Kinnock, when Leader of the Opposition, made a promise to return them, but in May 1997, as one of its first acts, the incoming Labour government rejected a request from the Greek government.

The sculptures, it was often said in the nineteenth century, could only be properly appreciated in their original architectural context on the Acropolis of Athens, in the bright clear sunshine and among the surrounding mountains and seas of Attica, where Art and Nature, the human and the sacred, the past and the present, were uniquely in harmony. On the other hand, it was argued less poetically, the Elgin Marbles had been legally acquired, they were safer in London than they would be in Greece, more people were able to see and study them there, and the Greek government lacked the resources, the museum space, and the skills to protect, conserve, and display what they already had. In recent decades, however, whatever may have been the case in the past, none of these arguments retains much validity. It has been a long time since anyone suggested putting the sculptures back on the building or exhibiting them in the open air. Greece, with access to international funds and international expertise, is as well able as other countries to conserve its archaeological monuments.

In the past, the case for return was usually made directly by the Greek to the British government. In recent decades the emphasis has shifted towards mobilizing international opinion with the aim of including the Marbles in some new general regime of postcolonial restitution. Visitors to the Acropolis are given leaflets setting out the Greek claim. The draft UNESCO Convention on the Means of Prohibiting and Preventing the Illicit Import, Export and Transfer of Ownership of Cultural Property, which Western countries with rich museums are reluctant to join, aims to prevent the theft and export of objects of especial local cultural significance, to discourage the illegal excavations which the market in antiquities encourages, and to make illegal trading more difficult. Although in law the Convention has no retrospective effect, and it is highly doubtful if the Elgin Marbles would be covered if it did, the question of the return of the Parthenon sculptures remains the central case around which such debates cluster.

By focusing on the physical possession of cultural objects within the territorial confines of a nation state, and by conferring on national governments the sole responsibility for deciding what to define as 'cultural property', the Convention is built on a narrow, materialist, notion of what constitutes culture.[9] The hope of reversing the wrongs of the past is joined with an assumption, seldom questioned, that the promotion of stories of national heritage in order to boost modern nation-building is a desirable political and cultural aim. As a result some people who might otherwise be sympathetic to the aim of reuniting the sculptures of the Parthenon find themselves unable to swallow the rhetoric in which the demand is presented.

On the other side of the dispute, those who actively support the status quo have quietly abandoned most of the arguments and justifications used in the past. Now the emphasis is mainly on variants of the slippery slope argument. If the Elgin Marbles were returned, so it is alleged, the museums of the world would come under pressure to send other artefacts back to their country of origin, and as international collections were dispersed, research would suffer.[10] Only the institutions of the West, it is argued, are strong enough to uphold honest scholarly standards and to resist pressures of the kind familiar to Lord Duveen to give the public only what they want to see and hear and pay for. If the arguments for return are still, essentially, nationalistic, the arguments for the status quo are still, essentially, variations of older claims to imperial trusteeship and responsibility.

The Parthenon, a building originally erected to celebrate the civic identity of the free citizens of the city of Athens, later became an affirmation of panhellenic supremacy, of the benevolence of the Roman Empire, of the triumph of Christianity (Greek Orthodox and then Roman Catholic), and of the triumph of Islam. In the nineteenth century it became the cultural focus of the Modern Greek nation, of the romantic ideal of perfection, and of the debt of Western civilization to its ancient teachers. In the twentieth century it is increasingly perceived and proclaimed as a monument to Western liberal democracy, although not yet to free-market economics. The Parthenon has provided a site where, for two and a half thousand years, the cultural, political, and ideological discourses of each succeeding age have met, clashed, been temporarily settled, and have shifted again. Its long history illustrates vividly the privileging of some periods of the past over others, the clutching at imagined visions, the assertion of fictional pedigrees of legitimation, the construction of group identities, the differences between heritage and history, changing notions of the purpose of art, and changing perceptions of the sacred.[11] Throughout its long history the Parthenon has been reinvented, re-presented, and reinterpreted, and at each of the many transitions, the concerns of the newcomers have turned out to have been largely unforeseen and unforeseeable by those who went before.

The time seems ripe for another shift. With the building of a new museum in Athens, the opportunity exists to correct what some regard as the worst aspect of the present situation, the fact that the surviving pieces of the Parthenon, which are fragmentary enough, cannot be seen or studied together. Now that the British Museum's stewardship of the Elgin Marbles turns out to have been a cynical sham for more than half a century, the British claim to a trusteeship has been forfeited.

Appendix 1
The Firman

The authority under which Lord Elgin and his agents removed antiquities from the monuments of Athens derived from a series of official letters giving permissions, known as firmans, sent by the Ottoman government in Constantinople to the local Ottoman authorities in Athens over a period of years. As described in Chapters 9 and 10, Lord Elgin's agents by a mixture of cajolery, threats, and bribes, persuaded and bullied the Ottoman authorities in Athens to exceed the terms of the key second firman and to permit removals from the Parthenon and other buildings. Subsequently, using similar means, as described in Chapters 12 and 14, official representatives of the British government obtained firmans to allow the export of the Parthenon sculptures and other antiquities outside Ottoman jurisdiction. Although the extent of Elgin's legal authority from the Ottoman authorities is by no means the only, or even the most important question which arises, it does appear that all the activities of Elgin's agents which took place over many years in Athens and elsewhere, including the many abuses, were thus officially legitimated after the event by the government that held the responsibility at the time.

The second firman, given in July 1801 is the only one of which a text is known to have survived. All accounts of this firman derive from a document containing an official Ottoman translation into Italian which was given to a representative of Lord Elgin in Constantinople at the time when the permissions were granted. The document, which is now in my possession, has not previously been published, although a translation into English has been available since 1816.[1] A full transcript, made with the help of Italian scholars, is published here for the first time along with a new literal translation.

The document consists of a single folded sheet of laid paper, watermarked with a watermark of three hats, with an unidentified symbol between them, and a V G countermark. This watermark identifies the papermaker as Valentino Galvani, who is known to have possessed paper mills in the Veneto and in northern Italy in the 1790s and to have exported to the Levant.[2] The text is written in a single, clear, careful hand, each line closely justified at each end against a margin and the edge of the paper, presumably as a precaution to prevent interpolations. In the case of some words it is difficult to judge whether an initial capital is intended or not. The handwriting appears to be that of Pisani, the official British dragoman. A file note on the outside of the document in the hand of Philip Hunt notes 'Kaimacam's Letter N°. 2. To the Governor of Athens.'

At the time of the first edition of *Lord Elgin and the Marbles*, a search for the original Turkish version was made among the Ottoman archives at Istanbul, unfortunately without success. When the Ottoman archives are more fully catalogued and made accessible, the original version may yet come to light, along with the texts of the other firmans, and perhaps some indications of Ottoman thinking.

The Text

Traduzione d'una lettera di S. E.ᵃ il Kaimecam Pascià, diretta al Giudice, ed Anche al voivoda d'Athene——.

Dop'il saluto, vi si fà sapere qualm.ᵗᵉ il nostro amico sincero S. E. Lord Elgin, Ambasc.ᵉ della corte d'Inghilterra presso la porta della felicità, avendo esposto esser notorio che la maggior parte delli corti franche, ansiosa di legger ed investigar i libri, le pitture, ed altre scienze delli filosofi Greci, e particolarmente i Ministri, filosofi, primati, ed altri individui d'Inghilterra essendo portati alle pitture rimaste dalli tempi delli d.ⁱ Greci, le quali si trovano nelle spiaggie dell'Arcipelago, ed in altri climi, abbiamo di temp'in tempo mandati degli uomini e fatto esplorare l'antiche fabriche, e pitture, e che di questo modo li abili dilettanti della Corte d'Inghilterra essendo desiderosi di vedere l'antiche fabriche e le curiose pitture della Città d' Athene, e della vechia muraglia rimasta dalli Greci, e ch'esistono nella part'interiore del d.° luogo, egli abbia commesso ed ordinato a cinque Pittori Inglesi, già esistenti nella d.ᵃ Città, che abbian a vedere, contemplar, ed anche a dissegnare [*following two words inserted*] le pitture rimaste 'ab antiquo', ed avendo questa volta expressamente suplicato acciò

[*New page*]

acciò sia scritto ed ordinato che ai d.ⁱ pittori, mentre saran'occupati col'intrar e sortire dalla porta del Castello della d.ᵃ Città, che é il luogo d'osservazione, col formare delle scalinate attorno l'antico tempio dégl'Idoli, coll'estrarre sulla calcina /osia sul gesso/ gl'istessi ornamenti, e figure visibili, col misurare gli avvanzi d'altre fabriche diroccate, e coll' intraprendere di scavare secondo il bisogno, le fondamenti per trovar i matton' inscritti, che fossero restati dentro le ghiaja, non sia recata molestia, nè apportato impedim.° dalla parte del Castelano, nè di verun'Altro, e che non si s' ingerisca nelle loro scalinate, ed instrumenti, che vi avranno formati; e quando volessero portar via qualche pezzi di pietra con vechie inscrizioni, e figure, non sia fatta lor'oposizione, vi s'è scritta e spedita col N N la presente lettera, afin che dopo compreso il soggetto della med.ᵃ essendo chiaro l'impegno dell' Excelso Impero dotato d'esimie qualità, acciò vengano favorite simil istanze, conforme richiedono l'amicizia, sincerità, Alleanza, e benevolenza ab antiquo esistenti, e colla vicendevol accettazione d'ambe le parti, manifestam.ᵉ crescenti frà la Sub.ᵉ sempre durevole Corte Ottomana, e frà quella d'Inghilterra, e già che non vi è alcun male che le Sud.ᶜ pitture e fabriche siano vedute, contemplate

[*New page*]

contemplate, e dissignate, e dop'essere state accompite le convenevoli accoglienze d'ospitalità verso li suriferiti pittori, in considerazione anche dell'amichevol istanza sù questo particolar avenuta, dal prefato Amb.,ʳᵉ e per esser'incombente che non si faccia opposizione al caminare, vedere e contemplare delli inedemi le pittur, è fabriche che vorranno dissegnare, nè alle loro scalinate, ed instrumenti, all' arrivo della presente lettera usiate Attenzione perchè conformemᵉ. all' istanza del d.º Amb.ʳᵉ mentre li soprad.ⁱ cinque pittori esistenti in codesta parte, sarann'occupati coll'entrare e sortire dalla porta del Castello d'Athene, che è il luogo d'osservazione; col formare delle scalinate attorn il tempio antico degl' Idoli; col estrarre sulla calcina /osia sul Gesso/ gl'istessi ornamenti, e figure visibili; col misurare i rimasugli d'altre fabriche diroccate; e coll intraprendere di scavare second'il bisogno le fondamenta per trovarc i matton' inscritti chc fossero restati dentro la ghiaja, non vengano molestati nè dal Castellano, nè da altri, e neppure da voi sovraccennati, non vi singerisca nelle loro scalinate, ed instrumenti e non si faccia opposizione al portar via qualche pezzi di pietra con inscrizioni, e figure, e nella sufferita maniera operiate, e vi comportiate.

/ Sottoᵗᵗᵒ·/Sejid Abdullah
Kaimmecam.

Translation

Translation of a letter from His Excellency the Kaymacam Pasha, addressed to the Justice and also to the Governor of Athens——.

After the greeting, you are informed our sincere Friend, His Excellency Lord Elgin Ambassador Extraordinary from the Court of England to the Porte of Happiness, having explained that it is well known that the greater part of the Frankish courts are anxious to read and investigate the books, pictures, and other sciences of the ancient Greek philosophers, and in particular, the Ministers, philosophers, leading men, and other individuals of England being inclined to the pictures remaining since the time of the said Greeks, which are to be found on the shores of the Archipelago, and in other climes, have from time to time mandated men to explore the ancient buildings, and pictures, and that in this way the skilled dilettanti of the Court of England being desirous to examine the ancient buildings and the curious pictures in the City of Athens, and of the old walls of the Greeks, and which now exist in the interior part of the said place, he has therefore commissioned and ordered five English Painters, already dwelling in the said City, to examine, contemplate, and also to draw the pictures remaining 'ab antiquo' [*a Latin phrase meaning 'from ancient times'*], and he has at this time expressly asked us that it may be written and ordered that the said painters while they are employed in going in and out of the gate of the Castle of the said City, which is the place of observation, with moulding from the ladders round the ancient temple of the Idols, and with copying [*literally 'extracting'*] with mortar (chalk or plaster) the same ornaments, and visible figures, and with measuring the remains of other ruined buildings there, and with undertaking to dig, according to need, the foundations to find inscribed blocks [*more literally 'bricks'*], which may have been preserved in the rubbish, that no interruption may be given them, nor any obstacle thrown in their way by the Governor of the Castle or any other person, and that no one may meddle with their ladders, and implements, which they use for moulding; and when they wish to take away some pieces of stone with old inscriptions, and figures [*this phrase in ungrammatical Italian*], that no opposition be made; the present letter has been written and sent it by N. N. [*conventional way of showing that the name of an individual is to be inserted later; in the translation given by Hunt to the Select Committee in 1816, Hunt rendered the passage as 'by Mr. Philip Hunt, an English gentleman, Secretary of the Aforesaid Ambassador' and it is possible that the name was included in the original Turkish version to which Hunt had access*] in order that as soon as the subject of the mediation is clear that it is the explicit desire and engagement of this Excellent Empire endowed with eminent qualities to favour such requests as the above mentioned, in conformity with what is due to friendship, sincerity, Alliance, and good will subsisting ab antiquo between the Sublime and ever durable Ottoman Court and that of England and which is on the side of both those Courts manifestly increasing, particularly as there is no harm in the said pictures, and buildings being examined, contemplated, and drawn, and after having fulfilled the duties of hospitality, and given a proper reception to the aforesaid painters in compliance with the urgent request of the said Ambassador to that effect, and because it is incumbent on us to provide that they meet no opposition in walking, examining or studying the pictures and buildings they may wish to draw, and in any of their works of fixing scaffolding, or using their various instruments, and on the arrival of this letter you use your Attention to act conformably to the request of the said Ambassador while the said five painters dwelling in that place shall be employed in going in and out of the gate of the Castle of Athens which is the place of observation; with making moulds from their ladders around the ancient temple of the Idols; with copying with mortar (chalk or plaster) in modelling (with chalk or plaster) the same ornaments, and visible figures; with measuring the fragments and vestiges of other ruined buildings; and with undertaking to dig according to need the foundations to find inscribed blocks among the rubbish; that they be not molested by the Governor of the castle nor by any one else, nor even by you the above mentioned, and that no one meddle with their scaffolding or instruments, nor make any opposition to the taking away of some pieces of stone with inscriptions, and figures, and in the aforesaid manner you should act, and comport yourselves.

Signed [*in the translation given in the Select Committee's report the phrase used is 'signed with a signet'*]
Seged Abdullah Kaymacam.

Subsequent Official Claims and Assertions

House of Commons, 10 April 1984

'. . . The collection secured by Lord Elgin, as a result of transactions conducted with the recognised legitimate authorities of the time, was subsequently purchased from him and vested by an Act of Parliament in the trustees of the British museum "in perpetuity".'

Sir David Wilson, then Director of the British Museum, interviewed by BBC Television, 15 June 1986

'To rip the Elgin Marbles from the walls of the British Museum is a much greater disaster than the threat of blowing up the Parthenon . . . I think this is cultural fascism. It's nationalism and it's cultural danger, enormous cultural danger. If you start to destroy great intellectual institutions, you are culturally fascist.'[3]

House of Lords, 17 February 1996

Lord Inglewood (Government spokesman, in reply to what appears to be a series of inspired questions deliberately tabled in order to enable him to make his statement): '[The] Parthenon sculptures . . . were legally exported from their country of origin . . . The title of the British Museum to the Marbles is unimpeachable.'

Appendix 2

The Damage to the Elgin Marbles: Extracts from Official Documents (hitherto witheld from the public)

Minutes of Sub Committee on the New Parthenon Gallery, meeting on 8 October 1938

'They did not approve the experiments made by Mr Coulette (in Lord Duveen's employ) in filling gaps made by breakages in the frieze either as regards his attempts to reproduce the colour and texture of the individual frieze slabs or the adhesive of the filling piece, and recommended that these should be cast in a uniform colour and texture and attached lightly so that the edges of the breaks should be easily accessible.'

Minutes of British Museum Standing Committee, meeting on 8 October 1938

'The Director reported that through unauthorised and improper efforts to improve the colour of the Parthenon sculpture for Lord Duveen's new gallery, some important pieces had been greatly damaged. He asked for a Board of Enquiry to consider the nature of the damage and the policy of the Trustees in regard to publication of the facts, to determine responsibility for the damage, and to advise upon the necessary disciplinary action.'

First meeting of the Board of Enquiry, 20 October 1938

Present were Lord Macmillan, Lord Harlech, Rt Hon. Sir Wilfred Green, and Sir William Brigg. Regrets for absence were received from Sir Charles Petrie.

The Board examined Mr Pryce, Keeper of Greek and Roman antiquities, Mr Hinks, one of the two Assistant Keepers, Department of Greek and Roman Antiquities, Mr Smith, Department of Egyptian Antiquities, Dr Plenderleith, Deputy Keeper in charge of the Laboratory, Mr Holcombe, foreman mason, Mr Fisher, mason, Mr Gorman and Mr Lovelock, mason's labourers.

Extracts from the Report of the Board of Enquiry, dated December 1938

'On the 16th of September Mr Pryce left the Museum on short holiday leave. The three pieces of sculpture were then in their proper place in the

Elgin Room. Before he went away Mr Pryce gave no instruction either to Mr Hinks, who took charge in his absence, or to anyone else with regard to either moving the sculptures or cleaning them beyond a direction to Holcombe to prepare a mounting for the Iris figure which involved its removal from the pedestal. The Director informed the Board that he had personally reminded Mr Pryce that this figure must not even be washed without the authority of Dr Plenderleith in view of the precarious condition of its surface. While Mr Pryce was absent it came to the notice of the Director on the evening of Thursday 22 September that tools had been used in the cleaning of the Parthenon sculptures. He instructed Mr Hinks on the afternoon of 23 September to see that improper methods were not being used. On Sunday 25 September the Director happened to have occasion to pass through the basement of the Department. He was surprised to find there the Helios group in process of cleaning. On the bench he observed a number of copper tools and a piece of coarse carborundum, and from the appearance of the sculptures he at once saw that the tools had been used on the sculptures. On Monday morning 26 September the Iris was found by Mr Hinks to be undergoing similar treatment in an annex to the new Duveen Gallery, and the Selene horse's head was in the Foreman Mason's workshop. The Director ordered all further cleaning operations to be stopped and instituted an inquiry into what had occurred. Mr Pryce returned to duty on Tuesday 27 September.

Although Holcombe denied that he had used any copper tool in cleaning the horse's head, which he dealt with himself personally, the Board are satisfied the copper tools were used by Holcombe and the labourers under him in cleaning all the three pieces of sculpture in question. Holcombe admitted that apart from the instruction to prepare the mounting for the Iris figure he had received no specific instructions from the Keeper or the Assistant Keeper either to remove or to clean the sculptures. He appears to have assumed that he was at liberty to proceed at his own hand with the process of removing and cleaning. He apparently obtained some strips or rods of copper from the store and had fashioned those into tools of various shapes by flattening and sharpening the ends. He said that he had used similar tools on other occasions for cleaning marble and he apparently regarded himself as entitled to use them on the Parthenon sculptures. No effort was made to conceal them and they were lying exposed to full view on the bench when the Director first observed them.

In the course of the evidence given by Holcombe and the labourers it emerged that they had used tools in cleaning the metopes and frieze on which they had previously been engaged for some time. The Board did not think it within their duty to make a detailed examination of the metopes and frieze with a view to ascertaining the extent of the damage done, but they were impressed by the fact that such improper methods of cleaning had been allowed to be in operation over so long a period.

The effect of the method employed in cleaning the sculptures has been to remove the surface of the marble and to impart to it a smooth and white appearance. Mr Pryce described the Selene's horse's head as having been "skinned". The surface of the sculptures, showing the evidences of two thousand years of exposure to the climate of Greece, was a document of the utmost importance. There being no possible doubt about the history of the Parthenon sculptures, they came to the Museum as authentic masterpieces of Greek work of the fifth century B.C. and for purposes of study and comparison they are of inestimable value. The damage which has been caused is obvious and cannot be exaggerated.'

[*There then follows a description of the Department of Greek and Roman Antiquities.*]

'All the officers of the Department knew several years ago that it is dangerous to let masons clean sculpture because they are inclined to prefer their own trade processes to our scientific ones.

Washing used to be done periodically by the labourers "with ordinary water and hard brushes" but in 1932 this procedure was stopped, and the Research Laboratory was asked to devise a safer and more effective method. Dr Plenderleith then prescribed a neutral solution of medicinal soft soap and ammonia, and trained one mason's labourer to apply this in the proper manner with the proper brushes and distilled water. No other person washed or cleaned sculpture for the next four years and no washing was done except by the Keeper's order and under his supervision.

It was the tradition of the department that the Keeper or the officer in charge made his round of the mason's shop his first duty in the morning. Important moving operations or work needing direction during progress often meant a visit from the Keeper several times a day.

The Board have been unable to obtain any satisfactory explanation of the grave departure in this instance from the proper practice of the Department. They have, however, ascertained from Mr Pryce that a foreman employed by Lord Duveen in connection with the new Parthenon Gallery had expressed Lord Duveen's desire that the sculptures should be made as clean and white as possible and this may very well have become known to the workmen.

While the damage to the sculptures was directly occasioned by the unauthorised actions of Holcombe, it is impossible to acquit the Keeper and assistant Keeper of serious dereliction of duty and most unfortunate slackness and want of system.'

Minutes of Board of Enquiry, meeting on 15 November 1938

'Holcombe (Foreman mason), Sinclair, and Simenton, labourers, were examined in regard to payments made to them through Mr Daniel, Lord Duveen's representative in the new building.'

Extracts from the Second Report of the Board of Enquiry,
dated 8 December 1938

'Sinclair stated that he had used copper tools in cleaning the Parthenon sculptures since June 1937. He also stated that Daniel, the foreman employed by Lord Duveen, had pointed out to him that one of the slabs chosen by Lord Duveen to show in his new gallery was not white enough and that Holcombe had previously told him to see if he could brighten it up. The slab was in consequence recleaned. Daniel commended him for getting it whiter. The incident is of importance only as showing that Holcombe and Sinclair and presumably the other workmen were aware of Daniel's desire that the sculptures should be made as clear and white as possible for Lord Duveen.

The Board learned from Holcombe, Sinclair, and Simenton, that a sum of two or three pounds had been given by Daniel to Holcombe to be distributed among himself and the workmen after they had performed some heavy work in moving the sculptures, and that this sum was shared among them. The Board do not associate this payment with the cleaning operations, except in so far as it was calculated to promote the readiness of Holcombe and the workmen to comply with Daniel's wishes.'

[*Possible disciplinary measures against Pryce and Hinks.*]

'As regards the question of apprising the public of what has occurred the Board are of opinion that a public statement need not be made. They have learned with satisfaction that remedial measures applied by the Director and Dr Plenderleith have mitigated to a considerable extent the evidence of the treatment which the three pedimental sculptures have received so far as the eye of the general public is concerned but to the expert the damage will remain discernible. In these circumstances the Board do not recommend any communication to the Press on the subject.'

Signed Lord Macmillan, Sir Wilfred Green, Sir Charles Peers.

Minutes of British Museum Standing Committee, meeting on
14 January 1939

Accepts resignation of Hinks. The Committee's earlier decisions on reprimand and loss of ten years' seniority to be rescinded.

Notes

Abbreviations used in the Notes

BL Add.   British Library Additional Manuscripts
BL Egerton   British Library Egerton Manuscripts
FO   Foreign Office Papers in the Public Record Office, Kew
HMC   Historical Manuscripts Commission
NLS   National Library of Scotland

Chapter 1: An Embassy is Arranged

1. Historical Manuscripts Commission, *Report on the Mss of J. B. Fortescue Esq. preserved at Dropmore* (1892–1927) (hereafter HMC, *Fortescue*), iv. 359, Elgin to Grenville, 4 November 1798. Another copy in FO 78/20.
2. HMC, *Fortescue*, iv. 380.
3. Grenville informed Spencer Smith at Constantinople of Elgin's appointment on 18 December 1798 (FO 78/20). William Gartshore told Arthur Paget of the appointment as early as 4 December 1798. *The Paget Papers: Diplomatic and Other Correspondence of Rt. Hon. Sir Arthur Paget* (1896), i. 140.
4. NLS 1055, fo. 120. Elgin also alludes to his discussions with the King at Weymouth in a letter in BL Add. MS 38266, fo. 5.
5. For details of the earlier history of the family and of Elgin's education see Sydney Checkland, *The Elgins 1766–1917* (1988).
6. For the Elgin Fencibles see the collection of letters in NLS 5085 and 5087. More material among the Elgin Papers.
7. HMC, *Fortescue*, i. 603.
8. Earl Stanhope, *Life of Pitt* (1861–2), iv. 400. For other aspects of Elgin's early diplomatic career see HMC, *Fortescue*, i, ii, iii; BL Add MS 38266, fo. 5; *Cambridge History of British Foreign Policy*, i. 206, 274.
9. HMC, *Fortescue*, ii. 184.
10. Ibid. iv. 276, 95.
11. See, for example, remarks in *The Journal of Elizabeth Lady Holland, 1791–1811, edited by the Earl of Ilchester* (1908), i. 86, 146.
12. Revd Robert Tweddell, *The Remains of John Tweddell* (1815, 1816), 49 ff.
13. HMC, *Fortescue*, iv. 425.
14. Lord Granville Leveson Gower, *Private Correspondence 1781–1821* (1916), i. 262.

15. Elgin told Grenville of his engagement on 21 January 1799. HMC, *Fortescue*, iv. 446.
16. The information about the Nisbet fortune is contained in a short contemporary biography of Elgin in the periodical *Public Characters*, volume for 1807. Much of the other information, except where it relies on William Wittman's *Travels in Turkey, Asia Minor and Syria* (1803), is inaccurate. An income of this size would put the Nisbets amongst the richest families in the country.
17. *The Trial of R. Fergusson, Esq.* (1807), 2. HMC, *Fortescue*, iv. 446.
18. The unpublished letters between Elgin and Lady Elgin among the Elgin Papers leave no doubt of the warmth of their relationship at this time.
19. That Elgin borrowed money in 1797 is clear from [Select Committee], *Report from the Select Committee of the House of Commons on the Earl of Elgin's Collection of Sculptured Marbles* (1816) (hereafter *Select Committee Report*), p. xiv, where he is recorded as asking in 1811 for interest for fourteen years. The Elgin Papers contain letters from the Dowager Lady Elgin about her son's financial difficulties at this time.
20. Colonel Anstruther to Elgin, 19 March 1799, Elgin Papers.
21. Hunt to his father, 2 April 1799, Hunt Papers. For Hunt's earlier and later career see Eric Stockdale, *Law and Order in Georgian Bedfordshire* (1982).
22. *Select Committee Report*, 31. [Elgin], *Memorandum on the Subject of the Earl of Elgin's Pursuits in Greece* (hereafter *Memorandum*), 1 f. B. R. Haydon, *Autobiography and Memoirs*, new edn. (1926), 206. B. R. Haydon, *The Diary of Benjamin Robert Haydon*, ed. W. B. Pope (1960–3), i. 86.
23. *Select Committee Report*, 2. Elgin to Lord Hawkesbury, 7 July 1801, FO 78/32. Elgin's Report on his Embassy, 27 July 1806, FO 78/54.
24. HMC, *Fortescue*, v. 91. The 'magnificent publications' are the works published by the Society of Dilettanti, especially the early volumes of *The Antiquities of Athens* (by James Stuart and Nicholas Revett *et al.*).
25. Farington, 22, 25, and 27 April and 23 May 1799. The offer to Robert Smirke is confirmed by his manuscript journal. See also Jonathan Mayne, *Thomas Girtin* (1949), 49, who quotes *Morning Herald* of 6 May 1799.
26. Quoted in Thomas Girtin and David Loshak, *The Art of Thomas Girtin* (1954), 38.
27. Farington, 27 April 1799.
28. *Select Committee Report*, 32.
29. A. H. Smith, 'Lord Elgin and his Collection', *Journal of Hellenic Studies*, 36 (1916), 166.

30. Lord Holland, *Further Memoirs of the Whig Party 1807–1821* (1905), 336. Porson told Samuel Rogers that the offer had not been properly made. *Recollections of the Table-Talk of Samuel Rogers to which is added Porsoniana* (1856), 319.
31. Robert Walpole, *Memoirs relating to European and Asiatic Turkey* (1817), pp. xv, 84.
32. *Gentleman's Magazine*, 69, p. 369; Carlyle Papers.
33. Elgin, *Postscript to a Letter to the Editor of the Edinburgh Review* (1815), 17.
34. The financing is described explicitly in Elgin's letter to Lord Liverpool. BL Add. MS 38266, fo. 5.
35. HMC, *Fortescue*, v. 72.
36. BL Add. MS 38266, fo. 5.
37. Hunt to his father, 28 August 1799, Hunt Papers.
38. HMC, *Fortescue*, v. 250.
39. Elgin to Dowager Lady Elgin, 10 September 1800, Elgin Papers.
40. Hunt to his father, 17 July 1799, Hunt Papers.

Chapter 2: Great Events in the Levant

1. FO 78/24. For the general political and military history in this chapter I have relied to a great extent on Christopher Herold, *Bonaparte in Egypt* (1962), an excellent and well-documented account. Additional information comes from the FO 78 series of diplomatic records relating to Turkey in the Public Record Office.
2. Quoted by Herold, *Bonaparte in Egypt*, 133.
3. C. A. Wood, *A History of the Levant Company* (1935).
4. FO 78/20.
5. The circumstances in which the Military Mission was sent are related in FO 78/25–7. Some details of its activities are in Wittman, *Travels*.
6. John Barrow, *Life and Correspondence of Admiral Sir William Sidney Smith GCB* (1848).

Chapter 3: The Voyage Out

1. *The Letters of Mary Nisbet, Countess of Elgin* (1926) (hereafter *Nisbet*), 7.
2. Hunt to his father, 16 September 1799, Hunt Papers.
3. Philip Hunt, *A Narrative of What is Known Respecting the Literary Remains of the Late John Tweddell* (1816), 11.
4. Hunt to his father, 16 September 1799, Hunt Papers.
5. Extracts from Morier's captured journal were published by the French in *Courier de l'Égypte*, No. 70, p. 1.
6. Hunt to his sister, 22 September 1799, Hunt Papers.
7. *Nisbet*, 12 ff.
8. Ibid. 17.

9. *Nisbet*, 19.
10. Ibid. 22.
11. Ibid. 25.
12. He bought it at Rome for £1,000, but soon afterwards he was obliged to sell it and it passed into the possession of the Duchess of Portland, and then to the British Museum.
13. A. Michaelis, *Ancient Marbles in Great Britain* (1882), 109 ff.
14. Ibid. 111, M. L. Clarke, *Greek Studies in England, 1700–1830* (1945), 186.
15. Smith, 'Lord Elgin and his Collection', 168.
16. Ibid. 169, and Elgin to Dowager Lady Elgin, 5 October 1799, Elgin Papers.
17. *Nisbet*, 30 ff.
18. Quoted in Smith, 'Lord Elgin and his Collection', 171.
19. There is an account of Theodor's extraordinary career by Karl Obser in *Ekkhart-Jahrbuch* (1930), 18. An engraved self-portrait is in the Victoria and Albert Museum. For this information I am grateful to Frau Margrit E. Velte of Karlsruhe.
20. Smith, 'Lord Elgin and his Collection', 171 ff. The drawings they made in Sicily are among the Elgin collection.
21. *Nisbet*, 75.

Chapter 4: Reception at Constantinople

1. Tweddell, *Remains*, 262. HMC, *Fortescue*, iv. 438. Smith to Nelson, 24 January 1799, quoted in Barrow, *Life of Admiral Sir William Sidney Smith*, i. 251.
2. Spencer Smith to Grenville, 30 October 1799, FO 78/22.
3. HMC, *Fortescue*, iv. 476 ff.
4. Ibid. v. 316.
5. Barrow, *Life of Admiral Sir William Sidney Smith*, i. 381.
6. *Nisbet*, 34 ff. Hunt letters among Hunt Papers.
7. FO 78/26.
8. *Nisbet*, 39.
9. Smith, 'Lord Elgin and his Collection', 182.
10. *Memorandum* (1815 edition), 35. Wittman, *Travels*, 65.
11. Walpole, *Memoirs*, 98.
12. Wittman, *Travels*, 65. Robert Walsh, *A Residence at Constantinople* (1836), i. 206.
13. The word, like many transliterated from the Turkish, appears in several Anglicized forms at the time which I reproduce as they stand in the documents. For the narrative I have used the modern Turkish spelling as it appears in, for example, H. C. Hong, *A Turkish English Dictionary* (1957).

14. *Nisbet*, 48.
15. Carlyle to Dr Paley, 10 December 1799, Carlyle Papers.
16. *Nisbet*, 56.
17. My account of Elgin's reception is drawn from several sources including Elgin's report and claim for expenses, FO 78/24, Lady Elgin's letters in *Nisbet*, 40 ff., a long and detailed letter from Carlyle to Dr Paley in the Carlyle Papers, and a letter from Hunt to his father, 9 December 1799, Hunt Papers. The Turkish yard was twenty-seven inches.
18. FO 78/24.

Chapter 5: The Smith Brothers

1. Spencer Smith to Grenville, 10 June 1799, FO 78/22. My main source for events in Egypt is again mainly Herold. Much information about the Smith brothers is in Barrow.
2. For Elgin's initial difficulties with Spencer Smith see a series of letters in FO 78/24 and 28 and others in HMC, *Fortescue*, vi.
3. Smith to Elgin, 17 December 1799, Elgin Papers. Navy Records Society, *Private Papers of George, Second Earl Spencer* (1913–24), iv. 85.
4. Ibid. iv. 90.
5. Elgin to Sir Sidney Smith, 17 December 1799, FO 78/24.
6. HMC, *Fortescue*, vi. 89.
7. Elgin to Grenville, 16 February 1800, FO 78/28.
8. Elgin to Nelson, 18 February 1800, FO 78/28.
9. Elgin to Grenville, 25 February 1800, FO 78/28. The Admiralty's letter to Lord Keith is published in *The Keith Papers* (Navy Records Society, 1927–55), ii. 203. The Kaymakam was the deputy to the Vizier.
10. Elgin to Grenville, 10 March 1800, FO 78/28.
11. Elgin to Grenville, 9 May 1800, FO 78/29.
12. Published by the French in *Courier de l'Égypte*, Nos. 70, 73, 74.
13. Grenville to Elgin, 28 March 1800, FO 78/28.
14. This was the view of the French in Egypt after the capture of Morier's papers, *Courier de l'Égypte*, Nos. 70, 73, 74, 79. See also Barrow, *Life of Admiral Sir William Sidney Smith*, i. 394, 400; ii. 50, 60.
15. *Correspondance de Napoléon I, publiée par ordre de l'Empereur Napoléon III*, viii. 315.
16. *Nisbet*, 249, 278, 289. BL Add. MS 38266, fo. 5.
17. By J. G. Alger, *Napoleon's English Visitors and Captives* (1904). I have not found Alger's source.
18. *Le Jeu de Whist. Traité élémentaire des lois . . . traduit de l'anglais et rédigé par un Amateur Anglais* (1819). Smith's name is given in the edition of 1838.

19. The pencil drawing by Lusieri of the Elgins entertaining the Captain Pasha to whist is reproduced in Checkland, *The Elgins*, 40.
20. Lady Elgin to her mother, Elgin Papers.
21. Lady Elgin to the Dowager Lady Elgin, 25 March 1802, Elgin Papers.
22. Examples in Checkland, *The Elgins*, 11 ff.
23. Ibid. 30.
24. The taking of mercury is noted by Checkland, *The Elgins*, 41, 55, although without drawing the implications. Elgin's appearance was sometimes compared to that of Sir William Davenant, the early seventeenth-century playwright, known from the engraved portrait which was included as a frontispiece to editions of his works. This portrait, which shows a pronounced notch to the nostril, presumably downplayed the visible damage as much as possible, perhaps by showing the better side. It is reproduced by Mary Edmond, in *Rare Sir William Davenant* (1987). As Edmond shows, there were many contemporary allusions to Davenant's pox and to his nose, some in his own works.
25. Checkland, *The Elgins*, 77. The cruel allusions of Byron (see p. 181) suggest that it was known that the son had a mental illness earlier than 1813, the first date given by Checkland.
26. Checkland, *The Elgins*, 105.
27. There is a long series of letters of complaint about the Smith brothers in FO 78/28, 29, 30. Others are in HMC, *Fortescue*, vi.
28. HMC, *Fortescue*, vi. 347.
29. *Nisbet*, 147.
30. Ibid. 101, 141, 210.

Chapter 6: Work Begins at Athens

1. 'Logothetes' was the title of an official responsible for collecting church revenues. By Elgin's time it seems to have been used almost as a family name, at any rate by foreigners, of members of the Chromatianos family who held the post in Athens for many years and who also held British appointments. Spyridon Logotheti was Consul in 1800. His son Nicholaos was appointed Vice-Consul by Elgin in 1802 and promoted to Consul in 1816: *Nicholas Biddle in Greece: The Journals and Letters of 1806*, ed. R. A. McNeal (Philadelphia, 1993), 138 note. The Logotheti whom travellers encountered at Livadia was of a different family.
2. For Athens in the early nineteenth century, see D. Sicilianos, *Old and New Athens*, trans. Robert Liddell (1960). Many of the travellers, including especially Hobhouse, also give a full description with many additional details. For an account of how the Greek provinces were in fact governed see Helen Angelomatis-Tsougarakis, *The Eve of the Greek Revival* (1990).

3. A wide range of estimates is given by the travellers. Angelomatis-Tsougarakis, with access to reliable sources, suggests 10,000. See also John Fuller, *Narrative of a Tour through some parts of the Turkish Empire* (1830), 542.

4. For an excellent summary of how Athens appeared in the early nineteenth century, with many illustrations, see C. W. J. Eliot, 'Athens in the Time of Lord Byron', *Hesperia*, 37 (1968).

5. Sicilianos, *Old and New Athens*, 137.

6. Edward Dodwell, *A Classical and Topographical Tour through Greece* (1819), i. 358.

7. A list of revenues of the Ottoman Empire is in FO 78/29.

8. J. C. Hobhouse, *A Journey through Albania and Other Provinces of Turkey in Europe and Asia to Constantinople* (1813), i. 293. Forbin gives the population as 12,000, but, to judge from the numerous views of Athens, this seems to be an exaggeration (*Voyage dans le Levant* (Paris, 1819)).

9. Sicilianos, *Old and New Athens*, 137. The right applied to all taxes other than the poll tax and the customs taxes, and on legal dues. Ibid. 135. His main income seems to have come from property taxes.

10. Ibid. 146.

11. For a summary of the later history of the various monuments see Lya and Raymond Matton, *Athènes et ses monuments* (1963).

12. See John Henry Merryman, 'Thinking about the Elgin Marbles', *Michigan Law Review*, 83 (1985), 1897. For evidence that Elgin's firmans applied only to public property see the comment by Smirke in 1803 quoted p. 95.

13. Some also had access to Spon (*Voyage d'Italie, de Dalmatie, de Grèce, et du Levant* (Lyon, 1688)). After 1800 there was a huge outpouring of books of travels in Greece in several European languages. After the publication of Hobhouse's book with its thorough researches into the history of Athens from ancient to modern times, the travellers were better informed.

14. See Manolis Korres, 'The History of the Acropolis Monuments', in *Acropolis Restoration* (Athens, 1995), 42.

15. Diane Harris, *The Treasures of the Parthenon and Erechtheion* (1995), 5. The name of the other room, the Hecatompedon, the 'hundred-foot room', was also used for the whole building.

16. For a fascinating attempt to reimagine the technology of construction see Korres.

17. Some were found as a result of Elgin's excavations and are now in the British Museum.

18. Some were found as a result of Elgin's excavations and are now in the British Museum.

19. The claim that Athens was autochthonous was a key point celebrat-

ing Athenian pride made in the speech of Praxithea in Euripides' *Erechtheus*. See C. Collard, M. J. Cropp, and K. H. Lee, *Euripides: Selected Fragmentary Plays*, vol. i (1995), 159.

20. See Ian Jenkins and A. P. Middleton, 'Paint on the Parthenon Sculptures', *Annual of the British School at Athens*, 83 (1988). On some of the architectural blocks in the Elgin collection on public show, substantial traces of the original painted meander design can still be clearly seen. See also Chapter 24.

21. Joan B. Connelly, 'Parthenon and Parthenoi', *Journal of the Archaeological Institute of America*, 100/1 (1996).

22. As the carving appears at present, the child on the right is often assumed to be a boy. This may be partly due to the damage which the piece has sustained since it left the Acropolis, see Chapter 24. James Stuart, a highly reliable witness who examined the piece in 1750 when it was in a far better state than it is now, saw and drew the figure as that of a girl, without suggesting that he had any cause for doubt. Since the piece arrived in London, having suffered a good deal of damage in the meantime, opinion has tended to be divided, with most Victorian and later observers assuming that the figure is that of a boy. Given the extent of the damage to the surface as it exists now, the question can only be approached by shedding modern assumptions about the naked human body and trying to reconstruct how the ancient Greeks, with their very different attitudes to art, to sexuality, and to the appropriateness of nudity, might have presented, perceived, and interpreted the figure. Approached this way, there is no problem in reading the figure as that of a girl. A fine grave stele of a young girl with pigeons in the Metropolitan Museum, New York, reproduced by Jenkins in *The Parthenon Frieze* (1995), 36, Richter, *Sculpture and Sculptors of the Greeks* (1970), 492, and frequently elsewhere, shows her, presumably at the moment of death, with ungirt peplos revealing her nakedness in much the same way as the Parthenon child does, and there are other similar examples of both boys and girls. If Connelly's interpretation is right, the fact that the third daughter is shown as so young, emphasizes the scale of the sacrifice and of the impending tragedy.

23. Colin Austin, *Nova Fragmenta Euripidea* (Berlin, 1968), and Collard, Cropp, and Lee, *Euripides*.

24. Plutarch's *Life of Nikias*, xxix.

25. Collard, Cropp, and Lee, *Euripides*, 159. In a few places I have adapted their severely literal translation.

26. Collard, Cropp, and Lee, *Euripides*, 173, their translation adapted.

27. Book i, x. Translation from the Loeb edition.

28. See Savas Kondaratos, 'The Parthenon as Cultural Ideal: The Chronicle of its Emergence as a Supreme Monument of Eternal

Glory', in P. Tournikiotis (ed.), *The Parthenon and its Impact on Modern Times* (Athens, 1995).

29. Life of Pericles, xii.
30. Manolis Korres, 'The Parthenon from Antiquity to the Nineteenth Century', in Tournikiotis (ed.), *The Parthenon*, 156.
31. R. Chandler, *Travels in Greece* (1776), 51. The latest exhaustive list of fragments is in Frank Brommer, *Die Skulpturen der Parthenon-Giebel* (Mainz, 1963), *Die Metopen* (Mainz, 1967), and *Der Parthenonfries* (Mainz, 1977), but not in *The Sculptures of the Parthenon* (1979). Still useful for the history of the dispersal of fragments are A. H. Smith, *The Skulptures of the Parthenon* (1910), and Michaelis, *Der Parthenon* (Leipzig, 1871); and *A Description of the Collection of Ancient Marbles in the British Museum* (1812–61). For the Vatican fragments see *Journal of Hellenic Studies*, 58 (1938), 276 and *Fasti Archaeologici*, ii (1947), item 243. For the Würzburg fragment see G. Rodenwaldt, *Köpfe von den Südmetopen des Parthenon* (Berlin, 1948), 13.
32. For Fauvel's biography see the series of articles by Ph.-E. Legrand in *Revue Archéologique*.
33. As I read the inscription in the 1960s:

    AUGUSTE DE CHOISEUL GOUFFIER
    FOUCHEROT
    FAUVEL
    1776 ET 1781.

34. Legrand, *Revue Archéologique*, 30: 57.
35. For the history of these pieces see ibid. 24 as corrected by 25 and 26.
36. J. B. S. Morritt, *Letters Descriptive of a Journey in Europe and Asia Minor in the years 1794–1796* (1914), 175, letter of 18 January 1795. *Select Committee Report*, 130.
37. A water-colour of the Erechtheion painted by Robert Smirke in 1803, in the Library of the Royal Institute of British Architects, London, shows this cart prominently in the foreground.
38. *Description of Ancient Marbles*, vii (1835), Advertisement.
39. There are excellent colour reproductions of those that are known in Tournikiotis, *The Parthenon* and Checkland, *The Elgins*.
40. One which he drew of Constantinople was eighteen feet long.
41. Fuller, *Narrative of a Tour*, 545. H. W. Williams, *Travels in Italy, Greece and the Ionian Islands* (1820), ii. 331.
42. Dodwell says he paid about the same time, 80 piastres a day just to draw, Dodwell, *Classical Tour*, i. 293. In the Ottoman currency there were 40 paras to a piastre, 500 piastres to a purse. The rate of exchange against the pound sterling varied from place to place, and the pound rose strongly over the period. In 1801–3, the time of the main removals, there were about 9 Turkish piastres to the pound. By 1814 there were about 20. At all times, even taking account of trans-

action costs, the exchange rate was extremely favourable to visitors from western Europe. For a full note see Angelomatis-Tsougarakis, *The Eve of the Greek Revival*, 158.

43. Pay rates from William Haygarth *Greece: A Poem in Three Parts* (1814), 175. Although the pay rates were extremely low, Haygarth reckoned that, because the prices of provisions were even lower, labourers in Athens had a higher standard of living, and much more leisure, than labourers in England.

Chapter 7: In Search of Ancient Manuscripts

1. J. Dallaway, *Constantinople Ancient and Modern* (1797), 23. The chief sources for Carlyle's activities are letters and other documents quoted in Walpole's *Memoirs* and Walpole's *Travels in Various Countries of the East* (1820). The originals of the letters to the Bishop of Durham quoted in Walpole, with some others, are preserved in the Ipswich and East Suffolk Record Office under reference ILA 174: 1026/68. Some of Carlyle's manuscript journals are in the British Library. Others are quoted in his (posthumous) *Poems* (1805). A short sketch of Carlyle's earlier life is in the short-lived periodical, *Public Characters* (1802/3). It is clear from a letter of Carlyle to Dr Paley in the Ipswich and East Suffolk Record Office that Carlyle was fully familiar with the work of Dallaway.
2. BL Add. MS 27604, fo. 5.
3. J. H. Marsden, *Memoir of the Life and Writings of W. M. Leake* (1864), 7, gives an account of the circumstances in which the journey was decided. The journey itself is described by Leake in Walpole's *Travels*, 185.
4. Early twentieth-century typescript of the lost original, Hunt Papers.
5. Carlyle, *Poems*, 13.
6. Ibid. 16. For Byronic themes before Byron see Terence Spencer, *Fair Greece, Sad Relic* (1954).
7. Walpole, *Memoirs*, 162.
8. Ibid. 185.
9. E. D. Clarke, *Travels in Various Countries of Europe, Asia and Africa* (1811–23). Clarke's antipathy to Carlyle is confirmed in letters quoted in W. Otter's *The Life and Remains of the Rev. Edward Daniel Clarke* (1824), 485, 497, 505. The quarrel was the talk of Constantinople in January 1802 (see *Nisbet*, 165) and of Egypt in April 1802 (see *Life of General Sir Robert Wilson*, ed. H. Randolph (1862), 163, 233). Clarke somehow managed to obtain some drawings by Lusieri, Elgin's artist in Athens, and used them in his book, although Lusieri was contracted not to work for anyone else, and since most of Lusieri's work for Elgin did not survive, they are of particular interest. Clarke, *Travels*, part II, section I, p. 82, 'Tomb of Ajax'; part II,

section 3, p. 12, 'Marathon Village'. The view of the plain of Marathon (part II, section 3, p. 14) is said on the engraving to be from a sketch by Lusieri: in Clarke's list of contents it is described as 'by the author'. Clarke also incorporated a drawing by Theodor the Calmuck (*Travels*, II/2: 598). Another, of the Voivode, may also be by him (*Travels*, II/3: 2).

10. Walpole, *Memoirs*, 138.
11. Hunt's account of Athos is in Walpole, *Memoirs,* 198 ff.; Carlyle's is in BL Add. MS 27604.
12. Elgin, *Postscript*, 17.

Chapter 8: The Conquest of Egypt and its Results

1. FO 78/30–1, FO 78/54. For the general history I have relied, as usual, mainly on Herold.
2. The Turkish army included the remnants of Koehler's ill-fated British Military Mission although Koehler himself and his wife had died some months before.
3. *Nisbet*, 116 f.
4. Ibid. 119.
5. Ibid. 119.
6. Elgin to Hawkesbury, 16 July 1801, FO 78/32.
7. FO 78/33.
8. FO 78/33. *Nisbet*, 117 ff.
9. FO 78/35. *Nisbet*, 162 ff.
10. Ibid. 249, 278. BL Add. MS 38266, fo. 5.
11. FO 78/33. An engraving appears in Walsh, *A Residence at Constantinople*, ii, frontispiece.
12. Ibid. 171.
13. BL Add. MS 38571, fo. 19.
14. *Keith Papers*, ii. 406.

Chapter 9: The Firman

1. For the first firman see Smith, 'Lord Elgin and his Collection', 181, 183, 188.
2. A fuller note on the various firmans obtained by Elgin is at Appendix I.
3. *Nisbet*, 92.
4. Quoted in Smith, 'Lord Elgin and his Collection', 190.
5. Ibid.
6. Quoted Hobhouse Journal, 6 January 1810.
7. Pisani [British dragoman] to Elgin, 6 July 1801, Elgin Papers.
8. *Select Committee, Report*, 141.
9. Ibid., p. xxiv.

10. As appears from the modern letters in the collection, at that time the Hunt papers had been examined by various scholars and publishers but none had identified the document in Italian as the firman.
11. Pisani to Elgin, 6 July 1801, Elgin Papers. Quoted in Appendix 1.
12. This emerges from a phrase in Elgin's letter to Lusieri of 10 July 1801, 'you have now permission to dig'. Quoted in Smith, 'Lord Elgin and his Collection', 192.
13. *Nisbet*, 97.
14. Elgin to Lusieri, 10 July 1801. Quoted in Smith, 'Lord Elgin and his Collection', 191.
15. Elgin to Lord Hawkesbury, 7 July 1801, FO 78/32. Hunt's instructions are among the Hunt Papers.
16. Smirke's Journal. He was in Athens in July 1803.
17. M. R. Bruce, 'A Tourist in Athens in 1801', *Journal of Hellenic Studies*, 92 (1972), 174.
18. These details are from a letter of Hunt to Elgin, 31 July 1801, among the Elgin Papers. Smith, although quoting much of the letter, makes no mention of them.
19. See the quotations from Gell's diary (*Narrative of a Journey in the Morea* (1823)) and the comments by Bruce, a source which was not known at the time of the first edition of the book.
20. A water-colour by Dodwell which also shows Lusieri's scaffolding is at Broomhall.
21. *Nisbet*, 123. Hunt wrote a similar letter on 21 August 1801 to Lord Upper Ossory, Hunt Papers.
22. *Nisbet*, 123.
23. Smith, 'Lord Elgin and his Collection', 197.
24. Ibid. 201.
25. *Select Committee Report*, 146.
26. Ibid. 143.
27. Ibid. 146.
28. Smirke's Journal, 21 July 1803. This piece of evidence has not, as far as I know, been noted before the present edition.
29. *Select Committee Report*, 144.
30. They were, for example, worried about being held to account if the political climate changed.
31. Journal for 21 July 1803.
32. Hunt to Lord Upper Ossory, 21 August 1801, Hunt Papers. Before telling the story of his success at Athens to Lord Upper Ossory, Hunt prudently asked Elgin's permission. 'I know there are envious people', he wrote ominously, 'who will not fail to represent what has been done here as a violence to the fine remains of Grecian sculpture.' Hunt to Elgin, 21 August 1801, Elgin Papers.
33. *Select Committee Report*, 41.

34. Smith, 'Lord Elgin and his Collection', 346.
35. Hobhouse, *A Journey through Albania*, 339.
36. Ibid. 196.
37. Ibid. 357, referring to *Revue Archéologique*, 24 and 26.
38. He had no reason to. A. L. Millin's *Description d'un bas relief du Parthénon actuellement au Musée Napoléon*, which was incorporated as an appendix in the 1811 and 1815 editions of the *Memorandum*, says that the slab was detached from the Parthenon, 'a été détaché'. After Choiseul-Gouffier's death in 1817 the sale catalogue of his collection emphasized that the metope was found on the ground, L. J. J. Dubois, *Catalogue d'Antiquités ... formant la collection de ... M. le Comte de Choiseul-Gouffier* (Paris, 1818).
39. *Description of the Collection of Ancient Marbles in the British Museum*, viii (1839), 97.

Chapter 10: 'The Last Poor Plunder from a Bleeding Land'

 1. Elgin, *Memorandum* (1815 edition), 15.
 2. See, for example, Williams, *Travels in Italy, Greece and the Ionian Islands*, ii. 316.
 3. Hunt to Elgin 21 August 1801, quoted in Smith, 'Lord Elgin and his Collection', 200.
 4. According to Sicilianos, *Old and New Athens*, 356, the Metropolitan at the time was Gregory III, 1799–1820, described as 'one of the worst'.
 5. *Select Committee Report*, 144.
 6. Elgin to Lusieri, 10 July 1801, quoted in Smith, 'Lord Elgin and his Collection', 207.
 7. Quoted ibid. 196.
 8. *Keith Papers*, ii. 405.
 9. Lusieri to Elgin 11 January 1802, quoted in Smith, 'Lord Elgin and his Collection', 209.
10. Lusieri to Elgin 8 August 1802, quoted ibid. 227.
11. Smirke Journal.
12. Quoted in Smith, 'Lord Elgin and his Collection', 205.
13. Elgin to Lusieri, 10 July 1801, quoted ibid. 207.
14. Elgin to Lusieri, 23 December 1801, quoted ibid. 207. At the time there was little to be seen above ground at Delphi.
15. Hunt to Elgin, no date given, quoted ibid. 201.
16. Lacy to Hunt, 8 October 1801, Hunt Papers.
17. Dodwell, *Classical Tour*, i. 322. Bruce, 'A Tourist in Athens', 175, notes that since Dodwell left Athens on 15 September 1801 he could not have seen all that he claims to have seen. Bruce also suggests that in 1801 neither Gell nor Dodwell felt the indignation which they showed later.

18. Clarke *Travels*, part II, section 2, p. 483. 'Telos' is printed in Greek in the original.
19. Canto II, stanza xii. See p. 182.
20. C and D of the west pediment in Brommer's classification.
21. Morritt, giving evidence to the Select Committee, p. 128.
22. One head appears to be still in place in the picture by Gell reproduced in the Goulandris Foundation catalogue, p. 65. See also Dodwell, *Classical Tour*, i. 325. Dodwell's remarks on this fragment seem to be confirmed by a letter of Fauvel quoted in *Bulletin de la Société Nationale des Antiquaires de la France*, 6 (1900), 245. The *Notice sur le Musée Dodwell* (Rome, 1837), lists seven architectural fragments from the Parthenon and a 'testa barbata prov d'Atene' but this is now believed to refer to the head of the centaur from metope 5 on the south side in Würzburg. That head was already missing in the time of Stuart and Revett. See Brommer, *Metopen*, i. 83.
23. Wheler, *A Journey into Greece*, 361, punctuation simplified.
24. Spon, *Voyage d'Italie*, ii. 147.
25. See *Revue Archéologique*, 31: 97. *Select Committee Report*, 24, 118.
26. See, for example, the letter from Hunt, February 1805, in *Nisbet*, 344.
27. E. D. Clarke, *The Tomb of Alexander* (1805).
28. Otter, *Life*, 505.
29. Clarke, *Travels*, part II, section 2, p. 475.
30. *Travels*, II/2: 475.
31. G. P. Stevens, *The Erechtheum* (1927), 502.
32. Chandler, *Travels in Greece*, 191.
33. E. D. Clarke, *Greek Marbles* (1809), 32.
34. Otter, *Life*, 505.
35. Clarke *Travels*, II/2: 784.
36. Quoted in Smith, 'Lord Elgin and his Collection', 206.
37. Otter, *Life*, 516.
38. Lusieri to Elgin 11 January 1802, quoted in Smith, 'Lord Elgin and his Collection', 209.
39. Clarke, *Greek Marbles*, 34 ff.
40. Elgin to Grenville, 3 July 1800, FO 78/28.
41. Elgin to Hawkesbury, 7 July 1801, FO 78/32.
42. *Nisbet*, 140.
43. Smith, 'Lord Elgin and his Collection', 211.
44. Lady Elgin to Elgin, 19 May 1802, Elgin Papers. Smith, who quoted other parts of this letter chose to omit this revealing passage. He also omitted other passages which throw an unfavourable light on Lady Elgin's character. For the protection documents which were later obtained, see Appendix 1.
45. Lady Elgin to Elgin, 22 May 1802, Elgin Papers. Omitted by Smith.
46. See p. 95.

47. *Nisbet*, 199.
48. Quoted in Smith, 'Lord Elgin and his Collection', 214; *Nisbet*, 187.
49. Ibid. 207; FO 78/36.
50. *Nisbet*, 210 ff.
51. Lusieri to Elgin, 16 September 1802, quoted in Smith, 'Lord Elgin and his Collection', 232. Smith connects this with the destruction of the cornice mentioned by Clarke and repeated by Byron. Clarke had, however, left Athens in December 1801.
52. Lusieri to Elgin, 28 October 1802, quoted by Smith, 'Lord Elgin', 235.
53. Hunt to Elgin, two letters sent on 28 November 1802, Hunt Papers. An extract from one in Smith, 'Lord Elgin', 237.
54. Sicilianos, *Old and New Athens*, 229.
55. Quoted in Smith, 'Lord Elgin', 230.
56. Ibid. 206. Hunt had also suggested seizing Fauvel's collection in letters to Elgin on 31 July 1801 and 8 August 1801, Elgin Papers.
57. Smith, 'Lord Elgin', 362.
58. *Nisbet*, 154.
59. Quoted by Smith, 'Lord Elgin', 209.
60. Ibid. 217. Cf. *Nisbet*, 195.
61. Quoted in Smith, 'Lord Elgin', 218. Cf. *Nisbet*, 196.
62. Sir E. A. Wallis Budge, *The Rosetta Stone* (1929).
63. Clarke, *Tomb* 38.
64. *Annual Register* (1859), 430.
65. Quoted in Smith, 'Lord Elgin', 233.
66. I use the ancient name which was readopted later in the nineteenth century. In Elgin's day the island was universally known as Cerigo, as it was called during the centuries when the island was part of the Ionian Islands ruled by Venice.
67. See p. 132.
68. Smith, 'Lord Elgin', 237. A slightly different version is in a draft among the Hunt Papers.
69. Smith, 'Lord Elgin', 239.
70. Ibid. 240. Captain Clarke's own account of the incident is given in a fine edition of William Falconer, *The Shipwreck*, ed. J. S. Clarke (1811), 207.
71. *Nisbet*, 232, 334.
72. For the estimated total costs see p. 144.
73. Elgin to Lord Hawkesbury, 13 January 1803, FO 78/38.
74. Quoted in Smith, 'Lord Elgin', 234.

Chapter 11: Prisoner of War

1. Hunt to Elgin, 19 December 1802, Hunt Papers. For the general story of the British prisoners in France see Michael Lewis, *Napoleon and*

his *British Captives* (1962). Many details of the Elgins' life at this time in *Nisbet*.

2. *Moniteur*, No. 130.
3. *Nisbet*, 286. The passport given by the French Ambassador in Naples to Lord Elgin and his party is among the Elgin Papers.
4. Elgin to King of Prussia, 24 May 1803, FO 27/68.
5. *Nisbet*, 239.
6. Ibid. 238 ff., 248 ff.
7. *Correspondance de Napoléon I*, viii. 387.
8. *Nisbet*, 263.
9. Ibid. 259.
10. Quoted in Smith, 'Lord Elgin and his Collection', 360. *Nisbet*, 259.
11. *Revue Archéologique*, 24: 92; 26: 238.
12. Ibid. 24: 88.
13. Ibid. 30: 389.
14. Quoted in full in Edward Smith, *Life of Sir Joseph Banks* (1911), 209. The subsequent story is told in Smith, 'Lord Elgin and his Collection', 358 ff.
15. Farington, 5 December 1806 (published).
16. *Revue Archéologique*, 26: 238. Favuel almost certainly wanted this marble to provide materials for the restoration of the Louvre slab ordered by Bonaparte. It was regarded as useless by Lusieri and there seems to be no other reason beyond spite why he should want to steal it from him.
17. Quoted in *Bulletin de la Société Nationale des Antiquaires de la France*, 6th Ser. (1900), 245.
18. *Nisbet*, 278.
19. Ibid. 249.
20. *Correspondance de Napoléon I*, viii. p. 315.
21. *Nisbet*, and a series of letters in FO 27/68.
22. The fullest account of this puzzling episode is Sir Walter Scott, *Life of Buonaparte*, chapter 129, which derived from Elgin himself (see NLS 3902, fo. 95). Other evidence is in *Nisbet* and BL Add. MS 38266, fo. 5. The 'confession' of the prisoner called Rivoire is in Lewis Goldsmith (ed.), *Recueil de decrets, ordonnances etc de Napoléon Bonaparte* (1813), i. 1054.
23. *Nisbet*, 296.
24. Ibid. 321.
25. Ibid. 351.
26. E. d'Hauterive, *La Police Secrète du Premier Empire* (Paris, 1908), i. 387.
27. Lewis, *Napoleon and his British Captives*, 183. For Ferguson see the two pamphlets, *The Trial of R. Fergusson Esq.* (1807) and *The Trial of R. J. Fergusson, Esquire* (1808). Also informative is the record of

the divorce trial, 11 March 1808, before the Commissary Court of Edinburgh in the Scottish Register Office in Edinburgh, and further details in Checkland, *The Elgins*. Ferguson was released because of his contributions to science—he was a Fellow of the Royal Society.

28. *Nisbet*, 240.
29. *Select Committee Report*, 43. The truth about Elgin's imprisonment at Melun is difficult to disentangle. Fouché's report to Napoleon of 26 September 1805 (d'Hauterive, *La Police Secrète*, ii. 101) reads: 'Lord Elgin, Macmahon, Henri Seymour, Lord Yarmouth, sont autorisés à vivre à Melun sur parole.' Since Lady Elgin had not yet left Paris this squares with Elgin's statement to the Select Committee that he was living with his family. On the other hand, two later reports, of the 10 February 1806 (d'Hauterive, ii. 257) and 26 February 1806 (ibid. 276) seem to bear on the incident. The first reports the arrival at the Turkish embassy in Paris of letters for Lord Elgin; the second reports that Elgin and others were publicly and ostentatiously giving help to Austrian and Russian prisoners. Lord Elgin might have been arrested for the activities reported in the second but, because the letters from Turkey arrived at the same time, he might have connected his arrest with them. This explanation does not, however, square with his statement to the Select Committee that the incident occurred in 1805 when he was with his family.
30. *Memorandum* (1815 edition), 93, Elgin to Spencer Perceval, 6 May 1811, BL Add. MS 38246, fo. 119; Elgin to Long, *Select Committee Report*, p. vii.
31. *The Times*, 16 December, 1805.
32. NLS 1709, fo. 202.
33. BL Add. MS 38266, fo. 5.

Chapter 12: Lusieri on his Own, 1803–1806

1. Hunt to Elgin, 29 December 1802, Hunt Papers.
2. Hunt to Hamilton, 13 December 1802, Hunt Papers. A copy of Gavallo's letter is also in in the collection.
3. Otter's *Life of Clarke*, 502, 505.
4. Lusieri to Elgin, 28 October, 1802, quoted in Smith, 'Lord Elgin and his Collection', 236.
5. Journal in Greece.
6. Smith, 'Lord Elgin and his Collection', 256.
7. In 1801 Morier published *Memoir of a Campaign with the Ottoman Army in Egypt*. That this was unauthorized and caused a breach with Elgin is clear from a letter from Lady Elgin to Dowager Lady Elgin, 12 June 1802, Elgin Papers.
8. See p. 110.

9. Elgin to Lusieri, 4 October 1802, summarized in Smith, 'Lord Elgin and his Collection', 235.
10. Lusieri to Elgin, 28 October 1802, quoted ibid. 236.
11. See p. 123.
12. *Revue Archéologique*, 30: 389.
13. Lusieri to Elgin, 26 September 1803, quoted in Smith, 'Lord Elgin and his Collection', 257.
14. Aberdeen's Diary.
15. The list of antiquities collected for Lord Aberdeen by Gropius includes 'un très beau pied d'un Hercule d'un des metopes du Parthénon à Athènes', and 'goettes et morceaux de Marbre des Temples d'Eleusis, de Minerva, et du Cap Sunium, et des Propylées'.
16. Lusieri to Elgin, 6 February 1804, quoted in Smith, 'Lord Elgin and his Collection', 258.
17. Ibid.
18. Lusieri to Elgin, 4 July 1805, quoted ibid. 261. See also Appendix 1.
19. Reproduced in Plate 3.
20. Lusieri to Elgin, 4 July 1805, quoted in Smith, 'Lord Elgin', 261. See also Appendix 1.
21. Lusieri to Elgin, 8 October 1805, quoted in Smith, 'Lord Elgin', 262. See also Appendix 1.

Chapter 13: Homecoming

1. The main sources for the break-up of Elgin's marriage are the two pamphlets of the Ferguson trial, and the official records of Elgin's divorce suit before the Commissary Court of Edinburgh in March 1808 in the Scottish Record Office, Edinburgh.
2. Quoted in *The Trial of R. Fergusson Esq.*, 6.
3. Ibid. 10.
4. Quoted in the Commissary Court Record.
5. Quoted in *The Trial of R. Fergusson Esq.*, 32.
6. Ibid. 19.
7. Besides the two pamphlets, see also Sir Walter Scott's letters to Lady Abercorn in *Familiar Letters of Sir Walter Scott* (1894), i. 92, 116.
8. *Nisbet*, 248.
9. Ibid. 306.
10. BL Add. MS 38266, fo. 5.
11. HMC, *Fortescue*, ii. 184.
12. *Nisbet*, 326.
13. Ibid. 161.
14. FO 78/54.
15. Smith, 'Lord Elgin and his Collection', 312.
16. BL Add. MS 38266, fo. 5.
17. Smith, 'Lord Elgin and his Collection', 312.

18. Sir N. H. Nicholas (ed.), *Letters and Despatches of Nelson* (1845–6), v. 478.
19. *Select Committee Report*, p. xi.
20. BL Add. MS 38266, fo. 5.
21. Hunt, *Narrative*, 4; and NLS 5645, fo. 210. For his work for Bedford prison see Stockdale, *Law and Order in Georgian Bedfordshire*.
22. Smith, 'Lord Elgin and his Collection', 295.
23. Ibid. 357. *Select Committee Report*, 44.
24. Minutes of meeting, 4 November 1806.
25. A point made graphically by Panayotis Tournikiotis, 'The Place of the Parthenon in the History and Theory of Modern Architecture', in *The Parthenon*, 203.
26. Elgin Drawings in BM Greek and Roman Department.
27. Smith, 'Lord Elgin and his Collection', 255. The Calmuck went to Paris in August 1805 'pour suivre une affaire contre Lord Elgin', d'Hauterive, *La Police Secrète*, ii. 45. Later he became court painter in Karlsruhe.
28. Some amusing stories of Italian restorations in J. T. Smith, *Nollekens* (1828), i. 10.
29. Quoted in Smith, 'Lord Elgin and his Collection', 227.
30. See David Constantine, *Early Greek Travellers and the Hellenic Ideal* (1984), and Suzanne Marchand, *Down from Olympus* (Princeton, 1996).
31. For an interesting discussion of who were the 'artists' see Manolis Korres, *From Pentelicon to the Parthenon* (1995).
32. *Memorandum* (1815 edition), 39.
33. Farington, 5 December 1806 (published).
34. Smith, 'Lord Elgin and his Collection', 297.
35. B. R. Haydon, *Correspondence and Table Talk* (1876), i. 256. Elgin was still talking about restorations as late as 1814: Smith, 'Lord Elgin and his Collection', 318.

Chapter 14: The Second Collection

1. Smith, 'Lord Elgin and his Collection', 266 ff.; *Revue Archéologique*, 30: 389.
2. BL Add. MS 40096, fo. 21. Elgin to Mulgrave, 16 February 1808.
3. Quoted in Smith, 'Lord Elgin and his Collection', 269.
4. Ibid. 269.
5. Ibid. 273.
6. Quoted ibid. 274.
7. Ibid. 276.
8. FO 78/67.
9. Quoted in Smith, 'Lord Elgin and his Collection', 279.
10. This seems to be the meaning of the entry for 29 April 1811 in Abbott,

Diary and Correspondence (1861). See also Sir Robert Adair, *The Negociations for the Peace of the Dardanelles in 1808–9* (1845), i. 272. The original of this letter and the letter to which it is a reply are in FO 78/64.

11. FO 78/68.
12. Smith, 'Lord Elgin and his Collection', 280.
13. Quoted ibid. 279.
14. *Select Committee Report*, 1.
15. Ibid. 4.
16. Ibid. 7.
17. Ibid. 7.
18. See especially the various books and articles by John Henry Merryman noted in the Bibliography.
19. John Galt, *Life and Studies of Benjamin West* (1816), ii. 75.
20. Quoted in Smith, 'Lord Elgin and his Collection', 280.
21. John Galt, *Autobiography* (1833), i. 159.
22. Hobhouse, *A Journey through Albania*, 292.
23. Ibid. 346.
24. See p. 180.
25. In Byron's letters Nicolo is referred to once as 'Lusieri's wife's brother', *Letters and Journals*, ed. Leslie A. Marchand (1973–82), ii. 10, once as the 'brother of Lusieri's should-be wife', ibid., ii. 29, and the 'brother of Lusieri's spouse', ibid. ii. 16. An apparently official document (quoted in *Revue Archéologique*, 30: 385) mentions among the French colony at Athens 'la veuve du sieur Giraud dont la fille a épousé un Italien sous protection anglais'. The references to Giraud in Byron's letters to Hobhouse leave no doubt about the nature of the relationship.
26. *Letters and Journals*, ii. 71.
27. Ibid. ii. 65 note. See also Leslie A. Marchand, *Byron: A Biography* (1957), i. 282.
28. Quoted in Smith, 'Lord Elgin and his Collection', 313.

Chapter 15: Artists and Dilettanti

1. Flaxman had, however, shown an interest in the fragment of the Parthenon frieze owned by the Society of Dilettanti, see Margaret Whinney, *Sculpture in Britain 1530–1830* (1964), 185, and in Choiseul-Gouffier's casts, see David Irwin, *English Neoclassical Art* (1966), 73.
2. Quoted in Smith, 'Lord Elgin and his Collection', 297.
3. Haydon's *Diary*, ii. 15. The figure, number D in the east pediment in Brommer's classification, long known as the Theseus, is now thought to represent Dionysos.
4. Henry Crabb Robertson, *Diary, Reminiscences and Correspondence* (1869), i. 395.

5. Farington Diary, 30 March 1808 (published).
6. Published as an Appendix to Elgin's *Memorandum*.
7. Farington, 2 March 1809.
8. Ibid. 27 February 1808.
9. Ibid. 6 June 1807.
10. Ibid. 27 February and 30 March 1808.
11. Turner to Elgin, 7 August 1806, Elgin Papers.
12. W. T. Whitley, *Art in England 1800–1820* (1928), 135.
13. Farington, 20 June 1808. There were 20 shillings in a pound. A guinea was one pound, one shilling.
14. Ibid. 29 July 1808.
15. Quoted in Smith, 'Lord Elgin and his Collection', 306.
16. *Memorandum* (1811 edition), 42. The figures, number K, L, and M in the east pediment in Brommer's classification, are now thought more likely to represent Hestia, Dione, and Aphrodite. The reference to Mrs Siddons was removed from the 1815 edition, perhaps as a result of some scornful remarks in Clarke's *Travels*, part II, section 2, p. 485.
17. Haydon's *Autobiography*, 66. When he was a boy Haydon bought an expensive anatomy book by Albinus in order to improve his knowledge of the human form.
18. Irwin, *Winckelmann*, 160.
19. Haydon, *Autobiography*, 68.
20. Ibid. 69.
21. Haydon's *Diary*, i. 15.
22. Ibid. i. 27.
23. Ibid. i. 28.
24. Ibid. i. 29.
25. *Quarterly Review*, 14: 533.
26. Richard Payne Knight, *An Analytic Inquiry into the Principles of Taste* (1805), 4.
27. Haydon, *Autobiography*, 207. *Select Committee Report*, p. v.
28. See p. 104.
29. Farington, 30 March 1808.
30. See especially Michaelis, *Ancient Marbles*.
31. *Select Committee Report*, p. xxii.
32. *Specimens of Antient Sculpture*, vol. i, p. xxxix.
33. William Wilkins, *Atheniensia* (1816), 119 f.
34. Lionel Cust and Sidney Colvin, *History of the Society of Dilettanti* (1898), 133.
35. *The Townley Gallery, British Museum* (1836), 12.

Chapter 16: Elgin Offers his First Collection to the Government

1. Sir George Jackson, *The Bath Archives* (1873), 409.
2. Quoted in Smith, 'Lord Elgin and his Collection', 306.

3. Farington, 11 December 1802 (unpublished).
4. A copy of the letter is in NLS 1709, fo. 204. Most of it is published in *Nisbet*, 328.
5. No figures are known for the print run of the first edition. 250, 500, or 750 is my estimate based on the norms of other such pamphlets. For the second edition Elgin printed 500 copies of which many were distributed gratis to a second list of potentially influential peers, other politicians, connoisseurs, and artists. Murray archives. See also Chapter 19 n. 7.
6. Smith, 'Lord Elgin and his Collection', 308.
7. 'Description d'un bas relief du Parthénon actuellement au Musée Napoléon', by A. L. Millin. *Memorandum* (1811 edition), 72.
8. *Select Committee Report*, p. viii.
9. See p. 144 for a breakdown of this figure.
10. BL Add. MS 38246, fo. 119.
11. BL Add. MS 38191, fo. 197.
12. Abbott, *Diary and Correspondence* (1861), ii. 330. Quoted in Smith, 'Lord Elgin and his Collection', 311.
13. Ibid. 313.

Chapter 17: Poets and Travellers

1. The main features of the early publication history are noted by Thomas James, Wise, *A Bibliography of the Writings in Verse and Prose of George Gordon, Lord Byron* (1933).
2. 'Ten or twelve' according to Byron's letter of 25 December 1822, *Letters and Journals*, x. 70. The reason for Longman's refusal is confirmed in a letter to Revd Mr Card, 8 May 1815, 'some of our friends were hardly treated in it'. Longman archives, University of Reading Library, 99/98.
3. Advertisements by A. and W. Galignani in copies of books published by the firm. Five guineas would imply a premium of over 2,000 per cent above Cawthorn's price of five shillings, itself not cheap.
4. *The Life of Percy Bysshe Shelley* (1858), i. 300.
5. They are still commonly found. Most were written in expensive morocco notebooks, and carefully reproduce the title-page, the preface, and the notes as well as the verse.
6. There are also fakes of the first edition, and of the third edition with paper watermarked 1808, copies in author's collection.
7. *Complete Poetical Works*, ed. Jerome J. McGann (1980–93), vii. 103. In Soane Notebooks, 13 August 1816. Another version is quoted by Ioannes Gennadios, *Lord Elgin and the Previous Archaeological Invasions of Greece* (1930), 77. The couplet was attributed to Martin Archer Shee but is not included in his *Rhymes On Art*. For Byron quoting it see also *Medwin's Conversations of Lord Byron*, ed. Ernest

J. Lovell Jr. (1966), 211. The attribution to Byron is made in some unreliable editions of his works. A short poem in Latin, *Complete Poetical Works*, i. 330, repeats the satire of the revenge of Venus which is among the main themes of *The Curse of Minerva*, discussed below.

8. Murray archives. Not previously published or known. Original spelling retained.

9. Ibid. Not previously published or known.

10. Byron to Hobhouse 31 July 1811, *Letters and Journals*, ii. 65.

11. Thomas Moore's *Byron* (1830/1), chapter xi.

12. That Constable was among the publishers who rejected *Childe Harold's Pilgrimage* is shown by Byron's reference to 'the Crafty', in his letter of 25 December 1822, *Letters and Journals*, x. 70, not previously identified as a reference to Constable as far as I know. For Constable as 'the Crafty' see Mrs Oliphant and Mrs Gerald Porter, *William Blackwood and his Sons* (1897 and 1898), i. 121, and J. G. Lockhart, *The Life of Sir Walter Scott, Bart*, one-volume edition (1893), 167.

13. Murray archives. In order to give the book-buying public the impression that the book was selling even more rapidly than was the case, Murray, by changing the title-pages, pretended that there were ten editions before the end of 1814, although there were only six. Murray archives.

14. William St. Clair, 'The Impact of Byron's Writings: An Evaluative Approach', in Andrew Rutherford (ed.), *Byron, Augustan and Romantic* (1990).

15. Canto II, 11–15.

16. See Terence Spencer, *Fair Greece, Sad Relic*, and the early chapters and appendix 1 of St. Clair, *That Greece Might Still Be Free* (1972), which describe, and to some extent quantify, the books and reading by which the philhellenic myth was consolidated and diffused.

17. See especially Fani-Maria Tsigakou, *The Rediscovery of Greece* (1981) and *Through Romantic Eyes* (Athens, 1991), and the many gorgeous illustrations in Tournikiotis, *The Parthenon*.

18. Without going back to the early editions, especially those published before 1816 when *Childe Harold's Pilgrimage, Canto the Third*, was published as a separate book, it is hard for present-day readers to recapture a reliable sense of how *Childe Harold's Pilgrimage, A Romaunt*, was read, appreciated, and understood in the years immediately after it was published. With the development, in Victorian times, of the romantic notion that it was only the verse part of the book which constituted the 'poem', most editions, including the *Complete Poetical Works*, have tended to cut back the long passages of accompanying prose or to treat them, anachronistically, if they

were equivalent to scholarly editorial annotations to a prime text. Many modern editions omit them altogether. At the time when the work was first read, *Childe Harold's Pilgrimage, A Romaunt*, with its voluminous factual supporting and illustrative information about the antiquities, the state of literature, the history, and the political options open to the Greeks, probably reinforced the impression that Byron was no mere armchair visionary or polemicist, but a careful, thoughtful, observer who had been to the places he wrote about and who knew what he was talking about.

19. Haygarth, *Greece: A Poem in Three Parts*, part II, ll. 222 ff.
20. *Childe Harold's Pilgrimage*, canto II. 'Papers referred to by Note 33'.
21. Ibid.
22. See, for example, C. M. Woodhouse, *Capodistria* (1973), and the documents in Richard Clogg (ed. and trans.), *The Movement for Greek Independence, 1770–1821* (1976).
23. In the 1970s a friend of mine doing research on the life of Lawrence of Arabia was taken to meet an old Bedouin who spoke confidently about Lawrence whom he gave every appearance of having known personally. It turned out that his information was derived from seeing the film.
24. Byron to Clarke, 19 January 1812, *Letters and Journals*, ii. 156. Marchand reads 'Grossius', but, having looked again at the manuscript, BL Egerton 2869, fo. 7, I believe that the true reading is 'Gropius'. Geog Gropius was Aberdeen's agent. Byron frequently made jokes on names but the manuscript suggests no such intention here. In *Childe Harold's Pilgrimage*, canto II, note 6, Byron says that Aberdeen completely disowned Gropius' collecting activities. It is clear, however, from a letter of Hamilton to Elgin (2 May 1809, Elgin Papers) that Aberdeen at that time was laying claim to the vases collected by Gropius. The occasion of Byron's apology to Aberdeen is described in BL Add. MS 43230, fo. 114.
25. In all editions after the first.
26. Byron to Clarke, 15 December 1813, *Letters and Journals*, iii. 199.
27. Clarke, *Travels*, part II, section 2, p. 484.
28. Ibid. II/2: 485.
29. BL Egerton 2027. *Complete Poetical Works*, ii. 48.
30. Michaelis, *Ancient Marbles*, 285.
31. BL Egerton 2027. *Complete Poetical Works*, ii. 49.
32. Ibid. 48.
33. F. S. N. Douglas, *An Essay on Certain Points of Resemblance between the Ancient and Modern Greeks* (1813), 89.
34. Dodwell, i. 324, 322.
35. T. S. Hughes, *Travels in Sicily, Greece and Albania* (1820), i. 261.
36. J. C. Eustace, *A Classical Tour through Italy* (1813), ii. 20.

37. Especially Pouqueville, *Voyage dans la Grèce*, iv. 36, 74; Bartholdy, *Voyage en Grèce*, 45; and Forbin, *Voyage dans le Levant*, 11.
38. Chateaubriand, *Travels to Jerusalem*, 3rd edn. (London, 1835), i. 187.
39. Hunt to Elgin, 22 May 1801, Elgin Papers.
40. William Black, *Narrative of Cruises in the Mediterranean* (Edinburgh, 1900), 295. Black gives the date 1806 which is clearly impossible.
41. See Eliot, 'Lord Byron, Early Travellers, and the Monastery at Delphi', *American Journal of Archaeology*, 71 (1967). For the name on the Monument of Lysicrates and the Erechtheion, not, as far as I know, found during the recent careful examination connected with the restorations, see N. Parker Willis, *Summer Cruise in the Mediterranean* (1853), 145 and 148.
42. Forbin, *Voyage dans le Levant*, 11.
43. Dodwell, *Classical Tour*, i. 353, and *Quarterly Review*, May 1820.
44. Hobhouse, *A Journey through Albania*, 345. Many other references.
45. Smith, 'Lord Elgin and his Collection', 220, quoting William Turner, *A Tour in the Levant* (1812), i. 347.
46. *Complete Poetical Works*, ed. McGann, vol. i, no. 151.
47. The suggestion in Moore's *Byron*, chapter lxv that Byron's decision was aided by a 'friendly remonstrance from Lord Elgin or some of his connection' is confirmed by a reference in the Journal of Edward Everett. Everett met Byron on 18 June 1815 shortly after Elgin's Petition to Parliament was debated. 'I asked him,' he wrote, 'whether his poem which he speaks of as "printed but not published" in the notes to the Corsair, would ever be given to the World. Oh No! he replied it was a satire upon Lord Elgin, which a particular friend of each had begged him to suppress.'
48. Byron to Clarke, 27 May 1812, BL Egerton 2869, fo. 10, *Letters and Journals*, ii. 178.
49. Rogers's copy is in the British Library. It seems likely that many more than 8 copies were printed.
50. *New Monthly Magazine*, April 1815, 'The Malediction of Minerva'. This version is very corrupt and bears the signs of having passed through several manuscript versions before reaching the printer. *The Curse of Minerva*, in its abbreviated form, also appeared in editions sold by the Paris pirate publisher Galignani.
51. A month after 'The Malediction of Minerva' was published in the *New Monthly Magazine* a correspondent had pointed out that the author was Byron, *New Monthly Magazine*, September 1815. Other versions of *The Curse* were published in London in 1816, 1818, and 1819. Full versions under Byron's name were published in the United States in 1815 and 1816.
52. [James and Horace Smith], *Horace in London* (1813), ode xv 'The Parthenon'.

53. John Galt, *Letters from the Levant* (1813), 112. Letter dated 1 March 1810.
54. Galt, *Autobiography*, chapter VII.
55. An edited version of the *Atheniad* was published in Galt, *Autobiography*. Another version appeared many years earlier in the *Monthly Magazine*, 49 (1820).
56. In a letter to Elgin on 17 September 1811 Hamilton wrote: 'I saw Mr. Hume a few days ago who called to give me the satisfactory intelligence that Mr. Gant [*sic*] had given up all idea of bringing to light the productions of his Muse, and that the absence of Lord Biron [*sic*] had given him time to reflect on the improper tendency of his former intentions', Elgin Papers. Hamilton's misspelling of the names of Galt and Byron shows how little known both men were at the time.
57. John Galt, *Life of Byron* (1830), 183.
58. For a discussion of this point see Terence Spencer, *Fair Greece, Sad Relic*, 247 ff., and St. Clair, *That Greece Might Still Be Free*, early chapters.
59. Kelsall. Name of the author from Spencer, *Fair Greece, Sad Relic*, 279.
60. Byron, *A Letter to **** ****** [John Murray] on the Rev. W. L. Bowles's Strictures on the Life and Writings of Pope* (1821), 25.
61. Byron to Hodgson, 25 September 1811, *Letters and Journals*, ii. 106. De Pauw and Thornton were authors of books contemptuous of the Modern Greeks.
62. This seems to have been Hamilton's explanation to Haydon. Haydon, *Diary*, iv. 594: 'October 27, 1839. Spent the greater part of the day with Hamilton—a delightful one. He let me into the secret of the opposition of Lord Elgin at the time. He said Lady Elgin's Friends who were Tories (the Manners) and Fergusson's friends who were Whigs were violent in the hatred of everything he did and made all that stir in opposition backed by the jealousy of connoisseurship.' Elgin's counsel accused Ferguson of deliberately attempting to misrepresent Elgin's public life in the divorce trial of December 1807. *Trial of R. J. Fergusson Esquire*, 9, and *Trial of R. Fergusson Esq.*, 8.
63. Mrs Spencer Smith, the daughter of Baron Herbert, Austrian Ambassador to the Porte, had made a dramatic and romantic escape when the French entered Venice in 1806. This was related by the Marquis of Salvo in a book published in 1807. She is described in enthusiastic terms in Byron's letters. In *Childe Harold's Pilgrimage*, she is:

> Sweet Florence! could another ever share
> This wayward loveless heart, it would be thine:
> But check'd by every tie, I may not dare

To cast a worthless offering at thy shrine.
Nor ask so dear a breast to feel one pang for mine.

Chapter 18: Later Years in Greece

1. See C. R. Cockerell, *Travels in Southern Europe and the Levant 1810–1817* (1903).
2. Ibid. 51.
3. I use Stewart's classification. He dates the period from c.500 to c.470: *Greek Sculpture: An Exploration* (1990), i. 131.
4. Cockerell, *Travels*, 55.
5. FO 78/77. An edited version is in Cockerell, *Travels*, 56. The remark about farming Aegina has been taken to refer to Lusieri. For years he had proposed that permission should be sought from the Capitan Pasha, the Ottoman official who acted as governor of the islands of the Aegean, to allow excavations there. But he was not in Athens at the time the letter was written. The reference is probably to Georg Gropius.
6. Quoted in Smith, 'Lord Elgin and his Collection', 283.
7. Gally Knight and Fazakerly were later to serve on the Select Committee appointed to advise on Elgin's collection.
8. See Cockerell and Papers on Aegina Marbles.
9. Smith, 'Lord Elgin and his Collection', 284, 314. HMC Report on the Laing MSS preserved in the University of Edinburgh (1914–1925), ii. 757.
10. Papers on Aegina Marbles.
11. Cockerell, *Travels*, 219.
12. Apart from the usual sources, see the two more friendly accounts of Lusieri's last years by John Bramsen, *Letters of a Prussian Traveller* (1818), and Fuller, *Narrative of a Tour*. I have also consulted the unpublished journals of Hanson and of Master.
13. Walsh, *A Residence at Constantinople*, i. 126.
14. Hughes, *Travels in Sicily, Greece and Albania*, i. 267.
15. Williams, *Travels in Italy, Greece and the Ionian Islands*, ii. 361.
16. Gennadios, *Lord Elgin and the Previous Archaeological Invasions of Greece*, 40, 77.
17. Richard Monkton Milnes, *Memorials of a Tour in Some Parts of Greece* (1834), 133, M. B. Poujoulat, *Voyages dans l'Asie Mineure* (Paris, 1840), 5.
18. Gennadios, *Lord Elgin and the Previous Archaeological Invasions of Greece*, 40.
19. See also Chapter 25.
20. See W. M. Leake, *Researches in Greece* (1814), 226, and the discussion in Angelomatis-Tsougarakis, *The Eve of the Greek Revival*, 118.
21. Notes to Childe Harold's Pilgrimage, *Complete Poetical Works*, ii. 201.

Notes to pp. 208–213

Notes to pp. 208–213   373

22. *Select Committee Report*, 144. See also p. 95.
23. *Select Committee Report*, 57.
24. For example Douglas, *Ancient and Modern Greeks*, 85, Hughes, *Travels*, i. 259, Dupré, *Voyage à Constantinople*, 36, and Williams, *Travels*, ii. 307.
25. Hobhouse, *Travels*, i. 348.
26. Hobhouse MS Journal. I have restored the abbreviations and modernized the spelling.
27. For example, Frederika Bremer, *Greece and the Greeks* (1863), i. 9. See also p. 324.
28. 'Notes on Travelling in the Levant', Hunt Papers. Benizelos, called Beninzello, is also mentioned by Biddle, *Nicholas Biddle in Greece*, 155.
29. Hunt Papers.
30. Gennadios, *Lord Elgin and the Previous Archaeological Invasions of Greece*, 2.
31. Hobhouse, *A Journey through Albania*, 347.
32. Stevens, *The Erechtheum*, 536 ff.
33. For example, the illustrations in *The Antiquities of Athens*, iii; Clarke, *Travels*, part II, section 2, p. 544; Lusieri's drawing in Smith; 'Lord Elgin and his Collection'; Pomardi, *Viaggio nella Grecia*, 146; and Cassas and Bence, *Grandes vues pittoresques*.
34. Hughes, *Travels*, i. 266.
35. Williams, *Travels*, ii. 316.
36. Peter Edmund Laurent, *Recollections of a Classical Tour* (1821), 110.
37. *Select Committee Report*, 24, 118. Michaelis, *Der Parthenon*, discusses the fate of these two heads. See also a letter of Fauvel in *Bulletin de la Société Nationale des Antiquaires de la France* (1900), 245. See also p. 103.
38. J. C. Hobhouse, *Recollections of a Long Life* (1909), i. 26.
39. *Revue Archéologique*, 31: 94. Forbin, *Voyage dans le Levant*, 14.
40. Two pieces of metope and one of frieze were presented by J. J. Dubois in 1840; a fragment of the frieze was bought at the sale of the Pourtales collection in 1865. Several pieces of the frieze from a private collection in Karlsruhe also came into the Museum's collection. A. H. Smith, *Catalogue of Sculpture in the Department of Greek and Roman Antiquities*, (British Museum, 1892).
41. Cockerell, *Travels*, 262, quoted also by David Watkin, *The Life and Work of C. R. Cockerell* (1974), 16. The piece was part of Slab I of the south frieze, according to Brommer's classification.
42. Smirke, Journal.
43. Quoted in Smith, 'Lord Elgin and his Collection', 287.
44. Walsh, *A Residence at Constantinople*, i. 125. *Adventures of a Greek Lady* (1849), 111.

45. Ibid., Caroline, *Voyages and Travels* (1823), 436 ff.
46. [Stanhope], *Travels of Lady Hester Stanhope* (1846), iii. 168.

Chapter 19: Lord Elgin Tries Again

1. Three drawings showing the Elgin Marbles at Burlington House in 1816 are in the Print Collection of the former Greater London Council. Two are reproduced in Plates 8 and 9. See also Haydon's *Diary*, i. 441.
2. See vol. iv, p. 25. Smith, 'Lord Elgin and his Collection', 317.
3. Apart from the piece of plain marble taken by Lusieri in 1803, see p. 124.
4. Choiseul-Gouffier, *Voyage pittoresque de la Grèce* (Paris, 1782–1809), ii. 85. See Smith, 'Lord Elgin and his Collection', 362. For the reference to the 'negotiant Cairac' which Smith could not explain see the quotation in Stevents, *The Erechtheum*, 593. Choiseul-Gouffier's fragment of the frieze was stored in his warehouse in 1789.
5. *Voyage pittoresque.*
6. *Memorandum*, (1815 edition), 78.
7. 750 copies were printed. Copies were sent to 'The Speaker, Vansittart, Arbuthnot, Charles Long, Banks, Castlereagh, Wynne, Abercrombie, Wm Scott, P. James, Haydon, Sir Thomas Lawrence, Croker, Flaxman, West, Knight, Hay, Nollekins, Chantrey, Smirke, Wilkins, W. Lawrence, Planta [*Librarian of British Museum*], Combe [*Keeper of Antiquities*], Sir Joseph Banks, Rossi, Thomson, James, Hamilton, Horner, Fazakerley, Wellesley, Clerk, Wallace, Davis, Dawkins, Huskisson, Douglas, and Aukland'. Murray archives.
8. Quoted in Smith, 'Lord Elgin and his Collection', 322.
9. Hamilton to Elgin, 13 February 1810, Elgin to Hamilton, 18 April 1815, and Aberdeen to Elgin, 16 April 1816, Elgin Papers.
10. Hansard, ccci. 828.
11. See 'The Art Confiscations of the Napoleonic Wars' by Dorothy Mackay Quinn, in *American Historical Review* (1945), summarized with a discussion of the legal implications by John Henry Merryman and Albert E. Elsen, *Law, Ethics and the Visual Arts* (New York, 1979).
12. Quoted by Merryman and Elsen, i. 37.
13. Ibid. i. 38. Translated from the French.
14. Ibid. i. 33. Translated from the French.
15. Examples quoted by Merryman and Elsen, i. 35. Translated from the French.
16. 'Two Memoirs read to the Royal Institute of France on the Sculptures in the Collection of the Earl of Elgin by the Chevalier E. Q. Visconti.' Printed with the *Select Committee Report* (1816).
17. Ibid. 46.
18. Quoted in Smith, 'Lord Elgin and his Collection', 333.

19. Haydon, *Autobiography*, 224. See also Farington, 22 November 1815 (published).
20. *Select Committee Report*, p. xxiii.
21. In the *Autobiography* this incident is put in February 1816 during the Select Committee sittings. It is clear from the *Diary*, i. 488 that the marbles arrived in December 1815.
22. Quoted in Haydon, *Autobiography*, 231.
23. Ibid. 231. The allusion is to comments by Payne Knight in *Specimens of Antient Sculpture*.
24. Abbott, *Diary and Correspondence*, ii. 564.
25. *Elgin and Phigaleian Marbles* (British Museum, 1833), i. 10.
26. Haydon, *Autobiography*, 226.
27. Ibid. 680.
28. Haydon, *Diary*, i. 439.
29. *Elgin and Phigaleian Marbles*, ii. 107.
30. Haydon, *Autobiography*, 223.

Chapter 20: Tweddell J. and Tweddell R.

1. *Edinburgh Review*, No. 50. October 1815.
2. *Christian Observer*, June 1815.
3. *New Monthly Magazine*, November 1815.
4. Quoted in Tweddell's *Remains*, following the title-page.
5. Haygarth, *Greece: A Poem in Three Parts*, ii, ll. 347 ff.
6. Tweddell's *Remains*, 15.
7. W. B. Dinsmoor, 'Observations on the Hephaisteion', *Hesperia*, supplement 5 (1941), 16. Dinsmoor notes that Tweddell's Greek epitaph is referred to by numerous travellers but the Latin version by none. He suggests that this reticence was due to the hostility of the travellers to anything connected with Lord Elgin. That the two versions did in fact exist side by side in the Theseum is, however, proved by a reference in the unpublished Journal of Revd Robert Masters.
8. *Naval Chronicle*, 23, quoted in Tweddell's *Remains*.
9. Elgin, *Letter to the Editor of the Edinburgh Review* (1815), 21 ff.
10. *Naval Chronicle*, January–June 1816; also July–September 1816.
11. Clarke, *Travels*, part ii, section 2, p. 533.
12. Ibid. ii/3: 389.
13. Byron to Murray, 20 February 1813, *Letters and Journals*, iii. 20. The poem referred to is [James and Horace Smith], *Horace in London* (1813), ode xv, 'The Parthenon'.
14. *New Monthly Magazine*, January 1815.
15. That Philalethes was Hamilton and that he did not guess the identity of T. is clear from a letter of Hamilton to Elgin 14 February 1815. Elgin Papers.
16. Elgin, *Postscript*, 32.

17. *Christian Observer*, August 1815.
18. *Quarterly Review*, October 1816.
19. *Naval Chronicle*, July–September 1816.
20. Revd Robert Tweddell, *Account of the Examination of the Elgin-box* (Manchester, 1816).

Chapter 21: The Fate of the Manuscripts

1. Clarke, *Travels*, part II, section 3, p. 389.
2. Hunt, *Narrative*, 46.
3. Otter, *Life of Clarke* (1824), 562.
4. The figure is not certain. Miss Carlyle gave thirty-seven MSS to Lambeth excluding the Eutropius but at least one of these belonged to Carlyle before his journey.
5. Walpole's *Memoirs*, 163, 183.
6. Ibid. 176.
7. Philip Hunt to Robert Liston giving a résumé of the whole story, 20 June 1817. NLS 5645, fo. 210. Some official correspondence, including a copy of Carlyle and Hunt's certificate to the Patriarch is in FO 78/83, 87, and 89.
8. Carlyle MSS. Undated Memorandum by Carlyle HA 174:1026/68/10.
9. A Charge made, for example, in *Quarterly Review*, April 1818.
10. H. J. Todd, *Catalogue of the Archepiscopal Manuscripts in the Library at Lambeth Palace* (1812), p. v.
11. Ibid., p. iv.
12. Carlyle, *Poems*.
13. The Account of the sale of the MSS is mainly in H. J. Todd, *An Account of the Greek Mss chiefly Biblical which had been in the possession of the late Professor Carlyle* (1820). Further information is in NLS 5645, fo. 210.
14. Todd, *Account*, 38.
15. NLS 5645, fo. 210.
16. Todd, *Catalogue*, p. iv.
17. Todd, *Account*, 68.
18. Walpole's *Memoirs*, 183.
19. Hunt's *Narrative*, 36. Thomas Lacy to Hunt, 20 June 1800, Hunt Papers.

Chapter 22: The Marbles are Sold

1. Hansard, xxxii. 577, 15 February 1816.
2. Ibid. 824, 23 February 1816. Reprinted in Christopher Hitchens, *The Elgin Marbles* (1987).
3. See H. H. Lamb, *Climate, History, and the Modern World* (1982), 239.
4. See p. 283.
5. *Select Committee Report*, 31.

6. *Select Committee Report*, 45.
7. Ibid., pp. vii ff.
8. Ibid., p. xvii.
9. Ibid. 67.
10. Ibid. 70.
11. Ibid. 81, 83.
12. Ibid. 90.
13. Ibid. 92.
14. The beetle can be seen in Plate 8 among the Parthenon Marbles outside the museum at Burlington House.
15. See Appendix 1.
16. Haydon, *Autobiography*, 232.
17. Ibid. 233.
18. Ibid. 239. See also Michaelis, *Ancient Marbles*, 148.
19. See also Appendix 1.
20. Farington, 10 April 1816. The Murray archives show that 750 copies were printed. The Report was widely summarized in the press.
21. *Quarterly Review*, 28 May 1816; Farington, 6 June 1816. Payne Knight replied in an anonymous pamphlet reproduced largely in the *Examiner*, 7 April 1816, and *Classical Journal* (1816), 98. Visconti's MS reply is in the Gennadios Library, Athens.
22. *Examiner*, 28 April 1816.
23. Ibid. 19 May 1816.
24. Farington, 10 April 1816.
25. Ibid.
26. Haydon, *Diary*, ii. 12. Entry for 10 April 1816.
27. Haydon, *Diary*, i. 442. Entry for 13 May 1815.
28. Smith, 'Lord Elgin and his Collection', 342.
29. Hansard, xxxiv. 1027–40. Reprinted in Hitchens, *The Elgin Marbles*.
30. Cap. xcix of 56th year of George III.
31. Smith, 'Lord Elgin and his Collection', 332; Whitley, *Art in England 1800–1820*, 261.
32. Elgin to Lord Liverpool, 18 April 1817, BL Add. MS 38266, fo. 5.
33. The account for Elgin's Embassy is among the Elgin Papers. Some details are in FO 78/89. A statement of the history of Elgin's finances dated 1 May 1835 is among the Elgin Papers.
34. Smith, 'Lord Elgin and his Collection', 365. See also *The Banks Letters*, ed. Warren R. Dawson (1958), 100.
35. L. J. J. Dubois, *Catalogue d'Antiquités . . . formant la collection de . . . M. le Comte de Choiseul-Gouffier, Paris* (1818). Elgin is called 'un spéculateur anglais, [qui avait] entendu vanter le prix des sculptures'.
36. *Description of the Collection of Ancient Marbles in the British Museum*, vii (1835), 28.
37. For example, R. C. Lucas, *Remarks on the Parthenon* (1845), 29;

E. Edwards, *Lives of the Founders of the British Museum* (1870), i. 384; and L. Pingaud, *Choiseul-Gouffier: La France en Orient sous Louis XVI* (1887), 162. Compare Smith, 'Lord Elgin and his Collection', 357.

38. NLS 45649, fos. 127–8.

39. Master, Journal.

40. Dodwell, *Classical Tour*, i. 353; Hughes, *Travels*, i. 260; and Black, *Narrative of Cruises in the Mediterranean*, 149.

41. Master's Journal notes that this letter arrived when he was with Lusieri on 13 June 1819.

42. Walsh, *A Residence at Constantinople*, i. 122.

43. Milnes, *Memorials of a Tour*, 130.

44. See St. Clair, *That Greece Might Still Be Free*, and Virginia Penn, 'Philhellenism in England', *Slavonic Review*, 14: 363.

45. e.g. NLS 1055, fo. 118 (1821); 1055, fo. 120 (1824).

46. *Specimens of Antient Sculpture*, ii (1835), p. liv.

47. Quoted in Cust and Colvin, *History of the Society of Dilettanti*, 173; in *Historical Notices of the Society of Dilettanti* (by Hamilton) (1855), 101; and Smith, 'Lord Elgin and his Collection', 368. The *Historical Notices* quotes another letter from Elgin on the same occasion.

48. R. A. Higgins, 'The Elgin Jewellery', *British Museum Quarterly*, 23 (1961).

Chapter 23: 'An Aera in Public Feeling'

1. Smith, 'Lord Elgin and his Collection', 351.

2. Well illustrated in the essays in Celina Fox, *London, World City* (1992).

3. *Thanksgiving Ode*, 1816. Quoted by Ian Jenkins in 'Athens Rising Near the Pole; London, Athens, and the Idea of Freedom', in Fox. Similar sentiments in the poet laureate Robert Southey's *The Poet's Pilgrimage to Waterloo*, 1816.

4. For example: *The Elgin Marbles . . . selected from Stuart's and Revett's Antiquities of Athens*, Burrow, *Elgin Marbles*, Combe, *Brief Account*, Sharp, *Elgin Marbles*, and Lawrence, *Elgin Marbles*.

5. Burrow, *Elgin Marbles*, p. viii.

6. The designs were mainly the work of H. Corbould. The engraving was done by a variety of leading engravers.

7. *Description of the Collection of Ancient Marbles in the British Museum* (1812–61).

8. *Ancient Marbles*, part VI (1830), preface quoting *Select Committee Report*, 27.

9. Byron's *Letter to **** ****** [John Murray] on Rev. W. L. Bowles's Strictures on the Life and Writings of Pope* (1821), 27, *Complete Miscellaneous Prose Works*, ed. Andrew Nicholson (1991), 134.

10. Some of the nineteenth-century swivels still form part of the present mountings, and some at least are still in working order.
11. Ian Jenkins, *Archaeologists and Aesthetes* (British Museum, 1992), 31.
12. Haydon's pupils were Charles and Thomas Landseer, brothers of Edwin, and William Bewick, unrelated to the more famous wood engraver. The placard on the right reads 'Exhibition of Drawings by Haydon's pupils Landseers and Bewick for the Cartoons and Elgin Marbles'. The placard on the left reads 'Chalk Drawings by Haydon's pupils Landseers and Bewick Private View'. The goose on the left, labelled 'WC', tramples on papers marked 'Cabal, Two octavo volumes W.C.' and 'Quack artist, Play W.C. WeatherCock.' W.C. is William Carey, who noted that a price of six pence for a catalogue and one shilling for admission was absurdly high for an exhibition consisting of only eight chalk drawings. At the time one shilling was equivalent to a day's wages for a working man. The geese on the right trample on 'Catalogue Raisonnée'. See also Haydon, *Autobiography*, 680. Haydon records that Goethe alluded to the drawings in a letter to him written just before his death. See also *Goethes Wohnhaus* (Munich and Vienna, 1996), 32. Marks's print is reproduced in colour in David Blaney Brown, Robert Woof, and Stephen Hebron (eds.), *Benjamin Robert Haydon, 1786–1846*, the catalogue of an exhibition arranged by the Wordsworth Trust (1996), 113.
13. Quoted by Jenkins, *Archaeologists and Aesthetes*, 34.
14. *Elgin and Phigaleian Marbles*.
15. Ibid. i. 10.
16. In a letter to Hamilton 1836 quoted in *Letter from W. R. Hamilton* (1836), 11. The exact nature of Elgin's proposal is not clear but he seems to have wanted the Marbles to be exhibited in some public place in the open air.
17. Cutting from the *Examiner*, date not found.
18. See especially Stelios Lydakis, 'The Impact of the Parthenon Sculptures on 19th and 20th Century Sculpure and painting', in Tournikiotis, *The Parthenon*.
19. Visconti, *Mémoires* (Paris, 1818).
20. Quoted by Constantine, *Early Greek Travellers*, 105, from *Kleinere Schriften*, ed. Walter Rehm (Berlin, 1968), 29. I have made a slight change to Constantine's translation.
21. Quoted by Constantine, *Early Greek Travellers*, 106, from *Werke*, ed. J. Peterson and H. Schneider (Weimar, 1949–), xx. 101–2. A slight change to Constantine's translation.
22. Ernst Grumach (ed.), *Goethe und die Antike*, 494, from *Italienische Reise*, quoted in English translation by Lydakis, p. 240. The drawings were those made for Sir Richard Worsley's *Museum Worsleyanum* (1794–1803).

23. Grumach, *Goethe und die Antike*, 500, from a letter to H. Meyer 28/9 October 1817, quoted in English translation by Lydakis, p. 240.

24. Haydon, *Diary*, entry for 31 December 1816.

25. Grumach, *Goethe und die Antike*, 502, from *Tag- und Jahres-Hefte* (1818), quoted in English translation by Lydakis, p. 240. Lydakis, following Grumach, p. 495, says that Goethe had already seen casts of the Parthenon frieze in a little museum set up by a man called Schleyermacher in the palace at Darmstadt, but since the letter quoted is of 22 October 1814, before any moulds were made of the Elgin Marbles, it is not clear which casts, except possibly casts from the two pieces in the Louvre, could have reached Darmstadt by that date.

26. *Select Committee Report*, 96.

27. The episode is noted by Ian Jenkins, 'Acquisition and Supply of Casts of the Parthenon Sculptures by the British Museum, 1835–1939', *Annual of British School at Athens*, 85 (1990), 103.

28. Ibid. 113.

29. William Sharp, *Life and Letters of Joseph Severn* (1892), 32.

30. 11 January 1818. Signed GLIRASTES. The *Examiner* carried other poems on similar themes by Horace Smith and others. Shelley's *Ozymandias* was not published in book form until 1820 and then only in a small edition.

31. Marchand, *Down from Olympus*. For the suggestion that the eastern origins of Greek civilization have been downplayed as part of modern racism see Martin Bernal, *Black Athena* (1991), and the replies in Lefkowitz and Rogers, *Black Athena Revisited* (1996).

32. Rupert Gunnis, *Dictionary of British Sculptors 1660–1851* (n.d.). Further information about Henning and the Elgin Marbles is in his evidence to the Select Committee on Arts and Manufactures. *Parliamentary Papers*, v (1835).

33. Notably the Monument to Sir William Ponsonby in St Paul's and the Pediment of the Royal Mews of Buckingham Palace.

34. For Pistrucci's Waterloo Medal see Cornelius Vermeule, *European Art and the Classical Past* (1964).

35. Report of the Select Committee on Arts and Manufactures. *Parliamentary Papers*, v (1835).

36. See David van Zanten, 'The Parthenon Imagined Painted', in Tournikiotis, *The Parthenon*, 258.

37. See, for example, Philip S. Marden, an author who is explicit about such attitudes, *Greece and the Aegean Islands* (Boston and New York, 1907), 92.

38. Jenkins, *Archaeologists and Aesthetes*, illustration after p. 48.

39. For Haydon see his *Autobiography* and *Diary*; for West see Grose Evans, *Benjamin West and the Taste of his Times* (1959).

40. J. T. Smith, *Nollekens and his Times*, i. 289.

41. The brother of the two Landseers who had exhibited drawings of the Elgin Marbles.
42. Lydakis, 'The Impact of the Parthenon Sculptures', in Tournikiotis, 236.
43. See J. Mordaunt Crook, *The Greek Revival* (1972).
44. His books were *Travels in Italy, Greece and the Ionian Islands* (1820) and *Select Views in Greece, with Classical Illustrations* (1829), a volume of engravings.
45. See Willmuth Arenhövel and Rolf Bothe (eds.), *Das Brandenburger Tor, 1791–1991: Eine Monographie* (Berlin, 1991).
46. Marchand, *Down from Olympus*, 68.
47. See especially Panayiotis Tournikiotis, 'The Place of the Parthenon in the History and Theory of Modern Architecture' in Tournikiotis, *The Parthenon*, 206.
48. Reproduced in colour in Tournikiotis, *The Parthenon*, 209.
49. For an example of the American claim to be the ideal commonwealth of Hesperia imagined by the ancients see Samuel S. Cox, *A Buckeye Abroad*, quoted by Stephen A. Larrabee, *Hellas Observed* (New York, 1957), 260.
50. Elgin to Peel, 27 August 1822, BL Add. 40350, fos. 193, 195, 199. See also A. J. Youngson, *The Making of Classical Edinburgh* (1966, 1988), 159. The words 'facsimile' and 'restoration' were used in the appeal document.
51. A picture of how the completed building would have looked is reproduced in Youngson, *Classical Edinburgh*, 161.
52. See *Letter from W. R. Hamilton; Second Letter*, and *Third Letter*.
53. Hamilton, *Letter*, 7.
54. For Victorian constructions of Hellenism see Richard Jenkyns, *The Victorians and Ancient Greece* (1980).
55. M. S. Watts, *George Frederic Watts: The Annals of an Artist's Life* (1912), i. 137.
56. Leighton, *Addresses*, 85.
57. Ibid. 89.
58. Quoted by Connelly, 'Parthenon and Parthenoi', 56.
59. Quoted by Jenkins, *Archaeologists and Aesthetes*, 199.
60. Ibid.
61. Ibid. 202.
62. *Examiner*, 16 June 1816.

Chapter 24: 'The Damage is Obvious and Cannot be Exaggerated'

1. For a summary of what is known about the history of the disasters and the repairs to the building, see Manolis Korres, 'The Parthenon from Antiquity to the 19th Century', in Tournikiotis, *The Parthenon*. The extent to which the sculptures may have been repaired in anciept

times is not known. Nor is it yet established how far and how often the building may have been re-coated in Roman or later times. Dr Korres has advised me that microscopic analysis suggests three layers, an ancient original with later layers from the Roman and from the Ottoman periods.

2. Drawings Collection, Royal Institute of British Architects, London. Some, including those of the Acropolis and of the Parthenon, were stolen before 1973 and have not yet been recovered. The coloured reproduction in *Acropolis Restoration*, 70 appears to be from a coloured engraving.

3. Drawings Collection, Royal Institute of British Architects, London.

4. Smirke's MS Journal.

5. Ibid.

6. Reproduced from the original in the Bibliothèque Nationale, Paris, by Fani Mallachou-Tufano in 'The Parthenon from Cyriacus of Ancona to Frédéric Boissonas: Description, Research and Depiction', in Tournikiotis, *The Parthenon*, 184.

7. Reproduced from Dupré's book by Fani Mallachou-Tufano in 'The Parthenon from Cyriacus of Ancona to Frédéric Boissonas', in Tournikiotis, 181.

8. Haygarth, *Greece: A Poem*. In the preface Haygarth stresses the accuracy of his illustrations but gives no other explanation for his choice of brown. The original sketches, of which over a hundred are in the Gennadios Library in Athens, are also done in brown ink and brown wash.

9. For the climate changes see H. H. Lamb, *Climate, History and the Modern World* (1982). Haygarth, 170, was amazed at the 'fiery redness' of the evening sun. The young Benjamin Disraeli, who was there in 1830, noted the 'violet sunset', Beaconsfield, *Home Letters* (1885), 98.

10. Dodwell, *Classical Tour*, i. 344. Quoted by Jenkins and Middleton, 'Paint on the Parthenon Sculptures', *Annual of British School at Athens*, 83 (1988), 184. The other books by Dodwell, some of which contain coloured illustrations, conform to this image. See also Walter Colton, 'autumnal tinge', *Visit to Constantinople and Athens* (New York, 1836), 240.

11. Many of the pictures are reproduced in colour by Fani Mallachou-Tufano, and by others, in the various articles in Tournikiotis. Other pictures have been reproduced in colour by Tsigakou in *The Rediscovery of Greece* and *Through Romantic Eyes*, in the Goulandris Foundation exhibition catalogue, and elsewhere. For coloured reproductions of Athens *c.*1906 see John Fulleylove, *Greece* (1906). The many original pictures which I have seen in public and in private collections tend to confirm the observation J. M. W. Turner, who never saw Athens, tended

to paint his Greek ruins nearly white; see, for example, his views of the Acropolis of Athens and of the Temple in Aegina reproduced in colour in John Blaney Brown, *Turner and Byron* (1992), 66, 67. Zographos, a Greek painter in the primitive style, who painted scenes from the 1822 siege of the Acropolis, shows the temple either white or nearly white, reproduced in colour in the Goulandris catalogue and elsewhere. These exceptions tend to prove the rule that it was mainly Western visitors who preferred to paint in brown. For an example of the mixing of deep browns and white by a foreign artist who visited the Acropolis soon after the final Turkish handover, see the *Peytier Album* (Athens, 1971).

12. *The Scientific Report on the Analysis of Surface Deposits on Marble from the Acropolis in Athens*, carried out by the British Museum Research Laboratory, January 1970, concluded that the surface colour 'develops by traces of iron in the marble gradually migrating to the surface, where they are oxidised'. Quoted by Jenkins and Middleton, who take a different view.

13. Quoted by Jenkins and Middleton, 187, from *Principles of Athenian Architecture* (second edition, 1888). The dates given by Penrose for the wars are a little inaccurate.

14. Bayard Taylor, *Travels in Greece and Russia* (New York, 1859), 40.

15. *Letter*, 11. The phrasing is a little ambiguous but the context implies that Canova saw metal on the frieze as well as on the Iris.

16. *A Description of the Collection of Ancient Marbles*, vi. 26.

17. Ibid. vi. 11. It is not known what Cockerell had in mind in making this observation, but there is no obvious colour today.

18. Ibid. vi. 2.

19. See the brief note by D. E. L. Haynes, 'A Question of Polish', *Wandlungen* (1975).

20. The metope shown in the picture of Fauvel in Dupré, sometimes taken to be the original, is a cast. This picture confirms that moulds could be taken of the metopes which are in high relief as well as of the frieze, while they were still on the building. It would have been difficult, perhaps impossible, to make moulds of the pedimental sculptures while they were on the building and I know of no evidence that this was done.

21. Haydon mentions 'the Theseus, Ilissus, Neptune's breast, and hosts of fragments, three or four metopes', *Autobiography*, 223.

22. Some of the pedimental sculptures were a challenge to the moulder's art. The deep folds of drapery were only reproduced by making large numbers of separate small moulds, some not much bigger than the top of a man's thumb, as can be seen from early casts surviving in London and Berlin which preserve the join lines on the surface. It was within these deep cavities that the patina was thickest and the

marble was blackest. A list of the pieces to be included in the sets of casts supplied at the time is quoted by Jenkins, 'Acquisition and Supply of Casts of the Parthenon Sculptures by the British Museum, 1835–1939,' *Annual of British School at Athens*, 85 (1990), 102. Not all the pieces on the list were in the event moulded at that time.

23. Quoted by Jenkins and Middleton, 186, from British Museum archives.
24. Neither the Helios group nor the Iris appears in the list made in 1819 of the pieces included in sets of casts supplied at that time. See Jenkins, 'Acquisition', 102.
25. Jenkins, 'Acquisition', 109.
26. See Jenkins and Middleton. The brush stroke is on figure F.
27. Sheila Adam, *The Technique of Greek Sculpture* (1966), 56.
28. For example, on the drapery of the girls carrying jugs, Slab III of the east frieze according to Jenkins's classification, Jenkins, *Parthenon Frieze*, 77. For the lucky survival of the patina on this slab see p. 310.
29. Adam, *Technique* 3, following Carl Blümel, *Greek Sculptors at Work* (1955).
30. See Adam, *Technique*.
31. Ibid. 51.
32. Korres, *From Pentelikon to the Parthenon*, 7.
33. Richter, *Sculpture and Sculptors of the Greeks*, 142.
34. Dodwell, *Classical Tour*, i. 344. The architectural piece from the Erechtheion which Dodwell saw is probably the ornamental band, or epicranitis, which ran round the outside wall. As the piece appears in 1997, most of the right part preserves a rich brown over the whole surface, whereas the left part is less brown. Since there is no obvious indication of scraping, the difference may not be the result of cleaning, and even on the right part much patina remains.
35. By Archibald Archer, reproduced in colour from the original in the British Museum in Jenkins, *Archaeologists and Aesthetes*, after p. 49. Another coloured reproduction of the same picture in larger size in Lydakis in Tournikiotis, 233. An earlier reproduction in *An Historical Guide to the Sculptures of the Parthenon* (*Elgin Collection*) (1962) [by D. E. L. Haynes] shows the Marbles rather darker, but colour reproduction was then less reliable.
36. By James Stephanoff, reproduced in colour from the original in Jenkins, *Archaeologists and Aesthetes*, after p. 49.
37. For the large-scale drawings which Haydon and his pupils made while the Marbles were in their various makeshift exhibition spaces he chose brown paper, picking out the occasional highlights in white. An example is reproduced in colour by Checkland, *The Elgins*, opposite p. 85. In Goethe's house in Weimar, the colouring of the pictures of the Elgin Marbles makes a vivid contrast with the bright white of the

Graeco-Roman statues and of the casts among which the drawings are displayed. Illustrated in colour in *Goethes Wohnhaus*. A glimpse of the drawings, which hang on the wall of the staircase, can be seen on p. 27. A friend who visited the house recently has confirmed the accuracy of the colour reproductions. Later examples showing the Elgin Marbles as brown in Jenkins, *Archaeologists and Aesthetes*, after p. 49, and on the cover of his book. Some of the oil paintings may have darkened since they were painted as a result of changes in the colour of the varnish, but the water-colours also show the Marbles as brown. A china plate in the author's possession, probably made in Great Britain in Victorian times or later, and whose colour is unlikely to have been affected by time, reproduces a horseman from the Parthenon frieze in honey colour.

38. The original is now in the Uffizi in Florence. A coloured reproduction is shown on the flap of Russell Ash, *Lord Leighton*, no date given [1996], an exhibition catalogue.

39. This emerges from his discussion of the qualities of different types of coloured marble in book vii of *Geschichte der Kunst des Altertums*.

40. *Johañ Winckelmañs Sämtliche Werke*, ed. Joseph Eiselein (Donauöschingen, 1825), iv. 56, quoted in translation by Irwin, 118. Irwin's translation modified.

41. For example, J. P. Mahaffy, *Rambles and Discoveries in Greece* (1887), 33; William Eleroy Curtis, *The Turk and his Lost Provinces* (1903), 370.

42. A point noted by Francis Hervé, *A Residence in Greece and Turkey* (1837), i. 129, who was enchanted by the 'orange tint', of the older buildings.

43. Jenkins, *Archaeologists and Aesthetes*, 45.

44. Quoted by Jenkins, *Archaeologists and Aesthetes*, 51.

45. Letter to the *The Times*, 2 May 1921, quoted by Jacob Epstein, *Let there be Sculpture* (1940), 205. Letter to the *The Times*, 19 May 1939, quoted by Epstein, 205, and by Hitchens, *Elgin Marbles*, 91.

46. A water-colour of *c*.1880 which shows the Demeter looking brown is reproduced in colour in Jenkins, *Archaeologists and Aesthetes*, 145. The photographic illustration reproduced in David M. Wilson, *The Collections of the British Museum* (1989), 23, seems to have been taken from a photograph which shows the statue as it appeared long ago, not as it is now or has been for many years.

47. See Appendix 2.

48. H. J. Plenderleith, *The Preservation of Antiquities* (British Museum, 1934), 26, 27.

49. See Appendix 2. See also Plenderleith.

50. *Description*, part vi (1830), preface quoting *Select Committee Report*, 27.

51. Quoted by Jenkins, 'Acquisition', from British Museum archives.
52. FO 1940/41. See also Jeanette Greenfield, *The Return of Cultural Treasures* (1996), 66.
53. Edward S. Forster, *A Short History of Modern Greece, 1821–1956, Revised and Enlarged by Douglas Dakin* (1958), 119.
54. A. H. Smith, *Memorandum on the Proposed New Elgin Room* (1938).
55. See Colin Simpson, *The Parnership* (1987), and S. N. Behrman, *Duveen* (1952).
56. Examples from Behrman.
57. Simpson, *Partnership*, 24–5, 164–6.
58. Quoted by Marjorie Caygill, *The Story of the British Museum* (1981), 51, no source given.
59. *Crawford Papers*, 537. Diary entry for 8 May 1931.
60. Jenkins, who has seen the official records, says that bribes were paid. *Archaeologists and Aesthetes*, 228.
61. See quotation in Appendix 2.
62. Roger Hinks, *The Gymnasium of the Mind* (1984), 57. Confirmed by my conversations with some of those who were well placed to know what happened.
63. Quoted by Simpson, *Partnership*, 3.
64. Conversation, 1997.
65. Hinks, *Gymnasium of the Mind*, 54. I have been unable to identify Forsdyke's informant, Sidney Smith.
66. See Appendix 2.
67. *Encyclopaedia Britannica*, 11th edition. Although information about the cleaning of the Parthenon sculptures has trickled out over the years since 1938, the fact that carborundum was used has not hitherto, as far as I know, been made public.
68. Minutes of Standing Committee, 8 October 1938, quoted in Appendix 2.
69. The Trustees included the Archbishop of Canterbury, who acted as chairman, the Lord Chancellor, and the Speaker of the House of Commons, as principal trustees, plus the First Lord of the Treasury (prime minister), the Chancellor of the Exchequer, and all the principal secretaries of state, the Lord Chief Justice, the Master of the Rolls, and other principal law officers and judges, the Bishop of London, the Presidents of the Royal Society, of the Royal Academy, of the Society of Antiquaries, and of other learned bodies, an appointee of the royal family, and a range of hereditary appointments, including the Earls of Elgin. The ex-officio Trustees elected fifteen others from outside. Marjorie Caygill, *The Story of the British Museum*, 7. In 1939 the Standing Committee consisted of the Archbishop of Canterbury, as chairman, the Lord Chancellor, and the Speaker of the House of Commons, Lords Crawford, Ilchester,

Baldwin, Harlech, and Macmillan, Sir Wilfred Greene, Sir Henry Tizard, Sir William Bragg, Sir Henry Miers, Sir C. R. Peers, Professor G. M. Trevelyan, F. Cavendish Bentinck, Professor Gilbert Murray, J. Stanley Gardiner, and C. H. St John Hornby. *Whittaker's Almanack for 1939.* The Board of Enquiry consisted of Lord Macmillan, Lord Harlech, Sir Wilfred Greene, Sir William Bragg, and Sir Charles Peers, but the reports were only signed by Macmillan, Greene, and Peers.

70. Conversation with Dr Plenderleith, January 1997.
71. Bernard Ashmole, *Autobiography* (1994), 69.
72. Holcombe's article in *Daily Express.*
73. Ibid.
74. For Baldwin's part see Crawford, 593.
75. Epstein, *Let there be Sculpture*, 214. Confirmed by conversations with some of those who were well placed to know what happened.
76. The Treasury, which at that time had departmental responsibility for all Civil Service personnel matters as well as for the financing of the British Museum, would have had to approve any dismissals, and might ask awkward questions.
77. Hinks, *Gymnasium of the Mind*, 54.
78. *Daily Telegraph*, May 1939, British Museum cuttings scrapbook. Not all the cuttings are precisely dated. The Director's statement was later partially contradicted by the minister in Parliament who implied that the retirements were a disciplinary response to the unofficial cleaning, see Hansard, 26 May 1939.
79. Letter to *The Times*, 25 May, 1939, quoted by Hitchens, *The Elgin Marbles*, 92.
80. Ashmole, *Autobiography*, 69. Ashmole's account does not square in detail with that of the reporter of the *Daily Telegraph*. Since the metopes were not intended to be displayed at eye level, it looks as if Ashmole's manuscript, which was never intended for publication, contains an uncorrected slip of the pen, and that what he saw in 1938 were sections of the frieze.
81. Illustrated in Jenkins, *Archaeologists and Aesthetes*, 226.
82. British Museum scrapbooks.
83. That Epstein felt condescended to because of his origins is evident from several phrases in the correspondence and in his book.
84. Letter to *The Times*, 20 May 1939, quoted by Epstein, 210.
85. Hansard, 26 May 1939.
86. For example, Hansard, 26 May 1939.
87. For example, Lieut.-Colonel Sir A. Lambert Ward asked 'Is it considered by the experts that any serious injury has been caused to these Marbles by this cleaning?' The question by Mr Edmund Harvey 'May I ask how the unauthorised cleaning took place. Who was responsible for it?' was not answered, see Hansard, 26 May 1939.

88. *The Times*, 20 May 1939, reporting the answer given by Captain Crookshank, Financial Secretary to the Treasury, the previous day.
89. Hansard, 26 May 1939.
90. Hitchens, *The Elgin Marbles*, 90.
91. Ashmole, *Autobiography*, 73, and the article by Dr Ian Jenkins in the same volume. A few more details in [Haynes], *Historical Guide* (1962), 18.
92. Letter to *The Times*, 9 September 1948, British Museum scrapbooks.
93. 'When the Elgin Marbles were redisplayed in the Duveen Galleries of the British Museum in the 1960s, they were again cleaned, this time only using a poultice made of Sepiolite (a naturally occurring magnesium silicate) and distilled water. This removed so much dirt that had settled on the stone from the notorious London smogs of the previous 30 years that, after cleaning, the sculptures appeared light against the darker background of the off-white gallery wall, whereas, before cleaning, they had appeared darker than the surrounding walls.' Oddy, 'The Philosophy of Restoration', 6.
94. *Works of Art in Greece* (HMSO, 1946), ii.
95. Jenkins in Ashmole. A meeting of the Sub Committee on Building on 9 November 1951 decided to give the Duveen Galley 'last place' in the British Museum's works programme, British Museum papers, volume 7.
96. The inscription reads THESE GALLERIES | DESIGNED TO CONTAIN | THE PARTHENON SCULPTURES | WERE GIVEN BY | LORD DUVEEN OF MILL-BANK | MCMXXXIX. The pre-war designs, reproduced Jenkins, *Archaeologists and Aesthetes*, 227, show a more imperial inscription about the sculptures executed 'by or under the direction of Phidias', having been saved from destruction by the Earl of Elgin, and now being the property of the British Government.
97. [Haynes], *Historical Guide*, 18.
98. 'Cleaning, even though no chemicals were used, did have an undesirable side-effect. The cleaned marble had a "milky" or "hazy" appearance because, on a microscopic scale, the removal of dirt had opened up the surface, which was no longer smooth. Before cleaning, the irregularities of the stone surface were full of dirt and the sculptures reflected light differently. This effect was largely mitigated by applying a 5% solution of polyethylene glycol in distilled water—a wax-like material which remains soluble and so is easily removed.' Oddy, *Philosophy of Conservation*, 6.
99. I include as examples, *A Short Guide to the Sculptures of the Parthenon (Elgin Collection)* (1949), [by Bernard Ashmole] with reissues until 1961; *An Historical Guide to the Sculptures of the Parthenon (Elgin Collection)* (1962), [by D. E. L. Haynes] with many reissues, first published at the time of the opening of the Duveen Gallery: 'The

gallery was completed in 1938, and an opening ceremony was planned for the following summer; but while the sculptures were still being transferred to their new positions, it became clear that war was imminent. In expectation of immediate air raids, the sculptures were hurriedly [removed to safety]', 17; B. F. Cook, *The Elgin Marbles*, British Museum booklets (1984), with many reissues, and still on sale: 'An opening ceremony was planned for the following summer of 1939, but the sculptures were still being transferred to their new positions when the imminence of war made it necessary to take steps for their protection', 68.

100. Jenkins, *Archaeologists and Aesthetes*, 1992.

101. 'This cleaning [of the 1930s] was carried out in the spirit of the times when the philosophy of many restorers was, as far as possible, to make the objects look like they did when they were first made.' Oddy, *Philosophy of Conservation*, 5.

102. Quoted by Greenfield, *Return of Cultural Treasures*, 73.

103. *The Times*, 6 January 1997.

104. Quoted in Hinks, *Gymnasium of the Mind*, 52.

105. Hinks.

106. I was allowed to see the brief formal minutes of the decisions of the British Museum Standing Committee, but was refused access to the papers which were before them as they took their decisions.

107. 'The real trouble is that there are security implications in that particular file. As you will realise, there was much discussion in 1939 about the evacuation of the Museum and most of the details happen to be in the same block of papers. We are constrained by the Public Records Act in this, and as I have had to refuse access to those papers on one or two occasions recently, I am afraid that I must stick by this particular regulation. I deeply regret that we cannot allow you to look at the papers but I trust you will understand that a rule having been made it must be adhered to.' From a letter from Sir David Wilson, Director of the British Museum, to the author, 31 May 1984.

108. 'I am afraid that I can only repeat that I have definite instructions from the Trustees that no privileged access is to be given to the volume of records in which you are interested. The volume contains papers which date from 1932 to 1967, and is therefore closed to the public under Sections 5(1) and 5 and 10(2) of the Public Records Act of 1958, as amended by Section 1 of the Public Records Act, 1967, and is not due to become open to the public until January 1988.' From a letter from Sir David Wilson, Director of the British Museum, to the author, 14 June 1984.

109. The claim about the use of the papers as 'corporate memory' is made in the letter quoted in n. 110.

110. 'It would be a matter of regret to the Trustees if you were to continue

to think that the collection of papers in question might have been manipulated in order to avoid the consequences of disclosure under the Public Records Act 1958 . . . The documents in these volumes, although they deal with a variety of subjects, are not a miscellaneous collection. They have the administrative function of being the complete record of the proceedings of all the Trustees' sub commit-tees. To keep such records together, not simply because they form the corporate memory of a particular part of the Museum's administra-tion, is standard administrative and archival practice. I hope you will appreciate, therefore, that—as our own legal advice has confirmed—it is not possible for the public to consult the volume.' From a letter from the Lord Trend, Chairman of the Trustees, to the author, 4 October 1984. '. . . none of the papers in the volume has as yet been the subject of an application to the Lord Chancellor for extended closure . . . Furthermore the Museum entirely deny any suggestion that these papers were purposely bound in this way to avoid access to the earlier papers, and emphasise that the assembly was created in the ordinary and proper course of the Museum's administration.' From a letter from an official of the Lord Chancellor's Department to the author, 3 June 1985.

111. Information supplied by the British Museum in a letter from the Lord Chancellor's Department to the author, 3 June, 1985.

112. David M. Wilson (ed.), *The Collections of the British Museum* (1989), 13.

113. Especially the photographs in the 'Large Collignon' taken early in the century.

114. See, for example, the colour photographs in Andronikos, *The Acropolis*, made before 1978.

115. See A. P. Middleton, 'Report of the Analysis of Some Coatings on the Surface of the Bassae Frieze Sculptures', appendix II to Ian Jenkins and Dyfri Williams, 'The Arrangement of the Sculptured Frieze from the Temple of Apollo Epikourios at Bassae', in Olga Palagia and William Coulson, *Sculpture from Arcadia and Laconia* (Oxford, 1993).

116. Figure O in Brommer's classification.

117. On the drapery of the girls carrying jugs, Slab III of the east frieze according to Jenkins's classification, Jenkins, *Parthenon Frieze*, 77.

118. For example, between Slabs IV and V which show the seated gods.

119. For example, the photographs by Boissonas published in the 'Large Collignon'. The breakage was at that time concealed with modern materials.

120. The phrase of Epstein, who saw them at work.

121. According to the Cambridge records this cast was purchased from the British Museum's moulder in 1884.

122. *Letter*, 42; *A Description of the Collection of Ancient Marbles*, vi. 9.
123. They arc clcarly seen in the photographs by Boissonas published in the 'Large Collignon'. Holcombe was proud that he had personally cleaned this piece.
124. A point emphasized in the rules for cleaning. See Appendix 2.
125. On public display in the Abguß sammlung, Schloßstraße, Charlottenburg. Because of the loss of the records, the date at which it arrived from London is not known for certain, but the piece is undoubtedly among the earliest casts known to have survived in its original state.
126. Something similar can also be seen on the Cambridge cast of the Amphitrite from the east pediment.
127. For examples see Adam, *Technique*, 16, 51.
128. Ibid. 28.
129. Ibid. 31.
130. Ibid. 78. Commented on by D. E. L. Haynes, 'A Question of Polish', in *Wandlungen* (1975).
131. The sources for such a study include the records of 1938, other internal records, photographs and slides, and recollections of those who, directly or indirectly, knew what was done. Pre-1938 casts of many of the Parthenon sculptures in the Elgin collection survive in museums and storehouses elsewhere in Europe and the United States, as well as in the British Museum's own store. A comparison of their surfaces with the surfaces of the originals, especially if it could be done by cold blue light or by electronic scanning, would be likely to yield further information about what has been lost.

Chapter 25: The Parthenon since Lord Elgin

1. Trant, *Narrative of a Journey through Greece in 1830*, 264. Also noted by Milnes, *Memorials of a Tour*, 127.
2. Manolis Korres, 'The Parthenon from Antiquity to the Nineteenth Century', in Tournikiotis, *Parthenon*, 156.
3. Quoted by Wolf Seidl, *Bayern in Griechenland* (Munich, 1970), 99 from Neezer's memoirs published in Athens in 1937. Also quoted in translation in *The Acropolis at Athens: Conservation, Restoration, and Research* (Athens, 1986), 12.
4. Edgar Garston, *Greece Revisited* (1842), i. 128.
5. See especially Charalambos Bouras, 'Restoration Work on the Parthenon and Changing Attitudes towards the Conservation of Monuments', in Tournikiotis, and Fani Mallachou-Tufano, 'The History of Interventions on the Acropolis', in *Acropolis Restoration*.
6. See Margarete Kühn *et al.* (eds.), *Karl Friedrich Schinkel: Lebenswerk, Ausland* (Munich and Berlin, 1989).
7. Von Klenze, *Aphoristische Bemerkungen* (Berlin, 1838), 386. Quoted

in translation in *The Acropolis at Athens: Conservation, Restoration, and Research*, 13.

8. Consisting, according to Aubrey De Vere, *Picturesque Sketches of Greece and Turkey* (1850), i. 78, of 'fragments, triglyphs, metopes, trunks of centaurs, heads of horses, manes of lions, cannon balls'. See also Garston, *Greece Revisited*, i. 123.

9. De Vere, *Picturesque Sketches*, i. 98.

10. Grosvenor, *Narrative of a Yacht Voyage in the Mediterranean* (1842), ii. 151. Similar lists in Cornelius Conway Felton, *Familiar Letters from Europe* (Boston, 1865), 220; Taylor, *Travels in Greece and Russia*, 39; Bremer, *Greece and Greeks*, i. 8; and elsewhere.

11. Letter of H. B. Young, 30 July 1833, previously unknown and unpublished. Young Papers. Young was in Athens on about 10 July 1833, having been with King Otho when he visited Aegina a few days earlier. Young, who was on the British admiral's staff, was shown round by Gropius and by Pittakis, the Greek archaeologist who was responsible for the excavations, and his account is likely to be accurate.

12. The metope, number 12 from the south side, one of only two metopes found on the ground, was already down by the time of Le Roy. See Brommer, *Metopen*, i. 95 and 223.

13. Some detached fragments also survive. See Guy Dickins and Stanley Casson, *Catalogue of the Acropolis Museum* (Cambridge, 1912–21), ii. 76.

14. Pittakys, *L'Ancienne Athènes* (Athens, 1835), 356. 'les bas réliefs des métopes sont colories ainsi qu'on peut le voir sur le métope qui existe dans le mur de la forteresse' (The high reliefs of the metopes were coloured as can be seen on the metope which is in the wall of the fortress). Brommer could find no traces of colour on any of the metopes.

15. Young, *Five Weeks in Greece*, p. 37.

16. Edward Giffard, *A Short Visit to the Ionian Islands, Athens, and the Morea* (1837), 141.

17. Charles Swan, *Journal of a Voyage up the Mediterranean* (1826), i. 116.

18. Ibid. ii. 165.

19. For example, Beaconsfield, *Home Letters*, 99.

20. Willis, *Summer Cruise in the Mediterranean*, 147. It is possible that the vandalism by a party of British midshipmen, c.1836, noted by Hervé, *Residence in Greece and Turkey*, i. 131, may refer to the earlier incident as recorded by Trant. Another version is in Milnes, *Memorials of a Tour*, 127. See also de Valon, *Une Année dans le Levant* (Paris, 1850), i. 275.

21. Letter of H. B. Young, 30 July 1833, Young Papers.

22. Noted, for example, by Grosvenor, *Yacht Voyage*, and Harry Gringo, *Scampavias* (New York, 1857). Camels are only rarely shown in

nineteenth-century pictures of Athens, perhaps because they offended against the Westernizing ideology. For an author determined to resist the clichés but not always succeeding, see [Francis Skene], *Wayfaring Sketches among the Greeks and Turks* (1848).

23. For the Indian trader see Gringo, *Scampavias*, 100.
24. About, *La Grèce contemporaine* (Paris, 1854), 267, story repeated by Reinach in G. F. Abbott (ed.), *Greece in Evolution* (London and Leipzig, 1909), 275. I know of no authenticated example of this having been done.
25. Reinach in Abbott, *Greece in Evolution*, 287.
26. About, *Grèce contemporaine*, 267.
27. See E. C. Johnson, *On the Track of the Crescent* (1885), 15. Unlikely to be true as told.
28. De Vere, *Picturesque Sketches*, i. 85.
29. John L. Stephens, *Incidents of Travel in Greece, Turkey, Russia, and Poland* (New York, 1838), i. 72.
30. Young, *Five Weeks in Greece*, 37.
31. Jenkins, 'Acquisition', 93.
32. Reinach in Abbott, *Greece in Evolution*, 278.
33. Jenkins, 'Acquisition', 97.
34. Larrabee, *Hellas Observed*, 204.
35. The ancient monuments in the town continued to be eroded—as late as 1875 a British visitor to the Acropolis saw 'a young gentleman practising with a pistol at a piece of old carved marble work in the Theatre of Dionysus'. Mahaffy, *Rambles*, 40.
36. For the nineteenth-century interventions see especially Charalambos Bouras 'Restoration Work on the Parthenon and Changing Attitudes towards the Conservation of Monuments', in Tournikiotis, and Fani Mallachou-Tufano, 'The History of Interventions on the Acropolis', in *Acropolis Restoration*. For a summary written in the condescending tones of the nineteenth century see Théodore Reinach, 'Greece Rediscovered by the Greeks', in Abbott, *Greece in Evolution*. For a few details of the pensioners see Gringo, *Scampavias*, 100. For a dissenting voice see William Mure, *Journal of a Tour in Greece* (Edinburgh, 1842), i. 67.
37. J.-A. Buchon, *La Grèce continentale et la Morée* (Paris, 1843), 65.
38. For example, Mahaffy, *Rambles*, 79.
39. For the alleged physical likenesses see Angelomatis-Tsougarakis, *The Eve of the Greek Revival*, 88. Similar remarks are to be found in the travel books later in the century.
40. Fallmerayer, *Geschichte der Halbinsel Morea wärend des Mittelalters* (Stuttgart, 1830, 1836). See also Douglas Dakin, *The Unification of Greece, 1770–1923* (1972).
41. Notes to Childe Harold's Pilgrimage, *Complete Poetical Works*, ii. 203.

42. A thought emphasized in the poem by Thomas Hardy, 'Winter Words in the Elgin Room'.

43. See the collection of documents in Clogg, *The Movement for Greek Independence*.

44. See St. Clair, *That Greece Might Still be Free*. For Greek patriotism and signs of preparation for a revolution in the decades immediately before 1821 see Angelomatis-Tsougarakis, *The Eve of the Greek Revival*, 98.

45. Colton, *Visit to Constantinople and Athens* (Dublin edition), 243. See also Larrabee, *Hellas Observed*. It is not clear exactly when Colton's visit occurred.

46. For example, Mrs Russell Barrington, *Through Greece and Dalmatia* (1912), 51, quoting John Addington Symmonds, and Lilian Whiting, *Athens the Violet-Crowned* (Boston, 1913), 1.

47. For the early missionaries see St. Clair, *That Greece Might Still Be Free*, 195 ff., and sources there quoted. For attitudes of the Victorian missionaries to the pagan past and to the beliefs of the Greek Church see, for example, Emma Raymond Pitman, *Mission Life in Greece and Palestine*, (n.d.).

48. A point made, for example, by Colton, *Visit to Constantinople and Athens*, whose account contains one of the fullest and most unthinking expressions of romantic philhellenism.

49. Pittakys, *L'Ancienne Athènes*, 377.

50. Gringo, *Scampavias*, 102.

51. For example, Young, letter of 30 July 1833, partly quoted above, and Garston, *Greece Revisited*, i. 132; Marcellus, *Souvenirs de l'Orient*, ii. 354; Milnes, *Memorials of a Tour*, 129; Field, *From the Lakes of Killarney to the Golden Horn*, 293; Beulé, *L'Acropole*, i. 75; Mahaffy, *Rambles*, 83; Moüy, *Letters Athéniennes*, 94; Barrington, *Through Greece and Dalmatia*, 52.

52. Taylor, *Travels in Greece and Russia*, 41.

53. A phrase used in speeches and newspaper articles when she visited London in 1986.

54. See Dakin, *Unification of Greece*.

55. Quoted in *The Acropolis of Athens: Conservation, Restoration, and Research*, 17.

56. For example, Christopher Wordsworth, *Athens and Attica* (1837), an extreme example, Mahaffy, *Greek Pictures* (1890), Fulleylove, *Greece*, and Mrs R. C. Bosanquet, *Days in Attica* (1914). Also noticeable in the Baedecker, Macmillan, and Murray's Guides. There were many topographies of ancient Athens on which such accounts drew.

57. A point made explicitly, for example, by O. H. Hardy, *Red Letter Days in Greece and Egypt* (1906), 15.

58. For example, Whiting, *Athens the Violet-Crowned*.

59. Quoted by Savas Kondaratos, 'The Parthenon as Cultural Ideal: The

Chronicle of its Emergence as a Supreme Monument of Eternal Glory', in Tounikiotis, *The Parthenon*, 46.

60. Barrington, *Through Greece and Dalmatia*, 57.
61. Taylor, *Travels in Greece and Russia*, 42. Quoted, not quite accurately, by Larrabee, *Hellas Observed*, 284.
62. See, for example, Curtis, *The Turk and his Lost Provinces*, 372.
63. Bouras, 'Restoration Work on the Parthenon', in Tournikiotis, 326.
64. *Acropolis Restoration*, 9.

Chapter 26: The Question of Return

1. For example, Hammersley, See p. 255.
2. Young, letter of 30 July 1833. Young Papers.
3. [Frederick von Suckow], *The Shadow of Lord Byron or The Voice of the Akropolis to the British Nation* (1835). A copy is in the Gennadios Library, Athens.
4. Pittakys, *L'Ancienne Athènes*, 379, spelling not corrected.
5. Jenkins, 'Acquisition', 90.
6. R. A. H. Bickford-Smith, *Greece under King George* (1893), 222.
7. FO, 1940/41.
8. Conversations with some of those who were asked to advise.
9. Discussed by Greenfield, *Return of Cultural Treasures*, and, more thoughtfully, by Merryman in the series of books and articles listed in the Bibliography.
10. An extreme version of this argument broadcast by a former Director of the British Museum when Melina Mercouri was in London in 1986 is quoted in part in Appendix 1.
11. See, for example, Savas Kondaratos, 'The Parthenon as Cultural Ideal: The Chronicle of its Emergence as a Supreme Monument of Eternal Gloy', in Tounikiotis.

Appendix 1: The Firman

1. *Select Committee* p. xxiv.
2. See G. Eineder, *Ancient Paper-Mills of the former Austro-Hungarian Empire* (Hilversum, 1960), Nos. 700 and 706. I am most grateful to Mr John Simmons, formerly Librarian of the Codrington Library, All Souls College Oxford, for making the identification and for other help
3. Quoted from transcriptions by Hitchens, *The Elgin Marbles*, 98.

Bibliography

Main Manuscript Sources

Elgin Papers

A large collection of original papers relating to the collecting and sale of the Elgin Marbles, and to the political, domestic, and business life of the seventh Earl of Elgin, in the possession of the present Lord Elgin. The full and authoritative article by A. H. Smith, 'Lord Elgin and his Collection', *Journal of Hellenic Studies* (1916), which contains many transcriptions of documents relating to the Marbles, was based on a thorough study of these papers. I have included some material not used by Smith, including a few key passages from documents which Smith seems deliberately to have omitted.

Foreign Office Archives

Official records of the embassy and other matters relating to British relations with Turkey in Lord Elgin's time, mainly in the FO 78 (Turkey) series, Public Record Office, Kew.

Hunt Papers

A collection of diplomatic and personal papers, the remnant of a larger collection, which belonged to Philip Hunt, chaplain to Lord Elgin's embassy, in the possession of the author.

Other Manuscript or Unpublished Sources Consulted or Referred to in the Notes

ABERDEEN, EARL OF, Diary, British Museum, Department of Greek and Roman Antiquities.
——List of antiquities shipped by Georg Gropius on Lord Aberdeen's account, British Library, Add. MS 43256, fo. 6.
'Papers on Aegina Marbles', Department of Greek and Roman Antiquities, British Museum.
British Library, Additional and Egerton Manuscripts.
British Museum scrapbooks, containing newspaper cuttings about matters of interest to the Department of Greek and Roman Antiquities, 1909– .
CARLYLE, JOSEPH, Letters and other papers relating to his search for ancient manuscripts, Ipswich and East Suffolk Record Office.

COCKERELL, CHARLES ROBERT, Diary of his travels in Greece and elsewhere, letters, and other documents, including letters from Lusieri and others, Department of Greek and Roman Antiquities, British Museum. Extracts were printed in C. R. Cockerell, *Travels in Southern Europe and the Levant 1810–1817* (1903).

EVERETT, EDWARD, Journal, Library of Massachusetts Historical Society.

Foreign Office papers, 1940/41, relating to proposed scheme to return the Parthenon sculptures to Greece. Public Record Office, FO 371/33195.

HANSON, JOHN OLIVER, Journal, British Library, Add. MSS 38591 and 38592.

HOBHOUSE, JOHN CAM, Portions of his Journal, British Library, Add. MS 56527. For Hobhouse's printed *Journey through Albania* which drew on this journal see below.

MASTER, REVD ROBERT, Journal of a Tour in Egypt, Palestine and Greece in 1819, British Library, Add. MS 51313.

John Murray archives, in the possession of John Murray (Publishers), Ltd.

National Library of Scotland Manuscripts.

ODDY, DR ANDREW, 'The Philosophy of Restoration—New for Old', text of a paper given at a conservation seminar in Berlin, 1997.

SMIRKE, ROBERT, Notes on a Journey in Greece, Library of the Royal Institute of British Architects, London.

SOANE, SIR JOHN, Notebooks, Sir John Soane Museum, London.

YOUNG, H. B., Letters sent to his family during his voyages to Greece and Turkey, 1833, in the possession of the present author.

Printed Books and Articles

ABBOT, CHARLES, LORD COLCHESTER, *Diary and Correspondence* (1861).

ABBOTT, G. F. (ed.), *Greece in Evolution: Studies Prepared under the Auspices of the French League for the Defence of Hellenism . . . translated from the French* (London and Leipzig, 1909).

ABOUT, EDMOND, *La Grèce contemporaine* (Paris, 1854).

The Acropolis at Athens: Conservation, Restoration, and Research 1975–1983, Committee for the Preservation of the Acropolis Monuments (Athens, 1986).

Acropolis Restoration: The CCAM [Committee for the Preservation of the Acropolis Monuments], *Intervention*, ed. Richard Economakis (Academy Editions; Athens, 1995).

ADAM, SHEILA, *The Technique of Greek Sculpture* (1966).

Adventures of a Greek Lady, the Adopted Daughter of the late Queen Caroline Written by Herself (1849).

ANDRONIKOS, MANOLIS, *The Acropolis: The Monuments and the Museum* (Athens, 1978).

ANGELOMATIS-TSOUGARAKIS, HELEN, *The Eve of the Greek Revival: British Travellers' Perceptions of Early Nineteenth Century Greece* (1990).

ASHMOLE, BERNARD, *An Autobiography*, ed. Donna Kurtz (1994).

AUSTIN, COLIN, *Nova Fragmenta Euripidea in Papyris Reperta, edidit Colinus Austin* (Berlin, 1968).

BARRINGTON, MRS RUSSELL, *Through Greece and Dalmatia* (1912).

BARROW, JOHN, *Life and Correspondence of Admiral Sir William Sidney Smith GCB* (1848).

BARTHOLDY, J. L. S., *Voyage en Grèce* (Paris, 1807).

[BAYNES, EDWARD DACRES], *Childe Harold in the Shades* (1819). The author was identified by C. W. J. Eliot.

BEACONSFIELD, EARL OF [BENJAMIN DISRAELI], *Home Letters... Written in 1830 and 1831* (1885).

BEHRMAN, S. N., *Duveen* (1952).

BERGER, ERNST, and GISLER-HUWITER, MADELEINE, *Der Parthenon in Basel* (Mainz, 1996).

BERNAL, MARTIN, *Black Athena: The Afroasiatic Roots of Classical Civilization* (1991).

BEULÉ, E., *L'Acropole d'Athènes* (Paris, 1853).

BICKFORD-SMITH, R. A. H., *Greece under King George* (1893).

Nicholas Biddle in Greece: The Journals and Letters of 1806, ed. R. A. McNeal (Philadelphia, 1993).

BLACK, WILLIAM, *Narrative of Cruises in the Mediterranean* (Edinburgh, 1900).

BLÜMEL, CARL, *Greek Sculptors at Work* (1955).

BOARDMAN, JOHN, *The Parthenon and its Sculptures* (1985).

BOSANQUET, MRS R. C., *Days in Attica* (1914).

BRAMSEN, JOHN, *Letters of a Prussian Traveller* (1818).

BREMER, FREDERIKA, *Greece and the Greeks... Translated by Mary Howitt* (1863).

BRÉTON, ERNEST, *Athènes, décrite et dessinée* (Paris, 1862).

BROMMER, FRANK, *Die Skulpturen der Parthenon-Giebel* (Mainz, 1963).

——*Die Metopen des Parthenon* (Mainz, 1967).

——*Der Parthenonfries* (Mainz, 1977).

——*The Sculptures of the Parthenon* (1979).

BRØNSTED, P. O., *Reise i Graekenland i Aarene 1810–1813*, ed. R. B. Dorph (Copenhagen, 1844).

BROWN, JOHN BLANEY, *Turner and Byron* [a catalogue of an exhibition] (1992).

BRUCE, M. R., 'A Tourist in Athens in 1801', *Journal of Hellenic Studies*, 92 (1972).

BUCHON, J.-A., *La Grèce continentale et la Morée* (Paris, 1843).

BURROW, REVD E. I., *The Elgin Marbles* (1817).

BYRON, LORD, *The Complete Miscellaneous Prose Works*, ed. Andrew Nicholson (1991).

—— *The Complete Poetical Works of Lord Byron*, ed. Jerome J. McGann (1980–93).

—— *Letters and Journals of Lord Byron*, ed. Leslie A. Marchand (1973–82).

[CANOVA AND VISCONTI], *A Letter from the Chevalier Antonio Canova: and Two Memoirs read to the Royal Institute of France on the Sculptures in the Collection of the Earl of Elgin; by the Chevalier E. Q. Visconti, . . .* (1816).

CARLYLE, J. D., *Poems* (1805).

CAROLINE, *Voyages and Travels of H. M. Caroline Queen of Great Britain by one of her suite* (1823).

CASSAS AND BENCE, *Grandes vues pittoresques des principaux sites et monumens de la Grèce* (Paris, 1813).

CASTRIOTA, DAVID, *Myth, Ethos, and Actuality: Official Art in Fifth Century B.C. Athens* (Madison, 1992).

[BROTHERS CAZENOVE], *A Narrative in Two Parts, Written in 1812* (1813).

CHANDLER, R., *Travels in Greece* (1776).

CHATEAUBRIAND, VISCOUNT DE, *Travels to Jerusalem*, 3rd edn. (London, 1835); 1st pub. in France in 1806 as *Itinéraire de Paris à Jérusalem*.

CHECKLAND, SYDNEY, *The Elgins 1766–1917: A Tale of Aristocrats, Proconsuls, and their Wives* (1988).

CHOISEUL-GOUFFIER, COMTE DE, *Voyage pittoresque de la Grèce* (Paris, 1782–1809).

CLARKE, E. D., *The Tomb of Alexander* (1805).

—— *Greek Marbles* (1809).

—— *Travels in Various Countries of Europe, Asia and Africa* (1811–23).

CLARKE, M. L., *Greek Studies in England, 1700–1830* (1945).

CLOGG, RICHARD (ed. and trans.), *The Movement for Greek Independence, 1770–1821: A Collection of Documents* (1976).

COCKERELL, C. R., *Travels in Southern Europe and the Levant 1810–1817* (1903).

COLLARD, C., CROPP, M. J., AND LEE, K. H., *Euripides: Selected Fragmentary Plays*, vol. i (1995).

COLLIGNON, MAXIME, *Le Parthénon: L'Histoire, l'architecture et la sculpture. Introduction par Maxime Collignon, 166 planches en photographie d'après les photographies de Frédéric Boissonas et W.-A. Mansell & Co.* (Paris, n.d., c.1912) ['The Large Collignon'].

—— *Le Parthénon: L'Histoire, l'architecture et la sculpture* (Paris, 1914) ['The Small Collignon'].

COLTON, WALTER, *Visit to Constantinople and Athens* (New York, 1836, and later editions).

COMBE, J. L., *A Brief Account of the Marbles collected by Lord Elgin at Athens* (1817).

CONNELLY, JOAN B., 'Parthenon and Parthenoi: A Mythological Interpretation of the Parthenon Frieze', *Journal of the Archaeological Institute of America*, 100/1 (Jan. 1996).

CONSTANTINE, DAVID, *Early Greek Travellers and the Hellenic Ideal* (1984).

COX, SAMUEL S., *A Buckeye Abroad* (New York, 1852).

The Crawford Papers: The Journals of David Lindsay, Twenty-seventh Earl of Crawford and Tenth of Balcarres, 1871–1940 during the years 1892 to 1940, ed. John Vincent (Manchester, 1984).

CROOK, J. MORDAUNT, *The Greek Revival: Neo-Classical Attitudes in British Architecture 1760–1870* (1972).

CURTIS, WILLIAM ELEROY, *The Turk and his Lost Provinces* (1903).

CUST, LIONEL, AND COLVIN, SIDNEY, *History of the Society of Dilettanti* (1898).

DAKIN, DOUGLAS, *The Unification of Greece, 1770–1923* (1972).

DALLAWAY, J., *Constantinople Ancient and Modern with Excursions to the Shores and Islands of the Archipelago and to the Troad* (1797).

DALTON, R., *Antiquities and Views in Greece and Egypt* (1752).

DARWIN, SIR FRANCIS SACHEVERELL, *Travels in Spain and the East, 1808–1810* (Cambridge, 1927).

A Description of the Collection of Ancient Marbles in the British Museum (1812–61).

DE VERE, AUBREY, *Picturesque Sketches of Greece and Turkey* (1850).

DICKINS, GUY, AND CASSON, STANLEY, *Catalogue of the Acropolis Museum* (Cambridge, 1912–21).

DODWELL, EDWARD, *A Classical and Topographical Tour through Greece* (1819).

—— *Views in Greece* (1821).

—— *Views and Descriptions of Cyclopian or Pelasgic Remains in Greece and Italy* (1834).

—— *Notice sur le Musée Dodwell et catalogue raisonné des objets qu'il contient* (Rome, 1837).

D'OOGE, MARTIN L., *The Acropolis of Athens* (1908).

DOUGLAS, HON. F. S. N., *An Essay on Certain Points of Resemblance between the Ancient and Modern Greeks* (1813).

DUPRÉ, LOUIS, *Voyage à Athènes et à Constantinople* (Paris, 1825).

[Elgin], *Memorandum on the Subject of the Earl of Elgin's Pursuits in Greece* (edns. of 1810, 1811, 1815).

—— *Denkschrift über Lord Elgin's Erwerbungen in Griechenland: Nach der zweiten englischen Ausgabe bearbeit. Mit einer Vorrede von C. M. Böttiger und Bemerkungen der Weimarischen Kunst-Freunde* (Leipzig and Altenberg, 1817).

ELGIN, LORD, *Letter to the Editor of the Edinburgh Review on the subject of an article in No. L of that journal on 'The Remains of John Tweddell'* (1815).

ELGIN, LORD, *Postscript to a Letter to the Editor of the Edinburgh Review* (1815). *Elgin and Phigaleian Marbles* (British Museum, Library of Entertaining Knowledge, 1833).

ELIOT, C. W. J., 'Lord Byron, Early Travellers, and the Monastery at Delphi', *American Journal of Archaeology*, 71 (1967).

—— 'Athens in the Time of Lord Byron', *Hesperia*, 37 (1968).

—— 'Lord Byron, Father Paul, and the artist William Page', *Hesperia*, 44 (1975).

—— *Notes on which to Construct a Short Biography of Edward Dacres Baynes (1790–1863)* (privately circulated, 1997).

EPSTEIN, JACOB, *Let there be Sculpture: An Autobiography* (1940).

—— *Epstein: An Autobiography* (1955 and later edns.) [some differences from the 1940 version].

EUSTACE, J. C., *A Classical Tour through Italy* (1813).

FALLMERAYER, J. PH., *Geschichte der Halbinsel Morea wärend des Mittelalters* (Stuttgart, 1830, 1836).

FARINGTON, JOSEPH, *The Farington Diary*, ed. James Grieg (1922).

—— *The Diary of Joseph Farington*, ed. Kenneth Garlick and Angus Macintyre, later volumes by Kathryn Cave (1978–   ).

FAUVEL, see Legrand.

FELTON, CORNELIUS CONWAY, *Familiar Letters from Europe* (Boston, 1865).

The Trial of R. Fergusson, Esq. for Crim. Con. with the Rt. Hon. Lady Elgin (1807).

The Trial of R. J. Fergusson, Esquire, for Adultery with the Countess of Elgin (1808).

FIEDLER, KARL GUSTAV, *Reise durch alle Theile des Königreiches Griechenland* (Leipzig, 1840).

FIELD, HENRY M., *From the Lakes of Killarney to the Golden Horn* (New York, 1877).

FORBIN, COMTE DE, *Voyage dans le Levant* (Paris, 1819).

FOX, CELINA (ed.), *London: World City 1800–1840* (1992).

FROMMEL, C. (ed.), *Ansichten aus Griechenland*, text in German and French (no date or place of publication given, *c*.1835).

FULLER, JOHN, *Narrative of a Tour through some parts of the Turkish Empire* (1830).

FULLEYLOVE, JOHN, *Greece Painted by John Fulleylove... Described by J. A. M'Clymont* (1906 and subsequent edns.).

GALT, JOHN, *Voyages and Travels in the Years 1809, 1810, and 1811* (1812).

—— *Letters from the Levant* (1813).

—— *Life and Studies of Benjamin West, Esq.* (1816).

—— *Life of Byron* (1830).

—— *Autobiography* (1833).

GARSTON, EDGAR, *Greece Revisited* (1842).

GELL, SIR W., *Narrative of a Journey in the Morea* (1823).

[GENNADIOS, IUANNES], Ὁ λόρδος ᾿Ελγιν καὶ οἱ πρὸ αὔτου ἀνὰ τὴν Ἑλλάδα καὶ τὰς ᾿Αθήνας ἰδίως ἀρχαιολογήσαντες ἐπι δρόμεις, 1440–1837, Athens, 1930 [*Lord Elgin and the Previous Archaeological Invasions of Greece*] (1930).

GIFFARD, EDWARD, *A Short Visit to the Ionian Islands, Athens, and the Morea* (1837).

GOETHE, JOHANN WOLFGANG VON, see Grumach.

Goethes Wohnhaus. Maul, Gisela, and Oppel, Margarete, mit Beiträgen von Erich Trunz, Katharina Krügel, Marie-Luise Kahler, *Goethes Wohnhaus* (Munich and Vienna, 1996).

[GOULANDRIS FOUNDATION], Αθηνα απο το τέλος του αρχαίου Κόδμου ως την ίδρυδη του ελληνικού Κράτους, Athens, 1985 [a catalogue of an exhibition].

GREENFIELD, JEANETTE, *The Return of Cultural Treasures* (2nd edn., 1996).

GRINGO, HARRY, *Scampavias fom Gibel Tarek to Stamboul* (New York, 1857).

[LADY GROSVENOR], *Narrative of a Yacht Voyage in the Mediterranean in the Years 1840–41* (1842).

GRUMACH, ERNST (ed.), *Goethe und die Antike: Eine Sammlung* (Berlin, 1949).

Haller von Hallerstein in Griechenland, 1810–1817 ... herausgegeben von Hansgeorg Bankel (Berlin, 1906).

[HAMILTON, WILLIAM RICHARD], *Letter from W. R. Hamilton to the Earl of Elgin in the New Houses of Parliament* (1836).

——*Second Letter from W. R. H. Esq. to the Earl of Elgin on the propriety of adopting the Greek Style of Architecture in the Construction of the New Houses of Parliament* (1836).

——*Third Letter from W. R. H. Esq. to the Earl of Elgin on the propriety of adopting the Greek Style of Architecture in preference to the Gothic etc.* (1837).

HARDY, O. H., *Red Letter Days in Greece and Egypt* (1906).

HARRIS, DIANE, *The Treasures of the Parthenon and Erechtheion* (1995).

HASKELL, FRANCIS, AND PENNY, NICHOLAS, *Taste and the Antique: The Lure of Classical Sculpture 1500–1900* (Yale, 1981).

D'HAUTERIVE, E., *La Police Secrète du Premier Empire: Bulletins quotidiens adressés par Fouché à l'Empereur* (Paris, 1908).

HAYDON, B. R., *Correspondence and Table Talk* (1876).

——*Autobiography and Memoirs*, new edn. by Aldous Huxley (1926).

——*The Diary of Benjamin Robert Haydon*, ed. Willard Bissell Pope (1960–3).

HAYGARTH, WILLIAM, *Greece: A Poem in Three Parts* (1814).

HEROLD, J. CHRISTOPHER, *Bonaparte in Egypt* (1962).

HERVÉ, FRANCIS, *A Residence in Greece and Turkey* (1837).

HIGGINS, R. A., 'The Elgin Jewellery', *British Museum Quarterly*, 23 (1961).

HINKS, ROGER, *The Gymnasium of the Mind: The Journals of Roger Hinks 1933–1963*, ed. John Goldsmith with a Foreword by Kenneth Clark and a Portrait Memoir by Patrick Leigh Fermor (1984).

HISTORICAL MANUSCRIPTS COMMISSION, *Report on the Mss of J. B. Fortescue Esq. preserved at Dropmore* (1892–1927).

HITCHENS, CHRISTOPHER, with Essays by Robert Browning and Graham Binns, *The Elgin Marbles: Should They be Returned to Greece?* (1987).

——Translation into Greek with a Foreword by Melina Mercouri and Prologue by Manolis Andronikos (Athens, 1988).

HOBHOUSE, J. C., *A Journey through Albania and Other Provinces of Turkey in Europe and Asia to Constantinople* (1813).

——*Travels in Albania and Other Provinces of Turkey in 1809 and 1810*, by the Right Hon. Lord Broughton, GCB (1858) [a new edn. of *A Journey through Albania*, with changes and additional material].

HOLCOMBE, ARTHUR, 'I am the man who cleaned the Elgin Marbles', *Daily Express*, 17 May 1939.

HÜBSCH, H., *Ansichten von Athen* (Munich, 1820).

HUGHES, REVD T. S., *Travels in Sicily, Greece and Albania* (1820).

HUNT, REVD PHILIP, *A Narrative of What is Known Respecting the Literary Remains of the Late John Tweddell* (1816).

——See also Stockdale.

INWOOD, H. W., *The Erechtheion at Athens* (1827).

IRWIN, DAVID, *Winckelmann: Writings on Art, Selected & Edited by David Irwin* (1972).

JENKINS, IAN, 'Acquisition and Supply of Casts of the Parthenon Sculptures by the British Museum, 1835–1939', *Annual of British School at Athens*, 85 (1990).

——*Archaeologists and Aesthetes in the Sculpture Galleries of the British Museum 1800–1939* (British Museum Press, 1992).

——*The Parthenon Frieze* (British Museum Press, 1995).

——and MIDDLETON, A. P., 'Paint on the Parthenon Sculptures', *Annual of the British School at Athens*, 83 (1988).

JENKYNS, RICHARD, *The Victorians and Ancient Greece* (1980).

JOHNSON, MAJOR E. C., *On the Track of the Crescent* (1885).

[JOLLIFFE, T. R.], *Narrative of an Excursion from Corfu to Smyrna... by the Author of 'Letters from Palestine'* (1817).

The Keith Papers, Selected from the letters and papers of Admiral Viscount Keith (Navy Records Society, 1927–55).

[KELSALL, CHARLES], *A Letter from Athens addressed to a Friend in England* (1812).

KLENZE, LEO VON, *Aphoristische Bemerkungen gesammelt auf seiner Reise nach Griechenland* (Berlin, 1838).

KORRES, MANALIS, *From Pentelicon to the Parthenon* (1995).

LARRABEE, STEPHEN. A., *English Bards and Grecian Marbles* (New York, 1943).

——*Hellas Observed: The American Experience of Greece 1775–1865* (New York, 1957).

LAURENT, PETER EDMUND, *Recollections of a Classical Tour* (1821).

LAWRENCE, RICHARD, *Elgin Marbles* (1818).

[LEAKE], MARTIN-LEAKE, WILLIAM, *Researches in Greece* (1814).

LEAKE, LIEUT.-COL. W. M., *The Topography of Athens* (1821; and 2nd edn., 1841).

LEFKOWITZ, MARY R., AND ROGERS, GUY MACLEAN (eds.), *Black Athena Revisited* (1996).

LEGRAND, PH.-E. 'Contribution à l'histoire des marbres du Parthénon'. *Revue Archéologique*, 3rd ser. 25 (1894).

——'Encore les marbres du Parthénon', *Revue Archéologique*, 3rd ser. 26 (1895).

——'Biographie de Louis-François-Sébastien Fauvel', *Revue Archéologique*, 3rd ser. 30 and 31 (1897).

LEIGHTON FREDERIC, *Addresses Delivered to the Students of the Royal Academy By the late Lord Leighton* (1896).

LE ROY, J. D., *Les Ruines des plus beaux monuments de la Grèce* (Paris, 1758).

LEWIS, MICHAEL, *Napoleon and his British Captives* (1962).

MAHAFFY, J. P., *Rambles and Discoveries in Greece* (1887).

——*Greek Pictures* (1890).

MARCELLUS, VICOMTE DE, *Souvenirs de l'Orient* (Paris, 1839).

MARCHAND, LESLIE A., *Byron: A Biography* (1957).

MARCHAND, SUZANNE L., *Down from Olympus: Archaeology and Philhellenism in Germany, 1750–1970* (Princeton, 1996).

MARDEN, PHILIP S., *Greece and the Aegean Islands* (Boston and New York, 1907).

MARSDEN, J. H., *Memoir of the Life and Writings of W. M. Leake* (1864).

MATTON, LYA AND RAYMOND, *Athènes et ses monuments du XVIIe siècle à nos jours* (Athens, 1963).

MERRYMAN, JOHN HENRY, 'Thinking about the Elgin Marbles', *Michigan Law Review*, 83 (1985).

——'Two Ways of Thinking about Cultural Property', *American Journal of International Law*, 80 (1986).

——'The Definition of Cultural Property', *U.C. Davis Law Review*, 21 (1988).

——'The Public Interest in Cultural property', *California Law Review*, 77 (1989).

——'The Nation and the Object', *International Journal of Cultural Property* (1994).

MERRYMAN, JOHN HENRY, and ELSEN, ALBERT E., *Law, Ethics and the Visual Arts: Cases and Materials* (New York 1979).

MICHAELIS, A., *Ancient Marbles in Great Britain* (1882).

——'Supplement on Marbles at Broomhall', *Journal of Hellenic Studies* (1884).

——*Der Parthenon* (Leipzig, 1871).

MICHON, E., 'Les Fragments du Parthénon conservés au Musée du Louvre', *Revue Archéologique*, 3rd ser. 24 (1894).

MILNES, RICHARD MONKTON (LORD HOUGHTON), *Memorials of a Tour in Some Parts of Greece* (1834).

MONCEL, TH. DU, *Vues pittoresques des monuments d'Athènes* (Paris, 1845).

MOORE, THOMAS, *Letters and Journals of Lord Byron with Notices of his Life* (1830/1).

MORRITT OF ROKEBY, J. B. S., *Letters Descriptive of a Journey in Europe and Asia Minor in the years 1794–1796* (1914).

MOÜY, CTE CHARLES DE, *Lettres Athéniennes* (Paris, 1887).

MURE, WILLIAM, OF CALDWELL, *Journal of a Tour in Greece* (Edinburgh, 1842).

NEILS, JENNIFER (ed.), *Worshipping Athena: Pantheneia and Parthenon* (Madison, 1996).

The Letters of Mary Nisbet, Countess of Elgin (1926).

OTTER, W., *The Life and Remains of the Rev. Edward Daniel Clarke* (1824).

PALAGIA, OLGA, AND COULSON, WILLIAM (eds.), *Sculpture from Arcadia and Laconia* (Oxford, 1993).

PENROSE, F. C., *Principles of Athenian Architecture* (1851; 2nd edn., 1888).

[PEYTIER], *The Peytier Album edited by Stelios Papadopoulos* (Athens, 1971).

PHILADELPHEUS, ALEXANDER, *The Monuments of Athens* (Athens, 1924; and subsequent edns. in Greek, English, and French).

PINGAUD, L., *Choiseul-Gouffier: La France en Orient sous Louis XVI* (Paris, 1887).

PITMAN, EMMA RAYMOND, *Mission Life in Greece and Palestine* (n.d., late Victorian).

PITTAKYS, K. S., *L'Ancienne Athènes* (Athens, 1835).

PLENDERLEITH, H. J., *The Preservation of Antiquities* (British Museum, 1934).

POMARDI, SIMONE, *Viaggio nella Grecia* (Rome, 1820).

POUJOULAT, M. B., *Voyages dans l'Asie Mineure* (Paris, 1840).

POUQUEVILLE, F. C. H. L., *Voyage dans la Grèce* (Paris, 1820–1; 2nd edn. with corrections and additions, 1827).

QUIN, MICHAEL J., *A Steam Voyage down the Danube* (3rd edn. with additions, Paris, 1836).

RICHTER, GISELA, *The Sculpture and Sculptors of the Greeks* (1929; final edn., 1970).

RIEDERER, JOSEF, 'The Decay and Conservation of Marble in Archaeological Monuments', in Norman Herz and Marc Waelkins (eds.), *Classical Marble, Geochemistry, Technology, Trade* (Dordrecht, 1988).

ROSS, LUDWIG, *Erinnerungen und Mittheilungen aus Griechenland* (Berlin, 1863).

ROTHENBERG, JACOB, *'Descensus ad Terram': The Acquisition and Reception of the Elgin Marbles* (doctoral thesis, Columbia University, New York, 1967; printed 1977).

ST. CLAIR, WILLIAM, *That Greece Might Still Be Free: The Philhellenes in the War of Independence* (1972).

SAYER, R., *Ruins of Athens and Other Valuable Antiquities in Greece* (1759).

SEIDL, WOLF, *Bayern in Griechenland* (Munich, 1970).

[SELECT COMMITTEE], *Report from the Select Committee of the House of Commons on the Earl of Elgin's Collection of Sculptured Marbles* (1816).

SHARP, WILLIAM, *Elgin Marbles: A Series of Outline Drawings* (1817).

SICILIANOS, D., *Old and New Athens*, trans. Robert Liddell (1960).

[SIMOPOULOS, K.], Χένοι Ταξιδιώτες ττήν Ελλάδα, Athens 1972–1975.

SIMPSON, COLIN, *The Partnership: The Secret Association of Bernard Berenson and Joseph Duveen* (1987).

[MRS SKENE], *Wayfaring Sketches among the Greeks and Turks* (1848).

SMITH, A. H., *Catalogue of Sculpture in the Department of Greek and Roman Antiquities* (British Museum, 1892).

—— *The Sculptures of the Parthenon* (1910).

—— 'Lord Elgin and his Collection', *Journal of Hellenic Studies*, 36 (1916).

—— *Memorandum on the Proposed New Elgin Room* (privately printed, 1938).

SMITH, J. T., *Nollekens and his Times* (1828).

Specimens of Antient Sculpture (Dilettanti Society, 1809 and 1835).

SPENCER, TERENCE, *Fair Greece, Sad Relic* (1954).

SPON, JACOB, *Voyage d'Italie, de Dalmatie, de Grèce, et du Levant* (Lyon, 1688).

STACKELBERG, OTTO MAGNUS VON, *La Grèce: Vues pittoresques et topographiques* (Paris, 1834).

—— *Schilderung seines Lebens und seiner Reisen in Italien und Griechenland, nach Tagebüchern und Briefen, dargestellt von N. von Stackelberg* (Heidelberg, 1882).

[STANHOPE], DOCTOR MERYON, *Travels of Lady Hester Stanhope* (1846).

STEPHENS, JOHN L., *Incidents of Travel in Greece, Turkey, Russia, and Poland* (New York, 1838, and later edns.).

STEVENS, G. P., *et al.*, *The Erechtheum* (1927).

STEWART, ANDREW, *Greek Sculpture: An Exploration* (1990).

STOCKDALE, ERIC, *Law and Order in Georgian Bedfordshire* (Publications of the Bedfordshire Historical Society, 61; 1982).

STUART, JAMES, AND REVETT, NICHOLAS, *et al.*, *The Antiquities of Athens* (Dilettanti Society, 1762–1816).

—— *The Elgin Marbles... selected from Stuart's and Revett's Antiquities of Athens... with Report of Select Committee* (1816).

SWAN, CHARLES, *Journal of a Voyage up the Mediterranean* (1826).

TAYLOR, BAYARD, *Travels in Greece and Russia with an Excursion to Crete* (New York, 1859).

THORTON, THOMAS, *The Present State of Turkey* (1807).

THÜRMER, J., *Ansichten von Athen* (Rome, 1823).

TODD, H. J., *Catalogue of the Archepiscopal Manuscripts in the Library at Lambeth Palace* (1812).

—— *An Account of the Greek Mss chiefly Biblical which had been in the possession of the late Professor Carlyle, the greater part of which are now deposited in the Archepiscopal Library at Lambeth Palace* (1820).

TOURNIKIOTIS, PANAYOTIS (gen. ed. *et al.*, *The Parthenon and its Impact on Modern Times* (Athens, 1995).

The Townley Gallery, British Museum (Library of Entertaining Knowledge, 1836).

TRANT, CAPTAIN T. ABERCROMBY, *Narrative of a Journey through Greece in 1830* (1830).

TSIGAKOU, FANI-MARIA, *The Rediscovery of Greece: Travellers and Painters of the Romantic Period* (1981).

—— (ed.), *Through Romantic Eyes: European Images of Nineteenth Century Greece From the Benaki Museum* [a catalogue of an exhibition] (Athens, 1991).

TURNER, WILLIAM, *A Tour in the Levant* (1812).

TWEDDELL, REVD ROBERT, *The Remains of John Tweddell* (edns. of 1815 and 1816).

—— *Account of the Examination of the Elgin-box at the Foreign Office in Downing-Street, on 7th November 1816, In a Letter to James Losh Esqe, Barrister at law* (Manchester, privately printed, 1816).

VALON, LE VTE ALEXIS DE, *Une Année dans le Levant* (Paris, 1850).

VISCONTI, LE CHEVALIER E. Q., *Mémoires sur des ouvrages de sculpture du Parthénon, et de quelques édifices de l'Acropole à Athènes* (Paris 1818).

WALKER, W., *Six Picturesque Views of Greece* (1804).

WALPOLE, REVD ROBERT, *Memoirs relating to European and Asiatic Turkey* (1817).

—— *Travels in Various Countries of the East* (1820).

WALSH, REVD ROBERT, *A Residence at Constantinople* (1836).

WATKIN, DAVID, *The Life and Work of C. R. Cockerell* (1974).

—— and Mellinghof, Tilman, *German Architecture and the Classical Ideal, 1740–1840*, (1987).

WATTS, M. S., *George Frederic Watts: The Annals of an Artist's Life* (1912).

WHELER, GEORGE, *A Journey into Greece... In Company of Dr Spon of Lyons* (1682).

WHITING, LILIAN, *Athens the Violet-Crowned* (Boston, 1913).

WHITLEY, W. T., *Art in England 1800–1820* (1928).

WILKINS, WILLIAM, *Atheniensia* (1816).

WILLIAMS, H. W., *Travels in Italy, Greece and the Ionian Islands* (1820).

——*Select Views in Greece, with Classical Illustrations* (1829).

WILLIS, N. PARKER, *Summer Cruise in the Mediterranean* (1853).

WILSON, WILLIAM RAE, *Travels in Egypt and the Holy Land* (2nd edn., 1824).

WINCKELMANN, see Irwin.

WITTMAN, WILLIAM, *Travels in Turkey, Asia Minor and Syria* (1803).

WORDSWORTH, CHRISTOPHER, *Athens and Attica: Journal of a Residence There* (2nd edn. with additions, 1837).

Works of Art in Greece, the Greek Islands, and the Dodecanese: Losses and Survivals in the War (London, HMSO, 1946).

WORSLEY, SIR RICHARD, *Museum Worsleyanum* (1794–1803).

YOUNG, JAMES FOSTER, *Five Weeks in Greece* (1876).

YOUNGSON, A. J., *The Making of Classical Edinburgh* (1966; reissued with some additions, 1988).

Index

Abbreviations used in the index: LE: Lord Elgin; EM: Elgin Marbles,

Abercromby, General Sir Ralph (1734–1801) 80
Aberdeen, George Hamilton Gordon, 4th Earl of (1784–1860) 137, 172, 189, 190, 191–2, 219, 251
About, Edmond 320
Acropolis, the:
  as Turkish military fortress 43–4, 47, 59, 61, 62, 65–6
  restored following Turks surrender 316–19, 321–2, 325–6, 330–1
  see also Parthenon, the
Adair, Sir Robert (1763–1855) 154, 155–6, 158
Adam, Sheila 288–9, 312
Aegina Marbles 201–4, 248
Ainslie, Sir Robert (?1730–1812) 7–8
architecture, EM influence on 273–6, 316–17
artists, EM influence on 162–72, 263, 272–3, 276–7
Ashmole, Bernard 300–1, 302, 387n.
Athenian Club 189–90
Athens:
  in year of 1800: 43, 46–7
  history of 47–9, 57–62
  Ottoman administration of 44–5, 95
  visitors to 62, 159–60
  and LE clock 206–7
  citizens of 208–10
  England as successor to ancient 262
  pollution in 284, 329–30, 331
  and war damage 292, 303, 314–16
  missionaries attracted to 324
  see also Acropolis, Parthenon
Austin, Professor Colin 55

Balanos, Nikolaos 328–9
Baldwin, Stanley (1867–1947) 299, 300
Balestra (draftsman engaged by Hamilton) 26, 84
Banks, Sir Joseph (1743–1820) 124
Barrington, Mrs Russell 327
Basilio, Menachini 132–3
Beaufort, Francis (1774–1857) 20
Benizelos, Ioannes 210
Berenson, Bernard (1865–1959) 294, 295
Berlin 273
Bonaparte, Napoleon (1769–1821):
  and conquest of Egypt 11–13
  and Battle of the Nile 14–16
  and siege of Acre 18–19
  dashes to France from Egypt 22
  and animosity towards LE 39, 125
  and strategy in Egypt 80–1
  issues prisoner of war decree 120–1, 122
  and Parthenon sculptures 123, 129–30
  orders LE's arrest 126
  and British diplomats 127–8
  releases LE 130
  abdicates 215
  escapes from Elba 218
  defeated at Waterloo 221
Boyer, General 126
British Government:
  funds Carlyle's mission 8
  allies with Ottoman Empire 16
  appoints Sir Sidney Smith 18
  accepts Convention of El Arish 38
  congratulates LE 84
  and possible invasion of Greece 90

British Government (*cont.*):
  refuses prisoner exchange for LE
    126
  devotes resources to help LE 158
  negotiates with LE 177–8, 179
  Select Committee, *see* Select
    Committee, House of Commons
  Act of Parliament transferring EM
    254, 255
  and question of cleaning EM 302,
    305, 387 n.
  and policy on return of EM 334
British Museum:
  considers buying EM 219
  receives EM 255, 261
  buys from Choisseul-Gouffier
    collection 257
  publishes engraving book 262
  requires more space 277–9
  cleaning policy of 291–2
  and Duveen gallery 293, 304–5
  and Board of Enquiry (1938) 296–8,
    342–5, 386 n.
  Standing Committee's reaction to
    findings 296, 299–300, 312–13
  and public records 306–8, 342–5,
    389–90 n.
Brönstedt, P. O. 202
Brougham, Henry Peter Brougham,
    Baron Brougham and Vaux
    (1778–1868) 245
Bruce, Lord (son of LE) 40, 41
Byron, George Gordon, 6th Baron
    (1788–1824):
  first visit to Athens of 159, 160–1
  English Bards and Scotch Reviewers
    180–1, 367 n.
  Childe Harold's Pilgrimage 182–4,
    186–92, 263, 368–9 n.
  Curse of Minerva, The 193–200,
    370 n., 371 n.
  and Greeks 208, 323
  and John Tweddell's tombstone 231

Canova, Antonio (1757–1822) 149,
    223, 224, 265, 311

Canterbury, Archbishop of (1805–28)
    241–4
Capitan Pasha 29, 40, 86
Carlyle, Joseph Dacre:
  engaged by British Government 8
  describes Sultan's audience chamber
    33
  in Constantinople 69–70, 75–6
  and notes on travelling 71–3
  travels in search of manuscripts 74,
    75, 76–8, 239–40
  returns home 79, 240
  death of 241
Carlyle, Miss (sister of Joseph Dacre
    Carlyle) 241–4
Cavendish, Lord George 218, 219, 221
Cawthorn, James 180–1
Chateaubriand, François-René,
    Vicomte de (1768–1848) 192
Choiseul-Gouffier, Comte de 13, 63–4,
    96–7, 112, 122–5, 216–17, 257
Clarke, Captain (brother of Edward
    Daniel Clarke) 117–18
Clarke, Edward Daniel (1769–1822):
  in the Troad 77, 355–6 n.
  as eyewitness to Parthenon removals
    102–3
  and Eleusis statue 104–6
  writes to Lord Byron 189–90
  receives copy of *Curse of Minerva*
    193–4
  and John Tweddell's papers 230,
    233–4, 238–9
Cockerell, Charles Robert (1788–1863)
    201–5, 212–13, 262, 275, 285, 311
Combe, Taylor (1774–1826) 204
Connelly, Professor Joan B. 54–5,
    353 n.
Coulette (Duveen's moulder) 295, 342
Crawford, Lord 294–5
Cruikshank, George (1792–1878) 254;
    Pl. 10

Dallaway, James (1763–1834) 68–9
damage to the Elgin Marbles:
  from taking mouldings 286–7

from their time at sea 289, 310
from cleaning 286, 291, 295–6,
   297–9, 305, 342–5, 388 n.
damage to the Parthenon:
   during conversion to Christian
      church 60
   during warfare 61–2, 304, 314–16
   from souvenir hunters 62, 95–6,
      211–12, 319, 393 n.
   from removal of sculptures 102–3,
      190, 134, 137
   by pollution 284, 329
Daniel (mason employed by Duveen)
   298, 345
Daniell, William 7, 164
Dilettanti Society 63, 170–1, 191,
   203–4, 214–15, 253–4, 260
Dodwell, Edward (1777–1832) 91, 102,
   138, 192, 283, 289, 358 n.; Pl. 2
Douglas, F. S. N. 192, 246
Drummond, Edward 135, 137, 138
Dundas, Henry, 1st Viscount Melville
   (1742–1811) 2–3, 42
Duveen, Joseph, 1st Baron Duveen of
   Millbank (1869–1939) 293–5,
   304–5, 344

Economakis, Richard 329–30
Edward VII, King (1841–1910) 294
Eglen, Captain (*Mentor*) 116
Eleusis statue 105–7
Elgin, Mary Nisbet, Countess of:
   marries LE 4
   suffers seasickness 20, 22, 109
   on Lord Nelson 21
   meets the Hamiltons 23
   is overjoyed with artists 27
   visits Troy 30
   describes Sultan 33
   and social life in Constantinople
      39–40
   first child is born 40
   and celebration of French defeat 82
   is received by Sultan's mother 83
   on second firman 89–90
   in Athens 107–9, 359 n.

third child is born 109
and Count Sébastiani 113, 125–6
uses feminine persuasion 114–15
and imprisonment of LE 120–1,
   126
and social life in Barrèges 122
returns to England 128
and Robert Ferguson 129, 140–1,
   173
and divorce from LE 141–2
Elgin, Thomas Bruce, 7th Earl of
   (1766–1841):
   early career of 1–4
   marriage of 4–5
   selects staff 5, 7–8
   reasons for collecting and studying
      antiquities 6, 101, 129, 134, 260,
      261
   instructions for embassy 11
   and voyage on *Phaeton* 10, 20–5
   meets Sir William Hamilton 24–5
   reaches Dardanelles 29
   at Sigaeum 30–1
   presents credentials to Sultan 31–4
   and Smith brothers 35–42
   and Convention of El Arish 37–9
   and disfigurement by syphilis 40–1,
      181, 192, 351 n.
   is honoured by Turks 83
   sends 'Memorial' to Government
      84–5
   and second firman 88–90
   wants architectural specimens 99
   visits Athens 107–9
   leaves Constantinople 118
   is interned in France 120–6, 128–9
   is imprisoned at Melun 126–7,
      129–30, 362 n.
   is released from France on parole
      130–1
   is refused further credit 138
   divorces Lady Elgin 140–2
   public career virtually over 142
   and financial situation 142–4, 256
   rents house for EM 145–6
   considers restoring EM 147–50

Elgin (*cont.*):
and shipment of second collection
152–4
furious at Lusieri's detour to Athens
154–5
and John Galt 158–9, 197–8
desires to call on Lord Byron 160–1,
181–2
remarries 173
publishes '*Memorandum*' 175–6,
367 n.
negotiates sale of EM 176–8
is attacked in *Childe Harold* 183–4,
187
is attacked by 'Eleusinian' Clarke
190
is disparaged by visitors to Athens
192
is attacked in *Curse of Minerva*
194–7, 199
suspects conspiracy against him
199–200, 371 n.
presents clock to Athens 206–7
and Dilettanti Society 214–15
is free to go to Paris 215–16
in index to Robert Tweddell's book
228
and Tweddell papers 229–37
as witness to Select Committee
246–7
sells EM 254–5
and Choiseul-Gouffier metope 257
decides he cannot afford Lusieri 258
death of 259–60
Elgin Marbles:
LE's reasons for collecting the 6,
101, 129, 134, 260, 261
removed from Parthenon 93, 108,
110, 134–5, 136–7
transport to England 113–15,
116–18, 158–9, 160
Mentor cargo sunk 116, 132–4, 310
second collection stranded at
Piraeus 139
displayed in temporary museum
145–6
and question of restoration 147–50

artists reaction to 162–72, 263,
272–3, 276–7
at Burlington House 178–9, 225–6;
Pll. 8, 9
mentioned in *Childe Harold* 184
second collection arrives in London
204, 214
inspected by Visconti 217–18, 374 n.
negotiations 219, 296, 299–300,
312–13
praised by Canova 224
discussed in Select Committee
246–51, 252–3
moved to British Museum 255, 261
public reaction to 264, 291
poets influenced by 269–71
casts of 265–70, 286–7, 383 n.
architecture influenced by 273–6,
316–17
cleaning of 286, 291–2, 295–6, 297–9,
305, 342–5, 388 n.
displayed in Duveen Gallery 293,
304–5
and rumours of damage 300–2
placed in storage 303, 388 n.
and question of return to Greece
332–6
Elphinstone, George Keith, Viscount
Keith (1746–1823) 38, 41, 85, 100
Epstein, Sir Jacob (1880–1959) 291,
297, 300, 301, 303
Erechtheion 47, 100, 135, 193, 211, 258,
315
Erechtheus 55–7
Euripides (*c.*480–406 BC) 55
Eustace, J. C. 192
Everett, Edward 370 n.

Fallmerayer, J. Ph. 323
Faraday, Michael (1791–1867) 286
Farington, Joseph (1747–1821) 164, 254
Fauvel, Louis-François-Sébastien:
held prisoner by Turks 14, 112
uses bribery 63–4
cart used by English 65, 112, 354 n.
seizes marbles 123–4
and struggle with Lusieri 136

tries to seize second collection 152
makes offer for Aegina Marbles 203
sells some of his collection 212
buries John Tweddell 229
knew Parthenon was painted 282
is refused permission to export 319
Fazakerly, J. H. 203, 246, 251
Ferguson, Robert 129, 140–2, 173, 200
firmans (official letters of permission):
  to enter Topkapi Serai 69
  for Hunt and Carlyle 76
  first one issued to LE's staff 86
  second one issued to LE's staff 87–92
  investigated by Select Committee 94
  issued for outside Athens 99
  and Lady Elgin's false story of 135
  to export collections 154, 155–8
  text of second firman 338–41
Fischer, Karl von 274
Flaxman, John (1755–1826) 149–50, 162, 214, 248
Forsdyke, John, *later* Sir John 295–6, 297, 300, 303, 343–5
Foster, John (?1787–1846) 202, 205
France:
  and conquest of Egypt 12–13
  at war with Turks 16
  and Convention of El Arish 36, 37–9
  defeated in Egypt 80–2
  makes peace with Turks 113
  makes peace with Great Britain 119
  resumes war with Great Britain 120
  interns LE 120–31
  forms alliance with Turks 151–2
  and return of art 221–4
Fuseli, Henry (1741–1825) 166

Galt, John (1779–1839) 158–9, 197–8
Galvani, Valentino 337
Ganteaume, Admiral 80–2
Gavallo, Pietro 132, 133
Gell, Sir William (1778–1836) 91, 93, 103, 138; Pll. 3, 6
Gennadios, Ioannes 333
George, Prince of Wales, *later* George
IV (1762–1830) 203, 204, 222
George V, King (1865–1936) 294
Giraud, Nicolo 160, 201, 365 n.
Girtin, Thomas 7
Goethe, Johann Wolfgang von (1749–1832) 263, 267, 380 n.
Greek Government 319–20, 321, 330–1, 333
Greek Nationalism 207–11, 218, 316, 322–3, 325, 336
Gregson (boxer) 164
Grenville, William Wyndham, Baron Grenville (1759–1834) 1, 2, 6–7, 37–8, 42, 130, 142
Gropius, Georg 191–2, 314, 369 n.
Guildford, Lord 207

Haller von Hallerstein, Baron Karl 202, 205, 274
Hamilton, Emma, Lady (c.1765–1815) 22–3
Hamilton, William Richard (1777–1859):
  engaged as private secretary to LE 5
  is sent to recruit artists 25–7
  secures Rosetta Stone 115
  and *Mentor* cargo 116, 132
  disagrees with restoration of EM 147, 148
  on Lord Byron 161
  suggests cuts to *Memorandum* 176
  as possible reference in *Childe Harold* 191
  on Athenians reaction to removal of EM 208–9
  opens negotiations on sale 219
  represents British Government in Louvre 223
  writes article praising LE 234
  and Carlyle manuscripts 242
  as witness to Select Committee 247–8
  is concerned about eroding colour of EM 286
Hamilton, Sir William (1730–1803) 23–4, 191

Hammersley, Hugh 255
Harrison, Thomas (1744–1829) 6, 170,
    275
Haseki, Hadji Ali 44
Haydon, Benjamin Robert
    (1786–1846):
  sketches EM 165–7, 214
  compares Phigaleian Marbles to EM
    225
  condemns Select Committee 251–2,
    254
  in satirical print 263, 379 n.; Pl. 11
  1816 diary entry 267
  and John Keats 268
  has moulds made of EM 286
Haygarth, William 188, 199, 231, 282
Hazlitt, William (1778–1830) 279
Helios group 285, 286, 296, 311–12,
    344; Pl. 12
Hemans, Mrs Felicia Dorothea
    (1793–1835) 262
Henning, John (1771–1851) 271
Hill, Sir George 301–2
Hinks, Roger 295–6, 300, 306, 343–4,
    345
Hobhouse, John Cam (1786–1869)
    103, 159, 182, 209; Pl. 5
Hogg, Thomas Jefferson (1792–1862)
    180
Holcombe, Arthur 292, 295, 297, 298,
    300, 311, 343–5
Hope, Thomas (?1770–1831) 191
Hughes, Thomas (1786–1847) 192, 211
Hunt, Philip:
  engaged as chaplain to LE 5–6
  financial situation of 9
  on the *Phaeton* 10
  has second thoughts 20
  at Yenicher 31
  travels with Carlyle 70, 71–3, 75,
    76–9
  draws up memorandum for second
    firman 87
  as witness to Select Committee 88,
    156–7, 251
  takes second firman to Athens 91–4

  suggests whole Caryatid porch be
    removed 100
  on diplomatic tour of Greek
    mainland 100–1
  organizes shipment of EM 116–18
  joins LE in Barrèges 122
  accompanies Lady Elgin to England
    128
  on Athenians' reaction to removal of
    EM 208
  and John Tweddell 235–6
  replies to Clarke's accusations 238
  and Carlyle's manuscripts 241–4
Hutchinson, General 115

Inwood, Henry William (1794–1843)
    273
Iris 52, 296, 311–12
Isocrates (436–338 BC) 58
Ittar, Sebastiano 26, 65, 146; Pl. 7
Iwanovitch, Theodor (Calmuck) 26, 65,
    93, 112, 146

Jenkins, Ian 287, 383 n.
Jerusalem, Patriarch of 76, 239, 241–4
Jervis, John, Earl of St Vincent
    (1735–1823) (Admiral) 14–16

Keats, John (1795–1821) 268–70
Keith, Lord, *see* Elphinstone, George
    Keith, Viscount Keith
Kinnock, Neil 334
Kléber, General Jean-Baptiste 36, 37,
    38–9
Klenze, Leo von 265, 274, 316–17, 318,
    321, 327
Knight, Henry Gally (1786–1846)
    203
Koehler, Brigadier General George
    Frederic (d. 1800) 17, 29–30, 36,
    41, 70, 73, 356 n.
Korres, Manolis 288

Lacy, Thomas 101–2
Laurent, Peter Edmund (1796–1837)
    212

Lawrence, Sir Thomas (1769–1830)
164, 248–9
Le Roy, Julien David 47
Leighton, Frederick, Baron Leighton
of Stretton (1830–96) 276–7, 289
Levant Company 16–17, 200, 233
Linckh (painter) 202, 205
Liverpool, Robert Banks Jenkinson,
2nd Lord Liverpool (1770–1828)
221, 256
Logotheti, Nicholaos 137, 208, 351 n.
Logotheti, Spyridon 43, 91, 93, 100
Long, Charles, *later* 1st Baron
Farnborough (1761–1838) 176,
178, 219, 223, 246
Louvre, the 123, 215, 221, 223, 268
Ludwig, Crown Prince of Bavaria 204,
225, 274
Lusieri, Giovanni Battista: Pl. 4
engaged by LE 24–5
recruits artists 25–7
and method of working 65–6 (*see*
Pl. 6)
and LE's clock 106–7
makes more removals from
Parthenon 134–5, 136–7
operations are halted 138
guards second collection 139
flees from Athens 152
returns to Athens 154–5
sails on *Hydra* 160, 201
mentioned by Lord Byron 187
duels with Gropius 191–2
provides tombstone for John
Tweddell 231
in old age 213
death of 258–9

McLean, Dr (Embassy physician) 10,
20, 25
Maltass, Stephen 153, 154
Manners-Sutton, Charles (Archbishop
of Canterbury) (1755–1828)
241–4
Mechanics Institutes 264
Menou, General (French Commander

in Egypt) 81–2, 115
Mercouri, Melina 306, 325
Middleton, A. P. 287, 383 n.
Montagu, Lady Mary Wortley
(1689–1762) 30
Morier, John Philip (1776–1853) 5, 21,
25, 36, 42, 135
Morosini, General (Venetian) 61
Morris, Captain (*Phaeton*) 9, 20, 21, 23,
29
Morritt, J. B. S. (1771–1843) 64, 251
Murray, John (1778–1843) 182

Neezer, Christoph 315
Nelson, Horatio, Viscount Nelson
(1758–1805) 14–16, 18, 21, 23, 124,
134, 143–4, 216
neoclassicism 147, 184, 186, 188, 282,
316–17
Newport, Sir John (1756–1843) 220
Newton, Sir Charles (1816–94) 279
Nisbet, Mr and Mrs (parents of Lady
Elgin) 40, 78–9, 86, 134, 236
Nollekens, Joseph (1737–1823) 164,
214, 248

Oswald, Elizabeth 173
Ottoman Empire:
declares war on France 12–14
receives LE 31–4
and Convention of El Arish 38
administration in Athens 44–5
celebrates French defeat 82–4
issues second firman 88–9
fully co-operates with Philip Hunt
99
gives LE letters of approval 110–11,
135–6
bans removals from Parthenon
137–8
at war with Russia and Britain
151–2
makes peace with Britain 156
and use of antiquities 157–8
Peloponnese governor shares spoils
205

Ottoman Empire (*cont.*):
  Lusieri makes deal with 206
  and Greek War of Independence
    314–15
  allows export of sculptures 332

Parthenon, the:
  construction of 49
  sculptural decoration of 49–51
    (illus.)
  painted surfaces of 51, 271–2,
    281–91, 309–12
  frieze 51–4, 57, 110, 134, 136–7, 212,
    310; Pl. 1
  removals from 93, 98, 102–3, 108,
    110, 134–5, 136–7, 212–13
  change in appearance of 103–4; Pll.
    3, 5
  as symbol of Greek national identity
    189, 324, 335–6
  colour of 281–5, 384–5 n.
  effected by pollution 284, 329–40
  restoration work on 316, 327–9
  see also damage to the Parthenon
Pausanias (2nd-c. AD historian) 47, 49
Payne Knight, Richard 167–72, 219,
    249–50, 253–4
Penrose, F. C. (1817–1903) 284
Perceval, Spencer (1762–1812) 177–8,
    179
Phidias (*fl.* 490–430 BC) 48, 49, 264
Phigaleian Marbles 204–5, 224–5, 248,
    309
philhellenism, ideology of 186, 187–8,
    189, 210–11, 259, 323, 324, 325
Pisani (official British dragoman)
    87–8, 337
Pitt, William (1759–1806) 2
Pittakis (ephor of antiquities) 321, 333
Plenderleith, Harold 295, 343–5
Plutarch (*c.*46–120) 59
poets influenced by EM 269–71
pollution 284, 290, 329–30, 331
Porson, Richard (1759–1808) 8
Preaux (painter) 229
Propylaea 47, 52, 61

Pryce, Frederick 297, 300, 342–4
public records of British Museum
    306–8, 342–5, 389–90 n.

Quincy, Quatremère de 223

Revett, Nicholas (1720–1804) 47, 51,
    53, 104, 170, 250, 282
Rhodes, Cecil John (1853–1902) 277
Rogers, Samuel (1763–1855) 194
Romanticism, aesthetics of:
  and question of restoration 148
  perception of EM 163–7, 268–73
  Payne Knight's opposition to 169
  supersedes previous aesthetic 172,
    200
  and colour of Parthenon 283
  influences EM display in Duveen
    Gallery 293, 305
  and beauty of Parthenon as a ruin
    327
Rosetta Stone 115
Ross, Ludwig 321
Ruffin (French Chargé d'Affaires)
    13–14, 84
Ruskin, John (1819–1900) 327

St Vincent, Admiral, *see* Jervis, John,
    Earl of St Vincent
Schiller, Johann von (1759–1805)
    266–7
Schinkel, Karl Friedrich 273, 316–17
Schliemann, Heinrich (1822–1890) 322
Scott, Sir Walter (1771–1832) 276
sculpture, techniques of Greek 288–9
Sébastiani, Count (Bonaparte's agent)
    113, 119, 121–2, 125–6, 151
Select Committee, House of Commons
    (1816) 7, 88, 94, 96, 129, 156–7,
    220, 246–53
Selene's horse 271, 296, 311, 344
Severn, Joseph (1793–1879) 269
Shelley, Percy Bysshe (1792–1822) 270
Siddons, Sarah (1755–1831) 164–5
Simenton (labourer cleaning EM)
    344–5

Sinclair (labourer cleaning EM) 344-5
Smirke, Richard 7, 164, 282
Smirke, Sir Robert (1780–1867) 7, 95, 134, 164, 282
Smith, A. H. (1860–1941) 257, 397
Smith, Horace (1779–1849) 194
Smith, James (1775–1839) 194
Smith, Sir Sidney (1764–1840) 17–19, 28–9, 36, 37, 41–2, 74–5
Soane, Sir John (1753–1837) 273
Spencer Smith, John 17, 35, 42, 126, 200, 230, 232
Spon, Dr Jacob 104, 250
Stackelberg, Baron von 202
Stanhope, Lady Hester (1776–1839) 159, 213
Straton, Alexander 42, 141
Stuart, James (1713–1788) 47, 51, 53, 104, 170, 250, 281–2, 283
Stuart, Sir John 152–3

Talleyrand-Périgord, Charles Maurice de (1754–1838) 13, 126, 131, 222
Taylor, Bayard 284, 325, 327
Theseum 65, 314–15; Pl. 7
Thornton, Thomas 229, 231–2
Thorwaldsen, Bertel (1768–1844) 204
Threed, William 271
Topkapi Serai library 68–9, 75, 76
Townley, Charles 170, 172, 178
Trant, T. Abercromby 314, 318–19
Turner, J. M. W. (1775–1851) 7, 164, 245

Tweddell, John (1769–1799) 227–37, 238, 375 n.
Tweddell, Robert 232–7

UNESCO 330, 335

Valhalla 274
Vansittart, Nicholas, *later* 1st Baron Bexley (1766–1851) (Chancellor of Exchequer) 220, 245, 246
Viollet-le-Duc, Eugène Emmanuel (1814–79) 326
Visconti, Ennio Quirino 215, 217–18, 219, 223–4, 264

Watts, G. F. (1817–1904) 276–7
West, Benjamin (1738–1820) 7, 163, 169, 176, 214
Westmacott, Sir Richard (1775–1856) 248, 265, 278–9
Wheler, Sir George (1650–1723) 47, 104, 250
Wilkins, William (1778–1839) 171–2, 251
Williams, H. W. (1773–1829) 211, 273
Wilson, Sir David 307, 341
Wilson, Harold (1916–95) 99
Winckelmann, Johann Joachim (1717–68) 147, 148, 162, 166, 168, 266, 289–90
Wordsworth, William (1770–1850) 261–2

Young, H. B. 317–18, 392 n.

OXFORD

MORE OXFORD PAPERBACKS

This book is just one of nearly 1000 Oxford Paperbacks currently in print. If you would like details of other Oxford Paperbacks, including titles in the World's Classics, Oxford Reference, Oxford Books, OPUS, Past Masters, Oxford Authors, and Oxford Shakespeare series, please write to:

UK and Europe: Oxford Paperbacks Publicity Manager, Arts and Reference Publicity Department, Oxford University Press, Walton Street, Oxford OX2 6DP.

Customers in UK and Europe will find Oxford Paperbacks available in all good bookshops. But in case of difficulty please send orders to the Cash-with-Order Department, Oxford University Press Distribution Services, Saxon Way West, Corby, Northants NN18 9ES. Tel: 01536 741519; Fax: 01536 746337. Please send a cheque for the total cost of the books, plus £1.75 postage and packing for orders under £20; £2.75 for orders over £20. Customers outside the UK should add 10% of the cost of the books for postage and packing.

USA: Oxford Paperbacks Marketing Manager, Oxford University Press, Inc., 200 Madison Avenue, New York, N.Y. 10016.

Canada: Trade Department, Oxford University Press, 70 Wynford Drive, Don Mills, Ontario M3C 1J9.

Australia: Trade Marketing Manager, Oxford University Press, G.P.O. Box 2784Y, Melbourne 3001, Victoria.

South Africa: Oxford University Press, P.O. Box 1141, Cape Town 8000.

CLASSICS

Mary Beard and John Henderson

This *Very Short Introduction* to Classics links a haunting temple on a lonely mountainside to the glory of ancient Greece and the grandeur of Rome, and to Classics within modern culture—from Jefferson and Byron to Asterix and Ben-Hur.

'This little book should be in the hands of every student, and every tourist to the lands of the ancient world . . . a splendid piece of work'
Peter Wiseman
Author of *Talking to Virgil*

'an eminently readable and useful guide to many of the modern debates enlivening the field . . . the most up-to-date and accessible introduction available'
Edith Hall
Author of *Inventing the Barbarian*

'lively and up-to-date . . . it shows classics as a living enterprise, not a warehouse of relics'
New Statesman and Society

'nobody could fail to be informed and entertained—the accent of the book is provocative and stimulating'
Times Literary Supplement

A Very Short Introduction

POLITICS

Kenneth Minogue

Since politics is both complex and controversial it is easy to miss the wood for the trees. In this Very Short Introduction Kenneth Minogue has brought the many dimensions of politics into a single focus: he discusses both the everyday grind of democracy and the attraction of grand ideals such as freedom and justice.

'Kenneth Minogue is a very lively stylist who does not distort difficult ideas.'
Maurice Cranston

'a dazzling but unpretentious display of great scholarship and humane reflection'
Professor Neil O'Sullivan, University of Hull

'Minogue is an admirable choice for showing us the nuts and bolts of the subject.'
Nicholas Lezard, *Guardian*

'This is a fascinating book which sketches, in a very short space, one view of the nature of politics . . . the reader is challenged, provoked and stimulated by Minogue's trenchant views.'
Talking Politics

A Very Short Introduction

ARCHAEOLOGY

Paul Bahn

'Archaeology starts, really, at the point when the first recognizable 'artefacts' appear—on current evidence, that was in East Africa about 2.5 million years ago—and stretches right up to the present day. What you threw in the garbage yesterday, no matter how useless, disgusting, or potentially embarrassing, has now become part of the recent archaeological record.'

This Very Short Introduction reflects the enduring popularity of archaeology—a subject which appeals as a pastime, career, and academic discipline, encompasses the whole globe, and surveys 2.5 million years. From deserts to jungles, from deep caves to mountain-tops, from pebble tools to satellite photographs, from excavation to abstract theory, archaeology interacts with nearly every other discipline in its attempts to reconstruct the past.

'very lively indeed and remarkably perceptive . . . a quite brilliant and level-headed look at the curious world of archaeology'
Professor Barry Cunliffe,
University of Oxford

A Very Short Introduction

BUDDHISM

Damien Keown

'Karma can be either good or bad. Buddhists speak of good karma as "merit", and much effort is expended in acquiring it. Some picture it as a kind of spiritual capital—like money in a bank account—whereby credit is built up as the deposit on a heavenly rebirth.'

This Very Short Introduction introduces the reader both to the teachings of the Buddha and to the integration of Buddhism into daily life. What are the distinctive features of Buddhism? Who was the Buddha, and what are his teachings? How has Buddhist thought developed over the centuries, and how can contemporary dilemmas be faced from a Buddhist perspective?

'Damien Keown's book is a readable and wonderfully lucid introduction to one of mankind's most beautiful, profound, and compelling systems of wisdom. The rise of the East makes understanding and learning from Buddhism, a living doctrine, more urgent than ever before. Keown's impressive powers of explanation help us to come to terms with a vital contemporary reality.'
Bryan Appleyard

A Very Short Introduction

JUDAISM

Norman Solomon

'Norman Solomon has achieved the near impossible with his enlightened very short introduction to Judaism. Since it is well known that Judaism is almost impossible to summarize, and that there are as many different opinions about Jewish matters as there are Jews, this is a small masterpiece in its success in representing various shades of Jewish opinion, often mutually contradictory. Solomon also manages to keep the reader engaged, never patronizes, assumes little knowledge but a keen mind, and takes us through Jewish life and history with such gusto that one feels enlivened, rather than exhausted, at the end.'
Rabbi Julia Neuberger

'This book will serve a very useful purpose indeed. I'll use it myself to discuss, to teach, agree with, and disagree with, in the Jewish manner!'
Rabbi Lionel Blue

'A magnificent achievement. Dr Solomon's treatment, fresh, very readable, witty and stimulating, will delight everyone interested in religion in the modern world.'
Dr Louis Jacobs, University of Lancaster

seated on stools, and chanting from immense books placed on music-stands, and having the notes scored in such gigantic characters as to be legible from every part of the choir. A few lights on these music-stands dimly illumined the choir, gleamed on the shaven heads of the monks, and threw their shadows on the walls. They were gross, blue-bearded, bullet-headed men, with bass voices, of deep metallic tone, that reverberated out of the cavernous choir.

To our right extended the great body of the church. It was spacious and lofty; some of the side chapels had gilded grates, and were decorated with images and paintings, representing the sufferings of our Saviour. Aloft was a great painting by Murillo, but too much in the dark to be distinguished. The gloom of the whole church was but faintly relieved by the reflected light from the choir, and the glimmering here and there of a votive lamp before the shrine of the saint.

As my eye roamed about the shadowy pile, it was struck with the dimly seen figure of a man on horseback, near a distant altar. I touched my companion, and pointed to it: "The spectre statue!" said I.

"No," replied he; "it is the statue of the blessed St. Iago; the statue of the commander was in the cemetery of the convent, and was destroyed at the time of the conflagration. But," added he, "as I see you take a proper interest in these kind of stories, come with me to the other end of the church, where our whisperings will not disturb these holy fathers at their devotions, and I will tell you another story that has been current for some generations in our city, by which you will find that Don Juan is not the only libertine that has been the object of supernatural castigation in Seville."

I accordingly followed him with noiseless tread to the farther part of the church, where we took our seats on the steps of an altar opposite to the suspicious-looking figure on horseback, and there, in a low, mysterious voice, he related to me the following narrative:

"There was once in Seville a gay young fellow, Don Manuel de Manara by name, who, having come to a great estate by the death of his father, gave the reins to his passions, and plunged into all kinds of dissipation. Like Don Juan, whom he seemed to have taken for a model, he became famous for his enterprises among the fair sex, and was the cause of doors being barred and windows grated with more than usual strictness. All in vain. No balcony was too high for him to scale; no bolt nor bar was proof against his efforts; and his very name was a word of terror to all the jealous husbands and cautious fathers of Seville. His exploits extended to country as well as city; and in the village dependent on his castle scarce a rural beauty was safe from his arts and enterprises.

DON JUAN
A SPECTRAL RESEARCH

"I have heard of spirits walking with aërial bodies, and have been wondered at by others; but I must only wonder at myself, for, if they be not mad, I 'me come to my own buriall."

SHIRLEY'S "WITTY FAIRIE ONE"

EVERYBODY has heard of the fate of Don Juan, the famous libertine of Seville, who, for his sins against the fair sex and other minor peccadilloes, was hurried away to the infernal regions. His story has been illustrated in play, in pantomime, and farce, on every stage in Christendom, until at length it has been rendered the theme of the opera of operas, and embalmed to endless duration in the glorious music of Mozart. I well recollect the effect of this story upon my feelings in my boyish days, though represented in grotesque pantomime; the awe with which I contemplated the monumental statue on horseback of the murdered commander, gleaming by pale moonlight in the convent cemetery; how my heart quaked as he bowed his marble head, and accepted the impious invitation of Don Juan; how each footfall of the statue smote upon my heart, as I heard it approach, step by step, through the echoing corridor, and beheld it enter, and advance, a moving figure of stone, to the supper-table! But then the convivial scene in the charnel-house, where Don Juan returned the visit of the statue, was offered a banquet of skulls and bones, and on refusing to partake, was hurled into a yawning gulf under a tremendous shower of fire! These were accumulated horrors enough to shake the nerves of the most pantomime-loving school-boy. Many have supposed the story of Don Juan a mere fable. I myself thought so once; but "seeing is believing." I have since beheld the very scene where it took place, and now to indulge any doubt on the subject, would be preposterous.

I was one night perambulating the streets of Seville, in company with a Spanish friend, a curious investigator of the popular traditions and other good-for-nothing lore of the city, and who was kind enough to imagine he had met, in me, with a congenial spirit. In the course of our rambles, we were passing by a heavy dark gateway, opening into the courtyard of a convent, when he laid his hand upon my arm: "Stop!" said he; "this is the convent of San Francisco; there is a story connected with it, which I am sure must be known to you. You cannot but have heard of Don Juan and the marble statue."

"Undoubtedly," replied I; "it has been familiar to me from childhood."

"Well, then, it was in the cemetery of this convent that the events took place."

"Why, you do not mean to say that the story is founded on fact?"

"Undoubtedly it is. The circumstances of the case are said to have occurred during the reign of Alfonso XI. Don Juan was of the noble family of Tenorio, one of the most illustrious houses of Andalusia. His father, Don Diégo Tenorio was a favorite of the King, and his family ranked among the *veintecuatros*, or magistrates, of the city. Presuming on his high descent and powerful connections, Don Juan set no bounds to his excesses; no female, high or low, was sacred from his pursuit; and he soon became the scandal of Seville. One of his most daring outrages was, to penetrate by night into the palace of Don Gonzalo de Ulloa, Commander of the Order of Calatrava, and attempt to carry off his daughter. The household was alarmed; a scuffle in the dark took place; Don Juan escaped, but the unfortunate commander was found weltering in his blood, and expired without being able to name his murderer. Suspicions attached to Don Juan; he did not stop to meet the investigations of justice and the vengeance of the powerful family of Ulloa, but fled from Seville, and took refuge with his uncle, Don Pedro Tenorio, at that time ambassador at the court of Naples. Here he remained until the agitation occasioned by the murder of Don Gonzalo had time to subside; and the scandal which the affair might cause to both the families of Ulloa and Tenorio had induced them to hush it up. Don Juan, however, continued his libertine career at Naples, until at length his excesses forfeited the protection of his uncle the ambassador, and obliged him again to flee. He had made his way back to Seville, trusting that his past misdeeds were forgotten, or rather trusting to his daredevil spirit and the power of his family, to carry him through all difficulties.

"It was shortly after his return, and while in the height of his arrogance, that on visiting this very convent of Francisco, he beheld on a monument the equestrian statue of the murdered commander, who had been buried within the walls of this sacred edifice, where the family of Ulloa had a chapel. It was on this occasion that Don Juan, in a moment of impious levity, invited the statue to the banquet, the awful catastrophe of which has given such celebrity to his story."

"And pray how much of this story," said I, "is believed in Seville?"

"The whole of it by the populace, with whom it has been a favorite tradition since time immemorial, and who crowd to the theatres to see it represented in dramas written long since by Tyrso de Molina, and another of our popular writers. Many in our higher ranks also, accustomed from childhood to this story, would feel somewhat indignant at hearing it treated with contempt. An attempt has been made to explain the whole, by asserting that, to put an end to the extravagances of Don Juan, and to pacify the family of Ulloa, without exposing the delinquent to the degrading penalties of justice, he was decoyed into this convent under false pretext, and either plunged into a perpetual dungeon, or privately hurried out of existence; while the story of the statue was circulated by the monks, to account for his sudden disappearance. The populace, however, are not to be cajoled out a ghost-story by any of these plausible explanations; and the marble statue still strides the stage, and Don Juan is still plunged into the infernal regions, as an awful warning to all rake-helly youngsters, in like case offending."

·While my companion was relating these anecdotes, we had traversed the exterior courtyard of the convent, and made our way into a great interior court, partly surrounded by cloisters and dormitories, partly by chapels, and having a large fountain in the centre. The pile had evidently once been extensive and magnificent; but it was for the greater part in ruins. By the light of the stars, and of twinkling lamps placed here and there in the chapels and corridors, I could see that many of the columns and arches were broken; the walls were rent and riven; while burnt beams and rafters showed the destructive effects of fire. The whole place had a desolate air; the night breeze rustled through grass and weeds flaunting out of the crevices of the walls, or from the shattered columns; the bat flitted about the vaulted passages, and the owl hooted from the ruined belfry. Never was any scene more completely fitted for a ghost-story.

While I was indulging in picturings of the fancy, proper to such a place, the deep chant of the monks from the convent church came swelling upon the ear. "It is the vesper service," said my companion; "follow me."

Leading the way across the court of the cloisters, and through one or two ruined passages, he reached the portal of the church, and pushing open a wicket, cut in the folding-doors, we found ourselves in the deep arched vestibule of the sacred edifice. To our left was the choir, forming one end of the church, and having a low vaulted ceiling, which gave it the look of a cavern. About this were ranged the monks,

"As he was one day ranging the streets of Seville, with several of his dissolute companions, he beheld a procession, about to enter the gate of a convent. In the centre was a young female, arrayed in the dress of a bride; it was a novice, who having accomplished her year of probation, was about to take the black veil, and consecrate herself to heaven. The companions of Don Manuel drew back, out of respect to the sacred pageant; but he pressed forward with his usual impetuosity, to gain a near view of the novice. He almost jostled her, in passing through the portal of the church, when, on her turning round, he beheld the countenance of a beautiful village girl, who had been the object of his ardent pursuit, but who had been spirited secretly out of his reach by her relatives. She recognized him at the same moment, and fainted, but was borne within the grate of the chapel. It was supposed the agitation of the ceremony and the heat of the throng had overcome her. After some time, the curtain which hung within the grate was drawn up: there stood the novice, pale and trembling, surrounded by the abbess and the nuns. The ceremony proceeded; the crown of flowers was taken from her head, she was shorn of her silken tresses, received the black veil, and went passively through the remainder of the ceremony.

"Don Manuel de Manara, on the contrary, was roused to fury at the sight of this sacrifice. His passion, which had almost faded away in the absence of the object, now glowed with tenfold ardor, being inflamed by the difficulties placed in his way, and piqued by the measures which had been taken to defeat him. Never had the object of his pursuit appeared so lovely and desirable as when within the grate of the convent; and he swore to have her, in defiance of heaven and earth. By dint of bribing a female servant of the convent, he contrived to convey letters to her, pleading his passion in the most eloquent and seductive terms. How successful they were, is only a matter of conjecture; certain it is, he undertook one night to scale the garden-wall of the convent, either to carry off the nun, or gain admission to her cell. Just as he was mounting the wall, he was suddenly plucked back, and a stranger, muffled in a cloak, stood before him.

" 'Rash man, forbear!' cried he; 'is it not enough to have violated all human ties? Wouldst thou steal a bride from heaven!'

"The sword of Don Manuel had been drawn on the instant, and furious at this interruption, he passed it through the body of the stranger, who fell dead at his feet. Hearing approaching footsteps, he fled the fatal spot, and mounting his horse, which was at hand, retreated to his estate in the country, at no great distance from Seville. Here he remained throughout the next day, full of horror and remorse, dreading lest he should be known as the murderer of the deceased, and fearing each moment the arrival of the officers of justice.

"The day passed, however, without molestation; and as the evening advanced, unable any longer to endure this state of uncertainty and apprehension, he ventured back to Seville. Irresistibly his footsteps took the direction of the convent, but he paused and hovered at a distance from the scene of blood. Several persons were gathered round the place, one of whom was busy nailing something against the convent-wall. After a while they dispersed, and one passed near to Don Manuel. The latter addressed him with hesitating voice.

" 'Señor,' said he, 'may I ask the reason of yonder throng?'

" 'A cavalier,' replied the other, 'has been murdered.'

" 'Murdered!' echoed Don Manuel; 'and can you tell me his name?'

" 'Don Manuel de Manara,' replied the stranger, and passed on.

"Don Manuel was startled at this mention of his own name, especially when applied to the murdered man. He ventured, when it was entirely deserted, to approach the fatal spot. A small cross had been nailed against the wall, as is customary in Spain, to mark the place where a murder has been committed; and just below it he read, by the twinkling light of a lamp: 'Here was murdered Don Manuel de Manara. Pray to God for his soul!'

"Still more confounded and perplexed by this inscription, he wandered about the streets until the night was far advanced, and all was still and lonely. As he entered the principal square, the light of torches suddenly broke on him, and he beheld a grand funeral procession moving across it. There was a great train of priests, and many persons of dignified appearance, in ancient Spanish dresses, attending as mourners, none of whom he knew. Accosting a servant who followed in the train, he demanded the name of the defunct.

" 'Don Manuel de Manara,' was the reply; and it went cold to his heart. He looked, and indeed beheld the armorial bearings of his family emblazoned on the funeral escutcheons. Yet not one of his family was to be seen among the mourners. The mystery was more and more incomprehensible.

"He followed the procession as it moved on to the cathedral. The bier was deposited before the high altar; the funeral service was commenced, and the grand organ began to peal through the vaulted aisles.

"Again the youth ventured to question this awful pageant. 'Father,' said he, with trembling voice, to one of the priests, 'who is this you are about to inter?'

" 'Don Manuel de Manara!' replied the priest.

" 'Father,' cried Don Manuel impatiently, 'you are deceived. This is some imposture. Know that Don Manuel de Manara is alive and well, and now stands before you. *I* am Don Manuel de Manara!'

" 'Avaunt, rash youth!' cried the priest, 'know that Don Manuel de Manara is dead!—is dead!—is dead!—and we are all souls from purgatory, his deceased relatives and ancestors, and others that have been aided by masses from his family, who are permitted to come here and pray for the repose of his soul!'

"Don Manuel cast round a fearful glance upon the assemblage in antiquated Spanish garbs, and recognized in their pale and ghastly countenances the portraits of many an ancestor that hung in the family picture-gallery. He now lost all self-command, rushed up to the bier, and beheld the counterpart of himself, but in the fixed and livid lineaments of death. Just at that moment the whole choir burst forth with a 'Requiescat in pace,' that shook the vaults of the cathedral. Don Manuel sank senseless on the pavement. He was found there early the next morning by the sacristan, and conveyed to his home. When sufficiently recovered, he sent for a friar, and made a full confession of all that had happened.

" 'My son,' said the friar, 'all this is a miracle and a mystery intended for thy conversion and salvation. The corpse thou hast seen was a token that thou hadst died to sin and the world; take warning by it, and henceforth live to righteousness and heaven!'

"Don Manuel did take warning by it. Guided by the counsels of the worthy friar, he disposed of all his temporal affairs, dedicated the greater part of his wealth to pious uses, especially to the performance of masses for souls in purgatory, and finally, entering a convent, became one of the most zealous and exemplary monks in Seville."

While my companion was relating this story, my eyes wandered, from time to time, about the dusky church. Methought the burly countenances of the monks in the distant choir assumed a pallid, ghastly hue, and their deep metallic voices a sepulchral sound. By the time the story was ended, they had ended their chant, and, extinguishing their lights, glided, one by one, like shadows, through a small door in the side of the choir. A deeper gloom prevailed over the church; the figure opposite me on horseback grew more and more spectral, and I almost expected to see it bow its head.

"It is time to be off," said my companion, "unless we intend to sup with the statue."

"I have no relish for such fare nor such company," replied I; and following my companion, we groped our way through the mouldering cloisters. As we passed by the ruined cemetery, keeping up a casual conversation, by way of dispelling the loneliness of the scene, I called to mind the words of the poet:

"The tombs
And monumental caves of death look cold,
And shoot a chillness to my trembling heart!
Give me thy hand, and let me hear thy voice;
Nay, speak—and let me hear thy voice;
Mine own affrights me with its echoes."

There wanted nothing but the marble statue of the commander, striding along the echoing cloisters, to complete the haunted scene.

Since that time, I never fail to attend the theatre whenever the story of Don Juan is represented, whether in pantomime or opera. In the sepulchral scene, I feel myself quite at home; and when the statue makes his appearance, I greet him as an old acquaintance. When the audience applaud, I look round upon them with a degree of compassion. "Poor souls!" I say to myself, "they think they are pleased; they think they enjoy this piece, and yet they consider the whole as a fiction! How much more would they enjoy it, if, like me, they knew it to be true—*and had seen the very place!*"

From *Wolfert's Roost*

LEGEND OF THE ENGULPHED CONVENT

A T the dark and melancholy period when Don Roderick the Goth and his chivalry were overthrown on the banks of the Guadalete, and all Spain was overrun by the Moors, great was the devastation of churches and convents throughout that pious kingdom. The miraculous fate of one of those holy piles is thus recorded in an authentic legend of those days.

On the summit of a hill, not very distant from the capital city of Toledo, stood an ancient convent and chapel, dedicated to the invocation of Saint Benedict, and inhabited by a sisterhood of Benedictine nuns. This holy asylum was confined to females of noble lineage. The younger sisters of the highest families were here given in religious marriage to their Saviour, in order that the portions of their elder sisters might be increased, and they enabled to make suitable matches on earth; or that the family wealth might go undivided to elder brothers, and the dignity of their ancient houses be protected from decay. The convent was renowned, therefore, for enshrining within its walls a sisterhood of the purest blood, the most immaculate virtue, and most resplendent beauty, of all Gothic Spain.

When the Moors overran the kingdom, there was nothing that more excited their hostility than these virgin asylums. The very sight of a convent spire was sufficient to set their Moslem blood in a foment, and they sacked it with as fierce a zeal as though the sacking of a nunnery were a sure passport to Elysium.

Tidings of such outrages, committed in various parts of the kingdom, reached this noble sanctuary, and filled it with dismay. The danger came nearer and nearer; the infidel hosts were spreading all over the country; Toledo itself was captured; there was no flying from the convent, and no security within its walls.

In the midst of this agitation, the alarm was given one day, that a great band of Saracens were spurring across the plain. In an instant the whole convent was a scene of confusion. Some of the nuns wrung their fair hands at the windows; others waved their veils, and uttered shrieks, from the tops of the towers, vainly hoping to draw relief from a country overrun by the foe. The sight of these innocent doves thus fluttering about their dovecote, but increased the zealot fury of the whiskered Moors. They thundered at the portal, and at every blow the ponderous gates trembled on their hinges.

The nuns now crowded round the abbess. They had been accustomed to look up to her as all-powerful, and they now implored her protection. The mother abbess looked with a rueful eye upon the treasures of beauty and vestal virtue exposed to such imminent peril. Alas! how was she to protect them from the spoiler! She had, it is true, experienced many signal interpositions of Providence in her individual favor. Her early days had been passed amid the temptations of a court, where her virtue had been purified by repeated trials, from none of which she escaped but by miracle. But were miracles never to cease? Could she hope that the marvellous protection shown to herself would be extended to a whole sisterhood? There was no other resource. The Moors were at the threshold; a few moments more, and the convent would be at their mercy. Summoning her nuns to follow her, she hurried into the chapel, and throwing herself on her knees before the image of the blessed Mary, "Oh, holy Lady!" exclaimed she, "oh, most pure and immaculate of virgins! thou seest our extremity. The ravager is at the gate, and there is none on earth to help us! Look down with pity, and grant that the earth may gape and swallow us, rather than that our cloister vows should suffer violation!"

The Moors redoubled their assault upon the portal: the gates gave way, with a tremendous crash; a savage yell of exultation arose; when of a sudden the earth yawned, down sank the convent, with its cloisters, its dormitories, and all its nuns. The chapel tower was the last that sank, the bell ringing forth a peal of triumph in the very teeth of the infidels.

Forty years had passed and gone, since the period of this miracle. The subjugation of Spain was complete. The Moors lorded it over city and country; and such of the Christian population as remained, and were permitted to exercise their religion, did it in humble resignation to the Moslem sway.

At this time, a Christian cavalier of Cordova, hearing that a patriotic band of his countrymen had raised the standard of the cross in the mountains of the Asturias, resolved to join them, and unite in breaking the yoke of bondage. Secretly arming himself and caparisoning his steed, he set forth from Cordova, and pursued his course by unfrequented mulepaths, and along the dry channels made by winter torrents. His spirit burned with indignation, whenever, on commanding a view over a long sweeping plain, he beheld the mosque swelling in the distance, and the Arab horsemen careering about, as if the rightful lords of the soil. Many a deep-drawn sigh and heavy groan, also, did the good cavalier utter, on passing the ruins of churches and convents desolated by the conquerors.

It was on a sultry midsummer evening, that this wandering cavalier, in skirting a hill thickly covered with forest, heard the faint tones of a vesper-bell sounding melodiously in the air, and seeming to come from the summit of the hill. The cavalier crossed himself with wonder at this unwonted and Christian sound. He supposed it to proceed from one of those humble chapels and hermitages permitted to exist through the indulgence of the Moslem conquerors. Turning his steed up a narrow path of the forest, he sought this sanctuary, in hopes of finding a hospitable shelter for the night. As he advanced, the trees threw a deep gloom around him, and the bat flitted across the path. The bell ceased to toll, and all was silence.

Presently a choir of female voices came stealing sweetly through the forest, chanting the evening service, to the solemn accompaniment of an organ. The heart of the good cavalier melted at the sound, for it recalled the happier days of his country. Urging forward his weary steed, he at length arrived at a broad grassy area, on the summit of the hill, surrounded by the forest. Here the melodious voices rose in full chorus, like the swelling of the breeze; but whence they came, he could not tell. Sometimes they were before, sometimes behind him; sometimes in the air, sometimes as if from within the bosom of the earth. At length they died away, and a holy stillness settled on the place.

The cavalier gazed around with bewildered eye. There was neither chapel nor convent, nor humble hermitage, to be seen; nothing but a moss-grown stone pinnacle, rising out of the centre of the area, surmounted by a cross. The green sward appeared to have been sacred from the tread of man or beast, and the surrounding trees bent toward the cross, as if in adoration.

The cavalier felt a sensation of holy awe. He alighted, and tethered his steed on the skirts of the forest, where he might crop the tender herbage; then approaching the cross, he knelt and poured forth his evening prayers before this relic of the Christian days of Spain. His orisons being concluded, he laid himself down at the foot of the pinnacle, and reclining his head against one of its stones, fell into a deep sleep.

About midnight he was awakened by the tolling of a bell, and found himself lying before the gate of an ancient convent. A train of nuns passed by, each bearing a taper. He rose and followed them into the chapel; in the centre was a bier, on which lay the corpse of an aged nun. The organ performed a solemn requiem, the nuns joining in chorus. When the funeral service was finished, a melodious voice chanted, *"Requiescat in pace!"*—"May she rest in peace!" The lights immediately vanished; the whole passed away as a dream; and the cavalier found himself at the foot of the cross, and beheld, by the faint rays of the rising moon, his steed quietly grazing near him.

When the day dawned he descended the hill, and following the course of a small brook, came to a cave, at the entrance of which was seated an ancient man, in hermit's garb, with rosary and cross, and a beard that descended to his girdle. He was one of those holy anchorites permitted by the Moors to live unmolested in the dens and caves, and humble hermitages, and even to practise the rites of their religion. The cavalier, dismounting, knelt and craved a benediction. He then related all that had befallen him in the night, and besought the hermit to explain the mystery.

"What thou hast heard and seen, my son," replied the other, "is but a type and shadow of the woes of Spain."

He then related the foregoing story of the miraculous deliverance of the convent.

· "Forty years," added the holy man, "have elapsed since this event, yet the bells of that sacred edifice are still heard, from time to time, sounding from underground, together with the pealing of the organ and the chanting of the choir. The Moors avoid this neighborhood, as haunted ground, and the whole place, as thou mayest perceive, has become covered with a thick and lonely forest."

The cavalier listened with wonder to the story. For three days and nights did he keep vigils with the holy man beside the cross; but nothing more was to be seen of nun or convent. It is supposed that, forty years having elapsed, the natural lives of all the nuns were finished, and the cavalier had beheld the obsequies of the last. Certain it is, that from that time, bell, and organ, and choral chant have never more been heard.

The mouldering pinnacle, surmounted by the cross, remains an object of pious pilgrimage. Some say that it anciently stood in front of the convent, but others that it was the spire which remained above ground, when the main body of the building sank, like the topmast of some tall ship that has foundered. These pious believers maintain that the convent is miraculously preserved entire in the centre of the mountain, where, if proper excavations were made, it would be found, with all its treasures, and monuments, and shrines, and relics, and the tombs of its virgin nuns.

Should any one doubt the truth of this marvellous interposition of the Virgin, to protect the vestal purity of her votaries, let him read the excellent work entitled *España Triumphante,* written by Fray Antonio de Sancta Maria, a barefoot friar of the Carmelite order, and he will doubt no longer.

From *Wolfert's Roost*

THE PHANTOM ISLAND

"Break, Phantsie, from thy cave of cloud,
    And wave thy purple wings,
Now all thy figures are allowed,
    And various shapes of things.
Create of airy forms a stream;
    It must have blood and naught of phlegm;
And though it be a waking dream,
        Yet let it like an odor rise
            To all the senses here,
        And fall like sleep upon their eyes,
            Or music on their ear."
                                —BEN JONSON

THERE are more things in heaven and earth than are dreamed of in our philosophy," and among these may be placed that marvel and mystery of the seas, the Island of St. Brandan. Those who have read the history of the Canaries, the fortunate islands of the ancients, may remember the wonders told of this enigmatical island. Occasionally it would be visible from their shores, stretching away in the clear bright west, to all appearance substantial like themselves, and still more beautiful. Expeditions would launch forth from the Canaries to explore this land of promise. For a time its sungilt peaks and long, shadowy promontories would remain distinctly visible, but in proportion as the voyagers approached, peak and promontory would gradually fade away until nothing would remain but blue sky above and deep blue water below. Hence this mysterious isle was stigmatized by ancient cosmographers with the name of Aprositus or the Inaccessible. The failure of numerous expeditions sent in quest of it, both in ancient and modern days, has at length caused its very existence to be called in question, and it has been rashly pronounced a mere optical illusion, like the Fata Morgana of the Straits of Messina, or has been classed with those unsubstantial regions known to mariners as Cape Fly Away and the coast of Cloud Land.

Let us not permit, however, the doubts of worldly-wise sceptics to rob us of all the glorious realms owned by happy credulity in days of yore. Be assured, O reader of easy faith!—thou for whom it is my delight to labor—be assured that such an island actually exists, and has from time to time been revealed to the gaze and trodden by the feet of favored mortals. Historians and philosophers may have their doubts, but its existence has been fully attested by that inspired race, the poets; who, being gifted with a kind of second sight, are enabled to discern those mysteries of nature hidden from the eyes of ordinary men. To this gifted race it has ever been a kind of wonder-land. Here once bloomed, and perhaps still blooms, the famous garden of the Hesperides, with its golden fruit. Here, too, the sorceress Armida had her enchanted garden, in which she held the Christian paladin, Rinaldo, in delicious but inglorious thraldom, as set forth in the immortal lay of Tasso. It was in this island that Sycorax the witch held sway, when the good Prospero and his infant daughter Miranda were wafted to its shores. Who does not know the tale as told in the magic page of Shakespeare? The isle was then

——"full of noises,
Sounds, and sweet airs, that give delight, and hurt not."

The island, in fact, at different times, has been under the sway of different powers, genii of earth, and air, and ocean, who have made it their shadowy abode. Hither have retired many classic but broken-down deities, shorn of almost all their attributes, but who once ruled the poetic world. Here Neptune and Amphitrite hold a diminished court, sovereigns in exile. Their ocean-chariot, almost a wreck, lies bottom upward in some sea-beaten cavern; their pursy Tritons and haggard Nereids bask listlessly like seals about the rocks. Sometimes those deities assume, it is said, a shadow of their ancient pomp, and glide in state about a summer sea; and then, as some tall Indiaman lies becalmed with idly flapping sail, her drowsy crew may hear the mellow note of the Triton's shell swelling upon the ear as the invisible pageant sweeps by.

On the shores of this wondrous isle the kraken heaves its unwieldy bulk and wallows many a rood. Here the sea-serpent, that mighty but much-contested reptile, lies coiled up during the intervals of its revelations to the eyes of true believers. Here even the Flying Dutchman finds a port, and casts his anchor, and furls his shadowy sail, and takes a brief repose from his eternal cruisings.

In the deep bays and harbors of the island lies many a spellbound ship, long since given up as lost by the ruined merchant. Here, too, its crew, long, long bewailed in vain, lie sleeping from age to age in mossy grottos, or wander about in pleasing oblivion of all things. Here in caverns are garnered up the priceless treasures lost in the ocean. Here sparkles in vain the diamond and flames the carbuncle. Here are piled up rich bales of Oriental silks, boxes of pearls, and piles of golden ingots.

Such are some of the marvels related of this island, which may serve to throw light upon the following legend, of unquestionable truth, which I recommend to the implicit belief of the reader.

The Adalantado of the Seven Cities

A LEGEND OF ST. BRANDAN

IN the early part of the fifteenth century, when Prince Henry of Portugal, of worthy memory, was pushing the career of discovery along the western coast of Africa, and the world was resounding with reports of golden regions on the mainland, and new-found islands in the ocean, there arrived at Lisbon an old bewildered pilot of the seas, who had been driven by tempests, he knew not whither, and raved about an island far in the deep, upon which he had landed, and which he had found peopled with Christians, and adorned with noble cities.

The inhabitants, he said, having never before been visited by a ship, gathered round, and regarded him with surprise. They told him they were descendants of a band of Christians, who fled from Spain when that country was conquered by the Moslems. They were curious about the state of their fatherland, and grieved to hear that the Moslems still held possession of the kingdom of Granada. They would have taken the old navigator to church, to convince him of their orthodoxy; but, either through lack of devotion, or lack of faith in their words, he declined their invitation, and preferred to return on board of his ship. He was properly punished. A furious storm arose, drove him from his anchorage, hurried him out to sea, and he saw no more of the unknown island.

This strange story caused great marvel in Lisbon and elsewhere. Those versed in history remembered to have read, in an ancient chronicle, that, at the time of the conquest of Spain, in the eighth century, when the blessed cross was cast down and the crescent erected in its place, and when Christian churches were turned into Moslem mosques, seven bishops, at the head of seven bands of pious exiles, had fled from the peninsula, and embarked in quest of some ocean island, or distant land, where they might found seven Christian cities, and enjoy their faith unmolested.

The fate of these saints-errant had hitherto remained a mystery, and their story had faded from memory; the report of the old tempest-tossed pilot, however, revived this long-forgotten theme; and it was determined by the pious and enthusiastic that the island thus accidentally discovered was the identical place of refuge whither the wandering bishops had been guided by a protecting Providence, and where they had folded their flocks.

This most excitable of worlds has always some darling object of chimerical enterprise; the "Island of the Seven Cites" now awakened as much interest and longing among zealous Christians as has the renowned city of Timbuctoo among adventurous travellers, or the North-east passage among hardy navigators; and it was a frequent prayer of the devout, that these scattered and lost portions of the Christian family might be discovered and reunited to the great body of Christendom.

No one, however, entered into the matter with half the zeal of Don Fernando de Ulmo, a young cavalier of high standing in the Portuguese court, and of most sanguine and romantic temperament. He had recently come to his estate, and had run the round of all kinds of pleasures and excitements when this new theme of popular talk and wonder presented itself. The Island of the Seven Cities became now the constant subject of his thoughts by day, and his dreams by night; it even rivalled his passion for a beautiful girl, one of the greatest belles of Lisbon, to whom he was betrothed. At length his imagination became so inflamed on the subject, that he determined to fit out an expedition, at his own expense, and set sail in quest of this sainted island. It could not be a cruise of any great extent; for, according to the calculations .of the tempest-tossed pilot, it must be somewhere in the latitude of the Canaries, which at that time, when the new world was as yet undiscovered, formed the frontier of ocean enterprise. Don Fernando applied to the crown for countenance and protection. As he was a favorite at court, the usual patronage was readily extended to him; that is to say, he received a commission from the king, Don Ioam II, constituting him Adalantado, or military governor, of any country he might discover, with the single proviso, that he should bear all the expenses of the discovery, and pay a tenth of the profits to the crown.

Don Fernando now set to work in the true spirit of a projector. He sold acre after acre of solid land, and invested the proceeds in ships, guns, ammunition, and sea-stores. Even his old family mansion in Lisbon was mortgaged without scruple, for he looked forward to a palace in one of the Seven Cities, of which he was to be Adalantado. This was the age of nautical romance, when the thoughts of all speculative dreamers were turned to the ocean. The scheme of Don Fernando, therefore, drew adventurers of every kind. The merchant promised himself new marts of opulent traffic; the soldier hoped to sack and plunder some one or other of those Seven Cities; even the fat monk shook off the sleep and sloth of the cloister, to join in a crusade which promised such increase to the possessions of the Church.

One person alone regarded the whole project with sovereign contempt and growing hostility. This was Don Ramiro Alvarez, the father of the beautiful Serafina, to whom Don Fernando was betrothed. He was one of those perverse, matter-of-fact old men, who are prone to oppose everything speculative and romantic. He had no faith in the Island of the Seven Cities; regarded the projected cruise as a crackbrained freak; looked with angry eye and internal heart-burning on the conduct of his intended son-in-law, chaffering away solid lands for lands in the moon; and scoffingly dubbed him Adalantado of Cloud Land. In fact, he had never really relished the intended match, to which his consent had been slowly extorted by the tears and entreaties of his daughter. It is true he could have no reasonable objections to the youth, for Don Fernando was the very flower of Portuguese chivalry. No one could excel him at the tilting match, or the riding at the ring; none was more bold and dexterous in the bull-fight; none composed more gallant madrigals in praise of his lady's charms, or sang them with sweeter tones to the accompaniment of her guitar; nor could any one handle the castanets and dance the bolero with more captivating grace. All these admirable qualities and endowments, however, though they had been sufficient to win the heart of Serafina, were nothing in the eyes of her unreasonable father. Oh Cupid, god of Love! why will fathers always be so unreasonable?

The engagment to Serafina had threatened at first to throw an obstacle in the way of the expedition of Don Fernando, and for a time perplexed him in the extreme. He was passionately attached to the young lady; but he was also passionately bent on this romantic enterprise. How should he reconcile the two passionate inclinations? A sim-

ple and obvious arrangement at length presented itself,—marry Serafina, enjoy a portion of the honeymoon at once, and defer the rest until
his return from the discovery of the Seven Cities!

He hastened to make known this most excellent arrangement to Don
Ramiro, when the long-smothered wrath of the old cavalier burst forth.
He reproached him with being the dupe of wandering vagabonds and
wild schemers, and with squandering all his real possessions, in pursuit
of empty bubbles. Don Fernando was too sanguine a projector, and too
young a man, to listen tamely to such language. He acted with what
is technically called "becoming spirit." A high quarrel ensued; Don
Ramiro pronounced him a madman, and forbade all further intercourse
with his daughter until he should give proof of returning sanity by
abandoning this madcap enterprise; while Don Fernando flung out of
the house, more bent than ever on the expedition, from the idea of
triumphing over the incredulity of the greybeard, when he should return successful. Don Ramiro's heart misgave him. Who knows, thought
he, but this crack-brained visionary may persuade my daughter to elope
with him, and share his throne in this unknown paradise of fools? If I
could only keep her safe until his ships are fairly out at sea!

He repaired to her apartment, represented to her the sanguine, unsteady character of her lover and the chimerical value of his schemes,
and urged the propriety of suspending all intercourse with him until he
should recover from his present hallucination. She bowed her head as
if in filial acquiescence, whereupon he folded her to his bosom with
parental fondness and kissed away a tear that was stealing over her
cheek, but as he left the chamber quietly turned the key in the lock;
for though he was a fond father and had a high opinion of the submissive temper of his child, he had a still higher opinion of the con-
servative virtues of lock and key, and determined to trust to them until
the caravels should sail. Whether the damsel had been in anywise
shaken in her faith as to the schemes of her lover by her father's eloquence, tradition does not say; but certain it is, that, the moment she
heard the key turn in the lock, she became a firm believer in the Island
of the Seven Cities.

The door was locked; but her will was unconfined. A window of the
chamber opened into one of those stone balconies, secured by iron bars,
which project like huge cages from Portuguese and Spanish houses.
Within this balcony the beautiful Serafina had her birds and flowers,
and here she was accustomed to sit on moonlight nights as in a bower,
and touch her guitar and sing like a wakeful nightingale. From this
balcony an intercourse was now maintained between the lovers, against

which the lock and key of Don Ramiro were of no avail. All day would Fernando be occupied hurrying the equipments of his ships, but evening found him in sweet discourse beneath his lady's window.

At length the preparations were completed. Two gallant caravels lay at anchor in the Tagus ready to sail at sunrise. Late at night by the pale light of a waning moon the lover had his last interview. The beautiful Serafina was sad at heart and full of dark forebodings; her lover full of hope and confidence. "A few short months," said he, "and I shall return in triumph. Thy father will then blush at his incredulity, and hasten to welcome to his house the Adalantado of the Seven Cities."

The gentle lady shook her head. It was not on this point she felt distrust. She was a thorough believer in the Island of the Seven Cities, and so sure of the success of the enterprise that she might have been tempted to join it had not the balcony been high and the grating strong. Other considerations induced that dubious shaking of the head. She had heard of the inconstancy of the seas, and the inconstancy of those who roam them. Might not Fernando meet with other loves in foreign ports? Might not some peerless beauty in one or other of those Seven Cities efface the image of Serafina from his mind? Now let the truth be spoken, the beautiful Serafina had reason for her disquiet. If Don Fernando had any fault in the world, it was that of being rather inflammable and apt to take fire from every sparkling eye. He had been somewhat of a rover among the sex on shore, what might he be on sea?

She ventured to express her doubt, but he spurned at the very idea. "What! be false to Serafina! He bow at the shrine of another beauty? Never! never!" Repeatedly did he bend his knee, and smite his breast, and call upon the silver moon to witness his sincerity and truth.

He retorted the doubt, "Might not Serafina herself forget her plighted faith? Might not some wealthier rival present himself while he was tossing on the sea; and, backed by her father's wishes, win the treasure of her hand!"

The beautiful Serafina raised her white arms between the iron bars of the balcony, and, like her lover, invoked the moon to testify her vows. Alas! how little did Fernando know her heart. The more her father should oppose, the more would she be fixed in faith. Though years should intervene, Fernando on his return would find her true. Even should the salt sea swallow him up (and her eyes shed salt tears at the very thought), never would she be the wife of another! Never, *never,* NEVER! She drew from her finger a ring gemmed with a ruby heart, and dropped it from the balcony, a parting pledge of constancy.

Thus the lovers parted with many a tender word and plighted vow.

But will they keep those vows? Perish the doubt! Have they not called the constant moon to witness?

With the morning dawn the caravels dropped down the Tagus, and put to sea. They steered for the Canaries, in those days the regions of nautical discovery and romance, and the outposts of the known world, for as yet Columbus had not steered his daring barks across the ocean. Scarce had they reached those latitudes when they were separated by a violent tempest. For many days was the caravel of Don Fernando driven about at the mercy of the elements; all seamanship was baffled, destruction seemed inevitable, and the crew were in despair. All at once the storm subsided; the ocean sank into a calm; the clouds which had veiled the face of heaven were suddenly withdrawn, and the tempest-tossed mariners beheld a fair and mountainous island, emerging as if by enchantment from the murky gloom. They rubbed their eyes and gazed for a time almost incredulously, yet there lay the island spread out in lovely landscape, with the late stormy sea laving its shores with peaceful billows.

The pilot of the caravel consulted his maps and charts; no island like the one before him was laid down as existing in those parts; it is true he had lost his reckoning in the late storm, but, according to his calculations, he could not be far from the Canaries; and this was not one of that group of islands. The caravel now lay perfectly becalmed off the mouth of a river, on the banks of which, about a league from the sea, was descried a noble city, with lofty walls and towers, and a protecting castle.

After a time, a stately barge with sixteen oars was seen emerging from the river, and approaching the caravel. It was quaintly carved and gilt; the oarsmen were clad in antique garb, their oars painted of a bright crimson, and they came slowly and solemnly, keeping times as they rowed to the cadence of an old Spanish ditty. Under a silken canopy in the stern sat a cavalier richly clad, and over his head was a banner bearing the sacred emblem of the cross.

When the barge reached the caravel, the cavalier stepped on board. He was tall and gaunt; with a long Spanish visage, moustaches that curled up to his eyes, and a forked beard. He wore gauntlets reaching to his elbows, a Toledo blade strutting out behind, with a basket hilt, in which he carried his handkerchief. His air was lofty and precise, and bespoke indisputably the hidalgo. Thrusting out a long spindle leg, he took off a huge sombrero, and swaying it until the feather swept the ground, accosted Don Fernando in the old Castilian language, and with the old Castilian courtesy, welcoming him to the Island of the Seven Cities.

Don Fernando was overwhelmed with astonishment. Could this be true? Had he really been tempest-driven to the very land of which he was in quest?

It was even so. That very day the inhabitants were holding high festival in commemoration of the escape of their ancestors from the Moors. The arrival of the caravel at such a juncture was considered a good omen, the accomplishment of an ancient prophecy through which the island was to be restored to the great community of Christendom. The cavalier before him was grand chamberlain, sent by the alcayde to invite him to the festivities of the capital.

Don Fernando could scarce believe that this was not all a dream. He made known his name and the object of his voyage. The grand chamberlain declared that all was in perfect accordance with the ancient prophecy, and that the moment his credentials were presented, he would be acknowledged as the Adalantado of the Seven Cities. In the meantime the day was waning; the barge was ready to convey him to the land and would as assuredly bring him back.

Don Fernando's pilot, a veteran of the seas, drew him aside and expostulated against his venturing, on the mere word of a stranger, to land in a strange barge on an unknown shore. "Who knows, Señor, what land this is, or what people inhabit it?"

Don Fernando was not to be dissuaded. Had he not believed in this island when all the world doubted? Had he not sought it in defiance of storm and tempest, and was he now to shrink from its shores when they lay before him in calm weather? In a word, was not faith the very corner-stone of his enterprise?

Having arrayed himself, therefore, in gala dress befitting the occasion, he took his seat in the barge. The grand chamberlain seated himself opposite. The rowers plied their oars, and renewed the mournful old ditty, and the gorgeous but unwieldy barge moved slowly through the water.

The night closed in before they entered the river, and swept along past rock and promontory, each guarded by its tower. At every post they were challenged by the sentinel.

"Who goes there?"

"The Adalantado of the Seven Cities."

"Welcome, Señor Adalantado. Pass on."

Entering the harbor they rowed close by an armed galley of ancient form. Soldiers with crossbows patrolled the deck.

"Who goes there?"

"The Adalantado of the Seven Cities."

"Welcome, Señor Adalantado. Pass on."

They landed at a broad flight of stone steps, leading up between two massive towers, and knocked at the water-gate. A sentinel, in ancient steel casque, looked from the barbican.

"Who is there?"

"The Adalantado of the Seven Cities."

"Welcome, Señor Adalantado."

The gate swung open, grating upon rusty hinges. They entered between two rows of warriors in Gothic armor, with crossbows, maces, battle-axes, and faces old-fashioned as their armor. There were processions through the streets, in commemoration of the landing of the seven Bishops and their followers, and bonfires at which effigies of losel Moors expiated their invasion of Christendom by a kind of *auto-da-fé*. The groups round the fires, uncouth in their attire, looked like the fantastic figures that roam the streets in Carnival time. Even the dames who gazed down from Gothic balconies hung with antique tapestry, resembled effigies dressed up in Christmas mummeries. Everything, in short, bore the stamp of former ages, as if the world had suddenly rolled back for several centuries. Nor was this to be wondered at. Had not the Island of the Seven Cities been cut off from the rest of the world for several hundred years; and were not these the modes and customs of Gothic Spain before it was conquered by the Moors?

Arrived at the palace of the alcayde, the grand chamberlain knocked at the portal. The porter looked through a wicket, and demanded who was there.

"The Adalantado of the Seven Cities."

The portal was thrown wide open. The grand chamberlain led the way up a vast, heavily moulded, marble staircase, and into a hall of ceremony, where was the alcayde with several of the principal dignitaries of the city, who had a marvellous resemblance, in form and feature, to the quaint figures in old illuminated manuscripts.

The grand chamberlain stepped forward and announced the name and title of the stranger guest, and the extraordinary nature of his mission. The announcement appeared to create no extraordinary emotion or surprise, but to be received as the anticipated fulfilment of a prophecy.

The reception of Don Fernando, however, was profoundly gracious, though in the same style of stately courtesy which everywhere prevailed. He would have produced his credentials, but this was courteously declined. The evening was devoted to high festivity; the following day, when he should enter the port with his caravel, would be devoted to business, when the credentials would be received in due form, and he inducted into office as Adalantado of the Seven Cities.

Don Fernando was now conducted through one of those interminable suites of apartments, the pride of Spanish palaces, all furnished in a style of obsolete magnificence. In a vast saloon, blazing with tapers, was assembled all the aristocracy and fashion of the city,—stately dames and cavaliers, the very counterpart of the figures in the tapestry which decorated the walls. Fernando gazed in silent marvel. It was a reflex of the proud aristocracy of Spain in the time of Roderick the Goth.

The festivities of the evening were all in the style of solemn and antiquated ceremonial. There was a dance, but it was as if the old tapestry were put in motion, and all the figures moving in stately measure about the floor. There was one exception, and one that told powerfully upon the susceptible Adalantado. The alcayde's daughter—such a ripe, melting beauty! Her dress, it is true, like the dresses of her neighbors, might have been worn before the flood, but she had the black Andalusian eye, a glance of which, through its long dark lashes, is irresistible. Her voice, too, her manner, her undulating movements, all smacked of Andalusia, and showed how female charms may be transmitted from age to age, and clime to clime, without ever going out of fashion. Those who know the witchery of the sex, in that most amorous part of amorous old Spain, may judge of the fascination to which Don Fernando was exposed, as he joined in the dance with one of its most captivating descendants.

He sat beside her at the banquet! such an old-world feast! such obsolete dainties! At the head of the table the peacock, that bird of state and ceremony, was served up in full plumage on a golden dish. As Don Fernando cast his eyes down the glittering board, what a vista presented itself of odd heads and headdresses; of formal bearded dignitaries and stately dames, with castellated locks and towering plumes! Is it to be wondered at that he should turn with delight from these antiquated figures to the alcayde's daughter, all smiles and dimples, and melting looks and melting accents? Beside, for I wish to give him every excuse in my power, he was in a particularly excitable mood from the novelty of the scene before him, from this realization of all his hopes and fancies, and from frequent draughts of the wine-cup, presented to him at every moment by officious pages during the banquet.

In a word—there is no concealing the matter—before the evening was over, Don Fernando was making love outright to the alcayde's daughter. They had wandered together to a moon-lit balcony of the palace, and he was charming her ear with one of those love-ditties with which, in a like balcony, he had serenaded the beautiful Serafina.

The damsel hung her head coyly. "Ah! Señor, these are flattering words; but you cavaliers, who roam the seas, are unsteady as its waves. To-morrow you will be throned in state, Adalantado of the Seven Cities; and will think no more of the alcayde's daughter."

Don Fernando in the intoxication of the moment called the moon to witness his sincerity. As he raised his hand in adjuration, the chaste moon cast a ray upon the ring that sparkled on his finger. It caught the damsel's eye. "Signor Adalantado," said she archly, "I have no great faith in the moon, but give me that ring upon your finger in pledge of the truth of what you profess."

The gallant Adalantado was taken by surprise; there was no parrying this sudden appeal; before he had time to reflect, the ring of the beautiful Serafina glittered on the finger of the alcayde's daughter.

At this eventful moment the chamberlain approached with lofty demeanor, and announced that the barge was waiting to bear him back to the caravel. I forbear to relate the ceremonious partings with the alcayde and his dignitaries, and the tender farewell of the alcayde's daughter. He took his seat in the barge opposite the grand chamberlain. The rowers plied their crimson oars in the same slow and stately manner, to the cadence of the same mournful old ditty. His brain was in a whirl with all that he had seen, and his heart now and then gave him a twinge as he thought of his temporary infidelity to the beautiful Serafina. The barge sallied out into the sea, but no caravel was to be seen; doubtless she had been carried to a distance by the current of the river. The oarsmen rowed on; their monotonous chant had a lulling effect. A drowsy influence crept over Don Fernando. Objects swam before his eyes. The oarsmen assumed odd shapes as in a dream. The grand chamberlain grew larger and larger, and taller and taller. He took off his huge sombrero, and held it over the head of Don Fernando, like an extinguisher over a candle. The latter cowered beneath it; he felt himself sinking in the socket.

"Good night! Señor Adalantado of the Seven Cities!" said the grand chamberlain.

The sombrero slowly descended—Don Fernando was extinguished!

How long he remained extinct no mortal man can tell. When he returned to consciousness, he found himself in a strange cabin, surrounded by strangers. He rubbed his eyes, and looked round him wildly. Where was he?—On board a Portuguese ship, bound to Lisbon. How came he there?—He had been taken senseless from a wreck drifting about the ocean.

Don Fernando was more and more confounded and perplexed. He

recalled, one by one, everything that had happened to him in the Island of the Seven Cities, until he had been extinguished by the sombrero of the grand chamberlain. But what had happened to him since? What had become of his caravel? Was it the wreck of her on which he had been found floating?

The people about him could give no information on the subject. He entreated them to take him to the Island of the Seven Cities, which could not be far off; told them all that had befallen him there; that he had but to land to be received as Adalantado; when he would reward them magnificently for their services.

They regarded his words as the ravings of delirium, and in their honest solicitude for the restoration of his reason, administered such rough remedies that he was fain to drop the subject and observe a cautious taciturnity.

At length they arrived in the Tagus, and anchored before the famous city of Lisbon. Don Fernando sprang joyfully on shore, and hastened to his ancestral mansion. A strange porter opened the door, who knew nothing of him or his family; no people of the name had inhabited the house for many a year.

He sought the mansion of Don Ramiro. He approached the balcony beneath which he had bidden farewell to Serafina. Did his eyes deceive him? No! There was Serafina herself among the flowers in the balcony. He raised his arms toward her with an exclamation of rapture. She cast upon him a look of indignation, and, hastily retiring, closed the casement with a slam that testified her displeasure.

Could she have heard of his flirtation with the alcayde's daughter? But that was mere transient gallantry. A moment's interview would dispel every doubt of his constancy.

He rang at the door; as it was opened by the porter he rushed upstairs; sought the well-known chamber, and threw himself at the feet of Serafina. She started back with affright, and took refuge in the arms of a youthful cavalier.

"What mean you, Señor," cried the latter, "by this intrusion?"

"What right have you to ask the question?" demanded Don Fernando fiercely.

"The right of an affianced suitor!"

Don Fernando started and turned pale. "Oh, Serafina! Serafina!" cried he, in a tone of agony; "is this thy plighted constancy?"

"Serafina? What mean you by Serafina, Señor? If this be the lady you intend, her name is Maria."

"May I not believe my senses? May I not believe my heart?" cried

Don Fernando. "Is not this Serafina Alvarez, the original of yon portrait, which, less fickle than herself, still smiles on me from the wall?"

"Holy Virgin!" cried the young lady, casting her eyes upon the portrait. "He is talking of my great-grandmother!"

An explanation ensued, if that could be called an explanation which plunged the unfortunate Fernando into tenfold perplexity. If he might believe his eyes, he saw before him his beloved Serafina; if he might believe his ears, it was merely her hereditary form and features, perpetuated in the person of her great-granddaughter.

His brain began to spin. He sought the office of the Minister of Marine, and made a report of his expedition, and of the Island of the Seven Cities, which he had so fortunately discovered. Nobody knew anything of such an expedition, or such an island. He declared that he had undertaken the enterprise under a formal contract with the crown, and had received a regular commission, constituting him Adalantado. This must be matter of record, and he insisted loudly that the books of the department should be consulted. The wordy strife at length attracted the attention of an old gray-headed clerk, who sat perched on a high stool, at a high desk, with iron-rimmed spectacles on the top of a thin, pinched nose, copying records into an enormous folio. He had wintered and summered in the department for a great part of a century, until he had almost grown to be a piece of the desk at which he sat; his memory was a mere index of official facts and documents, and his brain was little better than red tape and parchment. After peering down for a time from his lofty perch, and ascertaining the matter in controversy, he put his pen behind his ear, and descended. He remembered to have heard something from his predecessor about an expedition of the kind in question, but then it had sailed during the reign of Don Ioam II., and he had been dead at least a hundred years. To put the matter beyond dispute, however, the archives of the Torre do Tombo, that sepulchre of old Portuguese documents, were diligently searched, and a record was found of a contract between the crown and one Fernando de Ulmo, for the discovery of the Island of the Seven Cities, and of a commission secured to him as Adalantado of the country he might discover.

"There!" cried Don Fernando, triumphantly, "there you have proof, before your own eyes, of what I have said. I am the Fernando de Ulmo specified in that record. I have discovered the Island of the Seven Cities, and am entitled to be Adalantado, according to contract."

The story of Don Fernando had certainly, what is pronounced the best of historical foundation, documentary evidence; but when a man, in the bloom of youth, talked of events that had taken place above a century previously, as having happened to himself, it is no wonder that he was set down for a madman.

The old clerk looked at him from above and below his spectacles, shrugged his shoulders, stroked his chin, reascended his lofty stool, took the pen from behind his ears, and resumed his daily and eternal task, copying records into the fiftieth volume of a series of gigantic folios. The other clerks winked at each other shrewdly, and dispersed to their several places, and poor Don Fernando, thus left to himself, flung out of the office, almost driven wild by these repeated perplexities.

In the confusion of his mind, he instinctively repaired to the mansion of Alvarez, but it was barred against him. To break the delusion under which the youth apparently labored, and to convince him that the Serafina about whom he raved was really dead, he was conducted to her tomb. There she lay, a stately matron, cut out in alabaster; and there lay her husband beside her; a portly cavalier, in armor; and there knelt, on each side, the effigies of a numerous progeny, proving that she had been a fruitful vine. Even the very monument gave evidence of the lapse of time; the hands of her husband, folded as if in prayer, had lost their fingers, and the face of the once lovely Serafina was without a nose.

Don Fernando felt a transient glow of indignation at beholding this monumental proof of the inconstancy of his mistress; but who could expect a mistress to remain constant during a whole century of absence? And what right had he to rail about constancy, after what had passed between himself and the alcayde's daughter? The unfortunate cavalier performed one pious act of tender devotion; he had the alabaster nose of Serafina restored by a skilful statuary, and then tore himself from the tomb.

He could now no longer doubt the fact that, somehow or other, he had slipped over a whole century during the night he had spent at the Island of the Seven Cities; and he was now as complete a stranger in his native city, as if he had never been there. A thousand times did he wish himself back to that wonderful island, with its antiquated banquet halls, where he had been so courteously received; and now that the once young and beautiful Serafina was nothing but a great-grandmother in marble, with generations of descendants, a thousand times would he recall the melting black eyes of the alcayde's daughter, who doubtless, like himself, was still flourishing in fresh juvenility, and breathe a secret wish that he was seated by her side.

He would at once have set on foot another expedition, at his own expense, to cruise in search of the sainted island, but his means were exhausted. He endeavored to rouse others to the enterprise, setting forth the certainty of profitable results, of which his own experience furnished such unquestionable proof. Alas! no one would give faith to his tale; but looked upon it as the feverish dream of a shipwrecked man. He persisted in his efforts; holding forth in all places and all companies, until he became an object of jest and jeer to the light-minded, who mistook his earnest enthusiasm for a proof of insanity; and the very children in the streets bantered him with the title of "The Adalantado of the Seven Cities."

Finding all efforts in vain, in his native city of Lisbon, he took shipping for the Canaries, as being nearer the latitude of his former cruise, and inhabited by people given to nautical adventure. Here he found ready listeners to his story; for the old pilots and mariners of those parts were notorious island-hunters, and devout believers in all the wonders of the seas. Indeed, one and all treated his adventure as a common occurrence, and turning to each other, with a sagacious nod of the head, observed, "He has been at the Island of St. Brandan."

They then went on to inform him of that great marvel and enigma of the ocean; of its repeated appearance to the inhabitants of their islands; and of the many but ineffectual expeditions that had been made in search of it. They took him to a promontory of the island of Palma, whence the shadowy St. Brandan had oftenest been descried, and they pointed out the very tract in the west where its mountains had been seen.

Don Fernando listened with rapt attention. He had no longer a doubt that this mysterious and fugacious island must be the same with that of the Seven Cities; and that some supernatural influence connected with it had operated upon himself, and made the events of a night occupy the space of a century.

He endeavored, but in vain, to rouse the islanders to another attempt at discovery; they had given up the phantom island as indeed inaccessible. Fernando, however, was not to be discouraged. The idea wore itself deeper and deeper in his mind, until it became the engrossing subject of his thoughts and object of his being. Every morning he would repair to the promontory of Palma, and sit there throughout the livelong day, in hopes of seeing the fairy mountains of St. Brandan peering above the horizon; every evening he returned to his home, a disappointed man, but ready to resume his post on the following morning.

His assiduity was all in vain. He grew gray in his ineffectual attempt; and was at length found dead at his post. His grave is still shown in

the island of Palma, and a cross is erected on the spot where he used to
sit and look out upon the sea, in hopes of the reappearance of the phantom island.

NOTE.—For various particulars concerning the *Island of St. Brandan*
and the *Island of the Seven Cities*, those ancient problems of the ocean,
the curious reader is referred to articles under those heads in the Appendix to the *Life of Columbus*—W.I.

THE FRANCIS
PARKMAN READER
Edited with an introduction
and notes by
Samuel Eliot Morison
544 pp., 1 illus., 5 maps
80823-4 $17.95

HERE AT *THE NEW YORKER*
Brendan Gill
428 pp., 131 illus.
New introd. by the author
80810-2 $15.95

THE EDMUND WILSON
READER
Revised and Expanded
Edited by Lewis M. Dabney
808 pp., 1 drawing
80809-9 $18.95

IN THE SPIRIT
OF JAZZ
The Otis Ferguson Reader
Edited by Dorothy Chamberlain
and Robert Wilson
Foreword by Malcolm Cowley
327 pp., 1 photo
80744-0 $15.95

THE AMERICAN EARTHQUAKE
**A Chronicle of the Roaring
Twenties, the Great Depression,
and the Dawn of the New Deal**
Edmund Wilson
576 pp.
80696-7 $17.95

BATTLE-PIECES AND
ASPECTS OF THE WAR
Herman Melville
New introd. by Lee Rust Brown
282 pp.
80655-X $13.95

THE COMPLETE HUMOROUS
SKETCHES AND TALES OF
MARK TWAIN
Edited with an introduction
by Charles Neider
722 pp.
80702-5 $19.95

FACES IN THE CROWD
**Musicians, Writers, Actors &
Filmmakers**
Gary Giddins
288 pp.
80705-X $13.95

FRANZ KAFKA
A Biography
Max Brod
295 pp., 8 photos,
3 pp of Kafka's sketches
80670-3 $13.95

GEORGE WASHINGTON
A Biography
Washington Irving
Edited and abridged with an
introduction by Charles Neider
790 pp., 3 illus., 5 maps
80593-6 $18.95

HARDBOILED AMERICA
**Lurid Paperbacks and the
Masters of Noir
Expanded Edition**
Geoffrey O'Brien
216 pp., 137 illus. (8 pp. in color)
80773-4 $16.95

REVOLUTION OF THE MIND
The Life of André Breton
Mark Polizzotti
784 pp., 48 photos, 1 line drawing
80772-6 $20.95

RICHARD WRIGHT READER
Edited by Ellen Wright and
Michel Fabre
910 pp., 66 photos
80774-2 $22.50

SAINT-EXUPÉRY
A Biography
Stacy Schiff
559 pp., 40 illus.
80740-8 $18.95

THE GREAT WEST
**A Treasury of Firsthand
Accounts**
Edited by Charles Neider
460 pp., 94 illus., 3 maps
80761-0 $22.95

Available at your bookstore

OR ORDER DIRECTLY FROM 1-800-386-5656

VISIT OUR WEBSITE AT WWW.PERSEUSBOOKSGROUP.COM